Fiddler's Dream

Show card, "Roy, Lonnie, and John" ("The Boys from the Hills"), at radio KFAB, Lincoln, Nebraska, January 1939. L-R: Roy McGeorge, fiddler Lonnie Robertson, bassist John Montgomery. (Courtesy Henry McGeorge)

Fiddler's Dream

Old–Time, Swing, and Bluegrass Fiddling in Twentieth–Century Missouri

Howard Wight Marshall

UNIVERSITY OF MISSOURI PRESS
Columbia

University of Missouri Press, Columbia, Missouri 65211
Printed and bound in the United States of America
 First printing, 2017.

ISBN: 978-0-8262-2121-6
Library of Congress Control Number: 2017933621

∞™ This paper meets the requirements of the
American National Standard for Permanence of Paper
for Printed Library Materials, Z39.48, 1984.

Typeface: Garamond

Published with the generous support of the Missouri Humanities Council.

To the memory of Leroy (Red) Canaday.
He was *the* fiddler in my hometown.

Contents

Dancing a Virginia reel, the evening's opening dance and "ice breaker," at Hallsville, in 2013; this monthly dance, hosted by John and Betty White, draws more young people than old-timers to the dance floor. (Photo by Jean A. Fugate-Besalke)

Preface

Artistic snobbery is so ridiculous! Many an immortal tune has been born of the stable or the cotton field. *Turkey in the Straw* is a magic melody; anyone should be proud of having written it, but, for musical high-brows I suppose the thing is *déclassé*.

—John Philip Sousa, *Marching Along: Recollections of Men and Women and Music*

In 2012 *Play Me Something Quick and Devilish: Old-Time Fiddlers in Missouri* documented traditional fiddle and dance music from the early European settlement of the state down through the nineteenth century and into the early twentieth.[1] *Fiddler's Dream* begins where the 2012 volume ended, in the early-twentieth-century era of great excitement, anticipation, and innovation that would change American society, just as it would change "old-time fiddling." *Fiddler's Dream* thus picks up the saga of fiddle and dance music in the post–World War I era and the Roaring Twenties Jazz Age and winds down in the 1960s. Many themes and people appear in both volumes, for local history and vernacular traditions are not a straight line but more of a loop, looking back and forth through time, the past informing the present and previewing the future. A third volume is being considered, to continue the narrative.

In the 1910s, the 78 rpm record overtook the Edison cylinder in popularity. The 78 in turn was superseded by the 33 rpm long-playing (LP) record in the 1950s. Home recordings with reel-to-reel and then cassette magnetic tape became widespread in the 1960s, encouraging drastic changes in the fiddler's world because, suddenly, inexpensive home tape recorders were made available. Fiddlers could "tape" jam sessions, concerts, fiddlers contests, and their own playing as never before—and make copies of commercial recordings to pass around from musician to musician.[2]

Like the 2012 volume, *Fiddler's Dream* is a personal and impressionistic documentation and presentation of local history, cultural studies, and social history with old-time fiddling and fiddlers as its focus. It is prudent once again to say that this is not a book of musicological analysis. Nor is this book, despite endnotes and propositions, a theoretical treatise. I have been interested in the subject and accumulating information and ideas about it for several decades, and more and more I feel the way Nat Hentoff describes his quest to understand jazz: "Once you're inside the music you'll want to keep going deeper and deeper, because it is impossible to get enough of it."[3]

A sampler compact disc of Missouri tunes and fiddlers, produced by Voyager Recordings and Publications, is enclosed with this book, and an index provides information on the tunes and players. The CD offers audible snapshots of the music and musicians, and it augments the CD that accompanied the 2012 book *Play Me Something Quick and Devilish.*

"Here Lies the Most Famous Old Time Violin Player of Northwest Mo." Among many evidences of fiddlers of former times for whom we have little information is the tombstone of William Tibbs Lafever (1852–1924) of the Camden community in Ray County. (Photo by Jerry Garrett, 2007)

When the first book came out, I began receiving readers' questions about fiddlers left out. Dozens of names of musicians appear in the two books, but, due to limitations of space, only an arbitrary selection could be presented. The fiddlers who are profiled in the two books do not represent any sort of "hall of fame"; they are people about whom research (and sometimes recordings) is available. In many cases, particular fiddlers were included because of their relevance to a particular historical topic. One of the difficult jobs in the research and writing of this book was selecting fiddlers and musicians to include. Out of hundreds of possibilities, whose story would illuminate a historical theme or musical discussion? Who would be given only in cameo, and who would get fuller exposure?

I have often had to inform people that a certain fiddler was being "saved," as it were, for discussion in a further publication. A number of prominent names come up again and again in both books. Many names given a spotlight in *Fiddler's Dream* will be familiar to aficionados of fiddle history, such as Lonnie Robertson and Claude Williams. It has been a pleasure to bring a number of other fine fiddlers, who were scarcely known outside their communities, such as Bert Lewis and Bill White, to broader appreciation, as well as fiddlers known primarily in country music shows and the commercial music industry, like Zed Tennis and Ishmael (Ozark Red) Loveall. Even as this volume was being finished, I learned of fiddlers' names for which little information has come to light.

Transcriptions and Traditional Music

The sample transcriptions of tunes were prepared by Amber Gaddy, Gus Garelick, Sharon Graf, Jack Tuttle, Philip K. Vinyard, Stuart Williams, and Matthew Wyatt. Transcriptions are set in standard musical notation. The transcriptions were checked by Columbia violinist Rebecca Smith (thank you, Rebecca!).

In some cases, bowings are suggested as well as recommended chords for accompanists. Ingredients such as bowings are crucial to a fiddler's own style and musical personality, but like other pieces of the puzzle, a fiddler may very well change his or her bowings over many years of performance and in the never-ending creative tinkering with melody, phrasing, bowings, note choices, and more that is essential among the scores of fiddlers I have known throughout my life.

The chords that may be used by the fiddler's "backup," "second," "accompanist," and "rhythm" may also vary, according to factors such as the accompanist's knowledge of the tune, the accompanist's skill, the fiddler's preferences (which may change over time

Archives offer treasure troves of documentation, and sometimes a photo appears with scant but tantalizing notes; "Klein brothers, Sedalia, Mo., 1939," Vanishing Missouri Collection, Missouri State Archives. (Courtesy Missouri State Archives)

and even according to who is providing the accompaniment on what instrument), and the inherited custom for the chord changes (progression) in the locale where the music is recorded. An old-time fiddler may prefer a certain chord progression in an old tune like "Billy in the Low Ground," while a fiddler espousing bluegrass styles may prefer a different chord progression—and the swing fiddler yet another set of changes. All these things increase the importance of paying attention to the traditions of the region or town where the music is made and, for the accompanist, to beware the tempting facility of copying chords from Internet sites and tune books published about fiddling in other regions and traditions.

Personal variation is a cornerstone of folk music, so these musical examples should not be considered "the best" or "ideal" settings. Variation and improvisation have always been characteristics of fiddling, so the aim of these transcriptions is to capture the essence of a tune as played at one moment in time. Having said that, these examples are good ones to speak for the musicians and fit representations of their style and time period. Transcriptions serve as one sort of guide that can be used in learning and performing tunes. In a number of cases, the transcriptions are based on the recordings on the Voyager Recordings and Publications companion CD that comes with this book.

Remember that musical notes written down on a piece of paper cannot truly represent a player's versatility, depth, and music. Notation can represent only the way

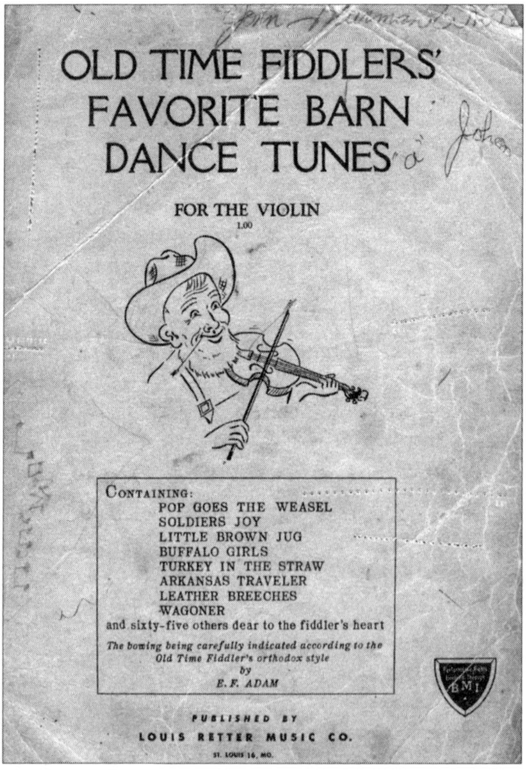

In 1929, among self-published volumes of tunes "dear to the fiddler's heart" included the St. Louis violin-maker Ernst F. Adam's *Old Time Fiddlers' Favorite Barn Dance Tunes*—prized by fiddlers who could "cipher the chicken scratches" or, perhaps, have a pianist friend pick out the melody. (Courtesy John T. White)

a fiddler played a tune on a given day and time in history, and it is well known that fiddlers seldom play a tune the same way again. With no orchestra conductor or sheet music to try to adhere to, in the hands of a traditional fiddler a tune may well change over time as it is played and tinkered with through the years. The notes on paper represent the bare bones, the skeleton; in live performance the notes become music.

The 2012 book discusses the matter of musical literacy and its spread among supposedly "self-taught" fiddlers. Many players of traditional music do not read music, of course, and are proud of it, assuming that illiteracy somehow provides a stamp of cool or "more traditional" on their playing. But since Victorian times, the number of note readers has been growing. This trend, more and more evident today, is particularly audible (and visible) among younger players because of the influence within the world of old-time music of star fiddlers who have had at least some formal training through Suzuki lessons or—usually "and"—classical violin lessons. Does the influence of the classically trained players—typically with superior violinistic skills of intonation, playing in tune, and bowing, especially in the influential venues of the fiddlers contest and convention stages as well as fiddle "workshops"—affect the presumably more traditional or folklike habits and expectations of performance style and repertoire? Certainly.

Fiddlers who are ear musicians, and who value the older generation's great personal variety in performance style, seldom play a tune the same way twice. For the transcriptions, remember that the moment when a recording was made may have been when the player was having a bad day or when he or she was in advanced years or poor health and not playing with the command and finesse celebrated in the younger days. Most transcriptions are made by listening to recordings, further distancing the transcription from live performance because the transcriber is not able to watch the fiddler or ask questions. In transcriptions, therefore, while the written basic melody is usually close to correct if not spot-on, such details as indications of up-bows and down-bows are difficult to prove perfectly correct. And remember that the notation is based on that one recorded or observed performance, which for old-time fiddlers would have been different, if only slightly, the next time the fiddler played that melody.

All these things, and other elements, mean that transcriptions are starting points but not blueprints to be slavishly followed. The transcription is a useful reference and inspiration for creativity and completion, like the floor plan of a house scribbled on the back of an envelope and handed to a carpenter. The transcription indicates a rough outline from which a fiddler or carpenter will employ his or her mind and tools at hand to bring the music or the building to life.

As a multidisciplinary study in local cultural heritage, in tone and style *Fiddler's Dream* seeks to encourage interest among general readers as well as researchers, scholars, and aficionados of American fiddling. This book and accompanying CD are a tribute to the musicians, family members, and friends who have loved this living heritage and carried it forward to new generations. I appreciate their generosity and willingness to share their stories and music.

Acknowledgments

I grew up in a family that loved telling stories about local history. They came to central Missouri from Virginia, North Carolina, Kentucky, and West Virginia. In each generation since the early 1800s, there have been musicians, from church choir tenors, dancing masters, and fiddlers to marching-band cornetists, ukulele-strumming flappers, a New York City opera singer, and one rock-and-roll star.

Although my academic focus has been vernacular architecture and material culture, I have always been a musician and interested in the documentation of fiddling and fiddlers. Many people helped me with advice, assistance, and inspiration, and I thank Paul Anastasio, Dave Barnes, Cathy Barton and Dave Para, Michael Breid, Kyle Brown, Jack Burlison, Leroy Canaday, Robert Cathey, David Cavins, Terry Cunningham, Linda Danielson, Larry Ellis, Amber Gaddy, Gus Garelick, Jerry Garrett, Cecil Goforth, Kathy Gordon, Sharon Graf, Dan Grotewohl, Greg Harmon, Mike Hartgrove, Warren Helton, Julie Henigan, Clifford Hill, Lew Holt, Donna Taylor Hook, Jim Hoots, Lonnie and Charlene Hoppers, Gerald Jones, Kelly and Shirley Jones, Mary Larsen, Billy Lee, Brad Leftwich, Rich Levine, Belinda Luke, Sharon and Nicole Marriott, Mike Matney, Jim McCarty, Homer McCullom, Jim McGreevy, Kelly McIniry, Ed and Blanche McKinney, Michael Mendelson, Jack Oliver, Jim Orchard, Dale Pauley, Russ Ravert, Dave Reiner, Jim Russell, Judy Scheurer, Geoff Seitz, H. K. Silvey, Larry Sledge, Don and Barbara Stevens, John G. Stewart, Janet Taber, Charlie Walden, Tom West, John R. White, Phil and Vivian Williams, Roger Williams, Stuart Williams, Musial Wolfe, and Matt and Allen Wyatt.

My colleagues Thomas A. Adler and Drew Beisswenger made important suggestions for improvement. Those who read early versions of parts of the manuscript and advised improvements include Terry Cunningham, Chuck Haddix, Lonnie and Charlene Hoppers, Gordon McCann, Ed McKinney, Jim Nelson, Dan William Peek, Russ Ravert, Heather Roberson, and Jim Ruth. I am grateful to David Cavins for assistance with digital photography, sound recordings, and website assistance. Voyager Recordings and Publications produced the companion music CD that accompanies this book, which is an essential part of the project.

Vivian Williams suggested useful changes as I completed the final draft. I thank Clair Willcox, Sara Davis, Mary Conley, and other staff at the University of Missouri Press for their patience, and I thank editor Annette Wenda for her many improvements to the final draft.

Some of the material in this book grew from articles in such journals as the *Missouri Historical Review*, *Fiddler Magazine*, *Missouri Folklore Society Journal*, *Devil's Box*, *Old-Time Herald*, and *MSOTFA Quarterly*.

I also wish to thank my children, Sandy, Holly, John, and Heather, for their encouragement, and my wife, Margot Ford McMillen, for advice and encouragement.

Abbreviations

Beisswenger and McCann	Drew Beisswenger and Gordon McCann, *Ozarks Fiddle Music: 308 Tunes Featuring 30 Legendary Fiddlers with Selections from 50 Other Great Ozarks Fiddlers*
Christeson 1	R. P. Christeson, *The Old-Time Fiddler's Repertory*, vol. 1
Christeson 2	R. P. Christeson, *The Old-Time Fiddlers Repertory*, vol. 2
Cole's	M. M. Cole, *One Thousand Fiddle Tunes*
Good Tune	Howard W. Marshall et al., *"Now That's a Good Tune": Masters of Traditional Missouri Fiddling*
Mel Bay	Mel Bay Publications, Pacific, MO
MSOTFA	Missouri State Old Time Fiddlers Association, Columbia
Play Me Something Quick and Devilish	Howard Wight Marshall, *Play Me Something Quick and Devilish: Old-Time Fiddlers in Missouri*
Ryan's	William Bradbury Ryan, *Ryan's Mammoth Collection of 1050 Reels and Jigs*

Fiddler's Dream

The Seitz Violin Shop in the old Carondelet neighborhood of south St. Louis is a magnet for violinists of all stripes, and old-time fiddle sessions are apt to break out when the occasion permits. Such places are informal people's museums as well as a source for instruments, repairs, and advice. Missouri has several violin shops of this depth and quality, including Wyatt Violin Shop on the west side of the state in Independence. (Courtesy Geoff Seitz)

Introduction

> **Our reception exceeded our expectations. We found nothing but civility, elegance, and plenty. After the usual refreshments, and the usual conversation, the evening came upon us. The carpet was then rolled off the floor; the musician was called, and the whole company was invited to dance, nor did ever fairies trip with greater alacrity. The general air of festivity, which predominated in this place, so far remote from all those regions the mind has been used to contemplate as the mansions of pleasure, struck the imagination with a delightful surprise, analogous to that which is felt at an expected immersion from darkness into light.**
>
> —Samuel Johnson (1775), quoted in Peter Levi, ed., *A Journey to the Western Islands of Scotland: James Boswell, the Journal of a Tour to the Hebrides*

This is a book about local history and the fiddle and dance music of people across our society for whom "old-time music" is part of lives and pleasures. It is marvelous to know that, in many ways, little has changed in the traditions of homemade music and hospitality since Dr. Johnson's rambles in Scotland 250 years ago. In continuing the saga from the 2012 volume, the time line in this book brings us from the 1920s into the early 1960s. Because the first book presents much of the historical and cultural framework, readers are encouraged to consult the 2012 volume for this contextual information.

Because this book begins where the 2012 *Play Me Something Quick and Devilish: Old-Time Fiddlers in Missouri* wound down—the 1920s—it will be helpful to recall major themes presented in that book. Let's review. A small, portable musical instrument, the violin/fiddle had already enjoyed a lively heritage by the time the American Midwest was settled; it was the most commonplace musical instrument on the trans-Mississippi frontier, just as it was back in Virginia and the Carolinas. In a chronology moving through periods of European and European-American settlement, the 2012 book introduced the fiddle and dance traditions brought to the Missouri Territory and state. Much of this music was inherited from Britain and Europe, and much of it had percolated through generations of experience and evolution, especially (but not exclusively) in the eastern and southeastern United States, before being transplanted to Missouri.

The early phase from the later 1700s to the very early 1900s was marked by the tendency of certain ethnic communities and settlement populations to add their folk dances and fiddle tunes to the growing profile that began, tentatively, in colonial French villages founded by Canadian French explorers, voyageurs, and miners along both sides of the Mississippi River, principally from the St. Louis area south to New Orleans. Few and fragile are the traces of the old French fiddle music, and it was supplanted in the early 1800s, first by the British Isles–related reels, jigs, and hornpipes flowing into Missouri with old-stock Americans from Kentucky, Tennessee, the Carolinas, and Virginia and then, a few decades later, by the addition of dances and tunes brought by German-speaking immigrants—the great couple dances such as the schottische, polka, and, especially, the waltz.

The 2012 book brought to light many other features of the fiddler's world that help us understand the influence of the fiddle/violin in daily life and in the broader changes taking place in society and culture. These things, all intertwined with "old-time fiddling" and dancing, include such elements as the rise in popularity and influence of military bands with their newfangled brass instruments during and after the Civil War era; the continuing evolution of the minstrel stage; the growth of musical literacy (notably with the many German-speaking music teachers coming to Missouri after the Civil War); the railroad boom with its many immigrants and Civil War veterans laying track and playing fiddle music at night in camp; the evolution of ragtime, early jazz, and Tin Pan Alley music publishing as new fulcrums for popular music composition and performance and the crossovers with old-time music; and, in the twenties, the vast changes brought through commercial recordings and radio broadcasting into even the most remote community.

By the 1920s there was access for the first time, by almost anyone, to a violin. From the late 1800s, mail-order catalogs were bringing affordable, serviceable violins in the thousands from European shops and companies. Violins, as well as commercial records, phonographs, radios, books of printed melodies, banjos, parlor organs, guitars, and countless other goods, flowed into Missouri homes in cities, small towns, and seemingly isolated residences. Imported European "factory Strads," modeled on old Italian master instruments, were typically sold in mail-order catalogs. These shop violins from Europe (mainly Germany, Austria, and France) were of varied levels of quality. Sold in the millions by a flourishing import market, these violins and bows helped democratize the violin and encouraged the spread of all sorts of performance styles and repertoires, from old to new, "square-dance fiddling" to jazz.

The vast majority of old violins we see today being played in Missouri, especially by older musicians, are mail-order catalog violins from Sears, Roebuck or from Montgomery Ward and made between 1880 and the 1930s. Unknown additional numbers of European violins came to the United States as war souvenirs as veterans returned from the First and Second World Wars. In addition, Missouri, like other states, always had many professional and amateur violin makers (a subject to be taken up in a future publication). The violin became the most popular and commonly played musical instrument in early Missouri and through most of the generations that followed, to be joined in the late 1800s by the upright piano and, finally in the World War II years, by the guitar as America's favorite instruments for people making their own music.

It was an exciting time. Inspired by hearing a recording of "Turkey in the Straw," "When Irish Eyes Are Smiling," "Lauterbach," or "Kansas City Kitty" on a 78 rpm record, or in a broadcast, a person could order the recording and the machine that would play it again and again and a violin on which to work out how to play the music for oneself. The mail-order catalog became everyone's "wish book," encyclopedia, and gateway—yesterday's Amazon, *Wikipedia*, and eBay.

One can appreciate the post–World War I era and the 1920s Jazz Age as a time of great change, and this is where I chose to close *Play Me Something Quick and Devilish* and continue the discussion in this further volume.

One of the lasting notions about the violin is that it is an instrument of the devil. The devilish connotations and contexts of fiddle and dance were not diminished with time; the Roaring Twenties and the Prohibition era (1920–33) would add greatly to the boozy and raucous stereotypes that many people continue to hold. The federal Prohibition legislation, meant to make liquor and its social problems go away, in fact had the opposite effect, with the nation's newfound love of alcohol and its racy context of illegal nightclubs and related activities. The thousands of doughboys returning from France after the German surrender at the end of World War I, having borne the terrors of trench warfare and mustard gas, and having also seen and sampled the wonders of nightlife in wide-open Paris ("Gay Paree," as songs described it), would no longer be shy, innocent farm boys, college kids, and factory lads; the widening liberties of the Roaring Twenties and the Jazz Age would suit most of them just fine.

It was commonplace for older fiddlers of my acquaintance to recollect those wild times of the twenties as a time of moonshine and fast living; a lot of fiddlers, like a lot of jazz musicians, felt it appropriate to consume quantities of alcoholic libations when performing at a dance or jam session. It is no wonder that a lot of church people began to excavate from dusty sermons the old fears and perceive anew the ancient devilish connections between social dancing and fiddling and alcoholism and delinquency.

AM radio proved to be one of the most influential forces in the continuing evolution of fiddle music. With the many stations that broadcast in the 1920s and 1930s, new arenas, new audiences, and a chance to earn a living performing music opened up for fiddlers with the right mix of skill and ambition. Lonnie Robertson, one of Missouri's best-known radio fiddlers, is prominent in this discussion. During the World War II years, Robertson teamed up with guitarist and singer Roy McGeorge to form "Lonnie and Roy," a duo who sang and played mandolin (Robertson) and guitar, typical of the so-called brother-duet style of the 1930s radio, concert, and recording scene. Roy McGeorge and Lonnie Robertson, as well as Howe Teague and Emmett Heath, offer good examples of the young musicians who sought careers in AM radio in the 1920s into the 1960s and became celebrities far beyond their native turfs.

Some Missouri fiddlers left for the West in the twentieth century. Missouri was prominent as the starting block and great funnel in pioneering the western United States following the Louisiana Purchase of 1803 and ensuing Lewis and Clark Expedition (1804–6), during the western trails period and decades of mining booms in the Civil War period, and once more during the Great Depression and World War II era in the mid-twentieth century. If we notice fiddlers who got their grounding in Missouri before heading to California or New Mexico or Washington State, the

Springfield's KWTO was a leading regional radio station and launching pad for country music stars and professionals. Four Missouri fiddlers on KWTO in the 1940s on shows such as "Korn's-A-Krackin" and "The Farm and Home Hour." *Left to right*: Lenny Aleshire, Buster Fellows, Slim Wilson (primarily a guitarist and vocalist), and Red Loveall. (Courtesy Michael Breid)

familiar generalization about Missouri's role in the history of the American West is considerably enhanced.

Fiddlers going west—whether in a steamboat thrashing upriver, nursing a Conestoga wagon and mule team, bumping along in an expensive stagecoach to the gold camps or open range or new farmland, aboard a steamship rounding Cape Horn for California, or later in a railroad carriage—took their music with them. Other new forces, depicted in Hollywood movies such as John Steinbeck's *The Grapes of Wrath*, moved displaced families of the Dust Bowl and Great Depression of the 1930s toward better circumstances and opportunities. The World War II years did the same, when people sought work in war matériel factories and shipyards on the West Coast. In this volume, several players are highlighted, such as Earl Willis, Ron Hughey, and Ishmael (Ozark Red) Loveall, who continued and evolved their music in the West and became known there as influential "Missouri fiddlers" and radio performers.

A chapter takes up fiddlers contests from the 1920s into the World War II years, when fiddlers' competitions sprouted across the nation. In the 1920s, fiddlers competed in live contests broadcast from the early radio station WOS (Watch Our State) in Jefferson City, and these broadcasts were heard as far away as Cuba, Hawaii, and Canada. This is the decade when fiddlers contests emerged from the occasional fish fry or county fair event to become a major force and influence in traditional fiddle music.

The 1920s impetus for contesting dwindled during the hard times and World War II years, but competitions surged back in the 1950s. Contests evolved in tandem with the Folk Music Revival of the 1960s, the resurgence of string bands (based on the classic 1920s and 1930s period of 78 rpm records and radio), the nascent cultural arts agencies (with state and federal funding for folk music programming), and the emergence of fiddlers' associations devoted to hosting contests as a way to try to help

Cultural Regions of Missouri. The sheer acreage of the Ozarks region makes it a substantial portion of Missouri's landmass, but Little Dixie is also a large cultural-geographic region; both regions represent broad fiddle styles and both regions feature a variety of other styles. In the late twentieth century, non-regional fiddle styles (swing, bluegrass) became prominent. (Walter A. Schroeder and Howard W. Marshall, refined by James D. Harlan, 1998)

conserve what the associations and contest promoters considered to be authentic old-time fiddling.

It is only in 2010 that the last of the live AM radio country shows in Missouri expired, Ron Lutz's *Rooster Creek Show* in Fulton. "Country radio" on the FM band has obliterated AM broadcasting, and FM has grown exponentially with the "Top 40"–style Nashville shows that seem to program the same list of country hits; to some listeners, the Nashville music is more akin to rock and roll and rap than old-time hillbilly music. The popular NPR show *Prairie Home Companion* brings regional musicians to a national audience, but only the small independent "community radio" FM stations broadcast community old-time music to help hold back the tide. In Missouri these include KDHX in St. Louis, KMST in Rolla, and KOPN in Columbia as well as broadcasting over the Internet.

The recording industry and the country music oprys, jamborees, "barn dances," and other kinds of shows helped spread fiddle music across the continent and far beyond. The country music show in the small-town theater is alive and in decent health in Missouri. And of course, an entertainment industry thrives in the neon Xanadus of "Branson U.S.A.," but much has been stored in the attic in the processes of modern reinvention, extreme professionalization, further commercialization, and homogenization of what people still call country music.

North Missouri glaciated landscape, North Fabius River, Schuyler County, four miles south of the Iowa border on US 36. (April 2015)

Bluegrass music evolved in the 1940s under the hand of its "father," Bill Monroe. Bluegrass is a complex amalgam of old-time fiddling, country blues, gospel-singing vocal styles, and an ensemble sound crafted more for the radio broadcast, record store, festival, and concert than the old-time dance. In its early years, bluegrass was programmed on opry shows and radio as hillbilly or country music. In the 1960s, bluegrass would solidify its identity as a separate but closely related genre of traditional music. Fiddlers aspiring to professional careers in hillbilly music and shows in the 1940s and 1950s needed to be versatile and adept at different styles of music—and bluegrass became one of them.

As seen in *Play Me Something Quick and Devilish*, early jazz and swing were important in the evolution of fiddling styles and repertoire. Many of us hold the stereotype of fiddle music simply as inherited relics of British Isles hornpipes and reels with dollops of German American dance tunes and waltzes. But the story is more complex. While many fiddlers did work to carry on their legacy of nineteenth-century fiddling, most older fiddlers of my acquaintance play many Tin Pan Alley compositions as well as versions of early jazz standards they heard on 78 rpm records by thrilling jazz pioneers such as Joe Venuti.

In the 1930s and 1940s, the jazz-influenced, musically literate musicians in "western swing" bands such as Bob Wills and His Texas Playboys made western swing a permanent cog in the nation's traditional musical genres. The fiddle was and remains the essential hub in a western-swing ensemble. Among Missourians who played important roles in the development of "Nashville" fiddling was Dale Potter. Potter grew up in the Bootheel region (not usually known for its fiddlers), fiddling for pie suppers, square dances, and live radio shows and competing in fiddlers contests. Potter became famous after he moved to Nashville and helped invent "country and western" fiddle styles as a session man on Hank Williams's hit records in the post–World War II years.

A Few More Words on Styles and Violinistic Skills in Old-Time Fiddling

There are many styles of old-time fiddling, perhaps as many as there are fiddlers. In *Play Me Something Quick and Devilish* in 2012, we spoke about efforts to identify and categorize the fiddling characteristic of Missouri's major cultural-geographic regions. There are broad patterns of style that can be seen as representative of certain regions, communities, and eras in history. These broad "old-time" fiddle styles in Missouri have been marked off with some measure of utility as Ozark style, Little Dixie style, and North Missouri (Missouri Valley) style. These regional styles evolved in the mid-twentieth century.

Other major styles hew less to region and settlement history and more to changes in vernacular music and society. These modern styles, which today represent their own columns of attention, include western swing of the 1930s (which owed much to musical literacy and recordings by jazz violinist Joe Venuti), bluegrass fiddling (indebted to blues and early jazz), the generalized superregional American fiddle style developing especially in the 1960s and 1970s and often called festival style (a.k.a. Appalachian or "mountain style"), and today's hyperperfect National Contest style (a.k.a. "Weiser style") with its debt to Texas and Oklahoma virtuosos and swing guitar accompaniment.

So, in the 1920s, the profile was well established for most fiddlers who performed in public and in contests and played for dances. At that time, commercial recordings and broadcasts were having an impact on how fiddlers played, and even on these there were smooth, "notey" fiddlers and there were "rough" shuffle-bow fiddlers. Nationally, there was a "smooth school" of fiddling, represented on the recordings by professional violinists such as Charles D'Almaine and Don Richardson, as well as by more stereotypical old-time fiddlers who also played smooth and notey, such as Eck Robertson and Lowe Stokes. In many cases, the professional violinist-fiddlers such as D'Almaine and Richardson opened up new worlds for local fiddlers when first they heard them on an Edison cylinder or a 78 rpm record of their fiddling.

This was the case with young Milo McCubbin of Cross Timbers (presented in the first book), who thrilled to Don Richardson's "Arkansas Traveler" and "Durang's Hornpipe" with piano accompaniment on 78 rpm records on his family's hand-cranked Victrola in 1916. McCubbin—and many other people—also listened to other Richardson recordings of well-known fiddle tunes such as "Red Wing," "Ricketts Hornpipe," "Mississippi Sawyer," "Heel and Toe Polka" ("Jenny Lind Polka"), "Miss McLeod's Reel," "Irish Washerwoman," and "Old Zip Coon" ("Turkey in the Straw"), and some fiddlers who heard these recordings began to seek to play in a smoother and more precise and single-string style than that of the more typical "rough school" old-time fiddler.

The early commercial recordings helped bring attention to the more "notey" melodic styles and the single-string bowing of trained commercial fiddler-violinists such as D'Almaine and Richardson, and other fiddlers began to admire technically superior skills of bowing, intonation, and playing in tune. One might even suggest that the early 1900s violinist-fiddlers were a strong link in the chain from the regional rough-and-ready, older styles of the local square-dance fiddler to the refined and polished skills in jazz, western swing, country music, and bluegrass as well as fiddlers contest champions. This helped lead to what can be called the two main schools of fiddling: the smooth school of old-time fiddling and the rough school of old-time fiddling. This formulation helps describe major approaches to playing fiddle music today.

While many adherents are devoted to the rough school, the smooth school appears to be winning out. The trend toward smooth, buffed fiddle techniques is given force by the importance of festivals, contests, and fiddle camps as prime venues where many young people and their parents may first encounter live fiddle music. Contests and festivals brought out the more creative and "hot" musicians; listeners who saw only the stage show or contest may have missed hearing other different styles of playing in parking-lot or campground jam sessions.

But, of course, music does not stand still. While this book focuses on the 1920–60 years, the music continues, and many of the stories in this volume go past the 1960s to the present. The ways old-time fiddle and dance music moved forward through the twentieth century and the ways fiddlers responded to change—rejecting, accommodating to, or fully embracing ineffable evolution—are really the focus of this book.

The Musslin Sisters, Gertrude (*Left*: violin and guitar) and Jean, when they were performing as a sister duet on WHB AM, Kansas City, in the early 1950s. (Courtesy Loretta Nye)

Radio Fiddlers 1

Radio must be considered, not as a form of art, but as a means of conveying art to the multitudes. When so considered, its invention may be counted as being as important as the invention of printing was to literature.

—Rupert Hughes (1903), quoted in Deems Taylor and Russell Kerr, eds., *Music Lover's Encyclopedia by Rupert Hughes*

The decades of the 1920s to the 1960s were marked by profound changes to cultural traditions, with the rapid expansion into American life of innovations like the telephone, automobiles, and movies, as well as new media like sound recordings and modern sheet-music publishing.[1] For music, radio was the great catalyst (even more than records), enhancing and popularizing existing community traditions while pushing forward their continuing evolution. Anyone with access to a radio—whether purchased or handmade—now could listen to a wide range of music from other places and other cultures, transforming tastes, attitudes, and traditions. For fiddlers, radio would come to mean a larger stage and vastly more cross-pollination of styles and tunes.

Broadcasts from across the continent could be heard on the early "radio sets" of all kinds from companies such as Westinghouse, Atwater-Kent, and RCA. In the early days, people could assemble their own sets from vacuum tubes, receivers, triode amplifiers, Bakelite dials, loudspeakers, headphones, antennas, and other accessories from a Sears, Roebuck or a Montgomery Ward catalog or from the local department store. Such radios were often powered by an automobile battery; electric service was still sparse and unpredictable in the early 1900s, especially in remote areas. Some people put together even more basic and inexpensive "crystal sets," which did not need vacuum tubes, separate sources of electricity, or elaborate parts.[2]

Newspapers ran columns about the new technology.[3] Just as with the spread of phonographs, automobiles, telephones, electricity, and impressive (but dangerous) new mechanized farm equipment, the language was as new as the machines. A handy individual with a few tools could wire his radio to his flivver. From the *Monroe County (MO) Appeal* in 1923:

Runs Radio with His Ford

With $32 worth of radio parts and a battery from his Ford car Emmett Bourne, near Fairview, listens on the world by day and by night, being in touch with stations which send out current news and entertainment numbers all the way from Cuba to the Pacific Coast, from Canada to the Gulf. . . .

Those who say the radio will revolutionize life for the farm are right. It revolutionizes his bedtime for a starter. Instead of going to roost with the chickens, he becomes a night owl, sitting at his instrument and reveling in entertainments, free of cost, by talent equal to the best of Chautauqua circuits.

. . . [T]he family sits down to such an entertainment bill of fare as it never dreamed of listening to a few years ago.

. . . [W]e supplement the battery that comes with the machine with the battery from our Ford car. (Electric lines had not yet reached his farm.) When it begins to run down we hitch it to the outfit with which our house is supplied with water (a windmill or a well pump) and give it a charge. My advice to every farmer is to get one of these outfits and bring the world to his sitting room.[4]

The sound of the human voice was exciting, and just as enthralling was the music, giving many people their first exposure to grand opera, dance orchestras, Irish tenors, gospel quartet, and old-time fiddling.[5] It became apparent that "popular" music in various forms would rule the airwaves, especially live programs featuring people and musicians from the radio station's principal listening area. Old-time fiddling exhibitions and early forms of swing and jazz music soon outgunned the symphony and the opera icon the Great Caruso, as local stations developed their own programs that sounded like entertainments of the past, such as minstrel shows, vaudeville routines, and fiddlers' frolics. The new technology meant that people could listen from distant places instantaneously and share the experience with family, friends, and fellow musicians. A fiddler listening to a radio program could pick up a telephone and alert others to an especially exciting performance. (While electric power would reach some communities only after World War II, most people had access to a telephone in the 1920s.)

Pioneer Radio Fiddlers

The first fiddler to perform on live radio seems to have been Fiddlin' John Carson of Georgia, over an Atlanta station in September 1922.[6] A railroad laborer, farmer, jockey, and moonshiner, John Carson made 78 rpm records for Okeh in 1923, soon after the first commercial fiddle records made for RCA in New York City in 1922 by Eck Robertson and Henry Gilliland. Carson played a violin his grandfather had brought from Ireland in 1800.

A number of string bands became popular on records and radio, including groups offering contemporary dance music of the times as well as familiar old breakdowns and waltzes. Fox-trots, rags, and blues music were becoming part of the old-time fiddler's repertoire, and old-time string bands often found themselves working the new dance tunes into their sets in order to stay busy performing and earning money. It was a lively time of experimentation. New branches of the old oak were budding. In 1925 the recording industry standardized the 78 rpm record, opening the way to the growth of commercial sound recordings in local stores and mail-order catalogs. The early radio fiddlers, like Uncle Jimmy Thompson, were followed by fiddlers such as Clark Kessinger, Curly Fox, Fiddlin' Arthur Smith, Dale Potter, Tommy Magness, Chubby Wise, Robert (Georgia Slim) Rutland, Howdy Forrester, Tommy Jackson, and from Canada Don Messer.[7]

East Tennessee radio fiddler Curly Fox (Armin Leroy Fox) had fiddled with vaudeville and medicine shows in Tennessee and began his radio career in 1932 in Atlanta. He performed on *The Grand Ole Opry* through much of the 1930s and 1940s and joined with Texas Ruby in the later 1930s to become a favorite duet on Saturday night. Fox was among the modern fiddlers whose intricate noting, double-stops, and bow movements separated their styles from most of the popular old-time fiddlers in the commercial arena. One of Fox's exhibition pieces was the venerable "Listen to the Mocking Bird" (also spelled "Mockingbird"), a dressed-up fiddle version of the Civil War–era ballad.[8]

During the 1930s, when fiddle music was still called hillbilly music, a West Tennessee–bred railroad worker named Arthur Smith, whose recordings and performances were heard on radio across the nation, became an early and lasting influence across the genres of old-time fiddling and country music. His recordings from the 1930s with musicians like the Delmore Brothers and Sam and Kirk McGee remain essential listening.[9] Known as "Fiddlin' Arthur Smith," he displayed much of the smoothness, elegance, and drive that would be important in the evolution of bluegrass fiddling during the World War II years. Although Smith made his musical career just before Bill Monroe hammered out "bluegrass," his thumbprints are all over bluegrass fiddling. His smooth and bluesy style, adding fast-paced, driving breakdowns, brought new things to fiddling, and his so-called long bow style (achieved as much through smoothness rather than long bow strokes) was much imitated.

Arthur Smith's 78 rpm records, such as "Blackberry Blossom" and "Red Apple Rag" (Smith's first record, on Blue Bird), followed by instrumentals such as "Fiddler's Dream," "Sugar Tree Stomp," "Smith's Reel," "Bill Cheatem," "Indian Creek," and "Peacock Rag," several of which he is credited with composing, went into the old-time and bluegrass fiddlers' repertoire.[10] Many of these classics were recorded on RCA Victor with the Delmores, sometimes along with popular vocal numbers and under the title "Arthur Smith Trio." Not everyone liked Smith's music, in part because his "modern" fiddling was so popular that his style began to drown out some local traditional fiddling styles, reflecting the sharp competition and jealousies between adherents of different fiddle styles heard in 1920s contests that continue today.

Several "Arthur Smith tunes" became popular on the fiddlers contest circuit in Missouri. "Fiddler's Dream" became the signature of Boone County champion fiddler Pete McMahan (see the 2012 *Play Me Something Quick and Devilish*); Pete had a sign over the gate to his front yard in Harrisburg with "Fiddler's Dream" on it. Columbia fiddler Aaron Oliver, a contest fiddler and in the generation before McMahan's, was a close student of Arthur Smith's radio broadcasts and records. Oliver's nephew Jack Oliver recalled in a 2013 interview that his uncle played a very similar style to Smith's and, when listening to Smith on *The Grand Ole Opry*, would comment that "he missed a turn" when Smith would play a wrong note or make a bowing slip or do something different or perceived as being different from the record or the way Smith played it over the radio broadcast a week or two before.

In the late 1930s, Arthur Smith performed for a time with two other young fiddling firebrands, Howard (Howdy) Forrester and Robert (Georgia Slim) Rutland, and a string band called the Tennessee Valley Boys. The combination of these three innovative fiddlers must have been a delight to behold; unfortunately, no commercial recordings exist. Smith was also a brilliant contest fiddler. He played in radio and vaudeville shows, where on several amazing occasions he, Clark Kessinger, Rutland, Natchee the Indian, Clayton McMichen, and other hot fiddlers performed in openly rigged contests, to the delight of their theater and radio audiences. Winners were decided by audience applause. Smith ranged widely in his ensembles and recordings. At one point, in October 1940, Smith made outstanding recordings of "K. C. Stomp," "Smith's Rag," "Peacock Rag," "Crazy Blues," and "Bill Cheatham" on Bluebird, with Clyde Moody (guitar), Bill Westbrooks (bass), and Tommy Magness (second violin), who were members of Bill Monroe's Blue Grass Boys.[11] Like many popular radio performers, Smith issued publications aimed at his fan base. He produced two song folios featuring songs from his recordings and appearances.[12]

Unlike other commercial musicians from Nashville, Arthur Smith was considered a "folk performer" during the Folk Music Revival in the 1960s and invited to folk festivals. Folk groups such as the New Lost City Ramblers helped bring attention to Smith, who, his performing career having evaporated in the 1950s, had been working as a carpenter in Nashville and was brought back to much acclaim. His "Peacock Rag," accompanied by the Delmores from their 1941 record, is included in an LP sampler, *"That's My Rabbit, My Dog Caught It": Traditional Southern Instrumental Styles.*[13] Thanks to New Lost City Ramblers cofounder Mike Seeger, Smith appeared with the McGee brothers at the 1965 Newport Folk Festival and was warmly received. In addition, Smith's fiddling was brought back through bluegrass bands such as Flatt and Scruggs and fiddlers such as Paul Warren and Tommy Jackson, who played many of Smith's fine instrumental pieces in their shows and on their recordings.

Tommy Jackson was well known as the staff fiddler on *The Grand Ole Opry* radio program and as a session musician, and he made more fiddle records than anyone in the 1950s and 1960s. Many consider Jackson the most influential fiddler of the era. His first release was a 78 rpm record in 1948 of "Black Mountain Rag" and "Fire on the Mountain." Much influenced by Arthur Smith, in 1953 Jackson began releasing the square-dance LPs that helped make him famous, producing some dozen LPs and thirty singles for the Mercury and Dot labels. These square-dance records, friendly to dance callers as well as musicians, are consistently mentioned by older fiddlers across the United States and Canada as important in their formative years for acquisition of both style and repertoire. Tommy Jackson's "clean, driving, straightforward style won a lot of admirers," and, very significantly, he also loved jazz and swing, listening to Stéphane Grappelli, Bob Wills and the Texas Playboys, and even the modern jazz Dave Brubeck Quartet.[14] Jackson may have wanted to branch out and play more than breakdowns for square-dance records and backup fiddle licks for country singers—but breakdowns and backup were Tommy's bread and butter.[15] Charles Wolfe felt that Jackson, more than any other fiddler, helped keep fiddling alive during the decades when country music was changing into the Nashville sound and "rock and roll threatened to engulf country and bluegrass."[16]

As for other commercial fiddlers whose music was embraced throughout the fiddler's landscape, Tommy Jackson's style could be characterized several ways—especially "old-time" and "bluegrass"—and, in his recordings and commercial career as a session player, he played all sorts of styles as the job or session indicated. Frank Maloy has written that Jackson's "clean, precise technique, and beautiful tonal quality, plus an individual style, made him instantly recognizable to fiddle music fans in all parts of the country."[17]

Tommy Jackson is high on the list of the most copied commercial fiddlers of all time, and his square-dance records and frequent *Grand Ole Opry* radio show appearances exhibited his straight-ahead, hard-driving hoedown style. When he worked as a studio musician for country artists, he altered his style accordingly and was one of the session fiddlers, along with Dale Potter, who helped develop the smooth double-stop fiddle style popular as backup and accent behind singers that has been carried forward by Nashville fiddlers such as Buddy Spicher. Potter (profiled elsewhere in this book) also performed with Red Foley's Pleasant Valley Boys, Ray Price's Cherokee Cowboys, and other prominent country groups.

With the popular country singer Ray Price, Jackson developed the "lonesome fiddle" sound by "spinning sympathetic counterpoints around Price's vocals." Richard Kienzle: "What made Jackson's fiddling so distinctive? Part of it was his abiding admiration for Bob Wills' breakdown fiddling, as well as the improvisational styles of the various swing fiddlers in the Texas Playboys." In order to keep playing open strings, which was part of the Ray Price sound, Jackson tuned higher when necessary, and, at other times, he used a violin capo that Price made for him from a guitar capo. It sounded like trick fiddling, and few fiddlers listening to the records were able to figure out how Jackson did it.[18]

Jackson's 45 rpm and LP records continue to be superb learning tools. He played it straight, and he played it great. In the late 1960s, as I was inching toward playing fiddle music, I nearly wore out two of Tommy's "square dances without calls" records. Jackson took classic tunes like "Cripple Creek" and made a person want to play them like he did. In those days, people loved tunes like "Cripple Creek." Moreover, on these records Jackson is not trying to impress anyone with hot licks; he is laying down strong, driving, clear fiddle music for square dancers.

Jackson was born in Alabama, and his family moved to Nashville when Tommy was one. He grew up in the lively country music capital and soaked up *The Grand Ole Opry* music. He was fiddling in local establishments at seven and playing professionally at twelve. At seventeen he headed his own band, the Tennessee Mountaineers, and soon was performing on the *Opry*. During World War II, Jackson was a B-29 bomber tail gunner in the Pacific theater. After the war, he played with Red Foley and began a steady career, performing and recording with stars such as Hank Williams, Ray Price, and Faron Young, as well as Foley and others. The difficulty of acquiring digital releases of Jackson's fiddling was rectified in 2010 by the British Archive of Country Music's CD *Tommy Jackson.*[19]

Meanwhile, Howdy Forrester was known as Roy Acuff's fiddler. Acuff and His Smoky Mountain Boys was a major *Grand Ole Opry* hillbilly radio band on WSM in Nashville and other stations from the 1930s into the 1980s. Acuff was a solid old-time fiddler and eventually shifted to the role of bandleader, leaving the hot fiddle solos to Benny Martin, Tommy Jackson, Forrester, and others who put in stints as the main fiddler in the group—and especially Tommy Magness.

While Tommy Jackson was in the service during World War II in 1943, Tommy Magness filled in for Jackson with Roy Acuff's band and remained until Forrester's return in 1951.[20] Tommy Magness, also from Tennessee, was the first fiddler to perform with Bill Monroe and His Blue Grass Boys on *The Grand Ole Opry* and had been with Roy Hall and His Blue Ridge Entertainers before working with Monroe.[21] Magness is credited with popularizing "Orange Blossom Special" in radio broadcasts. A 78 rpm album featuring Magness called *Old Time Barn Dance (Square Dances without Calls)* was drawn from a 1949 session of home recordings and is a classic presentation of eight "big" fiddle tunes—"Dance Around Molly," "Black Mountain Rag," "Pretty Little Widow," "Smoky Mountain Rag," "Grey Eagle," "Lonesome Indian," "Bully of the Town," and "Polk County Breakdown."[22]

Versions of "Dance Around Molly," "Black Mountain Rag," "Grey Eagle," "Lonesome Indian," and "Polk County Breakdown" remain solid in the Missouri fiddlers' tune kit. "Polk County Breakdown" is of such popularity in Missouri both as a square-dance tune and as a contest piece that most people assume it was named not for the county in Tommy Magness's home state of Tennessee but for Polk County, Missouri. "Pretty Little Widow" is a variant of the southern tune "Sugar Foot Rag" and usually played by Missouri fiddlers under the latter title. Fiddlin' Arthur Smith's "Smoky Mountain Rag" was later recorded by Kenny Baker, whose version is sometimes heard among bluegrass fiddlers; the old country two-step rag "Bully of the Town" was once well known across Missouri but has lately become a rarity. Tommy Magness's powerful, driving style was influential and carries through into today's bluegrass and contest fiddling, even while recordings are scarce and too few fiddlers are aware of Magness.

Howdy Forrester had played briefly with Bill Monroe and the Blue Grass Boys in the 1940s, before and after his service in World War II. His wife, Goldie Sue (Sally Ann) Forrester, had played accordion (yes, accordion) for three years with the Blue Grass Boys.[23] Howdy settled in a steady job with Acuff and appeared regularly on *The Grand Ole Opry* from 1951 to 1987, when he retired. I well remember being backstage at *The Grand Ole Opry* in the 1970s and being thrilled watching Howdy up close, whose relaxed manner, aplomb, and smooth professionalism were impressive, particularly onstage next to the hillbilly showmanship of Roy Acuff and Bashful Brother Oswald. Forrester's recordings continue to inspire with his power, accent, and superb bowing in the "single-string" and "long-bow" approach to fiddling. These are all characteristics common in some parts of the South, Texas, Missouri, and Canada as well as in the largely nonregional, modern National Contest fiddle style.

Robert (Georgia Slim) Rutland was a fiddler who reached audiences primarily through radio. From Tifton, Georgia, Rutland shared much with the creative, hard-driving "long-bow" fiddlers of the 1940s and 1950s such as Arthur Smith, Howdy Forrester, Tommy Magness, and Tommy Jackson, and he was a close friend of and performed with Forrester. A student of the innovative fiddling of Lowe Stokes and Clayton McMichen, Rutland is best known today for a set of spectacular solo home recordings in the 1950s, released in 1976 on an LP record called *Raw Fiddle*—one of the most interesting fiddle records of all time.[24]

A year after WEW began transmission in 1921 in St. Louis, WOS began broadcasting from the dome of the Missouri state capitol. High above the Missouri River in Jefferson City, this location was the highest in central Missouri and important for early radio transmissions. Beginning in June 1923, WOS routinely programmed live fiddle music, such as from the local champion Louie Barton, in 1924.[25] Other stations followed with old-time fiddling and country music, such as KLWT in Lebanon, KMOX in St. Louis, KFRU in Columbia, KDRO in Sedalia, KRLS in Mountain Grove, WHB in Kansas City, KBTC in Houston ("Keep Boosting Texas County"), KRMS ("K Robert M. Smith") in Osage Beach, KWPM ("Keep West Plains Moving"), KNCM ("K North Central Missouri") in Moberly, and KIRX in Kirksville.

The WOS studios were positioned in the highest point in central Missouri—the dome of the capitol building. (Photo by Jim McCarty, 2015)

Jefferson City's Louie Barton starred on WOS's "Barn Dance" program in 1924 and placed among the top winners in several of the fiddlers contests hosted by the radio station. Barton poses in the studio with George Schrimpf (bass) and guitarist Bryan Williams. (Courtesy Bob Priddy; The State Historical Society of Missouri, #026975)

WOS management let it be known that they would welcome fiddlers and string bands on their live Friday-night fiddling broadcasts as well as in the several contests aired live. Many fiddlers heard the early broadcasts and made appearances at the station, and legislative staff in the capitol may have encouraged fiddlers in their home districts to come to WOS. In time, more than two hundred fiddlers and ensembles would perform on WOS until its closure in 1933 due to the financial exigencies of the Great Depression.

The 1920s studio was primitive by today's standards. Musicians climbed a ladder to a small broadcast booth in the top of the capitol rotunda. Transmission equipment consisted of a single large electric microphone with limited fidelity. Some of the fiddlers who traveled to the capitol in Jefferson City to play over WOS came from distant towns, and some were from nearby; some were well known as contest champions and popular dance fiddlers, and many more were little known outside their own communities.

Elmer Schmutzler, Mount Hope

Among the local fiddlers who gave radio a try was Elmer Schmutzler (1910–96). Schmutzler was part of an old-line Bavarian-Saxon immigrant family in the Mount Hope rural community east of Jefferson City. As a boy, Elmer Schmutzler had taken violin lessons from Professor Oscar H. Petry Sr. (1890–1967), and he developed an appreciation for all kinds of music. Elmer enjoyed fiddling light classical pieces like "The Blue Danube" (Johann Strauss II, 1867), popular dance tunes like "Four Leaf Clover" ("I'm Looking over a Four Leaf Clover," Mort Dixon and Harry M. Woods, 1927), as well as the old square-dance standards such as "Turkey in the Straw."

As Elmer's son, Gary Schmutzler, observes, it was more common for young fiddlers to have some violin training than most people interested in "old-time fiddling" today realize.[26] Popular contest champions such as Daniel Boone Jones and George Morris from across the Missouri River in Boone and Callaway Counties, respectively, had formal violin training, but this deeply suggestive fact has generally been forgotten or, in some cases, purposely minimized (see *Play Me Something Quick and Devilish* for discussion of the increase of musical literacy among traditional fiddlers in early Missouri). Elmer's classical instruction increased his ability to play violin with superior tone and intonation; Mrs. Schmutzler would later tell their children that their father "made the fiddle sing while others played honky tonk style."

Columbia musicians Frank Oliver (guitar, *left*), Aaron Oliver (*center*), and their friend Daniel Boone Jones in a portrait made December 31, 1925, on the day the men drove thirty-five miles south to Jefferson City to compete in the December 31–January 1 two-day fiddlers contest broadcast live over WOS radio. (Courtesy Jack Oliver)

In the late 1920s, Elmer Schmutzler joined a string trio to enter one of the WOS fiddlers contests that were broadcast live from the capitol.[27] Schmutzler played his Hopf-model German-made violin in the contest, but at dances sometimes played mandolin as well as violin. The ensemble included a cousin, fiddler/violinist Herbert Schulz, who lived some two miles from the Schmutzler farm, and an older neighboring farmer, Herman Kraus (roughly age fifty), who played the upright bass. The upright bass (string bass or standup bass) had recently become a familiar part of orchestras and string bands, gradually pushing aside the cello in the role of "bass" accompaniment and rhythm. After the contest, the two boys hurried home to see how their performance sounded. "They performed flawlessly," but "family and friends who had gathered to hear the broadcast reported that all they heard was the bass."[28]

This string trio performed together on many occasions in Cole and Osage Counties, often joined by Elmer's sister Lillian Schmutzler Nichols playing piano accompaniment. During the 1930s Prohibition era, the group played Saturday-night dances in places such the KREBOL dance hall in Osage City, along with numerous barn dances and house dances (often centered on a birthday party). With the KREBOL hall as their home base, the trio was simply known as the KREBOL band. The income from playing dances helped Elmer acquire a series of smart Model A Ford roadsters. Eventually, Elmer Schmutzler went to work in the gasoline business, operating a Phillips 66 station with his wife across the Missouri River in Cedar City and retiring in 1968 from the Phillips Pipeline Terminal in Jefferson City.

While it may have been unusual to hear radio broadcasts from the dome of the state capitol, evolving technology allowed radio broadcasting from practically any location with electricity—even caves.

The geology of Missouri (known to many as the Cave State as well as the Show-Me State) features numerous caves. Some of them were found suitable for square dances and other community activities (as well as making moonshine during Prohibition). In Taney County where Silver Dollar City was developed in the 1950s, a vast cave called Devil's Den by early pioneers was renamed Marble Cave in the 1880s. The Marble Cave Mining and Manufacturing Company had hoped to mine marble there (no luck), but did mine bat guano for fertilizer. In the 1890s the cave was developed as an Ozarks tourist attraction. The cave's entry chamber, some two hundred feet high, is the largest in the United States. Inside the vast chamber, called the Cathedral Room, bleachers, a stage, and a dance floor were built, a piano lowered in place, and a variety of programs held. Marvel Cave hosted professional stage shows, operas, and piano recitals before it became a venue for hillbilly music shows and square dances in the 1950s. In 1956 Red Foley and the Ozark Jubilee from KWTO radio and TV performed for square dances in the Cathedral Room, and the music was aired live.[29]

North of Springfield in Greene County, Fantastic Caverns is another cave complex that developed into a tourist attraction, but with a more fragile geology than most other "show caves." Visitors ride in jeeps on a specified guided tour, and the current emphasis is on educational programs for young people. During Prohibition, an illegal tavern was located in the cave. In the 1950s and 1960s, various kinds of musical

In Taney County, the Herschend family developed Marvel Cave's Cathedral Room in the mid-1950s as a venue for square dancing, concerts, and live radio broadcasts. The "Annual Square Dance Festival" (today we might call it "square dance camp") lasted three days, with couples paying $10.00 to participate. At the festival, organized dance clubs put on demonstrations, and callers taught dancing using both records and live string bands with seasoned fiddlers from the area. (Courtesy Silver Dollar City)

shows were put on; programs in the 1970s were broadcast on KGBX-FM, a radio station in Nixa.[30]

In Shannon County, Square Dance Cave (or Fiddler's Cave), in Holmes Hollow, was a popular location through several generations, and it is also known locally as Knuckles Cave. The Knuckles family farmed on Blair's Creek bottomland near the mouth of Holmes Hollow. Fiddlers such as Bunk Williams, Howe Teague, Roy Wooliver, and Gene Goforth played for dances there (Goforth mentions the cave in comments on his *Eminence Breakdown* CD). Spelunking enthusiasts and naturalists from outside the region in the 1970s began calling it Cookstove Cave as it became a popular destination. While the entry is small and difficult, inside there is a large, high "room" with a natural limestone base that is level enough for dancing.[31] Other caves have also had a history as dance halls, such as Meramec Caverns (Franklin County), Pike's Peak Cave (a.k.a. Roubidoux Cave, Pulaski County), Rock Bridge Cave (Boone County), and probably several others unknown to me at this time.

"Barn dance" and "Frolic" became code for live old-time fiddle music, singing, and dancing. Such programs as Chicago's *National Barn Dance* and Atlanta's *Barn Dance* (broadcasting from 1934 to 1940) provided a variety of entertainment. There was as much "popular music" as there was "hillbilly" on some of these stations, but the hillbilly stuff was getting the nation's attention.[32] Audiences of rural farm folk and urban residents with rural connections were growing. In good public relations tones, an executive at Kansas City's KMBC radio praised what WLS was doing with their barn dance in Chicago:

> Among radio stations, WLS has been well known for the development of entertaining features that have grown into national institutions. Probably the most famous of all these is its Saturday night "National Barn Dance." From anvils to zither the barn dance runs the entire line of variety in music. Old fiddles sing, quartettes bring out their funniest songs, the harmonicas, banjos, guitars, and jews' harps join to make the *ole hayloft* ring with down-to-earth music—so dear to the hearts of rural thousands, and as has been shown time and again, a favorite of just anybody with music in their souls.[33]

Once some of the regional programs were picked up by national networks, such as NBC that picked up the WLS *Barn Dance*, the music could be heard around the world. Barn dances were created by small stations and new stations in other cities across the South and Midwest. The success of radio barn dances and hillbilly shows on stations like WLS, WSM, WWVA, and early Missouri stations such as WHB in Kansas City (beginning broadcasting in 1922) and KMOX in St. Louis (1925) influenced the development of country music. St. Louis was a crossroads for musicians of all kinds, just as it had always been for immigrants and pioneers in general, and St. Louis was a hot spot for radio stations. Several competing stations programmed country music and fiddle programs—sometimes at the same hour and sometimes with the same musicians popping back and forth between stations. While the programs took new sounds to fiddlers, they also helped strengthen the idea of regional styles and performers.

Among the "sister duets" in Missouri performing country and cowboy music on AM radio were the Musslin Sisters. From Sedalia, Gertrude and her sister, Jean, specialized in cowboy ballads and gospel songs on live Saturday-night radio shows broadcast over Kansas City AM radio station WHB in the 1950s. John Hunt was a familiar accompanist for several top central Missouri fiddlers in former days, such as Gene Wells of Fayette. Today, in her eighties, Gertrude, along with John Hunt, continues to compete in old-time fiddlers contests to participate in the fun. Ever the charming entertainer, and much to the audience's delight, Gertrude is apt to play (and sing the words to) "I Want to Be a Cowboy's Sweetheart" as her contest "fiddle tune of choice." The Hammer Sisters, from Neosho, were another popular sister duet in Missouri (see *Play Me Something Quick and Devilish*).

Gertrude and John Hunt at an old-time fiddlers contest in Boonville. (April 2010)

Generations and Violins: From Asa White to Jessie and Kellie

It is not uncommon to meet families who have been making their own music for generation upon generation. In many instances, old violins as well as the old melodies and stories are handed down, and the convivial context of family music and interaction continues. In the Blue Springs area, the White family's fiddling saga involves some expected ingredients—the love of certain old tunes like "Soldier's Joy" and "Down Yonder" and the enjoyment of old country music records. And their story contains some surprises, such as a great appreciation for musical literacy and today's younger family fiddlers bringing back to life the treasured violin their great-grandfather bought from a hobo in 1906.

In terms of performing on the radio, most fiddlers never tried their luck, but more often than we might expect, a fiddler came along who gave radio fiddling a whirl and found success. William E. (Bill) White (1912–99) was one of the many fiddlers who had a brief fling with being a radio entertainer. Bill White was born in his grandfather W. H. Montgomery's farmhouse north of Blue Springs in Jackson County, a few miles east of Independence and Kansas City. As a child, Bill was given private violin lessons in Independence. He was an apt pupil and augmented his lessons with study of violin books such as the multipart series by C. H. Hohmann *Practical Violin School* and *Progressive Course for the Violin* by Albert Harvey.[34] Bill began playing fiddle tunes at dances and jam sessions at seventeen, often with his father, Asa, playing guitar accompaniment.

Neither Bill nor his father, Asa, was exclusively an ear musician; they both learned from sheet music and transcriptions Asa made from the fiddling he heard at dances. Thus, Bill learned fiddle tunes both from printed transcriptions (as did his father) and from listening to other fiddlers play. Bill Buseer, part of an African American family whose farm was across the road and just north of the W. H. Montgomery place, played fiddle music, and the two young men traded tunes. Another neighbor, living on a farm on the south side of the Montgomery place, Steve Adams, played old-time two-finger five-string banjo with Buseer and White.[35]

Asa's father, Louis K. White, was born in Wheeling, Virginia (later West Virginia), and came to the Little Blue community in Jackson County at the end of the Civil War and married Mary J. Horn. The Whites' Montgomery and Clark ancestors fought in the Confederate army in the Civil War; a Clark served in Quantrill's Raiders and took part in Quantrill's notorious guerrilla raid on the federal town of Lawrence, Kansas, where one of Bill White's mother's ancestors was living at the time.

Asa E. White (1885–1913) was a musician who, while a farmer by profession, played cornet (and led the Blue Springs town band) as well as fiddle at local dances.

Bill White, 1975, with his father Asa's "Stradivarius" violin made in Germany, purchased from a hobo in 1906. (Courtesy John R. White)

Asa White liked the fiddling he heard at square dances and fiddle sessions, so he learned to play fiddle tunes by going to dances, listening to the fiddlers, and then returning home, where he "scored" the melodies on music ledger paper as he remembered them. He then memorized the tunes from his handwritten sheet music (transcriptions) and played them at dances and fiddle sessions. His son Bill learned fiddle tunes the same way.

In 1906 Asa White obtained his violin from a hobo, who carried it in a gunnysack. Asa bought the violin, a German import shop "Stradivarius" violin with elaborate purfling and inlay on the back, and his cousin Fred White bought the hobo's guitar.

Bill White's favorite square-dance tune was "Tennessee Wagner," which he played at a moderate tempo. He preferred to play two-steps (fox-trots) from the 1920s and 1930s popularized by dance bands and swing orchestras, like the 1923 Con Conrad song popularized on 78 rpm records by Billy Murray, Sophie Tucker, and others, "You've Got to See Mama Ev'ry Night (or You Can't See Mama at All)," a two-step played by other Missouri fiddlers such as Pete McMahan and Claude Williams.

Unusual for Missouri fiddlers, Bill White played medleys of tunes for round dances, such as combining "Peekaboo Waltz" and "My Wild Irish Rose." For a lengthy square dance lasting twelve minutes or more, White played a medley of "Cacklin' Hen" with "Leather Britches," "Sally Goodin," "Buffalo Gals," and "Black and White Rag." That is an unusually busy medley, with an uncommon number of tunes of different types and in different keys.

Commonplace in fiddling in the British Isles (especially Scotland and Ireland) and parts of the US Northeast and Canada, playing medleys of breakdowns at square dances was rare in Missouri. On occasion, an old-time fiddler in Missouri might play two tunes as a medley in the course of laboring through an extra long square dance, where repetition and rapid tempo became tiresome and even a source of stress and physical pain; changing to a different tune (sometimes in a different key) can provide some relief from the physical stress of fiddling through a long square dance. In more recent times, since the 1980s, some Missouri fiddlers adopted playing medleys of reels in large part due to the rise of the New England contra-dance movement in the Midwest (contra dancers and contra-dance fiddlers seem to like medleys).

Bill White and the Blue Ridge Mountaineers

Bill White played for square dances with his uncle Clyde Scarborough, who called the dances. In addition to fiddling for the dances, White played a prebluegrass two-finger, up-picking banjo style as accompaniment for other fiddlers. In 1939 he was playing fiddle in a western-swing cowboy band called the Blue Ridge Mountaineers, performing on KMBC and KCMO in Kansas City. Bill White was content with being considered an old-time fiddler or western-swing fiddler even while being a classical violinist. But when someone asked him if he played bluegrass music, he answered, "I don't play bluegrass. There's too much *crab* grass in it."[36] Another hillbilly radio band had a similar name, the Blue Ridge Partners, with fiddler Slim Hayter,

Bob McCubbin, and Ken Huckabee, a band that played on the *Brush Creek Follies* theater shows that were broadcast live on KMBC radio.[37]

Yes, we have no Blue Ridge Mountains in the midwestern United States. That landscape is back east, a province of the Appalachian Mountains chain running from Pennsylvania to northern Georgia, with famous sections in Virginia and North Carolina—from whence came a strong portion of Missouri's Scotch-Irish pioneers and their traditional fiddle and dance music. Although some string bands in Missouri chose to identify themselves with the Ozarks, or great rivers, or the prairies, Bill White's ensemble in the Kansas City area decided to make a link with the famous Blue Ridge Mountains and the influential traditional music of that vivid region.

The choice of "Blue Ridge Mountaineers" for the band was more apropos than one would first assume. There are numerous place-names in Jackson County, Missouri, with "blue" in them, related to the pioneers' settlement Blue Springs, and the Blue and Little Blue Rivers.[38] Furthermore, White's ancestors settled there along with many other people from Virginia's Blue Ridge Mountains region. Missouri's nonmountainous Blue Ridge is a series of low, undulating ridges, several miles in length, that begins in western Independence and runs southward along the east side of the Blue River (a tributary of the Missouri River), terminating in Raytown in the Kansas City metro area. At its lowest, the elevation here is 720 feet and, at its apex, 1,020 feet.[39] Even from the Blue Ridge Tower, the tallest building in the Kansas City metro area (beyond downtown), it is difficult to see much that is geographically distinctive about Missouri's Blue Ridge.

Images of mountains back east figure prominently in the presentation and mythology of old-time fiddling and old-time string bands. The Blue Ridge Mountains in Virginia, North Carolina, Tennessee, and Georgia by the 1950s were famous for old-time fiddlers and musicians. A number of early hillbilly bands used names with the Blue Ridge (Blueridge) in their band names.[40] The popular radio cowboy singer, recording artist, and movie star Tex Ritter performed with an ensemble called the Blue Ridge Mountaineers, and Virginia's early recording star Ernest "Pop" Stoneman performed as the Blue Ridge Mountaineer. One of the duos performing on Springfield, Missouri, radio KWTO was the station's own Blue Ridge Mountain Boys, featuring Virginians Jim Raines (plectrum banjo) and his father, Bob Raines (guitar). An early Missouri bluegrass band on AM radio in the early 1950s was the Blue Ridge Boys (Porter Wagoner, Urel Albert, Don Hoglen, Granville Nichols, and fiddler Don Russell). Numerous other generic formulations were adopted by hillbilly and western-swing bands, from "boys," "farm hands," "troubadours," "cowboys," "ramblers," and "rounders" to "playboys" and "ranch hands" as well as ensembles with "brothers," "sisters," or "family" in their names. Various Blue Ridge Mountaineer bands and entertainers were to be found on commercial records and radio programs in states far from and far flatter than the Appalachian Mountains, such as Michigan and Iowa.

Carrying It On

Many of Bill White's favorite tunes are played by the younger generation in the family, such as "Get Out and Get Under the Moon" (a song and two-step from the 1920s), "Soldiers' Joy" (Bill would first play this reel as a schottische and then shift it to a reel for square dancing), "Rufus Rastus Johnson Brown" (a Tin Pan Alley fox-trot based on "Whatcha Gonna Do When the Rent Comes 'Round"), "At a Georgia Camp Meeting," "Down Yonder," "Casey Jones" (Bill White's first fiddle tune), and "My Wild Irish Rose."

The White family music tradition, going back at least to Asa White, is being carried on by Asa White's grandson (Bill White's son) John R. White, who plays guitar, and John's four daughters. All four of Asa White's great-granddaughters have had music lessons and read music. Two of them, Jessie and Kellie, enjoy playing fiddle tunes. Their great-grandfather's violin was recently restored at the Wyatt Violin Shop in Independence for them to play.

A New Year's holiday music party in Independence: *Left to right*: Jessie White (with her great-grandfather Asa White's "Stradivarius" made in a German shop before 1905), Kellie White (playing her father John R. White's pre–World War II German import "Da Salo" violin), Samantha White (rear), and John R. White. (January 2015)

AM Radio and Old-Time Fiddlers

In Kansas City, the market for hillbilly music programs was as competitive as in the much larger city of St. Louis. Kansas City had the benefit of being the major city on the west side of Missouri, with little competition as an urban center west from there to Denver, Colorado, six hundred miles away. KMBC's *Brush Creek Follies* barn dance program was answered by KCMO with their *Cowtown Jamboree*, and both were popular Saturday-night live broadcasts that featured local talent as well as national recording and radio stars from the late 1930s into the 1950s. The *Cowtown Jamboree* lasted four hours and was aired live before large audiences in the public auditorium in the Ivanhoe Temple (Masonic Lodge 446) near downtown Kansas City. These and other stations presented strong competition to stations shunning popular forms of music, such as big band (dance orchestra) music and light classical fare referred to as "potted-palm music."

AM radio stations came to sizable towns such as St. Louis and Springfield, Jefferson City and Macon, Warrenton, Salem, and St. Joe. Signals covered the countryside and even competed (on a clear night) with signals like WLS from faraway Chicago. As country music emerged in the later 1930s and as strong drink, late nights, and long-distance trips by train or auto to perform in ballrooms and taverns became the norm, the more conservative musicians decided to stick closer to home. So many capable fiddlers stayed in their communities—and enhanced the music scene there.

By the mid-1930s, three-fourths of Americans owned a radio, even if it had to be wired to their automobile's battery. With the proliferation of local AM radio stations in the 1930s and 1940s, the town station became a venue for fiddlers and entertainers of all kinds. Very few fiddlers lived in locations so isolated that they could not travel to the county seat or railroad town with a radio station. Seasoned in the vaudeville show, house dance, fiddlers contest, or country tavern, many experienced old-time fiddlers were active in radio. Many gave live radio a try; an incomplete list of those names includes Jack Shockley, Shorty Prewitt, Orville Day, Zed Tennis, Buster Fellows, Blackie Lewis, Hoby Shepp, Eva Faye Washington, Bill Katon, Charlie Hiler, Buck Cuno, Uncle Billy Raines, Emmett Heath, Ralph Wrinkle, Red Loveall, Jimmy Gage, Ed Tharp, Clifford Hawthorne, Bert Lewis, Dusty Rhodes, John Hartford, Daniel Boone Jones, Gene Goforth, Milo McCubbin, Seth Bradley, Don Russell, Ansel Gore, LeRoy Haslag, Pete McMahan, Dale Potter, Slim Wilson, Bythel Friend, Dr. Jimmy Gray, Casey Jones, Leroy Canaday, Howe Teague, Aaron Oliver, "Boots Faye" (Grace Eloise Tartsch), Harold Leake, Roger Williams, Roy Wooliver, Uncle Jim Haley, Vee Latty, Bill (Junior) Perkins, Peanut Lynch, Ruth Hammer, Lloyd Lalumondier, Bert Lewis, George Morris, Bill Driver, Lee Roy Stoneking, Dolph Wilson, Nile Wilson, Lacy Hartje, Kay Smith, and Newell Looney.

Some of the radio performers were wizened elders fiddling the ironclads and old favorites (Daniel Boone Jones, Bill Katon), and some were spunky teenagers—like Dale Potter, the fireball creative fiddler from Puxico who would become famous in the Nashville recording business and can be heard on some of Hank Williams's first hit records. Some were also singers and formed ensembles. Many found that they had a knack for entertaining over the radio waves, developed careers "on the road" going from one station to the next, and went on to develop a semiprofessional or professional career. Some fiddlers who enjoyed the radio experience liked the fact that people could not see them. Some enjoyed the fiddling but were reluctant to speak over the air, such as *The Rooster Creek Show*'s Harold Leake.

According to Greg Harmon (a grandnephew), Kay Smith, a sister of Dallas County fiddler Floyd Smith, was a smooth, "modern" fiddler who performed with her sister, Wanda, on KWTO radio as the KWTO Country Gals.[41] Helen Evelyn (Kay) Smith (1923–2002) married Montana country singer Carson (Jack) Whittaker and, after touring the United States and settling in Billings, Montana, began performing as Country Girl Kay. After her husband's death, she married Bill Gardner; after his death, Kay moved to Washington State. Kay Smith sang her own rockabilly-style compositions on several Whitkay Records in the early 1960s, including "Arkansas Boogie," a popular if obscure 45 rpm record among western-swing enthusiasts.[42]

Other fiddlers who gave radio a whirl did not care for the lifestyle or did not stay with it. The fast-and-loose life associated with the traveling radio ensemble of "stars" became too much for the conservative and religious Ozark fiddler Bythel Friend. Likewise, Billy Lee of Wright City had an offer to travel with Bill Monroe's bluegrass band in the early 1950s, but would not leave his home and family. Roy Wooliver, one of Missouri's most gifted fiddlers but a bellicose and unpredictable character, played guitar and fiddle on the popular *Cousin Emmy* radio show on KMOX in St. Louis; in the oft-told story, Emmy fired Wooliver because he refused to wear socks when the show's cast performed for live audiences.[43] Some fiddlers, like Moberly's Leroy Canaday, would have continued in local radio jobs but came on the scene in the 1950s and 1960s era of AM radio's slow decline and replacement by FM.

After World War II, radio stations carried a wide variety of entertainment. Stations such as Warrenton's KWRE focused on programming country music and bluegrass, and these two styles of traditional music competed for listeners' attention. Roy Queen hosted a popular radio show on KWRE for several years as well as developing an opry venue in Warrenton (Warren County) that featured country music shows and fiddlers contests.

By the mid-1950s, most of the live radio barn dances had gone the way of the whalebone corset and buggy whip. A few programs run by skillful radio entrepreneurs with equally skillful and entrepreneurial musicians made it in television, including Springfield's *Ozark Jubilee* and Osage Beach's *Ozark Opry*, which was beamed live on Jefferson City's KRCG-TV. Television and shifts in national popular taste were pushing the media and country music in different directions. And by the mid-1950s, FM radio was beginning to compete with and rub out AM as the dominant broadcast format, a process generally complete by the late 1970s.

The Sunset Ranch Boys appeared on the *Roy Queen Show* on Saturday mornings on the Warrenton AM station KWRE in the early 1960s. Queen had begun his radio career in the St. Louis market and was a successful promoter. The ensemble comprised young musicians from Maries County, John Copeland on violin, John's

Studio cast at KOAM radio, Pittsburg, Kansas, an important regional station, ca. 1945. *Left to right*: Roy (Smoky) May, Lois Shook, Shorty Prewitt (born Ben Rockey, central Missouri; violin), Vi Clark (piano), guitarist Roy McGeorge in his comedic role as "Uncle Enoch," Webb Cardwell, Bill Squires, Earl Bledsoe. (Courtesy Henry McGeorge)

brother Verlin Copeland on electric lead guitar, and their cousin Elzie Helton, who sang and played rhythm guitar. The Sunset Ranch Boys managed to present music that appealed to both the "tear in my beer" country music crowd and the bluegrass and old-time fiddling "Katy Hill" crowd, with selections such as song hits "Love's Gonna Live Here Again" and "I'm Movin' On," together with fiddle instrumentals such as "Sugar in the Gourd," "Tomahawk," and "Sally Goodin."[44] Later, in the 1960s, KWRE's *Bluegrass Express* radio show became very successful under deejay Jeff Cook, a musician and founder of the Missouri Area Bluegrass Committee.

The radio shows were in large measure shunted offstage by a combination of homogenized FM radio programming and by changes in the styles of music people were listening to. Michael Breid, who produced and performed on radio shows, as well as being a professional musician and opry performer, commented in 2010:

> I've noticed that some of the country stations who have had a Saturday morning old time music show for a few hours have dropped them. They say they just didn't get the advertising $$$ they needed to support the show. Truth is, they moved the

shows from AM to FM, which doesn't go out as far, so people couldn't hear the shows. They don't hear the shows so they don't patronize the sponsors, therefore the sponsors don't pay for time on the air and the show is cancelled. Simple as that. The so-called "country" stations are just "too hip" for any of that nasal singing and old time fiddlin' and banjer pickin'.[45]

Early Radio and Fiddlers Contests

The year 1926 was the last time a state fiddlers contest was held in Paris. The reasons may be numerous. The St. Louis newspapers and sponsors may have moved on, and the live fiddling and contests held over WOS radio from Jefferson City stole a lot of their thunder. The Paris contests were popular, but the access and reach of WOS came to surpass the reach of newspaper stories, no matter how delightfully written and illustrated. The inexorable decline of newspapers was under way; the new magic of radio, talking pictures, and sound recordings was the hot new media.

As we have seen elsewhere, one of the first broadcast radio stations in the United States was clear-channel WOS in the capital city. The first program schedules included a daily fare that read: "8 P.M. Musical program. Speeches. General current news from late afternoon city papers."[46] WOS easily matched the reach and listenership of more famous stations such as St. Louis's KMOX and KSD and Kansas City's KMBC and WHB, not to mention major stations in other states.

No stigma seems to have attached to old-time fiddlers at the Paris contests who had American Indian blood. Indeed, one of the popular fiddlers of the omnipresent show tune that required an exhibition of wild Indian hollering, "Lost Indian," was Clate Ransdell of Moberly, substantially of Cherokee identity. So far as I can determine, it was not unusual for African American fiddlers and accompanists to compete in fiddlers contests—at least in central Missouri, where participation can be documented. Several African Americans performed over WOS, such as Bill Driver, Bill Burdick, and Bill Katon. Vernon Clatterbuck of Fulton, who knew Katon, remembered that fiddlers like Katon and Driver were well known in the area and many radio listeners recognized who they were by the music and styles they played over the air; a similar recollection by Earl Willis attested to Burdick's recognition.[47] From the 1920s into the 1940s, Driver competed in contests in the area of Miller, Cole, Maries, and Pulaski Counties, close to Jefferson City, and audiences at fiddlers contests recognized him as a WOS fiddler. It is likely that Driver's celebrity as a WOS radio fiddler helped smooth the way for his competing among white fiddlers in contests. Driver often won or placed high in competition with white fiddlers in the area he knew from picnics and sessions. People in Iberia recall fiddlers contests where the top three fiddlers consistently were Bill Driver, Henry Thompson, and Ike Helton.[48] Ike Helton and other Helton family fiddlers exchanged fiddle tunes with Driver.

From December 1925 to late 1929, WOS radio held nine major contests in their studios in the capitol rotunda, promoting them heavily, with several more contests into the early 1930s. Inevitably, the conditions of the Great Depression led to the station's decline, as with countless other radio stations, and to changes in management philosophy.[49] The contests aired over WOS from Jefferson City are famous, in part because people were mesmerized by the events, and a deep pool of anecdotes and recollections developed that continue down to the current day. Recently, the WOS contests were brought to wider attention by Charlie Walden's vivid 1983 article and in the work of Patrick Huber.[50] WOS programming, in tandem with the widely advertised major statewide old-time fiddlers contests in Paris, helped put Missouri fiddling on the map. Many of the successful contest fiddlers of the time, as well as popular dance fiddlers, performed at the radio station, including many fiddlers who did not take part in the state fiddlers contests. Walden and Huber, among others, have done extensive research and writing about the history of WOS and the fiddlers contests held in the capitol and broadcast by WOS. WOS was established as a public relations and informational arm of the Missouri secretary of agriculture's State Marketing Bureau. Signal was enabled by construction of a 500-watt Western Electric transmitter on the roof of the capitol. As Walden notes in his Internet article:

> The first airing of old-time fiddling on June 24, 1923, was very well received. The fiddler for this historic broadcast was Louie Barton, a Jefferson City local. He was accompanied by George Schrimpf on bass and Noland Wrightman on guitar. The program also featured a square dance caller, Tony Eveler, and Bryan Williams on mandolin. The combination of Barton, Schrimpf, and Williams (on guitar) came to be called "The Old-Tyme String Trio" and was the "house" band at WOS for some time. It is worth noting that this WOS broadcast of traditional American music predates WSM's Grand Old Opry (November, 1925) by more than two years. . . .
>
> It wasn't long before fiddlers and old-time musicians from across the state were making the trek to Jefferson City to play on WOS. Legislators may have served as "talent agents" for WOS by encouraging musicians from their home districts to play at the Capitol. Friday night at WOS was fiddlers' night and anyone who happened into the studio was welcome to play.

The landmark event for radio fiddling contests was the WOS-sponsored two-day event of December 31, 1925–January 1, 1926. Some eighty fiddlers were tested, including a number of fiddlers who were considered champions of their counties and regions. The method of judging was by audience response, following one of the two prevailing traditions for fiddle contest judging (the other being by a panel of judges). The results were debated and unsatisfactory to many people. As Walden wrote, "Judging for this and all subsequent WOS contests was by popular vote of the radio audience. A postcard was worth one point, a letter two, a telephone call three, and a telegram four. Fiddlers naturally encouraged their relatives and neighbors to cast votes for them. A tavern owner and fiddler in Northwest Missouri is alleged to have unsuccessfully offered funds to his patrons and kin to send in telegrams in his favor."[51]

The final results came in over the next two weeks, and more than five thousand votes were tallied. The ultimate individual winners were, first place, Tom Massie of Nevada; second, Daniel Boone Jones of Stephens; third, Louie Barton of Jefferson

City; fourth, Jess Burgess of Stoutland; and fifth, Aaron Oliver of Columbia. Their awards included cash amounts up to fifty dollars and gifts from local stores.

Virgil Smith of Montgomery City was one of many people who made the long journey by flivver to Jefferson City to watch and listen to the late 1920s and early 1930s fiddlers' gatherings and preparations for the contests held in the capitol. People enjoyed listening to the fiddlers warm up in various spaces in the building, and the contest could be heard over loudspeakers. On New Year's Eve in 1929, a state contest was broadcast.

> There was a guy by name of Jim Earnest lived over by Bellflower, a pretty good fiddler, and him and I used to do some jamming around. So we decided we'd go over to Jeff City to a contest, one time, on New Year's Eve. So we left about one o'clock, on New Year's Eve, and got over there . . . and parked right up by the capitol where them cannons used to be parked. . . . We stayed there all night, till about three o'clock in the morning. I think there was eighty-two fiddlers altogether, up there. Bunch of 'em, fiddling everywhere, you know.
>
> We got ready to come home—I had a Model-T Ford, a 1927 Model-T roadster. And we got in and started home. We got out there north of Jeff City . . . and ran out of gas. The thing quit on us. About ten above zero, about a foot of snow on the ground, well, there we were. Three o'clock in the morning. Well, we got out, started walking back toward Jeff City. Got to a service station at the end of the old bridge there was a guy down there by the name of Al Slush, had a service station there. . . . He had a '28 Chevrolet, so we finally got it started, so he run us back out there, got some gas and put it in, got it started, and then come back and filled it up with gas. So, but that was a very miserable night. Never will forget that.
>
> . . . Got home the next morning, at ten-thirty, and they were still playing in the contest over there. They didn't have judges. Everybody wrote a card; a postcard would count so many votes, and a letter would count so many, and that's the way they voted for the winner.[52]

As Virgil Smith recalled, the winners in the first WOS contest on New Year's Eve 1925 were decided by the audience, who sent postcards, letters, or telegrams to the station with their votes for first place. A postcard was worth one vote (one point), a letter two points, and a telegram three points. The contest attracted eighty-two contestants. It started at nine on New Year's Eve and paused at five in the morning for a break and some sustenance. The top fifteen fiddlers resumed butting heads at eight, and the contest ended at noon on January 1, 1926.[53] According to Nile Wilson's son, Garry Wilson, the story is often told that Dolph Wilson won first place in that New Year's Eve 1925 contest, based on the sheer number of responses sent to the station. However, since Dolph's fans sent postcards instead of the higher-vote-getting and more expensive letters or telegrams, Dolph Wilson finished further down the list.[54]

The 1925 event was reported across the state. An article in the *Houston Herald* (Texas County) includes a reference to the nagging problem of how the judging got

Virgil Smith (*left*) and Dwight Grover (Wellsville) swap tunes at Virgil's sixtieth wedding anniversary music party. (Montgomery City, 1993)

done. The article indicates some of the tunes played by local heroes Joe Rowden and J. A. Fleenor, and three others listed are ironclads of the Missouri fiddler's repertoire.

Old Fiddlers Contest

> One of the interesting features of Thursday night's radio program was the ringing of the Liberty Bell at midnight to give parting to the Old Year and welcome to the New Year. . . . Another attractive feature was the Old Fiddlers Contest at Jefferson City, in which two of our local manipulators of the resined bow took part with more than fifty other fiddlers of note. Texas County was represented by J. A. Rowden, of Tyrone, and J. S. Fleenor, of Solo. Joe Rowden played for his first number "Stoney Point," and for his second number "The Girl I Left Behind Me." Mr. Fleenor's first selection was "Arkansas Traveler." We feel assured that our Texas County celebrities will be considered among the leaders in the contest, but we are informed that the decision is made by radio fans sending in their votes in the popularity contest for their favorites, so the result will not be known until after January 13.[55]

The Rowden and Fleenor families continued to have musicians in their midst. Joe Rowden's son, also named Joe Rowden, was a fiddler, and Joe's great-great-great-granddaughter Allison Scheets has played fiddle in a West Plains–based bluegrass band called Sunnyside Up. Joe Rowden and Harold Rowden (Meta), a longtime Missouri bluegrass musician, were distantly related.[56] One of Fleenor's sons, Lowell Fleenor, was a classically trained violinist and taught music in West Plains for many years.[57]

On April 2, 1926, the WOS station followed its successful New Year's Eve contest with an even bigger event, an "Interstate Old Fiddlers Contest." In this contest, Missouri and its eight neighboring states held a series of preliminary contests to determine each state's official two top fiddlers. These two then contested as teams in the interstate match. Missouri's pair was Daniel Boone Jones and Louie Barton (replacing Tom Massie, unable to take part), who had been distinguishing themselves in fiddling competitions for many years and had placed high in the New Year's Eve WOS contest. In the WOS interstate contest, fiddlers from some of the other states seem to have been selected not by competition but by executive fiat: their governors picked them.

The list included some boldface names on the national scene. Uncle Jimmy Thompson of Tennessee had become famous through his groundbreaking performances over radio station WSM and *The Grand Ole Opry*. Other notable fiddlers with important reputations in their home states included Iowa's Frame Davis and Oklahoma's Sam Long, who appeared on 78 rpm records.[58]

"The Wilson boys" from Linn County were formidable contest fiddlers in the 1920s and 1930s. *Left*: Lester Wilson, Lester's brother Dolph, and Dolph's son Nile, who accompanied his father and uncle in the WOS radio contests and many others, and later became a fiddle champion in his own right. (Courtesy Nile Wilson)

Just as in other competitions of the times, the rules did not outlaw trick fiddling or show tunes. Several contestants played the familiar audience favorites "Listen to the Mockingbird" and "Lost Indian" (with war whoops). The only requirements were that the selections be "old-time tunes" and performed by the contestant with no more than one accompanist. Again, the radio audience was the judge. As Walden noted:

> To encourage listeners to cast their votes a variety of prizes were offered. All telegrams, postcards, and letters were numbered and placed in a huge box and the winners drawn by a blindfolded Governor Sam Baker. Premiums ranged from baby chicks to a house and forty-acre farm in Southeast Missouri.
>
> The success of this promotion is evidenced in the more than 250,000 communications received. The local telegraph office estimated that messages were being taken at a rate of 115 an hour. In Miami, Oklahoma, where voting was heaviest, some 500 telegrams were filed at one time. The Northwest and Canada turned in a large number of telegrams. Poor weather conditions accounted for the small number of returns received from the Southeastern United States.[59]

Results of the Interstate Old Fiddlers event were publicized two weeks later, with Missourian Daniel Boone Jones taking first prize. In the *Missouri Historical Review*, Patrick Huber summarizes much of the scope of the importance of WOS and its fiddler programs:

> This competition represented more than just a successful publicity stunt for the station. The Interstate Old Fiddlers Contest encompassed both Missouri's rural past and its modern present, and like so many other facets of the vibrant American popular culture that emerged during the Jazz Age, it embodied a complex interplay between traditionalism and modernism, between the march of progress and the backward glance of nostalgia, and—in the particular case of old-time fiddling—between the grassroots musical culture of the late nineteenth century and the commercial entertainment industry of the early twentieth century. In fact, the contest, a sort of *American Idol* of the Jazz Age, employed progressive publicity appeals[60] and state-of-the-art technology to promote what many contemporary observers considered an archaic and almost-forgotten music of a vanishing rural America. Ultimately, WOS . . . reflected a blending of traditional rural culture and modern urban sensibilities that characterized much of American popular culture in the 1920s.[61]

Whitty Elmore, "Champion of Dixie"

If most expatriate Missouri fiddlers made reputations on the West Coast, a few made reputations by moving east. The champion at the January 1926 Indiana and Kentucky Henry Ford contests was William Henry (Whitty) Elmore. Originally from Houston (Texas County), Elmore came from a long line of fiddlers and singers remembered as "the fiddlin' Elmores." Whitty's father, four brothers, fourteen nephews, and a son all played fiddle music, by ear. Elmore was reared north of Houston, where

Seth Bradley's loving cup. For the February 15, 1929, WOS radio contest, the state was divided into two chunks, north and south of the Missouri River—the state's traditional geographic and cultural division. Fiddlers entered a division according to where they lived. First place for fiddlers from north of the river was won by Bradley, the dance and radio fiddler and farmer in Callaway County who would be famous in later years on *The Rooster Creek* show on KFAL. Bradley's trophy, auctioned at a farm sale in June 2013, was engraved: Champion Old Time Fiddler / North Side Missouri River / Contest WOS / Feb. 15, 1929 / Seth O. Bradley / Mokane, MO.

his father operated a gristmill; his father enjoyed playing fiddle tunes while waiting for customers.

Whitty had relocated his family to Kansas and then in 1922 settled in West Baden in southern Indiana (an hour north of Louisville, Kentucky), where he made his living as a shoemaker, working in a stall in the famed West Baden Springs Hotel Spa and resort. Before leaving Missouri, Elmore had sold his violin and played very little for twelve years. However, in late 1925, "a wandering musician came through the spa where Elmore sits at his last and importuned Elmore to buy his fiddle for money with which the wanderer could buy food. In his arms the instrument awakened the memories of mountain melodies, and Elmore entered a local fiddle contest, which he won."[62] Encouraged, he competed in the necessary preliminaries before being selected to compete in the Louisville grand championship. Some 1,500 fiddlers in Indiana, Kentucky, and Tennessee competed in 114 preliminary contests. All but a handful had been eliminated.

Contests were inspired by, but not technically sponsored by, industrial magnate Henry Ford (see *Play Me Something Quick and Devilish*).[63] Paul Gifford documents Ford's promotion of fiddlers contests no earlier than August 1923, and Ford's activities seem to have peaked in late 1925 and 1926. Gifford has debunked "this myth" that Henry Ford sponsored fiddlers contests. Ford himself did not sponsor contests;

some of his car dealerships did, particularly in states such as Kentucky, Tennessee, and Indiana, where statewide contests in 1925 and early 1926 were the culmination of local and regional preliminary competitions.

Winners of the state contests traveled to Louisville to vie for Champion of Dixie at the Brown Theatre in January 1926. The contests were broadcast on radio and, in the days of high-wattage AM radio, were heard throughout the nation and beyond, including Elmore's hometown. The four winners at the Louisville finals—first place, William H. Elmore; second, J. L. (Bunt) Stephens of Tennessee; third, Marshall Claiborne of Tennessee; and fourth, Cooney Perdue of Kentucky—traveled to Michigan, their trips paid for by the Ford dealerships. In Detroit they fiddled an exhibition at a hotel banquet given in their honor by Henry Ford. They were taken on tours of the Ford factory (world famous for its assembly line and mechanical innovations) and given gifts. In some contests, Mr. Ford did donate loving cups as trophies for the winners.

No real "Henry Ford contests" were held in Missouri.

In the finals in Louisville, to win the crown of "Champion of Dixie," Whitty Elmore played "Red Bird," "Wild Goose," and "Hell among the Yearlings."[64] "Red Bird" is the usual title for the central Missouri tune "Waldo," attributed to Waldo Helton. "Wild Goose" is a tune that has slipped from the daily repertoire in Missouri (notwithstanding its appearance under a different title). The breakdown "Hell among the Yearlings" remains a standard at sessions, bluegrass festivals, and contests.

Elmore's prizes at Louisville included medals, a loving cup, cash, a new Ford touring car, train passage to Detroit to meet and entertain Henry Ford, and a slot in what was to be a "national" old-time fiddlers contest. In Detroit Whitty Elmore was to compete in the play-off contest between the regional champs in the several Henry Ford contests that had been held in various states, but this grand championship was never held.[65] The Louisville "Championship of Dixie" three-state affair was the largest of the regional contests (southern Indiana largely was culturally a branch of Dixie).

The *Houston Herald* picked up the Louisville account of Elmore's success on January 21 and made sure people knew he was a Missourian. Some people in Houston tuned in to the radio to listen to the contest; more would have heard him that day had they not been attending the funeral of a prominent citizen just as the contest was being broadcast.[66]

Henry Elmore Wins Big Fiddling Honors

The Louisville (Kentucky) *Herald-Post* of January 21 has the following regarding W. H. Elmore, or Henry as some Texas County folks know him, or "Whitty," as about everybody called him when he cobbled shoes and made the fiddle talk around Houston for his lifetime up to a dozen years ago, when he moved to Kansas and later to West Baden, Indiana, where he now resides.

W. H. Elmore was among fiddlers at the January 1926 Louisville contest who posed for the Caufield & Shook Studio. (Caulfield and Shook Collection #070112, Archives and Special Collections, University of Louisville)

The *Herald-Post* says:

Folks, meet W. H. Elmore, a darn good cobbler and a darn good fiddler. Last night at the Brown Theatre he was the recipient of the title of "The Champion Fiddler of Dixie." Be it known that the title was not borrowed, invented or assumed. It was earned. Earned in competition with several of the best fiddlers in Dixie—the finalist of 114 tournaments conducted by Ford dealers throughout Kentucky, Tennessee, and Indiana. Tonight "Dixie's Fiddling Cobbler," who is a native of the Ozark Mountains, but now a resident of West Baden, Indiana. . . . Tomorrow he receives a completely equipped Ford. Later he will be given a trip to Detroit to play in a National Tournament.

Another Louisville paper said:

Memories long since dimmed in the silence of the drifting years were revived where, before a capacity audience at the Crown Theater Wednesday night, William Henry Elmore, 63 years old shoemaker . . . playing the traditional tunes of his forbearers, was declared the "champion fiddler of Dixie." It is not hard to believe that the shades of long ago Elmores hovered over the theater rafters listening happily to their earthly successor playing "Red Bird," "Hell among the Yearlings" and "Wild

Champion of Dixie W. H. Elmore tries out a new Ford car at the Doss-Jones dealership in Louisville, KY. (Caulfield and Shook Collection #070161, Archives and Special Collections, University of Louisville)

The Louisville, Kentucky, winners, January 21, 1926. *Left to right*: J.P. Purdue (fourth place), Marshall Claiborne (third), Bunt Stephens (second), Whitty Elmore (first). The photo reminds us that most fiddlers choose their apparel when they sally forth to perform in public, whether that clothing is cleaned and pressed overalls or one's "Sunday best." (Caulfield and Shook Collection #070136, Archives and Special Collections, University of Louisville)

Goose," because as long as can be remembered the Elmores have been fiddlers. High up in the Ozarks they are called the "fiddlin' Elmores." The champion himself is the son, so he says, of a "natural born, left-handed fiddler." Then, too, were four brothers and in the present generation fourteen nephews—all fiddlers. So it is easy to understand why the heart of Mr. William Henry Elmore overflowed with happiness when he was told he won. He murmured, "They'll be glad." . . .

Both papers had pictures of "Whitty" and his fiddle. Friends at the old Texas County home are proud to learn of his good luck in winning over 1500 contestants in three states. . . . Henry and wife, sons and daughter now live at West Baden, Indiana, the children all married and all doing well.

John Farley circulated a letter of congratulations Tuesday to be sent to Champion Elmore and it was signed by a large number of old friends.

Congratulations from home folks to "Fiddlin' Whitty."[67]

Elmore went to Detroit. It turned out that there would no national contest, but, as promised, Whitty Elmore met the vaunted industrialist Henry Ford, who was "interested in the revival of old-time fiddling."[68] As he did with other invited fiddlers, Ford walked Elmore through his factories, hosted a banquet for Elmore and others, and spent time visiting with and listening to Elmore fiddle. Elmore played a few tunes on Ford's Stradivarius.[69]

Several Elmore descendants live in Texas County, and several are singers and musicians. As Ed McKinney notes, among the Elmore clan making names for themselves were brothers Willard "Lum" Elmore and Wilburn Elmore, who sang in a 1950s and 1960s gospel quartet called the Harmoniers, popular in the Houston area and on nearby Mountain Grove's radio station.[70] Whitty Elmore, aged sixty in 1926, is never known to have lost a fiddlers contest.

Columbia's Daniel Boone Jones was among fiddlers Ford brought to Detroit for similar tours, banqueting, and performances and was encouraged to sample Henry Ford's priceless old-master Italian violins. Dan Jones did not win any of the contests sponsored by Ford car dealerships, but he had won important contests aired internationally over WOS and fiddled on other high-wattage radio stations, so Jones's reputation extended across the continent. The *Columbia Daily-Tribune* headlined a report "D. B. Jones Plays for Henry Ford" in February 1929. "Mr. Jones, who has played over KFRU, WOS, WHO (Des Moines, IA) and other radio stations, is well known as a fiddler. He says Mr. Ford is interested in old-time music and has a choice collection of instruments."[71]

Depression Years and War Years

During the Great Depression, the major state and regional contests pulled back, due to difficulties in funding the substantial purses that were offered in the Roaring Twenties. Many small community contests, and certain of the major contests, managed to survive the hard times and war conditions that put a damper on many kinds of community events.

Many fiddlers contests escape notice entirely. Some are known by happenstance, in a family's shared memory or the luck of coming across an old newspaper story. For example, my grandfather Wiley Marshall, a retired one-room country schoolteacher and dance fiddler, once won a neighborhood fiddlers contest held a few miles east of our farm in eastern Randolph County. The modest contest was part of a community program held on February 1, 1944, in the Madison High School auditorium in honor of President Franklin D. Roosevelt's birthday. The event was like a miniature vaudeville show, with a cornet solo, tumbling and stunts by young pupils, a "reading," a "comic dialog," a short play, a vocal trio, selections by the girls' glee club, and a "contest for old fiddlers." "After the program, the audience enjoyed round and square dancing with the music by Mrs. J. B. Roberson, piano, and Lee Lepper, violin."[72]

A survey of fiddlers contests in Stoddard County in Southeast Missouri in the late 1930s gives us a feeling for a trend that edged contests out of the limelight for a time. Fiddle contests in the late 1930s offered entertainment and fiddling opportunities to many people, and Stoddard County had featured an annual round of contests just as had other regions of the state. The distance between towns like Puxico (home of young contest champion Dale Potter in the late 1930s) and the meager highways of the pre–World War II period meant that few fiddlers traveled north to the big contests in central and northern Missouri. Local contests were occasionally reported in the papers. A number of fiddlers competed at a contest in Dexter, located on Crowley's Ridge, in September 1938 at the annual Stoddard County Fall Festival and Agricultural Show. Most newspaper coverage in the principal organs in the area in Dexter and Poplar Bluff gave extravagant coverage to the youth agricultural and livestock exhibits, but they barely mention the fiddlers contest that was one of the culminating entertainments of the several-day festival. The 1938 contest did, however, receive good notice in one of Dexter's two papers, the *Dexter Statesman*. This paper included the contest in ads for the fall festival and invited all fiddlers from "S.E. Mo." to compete. In a page 1 story, the fiddlers contest and amateur show (talent show) are promoted: "Saturday will be Farm Bureau Day, and the program will be ended that night with a real rip snortin' fiddlers contest on the stage. There is no charge for entering the contests, so please get your fiddles down and your amateur stunts worked up, but don't fail to register early so that the committee can plan their program for everyone to have a place in the show."[73]

After the fair ended, the *Dexter Statesman* reported the results as part of a front-page article detailing the success of the festival. The fiddlers contest included a category for best string band as well as best individual fiddler, an uncommon category of competition in Missouri (but a category typical of many fiddlers contests in the southeastern United States):

> **Old Fiddlers Contest**
>
> In the old fiddlers contest Saturday night, the performers were Joe Russell, Puxico; James and Paul Cook, Dexter; Walter Palmer, Zeta, in the individual, with the Cotton Belt Ramblers and the Palmer group of Zeta fighting it out for the group money.
>
> Walter Palmer of Zeta won first prize money in the fiddling contest and the Cotton Belt Ramblers took first prize in the group contest.
>
> Uncle Ezra Frank put on a couple of skits that were well received.
>
> The big hand of the evening went to Tom Jackson, who is widely known as a dancer, and who put on a couple of lively numbers for the entertainment of the crowd.
>
> It was a real show and everyone was mighty well pleased with the fine performances.[74]

Most newspapers across the state in this period of time leading up to December 1941, when Japanese military forces attacked Pearl Harbor, were increasingly busy with stories of the emerging German domination of Europe, the evolving world war, Germany's aerial bombing of England—and front-page stories about the St. Louis Cardinals baseball team. Moreover, stories about President Roosevelt's Works Progress Administration (WPA) projects continued to appear, as projects such as highway paving continued (to be scaled back or halted when the United States became involved in the war). As war grew closer, fiddlers contests received less and less coverage, and many were folded into "Amateur Night" contests and variety shows at fall festivals, homecomings, and agricultural fairs. A great many of the young men who might have signed up for a fiddlers contest were entering military service.

In the 1930s and 1940s, another breed of fiddle contests was programmed by entertainment companies, radio stations, theaters, and others. These contests were not really competitions at all; they were well-crafted shows in which celebrity fiddlers were hired to put on a "contest" for an audience. To some ticket buyers, they seemed like vaudeville shows. Some of these staged contests were remarkable for their popularity and for their bringing together in mock combat major figures on the fiddle scene. On a circuit of theatrical fiddlers contests in the South, for example, the hired guns were stars of recordings, radio, and stage, such as Fiddlin' Arthur Smith, Clayton McMichen, Curly Fox, Clark Kessinger, Howdy Forrester, Georgia Slim Rutland, and Natchee the Indian. Most of those fiddlers have been tremendously influential through the generations, and their influences can be detected even in the turbocharged "National Contest style" of fiddling today. Occasionally, a popular local fiddler or a respected semipro was introduced into the lineup. There were also contests at these stage shows for string bands and yodeling. The fiddle bands often featured the fiddle contestants and were given such evocative names as Natchee's Tribe, the Mountain Melody Boys, Texas Cow Hands, and Trail Blazers.

In an interview with Jim Nelson, Howe Teague recalled one of these staged contests in St. Louis in 1940, between Natchee the Indian and Curly Fox. Teague heard about the contest on KMOX-AM radio. "Of course, Fox beat him." At KMOX someone interviewed Natchee and Curly on the air. Teague: "Old Natchee the Indian, he said he's going to scalp 'em that night. But Curly Fox got him—played the 'Mocking Bird' and goddam, he played every bird in the world, a-hollering' in there, and going on. And . . . Rubinoff or some great fiddler was there. And he said that Curly Fox put more notes in the fiddle than he knowed was *in* there. Quite a contest, I guess."[75]

Not really an Indian, Natchee was a Serbian immigrant (or was it Italian?) named Lester Vernon Storer.[76] In his stage persona as Natchee the Indian, Storer was a professional who fiddled on radio shows in the South and worked up a set of contest winners. He war-danced out onto the stage in full Plains Indian war bonnet and garb, with bells on his moccasins, waved his fiddle and bow around like a bow and arrow, and tore into audience pleasers like "Fire on the Mountain." If Ohio farm boys could get dressed up to imitate Arizona cowboys, certainly Storer could take the role of a wild Indian from the western plains. It was the old tent show beamed anew to the live radio audience. Rather than the serious proceedings of a 1926 contest in front of the county courthouse, these fiddle contests, promoted by Larry Sunbrock (a magazine writer), were more like folk theater or a carnival. Few considered them anything but entertainment. The fiddlers were typically required to play the same tunes, and these often included "show tunes" that were audience favorites but eventually banned by fiddlers' associations and contest committees—such as "Listen to the Mockingbird," "Orange Blossom Special," and cross-tuned "Black Mountain Rag" as well as "Back Up and Push."

Like those WOS radio contests, the judging was usually accomplished by audience applause. An electrical device called the applause-o-meter (clap-o-meter, an audience reaction indicator) was developed and refined in the 1950s and marketed to contests of all kinds, from political stump speeches to county fair queen contests to TV talent shows; the machine also found its way to the old-time fiddlers contest scene. Even an electric device that seemed to come from a Marx Brothers movie was worth a try. Attached to a microphone, the applause-o-meter would be set on the stage facing the audience. A dial and clock hand indicated decibel levels as people clapped for the performers. Fiddlers contest administrators were persuaded to use the machines because they were promoted as a more fair method of adjudication than the famously biased panels of judges historically used to sort the wheat from the chaff.

The emcee bounced around the stage, urging the crowd to greater decibels of approval. The entertainers could get not only theater crowds excited but "the folks at home" gathered around their radio sets as well.

But the applause-o-meter could be tricked. If a contestant had a large and loud throng of family and friends on hand, they were able to tilt the meter to favor their fiddler. So, before long, the applause-o-meter, while still found today (but not at fiddlers contests in Missouri), was discovered to be an easily manipulated machine and went out of fashion. The meter did indicate who was the most popular fiddler in the competition in that particular place on that particular day, but it did not indicate who was the superior musician among the players. Audience members of the kind normally bored (for example, reluctant children, inebriated men) found that the applause-o-meter inspired them to clap and cheer willy-nilly. Contest administrators went back to human judges, and efforts began to be made to find more judges with respected and serious knowledge of fiddling—all the better if the judges themselves were fiddlers or musicians—able and willing to try their best to be fair in sober conduct of their duties.

One's imagination of what these formidable soloists looked like as they were reared back and firing away into the microphone was fueled by colorful nicknames like Natchee the Indian and Big Howdy. Sometimes the results of these "showdowns" were rigged by the promoter before the show began. Sometimes the fiddlers themselves were not told who was to be the anointed winner for the evening, which led to post facto arguments and misunderstandings.[77]

Pete McMahan was among Missouri fiddlers of his generation who recalled enjoying these mock contests on the radio in the 1930s. McMahan admired the smooth and powerful fiddling exhibited by Natchee as well as the other influential commercial fiddlers he heard in the broadcasts, such as "Big Howdy" Forrester, Fiddlin' Arthur Smith, and Georgia Slim Rutland. Fiddlers knew good fiddling when they heard it, whether on records or radio or down at the neighborhood tavern.[78]

In terms of the hard-times economic environment, attending a local fiddle contest was a relatively inexpensive way to find some entertainment and pass the time. Contests continued after World War II and economic recovery in the 1940s, but by this time other forces were gaining people's attention and competing for their interests, including the explosion of radio programming, the growth of television, new forms of musical entertainment—as well as the importance of old-time fiddle-averse commercial country music, big-band music, and rock and roll—and the continuing popularity of country dance halls and taverns.

Fiddlers contests were held during the World War II years, but they were few and far between. World events of the era meant that many young musicians would be absent. The war ended in Europe in May 1945 with the Allies' defeat of Germany; the war in the Pacific ended in mid-August with Japan's surrender.

After Japan's surrender, one of many celebratory community events, an old-time fiddlers contest, was held at the National Guard armory in Columbia. Among the contestants were George Morris, Nolan Boone, Jake Hockemeyer, and Pete McMahan. McMahan had been drafted into the army in 1943 as a combat infantryman and had fought in North Africa and through the entire campaign in Sicily and Italy. Pete had just returned from northern Italy, where he was stationed when the war ended, and he was enjoying a forty-five-day furlough in Columbia before going to Fort Carson, Colorado, where he was discharged in mid-November. McMahan won the armory contest playing "Money Musk" and "Zig Zag Hornpipe" (in F), a tune he had learned from George Morris in the late 1930s, before going into the army after the attack on Pearl Harbor in December 1941.[79]

While vaudeville shows and amateur contests as well as dances and radio programs had provided fiddlers with public venues during the war, interest in fiddlers contests picked up in the late 1940s, notwithstanding the dampening effect of the Korean War. The resumption of contests coincided with and was helped by the national craze for square dancing and western movies and music. The Boone County Fair in Columbia, said to be the oldest county fair west of the Mississippi (having begun in 1835), resumed the long string of fiddlers contests that were often considered Missouri's most important competitions.[80]

Many young fiddlers cut their teeth on the repertory and style of the legendary contest fiddlers of the 1920s and 1930s, such as Henry Taylor, Vee Latty, Daniel Boone Jones, Ed Tharp, Casey Jones, Tony Gilmore, George Helton, and George

Morris, to name only a few. When the great revival of fiddle contests appeared in the jumbled 1960s era of change and crosswinds, a younger generation came to the stage, fiddlers who had been splicing touches of western swing and bluegrass into their playing and who would, in turn, have their contest styles and repertoires challenged and in many cases modified by the waves (gentle ripples at first, then the tsunami itself) of Texas-based and National Contest styles that gradually began to eat away at the bedrock of Missouri traditional fiddling in the 1970s and 1980s. Addressing that contentious and multihued history must await further study.

Lonnie Robertson of Springfield, Missouri, was a versatile and influential fiddler whose career flourished on AM radio. The careers of Robertson and his wife, Thelma, are celebrated in the Historium in the county seat at Gainesville. Robertson's favorite violin was a German-made "Maggini" copy from a mail-order catalog and, like many of his generation, he chose a stately Stetson western hat for his performances. (September 2014)

Lonnie Robertson

2

Lonnie Robertson. Here was the best Missouri fiddler I ever heard.

—R. P. Christeson, *The Old-Time Fiddler's Repertory*, vol. 2

Lonnie Robertson (1908–81) was among the best-known Missouri fiddlers who, with favorable circumstances and ambition, became prominent in the golden age of AM radio. Robertson saw the potential for building a career by promoting himself in radio studios up and down his core region on Missouri's western perimeter, as well as having a go at radio programs in the East.

In 1978 cultural historian and fiddle scholar Charles Wolfe wrote that, for many people in southern Missouri, "the name Lonnie Robertson has become synonymous with old-time fiddling."[1] Robertson is certainly among the most documented and recorded Missouri fiddlers, featured in Wolfe's research and writing, Drew Beisswenger and Gordon McCann's *Ozarks Fiddle Music* (with transcriptions of twenty-six tunes by Robertson), Kim Lansford's *Ozarks Mountaineer* article, and a variety of other publications, as well as in Robertson's many self-produced records from the 1960s to 1981.

R. P. Christeson, located in central Missouri, considered Lonnie Robertson to be Missouri's best, while Ozark folklorist Vance Randolph in Arkansas named Art Galbraith (Springfield) for the title. Christeson said of Robertson: "He knew an inordinate number of good tunes, could play them all well, and probably took more tunes to the cemetery than any other Missouri fiddler."[2] As my colleague Gordon McCann reminded me, I scarcely mention Robertson in my 2012 book, *Play Me Something Quick and Devilish*. Robertson, saved, as it were, for this book, is presented here as a leader of the twentieth-century parade of radio fiddlers.

Lonnie Robertson played violin and mandolin as well as guitar and sang and composed fiddle tunes. Determined to make his living as a performer, he worked on radio from the 1930s into the 1950s. Like other performers, his career was put on hold during lulls in activity and during a period when he fancied being a storekeeper in a small town near Springfield. He retired from radio in the 1960s.

Robertson was also well known because of his brief but fruitful partnership with guitarist Roy McGeorge. Typical of radio fiddlers and ensembles, Robertson, with his wife, Thelma, printed and sold song books, a helpful plank in the unsteady commercial platform with which professional and semiprofessional musicians struggled. Their 1940 songbook, *Lonnie and Thelma's Book of Beloved Hymns*, was issued while they were performing on Springfield's KWTO-AM and sold more than eight thousand copies at fifty cents each. Robertson was also active on the contest scene, as both competitor and judge, but did not derive much income from this notoriously tense and contentious activity. He preferred the role of radio fiddler and record producer.

Lonnie and Thelma, ca. 1955. The Down Home Folks enjoyed a long career, primarily on KWTO. Their harmony singing and handling of "heart songs" and gospel music were admired, and this reminds us that Lonnie Robertson was a skilled vocalist as well as an old-time fiddler. Other stations where they performed suggest efforts to make a living playing music, including KMA in Shenandoah, Iowa; WSVA in Harrisonburg, Virginia; WDZ in Tuscola, Illinois; and KDOA in Siloam Springs, Arkansas. (Courtesy Janet Tabor, the Historium)

Later, he took part in the 1960s and 1970s era of folk festivals and continued issuing self-produced and self-marketed records.

Lonnie Robertson was born on the family farm at Longrun, a village in the green folds of Ozark County some fifty miles southeast of Springfield and ten miles from Arkansas. The rocky soils and knobby landscape there favored livestock raising and forestry but discouraged row-crop farming. The Robertson family here began with Lonnie's grandfather coming from Georgia to Webster County in 1860. Lonnie's parents moved from just east of Springfield in Webster County south to Ozark County in 1900.[3]

A number of his family members, cousins, and in-laws played fiddle and dance music, including his father, Thomas Jarrett Robertson, and his brothers. Lonnie learned guitar at an early age by taking part in sessions and helping play for local dances. But as Ozark County historian Janet Tabor writes, it was when his father died when Lonnie was thirteen, and the lad inherited the family violin, that Lonnie got serious about learning to play fiddle music.[4] Born on January 8, 1908, Robertson loved to fiddle the old standard square-dance tune "The Eighth of January" (commemorating General Andrew Jackson's legendary victory over the British at the Battle of New Orleans in 1815, the last battle of the War of 1812) on his birthday.

The Robertson family violin had been played almost exclusively in an open tuning (scordatura or cross-tuning), which old Jarrett Robertson called "dischord," and this is the tuning in which Lonnie learned to play the instrument.[5] Playing in scordatura or open chords rather than in concert tuning (G–D–A–E) is often said to be more widely appreciated in the Ozarks than other Missouri regions, but it is difficult to test such a generalization. A very old tradition, scordatura appears in 1600s violin compositions, such as Austrian composer Heinrich Biber's "Mystery Sonatas" (1676). Dischord tuning appears to ultimately derive from the British Isles in the colonial period (if not before), and indeed it took centuries for violinists to somehow settle on what is now concert or standard tuning (G–D–A–E). As discussed in *Play Me Something Quick and Devilish*, scordatura (or chorded tunings) is known by several terms in Missouri, including "chording the strings," "chording up," "cross keys," "open tuning," "tuning up," "sawmill key," and "cross tuning," in addition to "dischord."[6] With the strings in an open chord, it is sometimes thought that a violin can produce greater volume and that the open strings reverberate impressively, giving not only volume but also interesting harmonies that to some ears echo the sounds of a bagpipe's chanter and drones. According to Paul Roberts:

> For young Lonnie the discovery of standard tuning was a revelation—a revolution even: "[with dischord tuning] You'd take both bass strings . . . make them blend with the A string. Or then you'd drop the E down, and you'd get a weary blend. Father played a lot of tunes that way, tunes I don't even remember today. . . . [M]any of those old-time fiddlers played only in cross-tune, not just because it's easier to play some tunes, but because, in those days before amplification, a cross-tuned fiddle has more volume and can be heard above the sound of the dancers. Anyway, I was playing fiddle in the store at Hammond the way my dad had played it, in dischord. Another fellow came in and picked up the fiddle and he tuned it up the other way. At that time I didn't know how to tune it the right way, in standard. Boy, I was a-listening close and when he tuned it that stayed in my ear until I got back home. So I tuned it up and went to learning to play that other way. It lets you play all sorts of different tunes.[7]

Learning to play music in standard violin tuning (concert tuning) as a teenager was critically important in Robertson's developing life as a career musician and entertainer. Without this new knowledge, self-taught fiddlers like Robertson would have found it tough going indeed when presented with chances to perform with musicians and ensembles with these skills and who were picking up music from Tin Pan Alley sheet music, piano compositions, tune books, and other written sources. Lonnie's chorded playing and, later, his learning to play in standard tuning made his experience much like that of other fiddlers, such as Columbia's Pete McMahan, Nile Wilson of Bucklin, and Gene Goforth of High Ridge. While it is notable that fiddlers like Robertson and Pete McMahan remembered fiddling only in chorded tunings as children, others of their generation in the same communities were well versed in playing in concert tuning as well as picking up fiddle tunes from written sources.

In terms of accompaniment, Lonnie learned to "beat the straws" or play "fiddle sticks" with knitting needles, to add accent and rhythm to a fiddler's music. Many other things can be used by the person doing the drumming on the fiddler's open strings while the fiddler is playing—stiff broom straws, bits of wire, wooden barbecue skewers from the grocery store, pencils, or chopsticks. This simple act of "beating the straws" can add to and enhance the volume and, in cases where no accompanist is available, can help a fiddler provide music for dances by him- or herself.

Lonnie Robertson also performed with reed-organ players. The reed organ (parlor organ) was available from local stores and mail-order catalogs, and many were small enough to be portable and could be transported in a farm wagon or buggy. Few people could afford pianos, guitars were rare, and banjos were only a bit less rare in this area of the Ozarks.

On the other hand, violins were plentiful, even if many were homemade and relatively poor quality mail-order instruments. Many violins had been brought in pioneer times from Virginia or Ireland and were cherished heirlooms to be handed down through the generations. Jim Orchard of Shannon County recalls that virtually every community and most families in his area had at least two fiddlers.[8]

Robertson also played "fiddle second" (or "second fiddle"), a tradition in which one fiddler plays accented notes or two-note chords under and supporting the other fiddler's melody. This tradition is rare today, but there are signs of its rejuvenation.[9]

In keeping with the experience of other Missouri fiddlers of his generation, Lonnie said his first tunes were big breakdowns for square dancing that every fiddler worth his or her salt was expected to be able to play: "Arkansas Traveler," "Tennessee Wagner," and "Soldier's Joy." Among tunes Lonnie learned in dischord from his father, Jarrett, were "Arkansas Traveler," "Fisher's Hornpipe," "Drunkard's Hiccups," "Cluck Old Hen," "Dry and Dusty," "and "Cotton-Eyed Joe."

Lonnie Heads North

At fifteen, looking for employment away from the family farm in Ozark County, Robertson traveled to St. Joseph to find work in a meatpacking plant. In St. Joe, he became acquainted with local musicians and before long was fiddling on a Sunday-afternoon live radio show over KFEQ, sponsored by Green Bag Feed.

Lonnie often said that he learned most of his fiddle technique and repertoire while fiddling at music parties ("jam sessions" is a newer term) and dances and at KFEQ radio in the St. Joseph area. He also learned some tunes from 78 rpm records by popular southern string bands and fiddlers such as Gid Tanner and the Skillet Lickers, Fiddlin' John Carson, Clark Kessinger, as well as Kentucky's Doc Roberts. As it turns out, features of Clark Kessinger's style as well as the styles of Lowe Stokes (the Skillet Lickers' principal fiddler) and Doc Roberts were palpably similar to features in the central and northwestern Missouri and Missouri Valley styles that Lonnie Robertson would become immersed in during his radio career.

Kessinger, Doc Roberts, and Lowe Stokes played in smooth, notey styles (with individual nuances)—as did Bob Walters and Casey Jones—that were helping evolve a principal fiddle style for professionals and a precursor to today's predominant fiddle styles in national contests, bluegrass, and country music. During this time, Robertson also listened to and learned bits from two more influential commercial fiddlers, Robert (Georgia Slim) Rutland and Rutland's friend Howdy Forrester. After his exposure to the northern playing of Walters and Casey Jones, he began working out the complicated, notey hornpipes so much evident in the old-time fiddlers' repertoire north of the Ozarks region and in Robertson's recorded oeuvre.

Robertson's style fits fairly comfortably with a northern stylistic profile, sometimes called "North Missouri style" or "Missouri Valley style," a principal fiddling style from the 1920s onward in areas in Missouri, Kansas, Nebraska, and Iowa, particularly but not exclusively along both sides of the Missouri River from approximately Kansas City (at Missouri's western edge) north into southeastern South Dakota. Among well-known exponents available on recordings were Bob Walters, Casey Jones, Amos Chase, Cyril Stinnett, and Lonnie Robertson, and all but Stinnett helped spread this style and repertoire through live radio shows from the 1930s into the 1950s. (Missouri's main stylistic categories are discussed in *Play Me Something Quick and Devilish.*)

Robertson's style defies easy categorization for those who place fiddlers in stylistic slots based on where they were born and learned to play music. His native turf was the lower Missouri Ozarks next to the Arkansas line. But his fiddling style, as attested by his admirer (and cousin) fiddler H. K. Silvey of Theodosia, Missouri, was not typical Ozark shuffle-bow fiddling—it was more like the fiddling in central and northern Missouri.[10] Yet when he played a hot square-dance tune, he could comfortably play at the greater tempos favored by influential Ozark dance fiddlers such as Howe Teague and Bob Holt.

When the Great Depression hit, Robertson and many others lost their jobs. While he made a bit of cash playing for Sunday-afternoon dances (as guitarist and fiddler), he could not survive financially. At this point, in 1931, Lonnie returned to Ozark County and married Thelma Jones. Still excited to be a radio performer, he telegraphed the manager at Yankton, South Dakota, station WNAX to offer his services as a fiddler. "Well, Lady Luck was smiling on this Ozark boy and back came a wire . . . saying 'come on.'"[11] He took the job and his music proved popular, and listeners wrote letters to the station asking for more Lonnie Robertson. At WNAX in 1933, Lonnie met Roy McGeorge, who would later become his singing and playing partner.

But with hard times pressing on his finances, Robertson left Yankton and WNAX and returned to the Springfield area, where he and Thelma operated a grocery store in the town of Brookline. Less than a year later, in 1937, Robertson contacted Roy McGeorge, who in the meantime was performing on radio in Pennsylvania. They decided to get together and look for work as "Lonnie and Roy," a "brother duet."

McGeorge moved to Missouri, and they were hired first in St. Joe at KFEQ and in 1938 moved to WAAW in Omaha. The year 1939 found them in Lincoln at KFAB and in 1940 at KFAB as well as performing at KOAM in Pittsburg and at KITE in Kansas City. While in Lincoln at KFAB, Lonnie and Thelma's son, Jarrett, was born.

Lonnie and Roy, a Brother Duet

Parallel to Lonnie Robertson's importance as a fiddler is his work in live hillbilly radio and the ensemble type called the brother duet. Lonnie Robertson and Roy McGeorge (1910–95) had met at WNAX in Yankton, South Dakota, in 1933 and as "Lonnie and Roy" performed together from 1938 until 1942.[12]

While they became quite popular together, Roy and Lonnie also had their ups and downs in the radio business. At WNAX Lonnie had been hired as a radio fiddler, but when he and McGeorge conceived of their brother act, Lonnie began playing mandolin and singing high-tenor harmony—the Bill Monroe to Roy's Charlie Monroe, as in the nationally popular Monroe Brothers. Lonnie's mandolin playing consisted of playing rhythm and taking solo melodic breaks, in the style typical of hillbilly mandolinists of the 1930s and 1940s. McGeorge sang the melody lead and provided guitar accompaniment. In addition to WNAX, Lonnie and Roy were heard on several other regional stations, such as WAAW (Omaha).

In the 1930s the brother-duet ensemble typically was two male vocalists (brothers, cousins, or other family members or colleagues) singing tight harmony and playing mandolin and guitar. Sometimes additional accompanists were included, and the ensemble became a trio or quartet. The singing was typically strong and clear, with most shows including at least one gospel song, and the instrumental accompaniment was usually spare, if elegantly performed. The brother duets reflected the fact that, often, musical abilities ran in families, and family bands and ensembles have always been part of the traditional music milieu. Many people feel that there is a special kind of communication and connection between brothers (or sisters) singing "close harmony" together, and many such duos had an almost sacred aura in their performances and representation of the good old days back on the farm when the old folks gathered around the woodstove in the evenings and sang together. Most radio stations programming hillbilly music featured such groups as one of the ensembles on a "jamboree" or "barn dance" show or in their own program.

Other well-known brother duets included the Blue Sky Boys, the Delmore Brothers, the Bailes Brothers, the Buchanan Brothers, the Louvin Brothers, Karl and Harty, and the Monroe Brothers (Bill and Charlie), the Kentucky duo featuring the tense, high tenor and mandolin playing of younger brother Bill, who in the later 1940s would help develop bluegrass music. Robertson and McGeorge covered songs on recordings and programs they liked, particularly songs from the Monroe Brothers and Karl and Harty, who were popular performers on the WLS *National Barn Dance*. Often, what began as two brothers or friends performing together evolved into full-fledged country or bluegrass bands in the 1940s.[13]

Robertson and McGeorge developed a comedy routine, to provide the jokes and patter expected in these radio shows. Robertson acted the role of "Etherham Hobbs" and McGeorge his foil, "Uncle Enoch." The comedy was a staple of live radio shows featuring hillbilly music, and the characters were developed to match up with the public's stereotypes, drawing on more than a century of minstrel stage, Toby shows, and "Arkansas Traveler" stage routines. Virtually every old-time string band featured at least one member filling the comedic role as rustic or rube, often in stereotypical hillbilly costume. Lonnie and Roy in part copied the nationally popular comedy duo Lum and Abner, heard across the continent in syndicated AM radio; their hillbilly sketch comedy was based on their hometown in Arkansas. Many bluegrass and country bands continue to include a member filling the role of rube, and the self-mocking comedy is as much fun in the 2010s as it was in the 1910s.

Roy McGeorge

McGeorge was born in Estill County, Kentucky, southeast of Lexington, and left home at seventeen to pursue a career in music. A good singer and guitarist, he developed a style of strumming guitar employing only his right thumb (with a thumb pick). In his guitar technique, he employed his little finger as a prop for his thumb-picking and strumming style, a style that sounded much like that of bluegrass guitarist Lester Flatt, complete with strong bass runs. As a child of nine, McGeorge had lost most of his first, second, and third fingers on his right hand in an accident while chopping firewood with his older brother Herb. He learned to work with his damaged hand and became a fine rifle marksman as well as a fine guitarist. When World War II broke out, McGeorge tried to enlist in the army but was refused because of his missing fingers; his son Henry recalls his father being upset at this rejection and stating to the army personnel that he was very likely a better rifle shot than any of the soldiers in the recruiting office.[14]

According to Henry McGeorge, one of his father's favorite melodies to pick on the guitar was a Hawaiian tune called "Kohala March," in which Roy played descending notes while Lonnie Robertson played ascending notes on mandolin. A number of commercial recordings of the tune had been released since 1914. Roy McGeorge could have heard any, or all, of these recordings and performances. The instrumental tune echoes the fashion for Hawaiian melodies and lap slide-guitar styles that were promulgated on 78 rpm recordings in the World War I years and ensuing years of popularity of Polynesian culture, food, and music, especially on the West Coast.[15]

In 1927 Roy McGeorge appeared on Louisville station WFIA, launching a career making music and performing. A year later, in 1928, he migrated west to WNAX in Yankton and moved for a time to KFNF in Shenandoah, Iowa. Like other musicians working live radio broadcasts, he moved around the region to work at various stations, including WDAY in Fargo, North Dakota; WOW in Omaha, Nebraska; KSTP in St. Paul, Minnesota; and KFEQ in St. Joseph, Missouri. Back at WNAX in 1933, Roy met Lonnie Robertson. Lonnie and Roy traveled to other regional stations, such as KFEQ in St. Joseph and Nebraska stations KFAB (Lincoln) and WAAW (Omaha). From 1939 to 1940, they stayed put as hired performers at KFAB in Lincoln. Lonnie and Roy typically used "Boil the Cabbage Down," the old favorite square-dance tune, as their theme tune on their shows, but they used other tunes as themes (such as part of an untitled fiddle tune on track 1 of the companion CD).

Lonnie and Roy's KFAB career was cut short. While performing on a live KFAB radio show at the fairgrounds, too much strong drink and an impudent remark got Lonnie and Roy fired. In one version of the oft-told episode, recorded by Ozark County historian Mary Ruth Luna Sparks in an interview with Thelma, it seems that Lonnie and Roy "had been celebrating Jarrett's birth and got to the KFAB program at the Nebraska Fair Grounds late. The announcer made a snide remark about Lonnie and Roy being late. 'So Lonnie hauled off and slugged him in front of the crowd and over the live radio. The end result was that the announcer, Lonnie, and Roy, and all were fired on the spot!' Thelma said." Another version of the saga has Lonnie, angry over the staff band's cornet player making romantic advances on Thelma, seizing the man and bashing him over the head with his cornet.[16]

Henry McGeorge with one of the transcriptions his father, Roy, recorded with Lonnie Robertson in Fort Worth, Texas, in 1941 for the Sellers transcription company. (At the Starvy Creek Bluegrass Festival near Conway, Missouri, July 2015)

"Greetings from Uncle Frank and His Hillbilly Cousins," promotional calendar with studio musicians at KOAM radio, Pittsburg, Kansas, 1941. Next to the announcer (*left, rear*), Roy McGeorge with his Martin guitar and Lonnie Robertson with a Gibson F-5 mandolin (popularized by bluegrass pioneer Bill Monroe), both men attired in western cowboy shirts and Stetson hats. (Courtesy Henry McGeorge)

Lonnie and Roy were soon blackballed from radio stations in the region. So in the fall of 1940, they decided to travel down to Fort Worth, Texas, to make radio transcriptions for broadcasting at stations subscribing to the service. Roy and Lonnie's wives went to Theodosia to stay with Thelma's parents. While in Texas, Lonnie and Roy went to Del Rio, where they performed live over the famous "border radio" station XERG, a high-wattage AM station people heard as far away as Canada.

A studio portrait of staff musicians at KOAM in 1941 indicates the kind of music that was presented. All of them were part of the overall group "Uncle Frank and His Hillbilly Cousins," and various members were subtracted to form smaller groups for various performances. The look is one of the Hollywood movie–influenced cowboy band, but, typical of the World War II years, one or two of the musicians were part of subgroups with "college kid" or "big band" images. The instrumentation included guitars (acoustic flattop and archtop), mandolin, tenor guitar, upright bass, plectrum banjo, and clarinet. Having the best instruments enhanced the quality and appeal of the music being made and, along with costumes appropriate to the genre of music being performed, were signals of professionalism. The announcer is costumed as the traditional vaudeville "professor," interlocutor, or master of ceremonies, and the young girl singer on the front row left is made up as the stereotypical freckled country bumpkin.

Several recordings of Lonnie and Roy exist of the radio transcriptions made in 1941 at the Sellers Transcription Company studio in Fort Worth. These transcriptions were mastered at the studio and copies then mailed to stations that subscribed to the service—including many high-wattage stations just inside Mexico as well as stations across Texas and stations such as Chicago's WJJD. Radio transcriptions ("transcriptions discs" or "electrical transcriptions") were twelve- or sixteen-inch phonograph records (typically wax or aluminum) ready to be plopped on a studio turntable and broadcast on the air. Radio stations appreciated the transcriptions because a prerecorded program could be broadcast in cases when performers were not able to get to the station; to the listener, the show sounded live. This same strategy was employed decades later via tape recordings of prerecorded shows, such as *The Rooster Creek Show* over KFAL-AM in Fulton, Missouri. Robertson played fiddle tunes on the transcriptions, but, along with some hillbilly comedy, the music was primarily smooth duet singing with mandolin and guitar.[17]

Later in 1941, the heat had died down, and Lonnie and Roy were able to get fresh radio jobs, this time at KOAM in Pittsburg, Kansas. KOAM (Kansas, Oklahoma, Arkansas, Missouri) began broadcasting in 1937 and became an NBC affiliate. The call letters represented their focus region, the lower Midwest and eastern Great Plains. A high-wattage station, KOAM could be heard at great distances and in many states. The duet was featured on a daily show, and Lonnie had his own fiddling show as well. Lonnie's paycheck came to twenty-two dollars per week.

In Pittsburg in 1942, Lonnie decided to disband the Lonnie and Roy duet in order to concentrate on developing his performing career with his wife, Thelma. Lonnie and Roy remained friends and would get together to "jam" and visit whenever possible.

Roy McGeorge remained in Pittsburg, where he raised a family and continued at KOAM radio as a professional musician and part of the studio's technical staff. Roy became a fixture of the regional radio scene, partnering with mandolinist Earl Bledsoe as "Roy and Earl" to continue in the brother-duet performance idiom. McGeorge retired in 1973 after three decades in hillbilly radio and television at KOAM.

Next, Lonnie set out to form a family pickin' and singin' group with his wife, Thelma.[18] They called themselves the Down Home Folks. Thelma would develop into a star performer in her own right—she had been a fine singer in church choirs for many years—and soon became vital in the success of the duo. Thelma was a sharp businesswoman and largely, it was said, responsible for whatever financial success they enjoyed.[19] Thelma Jones Robertson was from the Ozark County village of Theodosia (not far from Lonnie's hometown of Longrun) and sang alto. Thelma had debuted on live radio in 1942 at KMA in Shenandoah. In 1962 Thelma lost her eyesight through illness, and this was a factor in the eventual winding down of the "Lonnie and Thelma" traveling and radio performances. They did, however, continue performing and issued songs on their own label. Thelma died in 2000.

The KWTO Years

Lonnie and Thelma—the Down Home Folks—settled in as performers at Springfield's KWTO (Keep Watching the Ozarks) 560-AM, the powerhouse station in the region. KWTO had been founded by Ralph Foster in 1933. Starting a radio station in the depths of the Depression was risky, but Foster and his colleagues put together a successful blend of programs in a format that kept the focus on everyday people and life in the four-state Ozarks region.[20] KWTO was so successful and widely heard that young musicians from many states considered performing there to be a career launching pad. However, in this instance, growing older, Lonnie and Thelma Robertson considered working at KWTO a comfortable situation in Springfield, the most important and prosperous city in their region.

Many stars of country music got their start on KWTO, or appeared there, from Red Foley to Porter Wagoner and Chet Atkins. Local and regional country musicians who performed at KWTO in the 1940s and 1950s would make a long list: for example, the Goodwill Family, the Haden Family, Speedy Haworth, Slim Wilson (a fiddler as well as band leader), Doc Martin, Dusty Rhodes, Dale Sledd, Lonnie Hoppers, and fiddlers the likes of Zed Tennis, Buster Fellows, Lennie Aleshire, Dale Potter, Red Loveall, Don Russell, Michael Breid, and Lonnie Robertson. KWTO's programs and those of other AM stations led to the development of "opry" show towns such as those at Branson and to eventual televised programs.[21]

Lonnie and Thelma's only child, Jarrett Robertson (1940–93), was an essential part of the Down Home Folks on KWTO, singing in the trio and playing various instruments. Young Jarrett, named for his grandfather, was a budding fiddler, and even at age five was part of the show. Jarrett "came to the studio every day with his parents, bringing toys to entertain himself while they were performing. He would be called to the microphone at least once during a show, to sing something like 'Happy Roving Cowboy.'"[22] Eventually, after college in Springfield, Jarrett joined the army, served two tours in Vietnam, and rose to the rank of major general; he died in a helicopter crash in Germany in 1993.

For Lonnie Robertson, the invitation to come to Yankton, South Dakota, to play and sing on the radio in the 1930s had been life changing. There, as Kim Lansford notes, in the WNAX studios, he met the famous Nebraska fiddler Bob Walters (Walter) as well as the Missouri champion and radio fiddler Casey Jones. Jones and Walters played in the notey, elaborate northwestern Missouri style, a.k.a. "Missouri Valley style," often with longer and fuller bow strokes. Robertson began working this style into his fiddling as well as numerous ornate hornpipes (many of them coming from old printed books of fiddle tunes) and other tunes he was hearing.[23] Lonnie and Bob Walters became good friends, and on several occasions Walters visited Lonnie and Thelma in Springfield; Walters appeared as a guest fiddler on Lonnie's KWTO radio show.[24]

Caney Mountain Records

Robertson's numerous commercial recordings indicate the depth and range of his repertoire, breakdowns, rags, waltzes, schottisches, polkas, and fox-trots, drawn from many years of fiddling for dances, contests, and sessions. Schottisches were relatively scarce in his section of Missouri, and Lonnie had learned one of his favorites, "Tunes from Home," from listening to the soon-to-be-famous German American farmhand turned accordionist Lawrence Welk at the WNAX studio in Yankton in 1927.[25]

Some of Robertson's fiddling is preserved on the 45 rpm sides, recorded in his kitchen in Theodosia on a reel-to-reel tape recorder in the 1960s and pressed as Caney Mountain releases by Wayne Raney's Rimrock studio. (There is a Caney Mountain in the Missouri Ozarks.) Raney, a radio performer and country music star, for many years operated a firm in Conway, Arkansas, that provided self-produced recordings for country musicians and for Missouri fiddlers, such as Lee Stoneking, Cyril Stinnett, and Pete McMahan. This was during the postwar decades when folk festivals, collectors, scholars, and record companies were giving shape to the folk music record business, and Robertson decided he should try this emerging commercial opportunity.

There were seven seven-inch 45 rpm EP (extended play) records, accompanied by old-time banjoist Troy Wilson of Ava, guitarist Paul Jones (a cousin of Thelma's), and bassist George Rhodes (who performed with the Goodwill Family on KWTO in the 1940s). Several tracks from these 45s were reissued on the Rounder CD *Lonnie's Breakdown*, by Gordon McCann, a longtime friend and guitar accompanist of Robertson's. During the years he knew Robertson, McCann tape-recorded Robertson's fiddling on some seventy occasions.

The music on *Lonnie's Breakdown* is driving and powerful and gives us a sense of his wide-ranging repertoire. Like other fiddlers of his generation, such as Delbert Spray, Howe Teague, and Taylor McBaine, the breadth of musical genres and dance types Robertson fiddled may surprise a player today who may stay generally inside the dotted lines of modern genres such as bluegrass, swing, and contest fiddling. On the tracks taken from the 45 rpm records, the banjo playing by Troy Wilson is notable for being a pre–Earl Scruggs form of three-finger picking, not too unlike the parlor banjo backup style made famous by Lena Hughes (Casey Jones's sister, in northern Missouri; her pre-Scruggs "parlor style," finger-style banjo backup can be heard on several of Cyril Stinnett's self-produced LP records). As McCann writes in the notes to the Rounder CD reissue, Lonnie worked up original tunes when he put material together for the 45 rpm EPs.[26] The reissued tracks include such Robertson compositions as "Lonnie's Breakdown," "Mountain Reel," and "Untitled Reel in B^b," along with tunes taken from his other recordings such as "Caney Mountain Hornpipe," "Lazy Hills Waltz," "Taney County Breakdown," "Untitled Reel in D," "Unnamed B^b Waltz," "A and E Rag" (renamed "Buck Fever"), "Bluebird Waltz," and "Arkansas Stomp."

Robertson knew that the recordings would be used at square dances in cases where a live band was not available. Robertson was following the example especially of Nashville fiddler Tommy Jackson, whose "square dances without calls" records were hugely popular in Missouri. Of Lonnie's known compositions, several have successfully gone into repertoires of fiddlers today, such as "Taney Mountain Breakdown" and "Lazy Hills Waltz." Robertson also followed a trend among fiddlers issuing recordings of traditional tunes by creating alternate titles, such as "Country Man's Hornpipe" for "Countryman's Reel." In their album notes, McCann and Mark Wilson include a list of Robertson's radio repertoire, a fascinating indication of the vast number of traditional tunes and songs for vocal numbers as well as "pop" songs from the 1940s.[27]

Sometimes Lonnie's methodology as record producer could be unconventional. Some records resulted from fiddle sessions that Lonnie organized in the front room in his big frame house on North Benton in Springfield. I happened to be an incidental participant in the making of one such LP. In November 1975, I was dispatched to Missouri (at that time I was a museum research director in Indiana) by Ralph Rinzler at the Smithsonian Institution to record a sampling of Missouri fiddlers. Robertson was on a list of fiddlers to visit (along with Art Galbraith, Lee Roy Stoneking, Taylor McBaine, Glenn Rickman, Cyril Stinnett, and Pete McMahan), and after I visited with and recorded Art Galbraith in Springfield, Art said something like, "Hey, Lonnie's having a picking party tonight, and we're invited. Let's go." Go we did. When we got there, Lonnie had a reel-to-reel tape recorder and microphones set up in front of a semicircle of armless "pickin' chairs." Not long after the session, Lonnie issued the Caney Mountain LP with tracks with tunes and musicians at Lonnie's jam session that evening. In talking later with Galbraith, who played mandolin on several of these LPs, I found no one seemed to mind.

Robertson took part in the contest scene from the 1960s onward. Sometimes he competed, and other times he served on the judging panel. He often won first in contests in the Ozarks and amassed the usual array of trophies and ribbons. His fiddle style worked well in his own region, but, as he noted, his fiddling did not go over as well up north in Little Dixie and northern Missouri. As quoted in Charles Wolfe's 1978 *Devil's Box* article: "There are still some good old-time musicians in the area. But some of the best fiddlers are up in north Missouri. There's Cyril Stinnett, . . . Pete McMahan, . . . Dean Johnston over at Lamar—that's the best ones. And some of the best fiddling contests are in north Missouri. They're better about judging; you either play old-time fiddle up there, or you don't get *nowhere*. They don't allow no bluegrass, no trick fiddling; down here, they mix it up a little."[28]

Robertson made those comments at age seventy as he reflected on contest fiddling in the 1960s and 1970s. The contest scene was changing. Texas-influenced and fancier fiddling styles were bumping aside older styles that had, for two generations, defined Missouri fiddling. Old-time fiddlers who would find success in the evolving contest environment—precisely those fiddlers Lonnie named—accommodated themselves in performance style and repertoire to national, nonregional trends supplanting regional and local contest fiddle styles and repertoires. It is also possible that, up in Little Dixie or northern Missouri, Robertson's playing was "heard" by local contest judges as different, as Ozark style, despite his fiddling displaying features of central and northern Missouri fiddling. Judges in those days tended to favor fiddlers from their own regions (an aspect of contests that has not changed).

Changing Tempos

Fiddlers shift tempos for a variety of reasons. A fiddler may simply speed up in physical and emotional response to a lively and eager set of square dancers. A fiddler may be almost imperceptibly "rushed" by an eager accompanist who inadvertently increases the tempo. Or an accompanist may "drag" behind the fiddler's tempo, gumming up the works.

A fiddler may play a certain tune at a scorching speed to please a given group of square dancers. Bob Holt, the great Ava dance fiddler, tore along at blazing speeds (up to 144 beats per minute [BPM] for his signature "Ninth of January") that he developed in order to please "the Ava dancers" square-dance group led by Edna Mae Davis in Douglas County.[29] At other times, Holt played the very same tunes slower. Lonnie Robertson certainly "made 'em sweat" with his "Taney County Breakdown," but other fiddlers, such as Bob Holt and Bob's devoted pupils today, such as Liz Amos, Ashley Hull Forrest, and David Scrivner, play as fast—sometimes faster!—than their teacher Holt (who died in 2004).[30]

Every fiddler who plays dances experiences the process of trying to please the dancers and caller, and it affects his or her tempos as it also affects the amount of pleasure he or she may derive from being the fiddler. The fiddler and accompanists are, after all, expected to provide a beat for dancers to enjoy and not to put on a concert or exhibition. Fiddlers almost never get a signal from a caller in the midst of a square dance to "slow down."

Moreover, when a fiddler comes to the challenge of being recorded, for whatever purpose, he or she may tend to slow the tempo down, even if slightly and even if unconsciously. The musician's mind tries to instruct the body to perform well, to make no mistakes, rather than lay down rhythm for dancing feet. There are other ways a fiddler's tempo may change in playing the same tunes, as when a fiddler is in a jam session with accompanists or other fiddlers who are accustomed to a certain prevailing tempo for the tunes.

On *Lonnie's Breakdown*, Robertson rips through local square-dance tunes in the keys of D, C, G, and A, such as "Lonnie's Breakdown," "Taney County Breakdown," and "Caney Mountain Hornpipe" (a reel, despite its title). Robertson learned "Taney County Breakdown" from an unknown dance fiddler in Rockaway Beach and gave the tune its title.[31] Robertson's tempos for his square-dance tunes may sound ultra-fast. However, there is a surprising degree of variation in the square-dance tempos of Robertson and most other fiddlers.

Frisky Jim

Transcribed by Sharon Graf

as played by Lonnie Robertson (Etherham Hobbs) 1939

"Frisky Jim," by Lonnie Robertson with Roy McGeorge, 1939, KFAB, Lincoln, Nebraska (hear on the companion CD). This radio show is in the Digital Archive of the Country Music Hall of Fame, where Etherham Hobbs mistakenly is given as "Ether Ham Hobbs" and "Frisky Jim" as "Frisky Dan" (http://digi.countrymusichalloffame.org/cdm/singleitem/collection/musicaudio/id/237/rec/4). Christeson gives Bob Walters's 1949 version in his 1973 book (p. 4) and seems unaware of Robertson's 1939 recording. (Courtesy Henry McGeorge; transcription by Sharon Graf)

Lonnie's Breakdown includes several of his 1960s-era 45 rpm records as well as later recordings, and the tempo for each of the two dozen square-dance tunes ranges from 114 BPM for "Rosebud Reel," up to 137 BPM for "Taney County Breakdown," and 138 BPM for "Lonnie's Breakdown."[32] This seems like a puzzling range for square-dance tempos, but it can be explained.

Different kinds of tunes are suitable for square dancing, and the nature of the tune affects the tempo. It is customary in Ozark, Douglas, and Taney Counties and environs for most fiddlers to play hoedowns (reels or breakdowns) at a comparatively fast tempo for square dancers, in the 130-and-above range of beats per minute. This works for the driving old-time breakdowns and reels with comparatively spare melodic lines traditionally heard at square dances in the Ozarks of southern Missouri. As McCann has articulated, "This region boasts a fast, vigorous style of fiddle music and square dancing not readily encountered in the Midwest today."[33]

So when Lonnie Robertson began to soak up some of the complicated, stately hornpipes he learned in northwestern Missouri, Iowa, and Nebraska (especially from his radio years with fiddlers such as Bob Walters and Casey Jones), in order to "get it all in" and retain the character of the more notey, melodically complex hornpipes, the tempos became slower. When fiddlers play the notey northern hornpipes at too rapid a tempo, the music suffers and the fiddling tends to sound stressed. Derived especially from eighteenth-century British Isles dance music and its special solo step dance, the hornpipe has a more melodically complex structure and a slower tempo, distinctions still heard in Irish and Celtic music in Britain and Canada.

In American fiddling, however, through the generations the special character of the slower, more melodically complex, often "dotted," and often very "Scottish" rhythm of the hornpipe proper has been sanded down; the result is that, by the early twentieth century, the old hornpipes had evolved into "hoedowns" (reels or breakdowns) to be played fast for square dancing (discussed in *Play Me Something Quick and Devilish*). In many cases, one can spot a breakdown that started out life as a hornpipe. Some of these old hornpipes are now evened out and fiddled like hoedowns; they may even have "Reel" or "Breakdown" in their names. Among the hornpipe-like tunes in the Missouri repertoire that have become hoedowns are "Miller's Reel," "Devil's Dream," "Tom and Jerry," "Bill Cheatem," "Grey Eagle," "Angus Campbell," "Fiddler's Hornpipe," "Coming Down from Denver," and those great chestnuts played by every seasoned Missouri fiddler I have known, "Leather Britches" and "Marmaduke's Hornpipe" (hear on the companion CD).

Good examples of this process of rendering hornpipes slower are Lonnie Robertson's versions of "Rosebud Reel," a rare and comparatively difficult melody in B-flat (114 BPM), and "Lonnie's Hornpipe."[34] Robertson had learned "Lonnie's Hornpipe" from the northern Missouri radio fiddler Casey Jones; its true title was not known.[35] Lonnie played it so often on his KWTO radio that listeners assumed that he had composed it, and people began to call it "Lonnie's Hornpipe." Lonnie did not claim authorship and stated in the notes to *Lonnie's Breakdown*, "Not mine. I learned it from a fiddler up north." "Up north" remains a common signifier among some Ozark fiddlers that the tune being referenced is not an Ozark tune and we might expect a different tempo and stylistic treatment. When Robertson recorded the tune, however, he chose to let the title be "Lonnie's Hornpipe." The tune reminds us of several other central and northern Missouri hornpipes, and it clocks in at 116 BPM as Lonnie played it, a good deal slower than his lickety-split Ozark breakdowns.

Another element in the discussion of Lonnie Robertson's tempos is that he was making his way as a professional fiddler at a time when bluegrass music was evolving. Bluegrass became known for its ultrafast instrumental tempos that could showcase a particularly deft Scruggs-style banjoist or fiery fiddler. It appears that Robertson did not desire to move into bluegrass music, either to become an ensemble player or to form a bluegrass band of his own. In terms of the tempos of bluegrass music, a good portion of the bluegrass instrumental repertoire is notoriously quite fast. Few old-time fiddlers could, or would want to, play fast enough to suit a bluegrass band of what we called "speed freaks" in the 1970s.

For instance, the Missouri bluegrass banjo player Lonnie Hoppers of Springfield played and recorded with Bill Monroe and His Blue Grass Boys in the early 1960s and often played tunes made famous by Monroe. One of these is the instrumental called "Pike County Breakdown" (recorded by Monroe's band in 1952 with Sonny Osborne doing the banjo honors). Monroe's "Pike County Breakdown" clocked in at around 155 BPM. Hoppers's tempo on his own 1980 recording of "Pike County Breakdown" (Lonnie Hoppers & Friends, *Pickin' for Fun*), in which he plays much the same banjo solo as his friend Sonny Osborne, comes in at around that same 155 BPM. On the same CD, Hoppers's version of the banjo instrumental "Train 45" (recorded by Missouri's Dillards bluegrass band as "Reuben's Train") arrives at the depot at around 170 beats per minute, too fast for the chickens to get off the track and too fast for all but a wild fiddler like Scotty Stoneman (of the Stoneman Family, Tennessee) to hang on to. It is generally agreed that many old-time fiddlers continue to find the blazing speeds typical of bluegrass music to be uncomfortable. "Too fast to dance to" is often the remark made.

Hoppers offers an additional perspective on bluegrass and old-time fiddlers: "Most of those old-timers wouldn't have liked it. Because, in my experience around here, a lot of those old-time fiddle players, they didn't want anybody else to be *featured* at *all*. They wanted everybody to just sit back here and play one fiddle tune after another, for four hours, you know."[36]

Very few fiddlers will render a tune at precisely the same BPM time after time, year after year, whatever the occasion. Old age and a pinch of lumbago or tennis elbow will slow down all but the most speedy dance fiddlers; many fiddlers will start to play hoedowns a bit slower and resist fiddling those painfully lengthy contra dances and square dances that young fiddlers relish.

Caney Mountain, 2014.

Apart from the delight we find in Robertson's fiddling, one more point could be made about Lonnie, Roy McGeorge, and their colleagues in the formative days of AM radio. There was a goodly amount of interesting and influential music being made in the midwestern United States, and it is hard to know the impact it had. As Charles Wolfe says in "Caney Mountain Fiddler," "In the 1920s and 1930s most of the record companies, convinced that the only decent old-time music was in the South, generally ignored the Midwest in their search for artists, and there are dozens of influential musicians from this area who never set foot inside a recording studio." It is a subject worth pursuing, especially when we understand that all those farm-and-home fiddling radio broadcasts of Midwest fiddlers on clear-channel stations in South Dakota, Nebraska, Kansas, Iowa, Illinois, and Missouri were heard by people as far away as Cuba, Florida, California, New York, and Canada.

While people were buying 78 rpm records of southern string bands, they were equally apt to sit by a radio and listen to fiddlers from their own Midwest region perform on radio programs. We may never solve the "who influenced whom" conundrum from those early days of radio, when musicians soaked up all the music they could, whether bouncing through the air from West Virginia, Ontario, Louisiana, Kansas, or anyplace with a high-power transmitter.

Lonnie Robertson, a star of early hillbilly radio, continues to inspire fiddlers, including younger generations who are finding pleasure in the fiddle music Lonnie made on old-time radio and vinyl records. Of that, I am glad. And from that, I draw confidence in the future's appreciation of this music and its fragile history.

Joe Russell (Urbana), Bert Lewis, and Agnes Moss at a music party at Lewis's home, Urbana, Missouri, ca. 1950. (Courtesy Gladys Reser)

3 Music Parties

You boys got your music with you? If you do, play that "Knockin' at Your Door."

—John Hartford, recalling how he and others would be met when visiting fiddler Walter Alexander in Leasburg in the 1950s in his autobiographical remarks, on the CD *Eminence Breakdown*

The old-time music party is the great conservator of traditional music, a living vault of well-loved, old-standby melodies.[1] It is also the dynamic incubator for new music as players share old standards and tunes, and performance styles, recently learned from a radio broadcast, a record, an opry show, or a festival (or today, perhaps, a YouTube video or download). Older, seasoned players form the nucleus of the music, but new learners and youngsters are encouraged.

The music party (house party, picking party, jam session, kitchen sweat) remains the great testing ground for neophytes and apprentices and an intimate space where a master's genius can be closely studied and appreciated. The music party is where like-minded musicians perform informally for their own amusement and for the enjoyment of family, friends, and neighbors. No one cares if a melody is flubbed, or a tune title forgotten, but the action can be "as dramatic as any other mode of performance."[2]

As much as old-time neighborhood dances, the informal music party has always been the lifeblood of traditional fiddle music. While there are many variations on the character of old-time music parties, with or without an evening break for refreshments, most are held in private homes and typically unknown to the rest of the community. Some are carefully organized and some are freewheeling, but every music party has its "jam-session etiquette," the unwritten code of behavior that has evolved through the years. A session has to have a leader. Some musicians host music parties because they are senior or influential players—and by being the host, they can have a measure of control over the guest list and the format the session takes. Some musicians enjoy hosting music parties because it offers a chance to bring notable fiddlers and other musicians to their home for hospitality, fellowship, and the promise of an evening of fine music. In Urbana, Missouri, for several decades, "music party" meant that Bert Lewis would be there.

Bert Lewis, Local Hero

The music of Bert Lewis is unfamiliar to most fans of Missouri fiddling beyond the Dallas-Polk-Hickory-Camden County area. But Bert Lewis was one of the outstanding fiddlers in the upper Ozarks from the 1920s into the 1950s.[3] He was one of countless fiddlers of a retiring if not shy nature, content for his music to be comfortably situated in neighborhood dances and music parties, with an occasional foray to an old-time picnic, pie supper, or fair. Lonnie Hoppers: "Everybody around here considered him to be the best fiddler in the country. They said he could play all night and never play the same tune twice."[4]

Charles Albert Lewis (1895–1967) was born in Golden City (Barton County) and eventually settled at Urbana in Dallas County. Unlike many of his peers, he did not seek opportunities to pursue his music beyond informal events in his town and the surrounding rural neighborhood. He did, however, perform for a time on a radio show in Sedalia as part of an old-time string band, but he was not interested in becoming an entertainer of any kind. Nor was he a contest fiddler. Indeed, Lewis was a modest man of few words.

At twenty-two in 1918, Bert Lewis enlisted in the US Army, to lend his services to the Allies in World War I. He trained at Camp Jackson, South Carolina, where he was assigned to the Eighty-First Infantry Division. From Camp Jackson, Private Lewis shipped out to France on September 9, 1918, as a member of the American

Bert Lewis in US Army uniform, a snapshot believed to have been taken during training at Fort Jackson, South Carolina, 1918, before he was shipped to France. (Courtesy Alice Carneal and Gladys Reser)

Expeditionary Force, commanded by General John J. Pershing (from Laclede, Missouri). Lewis was injured two days after landing in France, but nothing is known of it today, and Lewis, like many veterans, did not speak of his war experiences. The war was winding down and ended in November 1918, and most of his year in France was spent guarding German prisoners. He came home in September 1919.

Like many World War I soldiers, Bert Lewis came home with a "doughboy fiddle." Many of these instruments, acquired in one way or another in war-affected areas, were high-quality violins, while others were typical factory Strads made in Germany or France. The violin Lewis found in France was one he knew he would not play—a three-quarter-size violin, too small for him—but he knew young people in the family might play it. The violin was modeled on a Stradivarius by the Thibouville Lamy (JTL) firm in Mirecourt, around 1900, and is labeled "Celebre Voisgen / Depose." Located in the Lorraine region of northwestern France, Thibouville Lamy exported thousands of violins to North America, and then World Wars I and II virtually obliterated Mirecourt's violin-making heritage.

Bert Lewis's favorite moments of music were music parties. The central ensemble at music parties Bert Lewis hosted in the 1950s typically was Lewis and a neighbor, Alice Johnson (piano); Lonnie Hoppers (banjo); and sometimes a guitar player. Bert Lewis shared a preference of many fiddlers of his generation for piano backup, as well as four-string banjo. Like many fiddlers in former times, Lewis appreciated all kinds of accompaniment, and he had the knack of fiddling on through his tunes no matter whether an accompanist knew the music or chords or not. "Bert, for sure, wouldn't have cared *what* you were playing, as long as you could stay in the right *key* and have fairly good *timing*. If he *did*, he wouldn't say anything, you know, just a *nice guy*. He played *pretty good*."[5]

Bert Lewis was typical of the majority of old-time Missouri fiddlers—then and now—in the way that the quintessential tune forms in his repertoire were the reel (hoedown or breakdown) and the waltz.[6] Lewis also liked swing and western-swing music and played tunes such as "Kansas City Kitty" and "Indiana" ("Back Home in Indiana") as well as the traditional reels and waltzes such as "Sally Gooden," "Grey Eagle," "Bill Cheatem," "College Hornpipe" (a.k.a. "Sailor's Hornpipe"), "Tennessee Wagner," "Eighth of January," "Durang's Hornpipe," "Listen to the Mockingbird" (with expertly rendered birdcalls), "Billy in the Low Ground," "Arkansas Traveler," "Haste to the Wedding" (jig), "Soldier's Joy," the obligatory Missouri classic "Marmaduke's Hornpipe," "Peekaboo Waltz," and "The Waltz You Saved for Me." Typical of Ozarks fiddling, Bert Lewis's "Blackberry Blossom" has no minor chords in the accompaniment, although minor chords are present in most northern Missouri versions, in bluegrass fiddling, and in recordings that helped popularize the tune.

He fiddled the ironclad "Lost Indian" and included the vocalized "hollering" and moaning. His title for the omnipresent breakdown "Lead Out" ("Getting Upstairs the Monkeys," "Too Young to Marry," "My Love Is but a Lassie," "Shelby's Mule," "Seneca Square Dance," "No Little Home to Go To," and others) was "Possum Up a Tree." Like other upper Ozarks and south-central Missouri fiddlers, Lewis played only a few

Another notable fiddler in Dallas County was Floyd Smith of the Wood Hill–Louisburg area. Like Bert Lewis, Floyd Smith seldom performed outside his home community. Smith's grandson Greg Harmon, a livestock producer, musician, and stringed instrument repairman in the Tunas community of northern Dallas County, poses with Floyd Smith's violin. The violin was acquired by Smith from Bert Lewis, and made in 1957 by luthier Philip Showalter in Louisburg. (October 2014)

schottisches and jigs; when asked to play a schottische, he would often play "Cumberland Gap" in schottische rhythm.

Among tunes of Missouri provenance are "Waldo" (from the Helton family, east of Lewis's territory, which Lewis may have heard Bill Driver fiddle on WOS radio broadcasts in the late 1920s), "Old Parnell," "Red Bird" (with pizzicato section), "Rock All the Babies to Sleep," "Canary Waltz," and "Mill Creek Blue Mule." The latter is a version of "Blue Mule" as Bert Lewis learned it by listening to Lonnie Robertson's fiddling on Springfield radio station KWTO; this is the typical Missouri "Blue Mule."[7] A different "Mill Creek" was fiddled by Floyd Smith of Tunas, a friend and mentee of Lewis's; Smith credited the tune, which to my ears is a version of Fiddlin' Arthur Smith's "Walking in My Sleep," to "old Tom Taylor" from the Eldridge community.[8] Mill Creek is a tributary of the Niangua River in northeastern Dallas County near the hamlet of Lead Mine. The pioneer village of Mill Creek was renamed Celt (pronounced "Selt") when a US Post Office was established in 1888. As many as six water-powered flour and sawmills were in operation in the community.

Bert Lewis enjoyed plectrum and tenor banjo accompaniment, and existing recordings of his fiddling feature tenor banjo as played by a friend from Kansas City, Frances Smith. Lewis also appreciated old-time chorded piano accompaniment and was often accompanied by a neighbor, Alice Johnson, and Agnes Moss; Lewis himself provided a capable piano backup.

Lewis's fiddle style represents what I choose to call the smooth school of fiddling. His repertoire was firmly grounded in the rough-and-ready hoedowns of earlier generations, from 1920s-era country rags and ornate and intricate hornpipes to swing tunes, country songs, and bluegrass tunes of later decades. Despite the tune, or the tempo, Lewis moves the melody with a smooth, notey, but very straightforward style typical of others of his generation and taste, such as George Morris and Lonnie Robertson.

Fifty or sixty years ago, Lewis performed on radio, if even briefly. Around 1950 Lewis, with brothers Ed, Jim, and Bill Maddox, performed on KDRO-AM in Sedalia (some sixty-five miles north of Urbana). KDRO encouraged hillbilly bands, such as Dick Bennett and the Missouri Playboys (with fiddler Peanut Lynch) and the Happy Millers (with fiddler Milo McCubbin, discussed in *Play Me Something Quick and Devilish*). Local businesses underwrote the programming. In the 1940s and 1950s, AM radio stations such as KDRO could be heard at great distances; how many people heard Bert Lewis fiddling in Kansas and Iowa, Arkansas and Oklahoma, as well as across Missouri? If few people today remember the name, in the processes of oral tradition, it is not impossible that some of Bert Lewis's fiddle music trickled into the repertoires of fiddlers in many places and is still heard many decades later. We know his influence was clear in his own community, in the playing of fiddlers such as Floyd Smith of nearby Buffalo, who learned "Old Parnell" at music parties with

Grasshopper Rag

As played by Bert Lewis

Transcribed by Amber Gaddy

"Grasshopper Rag," as played by Bert Lewis, 1955 (hear on the companion CD). Other unusual tunes of Lewis's include "Silver Bell Waltz," "Coffee Shop Rag," "Old Tom Rowland's Hot," "Cumberland Gap Schottische," "Ozark Valley Waltz," and "Old Bohemian Waltz." (Transcription by Amber Gaddy)

The Ozark Drifters, ca. 1954, at the skating rink in Hermitage, Hickory County, Missouri. *Left to right, front*: Donnie Agee (Louisburg, electric guitar), George Hoppers (Urbana, guitar), Bobby Crabtree (Urbana, bass); *left to right, rear*: Truman Bridges (Louisburg, plectrum banjo), Bob Pitts (Elkton, guitar), Bert Lewis (Urbana, violin). (Courtesy Alice Carneal)

Bert Lewis.[9] In his later years, hearing problems caused Lewis to cease performing in public.

Many musicians moved in and out of the Urbana-area music parties through the years. There were Noah and Alva Garrison, brothers who played music at dances. Lonnie Hoppers played backup banjo for them at dances as a teenager. Lonnie's father, George Hoppers, was among the sought-after guitarists. George Hoppers's father-in-law, Henry Reeves (Babe) Franklin, played old-time claw-hammer banjo. Noah Garrison was a fiddler in Dallas County who played the basic shuffle-bow "sawing" Ozark style, but who had great rhythm and drive and was popular at square dances; his brother Alva played guitar backup, finger style, and could play melodies on the guitar. Jim Smith (guitar) and his wife, Frances (tenor banjo, accordion), moved to the Ozarks in 1952 and immediately became fixtures at area music parties; Frances recalled that, in Dallas County, "there were fiddlers and musicians under every bush, it seemed."[10]

Of the many other fiddlers, there were Joe Pfeiffer, Floyd Smith, and John Buskirk. Frances Smith remembered that Buskirk, a neighbor, a good jig dancer, and a "mule man," for whom she played tenor banjo and accordion backup, was devoted to his violin. "He always said his fiddle was his *religion*. And in a way I think it gave a lot of joy to people over the years."[11]

Bert's daughter, Gladys, was interested in music as a child and enjoyed the music parties that happened most weekends at their house or the home of friends. Gladys took classical violin lessons with the French JTL three-quarter-size violin her father had obtained as a soldier in France. Later, when she moved into high school, Gladys

Gladys Lewis as a teenager, ca. 1939, with her father's German "Strad" violin, at home, Urbana. A carpenter, Mr. Lewis built the family's house.

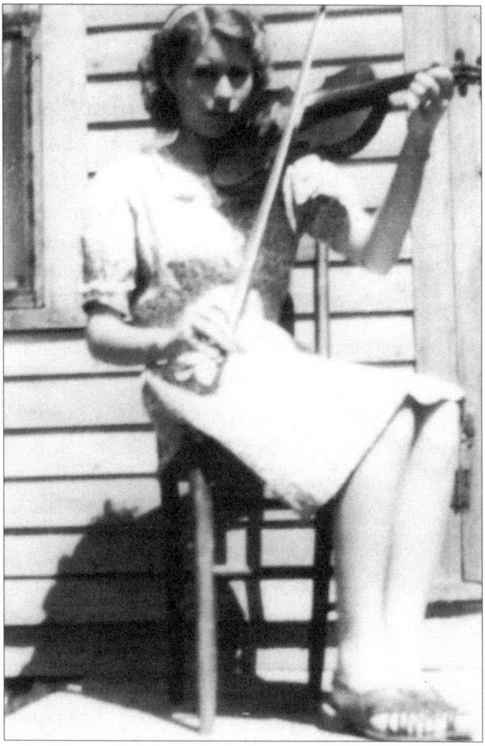

played her father's German-made full-size "Strad" in the school orchestra in Urbana. She says she was not an ear musician, played only from printed music, and did not learn old-time fiddling.[12]

A Region's Hot Shots: Cassity, Teague, and Wooliver

Orville Cassity, Roy Wooliver, and Howe Teague were drawn together by their passion for fiddle and dance music, and they were among the best-known fiddlers in their eastern Ozark landscape. Typical of most of the fiddlers in both this and *Play Me Something Quick and Devilish*, their experiences overlap in many ways and their stories encapsulate many of the topics in our discussion.

Like many fiddlers, their music does not easily fit the neat mosaic of genres and performance styles that researchers and students like to arrange. They were traditional and old-fashioned, but their music also wove through the great swells of early jazz, ragtime, and swing music. Their musical biographies reflect the broader history of tradition and change in old-time fiddle and dance music across the United States and Canada. They were creative, fully participant in the popular music of their times, while also conserving cherished square-dance hoedowns, waltzes, jigs, and schottisches that they inherited from their communities.

Orville Cassity

Orville Cassity (1889–1944) was a popular dance fiddler in the Ozarks in the early 1900s. He was a descendant of Irish Protestant immigrants who arrived by steamboat in nineteenth-century St. Louis and found a toehold there. The next generation moved down to Texas County near the Arkansas line and became laborers and farmers and fiddlers. There, where Orville was born, his father, James P. Cassity, was a well-respected dance fiddler.[13] As a young man, Cassity lived for a time in Arkansas and settled down in Reynolds County (two counties east of Texas County). He later moved to neighboring Dent County.

Cassity was among the young fiddlers of the Roaring Twenties with musical education and literacy who played smooth and enjoyed playing rags and pop tunes like "Wabash Fox Trot," "Forty Drops," "Dill Pickles," and other "uptown tunes" at dances.[14] Cassity's cousin Wiley Crandell often accompanied Cassity on old-time frailing banjo, as did the idiosyncratic fiddler and guitarist Roy Wooliver. Cassity's young protégé and pupil was Howe Teague of Salem, who became an influential fiddler at dances and contests and on radio and television.

By all accounts, Cassity was an outstanding and versatile fiddler who "had the gift." Howe Teague recalled that "Orville could damn near make you cry" with the beauty in his waltzes. Cassity was an effective contest competitor, too, playing complex hornpipes as well as popular tunes of the day. He was selected to represent Reynolds County in an invitation-only two-day fiddlers contest that was broadcast live on WOS from the state capitol in Jefferson City. As previously discussed, beginning on New Year's Eve, December 31, 1925, the legendary contest enrolled eighty-two contestants, going all through the night, and ended on New Year's Day.[15] Orville's guitar accompanist was his rambling companion Roy Wooliver. Cassity seems to have been so inebriated that he played poorly in the contest and won nothing.[16]

Cassity was interviewed by Salem artist L. L. Broadfoot, as Broadfoot was making a charcoal portrait of the fiddler. Cassity recalled how lively an evening could become when too much booze was consumed by folks at a country dance. Cassity's recollection (as written by Broadfoot) suggests that fiddlers as well as dancers enjoyed the high times.

> To me, this ol' fiddle is not only a musical instrument. I love its old tones. It will soothe and content me when everything else fails. I have spent many years fiddlin' for the old Ozark square dances, playin' the same old tunes my father used to play, beginning early in the evening to play for the dance and keep it up until the rooster crows the next morning.
>
> Gosh, but it's a lot of fun to see some of the old boys come wobblin' in about half shot on this wild mountain whiskey, an' when I make my old fiddle scream out on a tune like "Billy in the Lowlands" or "Stoney Mountain," they jump higher than a ten-rail fence, clap their heels together, the sweat pops out on 'em and they dance and holler till you can hear 'em a mile.[17]

When his first wife, a wealthy widow much older than he, died, Cassity inherited two large farms southeast of Salem on the West Fork of the Black River. Cassity's second wife was Dellie (Della) Teague, an aunt of Howe Teague's. As Howe Teague recalled, Cassity just "lived too high on the hog" and spent or traded it all away. He bought several new Model A Ford cars, driving drunk and wrecking one after another. Eventually, Cassity fell prey to the evils of alcoholism, and the dance tune everyone played, "Little Brown Jug," hit home; his best friend had, indeed, become his enemy. One of the anecdotes about Cassity's plastered adventures is recounted by Gordon McCann in the album notes for volume 1 of *Traditional Fiddle Music of the Ozarks* (Rounder CD 0435):

> Cassity's devotion to the bottle was quite serious. . . . One time he told Howe [Teague] of a wild night when he rode home with his equally inebriated brother after a night of fiddling. They passed some affluent farmer's estate and somehow decided in their confusion that it really belonged to them. In the harsh light of the next morning's hangover, Orville's brother muttered, "I believe I'll let my part of that farm go," but Orville, who had maintained a half pint in reserve, replied, "Oh, I'll just hold onto my share for awhile."

As Howe Teague remembered in talking with Jim Nelson, "the DTs" (deliriums tremens) hit his hands when Cassity tried to stop drinking, making smooth fiddling impossible. He died in Salem in early December 1944, age fifty-five. The death certificate spelled his name "Cassidy," listed the cause of death as a heart attack and his occupation as laborer, but no one remembers him as a hard worker. It was said of Orville Cassity that "he drank himself to death." A chronic, progressive disease like alcoholism should not define a person's life, but in the subculture of dance fiddlers from the Roaring Twenties into the late 1900s, too often it did.

Howe Teague

We know more about Howe Teague (1913–2005). He was born at Stone Hill, a farming community a few miles from Salem in Meramec Township of Dent County. Stone Hill, the area's oldest settlement, is said to have been settled in 1828. Howe Teague's paternal grandparents came from Ireland, via the "back way"—from the East Coast, through the Cumberland Gap, and across Tennessee to Missouri—in the 1850s as the tough years of the American Civil War were looming on the horizon. Howe Teague would not adopt the penchant for wandering of his mentors, such as Roy Wooliver; he would remain and enjoy a settled life in the same community in Dent County where his family had pioneered.

The family seems originally to have been located in Galway, Ireland, and eventually became Roman Catholic. They spread to Scotland, where the McTigues were a branch of Clan Farquharson and among the Catholic and Episcopalian families who fought for Bonnie Prince Charlie (Charles Edward Stuart) in his failed campaign to wrest the English crown from King George II; the disastrous loss to the English at the battle of Culloden near Inverness in 1746 ended "the rising" and led to suppression of the Highlanders and their culture and emigration to America and Canada. At some point, the McTigue family changed to being Protestant, perhaps in colonial America, perhaps through intermarriage. Like many other families with Irish and Scots names, theirs, MacTigue (McTigue), had been simplified somewhere along the way.

Howe's mother's people were Scotch-Irish and had been in Arkansas since the early 1800s. Members of the families fought in the Civil War. Like many other Ozarks counties, there was virtually no African American slavery in Dent, Reynolds, or Shannon Counties. It is timber country with poor soils for agriculture and had sparse population at the time of the Civil War.[18] Eventually, the Teagues settled on a large tract that his grandfather had inherited along the Meramec River, land that would be taken into Mark Twain National Forest. The Cassity family lived in the same rural neighborhood near the hamlet of Stone Hill. There is a fiddle tune called "Stony Hill" played by Wooliver, Teague, Cassity, Gene Goforth, the Heltons, and others in the upper Ozarks that may or may not make reference to the Stone Hill community in Dent County (there are other Stone Hills and Stony Hills). The Teagues were farmers, and the family built a large two-story hewn-log house in the customary type familiar among old-stock Americans in Missouri who were able to indicate a degree of prosperity and position in the county.[19]

The Teagues appreciated education and a well-sorted routine for the yearly round of work and leisure on their comparatively spacious livestock and grain farm. They fostered the minds and creative proclivities of their children, whom they treasured. Teague was fortunate to be comparatively uninterested in the booze and home brew that seemed to lubricate much of the nightlife and fiddling scene. He was known for his sunny disposition, and he had a generous and welcoming personality that would serve him well as a radio fiddler and solid citizen in his rural and small-town Dent County community.

Howe Teague lived his entire life in the Salem area, save for four years in the 1940s when he lived in St. Louis. He left high school after his freshman and sophomore years, farmed for several years, and made money hauling logs to lumber mills with a team of mules. In 1941 he married and moved to St. Louis to seek work on the Frisco Railroad. Unable to pass the railroad company's physical examination, Teague took a job in 1941 at the Railway Express freight office at Union Station in downtown St. Louis and worked there four years. After returning to Salem, Teague worked in highway construction.

Teague began his fiddling career in the days of ragtime and early jazz, what he called "the Charleston and Black Bottom days," and he played the tunes in the popular repertoire circulating through dance halls and heard on radio and records. Teague's repertoire was extensive and replete with the rich variety of tunes common in Missouri, from rags and marches to hoedowns, waltzes, schottisches, and jigs. His appreciation of the written page as well as the unwritten music in oral tradition in his community reminds us that many fiddlers loved all kinds of music. His versatility helped Teague become a popular dance fiddler and radio performer as well as a fiddler who was adept at improvising. The old saying that a fiddler never plays a tune the same way twice applied perfectly to Howe Teague.

Teague had played violin as a teenager in his uncle Latt Crandell's community orchestra in the 1920s. Latt's son, Wiley Crandell, was an old-time frailing banjo musician. There seem to have been no issues about satanic influences in the violin or conflicts with local churches, but the bias against dancing and fiddle music seemed to be on the increase, surely thanks to the wild times of the Roaring Twenties, followed by the grim times of the Great Depression. While he had no personal belief that the devil was in fiddle music, when he became a popular fiddler leading his own band at dances and on radio broadcasts, Teague decided to deflect offers to perform in church services. Teague "felt uncomfortable accepting invitations to play at church because of the historical animosity between the church and fiddle music."[20] The historic tension among conservative Protestant denominations across Missouri, and famously in the Ozarks among groups such as the Church of Christ, Assembly of God, and some Southern Baptist congregations, over the knotty doctrinal question of whether to welcome or ban musical instruments in church was evident in Howe Teague's community.

Howe's grandfather Wiley Teague played fiddle music, but Wiley "could barely touch a tune." "Barely touch a tune" is a way of saying that a fiddler's skills were average, at best. Wiley's favorite piece was "Getting Upstairs to the Monkeys" (a.k.a. "Shelby's Mule," "Seneca Square Dance," and "Moss Billy"; see *Play Me Something Quick and Devilish*). Howe's father, Odine Teague, did not play music, but Odine's sister, Dellie Teague Cassity (Mrs. Orville Cassity), was a pump-organ player and accompanied fiddlers in the area. Wayne Wingfield, an uncle on his grandmother's side of the family, had been a good fiddler who played for picnics and dances in the Salem.

As a child, Howe crafted violins from cornstalks: "Wasn't much of a fiddle, but it made a little streak of sound." A crude violin-like sound, squeaky and limited, can be produced by taking a roughly two-foot length of dry strong cornstalk and whittling out a narrow rectangular hole along one side of the shaft (while leaving some of the surface strands or fibers intact) that will become the top. The surface strands left intact will become the strings and are made to vibrate with a bow. One may then insert an inch of cornstalk for a bridge. The fiddler may employ another cornstalk as a violin bow; stiff weeds work, too, or a length of limber tree branch with a shoelace or sewing-thread horsehair, and a bit of fun may be had. Rosin to keep the bow on the strings and pull sounds can be made from pine-tree sap. Considered by most people in Missouri to be a folk toy of limited musical consequence and a child's pastime, cornstalk fiddles were, on some occasions, valued by would-be fiddlers with few other options and a cornfield nearby. Fiddle music, like nature, will find a way.[21]

Howe Teague was drawn to the violin at six or seven. At seven he acquired his first violin from his aunt Dellie Cassity in Salem. She had ordered a Sears, Roebuck violin—$3.98, case and bow included. Dellie had abandoned trying to learn the instrument and traded the outfit to her eager young nephew for a "runt pig" that he was

One of Howe Teague's radio bands that performed live over KSMO-AM in Salem in the 1950s. *Left to right*: Donna Stump (bass), Howe Teague, Dale Teague (guitar), and Woody Asbridge (guitar). Teague welcomed visiting musicians on his show and gave promising young musicians, such as Doug and Rodney Dillard, a chance to perform on the air. (Courtesy Jim Nelson)

raising at the farm. At first, the lad "just sawed around" on the runt-pig fiddle, until, one night, inspiration struck.

> I was sitting there one night, sawing away on that fiddle. And an old man was staying at our house at that time—my mother's cousin. And he'd sit there and chew his tobacco and I'd play the fiddle. And my dad and brother was possum hunting, you know. Oh, one night, I was really drawing that bow. And with nothing in mind, you know. But I was sawing on it. And he's sitting there about half asleep. And when I got through jerkin' that one off, he said, "Howe," he said, "you pretty nigh had a *tune* right there." That helped me a lot, you know.

Teague's first experience fiddling for a dance took place in 1914 at age nine. It was an unplanned rite of passage. As recounted in Beisswenger and McCann, the fiddler who had been hired to play the dance, Albert Hogan, had to cancel, and his accompanists were also absent. People at the dance knew the Teague boy was learning to play fiddle and asked him to take over and play for the dance, which he did, fiddling solo while sitting in a neighbor man's lap. Many fiddlers have similar memories of their first dance job as the fiddler in a band, but few went through the harrowing experience at nine years old—and fiddling solo for a roomful of eager dancers.[22] He survived.

As a teenager, Teague drew inspiration to concentrate on his fiddling when an itinerant laborer spent some time living with the family and doing farmwork. The itinerant laborer (whose name is not known) charmed the boy with two tunes that nicely bracket the entire history of old-time fiddle music in America, "Pop Goes the Weasel" (the English jig, country dance, and children's singing game from the 1600s) and "Swingin' Down the Lane (an Old-Fashioned Song with a Fox Trot Swing)," the pop song and fox-trot by Tin Pan Alley composers Isham Jones and Gus Kahn that became a jazz standard of the Roaring Twenties. Whoever this unnamed itinerant farm laborer may have been, he was fiddling complicated jazz music and popular tunes of the day—and helping stir an interest in this new kind of music in the young fiddler Howe Teague.

Could this itinerant laborer have been Roy Wooliver, the legendary rambling genius of old-time fiddling who inspired generations of players from Howe Teague to Cecil Goforth and John Hartford? If we were able to document Howe's hearing this unnamed fiddler play, we might suggest that he was familiar with the best-selling 1930 record "Swingin' Down the Lane," on the Brunswick label by the Isham Jones Rainbo [*sic*] Orchestra. The Isham Jones band was a fixture of the 1920s Chicago dance-club scene. Jones had worked in coal mines in Michigan as a child and taught himself fiddle and violin music and was one of the jazz pioneers who stressed the importance of hiring trained musicians in bands; As Jones said in 1923, "To start a jazz band of your own . . . [f]irst of all, you must have musicians—real musicians."[23]

The Teague family listened to records on their windup Victrola. They were especially fond of ballads and folk songs such as Vernon Dalhart's 1925 "The Death of Floyd Collins" and "The Wreck of the Old 97."[24] Teague played fiddle tunes absorbed from records, such as Doc Roberts's "Cumberland Blues," "Hell Broke Loose in Georgia" by Gid Tanner and the Skillet Lickers, Lowe Stokes's "Home Brew Rag," and Clark Kessinger's "Hell among the Yearlings" and "Forked Deer." When the family Victrola broke, Teague turned records with a finger so he could hear the music and learn it. Later on, his favorite radio fiddlers were Fiddlin' Arthur Smith and Curly Fox, from whom Teague learned the fine waltz "Georgianna Moon." Teague learned a peculiar tune, "Tulsa Hop," from an Arthur Smith record.

Teague also played five-string banjo in a style they called "frailing" ("like old Grandpa Jones," the *Grand Ole Opry* star), a principal style in the upper Ozarks, as elsewhere in Missouri. In frailing, one uses a downstroke with a cupped right hand, the backs of the fingertips brushing across the strings to produce rhythmic chords, and drams of melody if desired. This style of banjo, with nineteenth-century roots, makes fine accompaniment for an old-time fiddler. Teague played a few tunes, such as "Green Corn." But his first love was the violin. Accompaniment for others was often provided by someone chording "second fiddle" on a violin, by his aunt Dellie playing reed organ, or by someone playing "fiddle sticks" with darning needles for the fiddler.[25] Many of the square-dance tunes were played in chorded tunings. The guitar had not yet become commonplace in Missouri in the 1910s and 1920s.

Teague learned to read music and take tunes from books and sheet music. He took a US School of Music correspondence course from New York. Even though he ultimately decided that learning from books did not suit his goals, Teague continued to learn and play from tune books throughout his life. He also played by ear, imitating the traditional sounds he heard at dances and vaudeville performances, house parties and pie suppers. He had the good fortune to be able to absorb tunes and techniques from noted fiddlers and local characters Orville Cassity and Cassity's colleague Roy Wooliver. Both Cassity and Wooliver were known for their versatility and deep repertoires, and a number of young fiddlers were influenced by their performances. Teague's teachers included an uncle, the versatile musician, band leader, and fiddler Latt Crandell. Teague remembered:

> I had an uncle [Latt Crandell] that played from written music. He got a seven or eight-piece orchestra together that played orchestra music put out by Jenkins (the Kansas City music company). We had a clarinet and two fiddles and a cello and a bass horn. We played in his home and at church and school. He was the director and we all had our own music. I enjoyed it but I didn't like the sound of the music. Mostly marches and waltzes. . . .
>
> I heard people playing by ear that could get more expression than I could ever see written down on paper. Everybody that reads music gets the same expression in it. (However), you can make it sound happy or sad or whatever, according to what mood that that you're in. You can take a waltz like the old "Good-Night Waltz" or "Over the Waves" and you can put in a fast beat or you can tie your notes together and make it smoother and swell your notes up and down if you're tying them together. You can make people sit down and cry.[26]

While visiting in a Rolla music store around 1935, Teague leafed through the store's rows of sheet music. He discovered the sheet music to one of his favorite songs, the Stephen Foster classic "My Old Kentucky Home." Teague knew of no fiddlers who played the tune, so he stood in the music store and memorized its basic outline from the sheet music. Teague considered sheet music, found in piles in most people's piano benches, to be like a library, to be dug through for inspiration, recreation, and guidance. But he did not consider the printed notes to be sacrosanct. "The way they write it isn't very interesting to learn it, off of the paper. They have to cut out lot of stuff that you can't put in. . . . They leave out a lot of stuff. A real good fiddler like Orville Cassity and Curly Fox, if he don't like a tune, he'll put in something else he likes better."

Pie Suppers and House Dances

Communities supported and savored opportunities to get together. Pie suppers were for many years an important gathering time. Pie suppers (box suppers or "box socials" in other regions) were typically hosted at a local rural schoolhouse, a general store, or another public space. They were usually advertised as fund-raisers, with pies or dinners auctioned off and the proceeds going to a worthy community cause. Many of these events were held in public school buildings.

However, as local governments began to close the one-room schoolhouses in favor of larger centralized schools, many pie suppers were essentially rendered homeless. Some migrated to other places, but others simply ceased to exist. Today, events much like the old-time pie suppers continue to be held at venues such as saddle-club meetings, VFW halls, firehouses, church fellowship halls, or school gyms in town.

People could attend a pie supper practically every weekend in the autumn season, or later when the harvest was in, or coming in and there was leisure, but pie suppers could also be held in the springtime to help celebrate the close of the school year. People often danced to the music. The event usually started in the late afternoon or twilight, as people arrived and carried in food, tableware, and drink for a "basket dinner," "carry-in dinner," or "potluck."[27] Babies, teens, parents, and old folks all gathered for the rituals of visiting, shared supper, charity, general festivity, and reunion.[28] Such social events in the yearly round were highly anticipated in the rural community of former times.

The general outline of these events was similar across Missouri, but many variations and permutations were customary in different places. As the supper was concluding (sometimes entertainment by the young pupils came first), a teacher or local dignitary might offer welcoming remarks and promote the pie auction, which would commence at midevening. Funds raised by the auction were often devoted to the needs of the school—books, a microscope, roof mending—but during World War II much of the fund-raising was to benefit the Red Cross and the war effort. Before the auction might come performances by the young scholars—a scene from Shakespeare, a song, recitation of a patriotic speech, stanzas from John Milton or Sir Walter Scott, or a musical number (often this was a traditional ballad). A bedsheet or old quilt could serve as the stage backdrop, with curtains strung across the front on clothesline wire.

The highlight was really act 2, the auction of the homemade pies—that great and enduring symbol of hearth and hospitality. Pies for the auction were crafted and brought in cardboard boxes tied with string or ribbons, by eligible young women who wanted to participate and who were being "sparked" by an eligible young man. Most of the bakers wanted their pies to be won by their boyfriends; it usually worked, if the baker tipped off the beau about which box to bid on. The boxes were numbered and auctioned by number, with the contents of the boxes not visible to the bidders. Competition and jealousy could come into play if a bold young man tried to outbid a certain baker's boyfriend.

The successful bidder, hopefully the baker's choice companion, and the baker would then sit down together and enjoy the pie as their supper dessert. Howe Teague described these social events in 1988 during the recording session for the *Good Tune* project. "Well, the neighbors all brought in pies, you know, women, the girls, if they was wanting a feller. They'd sell them pies [auction to the highest bidder] to boys who was wantin' girlfriends, y'know. And that way, they sometimes mix up a match. Sometimes it'd cause a fight, [and] the girls wouldn't eat with the boys."[29] If alcoholic beverages were consumed, this activity took place out back and as quietly as possible.

A "Prettiest Girl" contest often followed the auction or was held as a break during the auction. People voted with a penny for their choice among those nominated, and the money collected added to the fund-raising pool. If time permitted, there might be other brief contests in good fun, such as "the dirtiest feet contest" (prize: a bar of soap) or "the most lovesick couple." Pie suppers often included a cakewalk (a kind of musical chairs), with dancers paying a sum to dance around the numbers in a circle and hope to land on their number when the music stopped. Cakes were the prizes, and the cakewalk would feature the musicians who would later play for the dance.

Fiddling and dancing commenced after the auction. At one pie supper Howe Teague played for, "an old man who could strike a tune on a fiddle, just barely . . . played 'Natchez Under the Hill.' He played with his eyes shut, boy he was *workin'* that *over*—and the curtains fell down on the floor! When he did open his eyes, the people were all staring at him in the audience, and he went out of there on *high*."

Jim Orchard, a bearer of local history, recalls 1940s and 1950s pie suppers in the one-room schoolhouses and villages in the deep hills of Shannon County, where the Red Cross was usually the recipient of the money raised. A pie supper would start just before dark, and people arrived in a horse-drawn wagon or on horseback. The stroke of midnight was typically the ending of the event. Old-fashioned ingenuity was on display in such elements as provision of ice. "We didn't have electricity, and didn't have any *ice*. But, you know, they'd go on the *bluffs* on the valleys, and that cold water'd drip and form those huge *icicles*. And take a *broad* axe and a wagon, and two or three stout men would put that ice in a wagon and haul that to a *sawdust* pile and bury that, and you'd have ice for the Fourth of July, so we'd have homemade ice cream and cake."[30]

The many pie suppers offered opportunities for fiddlers and musicians to play music, trying out their hand at entertaining audiences as well as making danceable music. In fact, pie suppers were a key phase in the long evolution of opry shows. With a bit more organization, planning, and securing the best musicians and singers in the neighborhood, an enterprising person could borrow or rent a hall and put on a show with a schedule, entertainment format, guarantee of good music (and often dancing), and, last but not least, a refreshment area for snacks such as hamburgers, cake, pie, coffee, and soft drinks.

House dances were another prime venue where people gathered and fiddlers performed. Furniture was carried out to the front porch or stowed away somewhere. Rugs were rolled up and shoved next to the wall. Kitchens were alive with chatter as people prepared the "midnight supper" or "snack" for tired dancers and musicians. Each set ("square") would have a member of the set do the calls for their dance, and usually the other set was dancing to a different set of calls by their own caller. Usually, there were two sets of dancers, eight people, dancing. Many of the square dances in the 1930s and 1940s had special callers who did singing calls while people square-danced.

House dances fitted well with the years of Prohibition (1920–33). Most visitors and musicians would be friends and neighbors, and a glass of moonshine or home brew could be taken, if desired, with comparatively little notice or complaint. Occasionally, a house dance became rowdy—someone would have a little too much doctored-up punch and make romantic eyes at another man's girl or otherwise get crossways with people. Howe Teague: "Pretty rough times, when the *moonshiners* was going then, you know. Most every steep holler around had a still in it. There was so many bootleggers that they kind of got to selling one another liquor, you know." Most invitation-only house dances began to die out after the repeal of Prohibition (1933) and in the 1940s when most of the boys were off to the war. Dances moved into towns and began to be held in public spaces that would accommodate larger crowds, such as in the city hall or a hotel ballroom. The rowdiness we associate with dances in this raucous era was more typical of late-night action at country taverns, dance halls, and sandbar parties along the rivers.

Teague Meets Wooliver

Howe Teague met Roy Wooliver at a pie supper at the Salem High School in the fall of 1932. Much older than Teague, Roy appeared to be "a little dried up feller" and cross-eyed. Teague had recently graduated from the high school and was asked to fiddle for the dancing. He lacked a "second" to provide accompaniment, so he secured the services of a cousin to play the piano with him. Someone had a guitar and handed it to Roy Wooliver, who had recently returned to the area after a term in the Missouri State Penitentiary.[31] Teague asked Wooliver to "help." Teague remembered that Wooliver played both finger style, picking out melodies, and with a flat pick to provide chords (both open chords and closed chords). "And oh, Roy was in for it *big*. Been anybody else, he probably wouldn't have played. He was *contrary* when he wanted to be. He liked me for some reason. We went in there and played whatever we was going to play, and [with] that girl, my cousin, playing the *piano*, she was pretty *good*. And got Roy to *pick* one, and he picked 'St. Louis Blues'—man, he could make that *cry*." That evening, Wooliver also finger-picked "Rainy Day Blues" and "The Desert Blues."

After the dance was over that evening, Teague, excited to meet Wooliver, invited Wooliver to the Teagues' farm to continue the music. Teague recalls saying, "Wish you could go over, stay all night with me," to which Wooliver replied, "Well, I guess I could." After taking his cousin home, Teague and Wooliver went to the Teague farm and had a memorable jam session. Their guitar that night was one that Teague had seen on the way home, resting in the yard under a cedar tree at the cousin's house, with strings rusty and out of tune. Teague took it home. "Old Roy, he took them strings off the guitar, got a pan of soap suds and washed them real good and put them back on it." Wooliver was a great guitar player, but Teague remembered, "You had to watch him like a hawk, he'd steal everything. He never did steal nothing off me, but he did my dad."

Howe Teague enjoyed the session and other sessions with Roy Wooliver, but Teague did not travel to dances and sessions with Wooliver. "I was afraid to go anywhere with him, he'd steal something, and get me into it." Perhaps by observing his elders and fiddle mentors Cassity and Wooliver, Howe Teague never enjoyed fiddling in taverns.

Teague became a popular radio personality in the 1940s, 1950s, and 1960s. At his first radio appearance in 1940, he was invited to fiddle on Cousin Emmy's 6:00 a.m.

show on KMOX in St. Louis. Roy Wooliver was playing fiddle for Cousin Emmy, and Wooliver had arranged for Teague to fiddle on the show—while Roy picked up a guitar and played some fancy licks. Up to that point, no one in Emmy's band knew that Wooliver played guitar, but he borrowed a Martin guitar from Bill Drake and accompanied perfectly Howe's fiddling "Blackberry Blossom." "My knees was knocking—KMOX was a big station at that time. But I done fairly well, I guess."[32] Teague also performed on KSD in the 1940s, with a "cute singer" called Daisy May in a Hollywood movie–style cowboy girl trio, the Ranch Hands.

Across the river, Teague played on the Cole Mason show that aired live from a theater in Granite City, Illinois—with thousands of people in the audience for a bond drive in the Washington Theatre. Among the many other programs on KMOX, country singer Pappy Cheshire had a popular radio show, with Wade Ray providing the fiddle music, and there was Roy Queen, who sang and played country music and was perhaps the most popular radio performer in the area ("Roy Queen was kind of king of the crawfish at that time").

Back in Salem in 1946, Teague went to work for a Springfield construction company contracting with the Missouri Highway Department. That led to employment with the highway department for "six bits an hour. . . . That meant twenty-five years of hard labor," five and a half days a week and some Saturdays. His foreman would relieve him of duties on Saturday mornings so he could do radio shows. Highway Department jobs were the best-paying jobs available to him and, like railroad jobs, carried benefits and a pension.

Teague first played on radio at KTTR in Rolla, in 1944, with blind guitarist Austin Wood's band. Wood sang cowboy songs, and Teague fiddled old-time and pop tunes. In the 1950s, Teague appeared in the Austin Wood band on Columbia's KOMU television. Eventually, Teague developed his own radio show at KTTR, and this program lasted two years. He then developed his Saturday-morning show on KSMO in Salem, a half hour's drive south of Rolla, and worked there sixteen years. Phillips Supermarket sponsored his Saturday-morning half-hour show all sixteen years, among other sponsors. Teague received requests in the mail to play tunes, and during one week in the 1950s he received some eighty fan letters.

Teague often included "pickup" musicians on his show, including musicians who asked to be on the show and Teague considered worthy and able. He relied on his son, Larry (born 1942), to play upright bass with whatever other musicians were there, as well as old friends like Ott Tate, Woodrow Asbridge, Dorothy Wright, and guitarist Sam Asbridge, who grew up near Teague in Dent County and played pie suppers with him. Sam Asbridge's stage name was "Cowboy Sam" when he performed in St. Louis. Asbridge's wife, Lillie Bell, played bass, and Les Gamblin played tenor banjo. In St. Louis, Asbridge studied music and performed on WEW with Roy Schaffer and the Carson Melody Roundup with Grandpappy Jones.

During a visit in Nashville, Tennessee, Teague met Zeke Clements ("the Dixie Yodeler"), a popular western-style country singer, songwriter, and a star of the *Louisiana Hay Ride* and *Grand Ole Opry* radio programs. Teague made fiddle records at Clements's

Gold Star Records studio. One of Teague's best-received records was "Ozark Mountain Fox Chase," a 45 rpm disc with Nashville studio musician and bluegrass banjoist Curtis McPeake. Clements's studio pressed several hundred copies, which Teague mailed to radio stations and then sold on air during his radio shows.

The 45 was followed in 1964 by an LP of square-dance music, *Square Dance Music/ Ozark Fiddlin'* (Gold Standard GS-SQ D.LP1, 1964). This project was an attempt to appeal both to consumers who liked fiddle music and to those taking part in the nationwide revival of square dancing. *Square Dance Music / Ozark Fiddlin'* has tunes on the A side, and the B side has the same tunes repeated but with square-dance calls added. The playlist echoes the evergreens familiar at practically any old-time dance in the South and lower Midwest: "Arkansas Traveler," "Eighth of January," "Chicken Reel," "Ragtime Annie," "Soldier's Joy," "Fire on the Mountain," "Sally Goodin'," "Gray Eagle," "Rye Straw," and "Cotton Eyed Joe."

For "Cotton Eyed Joe," Teague played a pre-western-swing version that he used as a square-dance hoedown or as accompaniment for a couple step dance. At the recording session, a visiting square dancer from California suggested that Teague fiddle tunes at a slower pace than his normal tempo in order to appeal more widely to the "western style" square-dance clubs. Recordings of square-dance music without calls had been popularized by Tommy Jackson. Because square-dance sets could go on for fifteen minutes or more, Teague played the tunes as a medley, one after the other, with no pause between.

More than twenty years later, Teague released his second LP, *Ozark Memories.*[33] This album featured Howe's son, Larry Teague, providing guitar as well as bass accompaniment in the studio production. *Ozark Memories* shows Howe Teague's emphasis in his repertoire on two-steps as much as on square dances, with titles like "Freight Train Moan," "Wabash Fox Trot," "Dreamy Georgiana [*sic*] Moon," "Homebrew Rag," "Darkness on the Delta," "Forty Drops" (from Orville Cassity), "Cotton Blossoms," and "Waiting for the *Robert E. Lee.*"

Howe Teague embraced bluegrass when it emerged in the late 1940s and 1950s. His versatility, as well as a sense of what audiences wanted, made him comfortable in bluegrass ensembles. Teague met a number of talented young musicians drawn to him through his KSMO radio shows and appearances at dances, such as Doug and Rodney Dillard, who with Mitch Jayne (working as a schoolteacher and part-time announcer on KSMO) and Dean Webb (from Independence) would form the immensely influential Dillards band.[34]

As the post–Folk Music Revival academics and collectors found their way to Teague's music, he began to be included in a number of projects. During his 1980s stint as a master teacher in the Traditional Arts Apprenticeship Program, Teague recorded some 160 tunes in sessions with his apprentice Clark Miller.[35] The 1989 University of Missouri documentary project *"Now That's a Good Tune": Masters of Traditional Missouri Fiddling* profiles Teague and includes recordings of his "Fourteen Days in Georgia" and "Forked Deer" as well as Charlie Walden's transcription of his unusual version of "Forked Deer" and "White River" (in scordatura, "tuned up" to Teague). Teague was among fiddlers who often carried a second violin with him, set in a "tuned-up" tuning

Wabash Foxtrot

As played by Howe Teague

"Wabash Fox Trot," by Howe Teague, 1986, with Howe's son Larry Teague (guitar and bass) (hear on the companion CD). (Courtesy Jim Nelson; transcription by Amber Gaddy)

(scordatura); other cross-tuned melodies he played included "Pretty Polly" and his take on a 45 rpm record by Texas Shorty (Jim Chancellor) of "Bonaparte's Retreat." In the 1990s, Teague began to play slower; partly because of poor health and a lack of the kind of accompaniment that inspired his fiddling, he lost interest in playing square dances. Larry had moved to Springfield.

Teague was featured in volume 1 of McCann and Mark Wilson's set of CDs of Ozark fiddlers, *Traditional Fiddle Music of the Ozarks*, with recordings of "Wabash

Fox Trot," "White River," "Nine Mile," "Everything," "Cluckin' Hen," and "Arkansas Hop." Beisswenger and McCann includes transcriptions of "Cluckin' Hen" ("Cackling Hen," from the soundtrack in a cowboy movie); "Marmaduke's Hornpipe" (the Missouri fiddler's anthem); from Orville Cassity the tunes "Wabash Fox Trot," "Everything," and "Forty Drops"; and from Roy Wooliver "Arkansas Hop," "Nine Mile," and the cross-tuned "White River."

Teague was also a fiddle-contest competitor and interested in the contest scene—where a measure of respect and acclaim, a bit of money, and perhaps a ribbon or trophy could come one's way. Contests were where many of the fiddlers in a region congregated, and the jam sessions backstage or in a motel room were memorable. But Teague was not what we call a "contest *fiddler*," one whose principal raison d'être was the competition arena.

Teague participated in his first competition in 1929 at age sixteen, with Wiley Crandell providing frailing banjo accompaniment. The contest was a fund-raiser put on by the vocational agriculture students in the Salem High School gymnasium. Although nervous to be competing against older fiddlers in the community, Teague did well and took second place, playing "Goodnight Waltz" and his version of Orville Cassity's "Wabash Fox Trot." A local fiddler in his nineties won first place, Wiley Blackwell; other prizes went to Latt Crandell, Sam Brockus, and a barber, Clarence Clark.

In contests Teague seems to have been able to keep a cool head and sense of humor about the fierce competition that could turn ugly. He recognized that, to be a consistent winner, most champions focused on and honed a very small number of well-known, powerful hoedowns, waltzes, and other tune types commonly accepted in the area as "contest tunes." A fiddler who played a rare or unusual tune in a contest ran the risk of confusing the judges and failing to clue them in to his or her real expertise.

Teague encountered his share of "sore losers" among the dozen or so "contest fiddlers," a sort of clique who devoted most of their time and effort to being successful in competitions instead of playing for pie suppers, square dances, or radio shows. Fed up with the pressures of performing under the scrutiny of judges and audiences who may or may not know much about fiddling, and frustrated by the quixotic and unfathomable judging in contests, Howe Teague wished for the old days when audience applause on an applause-o-meter would decide who was the best fiddler, rather than a panel of unqualified or crooked judges. Of course, he knew that an applause-o-meter was helpful only if a fiddler had enough fans in the audience to raise enough ruckus to make the meter needle mark off enough decibels to allow the fiddler to win something.

Roy Wooliver: Genius, Rascal

James Christopher LeRoy Wooliver was born in Reynolds County in 1896 and died in 1964 in St. Louis. But Roy, as he was known to all, left few traces—except (except!) in the legacy of fiddle tunes people play and the stories about his exploits they tell.

Throughout most of his life, Roy Wooliver wandered up and down the hills and hollows and along the rivers of his home territory in Shannon, Reynolds, Dent, and

Phelps Counties. Missouri's highest point, a forested ridge in a state park, Taum Sauk Mountain (1,772 feet), is in Iron County, Wooliver's territory. Here one finds great beauty, pure springwater, state and national parks that bring tourists, and Missouri's largest privately owned forestlands. For generations, there has also been widespread poverty and illicit drug manufacturing. Like other areas in the eastern Ozarks, once the Civil War took its toll, once the forests were cut down for railroad ties and construction lumber, and once the lead mines and plants closed, followed by the Great Depression in the 1930s and the demise of the railroads after World War II, the rough hills and few areas of good farmland led to the continuation of steady out-migration to St. Louis and other cities. There are few major highways in this part of the Ozarks, and the largest towns are county seats such as Eminence (population 591, Shannon County), Centerville (pop. 194, Reynolds), and Salem (pop. 5,009, Dent). Those who stayed put were often from pioneer families with established landownership or businesses. People with few advantages had a tougher time.

The Wooliver family in Missouri appears to be descended from the Wohleben family (Wolleben, Woolever, Woliver, Welliver), who came from west-central Germany to the American colonies in the early 1700s. The Woolivers were one of the "first families" of Dent County, Missouri. Roy's great-grandfather Daniel M. Wooliver came to Dent County from Tennessee in 1829 and settled along Spring Creek, making them among this area's first European-American settlers. Daniel's son Jacob was Roy Wooliver's father.[36] They made their living as farmers. Though little is known of them now, Howe Teague remembered Roy Wooliver's father and Roy's great-uncle Bob Wooliver (who served in the Union army during the Civil War) as good fiddlers. The paterfamilias of the Dent County clan, Daniel Wooliver, was said to have been a popular fiddler for dances in the community.

Only the basics of Roy's biography are known. Some information comes from census records and prison ledgers. He is mentioned in *Play Me Something Quick and Devilish* with regard to his influence on fiddlers like John Hartford and Gene Goforth and in discussion of the fiddlers in Missouri with a blend of old-stock American, German, and Cherokee ancestry.[37]

Said to be a loner and petty thief skittering along the edges of polite society, Roy Wooliver often scrapped for his meals and a night's shelter, depending on the good graces of the family of a musical acquaintance for sustenance. Roy knew where a hospitable farm family or a country tavern manager would welcome him and have a fiddle, banjo, or guitar handy (he seems never to have owned an instrument). In Wooliver's time, many farmers still grazed livestock in common, without today's marking off and fencing in of property; a person could cross creeks and walk miles of old trails and lanes, many of them from pre-European-settlement Indian times, without having to climb a fence or see inside a town. Wooliver's most reliable source of cash income was being hired to play for dances, and he often performed in these venues.[38]

The 1920 US Census indicates that Roy Wooliver was born in Dent County in 1895 (other sources suggest 1896) and was a resident of Cole County. Jefferson City is the seat of Cole County as well as the state capital; the state penitentiary is there, and

Roy's legendary several sentences in prison are well known to fiddlers and others interested. There seem to have been four times Wooliver served sentences in the Jefferson City prison. A file for 1920 in the Missouri State Archives indicates that Roy Wooliver was discharged from the Missouri State Penitentiary in 1920.[39] At age twenty-five, Roy and his mother, Melvina (born in Dent County in 1877), were incarcerated in the penitentiary at the same time. This would have been Roy's first time in the penitentiary, but we do not know the reasons he and his mother were there. In the 1920 census, Melvina "Woolliver" is listed as living in Cole County (nothing more). She was ill and would die in the prison in June 1920.[40]

In 1926 Wooliver was remanded to Jefferson City for a second sentence in the state penitentiary, this time for burglary. He stole a watch from the home of a citizen of Bunker named Black. The watch theft seeded a Wooliver legend, often recounted by Gene Goforth, Howe Teague, and John Hartford, who told stories about Roy's misadventures. These stories were not told in mockery or disdain but, rather, are the kinds of narratives people tell about inscrutable characters they admire. In 1987, while I was recording Gene Goforth in Hannibal for the University of Missouri project *"Now That's a Good Tune,"* Goforth recounted the cores of two of his favorite narratives about Wooliver. "Here's what he done. Of course, some of it's hearsay. I knew him since I was about thirteen years old. [Wooliver] used to play for some of them places, dances here and there. Roy got drunk and got his knife out and run them all off and went to bed. He was cross-eyed. He was a funny, odd guy. Little bitty guy, too. He stole a watch and they sent him up. And he got out and came back and stole the same watch."[41]

Howe Teague's recollection gives us the name of the purloined watch owner and offers a bit more narrative:

> I knew who he was, and everybody else did, I guess, because he'd been in the pen, in the penitentiary about three hitches already. They'd turn him loose and then have to go get him again. Stealing. Every time he seen something he wanted, he'd steal it. Well, he stole a watch *twice*. Went to the pen for stealing one watch.
>
> ["Old man Black, over at Bunker," owned the watch.] He was determined to have it. Then he shot some feller, in the shoulder, here. And that was his last hitch [prison sentence], I think. They dumped him again. . . . He didn't do nothing but play the guitar, in the pen, there. You see, Jeff City . . . WOS, and they had Saturday night entertainment on that radio, and they got a band out of the penitentiary. And of course that was just down *his alley*, you know, he played the fiddle then. And another feller over on Hudson Creek, some of his relations, I guess, he went up for something. And he called dances and Roy played the fiddle.[42]

The ledger indicates that Wooliver had been arrested (for the watch theft) on May 14, 1926. Having behaved well, and the paltry scope of the crime being obvious to the authorities, Roy was released three days later, on May 17.

As for Teague's mention that Wooliver was a member of a prison band taken around to perform in Jefferson City, that is probably accurate, even if yet to be documented.

Legends about incarcerated fiddlers and musicians being used by prison wardens or state governors for dances and parties around Jefferson City crop up from time to time. Certainly, if Wooliver was asked to fiddle for a party or dance (or even a fiddlers contest) while an inmate, this would have helped warm the authorities to an early release.

He had no such luck after going back to Bunker and stealing Mr. Black's watch a second time. It is not clear when Wooliver was incarcerated for the second watch theft, but he was released in July 1932.[43]

Petty thievery seems to have been part of Wooliver's life. As a local boy in the Reynolds and Dent County area living a rough life, who could do farmwork and was widely admired as a dance fiddler and musician, his pilfering and feisty personality could be forgiven or tolerated, most of the time. That is often how small rural communities function. But there are limits to a community's patience with one of their own who fails to learn from his or her mistakes. The straight-and-narrow path was not Roy Wooliver's.

In 1941, after Wooliver left Cousin Emmy's radio show and returned to Dent County, he found farm labor and room and board at the Odine Teague farm. The Teague family had been friendly to Wooliver and other itinerant workers and travelers for many years. One day Roy went into Salem and stole a book of government gas-rationing stamps (the war was on) from a woman who had the stamps—but no automobile. He also swiped gas-ration stamps from the farm truck of one of the Teague cousins.

Teague also recalled when Roy had been helping load hay on Doc Dillon's farm, next to the Teague farm. Roy wore a large overcoat everywhere, summer or winter. Back at the Teague farm, during the lunch break when the farmhands were having their meal, Howe Teague's mother became curious about seeing Roy with a new pair of buckskin gloves. Apparently, she saw the gloves in the pockets of Roy's big overcoat, and, in short, Roy had picked up the gloves, along with a measuring tape, from Doc Dillon's barn. Howe's father told Roy to just take them back where he found them. Then Howe's father discovered that Roy had stolen his new shoes, and that brought to an end the hospitality of the Teague farm. Roy was told not to come back. Whether deserved or not, most of the musicians around Wooliver thought they needed to keep an eye out for pickpocketing.

For his fourth and final penitentiary sentence, Roy's full name appears, for the first and last time: James Christopher LeRoy Wooliver. As Howe Teague recalled:

> He was pretty dangerous. You made him mad or something, he'd stick a knife in you, or shoot you. Like them two guys who was fighting in the highway over at Bunker one night, at a dance. Roy was staying there at that feller's house that was giving the dance. Them two guys out there, fighting on the road. . . . Roy knowed where the owner of it [the house] had his pistol. . . . There was a hell of a bunch out there, they said, watching that fight. And Roy run in there and got that gun, a *forty-four*, . . . and come running back out there and got right over 'em, and, hell he couldn't *see* nothing, and pulled 'er and it went off through that muscle in his arm. They called the *law*.

Roy Wooliver, ca. 1958. (Courtesy John Hartford, November 2000)

We do not know the details of his sentence, but Wooliver was paroled in 1952 after serving perhaps ten years.[44] A few years later, Wooliver was playing at tavern dances and jam sessions and being recorded by a young and eager John Hartford and Hartford's friends Marvin and Clifford Hawthorne.

For a character out of Twain or Faulkner, teasing out fact from oft-told anecdote continues to be challenging. Fiddlers like Gene Goforth developed the habit of having two violins at hand when they planned to see Roy. Thanks to Jim Nelson's interview with Howe Teague, we can bring into more clarity an outline of this tough and enigmatic, yet charismatic, man, whose bumptious doings and powerful music are part of the folk history of his region and beyond.[45]

Wooliver had the skills to become a professional musician on radio and recording sessions, but his temperament got in the way. He seems to have drunk whatever alcohol, moonshine, or beer anyone gave him, and although no one remembers him as a full-on alcoholic, drinking was part of his difficulties, just as it was for many musicians of his generation. Having a few too many drinks at a dance or jam session was common, but being drunk does not itself an alcoholic make. Hartford recalled an occasion where Roy was so drunk at a weekend-long music party in the village of Bourbon that he fell into the woodpile "and skinned up his nose."[46]

Howe Teague remembered that Wooliver "wanted to be *different* from everybody else." He rarely wore shoes and socks, and his shoes were perpetually worn out, and at one point Howe Teague's father bought Roy a pair of shoes and socks in Salem.

Roy did enjoy a year or so of success around 1940, performing with Cousin Emmy's radio show on KMOX as a member of her ensemble, the Kinfolks. As noted, Wooliver served as chief ensemble fiddler and played well any style and any tune on the playlist with little or no rehearsal. The attractive, flamboyant Cousin Emmy (Cynthia May Carver, from Kentucky) had worked in radio in various places, emceed the half-hour show, finger-picked five-string banjo, played some fiddle, did some hillbilly comedy, and sang with the group. Wooliver kept her banjo in perfect tune. But Wooliver was not part of Emmy's invited road tours; he could be unpredictable, or arrive onstage inebriated, or be improperly attired for a public performance. As Teague recalled, "He didn't care if the seat of his britches was out or not." Finally, Cousin Emmy dismissed Wooliver after he showed up for a performance at the radio station, where an audience had gathered to watch the show, wearing his typical run-down shoes and no socks.[47] Within a few years, Wooliver was back in the Jeff City penitentiary for the pistol incident at the Bunker dance.

By all reports, Wooliver made a point of being different and obstinate. Like Gene Goforth, Wooliver did not like to be recorded or interviewed on tape; they became restless and reticent and felt they did not play their best when faced with a microphone. Teague remembered that, at a dance at the house of a neighbor, Raymond Majors, "They wanted him to play 'Billy in the Low Ground' but he wouldn't play that for hell—just to be *contrary*. Said, 'I don't *know* that'!" He was "stubborn as hell."

His fiddle repertoire was deep, but he would rarely play a tune that someone requested. People enjoyed his playing at dances, and Roy's name as the fiddler would bring people out. But he did not like to be in the spotlight and, in part due to being cross-eyed, did not like to have his photograph taken.

On several occasions, Howe and Roy played house dances, with Roy playing guitar accompaniment for Howe, but Roy would rarely agree to accompany other fiddlers. On many occasions, people would come to the Teague house to hear Roy fiddle, and then Roy would not play what they asked him to play. "'I don't know it,' he'd say. He was just an *odd ball*."

John Hartford's telling of the pocketknife incident reflects Hartford's humor and eloquence and spices up the story. No exact date is known. Hartford had a way of lapsing back into rural Missouri dialect when telling these stories. "Old Roy he was playin' for a dance. . . . They said, 'Roy speed it up' and Roy, he just had one gait on the fiddle. They kept saying, 'Speed it up.' Old Roy, he got mad and said, 'You're a-wanting to dance like a bunch of people out in a field trying to kill a bunch of goddam snakes. By God, I ain't a-gonna play like that.' So he got out his knife and run 'em all off and went to bed."[48]

John Hartford, as a young bluegrass banjo player and fiddler in the late 1950s, traveled from his home in North St. Louis with his guitarist-friend Marvin Hawthorne to the eastern Ozarks and the Columbia area in central Missouri to meet and record some of the well-known and lesser-known old-time fiddlers he was hearing about. During the period, Hartford had been drafted and was stationed at Fort Leonard Wood, south of Rolla in Pulaski County and in the general territory of Howe Teague, the Goforths, Roy Wooliver, the Dillard boys, Don Brown, and many other musicians across the upper eastern Ozarks. And many were the army draftees delighted to find that "Fort Wood" was in the heart of a beautiful part of a state that was famous for old-time fiddling and bluegrass music. In 1958 Hartford's adventures took him to a country tavern, where he first saw and heard Roy Wooliver in action.

The encounter is among the many vivid anecdotes told by Hartford late in his life on some of his recordings, particularly in a CD of Goforth's fiddling produced by

Hartford, *Eminence Breakdown*, and a later CD of Hartford fiddling tunes he learned from Gene Goforth and Wooliver called *Hamilton Ironworks* (Rounder 0442, 2001). A number of the tunes recorded at this and other sessions, including "Hamilton Ironworks," were transcribed by Hartford in a series of articles in the now-defunct journal the *Devil's Box* and in *Fiddler Magazine*.[49]

On a cold evening in February 1958, John Hartford organized a music party with Wooliver and Gene Goforth. Hartford shrewdly and correctly understood that if he could get Gene Goforth—Roy Wooliver's number-one pupil and admirer—to come to the party, chances would be vastly improved that Roy would ease up on his well-known reluctance to be tape-recorded. John played tasteful backup on his Gibson "bow-tie" Mastertone five-string banjo, and his friend Marvin Hawthorne provided solid guitar accompaniment. What ensued was a remarkable evening of fiddle music. John recorded the session on what he called his "schoolhouse Wollensak" reel-to-reel recorder and microphone. This and other home recordings Hartford made have accrued mystical qualities through the years and have brought Wooliver, Gene Goforth, and also fiddlers such as the elderly Walter Alexander, an exceptionally interesting old-time hornpipe fiddler from Leasburg (Crawford County), to wide attention through the efforts of Charles Wolfe and Jim Nelson.[50] Wooliver's repertoire echoes that of other fiddlers of his generation in the eastern Ozarks, generally the counties of Reynolds,

Fiddler's Hornpipe

As played by Roy Wooliver

Transcribed by Amber Gaddy

Roy Wooliver's "Fiddler's Hornpipe," a breakdown in B-flat and F, familiar in central Missouri but rare elsewhere in the state, 1958 (hear on the companion CD). (Courtesy John Hartford; transcription by Amber Gaddy)

Dent, and Shannon, from old standards known everywhere to unusual and even rare tunes from this region. The tunes recorded that night in 1958 included Roy Wooliver's interpretations of well-known tunes like "Blackberry Blossom," "Paddy on the Turnpike," "Katy Hill," "College Hornpipe" (in B-flat, a.k.a. "Sailor's Hornpipe,"), "Bill Cheatem," "Forked Deer," "Grey Eagle," "Money Musk," "Cackling Hen," "Fisher's Hornpipe" (in F), and "Billy in the Low Ground." All those are in the repertoires of seasoned old-time fiddlers in Missouri in the mid-twentieth century. Wooliver also fiddled, in his flowing, smooth style, tunes that are less familiar in Missouri today, such as "Rocky Road to Denver" ("Rocky Road to Dublin") and "Up Jumped Trouble." But perhaps the diamonds in the session were tunes of local origins, with local place-names, or tunes known elsewhere that have localized versions in Missouri, such as "Ragged Bill" (B-flat), "Fiddler's Hornpipe" (B-flat), "Devil's Hornpipe" (B-flat), and "Hamilton Ironworks."

"Hamilton Ironworks" is a tune that Gene Goforth attributed to Wooliver. Typical of old-time fiddlers, Roy denied its creation, preferring to tell people he learned it from some old-timer years before, which is a way of adding luster and credentials to a tune in addition to diverting people's unwanted attention from the fiddler who has just played it. Beisswenger and McCann include Cecil Goforth's version in their *Ozarks Fiddle Music*; it is also in McCann and Mark Wilson's Rounder compilation CD *Traditional Fiddle Music of the Ozarks*, volume 1, *Along the Eastern Crescent*. Gene Goforth's equally robust version is on Goforth's CD *Eminence Breakdown* (Rounder 0388), and John Hartford's version is on Hartford's *Hamilton Ironworks*.

The site of the 1880s Hamilton Iron Works is in northern Washington County, near the railroad shipping town of Sullivan in lower Franklin County. The existence of an iron and copper smelting works there reminds us that this region of the eastern Ozarks is the famous Missouri "lead belt" of former times, a crucial driver of late colonial Missouri territory industry and settlement. The lead mines began to phase out in the early 1900s, and companies were forced out of business. The Hamilton Mine lasted only from 1873 to 1878 (a victim of financial difficulties), but the big stone smelters at the mill sites ("works") and shot towers there and in several other places continue to be important historical and archaeological sites.

Today, the remains of the Hamilton smelter (furnace) are conserved as part of Meramec State Park. The Sligo Iron Furnace was established in the 1880s and was located near the Teagues' and Woolivers' territory in northeastern Dent County. Like other mines and works, small communities of company workers grew up in the vicinity, typically along railroad lines serving the companies. Another of the 1800s ironworks has a fiddle tune named after it, the Moselle iron works, in the same upper eastern Ozarks quadrant of the Meramec River watershed.[51] Hartford's version of "Moselle" is on the Voyager CD with *Play Me Something Quick and Devilish*.

Hartford considered "Hamilton Ironworks" to have antecedents in older tunes such as a reel called "The Piper's Lass" in the 1883 *Ryan's Mammoth Collection* and the southeastern US tune "Cumberland Gap." We do not know whether Roy Wooliver may have developed his "Hamilton Ironworks" after hearing someone play "The

Hamilton Iron Works, Meramec State Park, near Sullivan, Franklin County, Missouri.

Piper's Lass" from Ryan's book or Cole's—such as his friend Orville Cassity, a musically literate and note-reading fiddler and admirer of tune books.[52]

Wooliver liked to read western cowboy stories in magazines and paperback books, but as he got older his vision deteriorated and he was nearly blind. Wooliver died in St. Louis of a heart attack in March 1964.[53] It is hoped that further research may contribute to a fuller understanding of the complex and illuminating story of Roy Wooliver.

The Duke City Cowboys. *Left to right*: Virginia Stallcup (bass), Marvin (Slim) Ervin (lead guitar), Mike Matney (guitar), and Bill Matney (violin), New Mexico State Fair, Albuquerque, September 1955. (Courtesy Mike Matney)

Missourians Out West

4

Missouri, stylistically, was the jumping off point. If they were raised in Oregon, their parents had come from those same places. It was a continuation of the mix that had gone on ever since Oregon Trail days. . . . Though they were raised in the Northwest, they still had vestiges of the various influences of styles found in the Pacific Northwest—Scandinavian, Western Canadian, New England as well as Missouri and Southern styles.

—Stuart Williams, quoted in Phil Williams and Vivian T. Williams, "Stuart Williams, Northwest Fiddler"

From the nineteenth-century waves of western migration to mining camps and new farms and ranches, several decades passed until new events uprooted other migrants in the tough years of the Great Depression and World War II.[1] The process is familiar though not universal: hard-pressed people pulling up stakes and transplanting the family to greener pastures, hoping for relief from the hard times. They looked for jobs in the busy timber industry, wartime defense industry, shipyards, and airplane plants of California, Oregon, and Washington. Some moved because they wanted to, others moved because the markets collapsed, and still others were displaced by the very programs designed to pull the country out of the Depression. Some moved because of the promise of relief from long, cold winters and health problems prevalent in the humid Midwest.

However they got to their new places of residence, they carried their traditions with them. Whether cooking, language, political preferences, or lists of favorite fiddle tunes, their Missouri past became part of their new present in states like Colorado, Arizona, Oregon, and California. Missouri fiddling took root easily in many places in the West. Evergreens from back home, like "Marmaduke's Hornpipe," "Rachel," "Tennessee Wagner," and "Grey Eagle" (tunes typically identified with Missouri even if most of them were found across the Upper South) became part and parcel of the fiddler's repertoire across many western states.

For some people, a sense of longing and nostalgia for a family tradition of music making in Missouri helped inform their lives, even if circumstances beyond their control wrested them from their native state before their lives could take root. R. D. Lunceford, 1997: "I'm a Missourian. I was born in exile. When people are forced to leave their native places, some of the few things they can take with them are their music and their stories." Thus begin Lunceford's notes to a CD of fiddle music; his family had moved to California from the Prairie Hill community in Chariton County in Missouri's Little Dixie region.[2] The spirit of musical memory, so important in our lives and so seldom articulated, has always been a hallmark of people moving to new places. According to Dr. Linda Danielson, when a fiddler moves west, "the culture and the memory of the old home sometimes become extra important."[3]

On numerous occasions, I have met fiddlers and other people in the West who have spoken of their heritage and roots in Missouri. To mention only a few who came from Missouri, there are Bill Matney and Jim and Larry Hoots of New Mexico; Roscoe White, Tony Boswell, Earl Willis, Earl Collins (by way of Oklahoma), Delbert McGrath, Ron Hughey, Allen Jennings, and Ed Neff of California; Solomon Northup, Jim Herd, Jess Essary, Chuck Morgan, and Ellis Cowin of Washington; Dave Frisbee, Don Gish, Almon Manes, Edna Jenkins, Guy Powell, Monte Stephens, and Duane Stephens of Idaho; and Alta Bance, Robert (Bob) Fast, Barney Alexander, Thelma Shepherd, and Lew Holt of Oregon. One of the founders of the California fiddlers association in 1966 was Floyd Chilton, a Missouri emigrant who was considered by many in California to be "the foremost authority on old-time fiddlers by Californians because of the number of old tunes he knows."[4]

Bill Matney (1903–69) played guitar in string bands in the Kansas City area. In 1928 Matney married Vera Shine and moved to Winchester, Kansas, where they opened a grocery store.[5] In 1937 Matney moved the family to a farm west of Humansville, Missouri (Polk County). He bought his first violin in a Kansas City pawn shop for five dollars and began teaching himself to play fiddle music for dances and house parties.

Matney left Missouri because of the dire economic conditions of the Great Depression and difficulties making a living on the farm. Growing row crops and raising livestock proved a losing prospect, and Matney began to lay a new plan—moving west to New Mexico. His two brothers had already moved to Albuquerque, and he had learned that he would also have the chance to play semiprofessional baseball there. As recalled by his son Mike Matney, in December 1940 his father sold the farm, loaded up his 1935 Chevrolet panel truck with his family's belongings, and headed west.[6]

In addition to playing semipro baseball in Albuquerque, Bill Matney found employment on the Santa Fe Railroad, and between baseball and his shifts on the Santa Fe, Matney also formed a string band called the Duke City Cowboys ("Duke City" was a nickname for Albuquerque), with Harold Browning and Frank Bobb, playing for dances in town halls and homes in the area. Band members at different times included Bill Matney on violin, Bill's sons Mike and Pat Matney, and Harold Browning, Frank Bobb, Virginia Stallcup, Marvin Ervin, and Tony Lewis. They performed into the mid-1960s for square dances, with callers providing "singing calls," and their repertoire ranged from fiddle tunes like "Cindy" and "Liza Jane," "Wagner," and "Up Jumps the Devil" to popular songs and swing numbers such as "Four Leaf Clover" and "Baby Face," as well as songs with a southwestern tint, such as the 1948 Peggy Lee hit song, "Mañana." His Missouri fiddling was evident in his music.

Johnny Luther (1908–60) was a fiddler from Sedalia who got his start in Missouri and found a degree of fame in Hollywood movies and in the 1930s and 1940s leading a cowboy band called Johnny Luther's Ranch Boys. Luther played the part of the fiddling cowhand and square-dance band member in B western movies such as the

Charles Sterrett films *The Fighting Buckaroo* (1943) and *Return of the Durango Kid* (1945) and the Hopalong Cassidy (Bill Boyd) film *Hoppy's Holiday* (1947), as well as musical westerns such as the Judy Garland film *Harvey Girls* (1946).[7] Luther died in San Pedro, California.

Earl Willis: A Boone Family Fiddler Leaves Little Dixie

Raymond (Earl) Willis (1901–95), a farmer from an extended family of musicians, lived his youth years in Missouri, soaking up the music scene and local influences before setting out west. From his family—which included descendants of the famous and famously musical Boone clan—he learned tunes and the culture of fiddling. From the many dances he played throughout the 1920s era (beginning at the age of twelve), he learned to play loud and to change tempo to suit the mood of the dancers. From a local African American fiddler Bill Burdick, he learned a syncopated bowing style and the use of ornamental slides. And in the 1940s, Earl Willis brought this music to Los Angeles.

Due to active fiddlers' associations, we have documentation of Missouri fiddlers who moved to the West Coast states of Oregon and Washington in the mid-twentieth century. Researchers and musicians paid attention when people spoke of where they had come from. As Oregon's Linda Danielson noted, in the Oregon Old-Time Fiddlers Project, fiddlers emigrated from two principal home states, Missouri and Oklahoma.[8] In her interviews, Professor Danielson asked fiddlers about their families and musical roots; the project is a treasure trove of documentation of vernacular music. Like many writers unfamiliar with Missouri's cultural geography, Danielson characterizes the fiddling of Little Dixie fiddler Earl Willis in terms of "the Ozarks."

> A third source of Oregon's immigrant fiddlers centers in the Ozarks region of Missouri and Arkansas, but on account of tastes, commonalities of repertoire and approach to playing that I observed among Oregon immigrants, I think of fiddlers from Oklahoma, Northern Texas, and Southern Illinois as also belonging with this group. The approach to bowing from this region often involves syncopating so as to imitate the banjo and fancy bow lick that Earl Willis called a "Missouri whipped bow." The use of ornamental slides testifies to the influence from African-American fiddlers mentioned frequently by Oregon immigrants from the area.[9]

The African American fiddler Earl Willis alluded to was Bill Burdick, from the Callaway County village of Williamsburg in the Little Dixie region of Missouri.

Willis was born at Mineola in 1901 on the western edge of Montgomery County above the Loutre River valley on the north side of the Missouri River, near the famed Booneslick Trail. Willis's family moved a few miles west to a farm near Williamsburg in 1905. Willis learned to play from a neighbor, Jack Fry, a farmer who played for dances, and Willis's Sailor cousins. Earl's first tune was "Buffalo Girls." He soon

Marmaduke's Hornpipe

As played by Stuart Williams, learned from Earl Willis.

Transcription by Stuart Williams

* The G chord (IV) provides a sense of movement even though it clashes slightly with the melody. This set of chords is known as "Missouri Rules" and is often preferred whether or not it fits exactly.

Variations on measures 3 & 4.

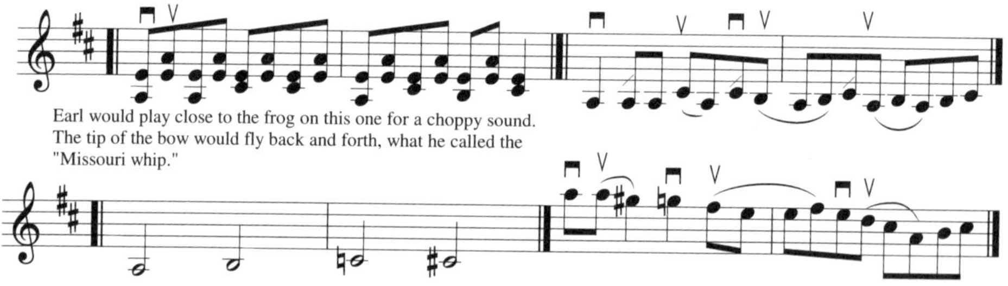

The first three of these were Earl's standard interchangeable licks for this type of tune. The last one is lifted from "Cricket on the Hearth." Also, try playing the 'A' part up an octave.

The classic Missouri tune "Marmaduke's Hornpipe," as played by Stuart Williams (Seattle, Washington) as he learned it from Earl Willis, who was Williams's mentor (Stuart Williams, *Evergreen Fiddler Tune Book*, 1:8). Williams first heard Willis in the early 1970s at a fiddle show where Willis was introduced by Wayne Holmes (Eugene, Oregon) as "the best damn hoedown fiddler there is." As Stuart Williams said on October 10, 2015: "I followed him around wherever he played, backed him up on guitar and piano at the Eugene Farmer's Market and other shows, visited at his home and taped his tunes to work on at home. All told, he was an important mentor to me and a huge influence in my fiddling." (Courtesy Stuart Williams) mastered the standards of the broadly current Missouri repertoire such as "Durang's Hornpipe" (his version sounds like versions of his contemporaries in Little Dixie Cleo Persinger and Taylor McBaine), "Soldier's Joy," "Billy in the Low Ground," "Mississippi Sawyer," "Girl I Left behind Me," "Wagner," "Stony Point," "Old Molly Hare," "Grey Eagle," and "Marmaduke's Hornpipe." Willis entered numerous fiddlers contests in the 1920s and early 1930s and recalled that "Grey Eagle" was the top contest tune in that era, played in the traditional two-part version.

Among Willis's favorite tunes of a Missouri application were "Brickyard Joe" (on the Voyager CD with this book), "Face the Wall," "Old Kitchen Floor," "Get Out of the Way (of the) Federals," "Walk Along John," "Sally in the Garden," "Crystal Stream Waltz" (learned from Vee Latty of nearby Fulton), and "Cherokee Strip" (the Boone family fiddlers' title for "Rachel"). Willis played tunes he learned from his contemporaries in Missouri, some of them learned in music parties, some from hearing fiddlers play over radio station WOS in Jefferson City in the late 1920s, and others from tapes and private-label LP records from the 1970s. Among these are "Willott's Hornpipe," a central Missouri hoedown with a "hornpipe" title often linked to Lee Stoneking of Clinton, and tunes from Lyman Enloe such as "Waldo" and "Oklahoma Red Bird." Willis learned a number of tunes in dischord (cross tuning) from his mother, including "Drunken Hiccups" and "Rye Whisky." The fiddlers Willis grew up with played several hornpipes in B-flat, such as "Lightning Hornpipe" and "Done Gone." All those are titles in the classic Little Dixie fiddle repertoire of the twentieth century.

In the 1920s and 1930s, Willis's mother taught him to play in dischord tunings. She also played reed organ, jew's harp or juice harp, and harmonica. Willis also learned tunes in dischord from Jack Fry, who many years before had taught Earl's mother cross-tuned tunes. Many tunes came from Earl Willis's Sailor family cousins, all musicians in the area, and Ellis would ride horseback to music parties with them. No one took time to teach young Willis particular fiddle techniques; he learned as many ear musicians learn, by watching, listening, and experimenting to get the music right.

Willis's grandmother was Delia Boone, one of the Boone clan, the most famous of whom was the pathfinder and Indian fighter Daniel Boone. Willis recalled that most of the Boone family played fiddle music, particularly the girls in the family, including Earl's mother. Three of his mother's uncles were fiddlers, Sam, Tucker, and Bud Boone. The Willises were English and Scotch-Irish. Most of the family—apart from his father, John (he jokes that his father "couldn't carry a tune in a sack with both ends closed")—played some sort of musical instrument.

> On the farm, and we'd be in at night, and banjo and fiddle and guitar and mandolin and everything, you know. Awfulest noise you ever heard in your life. Father worked hard all day and he'd come home at night . . . and he'd sit down to read his paper, and all that noise going on he'd (be in his) reading chair. He'd look up over the page and look at us and he never one time never said one word. And how he put up with it, I don't think there is another man on earth could have done it. . . . [G]uess he figured, "Well, let 'em go to it," you know. But he'd look up to see what's taking place—you'd think we was goin' to tear the house down.

Brickyard Joe

As played by Earl Willis

abbcbb and occasionally d

Transcription by Stuart Williams

"Brickyard Joe," by Earl Willis, Springfield, Oregon, ca. 1976 (hear on the companion CD). One of Willis's favorite old-time breakdowns, this is known as a central Missouri tune as well as a Kentucky tune. Willis may have heard it fiddled by players such as Tony Gilmore, who performed on WOS-AM radio in the late 1920s. (Transcription by Stuart Williams)

In the 1920s and 1930s, the Willis and Boone clan played a tune called "Face the Wall" for a square-dance figure by the same title. "[In the dancing] the women'd go one way and the men the other. Four women'd go this way and the four men that way, see. Then they'd turn and they'd come back, they'd face the wall, then turn and come back and go between each other. Then they'd go the other side, then they'd come back and then they'd dance." For comparison to Earl Willis's description of this dance, caller Steve Young of Taneyville (formerly of Winigan) calls a set called "Swing at the Wall," his variation of a dance found in publications like Lloyd Shaw's 1952 *Cowboy Dances*. Steve Young feels that Shaw's "Swing the Wall" is much the same as the Willis and Boone families' "Face the Wall." As Steve calls the figure:

> First couple out to the couple on the right,
> Around that couple and swing at the wall. (Outside the set, couple #1 separates and goes around behind couple #2 and swings)
> Through that couple and swing in the hall. (Couple #1 goes between Couple #2 and swings inside the square, while couple #2 swings also)
> Circle four, oh circle four,
> Docey-doe and away you go,
> Opposite by the right and partner by the left.
> The lady goes si and the gent goes do.
> Now on to the next you go. (Couple #1 goes to Couple #3 and repeats around the set back to home, then couple #2, 3, & 4 does the same)[10]

Willis learned "Face the Wall" from his mother in dischord tuning (A–E–A–C#), while his uncles played it in standard tuning and in the key of A. "Face the Wall," like "Sally Goodin," is found as both fiddle tune and square-dance call.[11] However, any good hoedown can serve as the music for the dance. "That's the Boone family. Sam Boone, and Tucker Boone, and Bud Boone—they all played those tunes."

Willis's second cousin Nolan Boone had fiddled over the 1920s WOS radio in Jefferson City and was a contest player from the 1920s through the 1970s. Another second cousin, Herman Boone, was a well-known dance fiddler in the Williamsburg area who had introduced young Pete McMahan to the art of fiddling for square dances.

Willis recalled African American fiddlers Bill Burdick and Bill Katon for Professor Danielson's Oregon collection. Willis knew Burdick personally but knew Katon only from his WOS radio performances. In the middle 1920s, the Willis family and other farm families would sometimes hire Bill Burdick and a friend who played guitar accompaniment to play music at their barbecues that were part of two- to three-day fox hunts.

> "He'd [Burdick] play a day and night. And one time I said—he was playing "Sally Goodin" in G. 'Course we always played it in A, see. I asked him if he ever played it in A, and he said, "No," he said, "I never did." He said, "Do you play it in A?" I

said, "Yeah, I do, Bill." And he said, "Well, play it for me." And I played it for him. And I don't think I've ever heard a human play it any better than he could, after he went to playing it in A. He was a fiddler.

Earl Willis learned several unusual central Missouri tunes from Bill Burdick, including "Jefferson City Blues." This is one of the Missouri tunes that, perhaps because of its difficulty or rarity, Willis seldom played after leaving Missouri. Similarly, Willis learned Bill Katon's tune "Old Kitchen Floor" from radio broadcasts, and this tune has also become rare. Earl admired Katon's fiddling just as much as Bill Burdick's.

Packed dance halls and the enthusiasm of the dancers late into the night demanded that fiddlers develop a forceful, powerful bowing arm with a lot of volume. Playing for dances like those had an effect on a fiddler's style. Willis played loud and "rough." His cousin Herman Boone played "smooth" and "sweet."

Missouri fiddlers' bowing was what Willis called "a free bow," a term I have not heard any other fiddler use. "Some of them old boys were pretty wicked with that bow, there, in Missouri, see, especially this one cousin I had (Herman Boone). Boy, his arm was just like a dishrag." Like many other young fiddlers, Earl Willis was fascinated and charmed by fiddlers and their music. He just had to do it himself. "I'd hear these guys play and I just wanted to play so bad, and I'd be out in the cornfield working, maybe riding the disc cultivator, and I'd be a-thinking all the time, 'How do you get that bow to work?'"

Earl Willis played his first dance in Williamsburg on Christmas 1913, when he was twelve. His brother played guitar accompaniment. Willis liked fiddling for dances and understood the value of dance fiddling in the process of ingraining in a musician's mind the fundamentals of dance rhythm and timing, as well as tunes. He was fortunate, like his cousin Nolan Boone, in being able to play loud for dancers in jam-packed halls in the days before electrical amplification. Another cousin, fiddler Herman Boone, was not in demand as a dance fiddler because Herman played "so weak and sweet, he just played so smooth he couldn't play loud," and dancers had trouble hearing him.

> 'Course playing dances was good for a kid. . . . I think it was in '28—I was real busy on the farm, and a guy wanted me to play for him, he had a roadhouse . . . and I agreed to play one night. I agreed to play one Saturday for him. He had a band there for the fiddler—he (the regular fiddler) didn't want to play . . . and he wanted me to take his fiddler's place—and I played for him five years. At that roadhouse. And that was during the Depression and he'd give me five dollars a night. In the summertime. And in the wintertime he'd give me three dollars a night. 'Cause we wouldn't have the big crowds, see. And in the summertime we'd have a fiddle, and guitar, and tenor banjo, drums, and saxophone. And all the people . . . we all knew each other, see. And it was pretty good, it was good playing. I just loved it.
>
> We'd play a square dance, we'd play about two squares, and then we'd play a waltz, then play about two more squares, then we'd play a fox trot. Then maybe a waltz,

too, see, that's the way they wanted it. That's the way they run in those days. About two squares. . . . That was '28—late '20s and the early '30s.

'Course you play a longer time. If you're playing a round dance you can quit any time you want to, if you're playing a square dance you can't. You got to play till they get this set through, and a lot of those sets are a lot longer than others, too. That was the advantage of playing for one caller. Now years ago when we was young and played dances, maybe this set'd be dancing, and the caller would be right on that set, the set over there, the other caller would be on that set. Each caller called his own set. . . . There was no amplification. And this guy would call the shorter set, maybe the one over there his set would be a lot longer—well you'd just have to play till he got through. And it was a lot of disadvantages to it. And the music was hard then, because you had no amplification, and you'd take six or eight or nine sets of dancing, and people were calling, it's hard to hear the music. That's one reason why I got more dances to play for than anybody, because I could play *louder*, I couldn't play as good as the other guy but I could play louder. And they used to tell us, "If we can't hear you, you just as well stay home," you know.

Along with other fiddlers in central Missouri, Willis played over WOS radio in the late 1920s; his group was called the Beacon Camp Fiddlers, sponsored by the owner of a service station in Callaway County called Beacon Camp where musicians would get together for music parties. The Beacon Camp Fiddlers made several appearances on WOS. Willis recalled that he enjoyed warming up with the band in the hallways of the capitol, but found the music less than satisfying when they crowded into the small studio space in front of the microphone and played live over the air.[12] The importance of radio as a source of fiddle music (and learning new tunes) during the Depression years cannot be overstated, since the dire economic straits meant that few people could afford to keep buying records for their record players.

In late 1929, the Chevrolet dealer in Montgomery City, operated by Thomas J. Weeks, sponsored a dance featuring Earl Willis and his band—violin, guitar, upright bass, and piano.[13] This was Willis's favorite ensemble, no doubt at least in part because of the tremendous accompaniment and rhythm that could be provided by guitar, bass, and piano. The event was hosted by Weeks to celebrate the unveiling of the first six-cylinder Chevrolet automobile, the AC International, a car designed to compete with the Ford Model A and appeal to the middle range of the market. Tom Weeks's father, also named Thomas, was a fiddle player and played a tune people called "Tom Weeks' Waltz," a tune that apparently was once familiar in the Montgomery City community and environs.

A large crowd gathered to listen to the music, visit, and have a look at the new Chevy car. A local "German accordion band" was hired to play a set of dance tunes while Earl Willis's ensemble took a break, had refreshments, and examined the automobiles.[14] This celebration took place a few weeks after the "Black Tuesday" Wall Street stock market crash of October 24—just as the enormity and implications of Black Tuesday were about to hit home. The good times of the Roaring Twenties were over for Tom Weeks as well as Earl Willis and many others at the celebration. The Great Depression was about to come crashing down.

In 1936, with the Depression full on, Earl Willis and some of his siblings decided they should leave the farm to find better means to make a living. There were no jobs, and the farm could not sustain the large family. The agricultural communities in the Williamsburg area were among many where farmers were going bankrupt. Without markets to buy their livestock, farmers were forced to slaughter their starving cattle.[15]

So the Willis boys moved to California. Earl wound up in Pasadena, and before long he was happily playing fiddle jobs in select venues. He found that most of the fiddlers were playing "western swing" and "hot fiddle"—and few were playing "down-to-earth hoedown" style. The Los Angeles area offered numerous venues for seasoned dance fiddlers who could handle some western swing as well as the hard-core breakdowns needed for square dancing.

On one occasion, Willis's cousin Herman Boone visited him in California, and while Herman played too softly for unamplified square dances back home, he got jobs thanks to the LA area's adoption of electrical amplification systems. Herman Boone spent a winter with the Willis family. "But he came to California . . . and spent a winter with me, and they just wanting fiddlers real bad, then, see. So I called up a guy, said, 'I got a good fiddler.' 'Oh,' he said, 'I want him.' He played for this guy all the time he was there. 'Course he had amplification and everything. Oh, gee, he just really fit right in the square dancing."

After service in the US Navy during the war, Earl Willis played for dances at naval functions in the late 1940s and early 1950s as well as performances at the Los Angeles County Fair and jobs to entertain at parties in the homes of people in the movie industry, such as those hosted by silent-film star Norma Shearer at her Santa Monica mansion, which was awash with celebrities. Willis particularly enjoyed the weekly Tuesday-night dances at the Terminal Island naval facility near San Pedro, where he and his brother, and a piano player, played. When the square-dancing fad took off in Los Angeles after World War II, Earl Willis fiddled for the popular dance caller Guy Spurlock in LA. "Yeah, we played square dances for 'em. . . . [Frank] Sinatra and all them guys would get together and square dance."

Willis recalled meeting jazz great Joe Venuti in Los Angeles:

> I was in contact quite a lot with a guy in California who'd been a violinist, and he turned over and went to playing other stuff on it. . . . And he did a pretty good job on it. In fact, we was recording one time and I was gonna record the hoedowns and he was gonna record some so-called singing calls. And this "Just Because" they wanted—he didn't know it. He said, "I haven't heard it. I don't know it." Said, "Run through it." So I run through it. He wrote it down. He put the notes down as I was running through it. He stuck it in his pocket. He was standing around there, and . . . (we) got ready to play and he still hadn't looked at it. . . . So he got ready to play, he just took it out of his pocket and put it under his foot, and I've never heard

such fiddlin' in my life! See, that's what you can learn by reading notes, if you got the talent to go with it.

Earl Willis was in awe of Joe Venuti's skill, and Venuti did not fail to recognize a great player in Willis. On hearing Willis play, Willis said Venuti remarked, "I'd give anything in the world if I could play them hoedowns like that." Willis replied, 'Well, if I could play the fiddle, the violin, like *you* can, I wouldn't care if I never heard another hoedown.' And I meant it." Such was the life of a fiddling Missourian who traveled so far from home to find himself rubbing elbows with a player with an entirely different set of skills—jazz. Willis: "But that's it—you want something you haven't *got*, see. But he could sure play."

Some thirty years later, Earl Willis moved to Macon, Missouri, and worked there until 1966. In 1966 he moved to Springfield, Oregon, where he died in 1995.

"Missouri Picnics" in Northwest Washington State: Ellis Cowin

Just as painful as the Great Depression is another factor that drove people from their land and homes: unforeseen consequences of government programs. One or another government program created with intentions of alleviating conditions of the Depression and helping people also forced people to leave their homes and farms. In an irony bitterly remembered by some people, thousands of small farmers and smallholders were ejected from their land by federal agencies set up to protect the environment, turn back the Dust Bowl, and create national forests to conserve remains of rapidly disappearing old-growth timberlands. These government projects often led to good things, and many benefited, but for those who were inside the map of the new federal land boundary, their story could end badly. Whatever the reason, numbers of people from Missouri found themselves in the Pacific Northwest. For those from farming families in the forested parts of states like Missouri, North Carolina, and Tennessee, their traditional skills of timbering and sawmilling were needed, and work was available.

Ellis Cowin was among many young men with the necessary skills who left their homes to find jobs in the timber industry during the 1930s and 1940s. Cowin was a square-dance fiddler from Van Buren, born in 1900 or 1901 and one of six children of Daniel and Viola Cowin (sometimes spelled "Cowen").[16] Van Buren is in the Ozark foothills of South Missouri's Carter County, an area taken by the federal government when Mark Twain National Forest was created in 1939 (and later Ozark Scenic Riverways National Park was added). Land in twenty-nine counties was taken into the national forest, representing some 11 percent of Missouri's forests. Famous for its timber, lumber mills, and railroad-tie industry, by the 1920s the forests were disappearing due to overharvesting and inefficient management practices, thus President Roosevelt's development of the national forest.

Ellis Cowin, at the annual "Missouri picnic" in 1966 in Lynden, Washington. The banjo player behind Cowin is Barney Munger, originally from Cincinnati, Ohio, who played in the Tall Timber Trio bluegrass band with Phil and Vivian Williams of Seattle. (Photo by Irwin Nash; courtesy Vivian Williams)

Along with former Missourians like Cowin, community picnics were gatherings of migrants from the Upland South and the Ozarks who had come to Washington State to work in the timber industry. Vivian Williams recalls the "Missouri picnics" at Lynden, in northwestern Washington near the Canadian border, where she and Phil Williams played music and met Ellis Cowin in the 1960s. Many musicians were "Tar Heel" timber workers from the vicinity of Silva, North Carolina, who came to the Darrington area of western Washington after World War II to work in the lumber industry. The Tar Heel picnics included many timber workers from Tennessee, West Virginia, and Missouri, and they were a tight-knit community. As Vivian Williams recalled:

> Everyone brought food, and although each group had their own table, it was kind of a potluck as well, since you were welcome to try food from other folks' tables. They had a pretty loose stage show, jam sessions, and probably family get-togethers as well. I don't recall any dancing, except perhaps a couple of drunks doing the "hillbilly jig" on a picnic table! Although there was drinking, it was mostly pretty civilized, these was definitely family affairs.
>
> The Missouri picnic was the same kind of thing, although since Lynden was a little more remote location, fewer "outsiders" showed up. But several of the regular

> Tarheel and other local bluegrass musicians did show up there. After all, they all played and jammed together all the time. I think the Missouri folks were a bit more sedate than the Tarheels.[17]

Among the tunes Cowin is known for in Washington State is a song-tune he brought from Van Buren called "Old Coon Dog." This is a different tune from the "Old Coon Dog" or "Best Old Coon Dog" that is a cousin of "Granny Will Your Dog Bite" and played in North Missouri by Nile Wilson, Albert Spray, Delbert Spray, and others.

Vivian Williams, who knew and performed with Cowin, feels that Ellis Cowin's "Old Coon Dog" "closely resembles" "Whoa Mule" or "Johnson's Old Grey Mule."[18] This tune appears in at least two tune books as played by Vivian Williams.[19] Cowin's "Old Coon Dog" was released on the 1969 Voyager LP *Comin' Round the Mountain*, along with music by former North Carolina and former Kentucky musicians.[20] Cowin sang a series of verses, some of which are "floater" lyrics found in minstrel stage and vaudeville songs. Cowin's "Old Coon Dog" is his version of a different song, one with humorous verses and a melody for which no parallel comes to mind.

After moving west sometime in the late 1930s or early 1940s, in 1943 Cowin married Wilhelmina Davie of Bellingham, Washington, a schoolteacher. Ellis Cowin lived in Lynden and died in 1982.

Walk Along John

from Ellis Cowan
Missouri & Lynden, WA

"Walk Along John," as played by Ellis Cowin in 1966 at the "Missouri picnic" near Lynden, Washington (hear on the companion CD) (Stuart Williams, *Evergreen Fiddler Tune Book*, 2:20). (Courtesy Stuart Williams)

Ishmael (Ozark Red) Loveall, Radio Fiddler

Born a few years after the first wave of fiddlers to go west in the mid-twentieth century was a youngster "too hot" to stay put in the old-time fold, Ishmael Wayne Loveall (1910–83). According to his niece Belinda Luke, her uncle Red was born in 1910 in the Linn Creek community of Camden County, along the Osage River in the Lake of the Ozarks area. Ishmael was reared by his maternal grandparents, Absalom Jacob Loveall, an Osage Indian who made his living trapping furs, and Elvira Ellen Langford.[21]

Ishmael learned to play fiddle music as a child from his grandmother and an uncle, Claude Loveall. His father played fiddle and his mother five-string banjo. Ishmael also played guitar, banjo, electric steel guitar, and other instruments and was a good singer. While still a child, Ismael Loveall performed at the Mainstreet Theater (a.k.a. Empire Theater), a famous vaudeville house in downtown Kansas City, playing five-string banjo in a comedy and string ensemble with the Weaver Brothers and Elvira. It was there that the gregarious red-haired lad acquired the nickname "Ozark Red."

A powerful performer, Loveall played the usual dances but flourished as an entertainer and contest fiddler. He admired classical music; as a child he saved his money so he could buy 78 rpm recordings by Fritz Kreisler. Loveall fiddled all the standards of the Missouri repertoire as well as pop tunes of the day and pieces of classical violin music pulled from records. Although this may seem incongruous for a country fiddler, many young players admired all sorts of music and sought to hear the famous violinists of their times, just as they listened to Joe Venuti's jazz records and the local hotel dance orchestra.

Loveall had begun competing in fiddlers contests while still in his childhood. While a seventh grader, he won a tough contest at Linn Creek, in which he had to play against some thirty-five other fiddlers, all of them older and more experienced than he. The first prize was a ten-dollar gold piece, which became Loveall's good-luck charm. When an illness struck in his teens, he moved in with his grandparents. Absalom Loveall was a trapper and taught young Ishmael the craft, trapping furs along the Osage River and its tributaries—rivers soon to be flooded with the building of Bagnell Dam and the Lake of the Ozarks. When the lake filled, no longer able to subsist by fur trapping and hunting, Red hired himself out as a hunting and fishing guide for tourists and turned to commercial fishing. In 1934 he married Wilma Cavin, the daughter of a resort owner.

The connections Loveall made with visiting fishermen and hunters helped him find his way to Kansas City. There in 1935 he performed with the KCMO radio band George Holstein and the Ploughboys. He worked at KCMO for eighteen months and, needing to recover from an ankle accident, moved back to the Ozarks. In 1936 he had the opportunity to play fiddle professionally again, with a group called the Happy Roving Cowboys, who performed on the southern Illinois radio station WTAD in Quincy. Loveall took the stage name "Cy" with the Happy Roving Cowboys and played with this old-time and western-swing combo for almost two years. He was making a name

Ishmael (Ozark Red) Loveall had a chance to meet his idol, Fritz Kreisler, at a concert at Drury College in Springfield, Missouri, in the late 1930s or early 1940s. Kreisler appreciated traditional fiddle tunes, and Loveall played several for him backstage after the concert. Loveall was also able to meet David Rubinoff, another classical violinist on tour in Springfield, and trade tunes on the maestro's 1731 Stradivarius. The Russian-Polish emigrant "Rubinoff" switched from classical performance to Hollywood movies and popular radio shows. (Courtesy Belinda Luke)

for himself. The band broke up in 1940, after Loveall suffered a broken leg in an automobile accident and spent weeks recuperating in a Jefferson City hospital.

About a year later, Loveall took a staff fiddler job at WSOY in Decatur, Illinois. From there, he moved on to WCBS and then WTAX, AM radio stations in Springfield, Illinois. Then, with Freckles Mattson, an old bandmate from the Happy Roving Cowboys days, Loveall went to work with touring musicians calling themselves the Rhythm Rangers, working for Cal Shrum, the popular radio and film entertainer. Cal and his brother Walt Shrum were born in Missouri and moved with the family to Colorado, where they developed careers as western-swing musicians in the Denver area. Later, Cal fronted a band appearing in several Hollywood B western movies.[22] When World War II broke out and men were being drafted in 1942, Freckles Mattson joined the navy. Loveall, whose poor health and numerous injuries kept him out of the draft, returned to the Ozarks. In 1943 he joined the staff at KWTO radio in Springfield. At this point, he returned to being called "Ozark Red."

Ozark Red became a celebrity on AM radio in the 1940s. In this case, the springboard was KWTO, where Loveall performed on the *Korn's-a-Krackin'* show and *The Ozark Farm and Home Hour*. *Korn's-a-Krackin'* was the first regularly broadcast program of its type in the midwestern United States and aired nationally over the Mutual Broadcasting System. *Korn's-a-Krackin'* also promoted "package shows," in which ensembles of performers from the radio program were offered by the station management for concerts and shows throughout the Ozarks region. This is the kind of package tour still popular today and promoted by country radio stations such as WSM (Nashville) and *The Grand Ole Opry*. In 1947, for example, *Korn's-a-Krackin'* packages were made available to towns with facilities with telephone service, so that a half hour of the one-hour live Saturday-night stage shows could be simultaneously broadcast over KWTO's feed to the Mutual Broadcasting System, taking the show to every radio station in the United States that subscribed to the Mutual service.

KWTO's entrepreneurial founder, Ralph Foster, had hit upon a smart marketing tool when he began publishing an occasional magazine called the *Dial*. Inspired by the extremely popular "movie star magazines" of the 1940s, the *Dial* gave readers, most of them paying subscribers, an inside peek at the radio station and its programs and performers. In a time when newspapers and magazines were essential in daily life, these little magazines prospered, if only for a while. In September 1944, Loveall was given substantial promotion in "The Spotlight" column in the *Dial*.

The packages were tailored to the town or theater being booked, in terms of both number of performers as well as format and type of country music presented—"spirituals, ballads, popular songs, hymns and musical gems."[23] One of the 1947 three-person packages was a trio made up of Ozark Red, Buster Fellows, and George Rhodes; Loveall was also in a four-person package with Dale Parker, Jerry Osborne, and Goo-Goo Rutledge. The byword of the promotional stories in the *Dial* was "all the finesse of Class A vaudeville."

One of the tunes of local connection Loveall fiddled was "Echoes of the Ozarks," a catchy melody he was playing by the late 1930s. A versatile tune, it can be played as a rhythmic fox-trot for couple dancing or with a bit more speed as a square-dance tune. Fiddlers heard "The Echoes of the Ozarks" and picked it up, either from Red's radio broadcasts or from hearing him at old-time fiddlers contests such as a contest in 1939 in the town of Bagnell in the Lake of the Ozarks area. Influential fiddlers such as Lee Stoneking, Luther Caldwell, Lyman Enloe, and Pete McMahan worked out their own versions of "The Echoes of the Ozarks," sometimes in different keys and sometimes with an alternate title.

After several years with KWTO, in the late 1940s, Loveall left Missouri and moved to San Francisco, California. The growing music scene on the West Coast was drawing many midwestern musicians, and people were being exposed to and taking part in the boom in country music radio, bluegrass, and early television broadcasting. Red Loveall's success at KWTO and on other radio stations, as well as the word within the professional grapevine, paved the way for access to jobs in San Francisco, some of them in posh venues playing the society circuit.

One of Loveall's professional jobs was in San Francisco—the city and region had been a magnet for Missourians since the Gold Rush era a century before—where Red was working with the Trailblazers. The Trailblazers were a hot western-swing band, with Dusty Dale, Mike O'Hearn, and Billy Salek playing piano accordion (enjoying a trend of popularity for that instrument in country and popular music). The Trailblazers were considered a topflight ensemble in the mold of the Sons of the Pioneers and played dances at such legendary venues as the Humoresque Club on East Fourteenth Street (International Boulevard) in Oakland.

In California in the 1950s, Loveall recorded and appeared with the country music star Farrell (Rusty) Draper—from Kirksville, Missouri. Draper's commercial records included 1950s hits such as "The Shifting, Whispering Sands" and "How Could You (Blue Eyes)." Among recordings with Draper is an instrumental "Ozark Kitchen Sweat." A "kitchen sweat" is an old-time house dance with a live band and plentiful food and libation, usually with some square dancing, with furniture moved to the porch or another room. For this recording, Loveall fiddled a medley of three

The Trailblazers at KPIX television studio in the Mark Hopkins Hotel on Nob Hill, San Francisco, ca. 1950. *Left to right*: Billy Salek, Dusty Dale, Mike O'Hern, and Red Loveall; the young ladies were models from San Francisco's Levi Strauss and Co., a sponsor and maker of the famous "Levi's" jeans. Performing here, a young fiddler from the Ozarks could very well feel as though he or she had made it in the music business. (Courtesy Belinda Luke)

traditional fiddle tunes he knew would be recognizable by his audience, tunes most Missouri fiddlers knew: "Red-Haired Boy," "Devil's Dream," and "Grey Eagle." Loveall's "Ozark Kitchen Sweat" is a medley worked up for the recording session and radio shows, and the set represents hard-core square-dance fiddling back in Missouri. Fiddle-tune medleys were unusual in Missouri in Loveall's time (and still are in most contexts excepting the contra-dance scene).

Loveall is credited with composing at least one fiddle tune, called "Raking the Leaves." This tune appears on only one known recording, as fiddled by Lyman Enloe in the 1980s. Enloe competed against Loveall in a fiddlers contest at the Lake of the Ozarks in 1939, and Loveall won first place playing "Raking the Leaves." After the contest, Lyman Enloe asked Red to play the tune for him backstage, and Enloe learned the tune on the spot.

Recordings of Red Loveall performing with Rusty Draper as well as at home jam sessions (reissued on CD in 2011) indicate a fiddle style that was clean, smooth, powerful, and modern in its western-swing solos and accompaniment as well as in his bowing and intonation that suggest his attention as a younger man to classical violinists. The recordings with Draper reveal Loveall's ability to move with ease between hard-driving hoedowns to carefully arranged accompaniment for Draper's country songs and the versatility of country music of the era in which an "old-time fiddler" could fit in with a jazz accordionist like the Trailblazers' Billy Salek or George Ceruti, who recorded blistering jazz solos in a recording of "China Boy" with Loveall's hot fiddle breaks. Red Loveall died in Carson City, Nevada, in 1983, where he was in semiretirement.

Ron Hughey: Mentor, Model, "People Pleaser"

Perhaps more than any other Missouri fiddler out west, with his many fiddlers contest wins, festival appearances, and essential 1970s LP record, Ron Hughey continues to be well known among fiddle fans back home. In the West he was the "Fiddler with a Million Friends and Hundreds of Tunes."[24] Ron Hughey (1914–74) was a gregarious farm boy from South Greenfield in the hills of Dade County, a few miles northwest of Springfield. His father bought a German-made "Ole Bull" factory violin from a mail-order catalog for him when he was seven years old for $4.50. Hughey played this violin all his life. Hughey's mother and sisters played piano, his brother played banjo, and his father and several uncles were fiddlers and square-dance callers.[25]

On the 1973 *Country Fiddlin' Ozark Style* LP, recorded in California, Ron Hughey told anecdotes about his early years in Missouri. The interview was recorded by M. Bryan Baker. With a mixture of recollected fact and dry humor, Hughey recalls his family: "I had six or seven uncles that fiddled. Dad's oldest brother, I guess, was about one of the best fiddlers. His name was Wyatt. His son, they both played. We used to go see them about once a year, and I really enjoyed that when I was a kid. . . . Uncle Ed—about all he did in the winter was stand around the stove, chew tobacco, and fiddle. And of course he eat pretty good, too, once in a while, about every thirty minutes."

Ozark Kitchen Sweat

as played by Red Loveall

Transcribed by Phil Vinyard

Red Loveall's "Ozark Kitchen Sweat," Chicago, 1939 (hear on the companion CD). Loveall fiddles a hot square-dance set with Rusty Draper (guitar) as the Sons of the Ozarks. Draper, from Kirksville in northern Missouri, had become prominent in country music in California. "Ozark Kitchen Sweat" is a medley Loveall put together of three big Missouri fiddle tunes, "Red-Haired Boy," "Devil's Dream," and "Grey Eagle." (*Rusty and Red: The Early Recordings of Rusty Draper Featuring Ozark Red Loveall* [British Archive of Country Music, CD D334, 2011]) (Transcription by Philip K. Vinyard)

In 1930 Hughey's family loaded up their Model T Ford and journeyed across Route 66 to Southern California, settling near Fresno in the Central Valley. The trip took a month, and the family was one of thousands of displaced midwesterners known collectively as "Okies" (many were indeed from Oklahoma) memorialized in the 1939 John Steinbeck novel and subsequent John Ford movie *The Grapes of Wrath*.[26] While the Hughey family were farmers back in Missouri, Ron sought a different life. Like many other young people surviving the ordeal of the Great Depression, he turned away from tilling the land and made his living as a welder and part-time musician.

Hughey became a familiar face at West Coast fiddling contests, as well as in local dance bands. He performed at dances and shows throughout the San Joaquin Valley, from Bakersfield to Sacramento, and played outside the valley in Santa Cruz and Oakland and other California cities. His various bands, such as the Arkansas Ramblers, the Texas Cowboys, Bill Thompson and the Ozark Mountain Boys, the Rangers, and the Air Raiders, were not as well known as the big "stars" of the day, like the

Ron Hughey of Fresno, California, with his Ole Bull violin, on the cover of his highly regarded 1973 LP, *Country Fiddlin' Ozark Style*. (Courtesy David Cavins)

Maddox Brothers and Rose, or the Sons of the Pioneers, but he was familiar with all their tunes and played them at music parties for years afterward. He also competed in state fiddling competitions, something he had done as a youngster in Missouri in the 1920s. Hughey's friend and fellow former Missourian Delbert McGrath was also a frequent competitor on the California contest circuit; both men had been state champions. Delbert M. McGrath (1918–2003) was from the Ozarks village of Day in Taney County, fiddled for square dances at age nine, and had been recorded by folklorist Vance Randolph in 1942 before McGrath emigrated to find factory work in Sacramento, California.

By the 1960s, Hughey was playing with mandolin player and fiddler Kenny Hall, western-swing guitarist Frank Hicks, and Fresno folk musician Pete Everwine, in the Sweets Mill String Band. In the mid-1970s, the California State Fiddle Championship was held in Fresno, and Hughey had already become a mentor to a whole new generation of younger fiddlers. It was in Fresno that he met fiddler and writer Gus Garelick, who at that time was producing a regular radio show about fiddling on KPFA-FM in Berkeley. Gus did several interviews at Ron's home in Fowler, outside Fresno, and some of the interviews included music by Ron's western-swing band the Sagebrush Symphony. Garelick recalls: "Ron Hughey was a dear friend back in the '70s and I learned a lot about old time fiddling from him. He was a real treasure in the California fiddling community in those days. . . . [T]he Sagebrush Symphony (with Hughey) (was) a kind of tribute to the Sons of the Pioneers. Ron Hughey did all the Hugh Farr parts, minus the bass singing, and came pretty close to getting that swing style note perfect."[27]

Hughey came to fame beyond the western states through the 1973 album *Country Fiddlin' Ozark Style*, which sold well through catalogs. The record contained an outstanding selection of tunes, among which were several Missouri ironclads, such as "Forked Deer," "Goodnight Waltz," "Cricket on the Hearth" (a.k.a. "Marmaduke's Hornpipe"), "Wagnor" [*sic*] (the first tune Hughey learned to play), "Dubuque," and "Missouri Waltz."[28] The album also featured two tunes Hughey learned from his uncles and considered "family tunes," "Yellow Gals" and "Sally in the Garden." Hughey's "Missouri Waltz" is unusual in that he includes the fugitive latter part of the tune that few musicians play. Hughey plays the tune in G, with this "Graveyard Waltz" part in E minor, much as some Missouri fiddlers play it in the present day.[29]

On the recording, Hughey plays his lifelong violin, the "Ole Bull fiddle," that he brought from Missouri. By this time, the Ole Bull had a hole through the back. Ron wore "overhauls," and he played with the violin held down against his chest (rather than tucked up under his chin). Years and years of playing had produced a hole in the violin, from its rubbing against the left strap button on his overalls. The violin's utility and sound seem not to have been noticeably affected, nor did Ron seem to mind.

"Yellow Gals" is an unusual tune. A modal tune, this one on Hughey's LP sounds Appalachian to my ears because of its comparative metrical alteration. This would be called a "crooked tune," due to its metrical shifts and the addition of measures, not unlike how other Missouri fiddlers of his era left out or added beats or measures.

Hughey said it was a family tune that he never heard outside his own family back in Missouri. I do not think this tune is connected to other tunes by similar titles, at least not in Missouri (for example, Bill Katon's "Walking with the Yellow Gal" as transcribed in Christeson's second volume). Transcriptions of "Yellow Gals" appear in two publications, the *Old-Time Herald* and Beisswenger and McCann.[30] The Kentucky tune called "The Yellow Barber" bears no resemblance to "Yellow Gals." The term "yellow" in Missouri in the years of Hughey's youth referred to a light-skinned African American person of mixed race, a mulatto. The title's reference was known, if not commonplace, and would not have concerned most Missouri fiddlers.

"Dubuque" is the same tune as "Old Dubuque," a familiar tune in Missouri. While it is still familiar in Missouri, it is not played often and has become rare. A close cousin is "Apple Blossom," played by Texas-style-based National Contest style fiddlers. The powerful eastern Ozarks fiddler Gene Goforth recorded his version as "Apple Time" on his 1974 private-label LP. The tune is also reminiscent of the Canadian reel "Snow Shoes," a tune popularized in Missouri in the 1970s and 1980s by fiddlers such as Pete McMahan and Kelly Jones. Ron Hughey's second part does not include the minor chord in the backup (preferred by Missouri fiddlers such as Art Galbraith, Johnny Bruce, Delbert Spray, Gene Goforth, and Kelly Jones). It sounds to me like his second part may have been unusual enough that his accompanists on the 1973 LP, while skilled and solid, were not exactly sure what to do and went with a standard chord progression, making the second part sound more like something from a different tune.

Tunes handed down from older fiddlers are often learned without titles. A swing piece called "Dad's Tune" ("Dad's favorite tune") is one of the tunes Hughey played at a jam session at his house in Fowler, California, in July 1973. The session, in which Hughey was accompanied by the Sagebrush Symphony, was recorded by Gus Garelick. Parts of the recording and interview with Hughey were aired on Garelick's radio program on KPFA in 1973 and 1974. "Rosetta" is a swing tune and represents that part of Hughey's musical life and repertoire. At dances in the 1930s onward, fiddlers like Hughey could be expected to play a broad repertoire that included the well-known swing tunes, two-steps, and songs of the day, such as "Kansas City Kitty" and "Limehouse Blues"; songs from the western-swing craze such as "Tumbling Tumbleweeds" and "San Antonio Rose"; as well as bluegrass pieces popularized on records, old standards, waltzes, and hoedowns for the periodic square dances that typically were included in the evening's dancing. This versatility is a hallmark of the seasoned, successful fiddler who performs widely and enjoys many kinds of music. As Baker's album notes for his 1973 LP said, Hughey was "a people pleaser."

"Stony Point" is a venerable reel from colonial times in the East and a standard among hard-core Appalachian-style fiddlers and some Missouri fiddlers. This was played by swing fiddler Hugh Farr and the Sons of the Pioneers. Farr had derived a tune he called "Indian Scout" from "Stony Point" by adding a third section, in the mood of the Indian-themed songs of the early 1900s and 1930s and 1940s cowboy movie music.[31] Gus Garelick writes about Hugh Farr: "Farr had a habit of taking a traditional tune and twisting it around to suit himself. By the time he recorded

'Indian Scout,' it sounded more like Hugh Farr than the original; furthermore, he never played it the same way twice, so there are several other recordings of the tune, and they're all different! . . . Ron obviously was a big fan of Hugh Farr and the Sons of the Pioneers. His 'Rosetta' is probably taken directly from Hugh Farr."[32]

Hughey's popularity was such that, after his death, a Ron Hughey Memorial Camp Out and Hoedown Fiddler's Contest was organized by District 2 of the California Old-Time Fiddler's Association. This is a Memorial Day weekend event held at the

Yellow Gals

Transcription by Gus Garelick
Digitized by Philip K. Vinyard

Ron Hughey, "Yellow Gals," a tune he identified as a melody from his family in Dade County, Missouri (hear on the companion CD). (Transcribed by Gus Garelick; digitized by Philip K. Vinyard)

rodeo grounds at Laton, south of Fresno. The event includes jam sessions, dancing, and a gospel music service on Sunday morning.[33]

A Fiddler with Wanderlust: Bob Fast

Bob Fast left Missouri to seek work in the Portland shipyards during World War II. But his decision to move reflected a lifelong search for adventure as much as the expectation of employment as an ironworker on the West Coast.

Robert Fast (1918–2002) was born on the farm in northeastern Missouri's Knox County. The nearest towns were the farm and railroad town of La Plata, a few miles west in Macon County, and the large railroad and farm town, with a state college, of Kirksville, a regional business hub. Knox County in the nineteenth century was known for fast-growing railroad towns such as Edina, where the Irish emigrant fiddle tune collector Francis O'Neill taught mathematics in the late 1860s.[34] The family is an old and large one in North Missouri. Their ancestors came to the American colonies from Europe in 1751 and changed the spelling of their name from "Faust" to "Fast."[35]

Late in life in Oregon, Fast would enjoy telling people at music parties, "I'm from way up in the prairie, northeast corner [of Missouri]. Thirty-five miles from Iowa and seventy-five miles from Illinois. All we raised around there was corn, hogs, and disturbances. [Fiddlers he remembers were] screechers and scratchers, but they was *good*."[36]

Bob Fast's father, Chrisley, was a fiddler known for playing at dances and music parties and for his occasional wins at contests. Chrisley and Laura Fast had nine children, all of them interested in making music. The Fast children became Chrisley's sometimes reluctant accompanists. The girls learned piano, an important instrument for backing up fiddle music as well as the customary instrument of well-brought-up females in musically literate families. His older brother Riley played tenor banjo, saxophone, and a bit of fiddle. In the teens and 1920s, the four-string banjo (tenor and plectrum) became a popular rhythm instrument in dance bands playing popular music of the era, and the four-string banjo sifted into the range of backup instrumentation for old-time fiddling.

After moving to the Kirksville area, Bob Fast grew up there playing tenor banjo and fiddle music for dances and jam sessions. The older children had claimed most of the available instruments, so Bob's mother ordered a twenty-five-cent harmonica for him from a mail-order catalog. The harmonica proved playable and enjoyable but eventually unsatisfying; Bob Fast wanted to be a classical violinist.

At about eight, and immersed in the community's fiddle and dance music, Bob Fast was drawn into the hobby of playing "rhythm" accompaniment for his father. Chrisley taught him to strum "three-chord" tenor banjo, the instrument his older brother Riley played. But, almost predictably, Bob found that sitting for hours chording the four-stringer was boring and tiring. According to Minnie Bennett in the Oregon Old-Time Fiddlers Association newsletter (and family members in Missouri), "Bob seconded for his father on the banjo, when he was very small. Sometimes he'd get so sleepy he'd start to nod; his dad would reach over and, with fiddle bow, crack him over the head to wake him up."[37] Rather than strum the tenor banjo with a flat pick, Bob taught himself to strum with the backs of his fingernails, his right hand

Chrisley Fast (fiddler, *left-center*) and friends at the farm on the occasion of Chrisley and Laura Fast's golden wedding anniversary, 1944. *Left to right*: John Fast, George Matthews, Guy Fast (banjo), Chrisley Fast, Perry Vandiver (*standing*), Loren West (banjo), and unnamed fiddler. In front of the stage are young Judith Smith Scheurer and an older cousin. Chrisley Fast insisted that he perform on some sort of stage (here, wooden planks arranged on sawhorses) in order to be heard. (Courtesy Dulcie Simler Fast and Judith Smith Scheurer)

cupped, making down strokes—the basic right-hand shape for the frailing and clawhammer styles of five-string banjo playing. Fast crafted a finger pick that he could tape to the first finger of his strumming hand (the right hand), to make it possible to strum long and loud without making his fingers sore.

In early jazz bands, before amplification systems, the tenor banjo had evolved as a rhythm instrument; it was built for volume, and a good player could lay down a solid, punchy accompaniment and be audible through the din in a noisy nightclub or dance hall. The tenor, and its longer-necked sibling the plectrum banjo, became part of the traditional musician's ensembles, too, adding rhythm and volume in unamplified venues such as the prolific house dances and music parties that were many fiddlers' principal venues. Many old-time fiddlers considered four-string banjo to be fine backup. At a typical square dance in someone's house, the fiddler and banjo player would stand in the doorway between the two front rooms (rugs rolled up, furniture shifted out), with a set of dancers in each room. In later years, Fast would admire the tenor and plectrum playing of professional banjoist Eddie Peabody, who made records and appeared on television programs such as *The Ed Sullivan Show*.

In his teenage years, Fast joined the school band in Kirksville, the nearest town with a secondary education system. This was his chance to be a violinist. The youngster "thought he was sick and tired of fiddle music. He liked symphony music. His family teased him and said he liked that 'symphotic' music. His Dad said, 'You'll come back to fiddle music someday.'"[38]

But Bob Fast finally was able to learn violin music and acquired basic technical skills through lessons with school orchestra instructor Homer Clough. Fast came into the band program to play violin as an ear musician with no music-reading abilities and no formal violin training. According to his wife, Dulcie Fast: "He tried taking band. His teacher, Homer Clough, had him play a sketch by himself one day. He couldn't do that, because he had just been playing along and couldn't read the music. That's probably when he had his few music lessons from Mr. Clough. His folks couldn't afford to continue the lessons and that was the end of his band."[39]

Fast lost interest in playing orchestra violin music—as well as finishing high school—and he joined the US Navy in 1937. Within a year, he was discharged for medical reasons, so in 1938 he joined the US Army. Stationed at the Panama Canal, Fast played violin in a dance band, but he lost his position because he was unable to read the band's musical scores. Fast became a cook and baker and was discharged in 1939 for a "nervous condition."[40] Still known as "Robert" back in Missouri, he had begun introducing himself as "Bob" Fast.

Out of the army, he returned to Missouri and began working in a Kirksville sheet-metal shop. Bob married Dulcie Simler (1922–2015), of Youngstown, a farm town west of Kirksville, in Kirksville in September 1941. When World War II

Bob Fast, at home, Oregon, 1970s. (Courtesy Tom West)

commenced for the United States with the Japanese attack on Pearl Harbor in December 1941, the shop owner closed the business and left for California to work in an airplane factory. Fast decided to do the same thing, but he was unable to get work because of his record of dismissals. He decided to enlist in the army a second time, but his previous navy and army records disqualified him, stamping "Reject" on his application; he was now classified "4-F," and further military service was excluded. After this, in 1943, the Fasts moved again, to Portland, where skilled workers were badly needed to support the war effort. He found work building military transports in the Willamette shipyards. He remained there for the duration of the war.

In 1945, after the war ended, Bob and Dulcie moved back to Kirksville and then to Quincy, Illinois, where Bob worked in sheet-metal shops. There, in 1955, Dulcie's chance acquisition of some records pulled Bob Fast back to fiddle music. Dulcie had found some Tommy Jackson records in a Quincy shop and brought them home. Soon Bob was listening to the records, sitting in front of their stereo outfit and trying to play a mandolin along with the music. Now he had access to one of the most influential professional Nashville fiddlers of the 1950s and 1960s. Tommy Jackson's music was appealing on many levels, from his articulate and driving square-dance style to his versatility fiddling swing music and playing backup for country music singers; his playing inspired countless fiddlers in the post–World War II era when fiddling was undergoing nationwide rediscovery. Along with players such as Tommy Magness, Dale Potter, and Howdy Forrester, Jackson was appreciated by classical violinists—another ingredient in Bob Fast's admiration for Tommy Jackson.

The fiddle music that had been resting quietly in the back of Bob Fast's mind sprang back to life; old Chrisley was right after all. And when he came back to old-time fiddling, Bob's playing displayed the studied bowing, intonation, and vibrato that he had learned as a teenager in Mr. Clough's orchestra.

In 1962 the Fasts moved for the last time, back to Portland. When Bob retired from sheet-metal work, he was finally able to concentrate on his fiddle. On a fishing trip with Dulcie, they happened to tune in on a live radio broadcast beamed from the National Oldtime Fiddlers Contest in nearby Weiser, Idaho. Dulcie Fast recalled:

> That done it! He started watching for contests. He would go and listen. Then we went to Weiser one Saturday. Next year we went on Friday. Then finally we went the whole week. We would go to the fiddle jams. He would join, only in the background corner. As he progressed, he made it to the front with the rest and also enjoyed playing in contests. We took part in Oregon's conventions. We also played a part in Oregon's camp out. . . . He really enjoyed our jams at home, playing with Bill Yohey, Rusty Modrell and Bus Boyk, Cactus Finley, Penny Mead, Don and Ruth Loring, and others.[41]

Based on recordings of Fast after moving to Oregon in 1962, he was a single-string player, with clean noting and intonation and selective application of vibrato.

Judicious use of vibrato in fiddle music—welcome in waltzes but typically distrusted in breakdowns—is often considered a sign that a player has had formal violin instruction, but this generalizing and typecasting can be misleading; many fine self-taught fiddlers, such as Ed Tharp, Cleo Persinger, Taylor McBaine, Pete McMahan, and Kelly Jones (all of them in central Missouri), worked hard to develop vibrato completely on their own.

Fast played a broad repertoire, with a lot of old swing and pop tunes among the old dance tunes, rags, and fiddle pieces from his youth in North Missouri. He liked fiddling in the keys of C, B-flat, and F. Facility in "the flat keys" has long been a marker for fiddling especially in central and northern Missouri fiddling and in bluegrass fiddling. Fiddling in B-flat and F (as well as the bluegrass key of B) is rare in the Ozarks and southern Missouri, where for many years I have often noticed older Ozark fiddlers' skeptical and desultory remarks when hearing a fiddler perform with good vibrato; surely, they think, there is a classical fiddler trying to play old-time music. A staple of old-time North American fiddling, "Fisher's Hornpipe" is generally played in the key of D (sometimes G) across the continent, but in central and north Missouri it has for generations been played in the arguably more difficult but rewarding key of F.[42]

Fast pondered his adventures playing fiddle and tenor banjo at those house dances and music parties back in Missouri. He developed his own versions of tunes from his childhood that he carried to the Pacific Northwest. Fast's version of "Vandiver's Jig," recorded on video at birthday parties in Portland in 1991 and 1993, gives us examples of tunes he carried to Oregon. "Vandiver's Jig" is from Knox County, attributed to fiddler and dance caller Perry Vandiver. As recalled by Moberly fiddler Tom West, Perry Vandiver was a brother of his great-grandfather Bert Vandiver, and his grandmother Bonnie Fast was one of Bob Fast's sisters. "Vandiver's Jig" illustrates the use of the vernacular term "jig" to represent standard hoedowns and square-dance tunes in common time, as well as jigs that are composed in 6/8 time, familiar today through the popularity of Irish music; "jig" was a term often applied to many kinds of fiddle tunes in former generations.

Fast put together a number of tunes that have percolated into the fiddle repertoire in the Pacific Northwest. These included dance tunes he composed in memory of people in Missouri, such as "Laura Corbin's Waltz," named for his mother. "Sassafras" is a country rag, and other compositions include "Windjammer" (1973), "Autumn Waltz" (1976), "Love Valley Waltz," and "Dance of the Fireflies."[43]

Fast's repertoire exhibited amazing breadth. At a music party, he would play tunes associated with northern Missouri, such as "Seamus O'Brien," "Old Parnell," and "Coming Down from Denver," and he fiddled a melody to the old ballad "Babes in the Woods" ("A sad tune! We used to sing that and just cry!"). He played old ironclads and evergreens familiar across the Midwest such as "Soldier's Joy," "Mississippi Sawyer," "Turkey in the Straw," "College Hornpipe" (a.k.a. "Sailor's Hornpipe"), "Cowboy Waltz," "Rochester Schottische" (a.k.a. "D and A Schottische"), "Golden Slippers," "Ragtime Annie," "Ricketts' Hornpipe," and "My Love Is but a Lassie" (in Oregon typically called "Chinkapin"). He played minstrel and vaudeville songs such as "Whistling Rufus" and "The Preacher and the Bear," sentimental songs like "My

Wild Irish Rose," and Tin Pan Alley pop numbers like "Oh How We Danced" (from Al Jolson), "Down Mexico Way" (from cowboy crooner Gene Autry), "Moonlight on the Colorado" (from a Hollywood movie), "Lara's Theme" (a.k.a. "Somewhere My Love," from the Hollywood film *Dr. Zhivago*), and "Somewhere over the Rainbow" (from *The Wizard of Oz*). Fast played country singer Hank Williams hits as well, such as "Hey Good Looking." He played tunes popularized on the fiddle contest circuit in the post–World War II years such as "I Don't Love Nobody." He played "Flop-Eared Mule" as a schottische rather than as a square-dance tune, as did most modern fiddlers—echoing its true origin as a nineteenth-century composition by Adam Couse, "Detroit Schottische" (1851)—and numerous tunes associated with the Pacific Northwest and Canada, such as "Rangers Waltz" (composed in the 1950s by a Quintin Ratliff, a saxophone player in a Spokane dance combo).

Young fiddlers today may be surprised and even perhaps confused that bona fide traditional fiddlers played such a remarkable variety of tunes and styles, but this has proved to be the case with the vast majority of fiddlers of Bob Fast's generation whom I have known.

Tom West remembers the last time he saw his uncle Robert Fast play fiddle music, at a reunion near Kirksville, around 1990. "The last time I heard him play the fiddle was at a family reunion a few years ago. He was sitting on a chair outside one of the shelter houses playing the fiddle. The ground was soft and the chair started tipping over. Several people rushed up to him to help. Bob just held out the fiddle to someone and said 'Don't worry about me, *just catch the fiddle!*'"[44]

Jim Herd, from Father to Son

James Burton Herd (1919–2002) grew up in the Eastview rural community of northeastern Taney County, near the Ozark County line.[45] Eastview was along Caney Creek, just south of McClurg (site of a long-running weekly music party). According to Beisswenger and McCann and Kathleen Oyen, Herd's family came from England in the eighteenth century (on his father's side) and Ireland on his mother's and established themselves in frontier northeastern Tennessee. Jim's grandfather was a fiddler in his Federal army unit during the Civil War. In 1904 Jim's parents came to Missouri and bought a farm.

Jim grew up playing for square dances, often tuning his violin in discord, as did his three brothers. After military service in World War II, Jim moved to St. Joe and then in 1951 to the farming community of Sunnyside in central Washington. While he was known as "Burt" in Missouri, he switched to "Jim" in Washington.

Herd spoke about his life and music in an interview in 1987 by Kathleen Oyen for the Washington Traditional Fiddlers Project. His experience followed the typical course of fiddling for house parties and square dances that went late into the night. In his part of Missouri, the vast majority of the dancing was to fast breakdowns, and people vigorously jig-danced to the music, while part of a square-dance set or solo took place to the side. There was only the occasional waltz or two-step at most dances.

Rosebuds of Avondale

As played by Bob Fast

Transcribed by Amber Gaddy

"Rosebuds of Avondale" as played by Bob Fast, 1970, with Russ Phillips, Stan Gleason (guitars), and unknown bass and mandolin players (hear on the companion CD). Published as "Rosebud of Allenvale" by Scottish composer-violinist J. Scott Skinner, ca. 1920. Other folk titles include "Rosebuds of Evermore" "Rosebuds of Avonmore," and "Rosebuds of Nevermore." "Rose of Sharon" was Howdy Forrester's title and is favored among some fiddlers. (Courtesy Judy Scheurer; transcription by Amber Gaddy)

> I was born and raised in the Ozark Mountains in southern Missouri, Taney County. I'm the youngest of a fiddling family, and the fiddling in my family goes back to my great grandfather, maybe farther, I don't know. He was born in 1789, and I still play some of the tunes that have been handed on down from father to son, now to the fourth generation. And the tunes that I play, I learned them from my father and my older brothers, we all played. It was something we was supposed to do, I guess. We never any of us, ever once went to a music school. I don't know anything about notes, I don't know one note from another. I play strictly by ear. I have played since I can remember, I don't really know when I started. It's been part of my life all along.

Herd pondered how to describe his fiddling style, a familiar situation for fiddlers as they travel beyond their home regions. Jim Herd called his style "Tennessee style," in large part because his father, from Sneedville, Tennessee, used that term, and also because many people connect old-time fiddling in the East Tennessee mountains with old-time banjo playing of the sort Herd liked.

> Dad said that back in Tennessee when they'd have a fiddle contest they'd always have a jig dance contest, and we did that in the Ozarks too. And you played a breakdown like I play here now and they jig danced. They called it jig dancing or buck dancing. It was practically the same step that the cloggers do today. And they always give prizes for the best jig dancer.
>
> I play a lot of the old time square dance tunes they played back when my grandfather was a young man. My grandfather Herd was a Union soldier. He carried his fiddle all through the Civil War, and played around campfires. It's been handed on down from one generation to another, and that's why I know that the style I play today was the style that they played back them days, because it was handed down from father to son, down to me. It's a lot of the same tunes, and the same style that they played back then. That's why I know it's particularly old time style fiddling.[46]

In Washington State, Herd soon became a fixture on the Northwest old-time dance, festival, and fiddle contest scene as both a competitor and a judge. He told people that he played the fiddle "in the exact style" as his father back in Missouri.[47] In 1991 Herd won the Senior Division at the National Oldtime Fiddlers Contest

Jim Herd. (Courtesy Vivian Williams)

in Weiser, Idaho. Like many fiddlers of his generation who had lived long enough to see their lifelong fiddle styles eroded by more fashionable fiddle styles, Herd was disdainful of the ultracomplicated contest fiddle style that had spread outward from Texas and Oklahoma in the 1970s. Speaking of his experiences and referring to fiddle contests, he said that, in former times, "they had people like Benny Thomasson as judges who knew about and liked the old-time fiddling. But now [he was speaking in the 1990s] it's all Texas all the way. They'll play a tune like 'Arkansas Traveler' and not one note in it will be in the old 'Arkansas Traveler.'"[48]

In 1999 Phil and Vivian Williams of Voyager Recordings and Publications, who had known Herd for decades, issued a CD of his fiddling recorded in Weiser during the June 1991 contest week, accompanied by Vivian (guitar), Phil (bass), and Laura Smith (claw-hammer banjo). The Voyager recording includes a representation of Herd's repertoire at age eighty, and he was still going strong: "Little Rabbit Where's Your Mama," "Tennessee Grey Eagle," "Tennessee Wagoner" ("There's probably been more square dances danced to them two tunes than any other tunes that you could bring up"),[49] "Smith's Waltz," "Old Hat," "Goldenrod Waltz," "Green Leaf Rag" ("Walking in My Sleep"), "Monkey in the Dog Cart,"[50] "Cumberland Gap" ("Me and my wife and my wife's pap, whipped all the rebels out of Cumberland Gap"),[51] "The Girl I Left behind Me," "Old German Waltz," "Katy Hill," "Chinese Breakdown," "Eighth of January," "Forked Deer" ("I played it ever since I was a little boy, and

Monkey in the Dogcart

hoedown

from Jim Herd
Late of Sunnyside, WA

Jim Herd, "Monkey in the Dog Cart" (Stuart Williams, *Evergreen Fiddler Tune Book*, 2:10; http://*www.wotfa.org*) (Courtesy Stuart Williams)

dad played it, and my grandfather, and probably my great-grandfather"),[52] "Katydid Waltz," "Durang's Hornpipe," "Gold Rush," "Turkey Creek Breakdown," "Zender Waltz,"[53] "Marmaduke's Hornpipe," "Chinky Pin" (a.k.a. "Chinkapin," "My Love Is but a Lassie," "Ten Nights in a Bar Room," "Lead Out," and others), "Hooker's Hornpipe," "Give the Fiddler a Dram," and "Old Coon Dog" (in the notes to *Old Time Ozark Fiddling*, Jim Herd said, "I played it ever since I was a kid. Dad used to sing it, he'd say 'Once I had an old coon dog, I wish I had him back; he'd run the old ones over the fence and the young ones through the crack'").

Jim Herd also appears on the third volume of the 2000 Rounder documentary *Traditional Fiddle Music of the Ozarks*, with his "Knock around the Kitchen" (an Ozarks version of "Richmond Cotillion" or "Richmond Polka"), "Twinkle Little Star," "Betty Lou Waltz," "Seabolt Quickstep," "Sally Johnson," "Hold on Bald While I Dance with Josie," "Durang's Hornpipe," and "Tennessee Gray Eagle" (a version of "Tennessee Wagner"). The session was recorded in 1997 by Mark Wilson and Kerry Blech at Herd's home in Sunnyside with Stan Jackson, a fellow Ozarks emigrant, providing guitar accompaniment. All but "Durang's" and "Twinkle Little Star" are transcribed in Beisswenger and McCann.

In the westward transmission of cultural heritage to pioneer Missouri—fiddle music included—from places like Virginia and North Carolina as well as from Europe (especially the British Isles and German-speaking Europe), a grand and complex musical tradition took deep root in the midwestern landscape. But the settlement story of a nation moves in waves through time, unending. It adds an intriguing perspective to our understanding of the fundamental history of cultural expression like fiddle and dance music if we bear in mind that traditions keep moving, as people move. Some old tunes carried in a fiddler's imagination and memory may remain much the same in California or Oregon—or indeed any other place in the world—while other tunes will change. People and their fiddle tunes do not hold still.

"Fiddling their way to Fame," Paris, Missouri, 1923, *St. Louis Globe-Democrat*, May 24, 1923. (Courtesy Donna Taylor Hook)

5 Contests

> **Who of you ever attended an old fiddlers' contest and listened to some of the old timers "hit 'er up" on the tunes your forefathers delighted in? What one of you is there who does not know the joy that comes in watching and listening to an aggregation of men of the old school of musicians as they struggle with "fiddle and bow" to prove to an audience their prowess and skill?**
>
> —*Moberly Monitor-Index and Evening Democrat*, December 27, 1921

Old-time fiddlers contests are a recurrent theme throughout this book and my previous book *Play Me Something Quick and Devilish*. These competitions have seen many changes, yet in many ways their embrace of competing goals (light entertainment or deadly serious competition) remains remarkably the same.[1] A fiddlers contest is a folk entertainment for an audience (which may not include knowledgeable listeners) to witness a brace of fiddlers and accompanists under pressure in front of microphones, working in or around arbitrary rules, trying to please a panel of presumably objective and qualified judges who must somehow divine who among these competitive individuals, often of quite equal skills, has performed his or her music the "best" in a particular time and place in order to "win" something of value or interest to take home for their emotional labors.

The typical farmer and small-town dweller enjoy nothing quite so much as a gathering, whether something taken for granted like Sunday church or a family reunion, or something special like a village fish fry, farm-equipment auction, county fair, or Fourth of July parade. Their city cousins have a fatter catalog of entertainments and pastimes, but many people there, too, perhaps in memory or nostalgia or on a day trip, enjoy "country" events. Contests, and the newer phenomenon of bluegrass festivals, became part of the summertime scene, and few events pull together more Norman Rockwell images of former times.

This chapter discusses contests in the exciting era of the 1920s, as contests of all kinds became a great pastime and passion for many people in the United States. Encouraged by the growth of local radio stations and a general national ebullience about being "American," fiddlers contests small and large sprouted across Missouri. They soon became a complex arena for performance, entertainment, and the testing of one's skills under stress against one's peers' skills under stress. This was a golden age for newspaper reporting, too, and generous use is made in this chapter of lively articles about contests. While it lasted—the 1929 stock market crash and subsequent Great Depression would cool off the excitements of the Roaring Twenties—it was a memorable time.

Seriously Seeking Competition

Uncle Aaron never missed a chance, even in old age, to play in a contest.
—Jack Oliver, April 18, 2013

Many fiddlers, having labored in the woodshed or parlor to reach competence, sooner or later find pleasure in sharing music with others. That is, they sometimes decide to become performers. Playing in front of an audience, perhaps at a neighborhood pie supper or talent show in the school auditorium or matching skills in a fiddling contest, helps ratify, demonstrate, and test a person's absorption of the music and command of the tradition.

Signing up for a contest shifts a player from one who plays in the house party or bluegrass festival campground (which can be competitive in various ways) to one who looks for direct, open competition. Playing in contests provides a process for a fiddler being vetted by his or her peers. Regardless of prizes or trophies, participation brings a certain kind of recognition and acceptance, and often mere participation brings a measure of respect from other fiddlers.

For some fiddlers, the process of competing is a passion, a Darwinian drive for supremacy and dominance. For many others, a fiddlers contest is a chance to bring home some much-needed grocery money. Some love trophies. Some focus on the chance to be around like-minded musicians and have no emotional investment in "winning" or "losing." The contest fiddler, while in many ways abandoning local old-time traditional playing aesthetics and repertoire and style, decides what and how to play the music, even though there are pressures to select tunes from the currently fashionable menu and perform in a currently fashionable contest style. Still others relish the opportunity to play the music they like—just as they like to play it—a sharp contrast to the compromise all players make when playing for a dance, on radio, or being a role player in a band or show; for these fiddlers, it is less about the money or trophies and more about emotion and personal satisfaction.

The first documented fiddlers contest in America was held in Hanover County, Virginia, on November 30, 1736. As noted in a frequently referenced article in the *Virginia Gazette*, published in Williamsburg:

> We hear, from Hanover County, that on Tuesday next, (being St. Andrew's Day,) some merry dispos'd Gentlemen of said County, design to celebrate that Festival, by setting up divers Prizes to be contended for in the following Manner (to wit), A neat Hunting-Saddle, with a fine Broad cloth Housing, fring'd and flower'd, etc., to be run for (the Quarter) by any number of Horses and Mares: A fine Cremona Fiddle to be plaid for, by any Number of Country Fiddlers (Mr. Langford's Scholars excepted), With divers other considerable Prizes, for Dancing, Singing, Foot-ball-play, jumping, Wrestling, etc, particularly a fine Pair of Silk Stockings to be given to the handsomest Maid upon the Green, to be judg'd of by the Company, At Page's

> Warehouse, commonly call'd Crutchfield in said County of Hanover, where all persons will find good Entertainment.[2]

That 1736 contest near Richmond was part of the region's annual celebration of St. Andrew's Day. St. Andrew is the patron saint of Scotland, from whence came many fiddlers and many fiddle tunes in colonial times. Contests today typically are part of a county fair, church picnic, fish fry, or fall harvest festival. The top prize in 1736 was a "Cremona Fiddle," in the era when fine violins were scarce and costly and Italian violins ("Cremonas") were sometimes awarded to contest champions; the tradition continues at some contests almost three centuries later. The contestants were treated to "liquor sufficient to clear their wind-pipes," but this custom has not been continued in modern times.[3] Patrick Henry and Thomas Jefferson (themselves fiddlers and owners of Italian violins) are said to have supported these events.

This contest in colonial Virginia barred trained violinists ("Mr. Langford's scholars"), a feature that would be welcome by many old-time fiddlers ("Country Fiddlers") today. Even in early times, people noticed that classically trained musicians playing practiced and memorized written music were apt to cart off most of the prizes. But little has changed in terms of the core of a fiddlers contest, an occasion to bring together musicians who play a few tunes at an event where some are recognized over the rest for the apparent quality of their musical performances and stage presence.

Competitions were everywhere in pioneer times, from rifle matches and footraces and horse races to informal competitions to bring in the best wolf or best honey on a bee hunt. An anecdote from the 1830s in Franklin County suggests how fiddling for a dance could seem to be a contest:

> At dances in Washington in the 1830s before many Germans had arrived, the music was usually provided by a single fiddler. Gert Goebel, one of the first Germans to settle in the town, described a dance where two fiddlers played. The two tried to play the same tune, but one played more slowly than the other. The American crowd was not bothered by the problem, but actually enjoyed the attempt of the faster fiddler to get further and further ahead of his partner. The crowd applauded him when he finished the tune well ahead of the other.[4]

One of the busiest decades for fiddlers contests was the 1920s. Contests and talent shows of all kinds became popular, inspired the Jazz Age dance craze, and, for some, by the alluring illicit behaviors of Prohibition, brought a delight in odd carnival-like happenings such as gold fish swallowing, dance marathons, and flagpole sitting. For a time in this contest-crazy era, competitions were held for the best square-dance callers and square-dance pairs. Traditions and styles of calling square dances were just as variegated and individualized as styles of fiddling; some callers clung to the ironwood of familiar turns and calls, but others adopted new and different calls and styles, setting up another example of the eternal tug between old traditions and new styles.

One such callers' and dancers' contest in the winter of 1923 in Monroe County featured fiddler Wood Brown, a local farmer and major force in contest fiddling. The event gave prizes for the best caller and the best square-dance pairs. The newspaper account illustrates what square dancing was like in this era, even while its language copies familiar romantic imagery and rural stereotypes.

> **JONES IS CHAMPION.**
>
> **WHILE FOUR COUPLES STEP TO LIVELY TUNES**
>
> **JONES WINS FIRST PRIZE AS DANCE CALLER**
>
> At the Opera House in Paris . . . Alva Jones won championship honors as a Monroe County dance caller while four couples stepped to old-fashioned tunes from an orchestra led by Wood Brown, the champion county and inter-county fiddler of North Missouri, for prizes offered to the most graceful dancers. First prize for style and grace went to Raymond McGee and Miss Vera Stephens, second prize to Joe Shearer and Miss Nell Williams. Other couples in the contest, all dancers of unusual merit, were Clarence Thompson and Miss Bertha Lou Williams and Ward Norfleet and Miss Georgia Norfleet.
>
> Ward Norfleet won second honors as a caller.
>
> The dancers gave exhibitions of grace and skill such as few people in the audience had ever witnessed. As the callers shouted forth their honor-your-partner, first couple the right will circle to the left, and other commands without number, sometimes shouting, sometimes singing, all the time clapping their hands and stamping their feet in time to the tunes. The four couples went through all the familiar mazes of the old-time square dance, to which they added a number of figures that the town people had never seen. The audience, all the while, was bobbing its heads, waving its hands, tapping its feet to the tantalizing music, the older members moving on memory's wings back to the days when they, too, stirred the sawdust at country picnics or swung their rosy cheeked partners on the puncheon floors in neighborhood homes.
>
> A contest between the prize couples last year and the winning couples this year for the county championship honors, with a similar contest between the champion callers, is being discussed. It would be an event of such novel and unusual merit that people would be attracted from far and near.[5]

Fiddling Contests in the Golden Age of Small-Town Newspapers

A town or city may become a fiddle contest epicenter by plan or happenstance. Paris was, for a few years, Missouri's fiddling-contest magnet, partly because the county and region sported a number of well-known fiddlers and also because of the town's famous newspaper. This was the home of the *Monroe County Appeal* ("We cover the news like the dew does Little Dixie"), founded in 1867. Today it is hard to appreciate the enormous influence and the role that newspapers had in daily life, especially those with sharp writing and energetic editors who enjoyed politics and the well-polished image of the old-time small-town newspaperman. Newspapering was particularly important in Missouri and competition between papers fierce; the nation's first school of journalism was founded at the University of Missouri in Columbia in 1908.

Reporters often competed to see who could print the most vivid accounts of fiddlers contests, and hyperbole and pseudonativism were much in evidence. Radio, their upstart media competition, was just beginning to take shape and would not seriously undermine newspaper readership for another decade. The stories feel very contemporary (although the language may not) for the issues around fiddlers contests that they reveal, a century later reflecting some of the same discussions about the nuances of competition, what tunes should be played, and how judging should be accomplished. In those days, the major St. Louis papers were read across Missouri, but particularly in the eastern and central portions of the state. Contending with the St. Louis papers were those in Kansas City on the western border, which covered the state well into the St. Louis papers' territory in central Missouri.[6] Local papers picked up story ideas from St. Louis papers, and vice versa; often the same story ran in several papers within days or weeks of each other.

Articles could stir interest in upcoming contests by highly inflated reports of supposedly bitter and fierce competition between top competitors (P. T. Barnum would have been proud). Among those often presented in stores as arch foes were Henry Taylor and Wood Brown, longtime friends, but Brown was from Monroe County and Taylor from Randolph County next door, so this invented rivalry did attract readers and contest audiences. The Paris paper also created a rivalry between Wood Brown and fiddler Uncle John Lewellen, a local character in nearby Florida famous for carving children's toys while telling stories about Samuel Clemens (Mark Twain).

Here is an example of the reporters' enthusiasm, at Paris in December 1921, six months before the town hosted the first state old-time fiddlers contest:

OLD TIME FIDDLERS "HIT 'ER UP" ON FOREFATHERS TUNES

HUNDREDS OF FEET THUMP FLOOR AT PARIS OPERA HOUSE

"CHAW" OF TOBACCO TAKES PLACE OF BATON

CONTESTANTS' JAWS KEEP TIME—WINNER LEARNED TO PLAY GOURD—ANOTHER WAS PUPIL OF OLE BULL

Special to *Monitor-Index*

The largest audience ever seen in a Paris, Mo., theatre sat spellbound Thursday evening through an hour's fiddling by just such old time musicians—men who have spent many a painstaking year in laborious picking out by ear here a chord there a little tune on their instruments in order that the pleasure loving portion of their neighborhood population might enjoy relaxation and merriment incident to an old fashioned "hoe down" or a community country square dance.

Was a Real Contest

No such contest as that held Thursday evening at the Opera House in Paris had ever been held in Monroe County.

. . . Never was there such a representative crowd from various county neighborhoods assembled in one place in the county.

Wood Brown, a farmer living southwest of Paris, fiddled through the contest to a place as winner of the gold medal given by the theatre management as first prize. Lute Riley, also a farmer, of south of Madison, came in for second and John Lewellen (Lewellyn) of Florida, sometimes called "Uncle John," took third. Second prize was a gold medal and third prize a silver one. Never was there such an aggregation of fiddling artists at one place in Monroe county, all but one of the five entered being veterans of many years standing and with reputations for fiddling that would be heard to beat anywhere in Missouri.

The setting arranged, an inside scene of a log cabin with a fireplace drying skins, a musket and other articles with which our pioneer ancestors were wont to adorn their dwellings, was an ideal one for the picturesque fiddlers as they sat grouped in a semi-circle around a log fire or came forward one by one to raise their fiddles to their shoulders, and saw out "The Lost Indian" or "The Arkansas Traveler," furiously chewing their tobacco in unison with the sound of their instruments and the tap, tap, tap of their feet beating out the time.

Feet Get Busy

As each one went to the front and took his seat or remained standing to play, applause shook the building, and as the music progressed, a rhythmical tap, tap, tap from hundreds of pairs of feet in the audience, keeping time with that of the fiddler, vibrated through the building from roof to foundation. The audience sat forward on seat edges, straining to catch and interpret every least harmonious sound.

Learned on Gourd Fiddle

Brown, winner of the contest, is 54 years old, a farmer and has been fiddling for 46 years, since he reached the age of 8, learning to play on an instrument made from a gourd, strung with very fine wire. All of his playing, as is that of the others who were entered in the contest, is by ear. The instrument on which Brown played Thursday evening is a Schweitzer made in Switzerland and is more than fifty years old. The first tune he learned to play was "Negro on the Way to Kansas."

Low of statue [stature], well moulded and jovial indeed, Brown gives the impression of an all round good fellow, even though he does stutter just a trifle. He gave a characteristic expression when asked as to his fiddling ability, saying, "W-w-well, isn't much. Lots of others can b-b-beat my time, but I make 'em sit and a-a-and take n-n-notice, eh?"

A Contest Veteran

Brown has been entered in innumerable community and township contests heretofore, having won prizes at Centralia, Sturgeon, Huntsville, Tulip, Middle Grove,

Madison, Florida and Moberly during recent years, coming away with the gold medal given for grand champion at the latter place. The three selections which Brown played Thursday evening were "The Lost Indian," "The Arkansas Traveler," and "Leather Britches."

The selection which brought the house down was "The Lost Indian" played as only Brown can play it, and interspersed here and there with the call of a lost Indian brave. Applause broke forth from all quarters whenever he gave out that call, to the accompaniment of a wildly patting foot and a slight swing of his body.[7] Brown is noted throughout Monroe, Randolph, and Audrain counties for his rendition of this one selection alone.

Riley's Fiddle Oldest

Lute Riley, winner of the gold medal given for second place, is also a farmer, 45 years old and has been fiddling for sixteen years. He learned to play through a singular circumstance. During the period of convalescence after a spell of sickness when he was 29, a neighbor brought to him an old fiddle, telling him to while away his idle hours picking out tunes. . . . Riley owns the oldest fiddle, being over a hundred years old, with a history dating back through his grandfather's time to an old southern negro from whom he bought it and who did not know the make or age of the thing. Riley also has a Stainer.

But for picturesqueness and the clamor of pioneer days, neither the winner of first prize nor that of second are noted, but the winner of third prize is all that could be desired. John Lewellen, better known as "Uncle John," from the village of Florida, the birthplace of Mark Twain, is one of the pioneer residents of this county and one of the most picturesque it has ever known. The oldest fiddler in the contest, three score and ten, with grayed hair and eyesight and hearing slightly impaired. . . . Always a strong partisan of Old John Barleycorn, as he himself says, he is still active and healthy, despite a life of hard work.

Pupil of Ole Bull

Lewellen, born in Hannibal, Mo., has been fiddling for sixty years, learning from an old violin maker, Ole Bull, in Hannibal during his boyhood. The fiddle on which he played Thursday evening is over forty years old and made by Bull.[8] Lewellen, after the death of his wife when he was thirty-two years old, took up residence in a small house mounted on sled runners which he moved from place to place as he wished, following his trade of carpenter and "Jack of All Trades." For the last 4 years he has lived in the historic little village of Florida, just across the street from the house in which Mark Twain was born, eking out a living by fashioning Mark Twain souvenirs from bits of wood salvaged from a lean-to which was torn from the house of Twain's birth recently. . . . Lewellen in his younger days carried away honors from many fiddlers contests in Hannibal and of recent years he has won prizes at many contests in the east part of Monroe County. In Lewellen's own words, he has "lived in a house by the side of the road, and been a friend to man."

The two fiddlers who did not place in the contest were Ralph Gallop, of Paris, and J. E. Allison, also of Paris. Gallop is a young man, 20 years old, a student of Brown's and entered more for the practice and experience than for anything else. Paris people were more than surprised to see that Allison, a prominent Paris business man, could even handle a fiddle. He proved to be very slightly less an artist than the winners of the prizes.

One unusual detail of the contest was a duet, played by Brown and Gallop, only one instrument being used, Brown doing the fingering and Gallop the sawing. According to old fiddlers, it was a very unusual exhibition of skill.

Five men, three of whom were also old fiddlers from all parts of the county, acted as judges of the contest. Experts when it comes to music that is intended for the "hoe-down" or the square dance, all declare that there never was and never can be such a contest in Monroe County again.

Among the selections played by the winners, in addition to those already mentioned, were "Mulberry Gap," "Sally Johnson," "The Grey Eagle," and "Matches from the Wood."[9]

Paris, 1923

Two state fiddlers contests were held in Paris, a town with a reputation for its fiddling contests and fiddlers. The contests were supported by local businesses as well as businesses and newspapers in St. Louis. The competitions were remarkable in several instances. Like the 1921 contest, the May 24, 1923, Missouri state contest received extensive coverage in the *St. Louis Star* and *St. Louis Globe-Democrat* as well as in local newspapers such as the *Monroe County Appeal*. The *Monroe County Appeal* was a prizewinning paper, its publishers and editors well connected in politics and business. The state contests in Paris would have had far less notoriety without the *Appeal*'s promotion.

Articles announced who had won crowns in other counties. The list grew heavy with names of well-known contest fiddlers back home, such as Daniel Boone Jones (D. B. Jones), who won the Callaway County contest; Macon County winner G. E. Cummins; and others. Several fiddlers wrote letters asking to be admitted to the contest, and they were approved—Mrs. Lem (Harriett) Waterman (Eldridge, Laclede County); L. B. Spurgeon (Conway, Laclede County); J. A. Oliver (James Aaron Oliver, Columbia, Boone County); H. K. Fountain (Centralia, Boone County); J. Wesley Murphy (Mexico, Audrain County); William Stalcup, P. E. Snider, and M. D. Richardson (Clarence, Shelby County); J. A. Hinds (Eldon, Miller County); W. R. Blankenship (Bevier, Macon County); Douglas Cook (Macon, Macon County); W. S. Harris (Kirksville, Adair County); Lute Riley (Middle Grove, Monroe County); and three fiddlers from Moberly in Randolph County, Bob Lilly, Clate Ransdell, and Aubrey Bradley.[10]

The same article in the *Monroe County Appeal* on May 11 says that Monroe County champion Wood Brown "continues to invite all ambitious fiddlers to the contest.

Postcard of left-handed fiddler and craftsman John Lewellen (1831–1931) in front of his movable dwelling and carpenter shop in Florida, Missouri. Lewellen carved gavels and other souvenirs from hewn logs salvaged from an addition to Mark Twain's birthplace to sell to visitors.

Sitting, standing, walking or flying across the landscape in a Ford, Wood can play any tune known to the fiddling fraternity without missing a note or mussing up the melody. His fame, coupled with a desire to hear him play, is partly responsible for the attendance that has been assured from a distance." The exaggerated rivalry between Wood Brown and Henry Taylor made good reading, and the newspapers pulled other contestants into the stories, too.

TAYLOR DEFIES WOOD BROWN

WINNER OF MACON CHAMPIONSHIP SAYS HE WILL FIDDLE MONROE COUNTY MAN TO A FRAZZLE

As the date for the state fiddling festival at Paris draws nigh those who have entered spend most of the time practicing on the old tunes and breathing out defiance to one another. Most of them are particularly aggressive toward Wood Brown, evidently because they believe he is the man they must reckon with when the Grand Championship of the great state dangles before their eager vision.

Henry Taylor, Randolph's premier fiddler, professes to fear that Brown will contract an attack of cold feet when autos and trains begin unloading their cargos of contestants at Paris, and says he will fiddle against Wood, even though it be necessary to follow him to the forks of the creek and force him to face the music. Taylor claims to have been born in a primeval forest and to have received his instinct for Nature's favorite music from the flocks of birds which sang about his cabin door.

> Brown scoffs at the idea of any Monroe County fiddler, especially one whose very name makes an ordinary performer frazzle up his chords from fear, as does the name of Brown, being intimidated by a man whose first name is a synonym for flivver. Nor does the fact that Taylor is a descendant of Zachary Taylor, a former president of the United States, mean anything to Wood.
>
> "I'll be right there when the bell rings and Taylor will be moaning worse than the Lost Indian when the Grand Championship of Missouri is pinned on my coat," says Brown.
>
> Defies and counter-defies of these famous knights of the bow are only samples of what is going on at long range between others. The fact that one woman, Mrs. Lem Waterman of Eldridge, Mo., has asked to be listed for the contest, means nothing to the masculine entrants. With a state championship trembling in the balance, gallantry will have to take a back seat and no favors, not even to a Baptist minister's wife like Mrs. Waterman, will be shown.[11]

That May 18, 1923, Paris newspaper article adds detail to what we know of the rules for the state contest. The afternoon preliminaries were open only to fiddlers aged sixty-five and above, but the evening finals were open to fiddlers of any age. It is not clear how fiddlers could have bypassed the preliminaries in a two-stage contest; such an outcome is unheard of today. The age limit fluctuated from contest to contest, with some competitions marking fifty as the cutoff.[12] The *Monroe County Appeal* picked up a story from the Clarence paper on March 23:

> **AFTER WOOD BROWN SCALP**
>
> **STATE-WIDE FIDDLIN' CONTEST TO BE HELD IN PARIS IN MAY**
>
> Clarence, Mo. Winning first prize . . . in the fiddling contest here Monday night, Henry Taylor of Cairo, Randolph County, looms up as a formidable figure in the state contest to be pulled off at Paris, Monroe County, Thursday, May 24. . . .
>
> Taylor has won the championship fiddle honors in Randolph County. He was victor in the big contest at Macon in September and now he has vanquished all comers at Clarence, Shelby County. The only world left for him to conquer is Monroe County, where "Jack" Blanton (editor of the *Monroe County Appeal*) is said to possess the best battery of old-time fiddlers on the continent, headed by Wood Brown.
>
> The "boss fiddler" does not look like an old-timer. He is about 50, dresses as neat as any business man, and lives on the farm where he was born. Fiddling runs in the Taylor family. . . . When Henry Taylor played "The Lost Indian," during the contest at Macon, it set the crowd wild. He gave the call, the long weird cry in the distance, and you could imagine the hand of time sweeping back a hundred years when this country was a limitless garden and the dawn came on a land glorious in its primitive beauty—as it was when the red men inherited it direct from the hand of the Creator.
>
> The activity of the old fiddlers in North Missouri the past year has excited nation-wide interest. The managers of the contest have received inquiries from almost every state in the union regarding the hoe-down dance calls, the names of the pieces and

rules for contests. A recent correspondent from South Wales, N.Y., writes for the rules for a contest, methods of publicity and the best time for holding a fiddle bout so as to get the most interest. He says he is an old time fiddler himself, and he wants to stage in New York state an event to be called "An Old Time Missouri Fiddlers' contest."[13]

On April 13, 1923, the next article to appear in the *Appeal* continues promoting the fame and feistiness of the local hero, Wood Brown, whose two sons, Bill and "Skeeter," were also fiddlers. Such statements no doubt were expected to encourage more and more people in the *Appeal*'s readership to come to the big doings. The quotes have a well-edited feel to them.

WOOD BROWN DEFIES THEM

MONROE COUNTY'S FAMOUS FIDDLER WILLING TO DEFEND AGAINST ANY FOOT-PATTER ON EARTH

"I see that Henry Taylor and other local fiddling champions from other parts of Missouri are coming to Paris, May 24, to gain championship honors at my expense. Well, let them come ahead; the more the merrier. I'm willing to meet any man on earth who pats his foot and moans over the Lost Indian when he plays. I want the *Appeal* to tell them I'm not only willing to meet them but that I defy them. Thus spoke Wood Brown, who has won more fiddling medals than any other man in North Missouri, to an *Appeal* man last Friday."[14]

The *Appeal*, April 27:

NOTED MEN COMING

MAYOR KIEL OF ST. LOUIS AND MAYOR CROMWELL OF KANSAS CITY ACCEPT INVITATIONS TO BE JUDGES

. . . Wood Brown, whose scalp all knights of the fiddle and the bow are eager to get, continues to defy them to get into the game. Evidence that the fame of the coming contest is spreading far and near comes from Eldridge, Laclede County, in the Missouri Ozarks. Mrs. Lem Waterman of Eldridge, . . . From St. Louis comes a letter from the city editor of the *Times*, asking for copies of the rules and regulations of the coming event. The *Times* began a campaign last week for a preliminary contest among the fiddlers of St. Louis County, the winner to be sent to Paris on May 24. . . . Two more champions have entered the ring, J. A. Oliver, champion of Boone County, and D. B. Jones, champion of Callaway County sending in their names this week.[15]

On May 23, 1923, the *Appeal* offered further promotion and added more names and an article accompanied by a photograph of Wood Brown. By now the St. Louis winners were known. Colonel Daugherty either did not make the cut or was unable to make the trip to Paris. The St. Louis contingent was being accompanied by newsreel photographers from Pathé News and International News as well as a *St. Louis Times* reporter. The article also helped spread a rumor that spare A strings would be in very short supply, should a contestant break a string and need a replacement.

READY FOR THE FIDDLINGFEST

As the *Appeal* goes to press Thursday old fiddlers are dribbling in from every direction; the mayors of St. Louis and Kansas City speeding towards Paris, accompanied by aldermen and friends, and delegations are sending word from all near-by points that they are preparing to join the throngs that will be attracted to the State Fiddling Contest, Thursday afternoon and night.

Harry T. Brundidge and Zachary Taylor, representing the *St. Louis Star*; B. J. Cope, staff man for the *St. Louis Times*; F. L. Maguire, camera man for the *International News*, and J. Harry Yeager camera man for the Pathe Weekly Film Co., arrived Wednesday afternoon.

Thursday's *St. Louis Times* contained a sensational story from Paris to the effect that one of the would-be fiddling champions had cornered the A-string supply so that any contestant who came without an A-string or who broke one while performing, would be unable to secure a new one and therefore would cease to be a rival. Rumors to this effect reached many of the fiddlers before they started from home. They brought along an extra supply. . . .

An old-fashioned fried chicken and country ham dinner will be given by local citizens Thursday evening. It will be served by the Ladies Aid Society at the Baptist Church. Mayor Evans will preside. The menu will include fried chicken, Country ham, peas, potatoes, fruit salad, hot rolls, strawberry shortcake, coffee and cigars. Visiting newspaper men, motion picture camera men and others from a distance will be guests. The magnificent trophy offered by the *St. Louis Globe-Democrat* as a championship prize has been on display in the window of Blanton's jewelry store all week. It was an object of profound admiration for everybody and especially for the old fiddlers.[16]

The May 24, 1923, state contest was backed by the *St. Louis Globe-Democrat*, guaranteeing widespread attention. A number of regional contests were held around the state to pick contestants for the Paris event, billed as the Missouri state contest, an extravagant claim but one that helped ratchet up the public's interest. Few readers who were fiddlers would take seriously the "state" claim, since it was impossible to get the top players from the far corners and neighborhoods of Missouri to attend. On June 1, 1923, the *Monroe County Appeal* published a full-page illustrated story on the May 24 proceedings. Employing photos courtesy of the *St. Louis Times*, the headline trumpeted, "Henry Taylor in Tuneful Triumph." Thus ended, temporarily at least, Wood Brown's top billing in his hometown paper, and thus a new layer of gold was added to Henry Taylor's reputation.

Unusual in Missouri fiddlers contests at that time, a young woman did very well competing against the men—Mrs. Lem (Harriett) Waterman, "queen fiddler of the Ozarks," won second place, with Wood Brown winning third.[17] Among contest fiddlers who competed were not only Wood Brown and Uncle John Lewellen, but several players who had become famous through their WOS radio performances and success in WOS fiddlers contests—Louie Barton of Jefferson City, Vee Latty of Fulton, and Thomas Jasper Massie of Nevada.[18] Numerous others competed, many unknown to researchers today, but important in their communities in the 1920s. While he did not win at Paris in the 1923 and 1926 state contests, George Morris of Columbia, a young man at the time, would go on to win many contests and have a long career in which he would be a major influence on many fiddlers of later decades (see below and elsewhere).[19]

HENRY TAYLOR IN TUNEFUL TRIUMPH

THE MAN FROM CAIRO CARRIED OFF STATE FIDDLING CHAMPIONSHIP.

MRS. LEM WATERMAN, SECOND. WOOD BROWN, THIRD.

Henry Taylor, of Cairo, Randolph County, was voted Grand Champion Fiddler of Missouri by the seven men who judged the great contest at Paris last Thursday night. The *St. Louis Globe-Democrat*'s magnificent trophy cup, a massive silver utensil eighteen inches high, embellished with the laurel wreath of victory, was awarded to Taylor, together with $25 in cash.

The contest really was between Henry Taylor, the Randolph champion, and Wood Brown, king bee of Monroe County fiddlers. Each man had scores of partisans in the crowd. Brown's admirers still insist that in another contest, with both men required to play the same sort of tunes, old Wood would land first. Taylor's admirers scoff at this claim. Another contest between them, with old time fiddlers as judges, is being agitated.

Mayor Kiel discussed music from a philosophic standpoint and said fiddling is a mode of expressing the human triumphs and sorrows that would live through the ages. Incidentally he denied that political aspiration had anything to do with his presence in Paris, saying that under no circumstances would he ever consent to the use of his name in connection with any other office than mayor of Missouri's metropolis.

Swept away by the tantalizing melody Capt. J. W. Adams, a 68 year old entrant from St. Louis and Mrs. Lucy Greenup, a widow of 66, joined hands, promenaded and jigged thru all the other measures of the old time hoe-down while motion picture cameras clicked and the crowd led by Mayor Kiel, applauded.

Henry Taylor, the Grand Champion, played "Sallie Gooden" and the American version of "Lost Indian" on the second. Wood Brown's initial selection was "Arkansas Traveler" and his closing selection, "Lost Indian." Both fiddlers interspersed their "Lost Indian" efforts with tuneful moans by way of adding a touch of realism to their art.

The other contestants and their selections were as follows:

Bob Lilly, Moberly—Fourteen Miles Below Leesburg and Dixieland.

A. Bradley, Moberly—Jenny, Are You There? And Snowbird on an Ash Wagon.

Mike McNearny, Kirkwood—Mississippi Sawyer and Turkey in the Straw.

"Champion of Missouri," Henry Taylor of Cairo, Missouri, received a loving cup from Paris mayor Clarence Evans (*St. Louis Globe-Democrat*, June 10, 1923). Three years later, Squire Taylor refused to compete in the April 1926 WOS contest because WOS contests were judged by audience vote rather than a panel of judges. (Courtesy Donna Taylor Hook)

H. K. Fountain, Centralia—Old Bell Cow, and Sadie.
J. W. Murphy, Mexico—Shortnen Bread and Never Get Your Money Back.
J. W. Adams, St. Louis—Aunt Sally Goodin' and Flowers of Edinburg.
Mrs. Lem Waterman, Eldridge—Soldier's Joy and Arkansas Traveler.
W. R. Blankenship, Bevier—Arkansas Traveler and Money Musk.
Douglas Cook, Macon—Irish Washerwoman and Natchez Under the Hills.
Lute Riley, Middle Grove—Arkansas Traveler and Old Sallie Johnson.
George Robinson, St. Louis—Chicken Reel and Cotton Eyed Joe.
John Lewellen, Florida—Gray Eagle and Mark Twain Special.
J. J. Oliver [J. A. Oliver], Columbia—Kansas City Rag and Soldier's Joy.
Ed Groom, St. Louis—Jenny Put the Kettle On, and The Rocky Road to Dublin.
Press Snyder, Clarence—Maggie and Money Musk.
George Sebastian, Clarence—Sally Goodin' and Arkansas Traveler.
John McCoy, Clarence—Arkansas Traveler and Leather Breeches.

Captain J. W. Adams of the 7th district fire department in St. Louis was one of the contestants. For 59 years he has played the fiddle. . . .

George Bachstein of Clarence, where most everyone plays the fiddle, has been a musician for 35 years.

John McKay, another contestant from Clarence, has played a fiddle for 30 years under the handicap of the loss of a finger on his left hand. Mr. McKay has the oldest fiddle in these parts, a Jacob Stainer instrument, its history dating back to 1563, when it was made in Scotland. Inside the instrument is a very interesting account of its long life. Mr. McKay got hold of the fiddle through the ignorance of the former owner as to its age and value. For many years it had lain in the man's barn and being in the way it was offered to its present owner at a bargain, after being remodeled the total investment being on $65. Mr. McKay would think a long time before letting his fiddle go for $1,000.[20]

The article reports that the afternoon preliminaries were won by Taylor, Brown, Waterman, Oliver, Groom, Selby, and Robinson. "They went to the second round with blood in their eyes." Another of the preliminary-round winners, though not fully noted in the article, was Clate "Peggy" Ransdell of Moberly. Ransdell, part Cherokee Indian, made his living as a coal miner. He was well known and won his share of contests—and he also specialized in playing and hollering "Lost Indian." Ransdell had lost a leg when a wall of coal collapsed on him in the mines near Huntsville, and he had carved his own artificial wooden leg—thus the nickname "Peggy."[21] It appears that Ransdell had gotten himself on the wrong side of Wood Brown, he of the high standards for what is and what is not old-time fiddling.

Ransdell, not to be counted out so soon, came back with "Hound Dawg Blues" and whistled an accompaniment. Brown protested to the judges that, "Hound Dawg Blues" and whistlin' by a fiddler wasn't old time music. Ransdell got away with it and whistled an encore while Brown fumed.

Mrs. Waterman's second bet was "Arkansas Traveler," which, she asserted before the beginning (of the final round), "ain't been played right yet." Play? Say, you fairly hear the traveler himself talking as the fiddle moaned, "Roof's leaking, why don't you fix it," says I. "Can't fix it when it's raining and when it's dry I don't need it," says he.

Then came Brown scowling at Ransdell. He played "The Lost Indian" and you could almost see the poor warrior straying through the forests as Brown tickled the cat gut. Then at the most mournful part of it, just to get even with Ransdell, Brown whooped, "Who-o-o-o-o." It was the Injun himself. A small boy shivered and the crowd yelled. But that one whoop was Brown's undoing.

Taylor stalked to the center of the stage, sat down, crossed his legs, patted time with his left foot and played the same tune, and he beat Brown at his own game, for he not only whooped twice, but threw in a holler to boot like this, "Who-o-o-o-o, Who-o-o-pe-yow." The crowd demanded an encore.[22]

> George Robinson, running strong, offered a novelty by playing "Cotton-Eyed Joe" with his fiddle resting on his head and he shouted the words: "Biggest fool I ever saw, came from the State of Arkansas, put his shirt on over his coat, buckled his breeches around his throat."

At this point, the second round finished up, and the six fiddlers were named as finalists. The judges asked each to play one tune in the third round. As in the other rounds, everyone seems to have played a fast breakdown or a round dance tune such as a fox-trot. One or two of the finalists decided to play novelty numbers and to include some singing while they fiddled. All the contestants fiddled solo, without any accompaniment.

> Then as was predicted, the judges announced that the winners would be picked from Taylor, Brown, Mrs. Waterman, Oliver, Selby and Groom. Right there the big battle started, for it was announced that each would have to play another tune. Mrs. Waterman, called upon first, picked "The Lower Edge O' Town," and announcer Major asserted that "This here woman will do her own marchin'." How she made that fiddle talk! How the feet patted! You could see a cabin in the Ozarks, a log fire and a crowd in blue jeans and calico patting to the time as she played. It made one hungry for hog meat and corn pone. "Lay on it" they shouted. "Bear down," "Pin the medal on her." Brown picked "Leather Britches" for his last appearance. The crowd patted and moaned. "Leather breeches, leather breeches, Mammy cut 'em out and daddy sewed the stitches."
>
> Taylor followed with "Sally and Her Crippled Chickens," chanting as he played: "Had a piece of pie, had a piece of puddin, gave it all away to little Sallie Goodin."[23] The crowd cheered, the winners were announced, flashlights boomed and the 3,000 fiddle fans patted their way back through the mud to Paris.[24]

It pays to advertise. The contest was a smashing success. After the dust settled, the *Monroe County Appeal* ran a short article on June 8 to acknowledge the fact that newspaper publicity was in "large measure responsible for the success of the Old Fiddlers Contest." The story notes that their series of well-timed and vivid articles in anticipation of the event had gotten very wide attention in city newspapers and had indeed helped advertise the merchants and city of Paris. "In due time the entire state was talking about the Fiddling Festival. In spite of rainy weather the event was the biggest kind of a success."[25] On June 10, 1923, the *St. Louis Globe-Democrat* ran a spread of evocative photographs taken that rainy day in May, "Fiddling Their Way to Fame."[26]

Paris, 1926: The Rematch

In May 1926, the citizens of Paris welcomed their second state old-time fiddlers contest. First came the April preliminaries, a county-wide competition to pick the

Fiddlers limber up on the courthouse lawn while the crowd gathers expectantly, a familiar kind of scene to fiddle contest attendees. Henry Taylor is at far right. (*St. Louis Globe-Democrat*, June 10, 1923); courtesy Donna Taylor Hook

fiddler for the state contest a month later. As they had done so well in 1923, the *Monroe County Appeal* crafted a campaign of articles to keep people interested. Of particular interest was rekindling the rivalry, manufactured by the newspaper, between Wood Brown and Henry Taylor. It was taken for granted that Brown would win the Monroe County championship and that Taylor would win in neighboring Randolph County and that they would butt heads at the state contest in May. The *Monroe County Appeal*, April 9, 1926:

WOOD ALL TUNED AND READY

> Wood Brown, Monroe County's champion fiddler, was in Paris, Wednesday, getting his instrument put in perfect condition for the coming contest. Wood was delighted that all hands would be required to play "Arkansas Traveler."
>
> "I am willing to fiddle against any man in the world on this old tune," he said to an *Appeal* man. "Just bring on Henry Taylor, Henry Ford, or Henry anybody else, and give us judges who know real fiddle music and you'll find me right there with the goods to defend my title."
>
> On account of impassable roads the county contest at Paris has been deferred to April20, at which time a number of ambitious knights of the rosined bow will undertake to deprive Wood of his laurels.[27]

The *Monroe County Appeal* on April 16, 1926, announced enthusiasm among fiddlers for the coming fracas for county championship, precursor to the state contest in May. Reigning champ Wood Brown was ready, having come to town to have his violin worked on to improve its sweetness and volume, but the paper said that "the other fiddlers say there never was a man so good but what someone else could be a little better." The paper was careful to say that no entry fee would be collected from fiddlers and that "judges will all be old fiddlers or square dancers." Once again the newspaper beat the drum of competition between Brown and Uncle John Lewellen. "I see Wood Brown says he ain't afeard of no fiddler," Uncle John Lewellen of Florida, one of the few left-handed fiddlers in existence, remarked Monday. "Well," he added, "you can just tell Wood that I ain't afeard of him either and that I'll be right there on next Tuesday for the county contest and I aim to carry away the honors."[28]

On April 23 the *Appeal* announced that Brown had come in first in the Monroe County contest, followed by Jim Clark and Frank Tanzy. Uncle John Lewellen tied with Tanzy but lost in a playoff round. "Judges of the contest were S. D. Crews, Centralia; Newt Turner, Clyde Masterson, Lake Trail; Rube White. Mr. Turner is blind. All of the judges are musicians." The article stated that the state contest winner would be given a recording contract in St. Louis and cash and that the *St. Louis Globe-Democrat* would offer prize money and "silver trophy cups" to the top three winners. The article also stirred the pot by claiming there was "a feud between [WOS] radio champions of Jefferson City" Henry Taylor and Tom Massie; the hype in the paper failed, however, to convince WOS radio managers to bring equipment to Paris to broadcast the contest.[29]

An article in the *Appeal* reported that Henry Ford had been invited to attend the Paris playoffs, but Ford did not appear.[30] This May 1926 state contest gathered special excitement because it followed the major contests aired over WOS radio in Jefferson City the previous New Year's Eve and previous April. Some people thought that the WOS radio contests were "state contests," but they did not have such official-sounding titles. Indeed, there was no mechanism for constituting anyone's contest as "the state contest." Paris merely saw the opportunity and took it.

The Paris paper predicted an audience of eight to ten thousand people for the 1926 state fiddlers contest, many times the population of the county itself. "No such aggregation of county fiddling champions has ever before been brought together in Missouri."[31] On April 30, two days before the May 2, 1926, state contest, the *Appeal* placed its culminating promotional article, announcing that "city champions" as well as "county champions" and "four state champions" would be in the competition. Some three hundred fiddlers competed in preliminary rounds across Missouri to derive the fiddlers competing at Paris on May 1. A special stage was built in front of the county fairgrounds grandstand, with "a huge amplifier" being set up—the same grandstand where the Mark Twain Old Threshers Association would hold fiddlers contests fifty years later.[32]

An impressive delegation of St. Louis business leaders, celebrities, and former mayor Henry Kiel came to Paris for the 1926 contest and were entertained by local politicians and community leaders. Mayor Kiel and Colonel F. M. Collins (president of Graham Paper Company) served as two of the four judges; the other two judges were John Prada of Paris and J. A. Oliver, the well-known fiddler from Columbia.

The *Monroe County Appeal* published many interesting articles about the affair. A blind fiddler from Harrison County in northwestern Missouri, S. F. Dutro, had become disoriented after the afternoon preliminary rounds and had left town, erroneously thinking he had been eliminated. The oldest fiddler in the contest year was T. H. Moss, at age eighty-five the St. Louis champion; he was called onstage to play in the prelims as soon as he reached the fairgrounds; exhausted from the travel, he was eliminated.[33] The majority of the contestants, in this early time of rough, unimproved roads and difficult travel—unless one lived near a railroad town with good connections—were from central and northern Missouri.[34] For many people, the trip would have been long and difficult.

Henry Taylor repeated his 1923 Paris victory by again being declared Missouri state champion in 1926, besting a field of thirty-one competitors.[35] He won two silver loving cups and one hundred dollars cash (including ten dollars donated by the *St. Louis Post-Dispatch*), impressive booty in 1926. Some confusion appears in the reporting of the winners' names: "George Morris, of Joplin, Jasper County," is named as coming in second, winning fifty dollars; however, this was the Columbia (Boone County) George Morris, a dominant fiddler of his generation who was a fiercely competitive young contest player and popular radio fiddler who specialized in difficult hornpipes in the flat keys.[36] The state champ was Henry Taylor. Fiddlers from nine states took part.

Thomas Jasper Massie's father was born in Virginia, his mother in Kentucky, and Tom was born in 1856 in Kentucky. After the Civil War, Tom Massie moved to Vernon County, Missouri, and worked as a day laborer. He died at age eight-four in 1940 after injuries sustained in a fall and ill with pneumonia. Massie was a champion who had won contests including the April 1926 Interstate Old Fiddlers Contest broadcast over WOS radio. Massie had placed in the 1923 Paris contest but did not make the top three finalists in 1926. He insisted that he was the reigning 1926 state champion because of his win at the WOS radio contest the previous April, to no avail.[37]

Henry Taylor had refused to compete in the fiddlers contests sponsored by WOS radio because the judging was accomplished not by a panel of appropriate judges but by popular vote of the audience. Radio audience members voted for favorites by paying for postcards, telegrams, or phone calls; fiddlers with numerous friends and relatives, or friends and relatives with monetary resources, did have an unfair advantage in such a judging system. Henry Taylor was right to question the judging technique, and the 1926 debate typifies continuing problems and debates today over how to best judge a fiddlers contest.

The afternoon preliminaries had different judges from the evening final round. The preliminaries had a panel of three judges who were well known and accepted old-time fiddlers, and this round saw the elimination of twenty-eight fiddlers. This is a telling detail. Later, the evening finals featured a playoff by the top three—Henry Taylor, George Morris, and Wood Brown. By the time of the evening finals, it would have been clear to the audience as well as other fiddlers that the judges had done their work, bringing forward three respected fiddlers. This fact seems to have allowed the evening judging to change into a more festive, but certainly more political and unprofessional, procedure: the judges for the finals were a mayor, a business executive, a local citizen, and J. A. (Aaron) Oliver, a Columbia champion and the only well-qualified judge on the panel. Oliver had played in the preliminaries, and, not being selected for the finals, in my opinion Oliver may well have been asked to help judge the evening final round perhaps to placate complaints about the other three judges' lack of qualifications to judge fiddle music.

The finals were so closely battled that the three top players, Henry Taylor, George Morris, and Wood Brown, were asked by the judges to try another round to settle the matter. The results were undoubtedly thought correct by many people but questioned by many others. But at least those three fiddlers, Morris, Brown, and Taylor, were recognized master players of traditional fiddle music. Second place was awarded to George Morris; third place went to Wood Brown.

As added prizes, the top two in the 1926 Paris state contest, Henry Taylor and George Morris, seem to have been invited to travel to St. Louis to make 78 rpm records for the Okeh label. The previous year in 1925, following the big New Year's Eve fiddle contest on WOS radio, Fiddlin' Sam Long of Oklahoma and George Morris had been offered recording contracts with the Gennett label in Indiana. Sam Long followed through; Morris did not.[38] Morris eventually may have made recordings, but Henry Taylor did not. This was a missed opportunity not only for Taylor and Morris but for the world of people purchasing 78 rpm records. Today, due to the vast numbers of 78 releases of fiddlers from other places, especially the southeastern United States, many have the notion that the top fiddlers of the 1920s were to be found only Down South. Not so. It was the fact, merely, that the New York City companies happened to head south.

An interesting sidelight into the contest scene is the "local favorite." Sometimes a local favorite and champion takes it all, or may place in the top group, or may find him- or herself entirely left out of the winning lineup. No doubt urged on by disappointed and loyal friends and neighbors in the Paris vicinity, within weeks of the May 1926 contest, Wood Brown sought a rematch with Henry Taylor. Another contestant, Frank Woods of Nevada, heard about the challenge and got into the act with a challenge of his own. The *Monroe County Appeal* in Paris reported that:

WOOD BROWN WANTS TO MEET H'Y TAYLOR

Wood Brown, champion fiddler of Monroe County and winner of third honors in the recent state contest, announced Saturday that he was considering a challenge to Henry Taylor, winner of first place, to a contest in which each man would put

> up a substantial sum of money, the entire purse to go to the one getting a majority of the judges' votes. Wood's idea was to pick one judge, and Taylor another, these two to pick the third man, then let the prize go to the one who got as many as two of the three votes.
>
> The day Brown made this suggestion Frank L. Woods not only made the same proposition at Nevada but actually posted $100 with the *Herald* as an evidence of good faith. His challenge was as follows: "I challenge the champion state fiddlers to a contest to be held July 4th. I propose that Henry Taylor, the winner of the contest at Paris May 1, Tom Massie, radio champion, and myself each put up $100 (mine is up) as a prize to the winner, the judges to be selected as follows: One by some St. Louis music house, one by some Kansas City music house, one by Henry Ford.[39]
>
> "Each contestant to play ten old-time square dance selections, one solo and one sacred piece, all by ear and neither contestant to be permitted a second." If Henry Taylor is willing to comply with these terms, or with others that may be agreed upon, or fiddle for a purse raised from other sources, the most unique event of them all may grow out of challenges Brown and Woods are making.[40]

Nothing is known or recorded about the answer, or lack of an answer, to the rematch challenges.

Why was Paris the location for the state fiddlers contests in 1923 and 1926? Perhaps the location was due to the high profile of Paris on account of the stature of its paper, the *Monroe County Appeal* (an influential paper with a strong Democratic Party bent), as well as this part of the Little Dixie region's importance in politics. Perhaps it was due to the enthusiasm and support of local sponsors (always a key ingredient in such an event). Paris was a robust, growing agricultural center in the mid-1920s. Also, Paris is just close enough to St. Louis to entice the curiosity of city folk interested in a day in the country, as well as the helpful attention given Paris by news media.

The state champion at Paris in 1923 and 1926 was a leading citizen of Little Dixie, Henry Taylor. Called "Squire," Taylor was part of a well-respected pioneer family with roots deep in the nation's history. His family farm was a landmark near Felps [*sic*] Chapel, a country Presbyterian church in the Levick's Mill farm community east of Jacksonville (the postal address was Cairo). Taylor was a popular citizen and for forty-two years justice of the peace of Salt River Township.

> I do know a bit about Henry and how he came to play the fiddle as I was told this by older family members I interviewed and this story was repeated more than once so I do believe it was so. The fiddle was his older brother Marion's and it was in a cabinet in the parlor. He would sneak it out to play when Marion was gone and he was a natural. Music was in his blood as Henry had an older half brother named Ferdinand (Uncle Ferd) and he played the fiddle as well. I don't believe any of them were as talented as Henry was.
>
> Most all of the (12) children with the exception of one or 2 were musically talented and at least 3 were very gifted. Uncle Ash, Uncle Frank, and Uncle Ep were the especially gifted ones. I found a pic of Uncle Frank with his fiddle. As Ep and Frank

> both fiddled I believe they already had fiddles. Ash played many instruments and actually made a couple that a family member has.
>
> They played at local dances quite often but great grandpa Henry never really approved of this and advised them against it as many of them there were moonshiners and drinking going on and he did not approve of this.[41]

My family members were dance musicians and not contest players, but in Randolph County Henry Taylor and his sons were the best-known fiddlers in Salt River Township. Taylor's renown was in part due to his prominence in newspaper stories about fiddlers contests. The Taylor family farm was in the same general district as my parents' farm, a few miles east of Moberly.[42] Taylor's father, James B. Taylor, came from Fayette County, Kentucky, to Randolph County in the same time period (1836) as my mother's great-grandfather James F. R. Wight, whose family came from neighboring Shelby County, Kentucky.

Macon, 1924: Fiddle Contests and Horse Races

Forty-five miles northwest of Paris, and some twenty miles north of Moberly, the railroad and coal-mining town of Macon held old-time fiddlers contests and jockeyed for the public's attention. Macon, seat of Macon County, was a growing town that had capitalized on its location along major railroad lines as well as its fortuitous landscape, beneath which were the newly developed bituminous coal mines. Macon is on the northern edge of the old Little Dixie cultural region and came to prominence not through Paris's heritage of agricultural and political importance in early Missouri, but through Civil War–era and postwar circumstances that favored its future—railroads, federal sympathies, mining.

Since the 1850s, Little Dixie towns—such as Paris, Hannibal, Columbia, Huntsville, Fayette—had been in competition. During the Civil War, which wrought dreadful hardships on civilians standing on both sides of the war, Little Dixie towns were often in open conflict with towns like Macon, Kirksville, and other pro-Union centers in northern and central Missouri. Macon was the location of a substantial Union army troop depot that was commanded by an infamous officer who was merciless in punishing pro-Confederacy civilians in the region they controlled, a name despised down to the present day among Missourians of a certain family heritage. Macon was a key city for the federal occupation due to the railroads intersecting there, and its location gave the federals quick access to pressure points in Little Dixie, an influential pro-South region. While the dominant prosperous farmhouse in Little Dixie was the tall Anglo-Southern "I house," just north in the Macon area it was the "temple-form house" type—known as "Yankee houses" to the Southerners. Such physical features on the land were a reminder to people of the very different heritages of towns that would, to an outsider, bear little of distinction.[43]

Paris was an old Little Dixie center of mules and horses, tobacco and hemp, and former Kentucky, Virginia, and North Carolina farmers. Though there were pockets of Northerners and abolitionists there, many people had owned African American slaves. The majority of the people of Monroe County and the broader Little Dixie vernacular region were old-stock Americans and African Americans. However, up in Macon County, the older population had been substantially modified through "Yankee" settlers, soldiers, railroad builders, and newer groups of Europeans who came to labor in the coal mines.[44] No love was lost between towns like Paris and Macon. Many years later, rivalries continued—in business, county baseball teams, high school sports teams, agricultural fair exhibitions and contests, horseshoe-pitching teams, and horse races. And fiddlers contests.

Macon also sought to make its mark in fiddlers contests, mounting competitions attracting some of the same fiddlers and audiences, just as their horse races did. Horse racing around quarter-mile ovals was, for many people, the signal event at any county fair or old settlers' reunion from post–Civil War days well into the twentieth century.[45]

Just as many small towns included a fiddlers contest in their Independence Day celebrations, Macon also held a July 4 fiddle contest. The Macon 1922 event included an age rule that was commonplace at the time, requiring fiddlers to be sixty years of age or older. Perhaps as a result of the age restriction, and certainly due as well to contests going on in other towns, the Macon administrators were disappointed to find that they had just two entries, J. T. Miles (aged sixty-two) and John Cromwell (eighty-two). Rather than going ahead with the contest, the judges wisely changed the program into a fiddling exhibition, which seemed to please all parties as well as the audience. "Each gave a fifteen minute recital that was enjoyed and cheered by all within hearing distance." The judges divided the ten-dollar first-place purse between Miles and Cromwell.[46]

Macon held another 1922 fiddlers contest, at the old settlers' reunion and festival in late September. It is believed that this Macon event aspired to be just as big a contest as the Paris state contest. On September 5, 1922, the Macon paper announced the forthcoming showdown. This time the administration altered the age rules slightly: "Open to persons above 50 years of age" and adding that each contestant was to play three tunes, "Arkansas Traveler" and two others of the fiddler's choice.[47] Many years later, "Marmaduke's Hornpipe" has become a sine qua non Missouri fiddle tune. A special division for the tune was developed for the 1989 Missouri State Fiddle Contest in Columbia.

Contest rules had not yet barred trick fiddling. In these 1920s contests, the concept seemed to apply to fiddlers who were adroit at showmanship and crowd-pleasing antics, such as playing the violin between their legs or behind their heads—commonplace stage tricks from the days of minstrel shows and vaudeville cutups. Henry Taylor seems to have been expert at fiddling with the instrument held behind his head. Such stage clowning has long been discarded at fiddle contests, and, perhaps as a result, it is rare to find a fiddler today who can accomplish these fine old gags.

Today, "trick fiddling" is applied to playing what are called, in this writer's opinion, "trick tunes"—tunes played with the instrument cross-tuned (see elsewhere) such as "Black Mountain Rag," and extravagantly wild show tunes like the radioactive "Orange Blossom Special." To ban or not ban tunes like this from contests is a theme that would trouble contest judges for many years, and continues to do so. In hindsight, it is ironic that contest fiddlers who could manage it did not mind using trick fiddling, or a fierce wild Indian holler, in their competition rounds. Yet some of the trick fiddlers strongly disapproved of judging the outcome by audience reaction.

A September 28, 1922, article in the *Macon Daily Chronicle-Herald* reported on the September 5 Old Settlers Day contest. Henry Taylor, probably the best-known contest fiddler in the region at this time, receives the limelight.

COUSIN OF BOB TAYLOR'S WON PRIZE

HENRY TAYLOR VANQUISHED FIELD OF 13 FIDDLERS

. . . The applause that followed his first selection, "The Eighth of January," showed that Taylor had made a big hit with the crowd. After the contest he was requested to play "The Lost Indian," which he did to the great delight of the big audience.[48]

Several contestants played "Arkansas Traveler," and several played "The Irish Washer Woman."[49] The contest paid four places. First went to Henry Taylor ($10.00), second to W. R. Blankenship of Bevier ($7.50), third to William Stalcup of Clarence ($5.00), and fourth to C. A. Terry of College Mound ($2.50).[50] After the contest, A. W. Selby, one of the three judges, and B. J. Simpson "gave an old fashioned dance, which created tremendous applause." Weeks later, two other articles, in October in the Macon paper and November in the *Moberly Weekly*, described more fully the September 5, 1922, event. Both articles are reprintings, with modest editing, of an article from the *St. Louis Star*.[51]

MEN OF THE FIDDLE AND BOW

MADE THE WELKIN RING ON OLD SETTLERS' DAY[52]

THE ART OF MUSIC MAKING AS PRACTICED BY MEN WHO INHERITED IT FROM THEIR SIRES

From the *St. Louis Star*.

It would have delighted the music-loving souls of Governor Bob and Alf Taylor of Tennessee to have witnessed the old-timers manipulate the "fiddle and the bow" at Macon Wednesday, Old Settler's Day. By chance it happened that Henry Taylor, winner of the first prize, was a cousin of the Tennessee Taylors, and his father John Belvard Taylor, was a nephew of Zachary Taylor, the twelfth president of the United States.

It may have been an announcement in a local paper that the *St. Louis Star* was interested in the contest that brought such a big line-up of old fiddlers out to take a hand in the contest. There were here 13 old fiddlers, every one of them an artist in the way of playing "The Arkansaw Traveler" and other classics of the fiddle. At the Monroe County contest last December there were five. Shelby County organized an old fiddlers contest in which seven took part. It was expected here there would be only six or seven at the most, and when 13 enrolled it was clear that something was going to happen in musical circles.

Chairman R. A. Guthrie started the contestants to sawing at 1:30 in a big tent hemmed with people, and though the races, with some of the best horses in the country, were started while the fiddlers were at work, not a person left the crowded tent. If you ever attended a fiddlers contest by old-timers you'll understand why. It's the individual characteristics of the performance. All keep time with their feet. Some sway their bodies backward, and forward and sideways. One man played "Whipping the Devil Around the Stump" with the fiddle back of his head. When Taylor played "The Lost Indian," he would inject a long, and mournful call sounding something like "Wa-h-e-e-e—wah-o-o-!" trailing off like a cry in the distance.

It was a day in Indian summer with scarlet tinted foliage creeping close to the big tents and exhibition building, and the incense of wood fires from nearby farm houses sifted through the air, suggesting long winter evenings soon to come, when the family would gather 'round the hearth and the gray haired father would take from its case the loved instrument of the pioneer and make the welkin ring. Under such conditions the old fiddler was born, and the melody he produces was placed in his soul at birth.

The fiddlers sat in an arena in the center of the big tent, the crowd packed densely around them.

As the music switched to a well-known lilt, the crowd would laugh. Not so the performers. They were a serious group, and no smile, overcast their features, even when doing their merriest airs. This winning of the fiddle contest with artists all around in the competition was no joking matter. It is an honor handed down from father to son, and to generations yet to come.

Some of the fiddlers were men with distinguished looks, long gray mustaches, keen blue eyes and well moulded features. There were others who looked the part of the old-time fiddlers as handed down in song and story. Such was Bill Harris, the blind musician of Adair County, who says he has been fiddling for dances and country celebrations for more than 50 years, and is good for goodness knows how many more.

The crowd really decides the winner when Henry Taylor of Cairo, Mo., took the chair and played "The Eighth of January." The applause that followed was quite as loud as that over on the race track, a stone's throw away, when the winning nag came under the wire. Taylor has eight fiddling trophies on his belt, some in contests where the kings of the bow were in the ring, and he played with a sureness of tempo that came from thorough confidence. Taylor said he began fooling with a fiddle when he was a lad of 8, and just "growed into it." Born May 6, 1865, still lives on the farm where the stork left him. He said people told him afterwards the birds were singing in the trees that day.

As Taylor sawed away with his bow, you could hear people in the Audience: "Watch that arm; never misses a stroke;" "Say, they'll have to hand it to that man!" "Boys, ain't he making that ole fiddle talk?"

When the performer shifted to "The Arkansaw Traveler" the crowd just yelled.

Most of the contestants were in their shirt sleeves, with their suspenders frankly in evidence. Some played with their knees crossed, and some hold their fiddles to their chins and others rested it alongside their heads.

A man in the audience said, "You can't lay down no rules for fiddlin'. I'm something of a fiddler myself, but I wouldn't want to go against that bunch—not since having heard that man Taylor. A fiddler plays whichever way is most comfortable to him. He don't pay no attention to what the book says—he just handles his old music bow the handiest. Why, if you'd tell these boys they had to learn how to play to notes and bars and scales they'd smash you."

"The Old Wagoner" seemed to be new to most of the crowd. It was played by Wm. Stalcup, and its beauty and fine rendition made for him a place with the winners.[53]

Some of the selections had quaint names suggestive of the grim humor of the old log cabin days. There were others that caused you to wonder just what they meant. Besides the pieces mentioned the contestants also played "Leather Britches," "Natchez Under the Hill," "Sail Away," "Bob Woods," "The Old Virginia Reel," "Old Dan Tucker," "Pop Goes the Weasel," "The Girl with a Hole in Her Stocking," "Charlotte Harris," "The Irish Washer Woman" and of course "Turkey in the Straw" was very much in evidence.

The performance closed with some old-fashioned dancing by A. W. Selby and B. J. Simpson, who gave an exhibition of intricate foot movements that set the crowd to cheering wildly.

It was stated in recent times in a well known musical journal that the old-time fiddler is dying out and that he has left no worthy successors; that "If there is to be a dance in the country now-a-days, a band or jazz orchestra has to be summoned from the nearest town, or else they get a piano and drums." One of the fiddlers who was there was asked about that.

"It may be true in the towns," he said, "but out in the country when they can get a fiddler for a dance they won't have any other kind of music. Jazz may do for some of the foxtrots and glides and shivery affairs, but when people who know what dancing is want to 'swing your partners,' they send for a fiddler every time. And when you 'shake the bushes' you'll find more fiddlers sticking around than you'd think. Look at the crowd here—thirteen in the contest and I'll bet there were twice as many in the audience. The fiddlers are not dying out—their tribe is growing."[54]

Much in that *Macon Daily Chronicle-Herald* article would bring a knowing nod from today's fiddle contest audiences and contestants.

Another report on this September 1922 Macon contest finds its theme in the hastening spread of jazz and its world of flappers, hard drinking, and nightlife, as well as new public roles for African American musicians, into every corner of the nations. This was the decade, remember, when jazz was becoming enormously popular and the jazz life seemed to be becoming a threat in many communities. Newspaper and magazine articles of the time often dramatized the perceived gulf between old-time music and emerging jazz music, and the gulf was deepened by the media reports.

An article by Edgar White in a November 1924 issue of *Musical Courier* provides a rare glimpse into the fervor and change going on in "old-time" fiddling in the Roaring Twenties—and the somewhat mixed feelings of observers about the potential loss of such hoary traditions that "ought to be preserved." The outsider's perspective and impression are apparent in the magazine editor's remarks preceding White's story, published in a journal read across the country. Visitors from St. Louis or other distant places might well be struck by the antique goings-on at an old-time fiddlers contest somewhere in the hills and prairies of northern Missouri. White reports on the 1922 Macon state fiddlers contest, and our friend Henry Taylor appears.

"JAZZ V. THE ARKANSAW TRAVELER"

BY EDGAR WHITE

This article is given space in the *Musical Courier* not because it has any musical significance but because it deals with a phase of American life that will probably soon disappear and be forgotten. It is not jazz that will push it aside, but civilization, rural development, opportunity. The solitude that made the fiddler of old is giving place to all sorts of pleasure, musical and otherwise, including the flivver and the radio, the talking machine and the picture theater, which so fill up the time of potential fiddlers that their mood is satisfied and need not the self-expression of the old time tunes. As our author says in this article, the old tunes ought to be preserved. But even in the preserving of them, the fiddle's spirit would be lost, and that is just as important and just as strictly a part of American history as the tunes themselves.—The Editor

Corn-shucking and fiddling-time are contemporaneous. They work hand in hand in making up the harvest.

Despite the declarations of a certain high-brow musical journal that the old-time fiddler had crawled into his hole and let "jazz" push him away from the footlights, nearly 3,000 enthusiastic fiddle-fans packed the grandstand the first night of the Macon (Mo.) fair and listened to thirty-two fiddledom stars of the log cabin days saw out "The Lost Indian," "Run, Nigger, Run," "Pop Goes the Weasel" and a hundred other soul-stirring classics of the bow.

Fiddlin' dead? . . . Goodness gracious, no! Why, at Macon these old-timers were the whole show. They came from everywhere in Missouri, and one fetched his old fiddle and bow all the way from Kansas. And the Jayhawker got three cheers and a tiger for the way he played "Rocky Mountain."

Before the battle of the bows began, manager R. A. Guthrie was called upon to lay down a rule.

"Yes, we will have no jazz in these here demonstrations." Said Bill Blankenship, of Bevier, holding up his fiddle threateningly.

"Jazz?" said Guthrie; "how can I tell?"

"It's like hanging a cat by the tail to a tree limb and shootin' at it . . . ," explained Bill logically.

All the boys nodded in assent. "Nothing but the old-time music goes," they declared in concert.

Seems that one of the fairs let some alleged "jazz men" get in and they won quite a round of applause from the youngsters who rather like the noise Blankenship so graphically described. Anyhow the fiddle and the bow vets organized and declared if anymore of that non-union jazz music got in they'd go on a strike. So to make a Macon holiday, jazz was banned.

"It's like this," said Henry Taylor, of Cairo, Mo., who won top honors in the world champion contest; "the fiddle men don't know anything about notes and bars and scales, and these fancy curves the jazz men put on. We play by sound, the old-time pieces that have been played for fifty years or more—that's all we know, and we think they're pretty good yet. There are 500 or more of those old melodies, and I guess every fiddler has his own peculiar way of playing them."

One man who listened closely to the performers up until midnight said: "Good gosh! Every man played the same piece."

An old-timer in the contest rail heard him and retorted: "The trouble with you is you don't know nothing about music."

The fun of an old-time fiddlers contest is in the absolute freedom of action. Some play with coats and vests off, their galluses (they call 'em) frankly in evidence, sleeves rolled up, sawing away for dear life while their stout shoes beat a lively tattoo on the floor.

When Taylor picked up his bow it seemed that every foot on the grandstand began tapping. Daintily dressed women in the private boxes delicately touched the floor with their French shoes. The effect was electrical. Taylor was awarded the top prize long before the judges announced their decision.

There were a dozen more "country champions" in the contest, some of whom had fiddled for fifty years.

Technically it would be a difficult job to decide such a contest, where no man has any technical knowledge. The judges have to pass on the melody, the harmony, the feeling a man puts into his work. Great musicians say there are no greater singers without great feeling. Sometimes a great sorrow puts into a singer's voice the one thing needed to perfect it. A certain historical instance is cited of a man who broke a woman's heart to give her voice the cadence necessary to make it sublime.

In a lesser way, perhaps, the old fiddler puts in his work pathetic touches because of the sorrow he has passed through, and of the autumn of life that silvers his hair. That must be it because one writer remarked as a curious circumstance that despite the fact that his hands grew stiffer, his body creaky and his eyes dim, the old musician's work became better and more melodious as the years drifted by.

The contest at Macon in September was the "round-up" of the fiddle events in Missouri during the year. The comeback of the fiddler occurred at Macon just a year ago. Small prizes were offered, because it was not expected more than five or six contestants would show up. Some didn't believe there were more than twenty old timers in the State. But the local paper began beating the brush and on the day of the contest twenty fiddlers showed up with their weapons of war. The surprised management had to hustle around pretty lively to get a tent big enough to accommodate the fiddlers and the large crowd that assembled to hear them.

Since then nearly every fair in the State has put on a fiddlers contest, and one of the events (at Paris) was attended by the mayors of St. Louis and Kansas City. There were twenty-four fiddlers in the ring. At Macon—the closing contest of the year—there were thirty-two. All the prize winners at other contests were present, and when the honors were accorded Taylor it was after he had gone against the greatest assembly of fiddling talent of his life.

Taylor is a cousin of former governor Alf Taylor of Tennessee, and of the late Bob Taylor. The Taylors were all famous fiddlers. Henry Taylor is nearly sixty, a tall, upstanding man, a great reader and well-educated. He believes that the old-time fiddler and his tunes belong to the history of the country and should be preserved. They represent a period of development that was characterized by peril and uncertainty. The old fiddle hanging over a wide hearth in the cabin made the solitude less dreary. To the moccasined frontiersman it spoke of the birds, the rustle of the wind, and the sound of the woodman's axe, the puffing of the steamboat—of life as he knew it. His problems, his joys, his sorrow were committed to it, and he found solace in the confidence bestowed.

"When you understand what the fiddle means to the old-timers," said Mr. Taylor, "you will understand why jazz has no place in their thought and ambitions."[55]

Edgar White's article, as well as his editor's preface, is fascinating, many layered. Its themes and tensions remain familiar at fiddle contests today. Then, the kind of new music competing with "old-time" was jazz, and this contest ruled that jazz would be banned. In the twenty-first century, debates tend toward whether "progressive fiddling" or "Texas style" (Texas-based National Contest style) should be acceptable in a Missouri "old-time" fiddling contest.

Salisbury, October 1929

Among other contests where Wood Brown and Clate Ransdell competed was a big contest in mid-October 1929 in Salisbury (Chariton County), west of Paris and Moberly. This was considered a "state contest." State champ Henry Taylor seems to have been absent from this event, and Columbia champions George Morris and Ed Tharp did not place among the winners. This major competition took place just two weeks before the stock market crash of Monday, October 28, 1929—an event that would bring hard times; the economic blight of the Great Depression would hamper sponsorship of fiddlers contests for a decade and more. As reported in the *Moberly Monitor-Index*:

WOOD BROWN WINS FIDDLING CONTEST

SECOND PLACE AT SALISBURY AFFAIR GOES TO CLATE RANSDALL, MOBERLY

20 CONTESTANTS VIE FOR $200 PRIZE MONEY

Salisbury, Mo., Oct. 11. Wood Brown of Paris, Monroe County, 62-year-old fiddler, playing a 125-year-old fiddle to accompaniment picked by his two sons on banjo and guitar, won the first prize of $100 in the old fiddlers contest here last night. Mr. Brown wore a medal stating that he had been declared a fiddling champion once before in a state contest held in his own home town.

Clate Ransdall [*sic*] of Moberly, who lost a leg several years ago in a mine accident and who also has a collection of trophies won by fiddling, won the second prize of $50. C. C. Kimbrell of Centralia, the oldest contestant, won third, $25. Aubrey Bradley won fourth, $10. Mrs. Clyde Steinbeck, the only woman contestant, was fifth, receiving $7.50. H. A. Janks of Hale won $5 for placing sixth, and Clarence Bennett of Salisbury won seventh prize of $2.50.

20 Fiddlers Compete

Thirty-seven contestants had registered in advance of the contest and were representative of all parts of the state. Owing to adverse road and weather conditions, only 20 were present to compete: George McCloud, Musselfork; Joe McDonald, Chillicothe; Giggs Vickery, Sweet Springs; C. C. Kimbrell, Centralia; George Morris, Columbia; Joe Anderson, Higbee; Everette Lynch, Sweet Springs; Clarence Bennett, Salisbury; Joe Lyons, Salisbury; Aubrey Bradley, Moberly; Ed Tharp, Columbia; Mose Slaver, Cowgill; Clate Ransdall, Moberly; C. E. Mitchell, Fayette; J. A. Janks, Hale; Wood Brown, Paris; J. J. Burger, Brookfield; Lee Magruder, Higbee; Miss Leona Lance, Columbia, a child; Mrs. Clyde Steinbeck, Mendon.

Each contestant was given a number in the order in which they registered and the numbers were put in a box and drawn out and contestants played in the order drawn.

Each contestant was allowed to play three pieces of his own choosing, and with exception of two all played accompanied by either banjo or guitar. "Eighth of January" seemed the most popular vehicle for the fiddling talent, as it was played by six of the contestants.

Other Popular Numbers

"The Hornpipe," "Leather Britches," "Money Musk," "The Old Hen Cackled," "Billy in the Lowlands" [today called "Billy in the Low Ground"], were also used many times. "Sally Gooding" ["Goodin"] played by Mrs. Steinbeck, if one judged by the response of the audience, was the most appealing selection played.

The event was managed by Raymond Cruse of Cruse Brothers, Salisbury's vaudeville team, and the business firms of the city were guarantors. Owing to bad roads the gate receipts did not pay expenses. All prizes were paid in full and satisfaction seemed to prevail among all the contestants except one, who having failed to get into the money in any of the seven places, publicly challenged the winners to another contest at his own expense but found no answering response.

> The judges were all Salisbury men, C. S. Johnson, jeweler; O. A. Yarbrough, section foreman; A. O. Prescott, rural mail carrier; Chas. Cruse, constable; and Jas. Mott, farmer.
>
> The affair brought together a very interesting cross section of life from many communities and most of them, if one would judge by swaying shoulders and tapping toes, were in thorough accord with the inspiring strains played by the perspiring musicians.[56]

The newspaper adds important details often neglected by the media. Some of the details prefigure development of agreed-upon contest rules when fiddler's associations were formed in later years—contestants played according to random drawing, they played three tunes of their choice, and the judging was accomplished by a panel of judges rather than by audience appeal—and we hope the judges were knowledgeable about fiddle music. All but two of the eighteen fiddlers were backed up by guitar or banjo, which at this time could have been either five-string or tenor banjo. "Eighth of January" in 1929 seems to have become more fashionable in fiddlers contests than "Arkansas Traveler," which had been the most played fiddle tune at contests earlier in the decade. The contest emcees and administrators were professional vaudeville performers from Salisbury.

Lee Mace led one of the first, if not the first, exhibition square-dance groups, on his *Ozark Opry* at the Lake of the Ozarks; cast members jig-danced while square dancing and wore heel taps, an innovation in the 1950s. *Left to right*: Mary Nichols, Goofer (Bill Atterberry), Belinda Williams Phillips, Perry Edenburn, Vicki Lombardo Sparkman, and Lee Mace. (Courtesy Dan William Peek)

Shows 6

Fiddler, speaking to the theater manager after the show: Nice place you have here. When was the last time I played here?

Manager: Tonight.

Barn Dance," "Jamboree," and "Hoedown" as well as "Jubilee" and "Opry" were among titles used for live, staged theatrical shows built around country music and comedy in the United States and Canada. In 1924 the *National Barn Dance* began live broadcasts on Chicago's WLS radio—a year before 1925, when *The Grand Ole Opry* began under its first title, *WSM Barn Dance.* The *WWVA Wheeling Jamboree* broadcast from West Virginia in 1933, and in 1950 Chicago had its black-and-white television *Windy City Jamboree. Don Messer's Jubilee* began airing across Canada on black-and-white television in 1957, helping spread country music and fiddling there. Missouri's *Ozark Jubilee* aired on television in 1955 from Springfield and a year later was being seen throughout North America on the ABC network. For a time, the word "hoedown" had its fans, with radio shows such as Canada's *Country Hoedown* and Philadelphia's 1948 *Hayloft Hoedown*, but "hoedown" did not have the right buzz. After Bill Monroe bought the theater (an old barn) in Bean Blossom, he continued calling it the "Brown County Jamboree."[1]

By the end of the 1950s, "barn dance," "jamboree," "hoedown," "jubilee," and the like were eclipsed by the catchy, evocative word "opry."[2] The formulation "grand ole opry," as used for a hillbilly music and comedy radio program, often with old-time dancing exhibitions, struck just the right tone with audiences. A gentle joke on the high-toned broadcasts of grand opera and classical music narrated in upper-class urban dialect in the early days of radio, the word "opry" had been used on WSM in the 1920s and had been in circulation since the 1700s.[3] "The opry" worked its way into the English vernacular to mean virtually any live stage entertainment for audiences that features country music (however defined).

The Shifting Sands of Country Entertainment

The live country music show continues, not only in the bright arenas of Branson but also around regional tourist and sportsmen attractions such as Mark Twain Lake and its Cannon Dam and the Hannibal area. A wide compass and heavy doses of nativistic patriotism are keys to their success. As Wayne Glenn writes, "To be successful, the Ozark Jubilee and the Ozark Opry were aiming at both rural and city folks for customers."[4] A country music show depends on the loyalty of its local fan base, and none of the small opry barns could stay in business without them. Larger enterprises with professional public relations budgets depend not only on the local audience but even more on attracting large numbers of visitors from cities and busloads of vacationers from distant states.

The "opera house" was a staple in many Missouri towns—especially prosperous railroad towns—and many provided an ambitiously decorated venue for all manner of theatrical and musical performances. Typically, these theaters, often situated upstairs over a department store on a prominent downtown spot, served many purposes, welcoming opry shows and political stump speakings as well as fiddlers contests, community theater performances, and concerts by touring artists and orchestras.[5] Some opry houses, such as the Farris Theatre in Richmond (Ray County), presented the town's first Hollywood movies as well as minstrel shows, vaudeville, light opera, orchestras, talent shows, dance recitals, band and orchestra concerts, and old-time fiddling. Built in 1901 by a consortium led by Samuel Dougherty, who had made his fortune in the Cripple Creek gold strike in Colorado, the Farris's premiere favored the town with Shakespeare's *As You Like It.* In 1911 the theater changed hands, with the Farris family taking over. The Farrises contracted for the town's first public sewer, dug in order to service the theater.

The Farris changed hands in 1915 and became a movie theater with the advent of silent films and then talkies a decade later; movies were a source for a number of what

The 1901 Farris Theatre, Richmond (Ray County), a fine "opera house" of the kind that graced prosperous farm and railroad towns in the glory days of vaudeville and variety show troupes and hosted country music oprys and shows for many years. (2011)

we think of as "fiddle tunes," many of them from the 1930s and 1940s musicals and B westerns. In the 1920s, Ray County's first radio programs were beamed from the Farris.

The movie theater function of the Farris ended in 1957 when newer purpose-built modern cinemas were built in the area, but the Farris reopened for country music shows developed by Byron Jones as well as productions of Broadway shows mounted by a local club; these lasted until the late 1980s. For a number of years, Leland Jones hosted the Country Pickin' Opry here. A citizens group called Friends of the Farris now owns the theater, promotes concerts of various kinds, including country music, and conducts restoration work.

The present-day show is an evolution of community entertainments of various kinds. The opry echoes the wagon shows, minstrel frolics, traveling circuses and carnivals, Chautauqua, and other kinds of professional and amateur entertainments popular across much of the United States. The vaudeville variety shows were often known as "Toby shows" and featured music, dancing, and comedy routines. "Toby" was a stock character costumed in hillbilly attire, topped off with a disheveled red wig. In these folk skits, Toby was the bumpkin who outsmarted the conceited, dapper city slicker—the ancestors of the Ozarker and lost city slicker in the "Arkansas Traveler" stage routine. Toby shows were a "major theatrical force responsible for keeping rural theatre alive in the early 1900s."[6] And Toby has not left the building.

Traveling circuses, called "wagon shows," worked their way across central Missouri on the Boonslick Trail as early as 1840. Although they focused on menageries and performances of exotic animals, especially elephants with names like "Hannibal," circuses included step dancers and comedy acts.[7] A circus that traveled to central Missouri, moving west from St. Louis to towns along the north bank of the Missouri River and returning back again along the south bank, included another stock character: a "clown who sang Negro songs and played a banjo."[8]

Often set up during summer weekends and autumn harvest time, the traveling circuses and stage shows were particularly important before modern technology began to remove entertainment from one's local park or carnival tent to commercial records, radio, television, and the Internet. Today's live stage shows and oprys lean heavily and appropriately on the nineteenth century. Despite the many decades of canned music and satellite-fed entertainment, our collective memory continues to spark with the imagery and nostalgia built into shows such as the now-defunct *Ozark Opry* in Osage Beach and Ron Lutz's *Rooster Creek* on AM radio, or in modern oprys such as the glitzy music theaters in the Branson area or, on a more modest scale, *The Big Creek Opry* in Pleasant Hill every Saturday night.

Is the Word "Opry" Obsolete?

Fewer and fewer people remember the glory days of AM radio and *The Grand Ole Opry*, when the family radio set was the gathering place in the living room on a Saturday night to hear live country music and cornball comedy. In fact, the first generation of people who could remember hearing Uncle Jimmy Thompson rip off a fiddle tune or DeFord Bailey wail a harmonica on the *Opry* in the 1920s are long gone.

In the early days of the development of such shows across the country in the 1940s and 1950s—*The Ozark Opry* in Osage Beach was Missouri's first and most famous example—the term "opry" worked well. People would drive into Osage Beach to see Lee Mace's *Ozark Opry* on a Saturday evening, then, back home again (or while driving home in their cars), they would switch on the radio to catch the last of *The Grand Ole Opry* broadcast from the Ryman Auditorium in Nashville—or the after-hours live show broadcast from the Ernest Tubb Record Shop (often with *Opry* stars as well as guests) from across the street.

Most of the small-town oprys, and later the big shows in Branson, played on the traditions of hillbilly radio and vaudeville personified in Nashville's *Grand Ole Opry.*

However, as the 1950s brought rock and roll into collision (and collusion) with country music, oprys, jamborees, and radio barn dances more and more were called "shows" as the events moved ever closer to some sort of accommodation to the relentless steamroller of rock music, or what some folks just called "Elvis."

Conservative people, the promoters and musicians in the many small-town theater music shows kept the term "opry" functional even as the old model was being changed by modern sounds and ever more electrified, rock-influenced country music in the 1950s and 1960s. Some in the business in Nashville called the new stuff "countrypolitan" or "the Nashville sound," as though such hip-sounding terms would become popular. Insiders began to call it "Nash-trash." Today, we can hear "Ameripolitan," meaning "music with prominent roots influence" such as "Honky-Tonk, Western Swing, Rockabilly, and Outlaw," that attempts to reach people younger than age fifty.[9] It will always be hard to nail down a name for the music.

In those decades, the Folk Music Revival was also happening. A few country music and bluegrass venues adopted the briefly popular word "hootenanny" for what had been "oprys" and "shows." "Hootenanny" did not catch on with conservative country and small-town people, however, to whom the word smacked of campus hippies, radical politics, protest songs, and California.

The word "opry" does continue to be used in some small-town theater shows across Missouri. But the word "show" rules in this entertainment genre. The promotional website http://www.mo-kanopry.com lists a number of venues in Missouri, Kansas, and adjacent areas of other states. We have venues such as Cline's Opry (Edgerton), Leland Jones's Country Pickin' Opry (Richmond), Barn Door Opry (Ravenwood), Black Diamond Opry (Macon), Darlington Opry (Darlington), and the Northtown Opry (North Kansas City). But venues with "opry" in their title are fewer than venues with titles such as Country Cabin Jamboree (Savannah), Old Town Jamboree (Hamilton), Holt County Hoedown (Holt), Country Music at the Lake (Warsaw), the Sally Mountain Show (Queen City), and Hazel Kinder's Lighthouse Theatre. There is nothing to argue for "opry" as the preferred term.

A cursory examination is instructive of the very long list of venues in Branson, the vast entertainment complex in the Ozarks that began with authentic country music (and is now minimally devoted to its roots). There are a few "jamborees," but one finds zero "oprys" on the official website.[10] "Show" is the predominant descriptor there, and few shows desire connection to country music or the region's cultural heritage. Among older shows with a heritage in Ozark authenticity, the Presley family calls their event a "jubilee." Many use a title describing their literal content, such as "Patsy Cline Remembered," "Sons of the Pioneers Branson Show," "Motown Downtown—a Tribute," "Linda Ronstadt and Jackson Browne Tribute Show," "Disney's Little Mermaid," and "The Golden Sounds of the Platters." It is of course difficult for a show to distinguish itself in the rush to please hundreds of thousands of tourists, from Wisconsin, Japan, and Mexico. Few shows present what most readers of this book would consider authentic country or old-time music.

Drew Beisswenger's 2006 video series on Ozarks jam sessions sheds light. Drew visited and recorded a wide array of events for Missouri State University. "Drawing the line between jam sessions, oprys, open-mike events, dances, community picnics, homecomings, fiddle competitions, festivals, and private house parties is not always easy." Beisswenger notes that "oprys differ from jam sessions in that the performances at the oprys are planned. Arrangements are made for specific musicians or groups to perform. Often, though not always, listeners are required to pay an admission fee and the bands are paid to play. Also, although an element of informality is often present, an M.C. ultimately controls the scheduling for the events." His focus was on the more traditional, less-formal events based on jam sessions rather than professional-style organized shows with fixed schedules at which a guest musician must make prior arrangement in order to perform. One "opry" is among those documented, the Webster County Opry, Fridays at the Rogersville Senior Center.[11]

"Jamboree" remains a viable term for the live music show with a variety of music genres and comedy routines. But the experiences, the music, and the popular culture of today's young people, and those to come, grow ever more distant from those ancient times of the live radio variety show. The word "show" has always been there, in the language, familiar and trustworthy. For one sitting in the audience in 2015 at two Missouri "oprys" (one deep in the Ozarks, the other in suburban Kansas City), it began to become clear that the old word "opry" is disappearing. The word "show" is the new "opry."

The Ozark Opry

Branson may be the center of today's opry universe, but it was not always so. In the 1950s, the Lake of the Ozarks and Springfield areas were prominent, and there were the 1930s and 1940s radio shows that beamed over the air from Kansas City, St. Louis, and throughout Missouri and other states; stations could be heard from as far away as Canada, New York, California, Mexico, and Cuba. But none of the shows was more influential, or finer, than Lee Mace's *Ozark Opry* in Osage Beach, Missouri, founded in 1953.[12]

Dan William Peek writes that the year "1953 is generally considered to be Year One in the history of the modern country music industry. It is significant that that same year marked the founding of the Ozark Opry, an entertainment concept that was the model for the industry's alternative dimension, now known as Branson-style venues." Peek's *Live! At the Ozark Opry* offers a glimpse into this groundbreaking opry show, its entrepreneurial founders, and its purposeful branding as fun-loving backwoods entertainment.[13] Peek based his book on interviews and original documents and offers insight into how the show was born at a key moment in the formulation of country music. *The Ozark Opry* carved out a versatile and attractive niche. The imagery and symbols of rural, backwoods culture and music of the era fed into the performance and appealed to broad audiences by incorporating contemporary country music and comedy.

With *The Ozark Opry* ensemble as regulars, radio station KRMS (Osage Beach) began to match the only rival in its broadcast area, Springfield's KWTO. The Springfield station had not had the programming uncertainties that Robert M. Smith's operation had experienced. Headquartered deep in the Ozarks, KWTO had gone country from the start.

A recording of a live half-hour 1955 *Ozark Opry* radio show on KRMS reveals that the opry format was in full bloom under Lee Mace's guidance and professional on-air mien. *The Ozark Opry* cast was performing throughout each week at a nearby

The Ozark Opry, ca. 1961. *Left to right*: Bob Penney, Lonnie Hoppers, Don Russell (violin), Lee Mace, Dillard Stamper, and Bob McCoy. (Courtesy Helen Russell and Dan William Peek)

hall, and these half-hour live shows could be unpredictable. While Mace worked up a play list for each show, a fiddler or banjo player might decide on the spot to play something else from their repertoire. On many of the early radio shows, the cast included only the several members whom Mace managed. One 1955 show featured Mace (bass player, vocals), Lonnie Hoppers (banjo), Billy Moore (violin, vocals), Dale Sledd (Dobro, vocals), and Bob McCoy (guitar, vocals); other cast members Dillard Stamper and the Hall Sisters were not on the show that particular day. The show went something like this:

1. Lee Mace makes opening comments and welcomes the listener, stressing the nightly performance schedule.
2. Gospel number, untitled, with vocals and fiddle break.
3. Mace promo for *The Ozark Opry* evening shows.
4. Mace introduces Hoppers—"He tears that banjo plumb *up*!"—and Hoppers plays a hot bluegrass instrumental of the era, "Pike County Breakdown" (as recorded in 1952 by Bill Monroe and His Bluegrass Boys, with Lonnie's friend, banjoist Sonny Osborne).[14]
5. Dale Sledd sings a popular Louvin Brothers song, "Poison Love."
6. Billy Moore sings and takes a fiddle break (solo), "I Don't Care If Tomorrow Never Comes."
7. Bob McCoy sings "Faded Love and Winter Roses."
8. Mace does another promo, and the show ends with Moore fiddling the iconic "Sally Goodin."

Billy Moore was a violinist from the southwest Iowa farm town of Red Oak who, at eighteen, had moved to Kansas City in 1954 or 1955 to make his way in professional music circles. Moore soon became enamored of bluegrass and country music in the exciting Kansas City scene and was hired by Lee Mace to be *The Ozark Opry*'s fiddler. Moore was among several classically trained violinists who converted to "fiddling" in the 1950s (today, the transition is common). Moore played on the opry three years. He was offered a job by the popular country duo Johnnie Wright and Jack Anglin to join Johnny and Jack's Tennessee Mountain Boys, and Bill Monroe also invited Moore to join the Bluegrass Boys, offers Moore declined. Lonnie Hoppers, a friend with whom Moore performed on *The Ozark Opry*, remembers Billy as "a good, slick fiddler with a good, big tone, like a Kenny Baker tone" and a fiddler who could also "play all those Benny Martin licks."[15]

While with *The Ozark Opry*, Billy Moore cut several "square dance without calls" 78 rpm records for Les Gotcher on Gotcher's Black Mountain Records label. Fiddle scholar Jim Nelson of St. Louis led me to one of Moore's records with "Poke County Breakdown" and "Cripple Creek" by "Billie [*sic*] Moore and the Ozark Opera Boys." "Poke County Breakdown" is a misspelling (perhaps intentional) of "Polk County Breakdown," popularized by Nashville fiddlers Tommy Magness, Tommy Jackson, and others. "Polk County Breakdown" is a tune popular among Missouri fiddlers and square dancers, especially in central and southern Missouri (where there is a Polk County). Les Gotcher was a popular square-dance caller who toured widely, teaching square dancing and putting on society dances during the post–World War II heyday of the square-dance revival.[16] Like other callers, Gotcher used the records on sound systems at dances where no live band was available or needed. Gotcher spent time in the Lake of the Ozarks area in Missouri in the mid-1950s and hosted square dances at Kirkwood Lodge, where Moore and other Ozark Opry musicians served as the band. On the record mentioned, the musicians included Lee Mace (bass, leader of the opry), Bob McCoy ("High Pockets"), Bob Penny, Dillard Stamper, and Sonny Newman, playing different kinds of guitars.[17] Gotcher liked the Missourians' music so much that he hired the group (including for one trip, banjoist Lonnie Hoppers) to travel west with him to do big square-dance events in Texas and California. In 1960, facing the military draft, Billy Moore enlisted in the US Air Force. He perished in an Air Force plane crash.

In bluegrass music, "Poison Love" and "Pike County Breakdown" remain staples of the well-versed, experienced band. The banjo instrumental as presented by Sonny Osborne and, later, Lonnie Hoppers was played ultrafast, in the mode then popular—but played too fast for all but the quickest fiddlers. While it made a good square-dance tune, "Pike County Breakdown" was composed for the lickety-split five-string bluegrass banjo, and it has not gone into the repertoires of fiddlers, notwithstanding the occasion when a fiddler is more or less forced to tear through a "break" in a band performance featuring the banjo. Lonnie Hoppers later recorded his equally fast version on his 1980 LP, *Pickin' with Friends*, and his tempo for "Pike County Breakdown" is virtually the same as when he played with *The Ozark Opry* in 1955 and the same as Sonny Osborne's 1952 tempo on the Monroe record, a blazing 155 beats per minute.

That set of tunes and songs typified virtually all hillbilly and bluegrass band performances of the 1940s through the rest of the twentieth century, a mix of classic instrumentals, one or two currently popular songs on the record charts, and at least one gospel song with harmony singing. *The Ozark Opry* was tapping the right chimes by proving that they were the real deal, grounded in old-time fiddle and dance music as well as adroit purveyors of popular Nashville country music of the day—and, with their gospel singing, were upright folk you would invite to Sunday dinner after church. All these ingredients mattered in a show's acceptance then, and still do today.[18] In addition, Mace spoke easily, in a fluid, basso northern Ozarks drawl that listeners connected with "real" hillbillies. *The Ozark Opry* formula has been carefully followed from the 1950s to today's "Branson" entertainment.

Joyce Mace remembered that Lee then got the idea to do a live show for the tourists. There was an old racetrack in Osage Beach to which the radio executives brought a flatbed truck with a little sound system for the stage. Lonnie Hoppers recalled that "it was set back off the road, and nobody would drive back there. It didn't work." They played to very sparse audiences, but Lee Mace learned from the experience. Undaunted, Mace and his comrades studied the landscape and zeroed in on the Lakeside Casino building, in the midst of the tourist action on the lake and along US Highway

54. Unfortunately, the room they rented was in a lower level of the building, not readily accessible, so Mace became the barker for the show, escorting tourists through the casino café and gift shop to the show and piloting his Pontiac, loudspeaker blaring, through the Bagnell Dam area on Saturday afternoons, inviting folks to come to *The Ozark Opry* that evening.

Born in nearby Miller County, and proud of his Osage Indian blood, Lee Mace was a fiddler, guitarist, bassist, and jig dancer in what he called "Ozark Mountain jig" style. Mace's parents were schoolteachers in Tuscumbia, and his father, Lucian, a fiddler, was elected to terms as Miller County sheriff and Missouri state legislator. Lee Mace had gotten his public performance start after service in World War II, when he played dances in fiddle bands at the annual three-day picnics along the Osage River in the Miller County seat of Tuscumbia—events fondly recalled by fiddle tune collector R. P. Christeson in his tune books and interviews.

Lee Mace made the upright bass his instrument in his role as leader of *The Ozark Opry* ensemble. Slap or "slam" bass style was important in country music, jazz, swing, bluegrass, and western swing. By the 1940s and 1950s, the bowed cello, which had been "the bass" in the 1800s and early 1900s at old-time dances, had been replaced when the upright bass or "doghouse" became popular and available.

In 1953 Mace's square-dance and jig-dancing group performed in Kansas City and New York on the *Ted Mack Amateur Hour* as the "Lake of the Ozarks Square Dancers." Soon after, Mace's dance ensemble danced on *The Grand Old Opry*'s wooden stage in the Ryman Auditorium in Nashville—under the amended title "*Grand Ole Opry* Square Dancers" required by *Grand Ole Opry* management. This was the first time that square dancers on *The Grand Ole Opry* wore taps on their shoes. The Mace group was the envy of many Nashville stars when they were invited to perform at such prestigious venues as the Chicago Fair in the summer of 1950 and the Blue Room nightclub in the famed Roosevelt Hotel in New Orleans, where the Lake of the Ozarks Square Dancers enjoyed high-society exposure among performers such as Frank Sinatra and Louis Armstrong. Three years later they set up their own opry in Osage Beach in the exciting and challenging years when the modern country music industry was being invented.

The Ozark Opry was a carefully configured alternative to the developing Nashville-style opry show. Joyce and Lee Mace were smartt in giving their show a distinctive and subtly different character. The Maces embraced the hillbilly stereotypes. According to Peek:

> What is most telling in the understanding of the Ozark Opry as it positioned in the emerging country music industry, is that Lee Mace embraced the term hillbilly. Through a marketing lens, the separate strategies of Nashville and Lee Mace become crystal clear. Lee saw that by positioning hillbilly music and dance as an exciting "new kind of entertainment" he could win audiences otherwise not accessible.
>
> In contrast, a voice from Nashville in the early 1950s might have proclaimed: "Ain't no hillbillies here. Call us country—practically suburbanites. Our music is

like pop music. Almost the same." This positioning, it was hoped, would win audiences for the newly minted "Country and Western" music.

Lee was selling "different" and Nashville was selling "same." Both would succeed.

Thus was the Ozark Opry founded in 1953 at the conceptual polar opposite of the conventional wisdom and wishes of the emergent country music industry, and it would remain so for the entire course of events.

Lee Mace knew his audience. Mace once told a reporter, "Folks were coming from Chicago and the first thing they wanted to see was the Dam, the next thing was a hillbilly. Well, we figured we would show them a hillbilly even if we had to go to Chicago and hire one."[19]

The Ozark Opry, on KRCG-TV, 1964. *Left to right*: Bill Atterberry, Jim Smith (banjo), LeRoy Haslag, Paulette Reeves (violin), Lee Mace, Darrel Gordon, and Pat Pryor. (Courtesy Haslag)

The success of *The Ozark Opry* attracted attention early on. Lonnie Hoppers recalled meeting the Mabe Brothers in 1955. The brothers regularly came to see *The Ozark Opry*, and, in 1959, the Mabes founded the first successful show in Branson, "The Bald Knobbers Jamboree." Hoppers remembered that the Mabes actually tried a show—prior to their Branson venture—at the Lake of the Ozarks, but the strong competition there may have encouraged them to try Branson.

Also in 1954, Dale Sledd, still a teenager, played his Dobro at one of the KRMS talent shows and was soon hired to join *The Ozark Opry* cast. Dale Sledd would go on from *The Ozark Opry* to perform as the rhythm guitar player and second tenor with the Osborne Brothers. "Sonny Osborne told me that Dale auditioned for them in a hotel room," Lonnie related. "He said they couldn't shake him, no matter what they played, he was right on top of it. Sonny said Dale was one of the best rhythm guitar players they had ever seen." Dale Sledd died in Warsaw, Missouri, in August 2016 at age seventy-nine.

The Ozark Opry was in some ways the most important of the early shows. The show closed for a brief time after organizer and leader Lee Mace's June 1985 death in an airplane crash, but resumed shortly under the management of Lee's widow, Joyce Mace, and with a new master of ceremonies to fill Lee's role. *The Ozark Opry* finally closed in 2005 fifty-three years after the rerouting of US highway 54. Joyce Mace would not have closed had the highway expansion not encroached on the opry building and parking lot.[20]

The crafting of showmanship is a venerable tradition through the long history of some people trying to entertain other people. Acceptance by the public, some level of celebrity, and a decent income are the intended results, but many entertainers do "put on the show" out of the sheer pleasure they find in the act of doing so. But learning the craft does not come easily for most people. An anecdote in the autobiography of Lawrence Welk, among the most successful of impresarios, makes the point: As a callow teenager just starting out in the 1920s, Welk found work playing accordion in a trio called George T. Kelly's Peerless Entertainers, playing shows and putting on dances in the conservative farm towns in the Dakotas. Welk admired Kelly and learned much of his stagecraft under Kelly's tutelage. One day George Kelly and his attentive apprentice, Welk, were having pie and coffee in a café in a town where the trio had performed and made a modest bit of profit. As paraphrased by Phil Williams:

> Welk was complaining loudly about the quality of the pie. He complained and complained. And the band leader (George Kelly) complimented the waitress and cook on the quality of the *coffee*. After leaving the restaurant, Welk asked his boss why he praised the poor quality of the meal. He told Welk, "listen to what you did in there—you criticized them for the pie, you didn't like it. I was complimenting them on the coffee. It wasn't that great a coffee, but who do you think they're going to hire back here? You always compliment people, they're trying to do their best—*and that's how you get along in life*.[21]

Like Lawrence Welk, Lee Mace's on-air style and charisma personified the best in live radio, TV, and stage work. LeRoy Haslag recalls that Mace admired Welk and patterned some of his own stagecraft after Welk's. Mace had met Welk on one of *The Ozark Opry*'s road trips to Minnesota, where the cast performed on the same bill as the Lawrence Welk orchestra, which by the 1960s had become a major force in show business. The Opry played the first set on a dinner show, and Welk's band followed.[22]

More than a hundred musicians served stints on *The Ozark Opry* at one time or another. The show's first banjo player, Lonnie Hoppers, went on to fame performing and making important commercial records with Bill Monroe and the Bluegrass Boys.

Dale Sledd began his career under Lee Mace's tutelage and went on to notoriety playing bluegrass with the Osborne Brothers and others; known mainly as a guitarist and Dobroist, Sledd also played violin, bass, and bluegrass banjo. Kelly Jones of Stover is a many-times Missouri state champion and professional country music sideman and entertainer. Veterans such as fiddler Mike Richardson, who has been in the cast of the Main Street Music Hall in Osage Beach, continued to perform with opry shows in the Lake of the Ozarks area well after the close of *The Ozark Opry* itself.

While many of the old-time local shows have disappeared, others have continued and some have sprouted. The spirit of these places endures in venues such as the Wilcox Opry Barn in Macon, Pleasant Hill's Big Creek Country Show, and many other shows. By the twenty-first century, generations of patrons have become accustomed to being audiences for entertaining shows put on for their pleasure. The entertainment has become part of the traditional music scene. If some of the now older people miss the old dance halls where they could square dance or waltz and enjoy an alcoholic beverage, younger patrons are usually unaware of those dance halls of former times.

During most of the 1950s through the 1970s, many kinds of venues claimed the attention of fans and audiences, from the neighborhood taverns and honky-tonks to the emergence of folk and bluegrass festivals and the revival of old-time fiddlers

The Ozark Opry is gone, but until recently the old neon sign still graced US 54, the superhighway funneling tourists from St. Louis and Chicago and points north into the Ozarks, eager for the kind of authentic "Ozark experience" provided in joyful abundance by *The Ozark Opry* for five decades. In 2015 the building was converted into a combination museum and Sears store. (Photo by Joy Peek)

contests. By the 1970s and 1980s, most of the taverns and dance halls where fiddlers had found work and camaraderie had become rough places; juke boxes with rock music drove away most of the musicians and dancers. The mythical honky-tonks beloved by Hank Williams fans almost disappeared. The aging of those war-years musicians was probably a factor, but the shift of rural taverns toward rock music, television sets, and a drug-related society meant that a lot of musicians were out of work. Some quit. Some turned to fiddle contests. Many, now long in the tooth, were content to sit in on jam sessions at senior citizens' centers.

Bluegrass fans have oprys and shows, too, even while most shows include a bluegrass number or two during the evening. Taken together with the bluegrass festivals around Missouri, and oprys that welcome bluegrass music, bluegrass fiddlers have more opportunities to perform than old-time fiddlers have. Even while they do not produce revenue or operate professionally, the monthly bluegrass music shows in the Kansas City area under the Heart of America Bluegrass and Old-Time Music Association function as organized events. HABOT events invite musicians and the public for evenings of informal jamming in back rooms, dinner, and an evening performance of bands that sign up for their allocated time onstage as the host and emcee see fit. Also in the Kansas City region, the Kansas City Area Bluegrass Music Club, founded in the early 1960s, has many features of an opry, but for many patrons it is the jam sessions in the back rooms that are the principal attraction of the KCABMC's monthly meetings.

Some shows take place in a town's firehouse or school auditorium as community fund-raisers. Many parks where major bluegrass festivals are held make arrangements for small shows, jamborees, and opry-style variety shows to help make good use of the property. Some shows include bluegrass but mostly present country music, such as the Cannon Dam Opry near Florida (Monroe County) and the Clinton County Opry near Plattsburg. Some oprys, such as the Ozark Music at the VFW Hall (Summersville) present mostly bluegrass music, with classic country music ("Hank Williams songs") added in. Most shows charge at least a nominal admission, and a few depend on goodwill donations.

In Missouri during the 1950s and 1960s, professional opry opportunities were limited, however, for the most part to locations in the general Ozarks uplands where the tourism environment and character of the music scene supported an ongoing show. While oprys existed and continue to exist in central and northern Missouri, these regions lack the colorful images and popular stereotypes of mountain music and hillbilly music that were honed to a keen edge in Ozarks locations such as the Lake of the Ozarks, Springfield, and the Branson area.[23]

Missouri fiddlers have tried their hands at opry performing since the emergence of the shows in the 1930s, often in tandem with live AM radio broadcasts. The list is long and would include such names, from the 1930s into the 1960s, as Andy Beaty, Seth Bradley, Bobby Joe Caldwell, Leroy Canaday, Larry Ellis, Audie (Buster) Fellows, LeRoy Haslag, Emmett Heath, Dale Hopkins, Kelly Jones, Billy Lee, Blackie Lewis, Newell Looney, Red Loveall, Milo McCubbin, Shorty Miller, George Morris, Red

Periman, Dale Potter, Paulette Reeves, Dusty Rhodes, Don Russell, Howe Teague, Zed Tennis, Bill Thornton, and Roy Wooliver. Most fiddlers who grew up from the 1930s into the 1960s, assuming that they had the necessary skills, performed at one time or another in some version of an opry show, radio program, or variety show.

Fiddlers with the requisite talent, ambition, and willingness to display their music and personae in front of audiences could seek steady work and even careers fiddling with an opry. The show provided a relatively stable venue, a predictable schedule, and an opportunity to young fiddlers who did not wish to travel with a touring band or relocate to one of the centers of the industry such as Nashville or Los Angeles.

It takes skill, ambition, and a measure of luck to be a successful and lasting professional musician. One must be comfortable crossing the borders between genres and styles, and a fiddler needs to be willing and able to alter and expand his or her fiddling skills to be versatile and salable. As Michael Breid (Arkansas Red), who began performing on oprys as a child in the 1950s, quips, "Music is my life—but I can't prove it." As John Hartford put it, "If you're clever enough, you might even get someone to give you money in return for your waltzes and breakdowns. Sometimes, it seems, however, that the fiddle is the most difficult instrument with which to earn a living—especially playing hillbilly style, or whatever you want to call it."[24]

The demands of the professional stage show or recording sessions mean that a fiddler becomes a member of a cast of musicians filling well-defined roles. A fiddler may play an entire show and play only accompaniment formulas such as kicks, tails, solos, riffs, fills, and runs to decorate and accent vocal numbers and the rest of the music. This is shaky ground for the typical old-time fiddler who is used to square dances, music parties, and fiddlers contests where the fiddler is the center of attraction rather than second banana.

Among problems fiddlers encounter when they test the waters with a professional show, dance band, or bluegrass band is whether to go ahead and jump in full-time. If they do so, they are often accused of selling out or going commercial, even while most "sidemen" like fiddlers are notoriously underpaid members of the music establishment.

Some of the influential players of former times, such as Don Russell, Lyman Enloe, Johnny Bruce, Delbert Spray, Pete McMahan, and Larry Ellis, were among those who were able to move back and forth between old-time fiddling and country music (and even bluegrass) without being branded—and most were gainfully employed with credible "day jobs." Enloe was a house painter, Bruce a family farmer and drainage tile installer, Spray a livestock breeder, McMahan a truck tire mechanic, Ellis an electrician.

If a fiddler becomes a working professional, as a role player in an ensemble, he or she tends to forfeit control over his or her own music. Fiddling may become less a thrilling artistic expression and quickly become more like *work*, with bosses, deadlines, long hours of rehearsal, difficulty saving money for retirement, travel fatigue, and potential family complications. Many talented young musicians who began such careers sooner or later decided to give it up; the old joke among musicians, "Don't give up your day job," is both dark humor and rueful reality. Others, like Dale Potter, Lonnie Robertson, and Michael Breid, became full-time working professionals in the music business, which can be an exciting and fulfilling trade, while enduring the ups and downs of performing for a living.

I asked Breid, who plays fiddle, banjo, guitar, bass, and other instruments as "Arkansas Red," what it takes to be a professional performer. Michael began his career at age seven in the 1950s on *The Brush Creek Follies* on Kansas City radio KMBC.

> Versiprosity (I don't think that's a word, but it's late). That's the key to being a successful show fiddler, guitarist, or spoon player. If a bluegrass style is wanted, study that style, as well as western swing, hot jazz fiddle a la Joe Venuti, and things like that. I'm always working because if they want bluegrass I can play that. If they want jazz or Merle Haggard country I can do that. Expose yourself to all sorts of music and learn just enough to make a fool of yourself and take the white folks' money. . . .
>
> Learn to be flexible. If you play a certain song in A and an entertainer who you have to play for says, "I sing it in B or B-flat," be able to play it in that key. Also listen to arrangements. Listen to intros and turnarounds. How many bluegrassers would be shocked if the guitar (rather than the fiddler) started the kickoff to "Uncle Pen" and the fiddler came in with a jazz intro that sounded like "Sweet Georgia Brown"?
>
> I would also say, "Be commercial." I love to play guitar behind the old time fiddle tunes, but one of my gigs requires that I do tunes by Elton John and James Taylor. I would say the words most associated with being a success in this business are "commercial, attitude, and flexible."
>
> I have known guitarists who insist that "da blues is the only music I like to play." That's fine if you can secure enough blues gigs to pay the rent, but what happens when "da blues gigs" are few and far between, your car payment is due, and you're hired to play with a band and the leader says, "Man, I hope you can play Bob Wills stuff, because that's what this gig is all about."
>
> I guess ambition or drive is a big part too. You have to appreciate nearly all kinds of music. I know my limits and I would not accept a gig playing heavy metal or rap. And it sure helps if you can read music too. I read music, but I don't sight read worth a damn. Luckily, like Glen Campbell I can read the number charts and chord charts, and have been lucky to have a pretty good ear. I worked a rodeo with Campbell once in Canada and I asked him about his music reading when he did sessions in L.A. and this is what he told me. "I can read, but not that well, but I can read chord charts, so when I have a certain part written out for me in musical notation I go over to the piano player and say, 'Man, this doesn't make sense to me. Did they write this correctly?' Usually the piano player will play it, and I'll say, 'OK, that's what I thought it said.' I've been blessed with a great ear, so when it comes to that part, I play it with no problem and pretend I'm reading it."
>
> Also having the right attitude. Don't walk into a gig thinking, "I can outplay any of these yokels." If you go to a session in Nashville, usually the musicians will *not* look like they just crawled out of a back alley Dumpster after an eight day drinking/

> drug binge. They look like they want to play the *session*, and producers like that. If they know the musicians know their instruments and are flexible enough to do what the producers want, then they will be invited back. The recording sessions I played in Springfield and Nashville were super because I went in with the attitude that this was a new experience for me and I was going to make the best of it. I found out that the other musicians had the same attitude.
>
> One other thing about being flexible: If the comedian gets sick, be able to fill in with a few jokes. If one of the singers suddenly gets ill on stage be ready to fill in with a song or instrumental. That was one of the great things I liked about working with Speedy Haworth when I was with Rex Allen. When Rex would get totally blitzed (which was most of the time) he would forget the words to a song or what song came next. If he forgot what song came next, he would turn to Speedy and say, "Play it Speedy," and Speedy would turn to the rest of us and say, "Wildwood Flower" or some such song and we would go right into it, just like it was part of the program. If Rex didn't come back on stage, Speedy would turn to me and say, "Grab your banjo." I'd go into a banjo standard, and then someone else would sing one, and then Rex would stagger back on stage and do "God Walks These Hills with Me," and no one but us would be the wiser. Attitude and flexibility are really the keys to success in this business. The old adage I love to use when people ask what kind of music I play, I reply with, "I'll play fish if you'll pay scale."[25]

Location had much to do with a fiddler's ability to join a show's house band. Zed Tennis (Christian County) and Ozark Red Loveall (Camden County) could easily travel to Springfield for KWTO radio programs and stage shows. LeRoy Haslag (Cole County) could easily travel from his home to the nearby tourist center at the Lake of the Ozarks to perform on Lee Mace's *Ozark Opry*. Many skilled performers had to make the tough decision whether to go on the road or move to Nashville or Los Angeles. In some instances, fiddlers relocated their families in order to take advantage of opportunities to perform on popular radio shows. Sometimes the relocation was modest enough to be compatible with a performer's family and long-range plans. Young single fiddlers were more apt to follow the music and jobs and move to Nashville, LA, or Las Vegas. The business has largely been seasonal, however, and some shows are shuttered during parts of the winter months.

A number of fiddlers were included in their show's recordings, and some produced their own private-label records to sell themselves. Jim Skiles (1918–2010), from Eldon, close to the Lake of the Ozarks, fiddled with the Lake of the Ozarks Square Dancers and the Valley Ranch Boys in the 1950s, performed over various radio stations, and later moved to California. Skiles's father was a violin maker. In the 1950s, Jim Skiles released his own 78 rpm recording of "Marmaduke's Hornpipe," representing a strong local dance fiddler cum show fiddler playing Missouri's most famous square-dance tune. Returning to Missouri, Skiles played bluegrass with the Gateway Bluegrass band for a time, but eventually, after a long trip home from a gig in northern Missouri or Iowa, "put the fiddle under the bed" and, because of family responsibilities, took no more trips to play fiddle.[26]

Bluegrass Fiddler Don Russell

Don Russell (1929–2000) of Winona (Shannon County) was among the first Missouri fiddlers in professional ensembles onstage and on radio to embrace bluegrass. Bluegrass music began to solidify in the middle 1940s under the influence of Bill Monroe and His Blue Grass Boys, and others. Bluegrass would become a global phenomenon. But in the early years, bluegrass was still thought of as "hillbilly" or "country" and performed in the traditional context of the opry show and radio program.

Russell was a guitarist and singer as well as a gifted fiddler. Don's father, James Walter Russell, was a fiddler in Shannon County. Don's brothers Amos and Bob Russell sang and played guitar, and other brothers played music, including Howard Russell. As Jim Russell recalls, Howard Russell was "the other fiddler in the family, nine years older than Don. I was told Howard learned to play young and did the 'medicine show' circuit."[27] Howard Russell played his father's violin.

In the mid-1940s, Don Russell formed a trio with Granville (Nick) Nichols and Urel Albert, all from Winona. They called themselves Urel Albert and the Rocky Road Playboys. Among their early attempts to make money having fun was fiddling for a medicine show for five dollars a night, promoting a patent medicine (a shin plaster), as recalled in a remarkable recording of "Orange Blossom Special" from a late winter 1966 fiddlers contest in Alton, Missouri, when Russell and Urel Albert performed again after many years (a recording conserved by Granville Nichols).

> *Urel Albert*: We was sitting over there at the house one day, pickin', like we always do. I had an old Kay guitar with a busted head and Don had an old fiddle with a big *man's head* on the end of it, with a couple glass *eyes*. And in walked a little old

At home in Winona, Don Russell with his friend and accompanist Urel Albert. (Courtesy Jim Russell)

man, from nowhere, just walked in the door, and says, "I wonder if you guys wanna *work*?" We said definitely *not*. He said, "Naw, I meant *playing music*." We said, "Well, now, we might try *that*." So he give us a job for five dollars a night at the medicine show, but it'd take ya all night to tell about it. Anyhow, that's the way *we* started.

Don Russell: Nineteen forty-seven, October.

In 1950 Don Russell and Urel Albert started performing with guitarist and singer Porter Wagoner, from nearby West Plains, in a bluegrass trio called the Blue Ridge Boys.[28] In addition to Russell, Albert, and Wagoner, the band included mandolinist Don Hoglen (who would later become a member of Larry Ellis's Greenside Up in Kansas City) and Granville Nichols (bass). In addition to performances live over KWTO radio in Springfield, the Blue Ridge Boys toured extensively in the region to promote KTWO's *Ozark Jubilee*. The band typically performed concerts wearing the homburg variant on the felted western hat emblematic of many country and bluegrass bands.

Jim Orchard, the pioneering bluegrass mandolin player from Shannon County, recalls being a high school student and finding his string trio almost comically up against the Blue Ridge Boys in a talent show in Winona. Wagoner, Albert, Nichols, and Russell were already well known, and all but Wagoner lived in Winona. Jim and two friends, Paul Brake and Jack Shockley, had formed a trio, and Jim signed them up for the talent contest at the Winona High School gymnasium to raise funds for the

As a youngster, Don Russell played guitar accompaniment for fiddlers and older musicians before staking out his own space as a fiddler, as custom has dictated for generations. At a music party in Winona: Russell (guitar, *second from right*), Urel Albert (mandolin, *left*), and others. (Courtesy Jim Russell)

Ozark Fiddler

Transcribed by Sharon Graf

as played by Don Russell 1960

"Ozark Fiddler" as played by Don Russell, 1960 (hear on the companion CD). (Transcription by Sharon Graf)

school: grand prize, fifteen dollars. Jack Shockley was a strong fiddler and guitarist, but Shockley did not like performing in front of an audience. Orchard talked him into it anyway; the boys had traveled a slow eighteen miles through winding hills and hollers to get to the contest, and they did love to play music.

> And we got over there, and guess who was on the talent show? Porter Wagoner and Granville Nichols and Urel Albert and Donnie Russell. I mean, they don't *come* any better than *that*!" Well, Jack said, "I'm not *playin*'!" They was back there in the back and you could *hear 'em*—man, they could *play*. Jack said, "I'm not playin'."
>
> You know what? We won it. 'Course we really *didn't*, but, *them* being *local*, they gave us the fifteen dollars [first prize], you know, and they got second place. . . . There's an underrated fiddle player, *Donnie Russell*. If he'd have stayed off of the sauce, you know—boy, *there* was a fiddle player.[29]

Don Russell then became the second fiddler on *The Ozark Opry*, following the departure of Billy Moore. Lonnie Hoppers recalls how Lee Mace "discovered" Don Russell. "Lee had lost his fiddle player [Moore]." Lonnie told Lee about Don living with his mother there. "Went down there and talked to him, and he played the fiddle for Lee, and Don just got in the car and come back with us, for the *Ozark Opry*."[30]

Among the recordings from that era are Don Russell's fiddling on a 45 rpm Starday record with Mace's subgroup, Lee Mace and His Ozark Opry Gang; Russell played versions of two classics of the old-time and bluegrass repertoire, "Steppin' in the Straw" (Mace's title for "Turkey in the Straw") and "Ozark Fiddler" ("Bill Cheatem"), with clog dancing.[31] On the record is the sound of jig dancing by Lee Mace, who was famous for his old-time steps. The group consisted of four musicians drawn from the larger cast to form a bluegrass band: Russell, Dale Sledd (banjo), Bob McCoy (guitar), and Mace (bass), all principals on the evolving Missouri bluegrass and country music scene.

After leaving *The Ozark Opry*, in 1963 Russell performed with Austin Wood's *Nashville Opry* in the Lake of the Ozarks, a show that competed for several years with Mace's show. Wood was a popular country music radio deejay and singer, blind, who had Nashville connections.[32] Russell played in another bluegrass ensemble in the same period, the Ozark Mountain Boys, with Dale Sledd, Urel Albert, Granville Nichols, Bobby Crabtree, and Lonnie Hoppers.

Leroy Canaday: A Night at Grandma's

While the opry entertainment thrived in the Missouri Ozarks, fiddlers in the central and northern regions of the state also had their days. For a number of years, before moving to Texas in 2005 to live with his daughter and her family, Leroy Canaday performed at a local show in northeastern Missouri called *Grandma's Country Music*. Little Dixie–style fiddler Canaday came up as a dance fiddler but was versatile and enjoyed entertaining people. He played in contests, oprys, radio shows, bluegrass bands, church services, and concerts.

Born in 1928, Canaday grew up on the family farm in the Maud community in the gentle prairie and woods of southwestern Shelby and northern Monroe Counties. Leroy's Irish father, Pierre, came to Missouri around 1900 from the vicinity of Oscaloosa, Iowa; his mother, Patsy Gertrude Palliser, was "mostly English" and from the Springfield area of Illinois. All of their children—Jewell Marie, Leonard Cecil, Orville Edward (Rooster), and Leroy Francis (Red)—had red hair, except for Leonard.

Canaday heard his first fiddling in the 1930s at the country store two miles up the road in Maud. At Tipton's store in Maud, as well as the nearby Granville community center, people gathered for sessions of fiddling and dancing. Electricity did not reach farms here until the late 1940s, so people came to listen to programs through the speakers of Tipton's battery-powered radio. People could tune in programs of an astonishing variety, from Canada to Mexico as well as the well-known Nashville shows and WOS in Jefferson City.

> The fiddlers, most of them, would get together at the old country store down there. That's where I learned some of my tunes, like "Soldiers Joy" and "Mississippi Sawyer" and "Ragtime Annie" and tunes like that. Used to be a Wright family of musicians who played for dances, they came up there. Had a saxophone, a horn, they played the fiddle, the banjo, about five or six of them. A couple of them would come up there on a Saturday night if they wasn't playing some place. The old storekeeper would give us a sody pop and a sandwich if we wanted and we'd sit there and play from the time they started till they quit.[33]

Leroy began playing at eight, using his elder brother Leonard's unused violin kept atop his mother's upright piano. "I'd sit there and look at it, and it got the best of me." Without a bow, Leroy made one out of a choke rod from a Model T Ford truck. Lacking horsehair for the bow, he rosined the metal choke rod. For violin strings, he used strings from a guitar. Finally, his father "got tired of listening to it, so he got the Sears-Roebuck catalog out and ordered me a fiddle bow." Canaday essentially taught himself to play "by trial and error." "When you say self-taught, naturally you learn by *watching*. You know, I'd go up to the old store and watch these guys. From observation, how they held the bow, try to figure out which one of them was holding it right and which one was holding it wrong. I had to learn that I had a little finger; it took a long time to learn that I had a little finger. You learn from doing." He learned to play guitar, chord the piano, and play chords on a plectrum (four-string) banjo, tuning it like the lower four strings of a five-string banjo.

Leroy's chief influences were the red-hot fiddlers on *The Grand Ole Opry* broadcasts. Canaday's idol as a teenager, Curly Fox, was known for exhibition pieces like "Johnson's Old Grey Mule" and "Listen to the Mocking Bird." He learned "Black Mountain Rag" in scordatura tuning (A–E–A–C#) from Tommy Jackson's 45 rpm record.

Leroy Canaday, Moberly, Missouri. (2000)

> Nashville. Grand Ole Opry. Listened to it *every* Saturday night, *every* Saturday night. At first, we didn't have a radio. One of the neighbors had one of those great big old boxes with the speaker sitting on top of it. There'd be four or five of the neighbors would gang up over there, and instead of having a TV party (like we do now) we'd have a Grand Ole Opry party, and have popcorn and like that. And I'll tell you, when the fiddle players come on, everybody better be quiet! The batteries would get weak, and you'd get your ears right down against the speaker and try to hear it. I think one of the first fiddlers I heard down there (on the Opry) was Curly Fox. The Fruit Jar Drinkers, The Gully Jumpers, they were all fiddle bands. That's where I got my inspiration. I *had* to learn to play the fiddle.[34]

Canaday won his first major competition in front of the courthouse in the county seat of Paris at age thirteen. As usual, his older brother Orville was his guitar second. He became an instant celebrity, a teenager competing with established master fiddlers in an area famous for its contest champions.

Leroy was not destined to be a farmer. He "didn't see much future in it," particularly after spending his childhood helping his family make their way through the Great Depression. His first paying job off their eighty-acre farm was at age ten in 1937, an after-school job nailing cheese boxes together in a plant in Shelbina for a penny each. He also worked at a service station while in high school and graduated from Shelbina High in 1946. In the fall of 1947, Canaday left the farm and moved a few miles west to Moberly. He was "following the fiddle."

Moberly was a prosperous railroad, manufacturing, and farm town, with opportunities for a good fiddler. Leroy met his future wife, Betty Ransdell, and they married in 1949. Leroy began playing in local dance bands, made some connections, and began earning money. A key acquaintance he made was band leader Virgil (Hap) Goodman. At Osterloh's Music Store, he traded the violin he got from his brother Leonard and fifty dollars cash for a good-quality factory instrument. "I had to play about a month and a half of dances to pay for it." Later, Canaday's number-one violin was a Guarnerius copy presented to him by an old friend, Kathryn Williams.

Canaday played fiddle and rhythm guitar in honky-tonk dance bands around Moberly and worked with Hap Goodman and the Shady Valley Gang on radio shows on KMMO (Marshall) and at dances across the region. Before their radio program at the Marshall station, they would play in Glasgow at the Highway Inn on Friday night and then drive an hour west to Marshall and do their half-hour Saturday-morning show, which they played from around 1948 to 1951. The band would then drive back to Moberly and play dances at the Dream Boat nightclub (formerly the Show Boat). "Never missed a Saturday night for five years." Leroy recalls that their theme tune was the old fiddle breakdown "Bile Them Cabbage Down." The band featured Hap Goodman and the Stuck brothers, with others sometimes taking part. Goodman did the talking and played guitar, banjo, and a bit of violin, bass, and a pedal steel guitar that he designed and built. Burl Stuck played five-string banjo, "flat top" (rhythm) guitar, and his brother Orville played steel and flattop.

Canaday also played in an ensemble that included pianist Edna Lewis and her brother Francis Strayhall on drums. Canaday chorded electric guitar (and played occasional lead) on the round-dance tunes and fiddled the hoedowns for the square dances. The square dances were called by callers hired by the dancers. Canaday played in fiddlers contests in the 1950s and 1960s, but left the contest scene and began playing in a bluegrass band. In the 1970s, with son Norman on banjo, daughter Kathy on bass, and guitarist Billy Brewer, Leroy formed the Shady Valley Grass, performing across Missouri and specializing in three-part "family harmony" singing.

For much of his working life, Leroy was an employee of Magic City Cleaners in Moberly, retiring from there in 1982, but he also worked in maintenance at the Moberly Regional Medical Center while developing his business, Leroy's Carpet Cleaning. He retired in 2001.

"Granny's Opry," as most call it, is located south of Paris on Mark Twain Lake. Some two hours from St. Louis, the Army Corps of Engineers reservoir attracts

Virgil Goodman and the Happy Valley Gang, 1950. *Left to right*: Leroy Canaday, Orville Stuck, Herman (Red) Vanderpool (replacing the absent Burl Stuck), and Virgil (Hap) Goodman with the triple-neck steel guitar he built. (Courtesy Canaday)

fishermen, campers, and tourists. Granny's is a metal-clad pole barn and opened for business in 1995 run by J. W. and Adelaide (Granny) Minor. There are theater seats, a stage and sound system, lights, and dressing rooms. The concession stand sells popcorn, hot dogs, coffee, cokes, cookies, and souvenirs such as T-shirts and baseball caps stitched with "Grandma's Country Music." Consumption of alcoholic beverages is against the rules; smoking is allowed outside the building.

I attended the opry one evening in December 2000 with Leroy and Betty Canaday. Leroy was the guest fiddler for the evening. A modest version of the big theater shows at the Lake of the Ozarks and Branson, Granny's has the benefit of a sharp, stage-savvy house band in western costume playing vintage instruments—a Gibson Les Paul electric guitar, Gibson "Barney Kessel" jazz guitar, Fender Stratocaster, Martin

Charlie Cook's Waltz

Transcribed by Sharon Graf

as played by Leroy Canaday

Note: The first time that Canaday plays the waltz is notated here. Canaday repeats the tune with slight variations, which are not notated (source:VRCD 353).

"Charlie Cook's Waltz" ("G Waltz") is a challenging but affecting tune composed by Mr. Cook (1910–60), from Boone County in the 1940s (hear on the companion CD). Virgil Smith, known for waltzes, said Cook's fiddling was "as smooth as a clock ticking" (December 3, 2001). (Transcription by Sharon Graf)

D-28 acoustic "rhythm" guitar, and a Rickenbacker bass guitar. Such instruments tell the audience that this show is likely to have professional-level musicians to match the fine instruments. The house band often includes an electric pedal steel guitar, an almost obligatory instrument for a classic country band. On occasions when Canaday is a guest performer, a violin completes the ensemble to a standard that Bob Wills would approve. The show starts at eight, and there are two sets of music separated by an intermission. The evening winds down around ten thirty.

The house band arrived around six to go through tunes and set up.[35] Saturday night was a typical evening of fiddling for Canaday. In years past, Canaday performed as a regular featured artist with the Dun-Ells, a popular country music band in central Missouri during the 1970s and 1980s and into the 1990s, featuring Fred and Phyllis Dunwoody and Warren and Pat Elliott, as well as with other such regional groups. Canaday was also active in bluegrass and old-time fiddlers contests.[36] Other theaters in northern and northeastern Missouri where Canaday fiddled include the Wilcox Opry Barn in Macon, Injun Joe's Opry near Perry, the Mark Twain Opry near Monroe City, and the Cannon Dam Opry. Name artists from Nashville are often a standard feature when budgets allow, and Leroy Canaday has performed with country stars Barbara Fairchild, Connie Smith, and Box Car Willie.

The repertoires of these shows run the gamut of classic country songs made popular by stars such as Roy Acuff, Hank Williams, Ernest Tubb, Faron Young, Ray Price, Kitty Wells, the Carter Family, Merle Haggard, Marty Robbins, Patsy Cline, and Bob Wills and the Texas Playboys. There are some classic rock-and-roll tunes as well as show tunes, jazz, swing, blues, and sentimental ballads, so the entertainment crosses a century of genres and hit music. The set lists in December 2000 included "Y'all Come," "Old Christmas Card," "Me and Bobby McGee," "For the Good Times," "St. Louis Blues," "Rock around the Clock," "Blue Christmas," "Faded Love," "Candy Kisses," "Crying My Heart Out over You," "Help Me Make It through the Night," "Jingle Bells," "Jingle Bell Rock," "Song Sung Blue," and "On Wings of a Dove." Canaday's "fiddle specials" were "Ragtime Annie," "Maiden's Prayer," "I Don't Love Nobody," "Red Wing," "Grey Eagle," "Down Yonder," "Westphalia Waltz," and Canaday's favorite, "Listen to the Mocking Bird." And yes, the emcee asked Leroy to play "Orange Blossom Special." The repertoire is eclectic but grounded in a classic country sound and instrumental arrangement, music that appeals to audiences, generally an older lot whose tastes tend toward hit songs from twenty or fifty years ago.

A show like Grandma's Country Music feels like the year 1950 or 1955, before the immense growth of rock and roll, the Folk Music Revival, nationalized progressive contest-style fiddling, and other forces began to move the walls around between different kinds of popular music. It was also a time before the sweeping popularity of FM radio, when people in northern Missouri could receive clear-channel AM stations. Musicians of Canaday's generation continue to remark on the importance of those radio stations in sparking their interests in music. Leroy Canaday died in May 2016.

One of the consequences of the popularity of radio, records, and shows is that traditional social dancing has suffered. While many early shows featured live square dancing by cast members and guests, dancing was becoming merely a cog in the machine for the seated audience. On the other hand, a wealth of new music was taken into the fiddler's world by these media and the venues. Many of today's ironclads therefore are not dance tunes but listening tunes. Listening tunes feed into the contest scene, with the result that set pieces and fancy performances competed for favor against old dance tunes among contest fiddlers, judges, and audiences. And it is notable that, while group and couple dancing is absent from the opry barn and stage-show scene, individual participatory jig and step dancing is a familiar sight, as people get up out of their chairs and jig to a fiddler's hot "Black Mountain Rag" or "Soldier's Joy." Such dancing lends a welcome air of serendipity to oprys and brings pleasure to both audience and band.

Rooster Creek: Missouri's Last Live AM Radio Opry?

Rooster Creek had a long, fine run. It sailed onto the airwaves of KFAL Fulton to great acclaim in 1958 and slipped away, barely noticed, fifty-two years later, in 2010. The show was an echo of the kind of playground of old-time dancing and music parties, gregarious musicians, and makers of imaginary home brew that nostalgia says typified old-time music in days gone by. It was also a bastion of live fiddle music, classic country songs, salty vaudeville humor, and improvised commercials for faithful sponsors.[37] People loved *Rooster Creek*, and they loved its King Arthur, Ron Lutz.

"Big Ron" Lutz was born in the rural Forest Green community of Chariton County in 1928, a fiddler, guitarist, trumpeter, harmonica player, and square-dance caller. Ron learned to play fiddle music from Bill Sharon, a well-known player in the Chariton and Carroll County area of west-central Missouri. Lutz recalls that Bill Sharon played a number of unusual local tunes, such as "Tobacco Worm's Eye."[38] Lutz was a born wordsmith and natural performer with a charm and charisma that made friends easily. He was also given a sonorous basso profundo speaking and singing voice, a voice made for radio. He gained the nickname "Big Ron" for good reason—he was more than six-foot-six and weighed in at 350 pounds when he started out as a young country music deejay at AM stations in Brookfield and Moberly (north-central Missouri) before moving to Fulton, the Callaway County seat east of Columbia famous for its radio fiddlers, such as Vee Latty, Daniel Boone Jones, Bill Katon, George Morris, the Cuno brothers, Keith Orchard, and Jake Hockemeyer.[39]

After moving to Fulton, Lutz put together country bands to play for fish fries, picnics, pie suppers, and family reunions. But most of all, Ron sang and played rhythm guitar with his band at dances at watering holes and halls such as Reed's Lake, east of Fulton; Hillbilly Village, west of Jefferson City; and the Pow Wow Lounge and the Rebel Room in Columbia, where Fulton's KFAL radio broadcast live shows on

Sunday afternoons. Such nightspots were magnets for country musicians, fiddlers, and dancers who did not mind the rough reputations of these post–World War II venues where booze flowed freely and a person (even a musician) was likely to get punched for staring too intently at another person's date.

In 1958 Lutz was playing a dance at Reed's Lake. During a break, he chatted with KFAL's Bob Nichols. Nichols and Roger Fox owned the station and suggested devoting some airtime to help promote Ron's dance dates. Ron said, "Fine, you let us do that, and I'll try to sell some advertising on the show," and Ron's radio show was born. The show was modeled in part on the farm-and-home daytime shows of the time. George Rutherford, Bubby Hayden, Bill Benskin, Russell Orchard, and Seth Bradley became regular musicians on the program. In other early versions of the *Rooster Creek* band, Seth Bradley (violin) and George Rutherford (lead vocalist, rhythm guitar) continued, Loren Gordon ("Cousin Loren") played lead electric guitar, Jack Brammer played drums, and, in 1961–62, the young John Hartford occasionally played fiddle and five-string banjo (and stashed his sleeping bag behind Ron's couch). After the death of Seth Bradley, fiddlers who became regulars on *Rooster Creek* included Francis Stephens, LeRoy Haslag, Rhonda Vincent, John Hartford, Bob Hagan, and Harold Leake, and there was a steady supply of visiting fiddlers who would take a turn, such as Bill Thornton, Keith Orchard, Bill Craighead, Win Kallenbach, Chris Brashear,

The *Rooster Creek* band on KFAL radio, ca. 1958. *Left to right*: Ron Lutz, George Rutherford, Loren Gordon, and Seth Bradley. At this time, the band was performing as the Rooster Creek Jamboree. (Courtesy John G. Stewart)

Charlie Walden, Chris German, Joe Hinkebein, and Howard Marshall. A number of bluegrass banjoists appeared as regular *Rooster Creekers* after bluegrass became more popular in the late 1960s, such as Steve Bode, Kevin Hendrix, and Dick Davis.

For the first several years, *Rooster Creek* was tape-recorded in the KFAL studio in the redbrick Palace Hotel on Fulton's courthouse square. In the 1970s, KFAL moved to a modest building on the northwest side of town. The studio building is small, and recording sessions were somehow managed by Ron, with a jostle of musicians and guests crowding around a microphone. During an unfortunate episode, *Rooster Creek* was evicted from the building, due to some shenanigans; new station management was displeased with the results of a rowdy recording session. It seems that some University of Missouri students from Columbia had visited the recording session in the studio and neglected to sweep up their empty beer cans and spilled ashtrays; as Bob Hagan recalls, "The cans and such were picked up by Ron who opened the place in the AM; but it was the crack in the glass front door that did it!"[40]

Rooster Creek sponsors stayed loyal to the program and liked the down-home and neighborly commercials. So "Ron and the boys" moved their evening recordings sessions and picking parties first to a friend's basement, then to a Davis Oil warehouse, and eventually to Ron's backyard at his farm east of town. An old trailer camper became the studio. Set up on blocks and provided with minimal climate control, the camper soon acquired the title "Rooster Nest" and grew crammed with rows of LPs and 45 rpm records, tapes, CDs, memorabilia, photos, instruments, chairs, and various new and old studio equipment and microphones.

Ron always sat back against the north wall in a massive wooden armchair built to accommodate his girth. Under the window along the east wall was positioned an old Formica kitchen table that supported the recording equipment and microphone. From his throne, Ron welcomed band members and guests and called the shots at the Thursday-night recording sessions. The Rooster Nest could hold only a few visitors, and only if they were willing to wedge themselves into a dusty corner or stand on the back porch and lean in through the doorway. Any visitor was likely to be invited to step up to the microphone with a song. The intimate space, with a fiddler's elbow likely to knock into a guitar or singer, was part of the ambience of the evening. The back of the camper had been enlarged with a small room for musicians' instrument cases, as well as space for an old, battered Philco refrigerator—that essential *Rooster Creek* accessory, bought from fiddler Bob Hagan for a dollar.

The Thursday-evening sessions began as musicians began to arrive. Visiting, informal singing and music, tuning of instruments, rerigging and testing of microphone cables and the cassette recorder, and discussions of the weather, cattle auction prices, guitar strings on sale somewhere, oddities of local politics, and so forth could take a few minutes or an hour. If family responsibilities, a truant cow, or a hay baler needed attention, some band members might arrive only just in time for the mid- to late-evening recording. The ensemble varied, and the informal music before and after the recording could last to midnight if there happened to be an inspired crew on hand. One of the pleasures of being a guest musician was that, if you passed muster, you were always invited back; once a *Rooster Creeker*, always a *Rooster Creeker*. Ron used to say, "Everyone is welcome, at least once." Bob Hagan remembers Ron telling a guest musician, "Welcome—do anything you think you're big enough to!"

A core of ready and reliable *Rooster Creek* Boys was necessary if Ron was going to be able to get on tape a usable session for airing on KFAL the next Saturday morning. If too few regulars or passable guest musicians were on hand, or if the mood of the core cast was not upbeat enough, recording would not take place; visiting and jamming simply continued, and a tape from a previous show would be aired the following Saturday. Ron always had "one in the can," just in case a taping did not go as expected.

Rebel Yell was the official relaxant and lubricant among *Rooster Creek* regulars. Rebel Yell is a bourbon made in Kentucky. Only one or two shops in Fulton stocked Rebel Yell, and a certain *Rooster Creeker* was tasked with bringing the evening's bottle. By the time *Rooster Creek* closed up in 2010, passing around the Rebel Yell and fetching beers from the Philco had become only a minor part of the event. Like the rollicking radio shows of the past, and the 1920s "Corn Likker Still in Georgia" images of old-time country music making, the taking of intoxicating beverages as part of the session was going out of fashion.

As a live program, recording *The Rooster Creek Show* could be wonderfully unpredictable. Songs and instrumentals were tried out in the early hours, and if something sounded good to Ron, he would tell Mark Olson (Ron's right-hand man) to "write it down." Others, including guest musicians, were welcome to chip in with a "Write it down, Mark!" when something sounded good. People often asked Ron to sing a favorite song among the many he sang well. The sets of music were scribbled on the tablet in the order they would be recorded. When Ron felt he had enough titles to fill thirty minutes, the recording commenced. There was always a mix of classic country and bluegrass standards and one or two fiddle instrumentals. If Ron was especially happy with a hard-driving fiddle breakdown, he would joyously start singing square-dance calls in the background—a delightful experience for everyone in the room. "Chicken Reel," a familiar old hoedown, always opened, and sometimes closed, the program.

Once the tape started rolling, the session was all business. The set list was recorded straight through, with no stops or retakes. If someone made a bobble or forgot some lyrics, the recorder kept right on recording. Whatever was recorded went on the air. The patter among musicians and guests crammed into the room could be spirited. KFAL station identifications and announcements were made at the station before the show came on. Following the Thursday-evening taping sessions, a band member took the half-hour cassette to the station on Friday, where in the show's final years the tape would be loaded into a computer and Saturday morning someone would push a button to broadcast the show at 11:25 a.m.

Commercials and announcements were presented without rehearsal by Ron and the boys—some of them were girls[41]—with guests joining in the fun, to plug an upcoming event, brag about a new CD, or mention a neighbor in the hospital. The ad-libbed commercials were often spiced with interjections by someone who had recently benefited from a sponsor's services. This sense of reality and immediacy, and the audience hearing that the *Rooster Creek* Boys endorsed the products, made the commercials very effective. Countless listeners declared "Ron sent me!" as they bought a set of tires, a load of lumber, or a new mattress or talked to Gary Sparks (a band member and friend of Ron's for more than twenty years) about purchasing a wheel-chair-accessible van. Some sponsors stayed with Ron, a genuine celebrity, from the beginning to the end of the show's career. Taco Bell became a sponsor because nearby stores were operated by Dick Davis, a five-string banjo player who appeared on the show and whose family business, Davis Oil Company, had been among Ron's first sponsors in the 1950s.

In the first generation of the *Rooster Creek* Boys, Lutz played trumpet and guitar and sometimes harmonica, autoharp, and acoustic guitar. The fiddler was Seth Bradley, rhythm guitarist and lead singer George Rutherford, lead electric guitarist Warren Gordon, and drummer Jack Brammer. Personnel shifted, and in 1960 or 1961 Francis Stephens joined the cast as fiddler (after the death of Seth Bradley), and Clyde Padgett joined the show as singer and rhythm guitar player. In the late 1960s and early 1970s, the regulars were Lutz, Rutherford, Russell Orchard, Dennis Schubert, and fiddlers Harold Leake and, on occasion, Bob Hagan.

Nashville stars on tour, such as Ernest Tubb, Jeanne Shepherd, and Cowboy Copas, sometimes stopped by the KFAL studio to say hello to Ron, and he became good friends with Tex Ritter. His daily country radio show on KFAL was called *Ron's Ranch*, and he used Chubby Wise's fiddle record of "Lost Indian" as his theme song.

Ron retired from KFAL in 1995.

Seth Bradley

Seth Bradley became Ron's first fiddler on the radio show. Bradley was a seasoned contest and dance fiddler known to radio audiences. In one sparkling instance in his youth, Bradley won a fiddlers contest that included the formidable George Morris of Columbia as well as other popular fiddlers.[42] Bradley's fiddling was smooth and his repertoire versatile, which suited the job of the radio fiddler. Fiddlers listening in learned tunes and improved their own versions of tunes by studying what Seth was doing. Among his specialties were "Mississippi Sawyer," "Lost Indian," and "Red Wing."

It was Bradley who was responsible for the *Rooster Creek* title. The legend began as a joke. Bradley's farm was located in southern Callaway County, on a branch of Auxvasse Creek, southeast of Ham's Prairie and north of Steedman. Ambrose Haley, a retired vaudevillian who had been an itinerant tent-show musician and singer and had performed on KMOX with Pappy Cheshire ensembles, was living in an old stone house on the Bradley farm.[43]

In 1957 Seth Bradley and Ambrose Haley decided to order 150 baby chicks in what was called a "straight run." An order of straight-run hatchery chicks is an even split between males and females; the valuable females become egg-laying hens. One spring morning, Ron was on Bradley's farm squirrel hunting along a small branch of a tributary of Auxvasse Creek that ran through the property. As the sun was coming up, Ron heard a great disturbance. Ron soon saw that there were 135 baby roosters strutting around learning to crow.[44] The branch running through Bradley's farm was small enough to step across and had no name, and on the spot Ron decided to call it "Rooster Creek"—and Bradley and Ambrose agreed. The following year, Ron named his radio show *The Rooster Creek Show*. Haley and the Bradley family had few eggs that winter—but plenty of fried chicken.[45]

As the years went on, more and more stations were swept up in the corporate homogenization of the music industry. Today the majority of country stations air a narrow selection of music selected in distant offices and downloaded from satellites to computers. The day of the local country music deejay on the small-town radio station is virtually over. Recent station breaks on KFAL announce "The Big 900, KFAL, your home for country legends and the stars of NASCAR racing."[46] The music now, by comparison to the old days, is largely a mix of rock-and-roll-style country and classic country, and KFAL is part of a media conglomerate.

In 2007 Ron recorded a CD called *Jack of Diamonds* with some of his favorite songs. Produced by Kirby Crane, the CD is a compilation of studio recordings and live on-air songs from *The Rooster Creek Show*. The songs range from "Silver-Haired Daddy" and "Dark as a Dungeon" to "Streets of Laredo" and "Amazing Grace."[47]

The final ensemble of the *Rooster Creek* Boys in 2010 included, in addition to Ron Lutz, Mark Olson of Fulton, Harold Leake of Millersburg (violin), Clyde Padgett of Fulton, Kyle Brown of Jefferson City, and Kirby Crane of Jefferson City. The last

A highlight of John Hartford's last visit to Fulton was a reunion with Ron Lutz, Hartford's radio mentor, and Hartford took part in the recording session for the show. Lutz, Hartford, November 2000. (Photo by Nyle Beatty; courtesy Mark Olson)

The Rooster Nest, where *The Rooster Creek Show* was taped. (2010)

session added guest musicians Dick Davis, Bob Hagan, Joe Hinkebein, Tish Hinkebein, and Kathy Gordon. Bob Hagan had been a regular Rooster Creeker years ago, and Davis, Hinkebein (mandolin, violin), and Gordon (acoustic bass) had been regular guests in recent years. These friends and musical colleagues continue to hold occasional jam sessions in the Rooster Nest, and broadcasting some special shows and reunion shows on KFAL has been discussed.

The final broadcast aired July 3, 2010. This show had been recorded several weeks before, in late May, when Ron decided that the end of the show was coming. Due to ill health (he died in 2011), Ron wanted a final show recorded and ready to go on the Saturday morning when he would ring down the curtain on Rooster Creek. In an unusual move, the May session had recorded more than one hundred minutes of favorite songs and tunes for the final program in July. Ron began the last show with a typical wisecrack in his deep bass voice: "Ladies and gentlemen, the following program is politically *uncorrect.*" As "Chicken Reel" was played in the background, led by Harold Leake, Ron then said, "Good morning, everybody! Once again it's time for country music on *The Rooster Creek Show.* We invite you to stay tuned because, after fifty-two years of Saturday-morning fun here on KFAL—we're gonna hang it up. I know it's a long time. We've had a lot of fun. But like the old country song goes, 'nothin's born to live forever.' Fifty-two years on 900, KFAL. I got it figured out, boys—it's somewhere around two thousand seven hundred and some-odd shows we've had on KFAL. And this brings us down to the final one."

This extralong show aired in its entirety on July 3, 2010. In his final sign-off, Ron bid farewell to his audience much as he had done for fifty-two years. "This is Ron saying, bye-bye, be good, be careful, and—*let's* come to dinner, boys."

Brochure from the Current River Opry at the Eminence Theater, Eminence, Missouri. (Courtesy Jim Orchard)

Opry Entrepreneurs and Born Showmen

7

What do you say to a fiddle player who's dressed in a three-piece suit?

"Will the defendant please rise."

—Larry Ellis, Big Creek Country Show

Evolution: "Riverways Opry" to "Ozark Music at the VFW Hall"

One of Missouri's best-known shows was the Current River Opry—in its infancy called the Riverways Opry. The show was mounted in several locations before it closed when management changed, but its successors evolved through four more locations. Despite the ups and downs, the spirit and pattern set by this creative and influential show continue. The story illustrates the lasting attraction of the concept—and the vital role of individual citizens to nourishing cultural institutions.

In the 1940s, the beloved pie suppers of former times had begun to evaporate with the consolidation of rural schools, where learning took place during the weekdays and on the weekends the buildings served as gathering places. With the desks moved aside, a square dance could be organized on a Saturday.[1] In 1948 Shannon County still had 110 one-room country schools; the last was shuttered in 1974.[2]

The Riverways Opry started on a Saturday night in May 1966 in an old red barn at a campground on the Current River, next to Big Spring State Park, south of Van Buren in Carter County.[3] "Riverways Opry" was an apt name. It referenced *The Grand Ole Opry*'s popularity and format, and it brought to mind the clear rivers, trout fishing, and recreational areas nestled in the spectacular Ozark Mountains. The region was evolving as a magnet for tourists and part of the newly organized Ozark Scenic Riverways National Park, formed in 1964 along the Jacks Fork and Current Rivers in Carter, Shannon, Dent, and Texas Counties. A boom in tourism was just on the horizon.

This was an era when talented local lads and lassies could imagine careers making music in one or another entertainment arena. After all, those boys from down the road at Winona had made it big on *The Ozark Opry* (Donnie Russell) and in Nashville (Urel Albert), and Porter Wagoner, from West Plains, was a rising star in Nashville. Those effervescent Dillard brothers from up in Salem put together a bluegrass band and were established in Hollywood, selling records, playing folk-music clubs, posing as "the Darling Boys" on *The Andy Griffith Show*, swapping songs with Bob Dylan and Joan Baez backstage at the Newport Folk Festival, and in their stage routines making the world aware of the comic nuances of maintaining Ozark privies and moonshine stills. Harold Morrison, from the mythical "High Lonesome" in Douglas County, took his banjo to Nashville and made it. Lonnie Hoppers up in Urbana made records and picked his Gibson "bowtie" banjo on *The Grand Ole Opry* with Bill Monroe and the Bluegrass Boys, for goodness's sake.

The Riverways Opry was organized by Ray Randolph. The first house band included Urel Albert, Gilbert (Arkie) Cannady, Clarence and Mary Ann Crider, Carolyn Burroughs, fiddler Clark Weaver, and Kenny Seaman, a promising young banjo player tutored in his Scruggs rolls by Michael Breid. Many of these musicians were from musical families and had started out playing pie suppers and talent shows; some were now radio performers, and others would find careers in the country music "theater" boom in Branson and other locations that would evolve in coming years, as well as in bluegrass music and bluegrass festivals.

By September 1966, the Van Buren location had outlived its purpose but had served well as the launching pad. Looking for a more comfortable, larger, and secure indoor site, Carl Seaman assumed ownership of the show and bought the old movie theater on Main Street in Eminence (population 600), the seat of Shannon County. Seaman moved the cast there and christened the show the Current River Opry. Seaman kept the opry momentum going, and, as his son Kenny writes, "It's

At the Current River Opry, Eminence. *Left to right*: Jim Orchard, Guy Stevenson, Kenny Seaman, Hubert Woolsey, and Andy Bressler. (Courtesy Jim Orchard)

doubtful that this particular show would have continued without Dad's purchase of the theater and bringing in regional and national guests. Ten-plus successful years really paved the way for all the following opry shows to continue." Seaman actively promoted the show, including securing local sponsors to air the Current River Opry on AM radio KXEN in St. Louis and Festus, broadcasting a weekly half-hour show that gave wide exposure to the show and helped establish a strong fan base in the St. Louis area.[4]

The Eminence Theatre seated up to 270, and most Saturday nights the house was packed, especially if a Nashville superstar was scheduled. Word had spread of this show in the heart of the Ozark Mountains. Nashville headliners such as Ernest Tubb, Roy Acuff, Stringbean, Flatt and Scruggs, Jim and Jesse, the McCormick Brothers, Jimmy Martin and the Sunny Mountain Boys, Benny Martin, and the Country Gentlemen (their first concert west of the Mississippi River) began booking appearances at the Current River Opry.

A bluegrass band grew out of the show, Kenny Seaman and the Current River Drifters, a popular ensemble at festivals and on records in the late 1960s.[5] Seaman, who had been the Eminence high school principal, moved to Fort Collins, Colorado, in 1975 to take a position teaching school and before long founded a new band there, the Bluegrass Patriots.[6]

After ten good years for the Current River Opry in the Eminence Theatre, in the fall of 1976 administrative complications, the death of Carl Seaman, and a fire in the theater—the furnace blew up—forced it to move. The new location became the Veterans of Foreign Wars (VFW) Hall in Eminence, and the show was mounted there from 1976 to 1993. Leadership and administration were taken on by Clarence and Mary Ann Crider. The Eminence VFW site did not prove entirely satisfactory, although the building and hall were excellent. Clarence Crider, one of the founders and star performers (a Chet Atkins–style electric guitarist), suggested moving to the VFW Hall in Summersville, some eighteen miles west on the Texas County line and a location drawing from the same Ozark region of fans and musicians. Thus, in 1993 the Current River Opry moved to Summersville.

The Current River Opry enjoyed a successful run at the Summersville VFW Hall from 1993 to 2010. The house band, Jim Orchard and the Bressler Brothers, was a popular ensemble that included Orchard (mandolin) and brothers Andy and Alvin Bressler of Eminence playing guitar and bass and singing bone-chilling close bluegrass and gospel harmony. Other members of the group were Clarence and Mary Ann Crider and, at various times, fiddlers Gene Roberts, Dean Von Allmen, and Odie Mullins. Jim Orchard at this time was switching back and forth between playing mandolin and violin. The show continued offering the mix of country, gospel, and bluegrass vocals and instrumentals, with at least one fiddle tune in each set, and guests were included.

The situation at Summersville changed. Clarence Crider (who was blind) was injured and could no longer perform regularly. The Bressler Brothers and Jim Orchard parted company. The Bresslers formed a new bluegrass ensemble with Alvin's sons,

Bruce and Scott; later, the band included mandolinist Harry Wagganer and fiddler Roger Williams.

With the Current River Opry at Summersville on the verge of shutting down in 2010, its administration was assumed by Sergio Ronzani, who had moved to the area from New Jersey and was an ardent country music fan. Because Clarence Crider prevented the newcomers from using the "Current River Opry" name, Ronzani decided to advertise the show as "Saturday Night Music." In official terms, the Current River Opry name was lost. But the concept continued. Jim Orchard stayed on as mandolinist and part-time fiddler; since the 1980s, Jim had been focusing on performing as a fiddler and alternated instruments. Clarence Crider hosted the show and led the band. There was no payroll for the band. Donations were received at the door to help defray the costs of keeping the hall open. Unfortunately, Ronzani was unable to keep the show going, and it was shuttered in November 2014.

At the same time the opry and then "Saturday Night Music" were happening Saturdays in Summersville, beginning in 2002 Jim Orchard helped organize a Friday-night show at Weaver's RV Campground with Larry Deatherage. Weaver's was located a few miles from Willow Springs on US Highway 60 about equidistant between Willow Springs and Mountain View, some twenty miles southwest of Summersville (in more populous Texas County). Jim named the show "Weavers' Pickin' Parlor," with Deatherage in charge. Depending on where a person lived, people informally called the show "the Willow Springs opry" or "the Mountain View opry." The house at Weaver's included, at different times, veteran musicians such as fiddlers Cliff Bryan and Dean Von Allmen from West Plains, Ed McKinney, Kirby Clark (mandolinist and fiddler), Jim Orchard, and talented youngsters Roy Bond, from Hartshorn in eastern Texas County (guitar), and Jasiah Shrode (banjo), from the Plato area in northwestern Texas County. Travis Hathaway from Boiling Spring was another young musician Jim Orchard encouraged. Various people filled in on bass, such as Sergio Ronzani (nicknamed "Sarge" by Orchard). Jim did not participate every week.

For Jim Orchard, the move to Weaver's presented an opportune moment to switch more completely from mandolin to violin as his principal instrument. Then, in his sixties, his time came at last to be "the fiddler in the band." The Weaver's RV Campground opry was successful. Then Weaver's changed hands. Once again, ownership and management issues plagued the show. There were debates over compensation for the musicians, and Jim parted ways with the new management.[7] Jim ceased participating in the Jamboree at Summersville in 2007 to take a larger role in managing the Weaver's show.[8]

In 2012 Orchard moved the Weaver's RV Campground show to Mountain View when Weaver's changed hands. The show, which Jim named the Jamboree, was mounted there from 2012 to 2014. In Mountain View, the show was held in the comfortable Chamber of Commerce building's public meeting space. During this time, folks at Summersville became interested in reviving the show there, and Orchard agreed to organize a reborn show, which would again grace the VFW Hall east of town. In November 2014, Orchard ended the Mountain View Jamboree. In January 2015, Jim returned to Summersville.

Jim Orchard explains a point of Shannon County history. (June 2015)

Jim Orchard, the Bard of Ink

James Woodrow Orchard Jr. was born in 1936 in Eminence, where his parents operated an ice business. After Jim's father acquired the farm in McHenry Hollow near Ink, the family moved to the farm in late 1939. McHenry Hollow is in "the Sunkland" area (a large geologic sinkhole basin), near the hamlet of Ink, on Spring Valley Creek (a tributary of the Current River).[9] The location is between Eminence and Summersville, and Ink families did most of their shopping and business in Summersville; even though just inside the Texas County line, Summersville was easier to reach than Eminence and fitted with more services and stores. But Eminence was the county seat of Shannon County, and Jim went to high school there. Jim recalls that "our *city* was Salem," forty miles north, the county seat of Dent County, with more plentiful services and larger population.

Jim Orchard's ancestors were early settlers in frontier times, most of them of "Irish" (Scotch-Irish) descent. He was a fan and performer of country and bluegrass music and later specialized in Bill Monroe–style mandolin, playing in bands that included some of Missouri's bluegrass legends.[10] His real passion was fiddle music and fiddle people, growing up in a family and cultural landscape where "fiddlers were everywhere." "The fiddle was always my favorite. There were fiddlers all over this place. The Shockleys, the Spurgeons, the Russells, the Goforths—all of 'em. Every community had at least *two* fiddle players. And they *could play*, you know."[11]

Jim's mother, Velma, liked music and gave him permission to go ahead and perform on radio programs, talent shows, oprys, and other places. But theirs was a family raised strict and regular churchgoers, and she had second thoughts about her eager young lad making his way into the world of music in which rough dance halls and honky-tonks were an alluring part. Some musicians are, by nature or ambition, apt to be drawn by the siren call to boisterous and murky venues. For young musicians, honky-tonks were not the same as pie suppers, talent shows, and oprys. On one occasion, his mother told Jim, with regard to the tavern their friends the Spurgeons operated in the lumber mill and river town of West Eminence, "If I ever catch you in that tavern, that'll be the end of your music career." Mom needn't have worried about her Jim.

On another occasion, Jim remembers his grandfather Roy Wallace, a prominent farmer in McHenry Hollow, "warning" him.

> I remember one time, I was probably in about the sixth grade, and my granddad—he wasn't much of a talker, kind of like Rich [Jim's brother Rich Orchard]. And he got me off to one side and he said, "Now I want to tell you something. I don't want you to think I don't like your music, I love it, you know I do, I sing in church, and I love it. And I love what you do. But," he said, "I just hope it don't take you places you don't need to go." And I haven't forgotten that.

In high school in the early 1950s, Jim and two friends, Paul Brake (guitar and mandolin, from Flatrock) and Jack Shockley (violin), played country music on radio station KSMO-AM in Salem. Jim played mandolin and guitar and swapped instruments with Brake for different tunes. Shockley was much older and had given Jim guitar lessons when Jim was in the third grade. At age seven, Jim had received his first guitar for Christmas in 1943—a Silvertone archtop from a mail-order catalog.[12] The new guitar did not come with a case, so his mother let him leave it on his bed, "like a favored house cat."

Jim Orchard, Paul Brake, and Jack Shockley called themselves the Booger County Ramblers. They secured a live fifteen-minute show at KSMO on Saturdays, sponsored by Coca-Cola. The Booger County Ramblers' show was followed by Mitch Jayne's *Hickory Hollow* show, which sometimes featured Rodney and Doug Dillard playing live music in the studio with their mentor, fiddler Howe Teague. Orchard jokes, "I couldn't understand why the Dillards got thirty minutes!" Doug Dillard's banjo playing was maturing and reaching a plateau of skill approaching his idol, Earl Scruggs. "Doug was a *hot cake!*" Three-finger syncopated bluegrass banjo playing was increasing in popularity but still unusual in mid-1950s Missouri, where the older banjoists Jim had heard at music parties and pie suppers were "frailers" and "drop-thumb pickers" who filled the traditional role of rhythm and accompaniment for fiddlers and singers.

When the fiddle bug hit Jim Orchard in the 1980s, he already owned violins and heard fiddle tunes percolating through his imagination. But the craft did not fall easily into his hands. He worked at it. Since childhood, his model had been the smooth *Grand Ole Opry* fiddler Curly Fox, whom Jim had seen perform with Texas Ruby at a concert in the Frisco railroad town of Winona (named for the Minnesota town by Minnesota lumber workers) in the late 1940s. Orchard well remembers the long path to becoming a fiddler. At a bluegrass festival many years ago, he was involved in a jam-session circle with the well-regarded old-time and bluegrass fiddler Garvin Lee. Jim was just starting to play fiddle in front of other musicians.

> When I got to messin' with the fiddle, Garvin Lee—Garvin's a great guy and a pretty good fiddle player, you know. Lee says, "Boy, you're gettin' better on the fiddle."
>
> And I said, "Well, I've spent hundreds of dollars on fiddles and they still *squeak*. And somebody suggested I probably needed better *bows*, and I started spending *thousands* on bows—and I'm still squeakin'."
>
> Garvin, he looked around and, there's eight or ten people sittin' there, he kinda snickered, and said, "I think I can help you. We've been friends a long time, it won't cost you hundreds or thousands."
>
> I said, "Well, you're the guy I'm *lookin'* for."
>
> He said, "Next time you go down to the store, it'll cost you a quarter—get two pieces of bubble gum and put 'em in your mouth, get 'em soft, and put one in each ear."

Orchard chose a career in public education. He taught school for thirty years, moving from the master of the one-room Flatwood School near Ink at age eighteen to teaching history and physical education and coaching sports teams at Eminence High School, to high school principal in the Houston and the Birch Tree–Mountain View systems.[13] Jim enjoyed his experience as a one-room country schoolmaster. He quips that Flatwood is "just a suburb of Flat Rock. But folks in Flat Rock would say the opposite." Orchard took retirement in 1985, although he enjoyed teaching and seeing the lights of literacy and knowledge appear in young people's eyes. "I *loved* to teach, but, I don't know—I coon-hunt eight nights a week, and I wanted to play music, and do sports with my kids. Life's just been too good to me, you know."[14] A natural archivist and scholar and proud of his "Ozarkian" heritage and country ways, Jim revels in local history and passing down the lore.

Orchard was active in the development of bluegrass festivals in Missouri in the early 1970s—those events are, after all, much like oprys and shows. The first bluegrass festival on his home turf had been started in Eminence in 1970 by Kenny Seaman. Orchard became a fixture and popular emcee at Bill and Mona Jones's "Pickin' Time" Bluegrass Festival at Dixon.[15]

Like other devotees of fiddling, Orchard studies the history of violins and violin making and enjoys discussing the pros and cons of different kinds of violins and bows. His repertoire includes a number of his own compositions—fiddle tunes named after local musicians, historical places, and cultural landmarks, such as Low Wassie—as

"Ole Fashioned Pie Supper & Musical Jamboree Featuring Jimmy Orchard & The Ozark Mountain Boys," newspaper ad, ca. 1972. (Courtesy Jim Orchard)

well as bluegrass and country favorites.[16] Jim's favorite among his fiddle compositions is "McHenry Hollow," and he continues to work out melodies with titles like "Flat Rock Hop." Fiddler, ballad singer, and raconteur Pete Counts is recalled in Jim's tune "Play Your Fiddle Uncle Pete" (*Old 'Ens an' New 'Ens*). Counts was a local character in Reynolds County who appears in artist L. L. Broadfoot's collection of the 1930s and 1940s, *Pioneers of the Ozarks*. As quoted by Broadfoot, Pete Counts: "I'm jus' a common ol' hill billy an' fiddler, an' here I am, singing' the 'Squallin' Cat,' 'Comin' through the Rye,' 'Hell Among the Yearlings,' 'Hell Up Skunk River,' an' all ov them there ol' tunes ye hear around in these hills."[17]

When Orchard brought the Saturday-night show back to the VFW Hall at Summersville in January 2015, his long experience with the vicissitudes of managing and performing proved valuable. He knew what was needed and saw that it got done, and the location was a good choice. The building is spartan and suitable; not too big and not too fancy, the hall seems to suit the audience and performers. Small is good.

The tried-and-true format still works. "Jim Orchard and the Boys" (Orchard, Jasiah Shrode, Roy Bond, Sherri Sue Sloan) start Saturday evenings at seven and, after a twenty-minute intermission, wind down at nine thirty. The band is augmented occasionally by Travis Hathaway, another young person with promising bluegrass skills (on mandolin and guitar), who comes onstage in the second half of the evening. The

VFW Hall, Summersville, Missouri. (June 2015)

show is called different names by fans, including "the Summersville opry," and many people still think of the show as "the Current River Opry." Jim Orchard's default word choice is "the show" and, when pressed for a name, calls it "Ozark Music at the VFW Hall" or "Little Carnegie Hall."

The show at Summersville includes the traditional features, from the well-practiced emcee's inclusion of audience members in jokes and anecdotes and a bluegrass and country music menu performed by musicians (expert and not so expert) to mixing young and older generations. The evening is often reminiscent of a family reunion. There are a small admission charge and a tin can for donations at the door; Jim distributes the proceeds to the house band, "so the boys can buy strings for their instruments." Newcomers and guest performers may be invited to the stage for a tune or song with "Jim Orchard and the Boys."

Food and drink are available in the kitchen. Although the venue is a Veterans of Foreign Wars lodge hall (a voluntary organization of military servicemen and servicewomen who have earned an overseas campaign medal), there is little or no flag waving, and there is little or no reference to the area's prevalent Bible Belt religious and political character. Orchard has added a nice touch: on the first Saturday of the month, the midevening break includes Jim recognizing everyone in the audience with a birthday that month, and birthday cake is enjoyed by all.

Young performers try their wings and gain experience in front of microphones and audiences as "working" entertainers, and Orchard, the fatherly musician, entertainer, and schoolmaster, is their mentor in more ways than one. Whatever arcs their paths will take, the youngsters can say that they got their start as bluegrass pickers and entertainers with the best—Jimmy Orchard.

At "Ozark Music at the VFW Hall," host and emcee Jim Orchard performs with youngsters from the area who are enthusiastic and skilled in their embrace of "classic bluegrass" as well as country music old and new. *Left to right*: Sherri Rose Orchard Sloan (Jim's daughter, Mountain Grove, bass), Jim Orchard, Jasiah (nicknamed "Hargis" by Orchard) Shrode, and Roy Bond. (June 6, 2015)

One more point. When we hear the old saw that it makes no difference whether a person gets involved in his or her community—"I'm just one guy. What can I do?"—it is good to remember that individuals matter in a healthy democracy. Jim Orchard cares about keeping the show alive and cares about the future of the music and its lore flowing through young people to future generations. So, at the VFW out on Highway 106, the old pattern for oprys continues. Next Saturday night, Summersville VFW, seven o'clock.

Tales of a Complete Fiddler: Larry Ellis

Larry Ellis of Lee's Summit is a seasoned fiddler whose broad interests and professional versatility make him welcome in virtually any venue. Many think of Ellis as a bluegrass fiddler, due to his work with Green Side Up and other bands, or as the fiddler in country music shows.[18] Larry Ellis is no purist—few fiddlers really are. He may play a violin through a sound system at a dance when needed and for many years has played a Zeta solid-body "Classic" model electric violin in what has been his steady gig since 1982, the Big Creek Country Show in Pleasant Hill. Country, swing, bluegrass, Cajun, folk, pop, rhythm and blues, rock, alternative (and other genre titles too numerous to sort out)—all are within Ellis's repertory of styles and genres as an entertainer.

The first of Larry's family in Missouri was William S. Ellis, born in Barren County, Kentucky. William and his wife, Eleanor Hughes Ellis (born in Tennessee), came to the Pilot Grove area of Cooper County sometime before 1830. Larry's great-grandfather Isaac Marion Ellis was born at the Cooper County farm in 1830. Known by his middle name, Marion, he and his wife, Millie Bailey, established a farm some ninety miles west in Cass County, near the border with Kansas Territory.

As the Border Wars heated up in the 1850s, Marion and Millie lived in an area of contested loyalties. The earlier settlers, many of them "Southern," along the Kansas territorial border south of Kansas City came into inevitable conflict with newer settlers in the adjacent Kansas region, the majority of whom were vigorous abolitionists from eastern states. The situation grew untenable for Missouri families when, in 1863 during a time of vicious guerrilla activities of the Civil War in Missouri, the Union army issued "General Order No. 11," a directive requiring anyone connected to or in sympathy with the Confederate cause to vacate their houses, farms, and property and within fifteen days leave Jackson, Cass, Bates and the northern portion of Vernon Counties.[19] Order No. 11 was issued within days of the infamous Confederate guerrilla raid on Lawrence, Kansas, by the western Missouri–based Quantrill's Raiders, in the most notorious of back-and-forth revenge attacks between the opposing forces.

Punitive raids by Union forces from Kansas (called "Jayhawkers") drove people from towns and farms and set fire to the majority of buildings and crops as they moved through the counties; the intention was to deprive Confederate guerrillas of support bases and sustenance. When the Ellises had to vacate, Marion Ellis moved his family east to his wife's family's area near Pilot Grove; they and most of their neighbors in southern Cooper County were pro-Confederate. In Pilot Grove, Marion Ellis decided to "join the Confederacy," as Larry Ellis puts it. Late in the war, in September 1864, Marion Ellis, who had been fighting with "Price's Army," came back to Cooper County, either to return to farming (having been released from service) or to recruit men for the Confederate forces, or both. Ellis says that "a Union-sympathizing group out of Boonville" captured Marion and summarily hung him from an oak tree near the family farm; Millie, twelve-year old Isaac, and his fourteen-year old brother, Bill, found the body, and Bill cut him down. "So that's some history there."

Born in 1939, Larry Ellis grew up on a farm south of Marshall in Saline County, northwest of Cooper County. His grandfather John Ellis was born on a Cooper County farm in the Buffalo Prairie area and played fiddle music at parties and dances in the neighborhood. Grandfather Ellis was the only musician (and fiddler) in the family until Larry came along.

Larry was inspired to learn to play violin at age ten in his one-room country school just south of Marshall. At a parent-teacher meeting at the schoolhouse, as Ellis recalls, Miss Kauffman, the schoolteacher, "got up in front of the people and said, 'I can

Larry Ellis tells a joke to Russ Ravert in a backroom fiddle session at the Kansas City Area Bluegrass Music Club, Kansas City. (May 2015)

teach violin lessons. If you have any sons or daughters that would like to take violin, I can teach it.'" So Larry and two of his friends began taking violin lessons from Miss Kauffman (Mrs. Dorothy Kauffman) at the Elgin school. The lessons lasted for a year, and then Miss Kauffman moved to northwestern Missouri to accept a teaching position in Princeton.

In one of the more interesting narratives about how one learns to play violin, Ellis says that Miss Kauffman would begin each lesson by getting her violin out, tuning up, rosining her bow—and fiddling "Chicken Reel." She said this helped "warm up" her violin. Then began the lesson, with sheet music and practice drills. So Larry Ellis started his fiddle journey as a note player but with fiddle music in his head. Ellis: "[I thought to myself], 'That must be *all right,* because I loved the fiddle music at the *square dances*—and, if *Miss Kauffman* can play it, that's what I want to do!' And after that, that's probably the only thing I *practiced* on—'Chicken Reel.'"

Larry began learning on his grandfather's mail-order-catalog "Stainer" violin. In high school in Marshall, he played classical and marching band music, starting out at the bottom of the second-violin section in the eighth grade and working up to third chair in the first violins in his senior year. One day in 1956 after orchestra practice, the director, Harold Lickey, called Larry aside: "'Lawrence,' he said, 'that violin is really not a good *tone* for an orchestra instrument—it's pretty *brash*.' And he says, 'I've got some fiddles back here, I'll sell you a couple of 'em, make you a good *price.*' So I tried both of them out, and I selected a John Juzek 'Artist' model, cost me *seventy-five dollars* that I'd saved up." Ellis still has the Juzek but prefers other violins for music he plays in bluegrass bands and country music oprys.

Larry liked the old-time dance fiddling of Hubert Skidmore, whom he heard at square dances around Marshall. "All the neighbors would gather in. The band consisted of a fiddle player and a guitar rhythm player. I *loved that sound.*" Skidmore operated a propane gas company in Marshall and constantly had a cigar in his mouth while playing fiddle music. Skidmore's standard fare for dancing were old favorites such as "Ragtime Annie," "Old Joe Clark," "Mississippi Sawyer," "Soldier's Joy," and "Eighth of January." His favorite waltz was "Over the Waves"—the only waltz Ellis remembers Hubert Skidmore playing. Skidmore did play two-steps and schottisches but did not play jigs.

At around age fourteen, Larry was fiddling for square dances at local affairs and branching out. He and some friends formed a string band and played square and round dances with country music and jitterbug hits.

Larry displays John Ellis's Stainer in a shadow box on the wall of the living room. John Ellis bought the violin in San Francisco around 1900, during a period when he was sampling life and work in the Bay Area. Larry eventually inherited the violin. When he moved to Lee's Summit in 1962 after his naval service, he decided to take "Grandfather's Stainer" to a respected violin expert and maker in Independence for an evaluation, Earsel Atchley. "And, he got a grin on his face, and he looked up the year 1900 *Sears catalog*—got it out, and still *grinning*, and he says, with his finger on it [the catalog illustration], 'That's your fiddle, right there.' And it was a copy of a Stainer, and the price was a dollar and half, and the case was seventy-five cents. Oh, the labor that went into such a small amount!"

Unlike most fiddlers documented in *Play Me Something Quick and Devilish* and this book, Larry Ellis did not grow up in a family listening to *Grand Ole Opry* radio shows or hillbilly records. His father liked classical music on records and radio, and Larry loved to sing the tenor harmony part in hymns in church. There was no fiddle or banjo music in their home. Singing in choirs and church was a great pleasure in his early years. "You need lots of good ear" and skill to sing the tenor part—or to fiddle the "twin part," which typically is a "third" above the melody notes (sometimes the twin line is below the melody). "I like playing twin fiddle harmony just as much as playing the melody."

Another aspect of Ellis's musicianship that differs from most other fiddlers is that he does not play any other instrument. Many fiddlers start out playing backup guitar or banjo for fiddlers, or piano. Many play mandolin (and vice versa)—it is tuned like a violin, has four pairs of strings, and the same scale (fingerboard length), and fiddlers can learn fiddle tunes by working out the melody on mandolin. When someone asks why he doesn't at least play mandolin, Larry answers, "My excuse is: If I ever get as good as I want to get on the fiddle, I'll start on the mandolin. I've never gotten bored with the fiddle."

Bye Bye Blues

Transcribed by Sharon Graf

as played by Larry Ellis 2012

"Bye-Bye Blues," as played by Larry Ellis, from *Fiddle CD #1*, an example of his swing fiddling. (Transcription by Sharon Graf)

Nor does Ellis do much fiddle teaching, which simply is too time-consuming. He has taught one person, his grandson, Devan Ellis, now in his thirties, and through the years has occasionally offered fiddlers advice.

Larry Ellis joined the US Navy in 1958 and served a four-year hitch. As a Seabee, he served in a powerhouse at the Naval Communication Station on Adak Island in the western Aleutians, near the US-Russian marine boundary. Larry performed in several country music dance bands to entertain his fellow sailors at recreational clubs, and these experiences brought him into contact with musicians across many genres. Larry liked swing music and absorbed a good deal of this music and began working out what would be a specialty of his in his musical career—playing double-stops and twin-fiddle harmony lines. His ability to "read," although rudimentary, helped him adjust to the needs of playing a vast array of different musical styles in dance bands.

After Adak, Larry's construction battalion was sent to build a helicopter base for the Marine Corps, called Futima, on Okinawa. In 1961 the battalion participated in an exercise cruise into the South China Sea off South Vietnam; the battalion never landed, and later it became known that the American warships passing along the coast were a show of force and a warm-up to what would occur in the Vietnam War.[20] Ellis was stationed at Camp Kubasaki naval base on Okinawa and performed in a dance band called the Cimarron Cowboys that mostly played western swing. "We played at enlisted men's or officers' clubs almost every night—and then worked every day."

Show Fiddler, Bluegrass Fiddler

Out of the navy in 1962 and back in Missouri, Ellis moved to Lee's Summit in Jackson County (in the Kansas City metro area), where he was able to start his long and successful career as an electrician at a Western Electric factory, where parts for telephones and other equipment were made. He found his first professional work as a show fiddler in nearby Sweet Springs in the cast of the Midwest Opry. The Midwest Opry performed in an old movie theater and represented the kinds of jamborees, shows, jubilees, and oprys that took root in the 1950s and 1960s. At this point, Larry got more serious about his fiddle playing and devoted himself to close study of the variety of styles and repertoires he would be expected to play, without hesitation and well, in a typical Saturday-night show. Around 1967, when he met Lonnie Hoppers and Howard Rash, Larry got interested in playing bluegrass music. While visiting at home in Marshall in 1967 or 1968, he went to a jam session and met banjoist Jack Deck.[21]

Soon after getting established in his position at Western Electric (the manufacturing arm of American Telephone and Telegraph), by chance Ellis met another young musician, bluegrass banjoist Lonnie Hoppers. Lonnie and his wife, Charlene, had moved from Urbana to Lee's Summit to find work as he was putting his bluegrass banjo career together. Later that same year, in September 1962, Lonnie Hoppers would become famous when he was invited by Bill Monroe to perform and record as a regular member of Monroe's Bluegrass Boys. While working at the plant, Larry along with guitarist Neil Griffith (also employed at Western Electric) began taking their work breaks and lunch hours to step outside to the employee parking lot, where they spent every spare minute playing bluegrass and country music, absorbing tunes and songs from each other, "pickin' an' singin'."

Hoppers loaned Ellis several Kenny Baker bluegrass fiddle albums, which Larry studied closely. Hoppers operated a wax-impregnation machine on the factory floor; Griffith was an electrician; Ellis as a master electrician roamed the factory maintaining equipment. Howard Rash, another hot young bluegrass player, also worked at the Western Electric Works, one of the better sources of employment in the region. In

1963, after his stint as a Bluegrass Boy, Hoppers came back to Lee's Summit and went back to work at Western Electric.

Another bit of luck for Larry Ellis was discovering the bluegrass and country music parties and informal shows hosted by the Kansas City Area Bluegrass Music Club, which had grown out of the informal Kansas City old-time fiddlers' club meetings. "Then I started going to *jam sessions*—Lonnie and Howard told me about them—at the Whatsoever Community Center, at 12th and Ewing—and that was the Kansas City Bluegrass Club, which still exists. A fine organization." Larry fell into sessions and pickup bands with the leading lights of the Kansas City bluegrass scene. Founded in the early 1960s by members of the Collins family, Jim McGreevy, Don Montgomery, Jack and Mae Burlison, and others, the Kansas City Area Bluegrass Music Club became a magnet for musicians, some of whom, like Lyman Enloe, came from old-time fiddling, some of whom, such as the Collinses, were already bluegrass devotees, and some, like McGreevy, who were coming to bluegrass from the hootenannies and folk-music scene. Several prominent bluegrass bands took shape at the monthly KCABMC get-togethers.[22]

Like the Collinses, McGreevy, and other Kansas City bluegrassers, Larry Ellis enjoyed and learned much from Lyman Enloe, of Raytown, who in music parties at the Whatsover Community Center taught Larry effective and strictly traditional versions

Green Side Up, 1974: *Left to right*, Keith George (bass), Rick George (guitar), Jerry Justice (mandolin), Dave Batson (guitar), Larry Ellis (violin), and Howard Rash (banjo). (Courtesty Larry Ellis)

of tunes such as the demanding "Fourteen Days in Georgia." "Wonderful man, Lyman. He was a house painter, you know. He painted houses so many years, that his right hand was *deformed*, from holding a paint brush" (between the right thumb and other fingers).

Green Side Up formed in 1971 and in 2016, at forty-five years, is the Kansas City area's longest-running bluegrass band. As Alison Campbell recounts in *Bluegrass Unlimited*, Larry Ellis named the band in reference to a joke heard everywhere in the 1970s and commonly told onstage at bluegrass festivals.[23]

> Green Side Up musicians work day jobs. One of those jobs included laying sod for a large landowner. These folks had never seen sod—where they were from sod grew from grass seed and rain. So as they were laying the sod, every so often, Larry and the gang would hear their boss call out "Green side up!" to remind them how to lay the grass. "Really, the original members of the band each offered a suggestion and then the band pulled a name out of a hat. My choice won—and I didn't cheat," swears Larry. "The idea is to keep things a little less serious, to loosen up and entertain."

The original Green Side Up included Ellis doing the fiddle work and singing harmony vocals, Jerry Justice (mandolin), Keith George (bass), Dave Batson (guitar), and Larry's friend from the Western Electric plant Howard Rash on five-string banjo. Rick George joined Green Side Up in 1972 and won fame by winning a national flat-picking contest at Winfield, Kansas, in 1974. For a brief time in 1972, Larry's old pal Lonnie Hoppers filled in as banjo player. In 1981 Green Side Up won first place in a contest among twenty-nine bluegrass gospel groups at Silver Dollar City. During this period in the 1980s, Larry and fiddler (and mandolinist) Don Hoglen played stunning twin-fiddle bluegrass pieces together. Hoglen, from West Plains and an important player in Missouri bluegrass history, had lived in Gladstone in the Kansas City suburbs at the time and now is retired and lives in Springfield.

Ellis is the sole remaining original member, and today the group includes Gary Bagley (guitar), Ty Green (banjo), Tammy Collins Fetters (bass), and Rob Collins (mandolin, a multi-instrumentalist member of the Collins bluegrass clan; Tammy Collins Fetters is a cousin). Through the years, Green Side Up has retained its reputation of a strong commitment to classic bluegrass sounds, avoidance of electric instruments, and like most bluegrass bands, inclusion of a gospel number in each performance.

Ellis's recordings include projects from his bluegrass-band days in the 1970s and 1980s with Green Side Up and tracks on the striking 1990 CD *The Missouri Session*, produced by Irl Hees and Joey Wieneman. In 2012 he recorded an album simply called *Larry Ellis Fiddle CD #1* that represents his many years playing swing and country music as well as acknowledgment of his bluegrass years with Green Side Up.[24] There are fiddle tunes in bluegrass and old-time stylings, such as "The Cuckoo's Nest" (hear on the companion CD). Some are of local reference: "Lee Sutton Special" (from a Tater Tate 1968 Rural Rhythm fiddle LP, *Fiddling Favorites of the U.S.A. and*

Canada), "Cheyenne," "Bully of the Town," "Sugar in the Gourd," "Whistling Rufus," "Black Mountain Rag," "Rutland's Reel," "Arkansas Traveler," "Back Up and Push," "Turkey Buzzard" (from the 1969 County Records LP *Joe Greene's Fiddle Album*), "Brilliancy," and "Redwing." Bluegrass ironclads on the recording include "Cheyenne" (the powerful twin-fiddling piece recorded by Bill Monroe and the Bluegrass Boys featuring Dale Potter and Bobby Hicks), "Arab Bounce" (composed by Alabama mandolinist Vernon Derrick), and Kenny Baker's "Kiss Me Waltz." There are compositions by Nashville session players such as "Scottsboro" (from Randy Howard) and bluegrass fiddler Blaine Sprouse's "September Waltz" (hear on the companion CD). There are standards of early jazz and swing: "Bye-Bye Blues," "Charmaine" (played as a two-step instead of in its original waltz time), and the steel-guitar western-swing classic Leon McAuliffe's "Panhandle Rag." The last track is the audience pleaser "Orange Blossom Special." On the old-time material Larry plays a standard violin, and on some of the jazz and swing he plays his Zeta electric. Ellis says he might have become "a better fiddler" had he not been just as interested in singing harmony and exploring harmony fiddle parts.

Ellis continues to lead Green Side Up—he is now the senior member of the ensemble—and plays with a gospel group as well as his "main gig," fiddling on the Big Creek Country Show every Saturday night.

No Time for Contests

Ellis competed in his share of old-time fiddlers contests through the years, but he does not consider himself a "contest fiddler" in terms of those who are dedicated, intense contest players. During the heyday of Missouri fiddling competitions in the 1970s and 1980s, Larry was too happily situated in bluegrass performances and opry shows to have much time for the contest circuit.

In 1981 Ellis did enter a contest at Silver Dollar City, sponsored by KWTO radio in Springfield, and won first place over eighteen other fiddlers; he was there with Green Side Up to compete in a gospel singing contest and decided to jump into the fiddlers contest as well. The event was billed as "The KWTO Ozark Mountain Talent Search, 1981, Silver Dollar City." In the runoff (between the three top contestants), Larry played "Dusty Miller" and "Black Hawk Waltz." The waltz is in the key of F, and the guitar second, Rick George, had his guitar capo placed on the wrong fret but kept on playing anyway, and it worked. Ellis's tunes in the elimination round were "Lime Rock," "Westphalia Waltz," and "Bill Cheatem."

Ellis occasionally agrees to help a contest promoter by serving as a member of the judging panel, and this is not a job he relishes. Like many fiddlers who value accepted customs of contest performance and adjudication, Ellis recognizes the current state of confusion and tension in contests (the debates over what is and is not "old-time" fiddling and the influence of modern "contest fiddling" styles). Like many other fiddlers, he prefers to stay out of the contest scene.

Larry Ellis (*left*) and champion contest fiddler and teacher Junior Marriot played "twin fiddle" (Ellis, harmony) after the Trail Days contest, Sedalia. (April 2015)

The Big Creek Country Show

En route to his many years with the Big Creek show, Larry Ellis performed with a number of other shows and oprys in the Kansas City area. In 1969 he worked several years in the house band for Byron Jones (an elder leader in the entertainment genre) at the Farris Opry House in Richmond. Larry then performed with Jennie Holloway's country show in Liberty and then two years with the Country Hayride Opry in Excelsior Springs.

Ellis joined the Big Creek Country Show in its first year, 1982, and has been with the show ever since.[25] Pleasant Hill is in Cass County, southeast of the Kansas City metro area and some twenty miles from the Kansas state line. Big Creek sounds like a generic name for the show, but there is a Big Creek here (a tributary of the Osage River to the south), and the town is situated on the rolling hills between Big Creek and Duncan Creek.

The Big Creek Country Show occupies the historic People's Theatre in downtown Pleasant Hill. The theater, which, with its small balcony seats 450 people, is owned by Cindy and Dennis Dittemore, who met as five-year-old child performers at the Union Mill Opry Show in Edgerton, some sixty-five miles north. After performing at the KC Opry, in 1982 the Dittemores decided to open their own show in Pleasant Hill. The year 2015 was their thirty-third year hosting the show in Pleasant Hill.[26] As Ellis recalls, the new show in Pleasant Hill was called a "show" in order to help separate

The People's Theatre is home to the Big Creek Country Show; in a historic district listed in the National Register of Historic Places, the theater underwent updating in 1948, with Art Deco motifs and neon lighting, but its original brick facade and layout are retained. (2015)

it from the several "oprys" in the region and perhaps because the term "opry" had become obsolete: "I think at one time [in the 1970s], the word opry was overused."[27]

Since joining the original cast with Dennis and Cindy Dittemore in 1982, Ellis has fiddled (and told thousands of jokes) on Saturday nights with the show, giving him opportunity to present and enjoy his several layers of fiddle skills and interests, from old-time hoedowns to covers of Nashville hit records, a pinch of bluegrass, and a good deal of popular and rock-and-roll songs from the 1940s onward.

In a typical show, emceed by Dennis Dittemore, Ellis plays two to four fiddle tunes. Ellis is also a vocalist, singing tenor harmony as the song at hand indicates. He opens the show with brisk fiddle tune and closes the first set ("first half") with another, and then, after intermission, his fiddling opens and closes the second half of the show. This position in the show's format reflects Larry's value as a longtime house-band stalwart, but having a fiddle tune start and end each set seems to be recognition of the historical central role of "fiddling" in entertainments like this one. On Saturday, May 9, 2015, here is Larry's set list, which he worked out a few days ahead: first of the show, "Washington and Lee Swing" and "Grey Eagle" (a contest tune that he had been asked by a fan to play on May 9); second half, "Dixie Hoedown" and "Leather Britches." "I try to end the show with an old-timey, square dance type fiddle tune."

If someone in the audience requests a tune during the show, Ellis feels it is important to honor the request. "People will request 'Black Mountain Rag,' 'Listen to the Mocking Bird,' or, *guess what*—'Orange Blossom Special.' Once in a while somebody will request 'Ashokan Farewell.'" Ellis positions himself in the center of the stage, behind the front row of microphone stands, and in front of the drum kit. He has a stool where he can sit for a breather and a foot pedal with which to pump up the volume when he takes a chorus on a song or plays a fiddle tune.

Every show has a cast member who does most of the planned joke telling, and Ellis plays the role on the Big Creek Country Show. Larry delivers his comedy at specific places in the evening show, with an occasional quip or repartee with a band member throughout the evening. He has an assigned slot in the show where he does back-and-forth jokes with Dittemore playing the straight man. As a safety measure, Larry has a list of the jokes he will tell taped to the back of his violin. "I'm not a musician, I'm just a fiddle player. However, I *am* a graduate of the Suppository of Music." Another: "What do you say to a fiddle player who's dressed in a three-piece suit? 'Will the defendant please rise.'" Many of the jokes are formulaic, recast jokes with different details, as in the second example—a banjo joke with "fiddle player" replacing "banjo player." Ellis says that in his Green Side Up bluegrass band performance, the jokes tend to be about banjo players; in country bands, they tend to be about drummers. "You can pick on any instrument."

Ellis does not assume the persona of the old-time vaudeville "Highpockets" or "Goofer" hillbilly clown, and this reflects the character of this "show" as broad and full of variety—it is not merely a "country" show. This is not an "opry." In his performance attire and demeanor, Ellis looks and comports himself as a seasoned professional musician who happens to like a good joke. Like the legendary radio and television comedian Jack Benny, Ellis is on the lookout for new jokes and humorous situations, and he maintains files of jokes at home. With a twinkle in his eye, he promises to publish a book of his lifetime joke collection. "I went downtown in Lee's Summit last summer—it was a nice Saturday afternoon, not too hot and not too cold, and I opened up my fiddle case and started playing, right there on the sidewalk. Pretty soon, an officer come up to me, and he says, '*Sir*, do you have a permit to play that violin here?' I said, 'No sir.' He said, 'Well, I'm afraid you're going to have to accompany me.' I said, 'Okay, what do you want to sing?'"[28]

At the Big Creek Country Show on June 27, 2015, the evening took the following outline. People began arriving at around seven for the eight o'clock curtain, with an audience filling the theater to capacity. The majority of the audience was made up of senior citizens, many of whom were bused to the show and are such regular attendees that they have seats assigned to them. The ticket price was twelve dollars. The ticket taker handed out a sheet of paper promoting the next few weeks' shows. A concession stand offered the usual range of refreshments, popcorn and candy bars, cold drinks or coffee. The old movie house, built in 1909, retains much of its original character; it appears to have undergone renovations in the 1930s or 1940s, with Art Deco moon-and-clouds neon figures hung on the side walls of the hall.

A few minutes before eight, folks were in their seats, visiting. Many were old friends or neighbors, and many seemed to have known members of the house band for years. Members of the cast came down from behind the stage and strolled up the two aisles, visiting with people and renewing acquaintances in the traditional "shake and howdy" audience courtesy.

The first half got rolling a few minutes after eight with emcee Dittemore's welcome and introductory remarks as the heavy red curtains drew aside and Ellis fiddled the first tune of the evening, a number announced as "Big Dog" (from a 2006 Byron

Larry Ellis sings "Americana," Big Creek Country Show, Pleasant Hill, Missouri. (June 27, 2015)

Berline fiddle CD). The vocal numbers began with Dennis Dittemore singing the Cajun-sounding country song "Chattahoochie" (Alan Jackson, 1993) and "This Is My Country" (the World War II–era song by Tin Pan Alley writer Don Raye, a favorite with high school choruses in the 1950s and 1960s) to set up the patriotic tone for this Fourth of July show. Vocalist Debbie Erickson (Debbie Martin), like Ellis an original 1982 cast member, joined in, playing rhythm on an Ovation acoustic-electric guitar. Erickson soloed on the 1981 country song recorded by Roseanne Cash "My Baby Thinks He's a Train" and Nanci Griffith's 1993 song "Night Rider's Lament."

Following this, Dittemore came to the center-stage microphones and worked as a straight man for several jokes with Larry Ellis. Pianist Phil Hilton was featured on two instrumentals, "One More Day" (the Diamond Rio country-rock song from 2000) and "Chariots of Fire" (from the 1981 Hollywood movie by the same title). Next, Erickson brought out a chocolate birthday cake with a few candles, and everyone sang "Happy Birthday" for Dennis Dittemore. Next guest vocalist Duke Mason of Webb City sang the rhythm-and-blues Roy Hamilton hit (1961, covered by Elvis Presley, 1974) "You Can Have Her" and "You Don't Know Me" (an Eddie Arnold country hit from 1955).

Guest vocalist Malena Rose (Malena Rose Marcase, from Blue Springs, a sophomore at Belmont University in Nashville) sang Chuck Berry's 1959 "Back in the USA" (the rock-and-roll song, covered by Linda Ronstadt, 1978), "Tennessee Waltz" (the Patti Page hit from the early 1950s), and "Wagon Wheel" (the 2013 Darius Rucker country-rock song, strumming her uke). Guest Kevin Jones (electric lead guitar, a performer at the Northtown Opry, North Kansas City, and eldest son of founder Byron Jones) sang the 1950s Flatt and Scruggs bluegrass standard "Rolling in My Sweet Baby's Arms" and "A Fire You Can't Put Out" (the 1980s George Straight country song).

Duke Mason sang Elvis Presley's 1970 version of "C. C. Rider," "If You Love Me Let Me Know" (the 1974 Olivia Newton-John soft-rock song as covered by Elvis in 1977), and "For the Good Times" (the 1970 Ray Price country ballad covered by Elvis, 1972). To signal intermission, Larry Ellis played a jazzy fiddle tune called "Foolin' Around," from a western-swing tune by fiddler Aubrey Haynie on his 1997 *Doin' My Time* CD.

After the intermission, during which cast members visited with audience members and took refreshment, the "second half" began with a fiddle tune by Ellis, "Leaving Rosine," another Aubrie Haynie tune from the 1997 CD. Kevin Jones presented several classic country songs, including "Love You a Thousand Ways" by country singer Lefty Frizzell (covered by Willie Nelson in the 1970s), and the 1970s John Anderson country song "Your Lyin' Blue Eyes."

Following Jones's set, there began a set of patriotic music—this was the "Fourth of July show" to celebrate Independence Day a week thence. Debbie Erickson offered comments and sang a medley of "America" and "God Bless America." Dittemore came out in an "Uncle Sam" costume with his saxophone and sang and played "Yankee Doodle Dandy" (as James Cagney sang it in the 1942 Hollywood movie about the life of George M. Cohan). Malena Rose returned and sang "You Ain't Woman Enough to Take My Man" (the 1966 Loretta Lynn country song) and, "for you veterans," the 1970s Lee Greenwood country song "God Bless the U.S.A." Ellis then sang the country music patriotic song "Americana" (1988, by Moe Bandy), fiddling a solo break.

Duke Mason returned and sang a country song, "It Keeps Right on a-Hurtin'," the George Jones country hit "He Stopped Lovin' Her Today," and Elvis's "American Trilogy" patriotic medley ("Dixie," "Battle Hymn of the Republic," "All My Trials"). This set was the evening's grand finale, with all the stops pulled and rousing, emotional musical arrangement. Dittemore then thanked the audience, made closing comments, and oversaw a drawing for thirty dollars in cash (a winning number is drawn and the price awarded; if no one has the winning number, the pot is increased, and the next drawing takes place at the next show). The show closed with Ellis fiddling a sparkling version of the old-time square-dance favorite "Tennessee Wagner." The show on this evening presented some thirty tunes and songs—thirteen of them classic country, six rock and roll, five pop songs, four fiddle tunes, and one bluegrass standard.

One marvels at the ability of cast members of shows like Big Creek County to seamlessly move through an evening playing and singing such a variety of music, crossing genres of classic country, honky-tonk, gospel, rock and roll, show tunes, fiddle breakdowns, big-band hits, and more. Almost nothing is off-limits to entertainers like these.

"Wah! Hoo!" (Cliff Friend, New York, Crawford Music, 1936) was a hit in repertoires of high-toned ballroom orchestras and western-swing bands; among early recordings were those by Bill Boyd's Cowboy Ramblers and Ray Whitley's Bar Six Cowboys.

Jazz / Swing / Western Swing 8

Back in the past and thrill packed days of the roaring west—the old frontier—loud with life and sudden death, overrun with warring redskins and ravaging whites, where it was the fate of many a brave man to feel the sting of hot lead or to swing at the end of a rope. Ha, but how things have changed! Today the sons of the old west are still killers, but killers of another variety. They are killing them with hot music and swinging them with swaying strains of rock-solid hot rhythm.

—Spade Cooley, opening narration for Hollywood ten-minute movie short *Spade Cooley, King of Western Swing* (1945)

Swing is often neglected in the saga of traditional fiddle music, but swing and its countrified cousin, western swing, are essential to see the whole story.[1] To some in the old-time fiddling community, swing may seem comparatively new, but it evolved in the 1930s. Gunther Schuller on swing: "1. A rhythmic element and a manner of playing (inflecting) rhythms peculiar to jazz. 2. A period in the development of jazz (1935–1945) characterized by the emergence and national popularity of 'Swing' bands; the Swing Era."[2] Schuller's definition is aimed at high-style and urban-centered swing dance music (Duke Ellington, Benny Goodman), but it applies well to what has become known as "western swing" as developed by cowboy-themed southwestern and western dance bands of the same period. Add Jean Ann Boyd's comment: "The western swing fiddler is more accurately a jazz violinist in a swing band."[3]

Differences between swing and western swing include western swing's continued focus on fiddles and guitar ensembles and embrace of old-time country music and dances, such as the square dance, polka, varsouvienne, and schottische. Most of the fiddlers who play tunes identified with "swing," such as "Charmaine" and "Kansas City Kitty," and tunes identified with "western swing," such as "San Antonio Rose" and "Faded Love," make no distinction between categories—and they may play these classics during what would seem to be a session of "old-time fiddling." The difference is as much, if not more, a matter of tunes people like to hear and play. If they like it, they play it.

Swing fiddlers, like bluegrass players, often started the adventure in old-time fiddling and moved to newer forms. The flow of dance music from the early 1900s into the western-swing music in the 1930s from "cowtown wranglers" and "prairie playboys" drew strength from old-time fiddling right alongside jazzier, swingier playing styles. They evolved as parallels, both based in old ways of making music on a violin for friends, dancers, listeners, and other musicians.

Venuti

Certainly as the lead instrument, the fiddler contributed greatly to western swing as it developed. Gary Giddins suggests that "take-off fiddling," in contrast to "breakdown fiddling," makes the old-time music into western swing.[4] With an old-time string band, a fiddler might play a break or solo, but in swing and jazz the soloist, on whatever instrument, launches a personal, creative, well-worked-out improvised and syncopated takeoff solo ("chorus"). The fiddler emphasizes single-string playing, with very few (if any) double shuffles or double-stops. Fiddlers in various genres were experimenting with takeoff solos in the late 1920s and early 1930s, but the takeoff solo became most associated with swing and jazz fiddlers.[5]

Improvisation is nothing new; much of it is evident in classical music and composers from Bach and Beethoven to Liszt and contemporary classical composers, as well as in the vernacular music of musical cultures around the globe. Improvising—"the art of composing in the moment, while performing without a written score"—requires the skill and discretion of a French chef.[6]

It is one thing to work in a different double-stop, drop in a rhythmic accent, or add a few notes, but it is another thing to develop a fully improvised solo. Here is where the swing fiddler is well served by knowing chords and a bit of music theory, because the chord progression is the platform for an improvised solo. While the backup musicians maintain the chords, the fiddler can swing out as far as he or she wishes, "improvising away from the tune." But the solo must follow the chord sequence (in particular cases, a solo may purposely antagonize the chord sequence), in order to descend safely back to earth. Knowing the tune's chordal structure is an absolute necessity.[7] The wisecracking gentleman who pioneered this music was Joe Venuti.

Philadelphia-born Italian American violinist Joe Venuti (1903–78) was the dean of swing fiddling. He moved the violin from a row of chairs in a dance orchestra to lead soloist, launching dramatic improvisational solos. His stunning 1920s recordings with guitarist Eddie Lang, his childhood friend with equal musical gifts, were popular around the world.[8] Venuti and Lang recorded with other young jazz players, such as the young Bing Crosby. Fiddlers and musicologists continue to try to figure out how Joe did it, and hot young fiddlers continue to mine his recordings like archaeologists at the Parthenon. Like other founders, Venuti was a classical musician who took to swing, and his "conservatory training made him as valuable to society bands as to hot ensembles."[9] Venuti is the name most frequently mentioned in conversations about swing's influence on other genres of fiddle music, such as country music and bluegrass.

New genres find proponents to explain what all the excitement is about, and Venuti tried his hand. In 1937 Joe published a slim instructional book of swing theory, *Joe Venuti Violin Rhythm: A School of Modern Rhythmic Violin Playing*. The volume stresses "syncopated rhythms, phrasing, bowing, blues, improvisation and tricks—all augmented with extensive explanations and exercises."[10] Venuti illustrates techniques such as four ways to play a "chorus" (solo): "straight," "rhythmic," "stylish," and "hot," and "Jazz Tricks" ("whip," "smear," "gliss" [glissando], and "flare").

Joe Venuti, swing fiddling's Prometheus, in the recording studio.

> *Straight*. That is to say, exactly as written.
> *Rhythmic*. [A tune] can be varied or modified rhythmically, but without using any notes not belonging to the melody.
> *Stylish*. This is another step forward, as the tune is not only rhythmically modified, but extra notes not occurring in the original melody, are added here and there. The melody, however, must remain clearly recognizable.
> *Hot*. Here the original melody may be disregarded, the player letting his imagination run freely. The rhythmical figures, however, must always be based on the foundation harmonies of the original melody.[11]

Venuti on double-stops is excellent and might have been written by master double-stop self-taught fiddlers such as Missouri's Dale Potter, Larry Ellis, Pete McMahan, or Roger Williams. "Double-stops may be used in any hot-chorus, but always keep in mind, you must only use them when you are sure they may be effective, and when the character of a tune calls for something richer, fuller, and more 'atmospheric,' than single-string playing. Double-stops should not be used to bolster up a weak phrase, for when a passage is not good enough by itself, double-stopping will certainly not do it, and quite probably, will make it worse!"[12]

Venuti on "blue notes" reminds us how useful it is to possess some knowledge of music theory. "A very effective embellishment in playing modern dance music is the use of 'blue' notes, which are the min. 3rd and min. 7th of the scale. In the key of C the 'blue' notes are E^b and B^b—in the key of D they are F and C and so on. . . . '[B]lue' notes should be used only sparingly." Venuti writes that the reason so much swing music is set in "keys with flat signatures" is to accommodate the "transposing instruments" of the orchestra, the "B^b instruments" such as tenor trumpet, saxophone, and clarinet. "Now the flat keys are by no means the easiest for the violin, but if he wishes to become an expert dance band player, he must accept the facts as they are and familiarise himself as thoroughly as possible with those keys." This is essentially the same as how old-time fiddler Pete McMahan explained learning to play in the flat keys in the 1940s and 1950s when he moved to Columbia from southern Montgomery County and realized he would need new skills to compete with the powerful F and B-flat hornpipe fiddlers such as George Morris and Ed Tharp; it sounds like Roger Williams, the great double-stop bluegrass fiddler in West Plains, too. Roger Williams takes special pleasure in working out double-stops: "To me, that is the best part of fiddle playing."[13]

Improvising on the chords maintained by the backup, rather than on the melody, means that the soloist can play just about any note and make it harmonize within the chord. This skill is often associated with experiments in Kansas City jazz in the 1940s by saxophonist Charlie Parker, with whom Claude Williams was performing (on guitar) in the Eighteenth and Vine district. If a fiddler "gets lost" out there in the Milky Way of glittering notes, he or she can always land on an appropriate chord and thus grab on to this lifeline to get through a solo. In other words, this is improvisation employing formulas founded on structure and pattern.[14] Writing about Joe Venuti's daring, complicated improvising, Aiden Massey writes that in "Summertime," "By bar 74, he seems to feel that it isn't going to go anywhere, so he abandons ship. He then teaches improvisers a good lesson: if things sound as if they are getting lost, throw off an impressive run, based on a dominant chord. You will soon find your way home!"[15]

Champion fiddler and classical musician Deena Bistodeau developed a valuable discussion of improv with regard to modern contest fiddling exemplified by the competition performances of Texas-based, swing-influenced contestants in venues such as the National Oldtime Fiddlers Contest in Weiser, Idaho, and Fiddlers Frolics in Hallettsville, Texas. Bistodeau explains "controlled improvisation" in this realm of Texas-style contest fiddling, and her comments apply to improv in swing fiddlers as well as bluegrass fiddlers like Larry Ellis. Controlled improvisation is the way "fiddlers manipulate basic themes to create multi strain variations."

Deena Bistodeau stresses features of controlled improvisation among Texas style–based contest fiddlers that situate this contest style as part of long-standing traditions;

"Controlled improvisation is a guarded oral tradition that has been passed down through the generations. . . . Elders of the tradition are revered as masters." Like Venuti's 1937 jazz tutor, Bistodeau underscores the necessity for the fiddler to have a very clear knowledge of the core melody of a tune (*with* its chord progression). Like Claude Williams and Charlie Parker, Bistodeau's fiddlers improvise on the chords, or what jazz musicians call "the changes." Bistodeau draws on such fiddlers and tunes as Terry Morris and his "Dusty Miller," transforming the old-time tune "into a multi-strain work that exhausts the fiddler's abilities in executing controlled improvisation."[16] Bistodeau also cautions against mechanical, slavish, perfect replication note for note and phrase for phrase of masterful versions because rote copying becomes clichéd and boring and is not part of the authentic tradition—no matter how such mimicry and perfection of memorized music may help a fiddler succeed in a contest.

One of the recurrent themes in swing fiddling is that the great players played smooth, working to avoid rough and raucous fiddling. Moving uptown was one of the essential results of the Roaring Twenties, so fiddlers interested in swing favored the "smooth school" of old-time fiddling in contrast to the "rough school" (see *Play Me Something Quick and Devilish*).

Farm-Town Cowboys and Uptown Hepcats

Swing and western swing emerged as clear genres of popular music during the Great Depression in the mid-1930s. Jazzy up-tempo fiddling and electric guitars backed by ensembles of horns, reeds, and drums, like Hollywood movies with beautiful people in beautiful clothes driving sleek autos, swing music and its dances brought needed diversion to people.

The term "western swing" is generally felt to have been coined by Spade Cooley's manager Foreman Phillips in 1944 or 1945 Los Angeles.[17] Spade Cooley's society dance orchestras filled the glamorous ballrooms of Southern California, and he somehow managed to bring forward the charm of old-time fiddle and square-dance music right alongside the big-band orchestra music of the era. The term "western swing" was not perfect; it discouraged the music's spread to New York and other regions distant from the South, Midwest, Southwest, and West, and it took a decade to catch on.

Cooley also liked the term "western jive," a term that really illuminates what was going on in popular music. Other bandleaders liked the terms "Texas swing" and "hillbilly jazz." Tony Russell:

> It was country, but not as The Carter Family knew it. There were fiddles and guitars, but the fiddles swerved through the tunes like drunken drivers, with little respect for the melody, and the guitars were hooked up to AMPLIFIERS . . . and on top of that brouhaha were instruments seldom heard in this context, clarinets and saxophones, bleating and blaring and generally making a whoopee alien to the Calvinists of Clinch Mountain.
>
> . . . [A] kind of hillbilly jazz is what much of it was, its key players ardent fans of Benny Goodman and Count Basie, Cab Calloway and Fats Waller. The fiddlers

cocked their ears to Joe Venuti and Stuff Smith . . . so they made it up as they went along. . . . [Many went west] turning themselves into Western equivalents of the Tommy Dorsey or Glenn Miller orchestras.[18]

Fans of Bob Wills (1905–75) and Milton Brown (1903–36) like to debate who should wear the mantle of father of western swing. No one would doubt that Joe Venuti was the father of swing fiddling and Bill Monroe the father of bluegrass, but as a movement western swing seems to have had at least two significant contenders for the crown.

As youngsters Bob Wills and Milton Brown had performed with Herman Arnspiger in the Aladdin Laddies and then the Light Crust Doughboys (sponsored by Burris Flour Mills) on Texas radio stations in 1931.[19] Brown did the singing, Wills played fiddle, and Arnspiger played guitar. In early 1932, Brown and Wills, with Milton's younger brother Derwood, made their first record as the Fort Worth Doughboys, "Sunbonnet Sue" and "Nancy Jane," with Brown leading the singing and Wills on violin.

In September 1932, Brown split off from Wills and Arnspiger and formed Milton Brown and the Musical Brownies with brother Derwood (guitar), Jesse Ashlock (violin), Fred Calhoun (piano), Ocie Stockard (tenor banjo), and Wanna Coffman (upright "slap" bass). This hot ensemble, with Brown's distinctive singing voice, quickly became a popular dance band and performed on radio stations such as KTAT in Fort Worth. In 1933 Brown brought in a jazz violinist with classical training, Cecil Brower. Soon Brower and Cliff Bruner were developing improvisational takeoff solos and twin fiddling. Brown was the "first Texas bandleader to use twin fiddles."[20] Twin fiddling had been heard on hillbilly records by groups such as Lowe Stokes and Clayton McMichen with Gid Tanner and the Skillet Lickers in the late 1920s, and twin fiddling would become a key ingredient in western swing and, soon, country and bluegrass as well.

Stacy Phillips and Paul Anastasio are among scholars and swing players who vote for Milton Brown as the father of western swing.[21] Anastasio:

> This band [Milton Brown], more than any other group, would come to define the musical hybrid that we now call western swing. Milton Brown and his Musical Brownies played old-time fiddle breakdowns, waltzes, and rags, but broke new ground by also performing the jazz and blues tunes of the day, not with horns, but with an ensemble of stringed instruments. Although violinists like Eddie South and Joe Venuti had been playing jazz violin since the mid-twenties, an entire band of stringed instruments playing jazz was really something new. . . . Cecil Brower, later joined by Cliff Bruner, supplied hot fiddle choruses, and folks all over Texas took to this new sound like ducks to water. Had Milton Brown not died in 1936 from injuries suffered in an automobile accident, it is quite likely that his band, not the band of his good friend, Bob Wills, would today be the best-known vintage western band. . . . [W]estern swing as we know it today would probably not exist had it not been for the groundbreaking work of Milton Brown and his Musical Brownies.[22]

Innovations in playing violin by such players as Cliff Bruner (an admirer of Joe Venuti), piano players such as Fred Calhoun (following Earl Hines and others), and guitar players such as Eldon Shamblin (following Eddie Lang, Django Reinhardt, Charlie Christian, and others) considered themselves jazz musicians, and they found the variant of swing and jazz called "western swing" suitable career paths. The jazz and swing knowledge and phrasing of such creative musicians, grounded in musical technique and theory, were essential in forming the sounds of the Milton Brown ensemble and, soon after, Bob Wills and His Texas Playboys.[23]

The Brownies were eclectic, their one-hundred-plus 78 rpm records running from old-time square-dance tunes to "Alexander's Ragtime Band," from cowboy ballads and swing and blues hits by Louis Armstrong, Duke Ellington, and Cab Calloway to "The Sweetheart of Sigma Chi." Dances were the group's principal venue and source of income, and their turf was small-town Texas. The repertoire had to be broad.

> If you want to know just what we got, we got good hokum and we serve it hot,
> easy ridin' papa, from Tennessee.
> We ain't good-lookin' and we don't dress fine, the way we whip it is a hangin' crime,
> easy ridin' papa from Tennessee.[24]

Bob Wills had left the Light Crust Doughboys to form his own band, taking vocalist Tommy Duncan with him. Milton Brown died in 1936, and within a few years Wills had incorporated Brown's innovations and become a swing band; the plowboys became playboys.[25] Wills and His Texas Playboys took the music to new heights on radio, records, dances, concerts, and Hollywood B western movies (part melodrama, part musical comedy) of the World War II era. In a typical film, Wills and his band act as wranglers called "the Bar W boys," packing Colt pistols and chasing bad guys—when they are not playing swing and singing at a dance, looking cool on horseback, and relaxing next to the old corral.[26]

The western-swing bands attired themselves in sartorial excellence matching their music. Playboys and singing cowboys are cool cats, not comic hillbillies (the comic hillbilly role in the Hollywood B westerns fell to the hero's sidekick), and cats wore Stetsons, hand-tooled boots, fancy shirts with pearl buttons, and tailored gabardine suits that would please Gene Autry or Roy Rogers. Their style was shared by many performers in country music and early bluegrass. The son and grandson of Texas dance fiddlers, Bob Wills seemed to wish for the image of Glenn Miller or Tommy Dorsey in his promotion of cool swing musicians at ease at the country club.

Band members often posed with knowing, ironic half-smiles. Strong drink was everywhere, even while pretending it was not. This is cowboy dance-hall music of the late Jazz Age and big-band era. Wills disliked the hillbilly image and cornball antics of many string bands of the time. Bob's signature Stetson beaver hat, grin, and cigar all added to an image of the country gentleman rather than the minstrel or vaudeville cutup, but people knew these musicians liked an alcoholic drink to be sociable. People at Playboys dances had a good time.

Many "Bob Wills tunes" went into the fiddler's repertoire, from "Faded Love," "Spanish Two-Step," "Maiden's Prayer," "Beaumont Rag," "Take Me Back to Tulsa" (hear on the companion CD, by Warren Helton), "Silver Bell," and "Twinkle, Twinkle Little Star" to his biggest hit, "San Antonio Rose"—the record that Bob said took him "from hamburgers to steaks."[27] Many of the Playboys' recordings include Bob's seemingly spontaneous interjections—a merry "Ah-haa!," "That's it, boys!," "Aw, turn it on, boy, turn it on!" and other punctuations. Milton Brown and other bandleaders of the time made similar comments and interjections in performances and on recordings, as did musicians and band leaders in jazz. Brown was fond of saying "Yeah!" in the midst of a hot takeoff solo by one of the Brownies, and this interjection of joy is familiar today in Texas-style fiddle sessions. Even Roy Acuff, playing "mountain music" in Tennessee with his overt hillbilly concert style, also gave out with hollers and quips ("Slap it, boy!") during performances and recording sessions.

In 1934 Bob Dunn, an innovative electric jazz guitarist (and lap steel guitarist) joined the Musical Brownies and completed the picture. Dunn's first session with the Brownies in 1935 marks the first commercial recording of an electrically amplified guitar. Other steel-guitar innovators included Leon McAuliffe and Zeke Campbell, who "played primarily in a jazz idiom, highly blues-inflected and invariably in a single-note linear style. As the electric guitar took hold, these bands became increasingly dominated by that instrument, to a large extent crowding out the fiddle. These bands also turned more and more to a jazz repertoire and instrumentation, adding trumpets and saxophones."[28]

The pedal steel took its place in the western-swing ensemble. This new instrument did not sit well with some fiddlers, because it can compete with the violin; the fiddler and "steel man" play similar solos and backup riffs and often in the same range. Some fiddlers, such as Leroy Canaday of Moberly, believe that the electric pedal steel guitar nearly drove fiddlers off the stage in the 1940s and 1950s because the electric steel could be cranked up and smother the fiddle—the same problem vis-à-vis fiddles that can be encountered in bluegrass music's use of the Dobro guitar. Despite the friction, fiddler Leroy Canaday's definition of a country band is typical: "A country band has to have a steel guitar or a good lead electric guitar and a fiddle or it isn't country."[29] The early "lap steel" was soon superseded by elaborate and more powerful versions that grabbed even more of the limelight. The problem of the fiddler being heard was only partly alleviated by the development of electric violin amplification devices. Many other fiddlers like playing alongside pedal steel guitars.

Eldon Shamblin of Bob Wills's band was an innovator in electric guitar jazz phrasing. Some feel that Shamblin's guitar accompaniment and takeoff solos made western swing what it is. Other guitar innovators included Billy Byrd of Nashville, who as a teenager listened to broadcasts of Django Reinhardt with jazz fiddler Stéphane Grappelli and the Hot Club de France (Europe's first jazz club) as well as records made by Benny Goodman's guitarist Charlie Christian.[30]

The 1920s had brought violin amplification by electricity, typically by clamping a device on the side of the violin or the violin bridge. The choice to plug in or not depends on the kind of music one is fiddling as well as the venue or demands of the performance setting. Through the 1930s, as larger jazz and swing bands incorporated horn sections of saxophones, trumpets, and trombones, the fiddler struggled more and more to be heard above the blast. Some fiddlers like the amplified sound, while others feel that amplification mars a violin's natural tone. Kansas City swing fiddler Claude Williams preferred unaltered sound and natural tone. At the same time, Williams recognized and accommodated to the trends and demands of jazz clubs and concerts, where he would play his acoustic violin amplified with a pickup connected to the sound system—often including electronic keyboard and electric guitar. As recalled by John G. Stewart of Columbia, who accompanied Claude Williams on guitar, Williams used a DeArmond bug for a period of time, then in the 1970s switched to a Barcus-Berry bridge (with a Polytone Mini Brute III amplifier), and in the 1990s changed to a Fishman setup. For a time, Williams experimented performing with a Boss OC-2 octave divider, "to create a second sound one octave below what he was playing on the fiddle." Stewart remembers that Williams "did his best to get it to sound like a sax."[31]

The process of larger and louder poked at old-time fiddlers as well as jazz and swing players, as they found themselves competing to be heard through the wall of sound put out by electric guitars and pedal steel guitars. Electric or electrified violins today are taken for granted in swing, jazz, rock and roll, and the myriad subgenres of alternative music, and even conservative old-time fiddlers sometimes use an attached amplification system in cases where they have difficulty being heard.

Just as Missouri, the crossroads state, had been the cradle of ragtime in the early 1900s, the state was part of the evolution of swing music in the 1930s, with St. Louis on the east side on the Mississippi River and, especially, Kansas City on the Missouri River on the west. Missouri fiddlers and musicians formed numerous ensembles—primarily dance bands. Many of these groups were successful on radio programs and shows, and their music prefigured the country and western music crafted in the 1950s. Missouri's old crossroads character continued right through the twentieth century as swing music was evolving.

Many Missouri fiddlers, rooted in old-time square-dance fiddling, stood aside from a full-on commitment to jazz and swing, even though all but the most conservative of people, if they danced, liked to dance to western-swing bands like Bob Wills's. Many other fiddlers—more than have been noticed—liked it too, even while continuing to be regarded as, and to continue to consider themselves, "old-time" fiddlers. Among them is Warren Helton.

Warren Helton: "Between Texas and Tennessee"

Warren Helton of Vienna (Maries County) exemplifies the enjoyment many old-time fiddlers find in a sojourn along other paths, such as bluegrass and swing.[32] Most if not all fiddlers of deep experience, especially those who played dances, who were active from the 1920s to the 1960s, played some swing tunes—even if sometimes they did not realize it.

Warren Helton (born 1937) is part of one those large pioneer clans that seemed to be full of fiddlers, banjo pickers, jig dancers, guitarists, and singers. The Heltons came from Kentucky or Tennessee to Maries County in 1818, before statehood. In these early decades in central Missouri, the vast majority of such pioneers were old-stock Americans, mainly English and Scotch-Irish. George Helton (Warren's uncle) and brothers Allen and Waldo Helton (cousins) are represented in the Christeson collections of fiddle tunes, and others of the older generations, such as Ike, Arch, and Oliver, are represented in repertoires of fiddlers such as Dean Johnston, Jimmy Gilmore, Lonnie Robertson, John Journagin, Lyman Enloe, and more. Other family fiddlers included Mose, Ben, Otto, and others in previous generations.

Warren (or "Warnie" as he is known) and his younger brother Wayne (born 1940) are keeping the legend alive. Warren Helton started out playing guitar—as many fiddlers did throughout the twentieth century. By age nine, he was seconding his father's fiddling not only on guitar but also sometimes on tenor banjo, which he played by strumming chords with a flat pick; this experience cemented tunes, solid rhythm, and chord changes in his memory. Many family members played old-time frailing-style five-string banjo. The Helton fiddlers also played old-fashioned "second fiddle" accompaniment for other fiddlers.

Brothers Warren and Wayne Helton play twin-fiddle tunes at a music party in Wayne's machine shop at his farm, Maries County, 2010. *Left to right*: Bobby Joe Caldwell (guitar), Warren Helton, John Copeland (a Helton cousin and fiddler, listening), Wayne Helton, and Elzie Helton (guitar).

Surrounded by music, fiddling was in his genes; his father, Vernon, his uncles, and several older cousins held sway as popular entertainers and dance fiddlers and musicians in the family's home area of Maries, Miller, and northern Pulaski Counties, south of Jefferson City. Like many young people, Warren absorbed numerous fiddle tunes from being in the presence of fiddlers at music parties. Among other venues, Helton family fiddlers played for dances in the American Legion Hall in the predominantly German American farming village of Brinktown in Maries County, where the dancers wanted the fiddlers to play waltzes faster than in the Anglo-American communities.

Warren Helton started playing fiddle music at nine years of age. One day he was trying to play the Kay guitar that his older half brother, Arlen, had left when he went into the army during World War II. Warnie's mother was afraid Warnie would scratch Arlen's guitar and took it away from the overeager child. Helton recalls that Bert Sims, a family friend who operated a bus line based in Washington, Missouri, had found a violin forgotten on a bus by its owner. Several years passed with no claim being made on the instrument, and Sims left it at the Heltons' for young Warnie to have—if the boy would learn to play it.[33] The same day his mother took Arlen's guitar away,

> I said, "Mom, I have got a mind to play." And I went in there and got that and played "Soldier's Joy." And I never will forget that. And Mom cried, she said, "I can't believe that." And Dad come home, she told him, [and] *he* cried. And he said, "Warnie, I hear you *played* a little bit—get that fiddle, play one." I said, "I'll play this little thing right here, it ain't very much, ya might tell what it is." And I played "Soldier's Joy." I never forget it. I had my first fiddle tune. I went from there. I was nine year old.

Years later, Jimmy Gilmore examined the instrument and found that it was a small viola.

Warren grew up around fiddlers who had made their marks in early radio broadcasts over Jefferson City's WOS, such as Bill Katon and Jimmy Gilmore. Those fiddlers were also powerful contest players in the region. Helton points to Jimmy Gilmore of Jefferson City as his principal mentor, beyond members of his own family. In long sessions at Gilmore's house in Jefferson City, Helton became more aware of swing fiddling, as this was one of Gilmore's focuses in his playing style and repertoire. They became good friends and played dances at the LoMo Club (near Lohman, west of Jefferson City), the Eagles Club, and other venues and wore fancy outfits when they played at dances. Warren never felt he played waltzes very well, because his mentor Gilmore play waltzes so well.

As demonstrated on the Voyager CD that accompanies the 2012 *Play Me Something Quick and Devilish*, Warren Helton's style is an elegant, subtle, smooth single-note style with fine accent and only occasional touches of double-stops and saw strokes. Listening to his playing "Soldier's Joy" and other standard breakdowns and waltzes

Jimmy Gilmore of Jefferson City, considered by those who heard him only in a fiddlers contest to be an old-time fiddler, also played swing and jazz; with Warren Helton, working out some tunes at Gilmore's home, 1963. (Courtesy Warren Helton)

like "The Waltz You Saved for Me," one might situate his style within what we usually call the Little Dixie style or central Missouri style. Maries County is considered an upper Ozarks county, and his fiddling attests to the fact that very few fiddlers stay put in the categories that scholars construct in analyses and comparative studies. Folk regions exist and serve to recognize distinctive cultural areas and matrices of traditions, but they are porous and borders should be considered outlines, not walls. Warren's style fits well into bluegrass, and he has performed with a number of bluegrass bands through the years, such as Harold Rowden and the Bluegrass Five and Ralph Withers and the Bluegrass Travelers.

Warren's younger sister, Leona Williams, is a strong country singer and songwriter. As a teenager in 1957, Leona had her own live radio show on KWOS-AM in Jefferson City called *Leona Sings*. She moved to Nashville and recorded for labels such as Hickory, RCA, Polygram, and MCA, scoring hits with "Once More," "Yes Ma'am, He Found Me in a Honky Tonk," "Country Girl with Hot Pants On," and "Broadminded." Leona also played upright bass and sang harmony for Loretta Lynn, traveling on tour with Lynn. Leona later recorded a hit record with Merle Haggard, "The Bull and the Beaver," and a duet album, *Heart to Heart*. Leona wrote several hit songs for Haggard, and they were married for several years. She then married songwriter Dave Kirby and moved back to Vienna and continued to tour and release records. In 1999 Leona joined Jean Shepard on the "Grand Ladies of Country Music" show in Branson and subsequently joined the Jim Stafford Theater. She then headlined the "Fall Creek Opry Show" in Branson. Leona recorded duets with George Jones, Jimmy Martin, Floyd Tillman, and other Nashville stars.

During the years that Leona was married to Merle Haggard, opportunities presented themselves for Warren to fiddle on country music shows with Leona and Merle in California and back home in Maries County when they were visiting. Warnie traveled with Leona as her fiddler on *Grand Ole Opry* package shows in 1971, 1972, and 1973, shows that featured Roy Acuff, Little Jimmie Dickens, Tom T. Hall, Hank Williams Jr., and other *Opry* stars. Leona and her group opened the shows. On one occasion, Leona opened the show at the annual Old Threshers Reunion in Mount Pleasant, Iowa, in 1974. At the last minute, Roy Acuff's Smoky Mountain Boys fiddler Howdy Forrester was unable to make the trip, and Acuff asked Helton to fill in for Forrester. Warren Helton knew all of Acuff's records and Howdy Forrester's tunes, and it worked out well. Helton's smooth, notey style reflected Forrester's.

Helton had the good fortune to perform occasionally with Tiny Moore and other legendary swing musicians, some of whom had, like Moore, been members of Bob Wills's Texas Playboys in former decades. Warren Helton: "We'd play all evening me and Jimmy and Tiny would. Out here at Mom's, you know. At different times. They'd stop by here, and park the bus out there, you know. We'd play over here at the Lake [Lake of the Ozarks], you know, we done a show over there. Boy, I'll tell you what, Tiny, that guy would make you want to *play*. I said, one time, 'Tiny you're sittin' on *ready*.' He said, 'Boy, I'm *sittin' on ready*.' Tiny, he played 'Sally Goodin' the best I *ever* heard it."

Warren Helton is strictly an old-time fiddler, even in a music party with Tiny Moore where swing and jazz were predominant. This echoes the experience of Lyman Enloe, Pete McMahan, and others of the old school whose style in performance remained essentially "old time" even while playing bluegrass or pop songs for a dancehall crowd. Warren often accompanies his sister Leona Williams in her Nashville appearances and Branson theater shows and has always been happy to do so, even though he does not play the sort of Nashville style that matches our stereotype of country music. Warren talks about fiddling with Leona's country band: "Leona said, we'd play some of them *swing songs*, like that, you know, and I can put *something in 'em*, you know [backup, fills]. She said, 'Warren, you never did like it—that's why you didn't *learn it*.' I said, 'You got it, you *got* it!' I like something like that 'Sally Goodin'—that's what *I like*, that's what I cut *my* eye teeth on."

For several years, Warnie and Wayne Helton both were members of the Strangers, Merle Haggard's band, and were known for their twin fiddling. Leona was one of Haggard's backup singers during the emergence of the country music landscape in Bakersfield, California—"Nashville West."

Through Warren's guest performances with Haggard and the respect his fiddling engendered, in 1982 he found himself featured in a book that Haggard and Tiny Moore published, *Swinging Texas Fiddlin': A Study of Traditional and Modern Breakdown and Hoedown Fiddling*.[34] This fascinating publication also included examples of the fiddling of Texas champion Vernon Solomon and Tiny Moore, who, along with Jethro Burns and others, had helped introduce electric mandolin to jazz and swing in the 1940s and 1950s. In 1970 Tiny Moore was part of Haggard's LP honoring

Left to right: Warren Helton, Merle Haggard, and Tiny Moore, Bentonville, Arkansas, 1972. (Courtesy Helton)

Bob Wills and Moore performed with Haggard.[35] In *Swinging Texas Fiddlin'*, Moore writes in a chapter titled "Warren Helton Style," "In comparing the styles of Vernon Solomon and Warren Helton, I think it might be said that Warren's style is the link between Texas and Tennessee."[36]

Nine of Warren Helton's tunes are transcribed in Moore and Haggard's *Swinging Texas Fiddlin'*: "Bill Cheatem," "Sally Goodin," "Grey Eagle," "Rag Time Annie" (with the "G part"), "Leather Britches," "Texas Picnic," "Katy Hill," "Billy in the Low Ground," and "Wednesday Night Waltz." All but two of these tunes are ironclads of the broad repertoire of Missouri fiddlers, from old-time square-dance players to swing and bluegrass fiddlers. Helton prefers to keep his fiddling traditional, remarking, in the example "Grey Eagle," that the "old-timers didn't put in extra parts." He plays it in the manner of his father's elder cousin Ike (Ikie) Helton (Waldo's brother) rather than the contemporary contest-derived and Texas-derived version. "I said [to myself], in my olden days, I'm going to play it like I heard it."

Warren Helton finally agreed to make a fiddle CD of his own in early 2014—at his family's request. *Warren Helton: Old Tyme Fiddler* features Warnie's fiddling accompanied by Leona Williams (guitar), Pat Coyne (bass), and Beverly Dillard (clawhammer banjo). Warnie's tune list covers the breadth of his experience and fiddling pleasures, with tunes such as the old family favorites "Billy in the Low Ground," "Ragtime Annie," "Grandpa Helton's Tune," "Marmaduke's Hornpipe," and "Bill

Texas Picnic

as played by Warren Helton

trans by Phil Vinyard

"Texas Picnic," as played by Warren Helton, 2010, one of Helton's tunes in the 1982 book by Tiny Moore and Merle Haggard, *Swinging Texas Fiddlin'*. The tune has elements of "Smith's Reel" in the first part and unusual bowing in the second, less familiar, section. Helton learned the tune from his grandfather Gib Helton in the 1940s: "Dad played it, George played it, they all played it." Despite the title, we are not aware of the tune being played beyond the Helton family musicians in and around Maries, Miller, and Pulaski Counties, Missouri. (Transcription by Philip K. Vinyard)

Cheatem"; breakdowns from Nashville fiddlers Arthur Smith ("Sugar Tree Stomp"), Tommy Jackson ("Acorn Hill Breakdown"), and Howdy Forrester ("Memory Waltz"); a tune from bluegrass star Kenny Baker ("Brandywine"); a Bob Wills swing tune ("Faded Love"); and Jay Ungar's much-loved "Ashoken Farewell." Helton's CD, recorded in his midseventies, speaks well of his music and for two centuries of Helton family fiddling in central Missouri.

"Ozark Cave Dweller" to "Texas Cowboy": Emmett Heath

While an avowed old-time fiddler like Warren Helton enjoyed swing music but remained steadfast in the old-time style in his family, other fiddlers transitioned smoothly into being swing players.

Emmett Heath (1918–59) formed "cowboy bands" in the 1940s, featuring his swing fiddling and his wife Rose's singing. Born in Rayville (Ray County), Heath played square dances, pie suppers, and country taverns in his rural neighborhood along the Missouri River east of Kansas City. Heath met his wife, Rose Washburn, of Princeton, when he was playing fiddle on KFRU radio in Columbia in the late 1930s where she was performing on a live show of her own as a cowgirl singer named "Carolina Katy."

Emmett and Rose Heath enjoyed the joyful western stage outfits popularized in the movies, mass culture, and many touring bands. They performed on various radio stations in Missouri in addition to KFRU and toured extensively in the South and Southwest. During the period when Heath fiddled on KFRU, Columbia-area fiddlers picked up tunes from his radio performances; Pete McMahan learned "Kentucky Blues" from Heath, and McMahan recalled that no other fiddlers seem to have played that tune.

Heath's daughter, Sharon Marriott, recalls some of his particular favorites, such as "Rocky Mountain Hornpipe," "Sailor's Hornpipe" (in the key of B-flat, a.k.a. "College Hornpipe"), "Durang's Hornpipe," "Fisher's Hornpipe" (in F), and "Ricketts' Hornpipe," along with ancient breakdowns such as "Wagner," rags such as "Black & White Rag," and the omnipresent jig "Irish Wash Women" ("Irish Washerwoman").

Emmett Heath's "Ozark Cave Dwellers" appeared on KFEQ radio in St. Joseph in the 1940s; they posed as cornball hillbillies to get jobs, but they were more cowboy than hillbilly. The instruments included a metal-body resophonic guitar and a homemade comic tenor banjo as well as violin. The announcer in the ten-gallon hat looks the part of the country squire, another familiar stereotype. (Courtesy Sharon Heath Marriott)

Sharon Marriott and her daughter, Nikki Marriott, protected several recordings made circa 1952 by Emmett and Rose with Garl Weaver (plectrum banjo). Garl Weaver was a barber and close family friend in Orrick, a few miles from Excelsior Springs, who in his spare time restored player pianos and clocks and built an occasional violin, including one with the scroll carved as a lion's head. The original recordings were made by Emmett Heath on a home recorder that produced one wax disc at a time. The recordings aptly demonstrate musicianship and command of a variety of tunes, from Roy Acuff's 1936 "Freight Train Blues" to the 1925 swing anthem "Sweet Georgia Brown" and fiddle tunes such as the 1790s tune "Durang's Hornpipe," the Texas tune popularized in 1923 by Eck Robertson "Done Gone," and Fiddlin' Arthur Smith's 1930s "Fiddler's Dream."

During Prohibition, the vast and sumptuous Elms spa and hotel in Excelsior Springs, an easy drive from Kansas City's Union Station, was a popular leisure getaway for shady characters such as Chicago mob boss Al Capone and other big-spending notables of the time. The Art Deco–style Hall of Waters building in the Elms compound was erected in 1936 by the federal government's WPA and now

Emmett Heath's "Texas Rangers" reflected the popularity and influence of the Bob Wills band as well as the nation's general embrace of Hollywood-influenced cowboy pop culture. Here the group is in Jackson, Mississippi, in 1939, where they performed on WJDX. The attire says success, and the band has the luxury of emblematic guitars of the era, an archtop (a favorite among swing players) for lead and rhythm guitar work and a Martin D-18. (Courtesy Sharon Heath Marriott)

Sweet Georgia Brown

Transcribed by Sharon Graf

as played by Emmett Heath 1952

recording begins mid-tune

Second time through is a slight variation of the first.

"Sweet Georgia Brown," Emmett Heath's version of the classic swing song, ca. 1952, with Rose (Carolina Katy) Heath (guitar) and Garl Weaver (plectrum banjo) (hear on the companion CD). (Transcription by Sharon Graf)

The Hall of Waters at the Elms hotel and spa in Excelsior Springs, where Emmett Heath died while fiddling for a dance in 1959. (Period postcard)

houses a museum and city offices. Mineral baths could be taken in the hall's well-appointed lower chambers. In the evenings dance bands like Emmett Heath's played music for patrons in various rooms in the hotel and Hall of Waters. In March 1959, at age forty-eight, Emmett Heath suffered a fatal heart attack while fiddling for dancers in the Hall of Waters ballroom.

Too Hot for Old-Time Radio: Zed Tennis

One of those who could have made it in Los Angeles or New York (or Nashville) was one of Missouri's best swing fiddlers—Zed Tennis. Almost too far out for acceptance in the conservative hillbilly radio broadcast scene in Missouri, Zed was, according to Gordon McCann, "too modern for the old-time fiddlers around here."[37]

Lowell (Zed) Tennis was born in the Christian County town of Nixa in 1912 and died at age fifty-nine in Springfield. Zed came up the usual way, learning fiddle tunes and playing for pie suppers, jam sessions, and dances. And then he got into swing music. This was the golden age of hillbilly records and radio, with 50,000-watt AM stations and touring bands carrying the new sounds across the continent. Trying his hand in the professional world, Tennis performed on AM radio stations in Kansas City as early as 1931, including WHB, and performed with a cowboy swing band called the Sophisticated Rangers on WOW in Omaha, Nebraska.[38]

Hank Penny's Radio Cowboys and Plantation Boys bands were among the first ensembles in the southeastern United States "to adopt songs and styles from their southwestern contemporaries" and take western swing to new audiences.[39] Penny was, in fact, rather like Tennis—a bit ahead of his time. When Hank Penny was invited to bring his band to *The Grand Ole Opry*, the performance was canceled by *Opry* leadership when they saw that Penny's band used drums and horns; the new music was drastically out of sync, and perhaps even threatening, in comparison to the well-groomed stereotype of "pure and rural" music promoted on *Opry* broadcasts. After this snub, Penny mused that his band stood no chance of being accepted in Nashville, because, "in those days (Nashville) was rank-and-file hillbilly."[40] Later, in 1944, Bob Wills had the same experience of being threatened with rejection by *Grand Ole Opry* managers; Wills was warned that "there will be no drums nor horns." However, Bob Wills refused to perform without his horns and drums, and he prevailed, and the *Opry* reluctantly aired its first real swing band, Bob Wills and the Texas Playboys.[41] The Hank Penny and Bob Wills bands were troublemakers in the eyes of *Grand Ole Opry* management, but by this time, during the zenith of big-band orchestras in the World War II years, the tide of swing and western-swing music would not be checked by grumpy antiquarians and shortsighted businessmen. Swing and western swing constituted the bulk of America's most popular music.

Zed Tennis left Missouri to perform as part of Hank Penny's Plantation Boys in 1941 when Penny was booked on the WLW *Barn Dance* in Cincinnati. There, Tennis worked up fancy twin-fiddle choruses with Carl Stewart and traded hot licks with takeoff lead guitarist Roy Lanham.[42] Their popularity on this and other radio stations made the band a success, and Zed became a contributor to western swing's development. In 1944 Penny and the Plantation Boys toured military bases in the southern states as a USO group. After the war, partly due to letters from his friend Merle Travis, who had served in the Marine Corps, Penny moved to California. "Travis said California was *the place* for a country entertainer: the money was good and the dance halls were begging for bands to entertain the thousands of defense plant workers and GIs in the Los Angeles area."[43]

After leaving Penny, Zed Tennis moved back to Springfield and found work as a staff musician at KWTO radio. Among the station's popular bands was a family ensemble, the Haden Family, and Zed fitted in with this ensemble. Ed McKinney remembers hearing the shows and thought Zed Tennis's fiddling was "very jazzy" and a step beyond what other fiddlers were presenting.[44] With Tennis providing much of the hot music, in the late 1940s the show's name became the Haden Family with Doc Martin and Zed Tennis. Tennis was often introduced over the air as "Zed Tennis, the prairie playboy," a nod to the influence and popularity of Bob Wills and the Texas Playboys. While Tennis was the Haden group's fiddler, he played mandolin as well, just as many fiddlers do. Tennis was among the first players to experiment with electric mandolins, which many listeners and fellow musicians found compatible with the evolving western-swing band sound.

Tennis composed several swing tunes, including "Finley Creek Blues," a bluesy country rag (two-step) that in successive years was popularized by old-time fiddlers such as Glenn Rickman, Art Galbraith, Lonnie Robertson, Jude Herndon, Emanuel

Zed Tennis with *The Penny Nichols Show*, KWTO-AM radio, Springfield, 1948. *Left to right*: Tennis, Luke McNeley (bass), Chuck Bowers (guitar), Penny Nichols, and Dale Parker (banjo). (*Dial*, November 1948, 20) (Courtesy Ed McKinney)

Wood, Bob Holt, and Jim Beeler, most of whom heard Tennis play the tune on KWTO and other shows.[45] Finley Creek is a tributary of the James River, which forks northeast and runs south of Zed's hometown of Nixa. Zed Tennis, unlike the Ozark old-time fiddlers who played the tune, was accompanied by a swing guitarist playing jazz chords, which gave a different and more fox-trot-like feel to the music. As recalled by Ed McKinney:

> Zed played mostly electric mandolin on their shows with a guy named "Doc" Martin playing steel guitar, but Zed usually put in one short fiddle tune per show. . . . The Haden's big thing was singing, although "Uncle" Carl H. played the harmonica occasionally, and Carl Jr. played rhythm guitar. At times daughter Elizabeth is posed in pictures either with an arched-top tenor guitar (Gibson) or with a mandolin (Martin two-point), but I don't recall hearing her play either of them. The next youngest son, "Smokey Mountain Jim," played stand-up bass in those days. Today, the next younger son, Charlie Haden, is a world-renowned bassist, traveling all over the world holding seminars and teaching classes on stand-up bass playing; he also records with high-priced bands.[46]

The Haden Family traveled the circuit of regional radio stations, performing for a period of time on live programs and then moving to other stations. In the early 1940s, they performed over NBC affiliate WOW in Omaha. At the WOW studio they recorded a series of transcriptions of their live shows.[47] Thanks to McKinney, we can hear transcriptions of live fifteen-minute shows that aired on WOW from August and September 1952. The programs were broadcast with Tennis, the "Cowtown Wrangler," fiddling with Doc Martin and the Hayden Family while the ensemble was performing under contract with WOW. A typical program, sponsored by Dexol

Bleach, Shina-a-Dish kitchen cleaner, and Perfex Super Glass Cleaner, looked like this one that aired August 29, 1952. The master of ceremonies was Doc Martin, and the play list is a nice mix of cowboy music, jazz, gospel, and traditional songs:

1. Theme tune, "Ride into Town" (up-tempo swing).
2. "It's a Sin."
3. "I'll Build My Castle in Heaven."
4. "Limehouse Blues" (instrumental; electric guitar first solo, then pedal steel guitar, then electric mandolin). Emcee says they have had listeners ask, "What is that instrument? Is it zither, or what?" Tennis: "Well, it's an electrified mandolin."
5. "Echoes from the Hills."
6. Emcee: "Now then, for all you old-time fiddle lovers out there, Zed Tennis, the flash from Nixa, is going to get his old Stradivicious up here, and he's going to give us a tune a lot of you have been asking for—Ida [pronounced "I'dee"] red and Ida blue, and I got stuck on Ida too!"
7. Thought for the day, "We are easily consoled, because we are easily afflicted."
8. Theme tune.

"Ida Red" is a well-traveled chestnut, appearing on early 78 rpm records of string bands in the Southeast, such as recordings by Fiddlin' Powers & Family (vocal by Carson Robison) in 1924, Riley Puckett with Gid Tanner and the Skillet Lickers in 1926, and under the title "Shooting Creek" by Charlie Poole and the North Carolina Ramblers in 1928.[48] The more familiar breakdown "Cripple Creek" is a relative of "Ida Red" as played in the South and Southeast. However, for swing musicians, and most Missourians of whatever stylistic persuasion, the "Ida Red" we have in Zed's fiddling is drawn from the tune's western-swing tributary of recordings, dance-hall appearances, and broadcasts of Bob Wills and the Texas Playboys. This is the version that served as the foundation for versions played by swing bands like Hank Penny's and swing fiddlers like Zed Tennis and many others. Tennis fiddles a chorus of "Cripple Creek" while playing "Ida Red" in the 1952 radio transcription. This is a good example of a Missouri fiddler representing traditions here, drawing on the inherited "Cripple Creek" and embracing more modern stylings of "Ida Red." What began as a breakdown became a standard two-step in dance halls across Missouri, Oklahoma, Texas, and points west.[49]

Zed's repertoire was as diverse as any lead player in a hot swing band. Often, on popular Roaring Twenties songs such as "Limehouse Blues" and "Yes Sir, That's My Baby,"[50] Tennis lofted takeoff solos on electric mandolin that would sound familiar to fans of Jethro Burns and Tiny Moore. The electric mandolin had just been developed and come into western swing largely through experimentation by Moore, a gifted swing player in California, a former Texan who had played with Bob Wills and the

Ida Red

Transcribed by Sharon Graf

as played by Zed Tennis 1952

"Ida Red," by Zed Tennis with Doc Martin and the Haden Family, August 29, 1952, broadcast from a prerecorded radio transcription (disc) over Omaha, Nebraska, station WOW-AM (hear on the companion CD). (Courtesy Ed McKinney; transcription by Sharon Graf)

Texas Playboys in the 1940s and recorded instrumentals with, among others, electric guitarist Eldon Shamblin and out-and-out jazz musicians like Shelly Manne.

Among others who remember Zed Tennis on KWTO in Springfield is guitarist and singer Michael Breid, who performed on the station with Tennis. According to Breid, "Zed was a hot Joe Venuti type fiddler. His big fiddle piece was 'Sunrise on a Guinea Farm.'"[51]

By the time of his death, Zed Tennis had been retired from the music business for many years. He had generally been forgotten by younger musicians, as the arc of western swing evened out with the popularity of competing genres such as bluegrass and rock and roll–influenced Nashville country. Zed's 1971 obituary in the Springfield paper barely touched his story as one of Missouri's most innovative and best-known jazz musicians. Nixa did, however, name a street after him.

Einstein of the Double-Stop, Dale Potter

> **Dale Potter's fiddling was so unique and impressive during the 50's and 60's on the Opry and on Chet Atkin's recordings, among others, that it wouldn't be too much of a stretch to suggest that it influenced every country/bluegrass fiddler who heard it.**
>
> —Peter Feldman, FIDDLE-L Internet discussion group, June 5, 2005

Dale Potter (1929–96) was a pioneer in the evolution of mid-1900s fiddle styles in western swing, "country and western," and bluegrass music. Versatile and gifted, Potter put a palpable stamp on today's bluegrass fiddling as well as western swing. A surprising number of older old-time Missouri fiddlers of my acquaintance were impressed by Dale Potter's fiddling, which for the most part they knew primarily through Potter's studio work in Nashville. Potter's smooth, complicated double- and triple-stops, backup, and fills and breaks are heard in some of Hank Williams's first recordings. Since the mid-1940s, Potter's inventive fiddling has been studied. He was always grounded in tradition, even his evolution of the now obligatory double-stop (and the rarer triple-stop) and including session work on Nashville stars' recordings, his tours with *Opry* star packages, and legendary gigs in Las Vegas.

Today double-stops are de rigueur for fiddlers in bluegrass, swing, and country music and the "old-time" player looking for ways to dress up a waltz. It was not always this way. Perhaps more than any other fiddler on the national scene, Potter set the pattern for smooth, flowing double-stops in fiddle music. Some say Potter invented the double-stop, but what Potter did was bring double-stops and harmony lines to a pinnacle of beauty and finesse that other players consider their model.

From the 1940s until the 1970s, Potter recorded with a who's who of country and bluegrass music, from Hank Williams, Carl Smith, Chet Atkins, Little Jimmy Dickens, Ray Price, and Webb Pierce to Bill Monroe and Mac Wiseman. Potter recorded with Bill Monroe's band, providing much-imitated twin fiddling with Benny Martin on Monroe's 1939 "Stoney Lonesome."[52] It is safe to say that every

Dale Potter with the Musical Millers, sponsored by Martha White Flour on Nashville's *Grand Ole Opry.* (WSM radio)

professional fiddler who played bluegrass, swing, or jazz in the 1950s and 1960s, whether Johnny Gimble, Benny Martin, Scotty Stoneman, Vassar Clements, Buddy Spicher, or Kelly Jones, owed a debt to Potter's vanguard. He was blessed with impeccable taste and burnished a swinging, jazzy style with perfect double-stops. Potter was an inventive player who played with a heavy bow stroke, and his style had appeal across musical genres.

As Paul Shelasky notes, Potter became a "legendary Nashville session fiddler whose early recordings with Chet Atkins, Jethro Burns, and other notables show his playing in the modern, jazzy style which made him famous, but he was a versatile musician who could adapt to any situation—witness his many recordings with Bill Monroe and the Bluegrass Boys."[53] Bill Monroe was, of course, the demanding boss man who hammered out his concept of bluegrass in the 1940s and 1950s by weeding through musicians to find those who could and would meet his vision of the music and who could command his respect. Monroe was hard to please, and it is a testimony to Potter's session skills in previous work with country stars like Hank Williams and Webb Pierce that Monroe said of Potter, "He was the only man I never had to tell anything twice."[54]

Dale Potter was born in 1929 in the farming community of Acorn Ridge east of Puxico (Stoddard County), a town named for a Shawnee chieftain.[55] The Bootheel region of southeastern Missouri is delta farmland, with drained swamps, forested flatlands, and bayou environment that had been converted into land suitable for cotton, soybeans, rice, and corn. The area is more Deep South than other parts of Missouri. It is on the Trail of Tears pathways by which Cherokee and other tribes from the Southeast came across Missouri, bound for the Indian Territory in northeastern Oklahoma; many citizens in the region have mixed ancestry. Acorn Ridge and Puxico are on the southern and eastern edges of the Ozark hills near a unique geological uplift called Crowley's Ridge. Crowley's Ridge runs from the Mississippi River just above Cape Girardeau and goes southwest past Poplar Bluff and to Helena, Arkansas, a landform that marks a natural boundary between the Ozark hills and the Bootheel delta.

Dale's father, John Potter, was a well-known fiddler in the community and taught Dale traditional fiddle tunes as a boy of nine. His first instruments were mandolin and guitar, and then, with violin, he began playing square dances and winning old-time fiddlers contests. Like Zed Tennis and many other youngsters with avid imaginations and broader horizons, Potter learned a lot of fiddle music from listening to records and radio shows—especially KVOO in Tulsa. Turning the knob to KVOO and other Oklahoma (and Texas) stations, instead of dialing WSM back east in Nashville, Tennessee, was significant, because doing so immersed the young fiddler in the sounds of emerging western swing, particularly the music of Bob Wills and the Texas Playboys. While successful in the old-time fiddling around him, Potter became fascinated by the swinging music.

Potter focused on learning the fiddling he heard on radio and records, with interesting limitations and results. As Nancy Cardwell writes in an interview with Bobby Hicks (a star pupil of Dale Potter's), as a boy Potter did not know that Bob Wills had two and sometimes three fiddlers playing the music he was hearing. Dale began to work out for himself how to play the multiple double-stops (and even triple-stops)—melody and harmony at the same time on two strings—in an effort to sound like the Bob Wills band's two and three fiddlers. This Potter accomplished, and his ability to play these harmonies and chords would eventually make him famous. His term for double-stop fiddling was "two string" playing.[56]

Before departing to forge a career as a professional, Potter played dances and competed in fiddling contests. He won the Puxico Home Coming contest in 1939 at age ten and then won the same competition the next two years. There were old-time fiddlers contests at county fairs and fall homecomings; Stoddard County had annual contests, and contests that Potter would have attended as a child were occasionally reported in newspapers of the later 1930s. However, in going through microfilm of newspapers in Dexter and Poplar Bluff in August and September 1939, 1940, and 1941, I found that Potter's name does not appear in the cursory coverage of fiddlers contests in those towns. Newspapers there appear not to have reported fiddlers contest results, although they advertised contests and reported extensively on other kinds of competitions in the community, such as WPA camp band contests, hog-calling contests, talent shows, and various beauty pageants.[57]

From 1939 through the World War II years, fiddlers contests had steadily lost the attention of newspapers, as critical issues of the Great Depression and then World War II captivated people's attention. Coverage of the fall agricultural festivals in Stoddard County concentrated on livestock and agricultural competitions—important farmwork with practical uses in a time of national uncertainty—almost to the total exclusion of reporting on entertainments such as the talent shows, vaudeville troupes, and fiddlers contests.

In high school in nearby Poplar Bluff, Potter was appreciated as a star musician in the community. School authorities granted him permission to leave class early each day in order to fiddle over the local AM station, KWOC, with Poplar Bluff country singer and guitarist Henry (Slim) Dortch and *The Ozark Jamboree*, a popular radio show. Other Missouri fiddlers performed over KWOC during this general time period in the late 1930s, including Gene Goforth, who played on the station in 1937 when Potter was eight years old. An old friend who attended Potter's funeral in 1996, Hank Jones, who performed with Eddy Arnold, recalled that, in a gem of understatement, "Dale would rather play fiddle than go to school."[58]

After working at KWOC, Potter traveled to Blytheville, Arkansas, some two hours' drive southeast of Poplar Bluff. There he fiddled with guitarist Thomas (Butterball) Paige over radio station KLCN. Paige and Potter were a popular duo, and they decided to move to Nashville to try their luck. There they went their separate ways, with Butterball Paige joining Ernest Tubb's Texas Troubadours and Potter fiddling with Milton Estes and His Musical Millers on *The Grand Ole Opry*. Potter found acceptance and success in Nashville; by the time Potter arrived, western swing was beginning to be taken seriously and programmed on even the more conservative country radio stations.

In January 1948, at age eighteen, Dale Potter made his first appearance on WSM's *Grand Ole Opry*, and he remained a regular on the *Opry*, performing with different ensembles, for the next thirty years, where numerous fiddlers studied his innovative double- and triple-stops.[59] Following his success on WSM, Potter began taking recording studio assignments, and in this highly prestigious (if underpaid) role he appeared on some of Hank Williams's first recordings, including the hit record "Wedding Bells." Some of country music's classic hits came from these Hank Williams sessions, such as "Lost Highway" and "Mind Your Own Business."[60] For country fiddlers and bluegrass fiddlers, Potter's "fills" and "licks" that serve as accent phrases and passages between vocal lines, and in other places in the song, as well as his rich double-stops, are still awe inspiring. In the early recordings with Hank Williams, we can hear the highly arranged tradeoffs between Potter and the steel guitar as well as the electric lead guitar. Other fiddlers would record with Hank Williams, and many others would be members of his band the Drifting Cowboys, such as Nashville session players Jerry Rivers, Chubby Wise, and Tommy Jackson, but Dale Potter set the standard.

Soon after his session work with Hank Williams, Potter went into the studio and laid down the fiddle track for Red Foley's "Sugarfoot Rag" (a retooling of a fiddle tune sometimes known as "Pretty Little Widow") with guitarist Hank (Sugarfoot) Garland. Following this, Potter took part in a session leading to a legendary 1952 record called *Jazz from the Hills*. This session includes Chet Atkins, Homer and Jethro (Homer Haynes and Jethro Burns), and steel guitar wizard Jerry Byrd in an informal group that became known around the music industry as the Country All-Stars. *Jazz from the Hills* included "Fiddle Sticks," one of Potter's best-known fiddling showcases; this LP remains one of the finest recorded statements of the innovative music being made by Potter, Atkins, Burns, and Byrd.[61] Potter also composed and recorded his signature tune, "Fiddle Patch," on RCA Victor, a standard piece in swing fiddling. Attesting to Potter's stature in both the "country" and "bluegrass" camps, "Fiddle Patch" appears in Stacy Phillips and Kenny Kosek's *Bluegrass Fiddle Styles*.[62] Based in Nashville, Potter performed with a variety of country singers and bands and traveled to other locations to perform, such as appearances over KWTO radio in Springfield, Missouri.

"Fiddle Patch" is associated today with Nashville fiddler Bobby Hicks. Hicks, who acknowledges that he learned his double-stop techniques from Potter, says, "Dale was king. He was the king fiddler around here [Nashville]. People like Jimmie Dickens and Webb Pierce—gosh, I don't know who all he recorded with—they would [wait to] record until he was back, if he was out of town or something. That's how good he was."[63]

Potter was drafted into the army during the Korean War and served in Korea in an engineer battalion. His hearing was damaged by his experiences in the army, but this partial impairment may have caused him to play more powerfully. After being discharged, he returned to Nashville and recorded and performed with Carl Smith, Kitty Wells, Web Pierce, Little Jimmie Dickens, Patsy Cline, Charlie Walker, Ray Price, Cowboy Copas (Lloyd Copas), Mac Wiseman, Faron Young, Bill Monroe and the Bluegrass Boys, and Boxcar Willie.[64] Dale found that things had changed in the industry while he was in Korea. Rock and roll was making heavy inroads into country music's audience and becoming an influence in the making of country music itself. Potter began to travel to perform with country shows in Las Vegas as well as in Honolulu and Dallas.

Among available recordings of Potter's fiddling is a set on a Rural Rhythm label compilation CD, *24 Fiddle Favorites*, which includes "Back Up and Push," "Las Raspa" (a.k.a. "Mexican Hat Dance"), "Gallopin' on the Fiddle," "Dill Pickle Rag," and "Corina" in addition to his signature piece, "Fiddle Patch."[65] His powerful versions of familiar tunes like "Back Up and Push" set the bar very high for other fiddlers. It is noteworthy that when Dale Potter put together his own albums of his music, he chose to include a pedal steel guitar player, recalling his recording sessions of the past. Potter was among few professional fiddlers who felt comfortable and artistically challenged when playing alongside the electric pedal steel guitar rather than feeling covered up or threatened. Some fiddlers today, such as Buddy Spicher and Kelly Jones, carry on Dale Potter's style of presenting tunes such as this.

Several examples of Potter's bluegrass fiddling appear on reissues of Bill Monroe recordings, such as *Mr. Bluegrass*.[66] Potter's smoothness and creative double-stops have continued to inspire younger professional fiddlers across the spectrum, from bluegrassers to Nashville cats to contest fiddlers to jazz players. Potter's first Rural Rhythm LP in 1963, *Dale Potter: World's Champion Country & Western Fiddler, Hoe Down!* (volume 1), includes a diverse list of country songs, popular tunes from his travels, fiddle tunes, and the obligatory gospel hymn, all played in a style that is still considered to be, a half century later, "wild" by many old-time fiddlers: "Draggin' the Bow," "Bully of the Town," "Let Me Call You Sweetheart," "In the Garden," "Rubber Dolly," "Faded Love," "Beaumont Rag," "Maiden's Prayer," "Hawaiian Sunset," "Westphalia Waltz," "New Carrol [*sic*] County Blues," "Twinkle Star," "Silver Threads among the Gold," "Big Ball in Town," "Aloha Oe" (the symbolic Hawaiian song from the 1890s), "Omie Wise's Tragic Romance," "Precious Memories," "Spanish Two-Step," "Don't Let the Deal Go Down," and "Gotta Travel On."[67] Such a wide selection of music from across the spectrum could help sell a recording, but in the case of a versatile fiddler like Potter, this was a set list of tunes he played in shows and enjoyed playing.

Potter moved back to Puxico in 1992, and his last years were spent in the Puxico–Poplar Bluff area. His music, however, traveled the world. As noted by Paul Wadey in an obituary in the London, England, *Independent*: "Many connoisseurs regard Dale Potter as the finest fiddler in the history of country music."[68]

Claude Williams on the cover of the University of Missouri alumni magazine, Columbia, 1984, featured in a story about his participation in the university's Missouri Cultural Heritage Center programs. He played a nineteenth-century German copy of an Amati violin and amplified it with a Baggs pickup system.

Born to Play Swing

9

It don't mean a thing if it ain't got that swing.

—Duke Ellington, 1931

Claude "Fiddler" Williams: A Jazz Life

If you ever want to hear the best jazz violin, look up Claude Williams out in Kansas City. I tell you this cat is great!

—Buddy Tate quoted in Mary Lee Hester, "The Cat's in the Fiddle," in *Going to Kansas City* (1980)

Perhaps Missouri's best-known jazz fiddlers in the formative years prior to the 1960s were Eddie South and Claude Williams, major recording artists as well as influential musicians.[1] Eddie South (1904–62) was born in the Mississippi River town of Louisiana, Missouri. South was African American and, although a violin prodigy and classically trained, found it difficult to find work in classical music. He traveled to France, as did many African American artists, writers, and musicians in those times. There, in addition to studying violin at the Paris Conservatoire, South began playing gypsy jazz and performing with Stéphane Grappelli and Django Reinhardt. Returning to Chicago, Eddie South continued to be an important innovator in jazz, Latin jazz, and swing.

Claude Williams, part of the same generation, fared better as an African American playing jazz and swing in Missouri, in part due to his location and work on the west side of the state in Kansas City's famous jazz and nightclub district. Williams was also blessed with longevity and lived to see a modern era that welcomed and took new interest in his music.

Williams was born in Muskogee, Oklahoma, in 1908, a son of blacksmith Lee Williams. As a boy, Williams listened to fiddle bands playing for dances and informal jam sessions in his Muskogee neighborhood of African American, old-stock American, and Indian families. That his family tree combined the cultural heritage of Cherokee, African American, and white European people was a source of pride to Claude Williams, and he often spoke of these elements in his life.

By ten Claude was playing pop and blues songs on guitar and mandolin with his brother and cousins in barbershops and hotel lobbies and for dances and had taught himself to play piano by ear.[2] While he was playing guitar in various venues, Claude was beginning to hear fiddlers, and the first fiddler that fired his imagination was Jack Skaggs, a believed-to-be-white blues fiddler from McAlester. Claude had been focused on guitar and playing melodies on the cello.[3] In a 1988 KOPN-FM radio interview with Susan Newstead, he recalled that, as a boy, like many other people, he pronounced the word "sel'lo."[4] Claude installed bass strings on his cello and plucked it as one would an upright bass, rather than bowing the cello. Williams would also occasionally play chords on a tenor banjo when additional rhythm was needed to shore up an ensemble. Williams's brother-in-law, Ben Johnson, "told my mama he was going to get me something that would never go out of style. He went downtown and traded that cello for a fiddle."[5]

Most accounts of Claude Williams's early days do not mention Jack Skaggs, focusing instead on his meeting with the charismatic and ebullient Joe Venuti. In 1928 Claude happened to hear Venuti perform with the Paul Whiteman Orchestra at a Muskogee fair. After hearing Joe Venuti fiddle "You've Got to See Your Mama Every Night or You Can't See Mama at All," within days Claude was playing the tune like Venuti.[6] Another important experience for young Williams was hearing Louis Armstrong play at a nightclub in Tulsa, an event that inspired Williams to learn to play diminished chords on guitar and violin and to improvise on the chord changes in tunes. Williams recalled, in remarks heavy with implications for what made his swing style distinctive: "'That's why I was a little ahead of other fiddlers. Now, Stuff Smith could swing, but he didn't know anything about changes and chords. All the cats wanted to jam with me because they knew they would hear *changes*, something different, not just jazzin' the melody.' Like other violinists such as Cecil Brower, Claude modeled his style after brass and reed instruments. 'That's because I mostly jammed with trumpets and saxophones.'"[7]

Williams began playing in the Muskogee-to–Oklahoma City circuit, often in a string band with Ben Johnson and other friends. At sixteen Williams performed with the Oscar Pettiford family band, another of the territory bands that traveled to cities within about a day's automobile drive from home. Pettiford was from Ocmulgee (some fifty miles from Muskogee), another northeastern Oklahoma town with a mixed Anglo, African American, and Indian community. Oscar Pettiford would later be famous as a bassist with jazz players such as Charlie Barnet and Coleman Hawkins and formed a 1940s bebop jazz ensemble with Dizzy Gillespie. Pettiford was also famous for playing jazz on the cello. Another of the territory bands was the Tulsa-based Terrance Holder band, and Williams joined this group in 1927. The Holder ensemble was called Holder's Dark Clouds of Joy and evolved into Andy Kirk's Twelve Clouds of Joy. Jitney dances (taxi dances) were one of the band's steady gigs.

> [At] jitney dances, the male patrons were required to pay a dime for the privilege of cutting a rug with one of the stable of dance-hall beauties. One jitney dance promoter in Tulsa made so much money "he'd give away a new Ford every Friday night," Williams said. "We'd never play a song for more than two minutes, then he'd blow a whistle and say, "Now we'll have a fox trot." At the end of each number, employees would encircle the dancers with a long rope, clearing them off the floor like cattle. To dance again, a man had to tear off another 10-cent ticket. "Union scale was a dollar and a half a night," Williams remembered. "We'd play for three, four hours with no intermission."[8]

The Kansas City Scene

In 1929 the Clouds' new leader, Andy Kirk, moved the band from Dallas to Kansas City, where they were booked at major dance and entertainment ballrooms.

Kansas City was the nearest major urban area with an active blues, jazz, and swing environment. There Andy Kirk and His Twelve Clouds of Joy became a formative swing and jazz orchestra. There was something very attractive about the music scene in Kansas City, a "wide-open town," where, in the Roaring Twenties, just about everything related to the entertainment business, and many other businesses as well, was controlled by crime syndicates. This was during Prohibition, and a lawless excitement permeated many neighborhoods, appealing to young people and others in these years after the hardships of the First World War and the 1929 stock market crash.

Among Kansas City's neighborhoods was a distinctive African American social, cultural, and business landscape in and around the blocks from Twelfth to Eighteenth Streets ("Eighteenth and Vine"). These were the "streets of dreams" where the "riff-based sound fueled by jam sessions in the district's crowded clubs" that were a principal "cradle of jazz."[9]

Like New York's Harlem, Chicago's South Side, and San Francisco's Tenderloin, Eighteenth and Vine was a relatively self-contained and self-sustaining cultural region, transformed by the influx of African American migrants in the early twentieth century from Old South areas to cities in the Midwest and North, typically railroad hubs and industrial centers, where jobs were waiting. Eighteenth and Vine became an incubator for jazz and swing, as other cities and railroad towns such as Joplin, Sedalia, New Franklin, and Moberly had been incubators for piano and ragtime in earlier decades.[10]

African American musicians, like their white colleagues, were performing live on AM radio in Kansas City. Bennie Moten's orchestra performed on WHB in 1923. "Count Basie had a regular slot on WHB playing the organ in the mid-1930s and WHB broadcast the Vine Street Varieties from the Lincoln Theater around the same time."[11] WHB in these years was a principal purveyor of swing, western swing, and jazz; the station later switched to Top 40 rock and roll. Such radio performances greatly helped the spread of jazz and even, as Nathan Pearson suggests, the development of jazz styles.[12]

Musicians came together in dance bands, nightclubs, and late-night sessions at after-hours spots to evolve what would be known as "Kansas City jazz," a style combining blues and swing and heavy on improvisation and individual artistry. Claude Williams's description of improvisation: "Taking the chords of a song and adding to that."[13] Among the many records produced was the Kansas City–born pianist Bennie Moten's remodeling of the old standard written by Thamon Hayes, "South," in 1928 (Victor 24893)—a tune played by old-time fiddlers as a two-step (fox-trot) today.[14] Bennie Moten had studied ragtime piano with two of Scott Joplin's students, and, with a modernized swing band under his baton that featured inventive young

Fox's Tavern, corner of Eighteenth and Vine, Kansas City, ca. 1945, one of the "jazz joints" in the district. (University of Missouri–Kansas City Libraries, Dr. Kenneth J. LaBudde Department of Special Collections)

musicians such as Count Basie, Walter Page, Ben Webster, and singer Jimmy Rushing, his orchestra was Kansas City's top dance band in the late 1920s—and the first to make jazz records.

As Claude Williams often said, "Kansas City had a different style, it seemed," and "jazz fiddlers don't play the tune the same way twice." "[Jazz is] music that, I've heard different fellows say, will cause you to start patting your foot. Kansas City was something like Vegas, then. Nobody'd go to bed at any time."[15] Kansas City was such an important center for jazz and swing that Williams felt that, in order to make it big in New York or Paris or LA, musicians first needed to come to Kansas City and spend some time in the Eighteenth and Vine scene. "The best musicians in the world have come through Kansas City. . . . Come to Kansas City and get the stamp on you, and then you can go anywhere."[16]

In 1929 Williams began recording with Andy Kirk's band, playing tenor guitar as well as violin. Williams appeared on the Clouds' first records for Brunswick and Vocalion, "Mess-a-Stomp," "Blue Clarinet Stomp," and "Cloudy."[17] After leaving the Clouds of Joy in 1930, Williams looked for work and spent a year playing tenor banjo in a dance band at jitney dances; the club owner had informed Williams that, if he wanted a job, he would have to play tenor banjo in the orchestra.[18]

Claude's prowess on the violin became evident, and he became Kansas City's leading jazz violinist. Playing in concerts and clubs in the Eighteenth and Vine neighborhood gave him opportunities to jam with touring artists like fiddler Stuff Smith and saxophonist Lester Young. Williams developed a lifelong affection for jazz saxophone and later included sax in his own recordings. Ironically, as the years went by, horns, especially saxophones, tended to replace violins in swing and jazz ensembles.

In Kansas City, Williams became a mentor to teenage saxophonist Charlie Parker. Experts have suggested that Claude's "fat" "hornlike" violin sound developed at least in part from his close relationships with Young, Parker, and other saxophonists. Stanley Crouch: "Williams is one of the unsung heroes of jazz violin; his control of the instrument allows him to get colors that are now nasal, now guttural, now frail and blistered by romance, now surging with the pulsation of perfectly conceived and executed riffs."[19]

In the mid-1930s, Williams injured a leg while on tour and, unable to function normally, was dropped by the Andy Kirk organization. Recovering, Claude went to Chicago to play violin and guitar with the Eddie Cole Trio and, returning to Kansas City in 1937, with the Count Basie Orchestra—major artists giving Williams exposure and increased reputation. Williams then moved to New York City with the Basie Orchestra and appeared on the Count Basie 1937 hit records "Honeysuckle Rose," "Pennies from Heaven," "Swinging at the Daisy Chain," and "Roseland Shuffle."[20]

At the same time he was asked to play guitar by Count Basie, Williams was among the few jazz players to make a reputation with the violin—the "rarely fashionable" instrument Williams had always preferred.[21] While performing in Basie's rhythm section at the William Penn Hotel in Pittsburgh, Basie let Williams go, having decided to bring in a new guitarist, Freddy Green, who would be satisfied principally playing rhythm guitar. Mary Lee Hester's interview with Williams indicates how deeply Claude was hurt by being fired by Basie, but said that it was part of the plan by John Hammond, Basie's producer, who did not like Claude's fiddling. Hammond no doubt realized Claude's love of fiddling would prevent him from focusing on guitar in the Basie rhythm section. Claude graciously taught his less experienced replacement guitarist, Green, a great deal before leaving New York.[22]

Claude moved back to Kansas City and formed a trio playing at nightspots in the Eighteenth and Vine jazz district. Later, Williams played with bands such as Buddy Tate and Lloyd Glenn and developed a long association with Jay McShann (also from Muskogee, Oklahoma), with whom Williams performed at the Newport Jazz Festival, and formed his own ensembles.[23]

Williams moved to Flint, Michigan, in 1938, where he played with a WPA band. When World War II broke out in 1941, Williams took a job as a welder in a tank factory. Also during the war, Claude served in the US Naval Reserves but was discharged due to sinus problems. After the war ended, Williams moved about the country playing with several bands and eventually returned to Kansas City, where he resumed working in the Eighteenth and Vine jazz clubs. But the once wide-open Kansas City scene was changing. The infamous Pendergast political machine, a vast organization that for many years had supported speakeasies, nightclubs, and quasi-legal entertainment venues where jazz flourished, went into decline during the World War II years. The lively nightclub district that had harbored and nourished jazz faded as Kansas City was "cleaned up"; the long, painful process of urban renewal and the hop-scotch of gentrification had begun.

A key driver of this governmental cleaning-up process was urban renewal (authorized nationally in the Federal Housing Act of 1954 and other actions). Urban renewal projects identified and helped fund demolition of "blighted areas" deemed incapable of repair, rejuvenation, and continued use—attempting to create "cities without slums" in the terminology of the time. Kansas City was only one of many American cities with swaths of ethnic and inner-city neighborhoods judged by city leaders and planners to be too run-down to save, and urban renewal hit hard. While several blocks in the Eighteenth and Vine jazz district were spared, many blocks on all sides were heavily impacted, and in some cases only the historic front wall and storefront remained. Numerous business buildings and private homes were razed and the area carved up by new roads, vacant lots, and interstate highway construction. While many of the buildings removed were marginally functional, poorly built, and in need of rehabilitation, many good, solid buildings were removed. Families moved away; businesses relocated. The neighborhood was never the same.[24] As businesses and clubs were closed or cleared away, the musicians' union (once known as the "colored" Local 627) and Mutual Musicians Foundation took on new importance by becoming a new center for jazz musicians to gather and hold jam sessions, broadcast music on their own FM station, and function as a museum of Kansas City jazz history—and tourist destination.

In the 1940s and 1950s, Claude Williams had traveled to perform with different bands. Then from 1952 on, he worked from his permanent base in Kansas City, making trips to play in Denver and Las Vegas and in Kansas City continuing to perform with the Jay McShann ensemble. Jazz of the sort Claude Williams and Charlie Parker played hit a low spot in audience popularity in the 1960s. The increasing popularity of rock and roll and rhythm and blues, as well as the new "free jazz" and "cool jazz," particularly after the impact of the late 1950s records of jazz innovators such as Miles Davis, Chet Baker, John Coltrane, the Dave Brubeck Quartet, Charles Mingus, and other far-out cats, began to change the general public's tastes and capture more interest among everyday white audiences and open a new gateway to jazz, especially among white college audiences.[25]

Claude Williams kept playing the kind of Kansas City jazz he loved. By 1971 Jay McShann's band consisted only of McShann (piano), drummer Paul Gunther, and Williams—who alternated between violin, guitar, and bass in the trio.[26] In the 1970s, Williams appeared at festivals in Montreal, Newport, and Denmark and in 1979 appeared in Nice, France, with fellow jazz violinists Svend Asmussen and Stéphane Grappelli.

The Era of Arts-and-Culture Agencies

In the 1970s and 1980s, arts programming and opportunities developed in the wake of the Bicentennial and new public funding for programs, museums, local historical agencies, and festivals of all kinds. In 1982 Williams performed at the Smithsonian Institution's Festival of American Folklife, in 1983 at the Frontier Folklife Festival in St. Louis, and at the New Orleans World's Fair in 1984.

In the 1980s, Claude Williams became a master in the Missouri Traditional Arts Apprenticeship Program (with National Endowment for the Arts, Missouri Arts Council, and Missouri Cultural Heritage Center funding). His first apprentice was Geoff Seitz of St. Louis. During 1994 and 1995, Williams took part in national tours called "Masters of the Folk Violin," organized by the National Council for the Traditional Arts, during which he performed his signature style of playing "jump blues" with guitarist John G. Stewart and others and performed his old Joe Venuti favorite, "You've Got to See Your Momma Every Night" (a commonplace variant of the authentic title).[27] Claude enjoyed swapping tunes and jamming with the other fiddlers on the tour, including Missouri old-time fiddle champion Charlie Walden, bluegrass fiddler Kenny Baker, and Cape Breton fiddler Natalie McMaster.[28]

John G. Stewart, the Columbia guitarist and jazz scholar who accompanied Williams in 1980s and 1990s performances, recalls occasions when Claude had an opportunity to fiddle with white old-time players.[29] One such occasion, in which I was involved, was in 1984 at a Missouri Arts Council conference at the Lake of the Ozarks. There participants in the Missouri Touring Program and Traditional Arts Apprenticeship Program gathered to receive awards, trade stories, jam, and offer "showcase" performances.

One of the informal performances at the conference found Claude joining Columbia old-time fiddler Taylor McBaine in front of the microphones. McBaine and Williams were nearly the same age (Williams was one year older), and both were intellectually curious and versatile musicians with broad repertoires that included Tin Pan Alley songs and pop tunes from the days of ragtime and the Roaring Twenties. The performance went fine. To everyone's delight and relief, Claude Williams and Taylor McBaine enjoyed fiddling together—both men were naturally outgoing, cheerful people. Later, in a jam session in the hotel lobby, Claude and Taylor fiddled "Sweet Georgia Brown" together. McBaine had inherited a quirk in his fiddling—a habit of leaving out beats, sometimes a measure or more, in certain tunes. McBaine left out two measures in "Sweet Georgia Brown," and with a twinkle in his eye Williams gently brought this to McBaine's attention and then illustrated how those missing measures went. McBaine grinned and corrected his timing, and they finished the tune together. In visiting with McBaine weeks after, I discovered that, not surprisingly, McBaine had returned to his old habit of leaving out those two measures in "Sweet Georgia Brown."

Stewart relates an anecdote about Claude Williams meeting old-time fiddler Pete McMahan in the early 1990s at Port Townsend, Washington, at the Festival

Old-time fiddler Taylor McBaine of Columbia (*left*) and jazzman Claude Williams share an impromptu tune at a Missouri Cultural Heritage Center–Missouri Arts Council program, Lake of the Ozarks, 1984. John G. Stewart (guitar) and Kevin Hennessy (electric bass guitar). (Missouri Cultural Heritage Center)

of American Fiddle Tunes. McMahan, famous for his hard-driving, powerful breakdowns and who grew up with strong racial biases, was somewhat skeptical about Claude Williams's abilities. The two men happened to be assigned to the same dormitory. In an impromptu session during breakfast and coffee one morning, when Pete asked if Claude played any fiddle music, Claude began playing "Tennessee Wagner," an ironclad of the old-time repertoire and a tune often played poorly. First Claude played it in the usual key of C, then modulated into F and played the tune, then modulated into E-flat and played it perfectly again. All doubt lifted from McMahan's face after Claude's off-the-cuff tour de force. What McMahan did not know is that Claude Williams grew up playing string-band music and square dances for white people in Muskogee; Claude knew this music.

Unflappable Master of Cool Jazz

Claude's style was the essence of tasteful, graceful jazz. He rarely played open strings. As John Stewart explained to me, Claude played "fingers down." That is, he kept his left fingers in such a position that he could easily move notes and his melody through virtually any key by shifting his hand, and he could modulate to other keys with relative ease. He did this by positioning his middle finger on the root note of the chord in the key the tune begins on. He then could shift his left hand and fingers to deftly "find" whatever notes he felt like playing, in whatever key was desired. This skill also enabled Williams to easily play along with an accompanist who might be out of tune.

Claude Williams never wanted to "play over people's heads," even while he participated in jazz's far-out bebop period in the 1940s and early 1950s. "I never did want to play the modern stuff. I didn't want to play over people's heads, I wanted them to know what I'm playing."[30]

Williams's settings of "How High the Moon," "Cherokee," and "Indiana" (commonly called "Back Home in Indiana") are among several tunes that describe his approach to jazz.[31] "Cherokee" (composed by British bandleader Ray Noble) was recorded by Williams's colleague Charlie Parker in Kansas City, Kansas, in 1941. The tune was further popularized by Glenn Miller, Tex Beneke, and others, and the tune was a hit again on a 1950s record by Charlie Barnet.[32] "(Back Home Again in) Indiana" was composed in 1917 as a "one-step" couple dance in the key of G by Tin Pan Alley song writers Ballard McDonald and James F. Hanley. The first recording of "Indiana" was a 78 rpm record by the Original Dixieland Jass Band of New Orleans (Columbia Graphonola A2297), a vaudeville and nightclub ensemble credited with making the first commercial jazz record ("Livery Stable Blues"), produced before the word "jazz" was formalized and widely accepted. The great dance tune and song "Darktown Strutter's Ball" was issued on the B side.[33] Both these tunes are well known among seasoned old-time fiddlers and swing fiddlers, while "Cherokee" is rarely played, at least in my experience in the state of Missouri.

In Kansas City, one of Claude's standard venues was the Plaza III on the fashionable Country Club Plaza. In the 1990s, Nashville fiddler and violinist Mark O'Connor invited Claude to his Tennessee fiddle camp to teach young people about jazz. Williams traveled to Washington, DC, on several occasions in the late 1990s to perform at the White House during the jazz-friendly Clinton administration. In 1997 Williams was inducted into the Oklahoma Music Hall of Fame, along with Merle Haggard, Patti Page, and Woody Guthrie. In 1998 Williams was awarded a National Heritage Fellowship by the National Endowment for the Arts. Williams died in Kansas City in 2004 at the age of ninety-six.

Williams had traveled the world as an unofficial goodwill ambassador for Kansas City and Kansas City jazz, bringing his fiddling to festivals and clubs from Monterey, California, to Paris, France. In Paris Williams performed at the Hot Club of France, the nightspot made famous in the 1930s by jazz combos such as those of Stéphane Grappelli and Django Reinhardt. Writing about formative players in jazz, such as Eddie South, Julie Lyonn Lieberman notes that Williams was one of the few fiddlers still working in the early twenty-first century who "witnessed the evolution of the violin from the black blues lineage, across the early jazz violin years" to the present time.[34] Many felt Williams was the "last known active musician to have recorded in the 1920s."[35] At a performance of his Hot Swing jazz quartet in Columbia in January 2010, Mark O'Connor spoke of Williams's popularity as an instructor at his fiddle

Back Home In Indiana

as played by Claude Williams

Transcribed by Jack Tuttle
Digitized by Phil Vinyard

2 Back Home In Indiana

Claude Williams, "Indiana," by Jack Tuttle for Mary Larsen's article in *Fiddler Magazine*; reset by Philip K. Vinyard. A sound clip is available on the Arhoolie Records website at http://*www.arhoolie.com*. (Transcribed by Jack Tuttle; courtesy Mary Larsen)

camps. O'Connor played a "ballad" he composed as a memorial to Williams, "Fiddler Going Home," and followed it with one of Claude's favorites, "Honeysuckle Rose."[36] No one brought the old classic Kansas City jazz and swing fiddling to more audiences than Claude Williams.

Bobby Joe Caldwell: "Play It like You Sing It"

While Claude Williams found his venues in urban clubs and dance halls, often as a section player in a large orchestra, and his audiences in the global fan club built around commercial recordings, swing fiddler Bobby Joe Caldwell (and his father, Luther) found their natural venues to be the small-town taverns, roadhouses, and "country" dance halls that dotted the state outside of the big cities, playing gigs in their spare time and never being commercially recorded.

Caldwell is perhaps Missouri's best-known swing fiddler that people outside of Missouri, and outside the clannish world of swing jam-session players, have never heard of. Bobby Joe Caldwell (1931–2012) of Columbia was a premier swing player. He had the ability to make his music swing, even when—especially when—playing the tune simple and straight. He began his long career in music by playing guitar accompaniment for the fiddling of his father and then began playing fiddle himself. Bobby Joe's sister Margaret Anna played piano and his brother Luther Jr. banjo.

His Mentor Was His Dad

Bobby Joe's father, Luther B. Caldwell, worked as a postman and maintenance foreman on the University of Missouri campus. Luther was a well-known dance fiddler in the Columbia area. He lost his right arm at the shoulder in an accident in 1938, when Bobby Joe was seven. A tree fell and nearly killed Luther; both arms were broken, his spine was fractured, and a lung was punctured.[37] Luther tried various methods of holding the bow (with his legs, with his foot) and found that he could operate the violin bow by wedging it into a door jam and moving the violin back and forth with his left arm, but this proved unworkable when the bow broke. Bobby Joe began to work with his father to be his bowing arm, sitting or standing next to or behind his father and bowing the violin strings. Luther Caldwell was a smooth fiddler, and Bobby Joe absorbed his father's bowing style in such tunes as "South" (hear on the companion CD) from this practice of teaming up. Luther began searching for a bowing device similar to those he had seen in nickelodeons, orchestrions, and other machines in which violins played mechanically; a store in Columbia called the Oriental Bazaar had such a device (made in Italy) displayed, and Luther had learned to play "Whispering" one-armed by watching and listening to it.

In 1947 Sam Burnett, a friend and retired University of Missouri electrician, built an aluminum-framed device that allowed Luther Caldwell to bow the violin by attaching the bow to a treadle that he could operate with his right foot, and this "contraption," as he called it, worked well. Caldwell's one-armed fiddling became famous, in part due to steady coverage by Columbia's two newspapers and continued fiddling

Luther Caldwell, promotional photograph, ca. 1950. The "contraption" is in the collections of the Boone County Historical Society. (Courtesy Matt Wyatt)

at various events. He was a versatile fiddler but most enjoyed playing swing tunes; one of his old-time tunes, "B-flat Hornpipe," is in R. P. Christeson's 1984 tune book. Caldwell judged as well as competed in (and won) fiddlers contests, and he appeared on *Ted Mack's Original Amateur Hour* on television in 1960. Luther's principal venues became county fair shows and dances. Among these were several performances in 1952–53 with the "Hillbilly Jamboree," a variety show at the Boone County Fairgrounds. Newspaper writers continued to discover Columbia's one-armed fiddler, and periodic stories appeared, including a 1968 photo story by a journalism student a year before Luther Caldwell died.[38]

Bobby Joe

Bobby Joe Caldwell grew up during a time when different styles of music and guitar accompaniment were popular. Jazz, big band, western swing, and swing caught the attention of fiddlers who, in previous times, would have centered their attention on old-time fiddle styles, dances, and repertoires. Like his father, Bobby Joe leaned toward swing. His guitar playing was devoted to jazz chords, closed chords, and shapes that would fit with swing and western swing. He never learned or particularly liked the open-chord (straight-chord) guitar style that was more familiar in the "old-time" fiddle circles in the Columbia area.

Bobby Joe Caldwell bows the violin for his father, Luther, ca. 1948. (Courtesy Bobby Joe Caldwell)

While a student at Hickman High School in 1948–49, Caldwell built a solid-body electric guitar as well as a lap pedal steel guitar in shop class. The teacher, Benton Deckard, played electric guitar and pedal steel and supported Bobby Joe's and other boys' guitar-building projects. Caldwell affixed a DeArmond pickup to the guitar to provide amplification. About this time, Bobby Joe purchased his first guitar, a Gibson archtop single-pickup electric, at Bussinger Music Store in downtown Columbia. Benton Deckard went to the store with Caldwell and guaranteed the time payment, and Caldwell paid off the guitar at nine dollars a month for a year.

At this time a high school sophomore, Caldwell played swing guitar in a dance band called the Melody Ramblers, along with his friends Tommy Wirt (fiddle), Johnny Willingham (bass), and Joe Daly (mandolin). Despite their youth, the Ramblers played at dance halls and nightclubs as well as venues such as the Missouri State Fair and openings of MFA Insurance offices in towns in central Missouri. Caldwell recalled with a laugh, "We actually made money at it."[39]

Caldwell did learn to play many of the standard hoedowns common among fiddlers that he would need for a square-dance set or schottische at dances, such as "Ragtime Annie," "Red Wing," and an Ed Tharp schottische called "Molly Brown." But while he acquired pieces of the old-time repertoire, his forte was swing, and in the playing of swing music his taste and sound were indelible. Bobby Joe often told me that he did not have an "ear" for hoedowns, while swing tunes were easily embraced in his imagination. In part because of his father's many dance jobs, Bobby Joe soaked it up and reveled in it. He acquired numerous tunes from his father, but he also learned tunes fiddled by his father's cronies, such as Ed Tharp, Charlie Cook, Bill (Junior) Perkins, and other versatile and smooth dance fiddlers in the area.[40] As Caldwell often said, swing is in the bowing, and his bowing was svelte; your bow movement has to be "pure," clean, and smooth.

Bobby Joe Caldwell was adept at playing twin fiddle and enjoyed jam sessions with fiddlers who shared his ability to "play twin fiddles" and "harmony fiddle." Caldwell's advice for playing "harmony" (twin fiddle) was "Play it like you're singing it."[41] Some of his favorite tunes were old standards passed down from Tharp and his father, Luther Caldwell, such as "Sunrise on the Guinea Farm" (which may have been an Ed Tharp tune), "Charmaine," "September in the Rain," "Little Coquette," "Maggie," "Faded Love," "Darling Nellie Gray," "Kansas City Kitty," "Confessin'," and "Rose Room." Many of these are Tin Pan Alley songs, big-band songs, Broadway show tunes, and hit-parade songs now considered part of what is sometimes called "the great American songbook" of hits from records and radio—like Benny Goodman, Guy Lombardo, Bing Crosby, Frank Sinatra, Patti Page, and others.

"Charmaine" is among the swing pieces commonly played in old-time fiddlers'

Bobby Joe Caldwell at a fiddle session at the Boone-Walters Historical Museum, Columbia, Missouri. (December 2009)

sessions in the Columbia area in the 2010s, an era when many old-time and contest fiddlers, especially those in middle age and beyond, seem to be opening up that chamber in their minds and memories where swing tunes dwelled unnoticed for many years. Composed in 1926, "Charmaine" was the theme music for a Hollywood silent movie about US Marines fighting against Germans in World War I France. The plot, starring James Cagney and Victor McLaglen, involves the men's rivalry over the affections of a French girl—"Charmaine de la Cognac" (acted by Delores del Rio). As background music for a silent film, the sheet music was distributed across the nation to every theater that screened the movie. All sorts of local musicians played the music "live" during the screening of the movie—from a pianist or organist perched in a corner with a view of the screen to small ensembles to substantial orchestras with maestros in an orchestra pit below the screen—and this helped ingrain the tune into repertoires of popular music in countless places.

Today, "Charmaine" is performed by some Missouri fiddlers both in the original waltz time and as an up-tempo fox-trot (two-step). The first recording to become a hit was as a waltz by the Guy Lombardo Orchestra in 1927 followed by other big-band records by Harry James in 1944, the Mantovani Orchestra in 1951, the Billy May orchestra in 1952, and Frank Sinatra in 1962. Some Missouri fiddlers play "Charmaine" in fiddlers contests as a waltz and alternately as a "tune of choice" (any kind of tune other than a hoedown or a waltz).[42] Very few tunes are played dually, as a waltz and as a fox-trot; one other example among Missouri fiddlers is the 1894 waltz composed by Anita Owen "Sweet Bunch of Daisies," which fiddlers such as Benny Martin and Kenny Baker recorded in waltz time and, midrecording, switched to up-tempo two-step. New Orleans jazz bands sometimes perform "Charmaine" as a two-step, as did Bill Haley and the Comets in the 1950s, the Irish pop-rock group the Bachelors, and country singer Hank Thompson, and recordings such as these from the 1950s and 1960s suggest the transition of "Charmaine" from moody waltz to up-tempo two-step.

"Kansas City Kitty" is played by old-time fiddlers, honky-tonk players, contest fiddlers, and even bluegrass players, but western-swing fiddlers glory in this ironclad of the repertoire. It has the qualities that make it ideal for improvisation—a rather simple, straight melody and set in a key (G) that offers latitude for creativity and upper-position improvisation. "Kansas City Kitty" was published in 1929 by Walter Donaldson (lyrics, Edgar Leslie) and the fox-trot was popularized by recordings by the Midnight Merrymakers and Billy Murray. Perhaps the best-known version is by the Kansas City jazz band Coon Sanders' Nighthawks (Victor 21939-A; Harry Silverstone, violin), a white band formed by Carleton Coon and Joe Sanders that performed over WDAF radio and at numerous high-society dances.[43]

Less commonly heard as a fiddle tune today is "I Love You So Much It Hurts Me," a country song written and recorded by Floyd Tillman in 1948. The 78 rpm record (Columbia 20430) was a best seller and soon covered by Jimmy Wakeley (1948) and by the Mills Brothers (1949), and recordings were released by numerous other singers through the years, from Patsy Cline to Andy Williams. "I Love You So Much, It Hurts" is one of a remarkable set of tunes Bobby Joe Caldwell recorded in an informal

Under the Silvery Moon

as played by Bobby Caldwell

Transcribed by Matthew Wyatt

*The suggested bowings are based on this recording & many other times hearing him play this song.

"Under the Silvery Moon," by Bobby Joe Caldwell, 2006, recorded at Caldwell's home in Columbia by Matt Wyatt; accompaniment by Wyatt, playing a 1949 Epiphone Triumph archtop guitar (hear on the companion CD). (Transcription by Matthew Wyatt) house session in Columbia with guitarist Matt Wyatt (playing a vintage Epiphone archtop) in 2006.

The Caldwell list included numerous western-swing classics from the 1930s forward and the omnipresent "Bob Wills songs." Like other swing fiddlers, Caldwell admired the fiddling of players such as Bobby Flores, a top western-swing fiddler, guitarist, and session musician from Texas, and Johnny Gimble, his favorite.

Out of high school, Caldwell served a hitch in the army. After his release from active duty, he began a long career as a carpenter with the B. D. Simon construction firm in Columbia. During these years, married and raising a family, he largely left the guitar and violin untouched. In the 1980s, Bobby Joe returned to music and began fiddling at Good Time Country, a rural dance hall and nightspot operated by the Terry Sapp family a few miles south of Columbia in the Pierpont area. This opry and nightclub was a major stop for touring country music performers from Nashville. While many of Caldwell's friends participated in the growing fiddlers contest scene in the 1960s, Caldwell himself steered away from entering contests and kept his focus on swing music.

In retirement, Bobby Joe Caldwell participated in weekly jam sessions in the Columbia area with old friends, such as Columbia fiddler Dale Pauley and guitarist Ivan Crane. (Hear Pauley's "Anniversary Waltz" on the companion CD.) The

Matt Wyatt (guitar), Bobby Joe Caldwell, and Bud Wyatt at a music party at the Wyatt Violin Shop, Independence, Missouri. (2008)

Tuesday-evening music parties rotated to different members' homes, and a typical evening included a mix of old-time fiddle tunes and swing and western-swing music.

With the resurgence of interest in swing, helped by contest fiddlers today who may play a swing tune as their tune of choice in competitions, younger fiddlers have come to appreciate Bobby Joe Caldwell's playing in new ways. Among the best of Missouri's younger swing fiddlers are Matt Wyatt of Independence and Justin Branum (now working professionally in Nashville), who learned tunes from Caldwell and include them in performances by their St. Louis–based ensemble, Swing DeVille. The swing and western-swing fiddling of players like Luther and Bobby Joe Caldwell is increasingly seen not as a niche or sidetrack but as a principal parallel line running throughout Missouri's multifaceted fiddle traditions.

Bill Monroe and His Blue Grass Boys in concert, Brown County Jamboree, Bean Blossom, Indiana, October 1962. *Left to right*: Roger Smith, Bill Monroe, Jimmy Maynard, and Lonnie Hoppers. Hoppers was the first Missourian to be a full-fledged Blue Grass Boy. (Courtesy Hoppers)

Bluegrass Time in the Show-Me State

10

And to be a good bluegrass fiddler, you're in a higher class of fiddle music than you would think about. It's not like the old-time square dance numbers that was made 30 to 40 years ago. With having the blues and everything that's been added to the blue grass, if he plays a good blue grass fiddle, he's on the up, you know—he's really a good fiddler.

—Bill Monroe quoted in Doug Benson, "Bill Monroe, King of Blue Grass Music," in *The Bill Monroe Reader*, edited by Tom Ewing (2000)

It is likely that in Missouri today, there are at least as many fiddlers who think of themselves as bluegrass fiddlers as "old-time" fiddlers. For the average listener, in fact, "bluegrass" is the most familiar term for fiddling. Like swing and western swing, bluegrass emerged to become a major force in American vernacular music and is rooted in older styles and genres, with strong elements of blues, gospel singing styles, early jazz, and swing.[1] This chapter presents a view of bluegrass music in its early period, for working purposes from the 1940s into the early 1960s; this is the era many remember as the era of "classic" bluegrass, an exciting time when the bluegrass sound was being formulated, tinkered with, and transplanted around the globe.

While originating in the Upland South, bluegrass evolved into a largely nonregional, international music nourished by international marketplaces, professional players with great musical sophistication (if not classical training), promoters, festival audiences, recording companies, and especially quickly changing global digital media. Much of the bluegrass repertoire came not from old-time standards but from contemporary country music and fresh composition. The same point was made previously about the sources for many of the fiddle tunes now considered "old-time" or "folk" music bubbling forth from anonymous ancient jam sessions, from "Durang's Hornpipe" (Hoffmaster, ca. 1785) to "Listen to the Mockingbird" (Septimus Winner, 1855), "Over the Waves" (Juventino Rosas, 1898), "Red Wing" (Kerry Mills, 1908), and "Missouri Waltz" (Jelly Settles, 1914)—composed music that percolated into the folk repertoire after first seeing daylight from known authors, Tin Pan Alley sheet-music publishers, and commercial records.

Bluegrass developed as concert music for small ensembles performing on radio, records, and stage for seated audiences. The music was not intended to be dance music. It is primarily listening music, on one hand, while, on the other hand, it is exceptionally participatory; most bluegrass fans also play the music. Just as conservative listeners decried the incursions of ragtime and early jazz into traditional fiddling, when bluegrass came along in the 1940s and 1950s, it was so slick and powerful that many people rejected it. Alan Lomax, the influential Library of Congress scholar and collector of folk music, called bluegrass bands "bluegrass orchestras" that "reign supreme" at folk festivals. "Here at last the British-American tradition has given rise to its own orchestra, a sort of five-piece Dixieland string band, certainly as virtuosic as any Gypsy orchestra, and they're playing what I call 'mountain music in overdrive.'"[2]

Bluegrass largely depends upon oral traditional learning and informal apprenticeship, and often its adherents proudly (if somewhat deceptively) disavow, and sometimes scorn, formal music training, classical music, and musical literacy. While this is the case, curiously, bluegrass encourages formal composition of new tunes and songs with authors and copyrights. While swing and western swing interacted with popular music and jazz and accommodated to horns and other orchestral instruments, bluegrass stuck close to accepted customs in string-band music and its three primary instruments—fiddle, banjo, guitar.

Most fiddlers who say they are bluegrass fiddlers play tunes and songs from the old-time repertoire and swing repertoire, even if other bluegrass fiddlers disavow any interest in old-time music or swing. However, while bluegrass fiddlers may acknowledge their debt to jazz and swing players such as Venuti and Grappelli, this is not the case with bluegrass guitar accompaniment. In the early years, bluegrass guitar players hewed to older, traditional, spare, straight-chord rhythm guitar styles (albeit with bass runs, occasional solos, and instances of innovative swing-like solos), rather than adopting the closed-chord, swing guitar styles that are essential in swing and western swing. But in the 1960s, bluegrass guitarists began playing jazz-like, controlled-improvisational takeoff solos, influenced at least in part by blues, swing, and rock and roll. Among influential guitarists in this regard were Doc Watson, Clarence White, and Dan Crary. By 1970 aspiring bluegrass guitarists were expected to be able to take a break and essentially mimic White, Watson, or Crary on instrumentals such as "Salt Creek" and "John Hardy" (hear on the companion CD). Many bandleaders were primarily singers, rhythm guitarists, and impresarios, but not hot guitarists, and began bringing an additional guitarist (typically a fiery young player) into the band to cover the obligatory guitar breaks.

One cannot speak of bluegrass music without spending some time with Bill Monroe, "the father of bluegrass." After recording and performing as a duet with his older brother Charlie on records and radio—making a reputation as an outstanding brother duet—in 1938 Bill decided to start his own band with which to articulate his vision of hillbilly string-band music. Bill began appearing on *The Grand Ole Opry* with his own band in 1939. His first banjoist, David (Stringbean) Akeman, came from the minstrel tradition of banjoist as purveyor of comic routines. Monroe provided much of the hot solo work on his mandolin. Monroe shaped what would be known as bluegrass music by bringing together ingredients of three venerable American vernacular music traditions: old-time Upper South fiddle music (as expressed in his uncle Pen Vandiver's "Scotch-Irish fiddling"), African American blues (including early jazz and swing), and southern gospel harmony singing.[3]

Monroe credited his childhood guitar mentor, an African American fiddler and guitarist, Arnold Shultz, in Monroe's western Kentucky home area around Rosine, with teaching him the blues music that worked its way into the otherwise very Anglo-Saxon–dominated (a.k.a. "white" or "Scotch-Irish") bluegrass.[4] Monroe made much of his Scottish and Scotch-Irish ancestors and the importance of old-time fiddling in his family heritage, the same heritage that underpins a large portion of old-time fiddling in America; he often used the term "Scotch-Irish fiddling" the way others would use "old-time fiddling." The singing reflects older North British and Gaelic singing styles filtered down through time in Protestant church choirs and hymn singing in the American Southeast, which includes good measures of African American stylings.

Bill Monroe and colleagues performed the first full-fledged bluegrass music in late 1945 in a quintet composed of mandolin; violin (Chubby Wise, who had replaced Howdy Forrester in 1943); guitar (Lester Flatt); five-string resonator banjo played in a three-finger, syncopated chord-based style (Earl Scruggs); and standup bass (Birch Monroe or Howard Watts). This ensemble thrilled audiences everywhere they went, playing tent shows, halls, and radio. Chubby Wise had played swing music before joining Monroe and helped bring clean, articulate, syncopated, smooth bowing with vibrato in just the right places into the evolving bluegrass sound.

Of great importance in that remarkable 1945 Monroe band were the young North Carolina banjoist Earl Scruggs, who took earlier two- and three-finger up-picking styles and crafted his own style that added tremendous drive and syncopation, and the distinctive singer and rhythm guitarist from Tennessee, Lester Flatt. As Chubby Wise recalled, in a humble downplay of his own influential fiddling, "Earl and Lester and Bill just tore 'em up every time they'd hit the stage."[5]

Another key instrument in bluegrass was the mandolin as Bill Monroe worked it. As a child, Monroe had wanted to be a fiddler, but his older brother Birch had claimed that instrument and older siblings Charlie and Bertha played guitar. Bill based his mandolin playing on old-time fiddling and gave the mandolin a new, muscular, voice. He picked strong, bluesy notes in melodies and developed a jazzy, bluesy, and aggressive "bluegrass chop" with closed chords up and down the neck, nailing in the back-beat accents and syncopation. Bill was a creative soloist in his breaks in songs, whether in presenting fiddle tunes or various kinds of formulas that helped add drive to the ensemble sound. Monroe took the mandolin to a new plateau of power and creativity in forging "bluegrass style." Monroe bought his secondhand mandolin, a Gibson F-5 model made in 1923 by Lloyd Loar for Gibson in Michigan, in a Florida barbershop in 1946. No other mandolin would have been up to the task in terms of volume, power, and quality suited to bluegrass.

Monroe named the group His Blue Grass Boys—referring not to a musical genre but to Monroe's home state of Kentucky, "the Bluegrass State."[6] Before Monroe linked up with Lester Flatt and Earl Scruggs, he said he played old-time music and hillbilly music.

The term "bluegrass" meant little until the mid-1950s.[7] The gradual process of becoming known as "bluegrass," and marking off its own territory, certainly improved its chances of attracting the interest of fans and musicians who were not fans of "hillbilly" and "country music." The distinction may seem strained today, but it was important in the 1950s. Signifying only the home base of the band were groups like Charlie Poole's North Carolina Ramblers, Roy Acuff and the Smoky Mountain Boys, Clayton McMichen's Georgia Wildcats, Tex Ritter and the Blue Ridge Mountaineers, and the Ozark Mountain Boys in Missouri. In an interview with Lester Flatt, prominent in forging the Blue Grass Boys' singing and rhythm guitar sound in the 1940s, Flatt offered his view on the subject:

> And 'course it's fine with me if they want to call it *bluegrass*. I go along with it, y'know. Just overnight the deejays started calling it bluegrass music. Bill Monroe and the Bluegrass Boys. And if he'd had the green grass boys, that's what it'd been, *green-grass* music. . . . But, 'course, when Earl and me went to work with him, it was a little different sound than what he has now. 'Course I'd never heard anybody pick that style banjo [Scruggs]. And 'course in '44 when I went to work with Bill, he had an *accordion*, and a guy playin' electric guitar, and Stringbean [David Akeman] playin' the five-string banjo. It seems to me you can have a group, and as long as you don't have a banjo in it, why it seems like they call it *country*, you know, *hillbilly*. But if it's got a banjo style like Earl [Scruggs] was pickin' at that time, it's called *bluegrass*.[8]

The "blue" in the word "bluegrass" is significant because, apart from referring to Monroe's home state, "blue" emphasizes the influences of blues and swing in both style and repertoire.

In the 1950s bluegrass competed hard to get recognition. Monroe kept honing the music to match his evolving blueprint and experimented as he went along. Some trials clicked—swing fiddling and slap bass—and other experiments were short-lived, such as the accordion, played by fiddler Howdy Forrester's wife, Wilene (Billie) Forrester, who was given the stage name "Sally Ann" by Monroe and played accordion and sang with Monroe's band during World War II.[9]

Monroe could be a difficult captain. He hired, fired, and lost the talents of numerous band members in the early years, when good paychecks and steady bookings were scarce. In those days, Bill was not as particular about his accompaniment as when he made it big in the 1960s and 1970s. In the early 1950s, occasionally Monroe would arrive in town to put on a show in an opry house, theater, or county fair tent with only one or two Blue Grass Boys, and he would contact a local musician to fill in for that concert.[10] This usually worked, if sometimes it was uncomfortable for the other band members, but Monroe "discovered" excellent young musicians this way. Some of them who started as "fill-ins" would eventually be invited into the fold. Monroe paid his band by the concert rather than by salary. This financial uncertainty was difficult to manage, and some musicians left because of it. If a musician was lucky enough to have even partial rights to a tune or song that was registered and released on a record by Bill Monroe and His Blue Grass Boys, that at least ensured a trickle of income over time.

The Blue Grass Boys often performed wearing "country gentleman"–style hats and white shirts, with khaki riding breeches (jodhpurs) and black equestrian boots, and in later years they wore western-style cowboy hats with dress shirts and neckties. The hat was generally in the form of the Open Road model by Stetson. Similar models were also bought for band members.[11] While people today often say that Bill Monroe insisted on white hats for his band, other light colors were also purchased for them. Lonnie Hoppers's Resistol is light gray. "The hat he bought me was a Resistol 'Lariat XX.' He bought it in Omaha, Nebraska at Wolfe Brothers in Sept. 1962. I don't remember if they had Stetsons or not, we just picked the hat we liked. We were playin' a show in Omaha that night, & were stayin' at a hotel right across the street from Wolf Bros. Bill & the B. G. Boys did wear the Stetson 'Open Road' hats back in the '40's, as did the Stanley Bros. & I believe even early Flatt & Scruggs. We called them funeral parlor hats!"[12]

The look was in part a nod toward western cowboys and their romantic stereotyping during the World War II years but was also a deliberate nod to the Stetson Open Road. This hat shape in its several variations was preferred by successful farmers, livestock raisers, and local politicians in the 1940s and 1950s from Maryland and the South all the way across the United States. The "Sunday-best" Stetson was kept clean and proper, and most wearers also had a "work hat" of the same type for everyday hard use. Stetsons came in different grades (by softness and quality of the felt), and the higher-grade models (marked inside with more *X*s) were expensive. Beaver fur was originally used for the felting material, but today felted wool or rabbit fur is more common. Hats by the John B. Stetson firm were world famous, like Levi-Strauss blue jeans and Pendleton wool shirts and blankets, a sterling success in the history of marketing. President Harry Truman wore Stetson Open Roads, as did Presidents Franklin D. Roosevelt before him and Dwight D. Eisenhower after and many politicians and community leaders during the time period—a time when most men wore hats as part of being properly attired in public, whether going to church or the grocery store.[13] The majority of these "stockman" and "rancher" hats were not white but a light shade of tan, brown, or gray ("silverbelly"). In Missouri light gray is dominant. In the heat of a summer festival or concert, Bill Monroe and others wore lightweight "Panama" plaited-palm or straw versions of the same style hats (most of them imported not from Panama but from Ecuador, where they originated).

Bill Monroe's marketing acumen worked. His look sent the signal that Monroe's music was not to be mistaken for the hillbilly music of radio, boozy country dance halls, B western movies, and oprys of the 1930s and early 1940s. This music was to be respected in every way. Many other bluegrass bands since then have proudly worn similar hats. The hat style (especially the Stetson Open Road) was adopted by countless old-time and bluegrass fiddlers across Missouri who understood the values of the talisman. The widths of brims and heights of crowns of Bill Monroe's own hats varied through the years (he liked the homberg shape at one point in the 1940s), but some version of the quintessential Open Road was his prevailing choice.

Many new bluegrass bands were formed by former Bluegrass Boys. Veterans often considered being a Bluegrass Boy as the high point in their lives as well as their careers. Those of a reflective bent, such as New York fiddler Gene Lowinger, guitarist Jim Rooney, and banjoist Bob Black, have written fascinating memoirs of their life-altering careers with "Mister Bill."[14] Others viewed a stint with Monroe more as an apprenticeship with the gods on Olympus, a springboard to recognition that would help when they left to form their own bands or join other bands. Hundreds of musicians performed with Bill Monroe over his many years in the business. There were regulars and fill-ins. At the top of the pecking order were the regulars, engaged as ongoing ensemble members and provided with the obligatory well-kept western hat. Some regulars worked a few months, while others stayed with Monroe for years.

Fill-ins performed briefly, when Monroe would play a concert, tour, or festival with a regular ensemble member absent (or no longer in hire). The actual number of fill-in Bluegrass Boys and guests may never be known. A guitarist or singer or banjoist may have played only once, at a festival somewhere long ago, with no recording or documentation of the appearance. Missouri fiddler Bythel Friend filled in for Benny Martin at four Missouri Ozarks concerts in 1948. Sixty to seventy fiddlers served at one time or another with Monroe.

In another bracket were musicians whom Monroe would invite onstage to play a tune with him at a concert or festival, and many have experienced that exhilarating moment. Monroe would often bring the host or festival promoter to the microphone, if he or she was a musician. There were musicians Monroe knew and with whom he liked sharing a tune when the band was appearing in their area, such as Missouri fiddlers Delbert Spray, Lyman Enloe, and Gene Goforth. At festivals with several bands on the card, Monroe enjoyed bringing up a top musician from a different band to play a tune or two, such as banjoists Doug Dillard and J. D. Crowe and fiddlers such as Vivian Williams and Tex Logan. A few musicians of exceptional reputation were invited to come to a studio date in Nashville to make records with Monroe, such as Dale Potter and Tommy Jackson.

Fiddle and Banjo, the Crux of Bluegrass

The violin and banjo form the nexus of nearly all genres of traditional Missouri fiddling, from old-time music to early jazz, early swing, bluegrass, and until the 1980s, contest fiddling as well. For bluegrass, since its gradual formulation in the 1930s and flowering in the 1940s and 1950s under Bill Monroe's stern hand, these two instruments have been the pillars of the genre, a partnership of creativity and beauty.

Unlike other musical instruments that may make up a string band or bluegrass ensemble—violin, guitar, mandolin, upright bass—the banjo does not come from centuries of European-American history. The violin is the product of five hundred years of evolution in stylish European artisanship, supported by royalty and aristocracy; the banjo is an American development drawn from African and Caribbean folk music, plucked banjo-like instruments of everyday music and minstrelsy.

Banjos are often homemade and may be curated in museums because of the supposed charm of seeing instruments made of crude materials and possum or rabbit hides for heads. Many other banjos are artfully designed and built luxuriously by some of the world's best craftsmen (with prices to match). Like guitars and mandolins, but unlike violins, a known logo or maker's name on a banjo is reasonable assurance of prestige and status and a signal (even if unreliable) that its owner may have skill in performance. A small number of innovative early builders and manufacturers, such as Stewart, Paramount, Orpheum, Vega, Bacon, and Gibson, set the standard for quality and collectibility. There are two basic kinds of banjos in American vernacular music: those with four strings and those with five—the fifth string was added in the 1840s.

The violin has remained much the same in design and construction as when it reached its zenith in the Renaissance shops of Italian masters such as Stradivari and Guarneri. The banjo as we know it in bluegrass is a twentieth-century artifact that depends heavily on modern materials, manufacturing processes, and acoustic design.[15]

Missouri had its share of creative, influential bluegrass banjo players in the early years of the genre. Among them were Harold Morrison from High Lonesome (Douglas County),[16] Lonnie Hoppers from Urbana (Hickory County), Dale Sledd (Warsaw), John Hartford (St. Louis), and Doug Dillard (Salem), followed soon after by players such as Michael Breid (Arkansas Red, originally from Missouri), Frank Jones (Richland), and Kenny Seaman (Eminence).

A bluegrass jam session, May 1958, Eminence. *Left to right*: Jim Orchard, Kenny Seaman, and Rich Orchard. (Courtesy Jim Orchard)

One of the best-known Missouri banjo pickers is Lonnie Hoppers of Springfield, who was born in 1935 in Urbana, when the five-string banjo was still comfortable in its traditional role principally as accompaniment in string bands and square-dance bands and as the minstrel and vaudeville entertainer's instrument. In this regard, since the days of minstrelsy the five-string banjo kept a central position in old-time music. Five-string banjos in most cases were not lead instruments but ensemble instruments for accompanying fiddlers and singers.

The four-stringers (tenor and plectrum) had their day as exciting new rhythm instruments in early jazz and ragtime dance bands, but by the 1930s technology and electrical amplification had signaled the end of the banjo's place in a dance band's rhythm section. There had been an uptick in interest in tenor banjo in the 1920s and early 1930s, and for a while it was a favored backup for such as Milo McCubbin and Art Galbraith, whose careers are outlined in the 2012 *Play Me Something Quick and Devilish.* By the 1940s, most tenor and plectrum banjos were stacked in closets—except in places where folks appreciated four-stringers.

Lonnie Hoppers: From Four Strings to Five

A brief look at Lonnie Hoppers's career illustrates the changes taking place in the role of the banjo as time-honored partner to the fiddle and the transition in his life from a youngster backing up old-time fiddlers at music parties in the upper Ozarks to professional bluegrass five-string player with Bill Monroe and the Bluegrass Boys on *The Grand Ole Opry.*

Hoppers is a rare bird, able to make his career playing bluegrass banjo—and the first to do this in Missouri. His first professional work came in 1953 at the age of seventeen with the Ozark Opry at the Lake of the Ozarks, followed in 1962 with his breakthrough work performing and making a dozen influential records as a member of Bill Monroe and His Blue Grass Boys.

Hoppers formed other bands through the years, including Lonnie Hoppers and New Union, and continues to perform and teach banjo. As many bluegrass musicians do, Hoppers released an album of gospel-song instrumentals, and he chose to record in the "fiddle and banjo" duet style important in the music and a sentimental nod to former times. A track from a 1992 album with fiddler Jamie Haage, *Old Country Church,* represents the format and conveys the mood (hear their "Unclouded Day" on the companion CD).

As a child in Urbana growing up around old-time banjo players and fiddlers in the early 1940s, Hoppers had experimented with playing drop-thumb five-string banjo in the manner of his grandfather Henry Reeves (Babe) Franklin, who called his style "knocking." But Lonnie preferred the rhythmic sound of the plectrum banjo, in which chords are played with a flat pick up and down the banjo neck.

Lonnie's father, George Hoppers, had an old open-back tenor, and Lonnie began experimenting with plectrum-style playing on his dad's banjo. Lonnie tuned in "open" G tuning, providing the same notes as the four low strings on a five-string banjo. The familiar D–G–B–D notes (low to high) of the four strings make an open G chord, and this is the principal traditional first banjo tuning in Missouri. (Standard tenor banjo tuning is C–G–D–A.) Lonnie also learned to tune the tenor D–B–G–C, providing a C tuning. Banjos can be tuned in many different ways, and in Missouri "G tuning" is the starting place for old-time and bluegrass five-string players (the fifth string is a high G), just as "C tuning" is usually standard for tenor and plectrum players.

While Lonnie was learning at home with his grandfather's five-string and his father's tenor banjo, his father began taking him to visit Truman Bridges, the community's primary banjoist, a plectrum player, and a cousin. Bridges had an inexpensive five-string banjo with the fifth string removed, making the instrument a plectrum. "He was playing it plectrum style in open G tuning. He knew all the major & seventh chords the length of the neck. That gave me something to do with my left hand! Truman was a good man & enjoyed showing me what he knew. Interestingly in later years as I improved with my right hand three-finger picking, Truman started changing to that style!"[17]

Playing plectrum banjo with Truman Bridges at music parties and dances gave Lonnie experience learning the chords and scales on the neck. He continued learning accompaniment and chording with fiddlers, but Lonnie also learned to pick out melodies with the flat pick. The tunes he was absorbing included a lot of swing music and two-step tunes he was learning from Truman Bridges, such as "Johnson's Rag," "South," "Birth of the Blues," and "Blues Stay Away from Me," in addition to the old-time tunes fiddlers played when people wanted to square dance. "So I learned a lot of old tunes that weren't bluegrass tunes, which was *good*, because I was learning how to play the *banjo*. Learning my *neck*."

> It was good for me, because I played on a lot of country music shows, too, later, and so I could fall right into a lot of that stuff. A lot of bluegrass banjo pickers are pretty heard-headed—kind of like bluegrass *fiddle* players, somewhat—bluegrass *anything*, you know. Some of 'em's really hard-headed, especially the older ones, you know. They don't want nothing to do with country music, a lot of them doesn't, they just turn up their nose at that. But I have always *liked* country music, because I had a good start in it. And I appreciated it. I appreciate *any* music as long as it's *good*, you know. That helped me get *work*, for one thing (being versatile).[18]

In the 1950s, Hoppers had the good fortune to be able to learn in the friendly and low-stress environment of house parties and pie suppers, but, as mentioned previously, even more important was the Urbana old-time fiddler Bert Lewis, who served as his guide into accompaniment for fiddling. Bert Lewis played the range of popular music of the day, but he was grounded in the firm territory of old-time dance fiddling of central Missouri. Like many fiddlers of his time, Lewis liked piano accompaniment, and a typical anchoring ensemble at house parties and dances would be Lewis, pianist Alice Johnson, and young Lonnie Hoppers. He enjoyed playing in all the expected keys and the flat keys of F and B-flat as well and encouraged Lonnie to try anything. This is the time-honored path for a musician who eventually forges a career—sitting through long nights of music as an accompanist, absorbing a myriad of tunes and styles and chords and ideas. Unlike many fiddlers, Bert Lewis was generous—he enjoyed and appreciated other musicians taking lead roles in the music they played.

> I'd go, try to play what little banjo I knew—mostly it was before I really got into bluegrass. And I was *trying*, you know (playing five-string banjo) more like my *grandpaw—more of a two-finger lick*. And sometimes I'd try a little still strumming with chords a little bit with a *flat* pick, because I was in a transition period. I was probably better at *chording* with a *flat* pick, mostly, at that time. Then I was *wanting* to do *this*, too (bluegrass banjo), so I probably did *both* with him. But *Bertie*, anything was fine with him. Bert, for sure, wouldn't have cared *what* you were playing, as long as you could stay in the right *key* and have fairly good *timing*. If he *did*, he wouldn't say anything, you know, just a nice guy.

With bluegrass on his mind, Lonnie began wishing for a five-string with a resonator, and his first one was a brand-new Bacon Belmont his father ordered in 1950

Lonnie Hoppers (age fifteen) plays his Bacon Belmont five-string banjo at a music party at Byron and Alice Johnson's farm near Urbana, 1950. *Left to right*: Bob McCoy (guitar), Orville Day (violin), "Bashful Bob" Penny (mandolin, *back to camera*), Byron Johnson (*listening*), Kenneth Pitts (guitar), Alice Johnson (piano, *hidden from view*), and Hoppers. (Courtesy Lonnie Hoppers)

Jim Walters Jubilee, 1961, Joplin television KODE Channel 12.0. *Rear*: "Bashful Bob" Penny (with Gibson ES175), Jan Maguire (vocalist, Kelly Edwards's daughter), and "Cousin Kelly" Edwards (Harmony electric lap steel guitar and bass). *Front*: Lonnie Hoppers with his 1954 Gibson "bowtie" Mastertone banjo, Dude Fellows (violin), Dean Webb (1956 Gibson F5 mandolin), and Eastman (Len) Willie (Martin D-28 guitar). Penny and Edwards did the comedy routines; Edwards called his lap steel guitar a "steam-heated biscuit board." Hoppers: "We were trying to make a living, so we threw everything we had at 'em!" (June 23, 2015); photo by Charlene Carson Hoppers

from the Sears, Roebuck catalog. "Once I figured out they were playing a *five-string*, that's what I really started talking to Dad about, you know—see what he could come up with. So I came home from school one day and he had that new Bacon Belmont laying on the table, and it had one of those soft chipboard cases, it was laying open. And it had a *case* and everything, you know. And there it was. *Man*. And I didn't let go of that until *midnight*, . . . before I had to get up and go to school the next day."

Hoppers knows the importance of fiddle tunes in the evolution of bluegrass banjo playing. "Tunes like that are really good to force you to try to be able to play the *melody* notes, all the *melody* notes that you can get and still try to get a decent sound and *roll*. And a lot of 'em, what they do (some banjo players) is they skip over way too many melody notes."

In 1954 Hoppers was able to order a new Gibson RB250 "bowtie" Mastertone from the Harry Vernon Music in Eldon. Lonnie borrowed the $238 from his father to pay for the banjo, with a Lifton hardshell case, and it arrived in June 1955. Lonnie then sold his Bacon Belmont five-string to his old friend and mentor Truman Bridges, who played it as a plectrum—with the fifth string removed. The proud owner of the bowtie Gibson, Lonnie Hoppers advanced quickly to become one of the nation's most respected bluegrass players, one whose style is rooted in the classic 1940s Earl Scruggs style but graced with Lonnie's own inventions and personal style. Hoppers exemplifies the professional bluegrass player "in the life"—completely devoted to the music and all its social and cultural heritage.

To Be or Not to Be a Bluegrass Fiddler

Discussions about the relationship between bluegrass and old-time fiddling draw a variety of comments. At a session at old-time dance fiddler Lee Stoneking's house in Clinton that I recorded for the Smithsonian in 1975, we drifted into the topic:

> *Mrs. Stoneking*: Bluegrass is good listening music, but *this* is *dancing music*. If you got any rhythm in your body, you can dance to *this*.
> *Lee Stoneking*: I'll tell you one thing about bluegrass music, I think it's beautiful. But they *chop it up* an awful lot. The old-time music is something that's a little smoother, it don't need to be chopped up but it's still smoother, see.

Earl Ball of Humansville spoke on the matter in a music party at his house with Forrest Enloe (guitar), Ron Ray (guitar), and Kathy Gordon (bass) in February 2008. Ball began playing bluegrass during the festival boom in the 1960s. Earl and Helen were regulars at Dixon, Starvy Creek, and Clinton, where their camper was a valued and welcoming oasis for fiddlers. At Earl and Helen's camp, old-time and bluegrass style fiddlers met, visited, compared instruments, and swapped tunes. Earl favored the smooth fiddling and big tunes of Arthur Smith and Tommy Jackson, but he grew up with and dearly loved the old and rare Missouri tunes, which he thought youngsters should be learning along with the latest bluegrass number.

Ball wanted to expose new and young bluegrass fiddlers to the ironclads in the older repertoire that continue to be the bedrock underpinning and nourishing modern bluegrass fiddling. "I still play the same old stuff I used to, you know. But about all you play in bluegrass is a break on a song or something, you know. Not many people want to sit and play *fiddle tunes*. There's a guy from Arkansas, he's kind of a crackpot—a *kid*, you know—[who] said, 'About two or three of those fiddle tunes is all I can stand.' Somebody sitting there by me at our camper said, 'Boy, then you're in the *wrong place!*'"

Old-time fiddling had significant influence on Bill Monroe's vision, and he often spoke of it. In his experiences as a youth, the fiddler was the featured performer. But many would say that no less important in bluegrass, if not more important, than the fiddle were the fetching innovations of Earl Scruggs's banjo playing. For years the banjo was more familiar in the expected bluegrass ensemble even than the violin. A few important bands had no regular fiddler, such as the Dillards, the Country Gentlemen, and the Seldom Scene. In some bands the fiddler's role was to provide a periodic hoedown and steady backup work, such as the Stanley Brothers and Jimmy Martin and the Sunny Mountain Boys. Some bands brought in a fiddler as a guest on a recording project. Several talented bluegrass fiddlers functioned essentially as independent musicians, moving from gig to gig and being featured at festivals.

Bluegrass instrumentals are often said to be too fast to dance to, but this notion does not really hold water. Many square dancers welcome a bluegrass fiddler blasting away on "Katy Hill" or "Sally Goodin," and many stereotypical old-time Missouri dance fiddlers of my acquaintance, such as Johnny Bruce, Lonnie Robertson, Lyman Enloe, Bob Holt, and Billy Lee, appreciated and played bluegrass, and they could play at hyperspeed. And even though bluegrass bands perform for seated audiences, dancing finds a way to happen. Solo jig dancing often breaks out at bluegrass shows and festivals when people rise from their chairs and flatfoot or jig (clog) along with spirited fiddling.

Bluegrass is a genre with unlimited permutations, and the music does not stand still. Almost from the beginning, individuals took different tacks in giving their ideas shape to help bluegrass. There are debates between conservative players of classic or roots bluegrass and those who prefer the modern or progressive "newgrass" styles that old fogies see as sketching too far outside the lines—not unlike the debates among swing musicians or old-time fiddlers.

The Ozark Mountain Trio, formed in 1960, was one of the early bluegrass bands in Missouri. Original members were Don Brown (mandolin), Norman Ford (guitar), John Hartford (banjo), and fiddler Paul Tinnon. Brown, founder and leader, learned mandolin by listening to Bill Monroe on Saturday-night *Grand Ole Opry* broadcasts. Bands like the Ozark Mountain Trio were helped by the many festivals that provided performance opportunities to supplement other venues, such as radio shows, oprys, and theater concerts. The group won the band contest at Bill Monroe's Bean Blossom, Indiana, festival in 1970 and other contests at places like Hugo, Oklahoma. Not only did Don Brown play "Monroe style" mandolin, but his high, nasal tenor voice also resembled the intensity of Monroe's. Brown often spoke of the importance of the singing style and the close harmony of voices, and many have commented that "southern" vernacular voices in bands like the Ozark Mountain Trio (from south-central Missouri) made bluegrass distinctive and attractive beyond the South and Midwest hearths. Brown noted that the instrumental work in bluegrass bands could sound much the same across the country, but not so the singing.[19]

Missouri was one of the first states where bluegrass flowered. And speaking of flowers, in the sixties, when bluegrass truly arrived, bluegrass music was as much part and parcel of the flower-child hippie scene as rock and roll or old-time fiddling. Bill Monroe said on several occasions that Missouri was a key state in sales of his first commercial recordings. In June 1974, Monroe told me that Missouri was where the 1940 Bluebird 78 "Mule Skinner Blues" (a new and faster version of a Jimmie Rodgers recording) "took off."[20] Missouri's cultural and musical heritage made it a receptive state to bluegrass. And, of course, Monroe's concerts and tours in Missouri and his long association with festival promoters and musicians increased his stature and reputation in the Show-Me State.

In Missouri bluegrass caught on after World War II first in places where there was already a long tradition of hillbilly and string-band music both in the community and on area radio stations. In Springfield, Kansas City, the St. Louis area, and the central Ozarks counties south of the Missouri River, certain towns became known for their radio stations programming bluegrass. By the 1970s, FM had swept away most AM stations, but in the 1960s AM was still relevant. Some AM stations survived by focusing on the farming business in their rural areas, and country music and bluegrass were considered fare for their audiences.

Warrenton's KWRE-AM programmed several bluegrass shows in the 1960s, and their broadcasts could be heard as far away as Hannibal, Jefferson City, and Moberly. The deejays on these shows were fans, and often bluegrass pickers themselves, and aired the latest news of festivals and concerts as well as new records. Regional and local bands were often featured. As the FM radio band took over the airwaves, the development of community radio and public broadcasting networks helped fill the lacuna left by the evaporation of AM transmission.

Several music stores in different parts of the state (especially if they sold Martin and Gibson instruments) became fixed in people's mental maps as places to stop off when traveling, to check out the instruments and jam sessions and bask in the bonhomie of kindred spirits. Occasionally, a violin shop would become interested in bluegrass and old-time fiddling, and become a gathering place and ad hoc music-party site. A few violin shops became more fiddler friendly in the mid-1960s as fiddlers contests became more familiar—and after fiddlers from Missouri came back from national and international contests with trophies and stories. Enlightened violin-shop owners began to understand that an old-time fiddler from a hamlet in the sticks, who may wander in wearing overalls or a feed cap, was just as likely to desire and be able to purchase an expensive violin, bow, and case as an orchestra violinist.

Bluegrass offered a new environment for fiddlers who looked for a path into concert-oriented show music. In bluegrass, just as in country music, the fiddler has to rethink his or her role and shift from essentially a soloist in front of dancers to being a role player in a concert ensemble. The bluegrass player's first responsibility is sideman in an ensemble that includes singing as much or more as instrumental music. A bluegrass fiddler spends much of his or her time playing backup, with specific solos (breaks) during a vocal number or when featured with a "fiddle tune." Other instruments are given breaks, too, and sometimes breaks are divided between the fiddler and the mandolinist, banjoist, guitarist, or Dobro player. A bluegrass fiddler needs to be able to provide all kinds of background, kickoffs, fills, licks, and tags that support and add accent, rhythm, harmony, and depth to the group's sound. Ed McKinney, an Ozark historian and bluegrass musician, feels that the new, limited role of a fiddler was "one of the factors holding back fiddlers from performing in bluegrass bands—they for the most part played hoedowns and waltzes. Many fiddlers in this area had no experience in doing any or all of the background inputs, and therefore tended to shy away from bluegrass performances. When outstanding bluegrass fiddlers like Kenny

Baker and Paul Warren (and others) became well known then many fiddlers in this area began to attempt a bluegrass style of performing."[21]

Old-time fiddlers coming into bluegrass had an additional challenge of fiddling what were essentially banjo tunes, in which the melody could be somewhat hard to get a fix on, as a banjoist played complex and elegant chords in and around the melody of a tune. Whether a fiddler can handle, and can be happy in, this role as team player and backup specialist has a great deal of bearing on whether the fiddler will succeed in the bluegrass world. Unlike the fiddler's role in old-time dance fiddling, in bluegrass the fiddler is not necessarily the default leader but one of several people in an ensemble.

"I Want You to Play the Old Time": Delbert Spray

Delbert E. Spray (1923–2001) was a farmer in the prairie and forest country of Clark County in extreme northeastern Missouri. Delbert was born into a family of farmers who grew crops and raised livestock near North Salem, to the west in Linn County. His Scotch-Irish and English ancestors had come to Sullivan County and Linn County from Kentucky and Ohio in the 1840s.

Delbert's grandparents' generation thought playing fiddle music was inappropriate. "They looked down toward a fiddler. They thought you should be an opera singer, or a concert pianist, and all that."[22] However, Delbert's father, Albert Ross Spray,

Albert Spray, ca. 1965, a left-handed fiddler who liked to play with the violin resting against the upper sill (above the keyboard) on an upright piano. (Courtesy Pat Davidson)

became a well-known fiddler. Albert played by holding the instrument vertically and resting it on a tabletop, upright piano keyboard sill, or his knees and bowing the violin like a cello player. He had no physical impairment to cause him to hold the violin that way, but somehow he had adopted the unusual playing position and even bowed left-handed. Albert Spray was much in demand at dances, where his favorite accompaniment was the piano backup by his son Delmas Spray. Albert was also a successful contest fiddler.

Delbert began learning to play fiddle and guitar music at age six and learned to play fiddle for square dances. Following in his father's footsteps, his first tunes for square dances were ironclads like as "Liberty," "Ragtime Annie," "Mississippi Sawyer," and "Bully of the Town" as well as the range of jigs, schottisches, waltzes, and two-steps expected of a good dance fiddler. Delbert grew up around some of the finest of the hornpipe and long-bow style fiddlers in the three-state area of northeastern Missouri, southeastern Iowa, and western Illinois. Delbert's first fiddlers contest victory was at age sixteen in 1937 in Keytesville, where he beat Dolph Wilson and Delbert's father, Albert.

After high school, Delbert joined the army in 1944, during World War II. In the Pacific theater, he served with the First Cavalry Division on New Guinea (a campaign lasting until the end of the war on August 15, 1945) and contracted malaria. He also worked as a barber in Special Services for a time. After his tour of duty in New Guinea, Spray was being transported to take part in the Luzon campaign, but his troopship was sunk by a Japanese submarine; many soldiers and sailors died. Delbert was rescued, but he lost his violin. After the war was over, later in 1945 Private First Class Spray transferred to Tokyo, where he performed in Special Services bands to entertain Allied troops of occupation and play dances. One group was a swing orchestra in which he played rhythm guitar, and the other was a string band in which he played country and old-time fiddle. He had heard and admired Bill Monroe and the Bluegrass Boys over radio broadcasts and on records, and Delbert would always be proud that, to the best of his knowledge, in that army string band in 1945 he had been the first American fiddler to play bluegrass music in Japan.[23]

Out of the service and home in Browning in May 1946, Delbert married Erma Brookhart of Clark County in Kirksville, where they were in college at the state teachers college (now Truman State University). Delbert and Erma's first date was at a square dance in a barn loft near Winigan, where Delbert's father, Albert, was the fiddler that night. This barn still stands, and in the early 2000s Steve and Debbie Young, whose family owned the farm, held square dances in the same barn loft.

Delbert attended the college two years, and Erma graduated in 1948 with a teaching degree combining business and English. Erma taught schools ranging from a local one-room school to high school, and her exceptional writing and organizational talents would be put to good use many years later when they helped organize bluegrass festivals and write grants for arts-council funding. After the war, Delbert Spray put fiddling on hold while he farmed and helped Erma raise their family. A friend, Gene Calvert, talked Delbert into resuming his fiddling. In 1961 Delbert had suffered a farm-machinery accident that affected his music for a while. He caught his left

Delbert Spray playing rhythm guitar in a US Army special services unit "swing orchestra," Tokyo, Japan, 1945. (Courtesy Pat Davidson)

The Young family's early 1900s barn near Winigan during a square dance in the hayloft, ca. 2002, where Delbert and Erma Spray danced on their first date in 1946. As vernacular architecture, the barn type is a "transverse-crib barn" and emblematic of central and northern Missouri farms. The ways people in regions build traditional barns, houses, and other structures are, like styles of fiddling, often indicative of deep cultural meanings and heritage customs (see Howard Marshall, *Folk Architecture in Little Dixie* and *Vernacular Architecture in Rural and Small Town Missouri* [1994; http://missourifolkloresociety.truman.edu/marshall.html], and *Barns of Missouri* [2003]).

hand in the spinning belt of a combine, and his left index finger was shorn off at the knuckle. Within months Delbert was fiddling again, and most people did not realize he was missing a finger.[24]

Erma began playing backup guitar for Delbert's fiddling in her sixties. A bright and strong lady, Erma held her own among the gentlemen. Erma and Delbert did not play for the rowdy dances in the area, however. At the farm near Kahoka, Clark County, they raised Hereford cattle and then Shorthorn and Angus crossbreds. Their cattle enterprise helped forge a friendship with Bill Monroe and Kenny Baker, whom Delbert and Erma had met at one of Monroe's Bean Blossom festivals in the 1970s. Based on Delbert and Erma's recommendation, Monroe and Baker drove a truck to Missouri to buy Shorthorn bulls from the Miller farm near Hannibal.

Delbert Spray, ca. 1970. (Courtesy Pat Davidson)

In August 1972, Delbert and Erma established an annual bluegrass festival in Kahoka, where Monroe's band, and Baker, performed. The Sprays were part of a small group of bluegrass enthusiasts, including their children, Patricia Spray Davidson and John Spray, who lamented the dearth of festivals and concerts in their region and decided to start their own. The Kahoka festival became one of the largest bluegrass festivals in the region. Many campers would arrive days early and stay days after the official closing. The Kahoka festivals, like all the best bluegrass festivals, had the feeling of a family reunion, old-time neighborhood picnic, and harvest celebration. Delbert and Erma made the festival grounds inviting; each morning, they made fresh country biscuits and gravy in the festival grounds' cook shack known as the Fiddler's Inn.

Always mindful of the violin's importance in bluegrass music, the festival held an open-mic "fiddler's frolic" onstage Friday night, with fiddlers from featured bands taking a turn to play a tune alongside local fiddlers. Some amazing impromptu fiddling took place on those occasions, and many "campground fiddlers" thrillingly found themselves standing next to fiddle stars like Kenny Baker or Kirk Brandenberger, whose father, Ernie Brandenberger, was a fine old-time fiddler and friend of Delbert's. On Saturday the results of the annual "Miss Kahoka Bluegrass" competition were announced, a county fair–like ingredient in the festival that helped bring local support and family participation. A few of the Miss Kahoka Bluegrass contestants turned out to be promising young fiddlers and musicians in addition to their more obvious attributes (Rhonda Vincent won the title twice).

In 1978 the Sprays' festival group founded the Tri-State Bluegrass Association (TSBA), which sponsors festivals and concerts in Missouri, Iowa, and Illinois.[25] Their principal events became the annual November and February indoor festivals in Hannibal, to offer off-season venues following the August festivals at the Clark County Fairgrounds at Kahoka. The TSBA continues to produce an annual bluegrass festival "blue book" and band guide. For a time, November and February festivals were held in Quincy, Illinois, a major town in the group's core interstate territory. Following Erma Spray's death in 2009, Spray's daughter, Pat Davidson, assumed management of the festival guide and website (http://www.tsbafestivals.org). The TSBA issued one LP record of music drawn from the Kahoka festival, spotlighting bands that had not been recorded on commercial labels.[26]

For a number of years, the TSBA hosted a Land of Mark Twain Fiddle Championship in Hannibal in November. This contest had an attractive purse, with assistance from the Missouri Arts Council, and attracted top contest fiddlers from many states. However, the November fiddlers contest eventually devolved into a standard bluegrass festival. There were too many competing interests and complexities to keep the contest and festival functioning together. Part of the reason for the demise of the Hannibal contest was predictable: a small clique of seasoned, expert "contest fiddlers" won year after year. Increasingly, most of the top players emphasized what was being called "Texas-style" or "progressive" or "National Contest style" fiddling, tune selection, and accompaniment rather than the bluegrass fiddling or old-time fiddling that festival audiences and first-generation bluegrass fans and performers knew best. Only a few major events, such as the autumn Tennessee Valley event in Athens, Alabama, have managed successfully to continue combining a bluegrass and old-time music festival with a fiddlers contest.

Delbert Spray was a fixture at all these festivals, impeccably dressed and sporting his Bill Monroe–style Stetson and a well-trimmed mustache, looking the part of the benevolent country squire, festival bossman, and master fiddle player that he was. Late into night, when most of the festivalgoers had retired and most other musicians had given out from exhaustion, we could find Delbert in the midst of a knot of pickers, playing away at his favorite tunes and happily answering requests. In those moments of freewheeling music parties, Delbert was not only unwinding from a long day of helping run the festival but also offering up his own fiddling for the enjoyment of others and typically adding a local tune into the mix that was handed down from previous generations.

Another feature of Delbert and Erma's role in bluegrass festivals was their encouragement of aspiring musicians and bands just getting started, particularly younger musicians. Many of the bands that received encouragement, and exposure to new audiences, at the TSBA festivals were the Faris Family (from Kansas), the Bob Lewis Family (from southeastern Missouri), the Martin Family (Warsaw and Jefferson City), and the family band the Cherryholmes (who left Los Angeles in 2002 to pursue their career in bluegrass at Midwest festivals). Delbert Spray was never too busy to step aside and find a quieter corner to coach and encourage a young fiddler. Many of the TSBA festivals in Hannibal included a fiddle workshop that featured both seasoned pros and aspiring young fiddlers.

In the 1980s, the University of Missouri's Missouri Cultural Heritage Center developed the state's Traditional Arts Apprenticeship Program, to pair seasoned "masters" with appropriate, and usually young, "apprentices" who could learn and carry on the music of the masters. The program was developed and funded nationwide by the National Endowment for the Arts, in league with the state arts council (in this case, the Missouri Arts Council, which also helped fund TSBA festivals). In the mid-1980s, Delbert Spray taught fiddle in the program, partnering with a young student from Kirksville named Michelle Ogle. Ogle was an interesting pupil, as a person with classical violin experience who had been experimenting with fiddle music and entering fiddlers contests. In addition to the help from Spray (and guitarist Jim Lindsey), students like Ogle were able to understand the importance Delbert Spray put on old-time fiddling and tunes from their region as well as simply learning fiddling technique. While Delbert's favorite music was bluegrass, he knew his history and encouraged learners to play the old-time and older tunes as well as bluegrass pieces. In his later years, Spray began teaching his great-granddaughter Ashley Foti to play fiddle music, and eventually she inherited his favorite violin.

Spray played a number of rare local tunes, some attributed to local fiddlers. "Best Old Coon Dog" was one of his dad's tunes—a G hoedown offering opportunity to illustrate bowing subtleties and syncopations. "Best Old Coon Dog" is typical of the tunes and style that drew professional fiddlers such as Tater Tate, Benny Martin, Kenny Baker, and John Hartford, as well as Bill Monroe, to Delbert Spray's fiddling. Among other tunes seldom heard outside northern Missouri were tunes Delbert's father, Albert, played, including "Best Old Coon Dog," as well as "Mag Brown," "Crippled Turkey," "Hogs in the Corn Field," "Sadie's in the Kitchen" (hear on the companion CD), "Bucks in the Brush," and "Muir's Hornpipe," which he learned from fiddler Wes Muir. "Best Old Coon Dog" and "Crippled Turkey" were recorded on a highly regarded Global Village LP in 1987 by Iowa fiddler, guitarist, and long-time friend Al Murphy, from Iowa City, Iowa, who recorded several relaxed music parties where Delbert Spray dug into his memory bank and played the old tunes for appreciative friends.[27]

Spray took to bluegrass with gusto. His fiddling abilities allowed him to render the old standbys and elaborate hornpipes of his region right alongside the emergent bluegrass fiddle style he admired so much. Spray composed tunes but never got around to producing a recording of his own fiddling. He did make a guest appearance on a private-label LP in 1983, called *Hard Times* (Triple Tree 83-002), produced by Spray and W. E. Stuart and recorded at Ozark Opry Records at the Lake of the Ozarks. The album featured the Iowa bluegrass group Pathfinder. Delbert played his composition "Harmony Pines Waltz" ("This lovely melody was created by Delbert while attending Oliver Smith's Harmony Pines Festival in Gilson, Illinois"). On one occasion, he had composed the low part of a tune called "Kentucky Memories." Delbert played it for his friend Gene Goforth, who liked it and added a high part to complete the tune with Delbert.[28] Among tunes never released on recordings is Spray's "Shorty's Tune,"

Delbert Spray's version of a northern Missouri tune, "Mag Brown," learned from his father, Albert Spray. (Courtesy Al Murphy; transcription by John Hartford, re-set by Philip K. Vinyard)

in honor of a friend and fan, Shorty Terrill, as well as songs he coauthored with Erma, such as "In the Land of Mark Twain."

For much of his fiddling life, his companion and backup guitarist was Jim Lindsey of Newark (see *Play Me Something Quick and Devilish*). Delbert and Jim traveled many times to Nashville, where they were treated to hospitality and nonstop jam sessions by Monroe, Tater Tate, Kenny Baker, Josh Graves, and Benny Martin. Lindsey, who had begun as a fiddler in childhood, had a knack for providing outstanding guitar accompaniment, and Jim appeared on *The Grand Ole Opry* several times as a guest guitar accompanist. Delbert, Erma, and Jim and Edna Lindsey also traveled to Nashville for John Hartford's New Year's house parties.

At a Monroe appearance in 1983 at a concert at McBride Auditorium in Iowa City, Iowa, Monroe composed a fiddle tune in Delbert's honor, "Delbert's Breakdown." It is a very Monroe-esque tune in the modal-sounding key of A minor (with the bridge in D). Bill brought Delbert to the stage and said,

> *Monroe*: Now I want you to listen close. [audience laughter] You know, I'm not bragging or anything. But sometimes I can put a mandolin number or a fiddle number or some banjo numbers together in a half a minute. And we's backstage and I just put this number together and I titled it "Delbert's Breakdown." [brings Erma forward to the mic] That's his wife, she kind of guides him and tells him what to do and everything. [audience laughter] [Bill and the band play the tune.] There you have it, boys.
>
> *Spray*: Thanks, Bill, I really love that, it's a good one.
>
> *Monroe*: Well, I think it's fine.
>
> *Spray*: Yes, sir.
>
> *Monroe:* Thank you. And I just want you to know that and that's the first title I thought about.
>
> *Spray*: Good! It's got a good title, you bet. I love that title. Now if I could just learn it, I'll be right in shape, won't I.
>
> *Monroe*: I'll put it on a tape for you. *I want you to play the old time*, you know, let your old time fiddle ring out, everything. Like this right: [Monroe picks a few notes of the melody] Really be pretty there with the fiddling coming in there.
>
> *Spray*: I like the bass part, too. That's a great song, thanks a million.
>
> *Monroe*: Delbert—thank you so much.
>
> *Spray*: Thank you a million.[29]

For Delbert's generation, pointedly playing "the old time," as Monroe often put it, there was no confusion of terms with "bluegrass." Old-time to these progenitors of the music was the music in its purest original form (to them)—what is now often called "classic bluegrass" as the music became internationally important from the 1950s into the 1970s. Monroe assigned part of the royalties for "Delbert's Breakdown" to his old friend Spray. In 1988 Spray gave the tune to Karl Shiflett's bluegrass band, a classic ensemble widely known in Missouri and the Midwest. "Delbert's

Breakdown" was recorded the next year on the CD *The Karl Shiflett & Big Country Show* (Rebel 1752). The fiddler with the Shiflett ensemble at the time was none other than Kirk Brandenberger, from Keokuk, Iowa, who grew up at Delbert and Erma's bluegrass festivals and learned much from Delbert's fiddling. Brandenberger, whose style is much like that of Kenny Baker, did the tune justice. Much to Delbert and Erma's surprise, in due course a royalty check soon arrived from Bill Monroe Music/BMI in Nashville.

Bill Monroe often called Delbert and Erma to visit about cattle and the old days. His favorite topics were always the same, how the times have changed, cattle, and foxhounds. Around Christmastime Monroe would phone Delbert and Erma and begin the conversation by singing into the phone, "Christmas time's a-comin', Christmas time's a-comin'"—and they knew it was Bill.[30] At Delbert Spray's funeral in Kahoka in 2001, musicians played and sang in the lobby before the service—Al Murphy, Rhonda Vincent, Kirk Brandenberger, Steve Head, Pat Sharman, Bob and Barb Lewis, and Bob Black; Johnny Vincent sang "Uncle Pen" and "Footprints in the Snow," and the Lewises sang "Go Rest High on the Mountain." Delbert and Erma's nine-year-old great-granddaughter, Ashley Foti, fiddled "Faded Love" on Delbert's violin.

Lyman Enloe's *Fiddle Tunes I Recall*, private-label LP with Kansas City's Bluegrass Association (1978, reissued by County Records in 1993), was widely praised and influential; the record illustrates the good music, mutual respect, and excitement that were possible when a strong old-time fiddler and an equally proficient and open-minded bluegrass band chanced to come together in the hospitable and heady atmosphere of a sixties folk music club.

Family Tradition 11

If there is any area of human achievement in which it pays to have adequate or lavish genetic background, music would be a formidable contender.

—Howard Gardner, *Frames of Mind: The Theory of Multiple Intelligences* (1983)

Music runs in families. That cliché, like all clichés, is built on truth. The notion of music being "in the blood" is ancient, just as in families with generation upon generation of bankers or coal miners, sailors or schoolteachers, artists or athletes, a pattern that seems to be breaking apart in modern times as families scatter across the nation. Whether the final answer is "nature" or "nurture" (most likely it is a combination of the two), it is one of the happy ingredients of fiddling that the gift often flourishes in families. A baby in the womb hears and learns, and tunes are imprinted just as is a mother's voice.

Many say that exposure to traditional music in childhood is vital, because the travels and trials through one's life may keep a person from doing things like playing the fiddle or banjo; people for years too busy in retirement rediscover youthful hobbies or unfulfilled plans that become possible only after the work is done, the last commute home is taken, and time becomes available. However may the geometry of opportunity, exposure, family support, and desire come into a person's drive to play music, being part of a family that values self-made music for the love of the music itself describes many fiddlers in this book.

Lyman Enloe: "I Like 'Em Just as Straight as Can Be"

Lyman Enloe was a person who wanted to be sure his music and the old tunes handed down to his care by the old-timers were passed to younger generations, and he made efforts to see it done.[1] Although reluctant to give formal lessons, he chose to work with several younger musicians who could learn his tunes and techniques, including Rusty Dutton, Dale Hopkins, Clifford Hill, Al Murphy, and Dan Grotewohl. Many others, such as Bill Shull and Charlie Walden, absorbed some of Enloe's music through visits and music parties as well as his recordings and appearances at fiddlers contests and bluegrass festivals, where he would be found in the middle of a nest of musicians in a campground jam session.

Of Irish and Dutch ancestry, Lyman Enloe (1906–97) was born on the family farm in Cole County, about halfway between Jefferson City and Eldon in the upper Ozarks. He was part of a large extended family. As a child, Enloe's love of traditional violin music was inspired by his older half brother, Wade, and by his father, Elijah (Lige) Enloe. Both played the fiddle and dance music of the region. Although Wade played only at home, his interest in the instrument was an important influence on Lyman Enloe, who thought the world of his older brother. Elijah, on the other hand, was one of the better-known fiddlers in central Missouri; Lyman was often at Elijah Enloe's side, playing rhythm guitar as tune after tune welded themselves into his memory.

As a young man, Enloe had also played banjo accompaniment for fiddlers in a two-finger (thumb and index finger) pre-bluegrass style. Enloe enjoyed playing "rhythm" guitar, and he started out playing with a thumb pick and forefinger and later adopted the use of a plectrum (flat pick or straight pick) that was more common among bluegrass musicians.

Lyman Enloe learned many tunes while accompanying Jefferson City fiddler Tony Gilmore in sessions, at dances, and on live programs on WOS radio. Enloe's first appearance on WOS was accompanying Wade in a fiddlers contest at WOS. Tony Gilmore was in the contest and afterward introduced himself to Lyman and asked the youngster to play guitar for him. After Lyman began accompanying Gilmore on WOS, eventually WOS staff found out that Lyman was learning to play fiddle music, too, so Lyman began bringing his violin to play a tune or two on the radio shows. By 1928 Enloe was playing fiddle on WOS on a weekly basis.

Enloe felt that he had an advantage because he had been playing rhythm guitar for his father, his uncle Pink, and Jim and Tony Gilmore, so he knew the tunes. "I didn't have to learn the tunes, all I had to do was learn to play them."

Tony Gilmore frequented the contest circuit with Enloe as backup guitarist. While playing guitar for Gilmore on WOS radio in Jefferson City in the late 1920s, Lyman learned the intriguing local tune called "Kansas City Rag." By that time, Tony and Jim Gilmore of Jefferson City were advanced, proficient players and helped Enloe out when he got started playing fiddle music. The rest was "mainly strength and awkwardness." Once he got started, it took Enloe nearly a year before he would play in front of Tony Gilmore.

Enloe grew up with equal exposure to the dance tradition and the contest tradition. There were few fiddlers in Cole County up to the Enloes' standards, so his father played for most of the dances. A cousin of Lyman's, Forrest Enloe of Humansville, recalled that, at numerous local dances, the music was provided by a trio with Lyman on guitar, while Lyman's brother Wade played bowed cello accompaniment.[2] All these experiences would be helpful in later years when Lyman fiddled for a dance that boasted thirty-two sets of square dancers on the floor, awaiting his music.

Lyman married Myrtle Howser in 1925. They lived in Jefferson City. After Lyman had worked in a shoe factory for several years, they moved to the old Enloe farm. After spending some ten years trying to be a farmer (as Lyman would say), he decided to leave farming and shift his energies to a more satisfying occupation: painting houses. In 1947 the Enloes, with seven daughters and two sons, moved to Raytown, on the southeast side of Kansas City's metro area. Enloe joined the painters' union and hired on with a contractor for several years until he and his son opened their own business in 1955.

Lyman started learning fiddle more seriously at age twenty-two.

> My wife was sick and I had to stay home from work. My dad had given me an old little fiddle, it was almost full sized. And I just had it hanging on the wall, never dreamed of ever playing it. I was sitting around the house like that and all of a sudden I looked at that little old fiddle and I told my wife, I said, "I believe I'll get that thing down, tune it up and learn to play it." She laughed at me, said, "That'll be the day," because I would never quit playing guitar, and I didn't think I would. I did just that, and got hooked on the damn thing and I've been playing fiddle ever since.

Lyman Enloe was, like Garvin Lee, Delbert Spray, Roger Williams, and Gene and Cecil Goforth, one of the generations who grew up in "old-time fiddling" who, as young men, were attracted to the excitement and pleasures of bluegrass music. However, whether Lyman Enloe, or the other names mentioned, can or should be filed away in one box or another is moot. The categories drawn by fiddle scholars and experts to classify a fiddler's "style" continue to be debatable (and even contentious) and a subjective exercise perhaps best suited to graduate seminars and scholarly papers (I know whereof I speak).[3] Yet to talk about the history and variety of fiddle tunes,

Lyman Enloe with the Bluegrass Association, among the most influential bands in the formative years of bluegrass music in Missouri. (Courtesy Jim McGreevy)

rocks, languages, or wheels, one needs to somehow sort out studiable blocks based on their perceived elements of expressed identity and personality.

The fiddler who has most influenced Enloe's mature style was bluegrass powerhouse Kenny Baker, whom he met at Bill Monroe's bluegrass festivals in Bean Blossom, Indiana, in 1970. Enloe was impressed by Baker's smooth use of the full length of the bow and worked hard to develop the skill.

One of the reasons Enloe enjoyed bluegrass festivals is that he disliked the hypercompetitive, intense atmosphere of the contest scene and instead appreciated the laid-back, informal scene in the festival campground. Enloe swapped tunes with Kenny Baker at festivals, during the period that Enloe was playing fiddle with Kansas City's highly praised Bluegrass Association band. Baker's composition "Festival Waltz" owes its title to Lyman Enloe. As recalled by Clifford Hill, an Enloe pupil and protégé, the tune recalls one of Kenny Seaman's bluegrass festivals at Eminence around 1970, where Enloe and Baker were visiting and swapping tunes. Baker told Enloe he had a new waltz but didn't know what to call it. Enloe listened to it and said, why not call it "Festival Waltz"?[4] When Nancy Cardwell asked Baker about Enloe, Baker emphasized Enloe's smooth playing and insistence on playing each part of a tune correctly: "Lyman Enloe is one of the finest old-time fiddlers I ever ran into. . . . When I hear him, I don't have to guess who it is."[5]

In 1966 Enloe had begun playing fiddle with the Down Home Folks in Kansas City, a group that evolved into the Bluegrass Association. Members of the original group were Chuck Stearman (mandolin), Jim McGreevy (banjo), John Bennett (guitar), and Don Montgomery (upright bass). Don Montgomery was also a fiddler and learned many of Lyman's tunes. In addition to his finesse playing his version of Scruggs-style banjo, Jim McGreevy also plays old-time frailing-style banjo. Enloe's daughter Audrey sang with the group on a regular basis. McGreevy and Montgomery later joined Mae and Jack Burlison's Bluegrass Brigade, and this band continues to perform (Montgomery does the fiddling with this group).[6] These and many other musicians came together at 1960s jam sessions at "the old fiddler's club," in a local ironworkers' union hall in Kansas City.

For fiddle players, Lyman Enloe's LP records with the Bluegrass Association became collector's items. These albums include Enloe playing several fiddle tunes on *One Tin Soldier* (Cavern Custom USR 4122, 1973) and *Strings Today . . . and Yesterday* (Cavern Custom 42419, 1974), and his all-fiddle albums *Rugged Road* (Society for the Preservation of Bluegrass Music, 1976) and *Fiddle Tunes I Recall* (1978).[7] A 2005 CD by County Records includes several tracks from Enloe's 1978 LP (with Casey Jones and Cyril Stinnett), *Three Fiddlers from the Show-Me State* (County CO-2739). Jim McGreevy comments on Enloe's style in the 1989 Cardwell article: "Lyman always had every tune pretty well structured. It was established how to play the tune well in advance and practiced and for the most part there was not a deviation. . . . That's how it was to be played *every* time it was played.' Later on, the bluegrass style of playing back up and improvising 'instant arrangements' developed, and 'that just didn't fit in with forty or fifty years of structured playing,' McGreevy says."[8]

Like most old-time fiddlers who become interested in bluegrass, Enloe pondered the differences between bluegrass and old-time. As Enloe put it during the recording session for *"Now That's a Good Tune"*: "When they [bluegrass fiddlers] take breaks or play a backup after the verses like that, it's just completely different. You know, they fill in and put in a lot more in it, a lot more fiddling in it than just the old-time fiddle tunes. Old-time fiddling has a lot more noting. A backup [bluegrass] fiddle player, when the song is going, he's filling in . . . but I've always stayed out of that because I just can't do it."[9] Lyman's comments largely echo those by many other fiddlers. However, unlike other old-time fiddlers bridging the two genres, Lyman did not particularly like, and did not adopt, the techniques to play backup fills, riffs, and chops that are part of the complete bluegrass fiddler's tool kit.

In the early 1980s, Barry Bergey's Friends of the Folk Arts brought Lyman Enloe to the Frontier Folklife Festival in St. Louis. He also participated in the University of Missouri's *"Good Tune"* project in 1989 and included his interesting versions of the rare tunes "Spotted Pony" (from Andy Beaty and Carol Beaty Hascall), "Waldo" (from Jim Gilmore and the Helton family), "Hanging around the Kitchen" (an alternate title Enloe used for "Richmond Cotillion" and "Richmond Polka"),[10] "The Rough Scotsman," "Call Your Dogs and Let's Go Hunting," and "Forgotten Waltz" from his father and Lee Carpenter.[11]

Many of the tunes that Enloe knew were passed down to his father from fiddlers like Ben Hines, Gum Messerschmidt, Lee Carpenter, Lou Hart, and Lawrence (Dutch) Noah, from whom he learned "Dutch's Waltz" (a version of "Canary Waltz").

One of Enloe's favorite tunes was "Echoes of the Ozarks," which he had learned from champion fiddler, violinist, and music-store owner Henry Thompson (Iberia), who played it in B-flat; Enloe, however, played it in G. Lyman's uncle fiddler Pinckney (Pink) Enloe also played the tune, having learned it from Ishmael (Ozark Red) Loveall, who helped bring the tune to prominence in the 1930s along with Fiddlin' Sam Long of Oklahoma, the Kansas-born fiddler who had lived in Joplin, Missouri, and had won fiddlers contests and in 1926 made a 78 rpm record of "Echoes of the Ozarks" in Richmond, Indiana, for the Gennett firm. Lyman Enloe often called the tune "Echoes of the Past," the title used by his uncle Pink.[12] Columbia fiddlers such as Ed Tharp and Luther Caldwell played the tune in B-flat and under the title "Traveling Back to Dixie."

Enloe learned an unusual tune, "Raking the Leaves" (issued on the companion CD with the 2012 *Play Me Something Quick and Devilish*), from Red Loveall at a fiddlers contest at the Osage River village of Bagnell in 1939. Lyman learned "Hooker's Hornpipe" and "Old Melinda" ("Malindy") from northern Missouri fiddler Casey Jones (whom Enloe listened to over the Pittsburg, Kansas, AM radio station KOAM) and helped spread the tunes throughout central Missouri.[13] "Taters" came from jam sessions with Cleo Persinger (who probably learned it from George Morris, "the Fiddling Sheriff"—see *Play Me Something Quick and Devilish*), and "Sunflower Hornpipe" and "Soapsuds" came from sessions with Kansas City's John Journagin. An unusual tune Lyman played called "Visha," a dialect form of "Vichy," came from the

Helton family in Maries County, the title commemorating a village in the southern quadrant of that county named after the French resort. Much of this information about Enloe's more obscure repertoire was documented by Al Murphy of Iowa during their fiddle apprenticeship together in 1989–90. (Murphy traveled to Enloe's apartment in Lee's Summit for their sessions.)

In 1990 Lyman Enloe participated in a marathon session concocted by Joe Wieneman and Irl Hees. Called *The Missouri Session*, the CD featured some thirty musicians and singers, including fiddlers Kirk Brandenberger and Larry Ellis as well as Lyman Enloe, and included some of Missouri's best-known bluegrass vocalists Don Brown and Andy and Alvin Bressler. The project was conceived of as a typical bluegrass-festival jam session, a nod to the continuing role of summer festivals in the music. Enloe fiddles "Dixie Hoedown" with stunning harmony fiddling by his younger colleagues Brandenberger and Ellis (hear on the companion CD).[14]

Recognition came to Lyman Enloe from various quarters, such as his being named Fiddler of the Year in 1984 at the Society for the Preservation of Blue Grass Music in America (SPBGMA) awards ceremony; there were two divisions for the fan balloting—Bluegrass Fiddler of the Year and Old-Time Fiddler of the Year (Lyman

"Forgotten Waltz," by Lyman Enloe, from the 1989 University of Missouri documentary *"Now That's a Good Tune."* (Transcription by Philip K. Vinyard)

was the latter). He was included in the University of Missouri's documentary *"Good Tune"* project, a finalist for two Grammy Awards (best album notes; best documentary). In 1995 Lyman was awarded a prestigious National Heritage Fellowship by the National Endowment for the Arts.[15] Perhaps the finest kind of acclaim is the fact that today, at bluegrass festivals in Missouri and elsewhere, people continue to play "Lyman tunes" such as "Oklahoma Redbird" (a demanding hornpipe in B-flat), "Forgotten Waltz," and "Down Home Rag."

Enloe appreciated good timing, intonation, and smoothness and stressed the importance of expressing one's personality in the music. He was also aware of the need to be a team player and entertainer onstage, to let an audience know that he enjoyed what he was doing. He looked askance at fiddlers with "big egos" who could not conceal how pleased they were with themselves: "It's not a good idea to get conceited in your music playing." Anyone who knew Enloe was struck by his imperturbable courtesy and gentility. He disliked the tense, feisty, and argumentative atmosphere at fiddlers contests, and, as a result, Lyman competed in and helped judge very few contests. As part of a judging panel, he would fret that he might score a deserving fiddler just off enough to knock him or her out of the running. One night before a contest, he could not sleep, worrying about having to judge the next day. That was Enloe's last contest judging.

In 1988 Enloe remarked on the fact that many of the strong young fiddlers were more interested in the "progressive" style of fiddling (today more often called "contest style") rather than the old-time traditions as he had inherited them. In his older years, he became more and more concerned with what seemed to be the steady loss of older fiddle tunes and, as people died, older playing styles that had become dated or rare. As a student of Enloe's in the middle 1980s, after Enloe resumed his fiddling, Rusty Dutton of Independence, already a seasoned musician, studied with Enloe as his apprentice in the Missouri Traditional Arts Apprenticeship Program and performed with him at festivals such as the Chicago Folk Festival (January 1986, 1990) and the National Folk Festival in 1990. Enloe's health was in decline, and Dutton helped Enloe remember tune titles and, in some cases, helped Enloe start a tune that had slipped his memory and in this way supported Enloe as his days were becoming fewer. Enloe was immensely proud of the fiddling of all of his students.

Clifford Hill of Eldon played guitar accompaniment for Lyman Enloe on many occasions, and, as a fiddler, Hill absorbed much of Enloe's approach. Hill, a fiddler originally from Miller County, whose paternal great-grandfather came from Tennessee before the Civil War and fought in the Union army during the conflict, operates a violin shop at his home and does high-quality repair work. With an analytical turn of mind, in addition to studying the work of other luthiers and reading books and manuals, Clifford Hill learned some of the ins and outs of violin repair through his association with Enloe and through his own trial and error working on instruments. Hill shared with Enloe dissatisfaction with the reluctance of the average bluegrass bands to ask the fiddler to play anything other than kickoffs, backup fills, and an occasional hot breakdown. Hill complains, "They never let you play a waltz." In one bluegrass band Hill played in for years, he was continually told *not* to play waltzes.[16]

Dan Grotewohl is a fiddler now living in Lawrence, Kansas, who, as a teenager and neighbor of Lyman Enloe's in 1963, became a devoted pupil. Grotewohl became the first youngster to work methodically in fiddle lessons with Lyman Enloe.[17] Enloe did not consider himself a fiddle teacher, but, as Nancy Cardwell writes in her *Bluegrass Unlimited* article on Enloe, he was proud of the progress of Dan Grotewohl. "I didn't teach him all that he knows now, but just got him started to know what it's all about."[18]

In 2015 Grotewohl wrote me about his experiences with his mentor, a statement rich with information and insight into many parts of being a "fiddler" as well as the near-mystical relationship that can accrue between the right young person and the right older person of generous spirit. Dan Grotewohl's remarkable memoir is worth quoting from at length:

> I first met Lyman when I was twelve or thirteen (1972–1973). We had moved from Topeka, KS to Kansas City, MO. My brother, Chris, had started playing five-string banjo the year or two before and we had already been listening to Bluegrass music for a number of years already (we went to the very first Walnut Valley Festival in Winfield, KS, as well as the next many each year thereafter). All along, I struggled to find the instrument right for me—one that I felt drawn to, that is. Then a cousin visited us in KC with his fiddle, and the first time I held the instrument in my hands I felt something special just in the way it looked and felt. I expressed some interest to my dad, who in turn inquired around local music stores about anybody teaching fiddle. They mentioned Lyman, prefacing it that he didn't give lessons, but maybe he might know someone who did. My dad contacted Lyman, who expressed reluctance, but he finally agreed to at least allow my dad and me to stop by. Conveniently, Lyman lived about a half mile away from us in Raytown.
>
> The first visit was quite simple. Lyman greeted us at the front door, introduced us to his wonderful wife Myrtle, and then led us into the kitchen where he had a couple fiddles sitting on the kitchen table. He told us that he had given a few pointers to his grandson, David, but that he had never even thought of giving anybody a real fiddle lesson. Anyway, we finally got seated. Lyman, in his easy going and gentle way, handed me a fiddle and helped me position it beneath my chin while offering a few suggestions about placement of my hand, handed me the bow and showed me how he held it, and then sat across from me. One note at a time, he demonstrated first how to make a sound, waited for me to try, struggle, before he played a couple more notes, struggle, and repeat until I made the adjustments and finally some semblance of sound. Probably after about thirty or forty minutes, I was spent.
>
> Lyman seemed to think that I showed some potential, and at the end of our evening together we asked him if he'd be willing to do it again. He agreed with a laugh. And that was the beginning of a few years spent learning fiddle with Lyman. Lyman's approach with me was purely by ear. He taught me a couple basic scales, had me

practice those for a few days and then finally taught me my first tune, Red River Valley. Each time I visited him at his house, we'd sit in the kitchen directly across from each other, our fiddles maybe a foot apart. I would try to copy each note and each sound, and Lyman, as I described above, would play a note or two, wait for me to find them, before he'd move forward with a couple more notes. It was purely trial and error for Lyman, and I think he took this tack because it made sense—call and answer, call and answer. Myrtle would sit in the living room watching shows, but she always kept one ear attentive to our playing in the kitchen, and sometimes she would offer praise from her place in the living room.

I don't even know if Lyman charged my dad any fee for helping me. Lyman was pure country goodness, where his word meant everything, where his handshake was worth more than a contract. Lyman's approach with me on fiddle was one of constant gentleness, compassionate suggestions, and complete non-pressure. And humor!! He quickly recognized that I was incredibly shy. We had just moved to a new area, I had hit puberty, everything emotional and physically was changing in me, and Lyman and the fiddle came along at such a vulnerable time for me.

Lyman was never only my fiddle teacher, instead, he took me under his wing and nurtured me as a person just as much as a player, and he also became a dear friend of mine. After a while, I probably went to his house several times a week to learn tunes and work on various aspects of my playing. And he told many stories about his life, and his playing. Sometimes we played very little and instead just chatted, or he would share with me his latest project repairing or restoring a fiddle.

My dad found an old beater fiddle to buy—it might have been $25, maybe $50, but it was a place to begin. That fiddle had those guitar-type tuners which I hated because part of the allure of the fiddle for me was staring down the fingerboard and seeing the beautiful wooden tuning pegs. I never did like my first fiddle. Eventually, as I improved, Lyman found a better fiddle for me and a better bow. And steadily I made improvements in my playing. Admittedly, I was also not always the best at practicing. Sometimes I would show up at Lyman's house somewhat ill-prepared. Never once did Lyman show any frustration; instead, he offered gentle reassurance that practice was usually the best way of getting better.

Lyman gently coaxed me into entering into a fiddle contest at some local bluegrass festival, the name I can't recall. I was petrified. But I did it because Lyman asked me to, explaining that it was important that I push the boundaries a bit and learn how to play on stage. Gulp! I have no memory of what I played, probably something like Fireball Mail, Over the Waves waltz, and maybe something like Red River Valley. I likely bombed! But I remember seeing Lyman standing back in the crowd just beaming. That I made him proud meant the world to me. That I played well or played poorly wasn't the point with Lyman, but that I got up there on stage exposed and tried my hardest. At another fiddle contest, I recall getting on stage, stepping up to the mic and being so distracted by worrying that the audience could see my knees shaking. I got stuck on one tune and had to keep stopping and starting, finally stomping my foot loudly and grunting in exasperation before stumbling through the trouble spot. Of course, I bombed yet again, but the crowd cheered loudly. During those years, every emotion, every struggled note and bobble in my playing was clearly documented on my face—tongue twisting, grimacing face, mouth and lips jerking about in their own struggle! And Lyman just laughed, not at me but with me. I might add that Lyman wasn't a fan of fiddle contests. He viewed them as far too political and fixed in favor of the local fiddler.

Another time while at Lyman's house, he handed me his prized fiddle—the same one he played on *Fiddle Tunes I Recall* (which to this day remains a real testament to the excellence in Lyman's playing). He had just made some adjustments to this fiddle, and as was his habit, he would ask me to play his fiddles so that he could hear the sound away from his own ear. We were standing in his kitchen, he came from upstairs with his fiddle, handed it to me—and I dropped it! I dropped his favorite fiddle! It landed squarely on the tail pin and bounced off of the linoleum floor! We had just a split second where we all stood there stunned. I was horrified. Lyman—laughed! We picked the fiddle up and Lyman inspected it carefully, put it beneath his chin and played it. Now, whether any damage had occurred, I'll never know. Lyman said nothing was wrong, that his glue work was strong, the sound post was still as he had placed it, etc. If something of damage had happened he would never let on.

In time, I built up a collection of Lyman tunes in my repertoire—things like Florida Blues, Oklahoma Redbird, and the like—and Lyman had the occasion to play on the radio in Lawrence, KS. He asked me to join him. Naturally, I was petrified. As I recall, at one point I was taking a bit of a solo on some remedial fiddle tune, the radio DJ had stepped away from his mic, and after I played the tune twice I just stopped playing! It made sense to me because I had finished the tune! I don't think at that point Lyman had taught me any endings to tunes so once the tune was done I simply stopped. Everyone in the recording booth stared at me for a moment in dead silence, the radio DJ was nowhere to be seen—dead radio silence. Then the DJ dashed around the corner and onto the mic. Lyman broke out in laughter.

Yes, I painted houses with Lyman two summers while I was in high school, and part of another summer while in my first year of college. And yes, Lyman believed that painting houses as we did, the old brush on style, complemented his bowing style. He was very particular that I not leave brush strokes in paint, so he taught me how to feather the paint brush on the front side and back side of any stroke. In some ways, it was very much like the Karate Kid movie, where actions seemingly unrelated to another action actually tied intimately together. Lyman believed, and I also believed, that the house painting taught me a lot about the fiddle bow stroke. We worked really hard during the summer months, dripping with sweat up on ladders, but Lyman made it fun every single day. He had this habit where when I was high up on a ladder painting, he would walk by and whack the ladder with his scraper. Naturally, it would give me quite the shock. Lyman would laugh. Later, I'd reciprocate the favor. Painting time was also filled with conversation about most anything. Lyman was a wonderful teacher even beyond music. He became a powerful role model for me, too. During those summers, Lyman paid me a really nice wage (darn near as much as I make now!) at the end of each week, then we would each be away on weekends at bluegrass festivals across the central US playing in our bands—Lyman with Bluegrass Association, and me with Cedar Creek.

I understand how you are choosing to categorize Lyman as a Bluegrass fiddler. I can't really categorize Lyman's playing because he was a hybrid player in so many ways. On one hand, where he was genuinely an old-time Missouri-style fiddler. Yet, he played in a bluegrass band and was at the center of so many epic bluegrass jam sessions where he and other famed fiddlers would be playing twin fiddle surrounded by a whole host of world-class musicians in on the mix. On the other hand, he didn't know how, nor did he really attempt, to play bluegrass back-up or take bluegrass fiddle breaks on vocals. His strategy with Bluegrass Association was to sit on a tall stool plucking his fiddle during vocals, then step to the mic when it was his turn to play one of his bring-down-the-house fiddle tunes like Lonesome Train Blues. So when I branched out from playing strictly fiddle tunes to playing bluegrass fiddle with bands I had to teach myself, which I did by studying carefully Kenny Baker and Byron Berline, who at the time were my two other favorite fiddlers.

"Bluegrass Kind of Got Me Hooked": Roger Williams

Roger Williams was born in August 1935 on the family farm on a low hill between Cureall and Pottersville in Howell County. This area, west of West Plains, is in the rolling farm country between major uplifts to the west and east that are more typical of the Ozarks. Roger's family is of Scottish, English, Irish, and Cherokee Indian heritage, and there are many musicians in the clan.[19] Roger's grandfather John Hollister Williams came west to Missouri from Canton (Hardin County), Ohio, in the late 1800s with several brothers and homesteaded a section of 640 acres of farmland near Pottersville, where they established "the home place." John Hollister Williams married Lucy Ellen McGoldrick, the daughter of Thomas McGoldrick, who came from middle Tennessee to the Cureall area, near Pottersville.

Roger began playing violin at age six, inspired by his elders and the older children in the family and the excitement of house dances and the music of other fiddlers in the neighborhood. Among the many musicians in the family were his maternal uncle Clyde Briggs, his father, various older cousins, and his three older brothers, Joe (mandolin), John (guitar), and Paul (bass). Roger's father, David Noah (D. N.) Williams, played upright bass and guitar. Roger's younger brother, Clyde (a.k.a. Dan O'Day), is a bluegrass fiddler and lives in Springfield, where he is a leader of the Greater Ozarks Bluegrass Society (http://www.gobluegrass.org).

Most of the family members were singers as well as instrumentalists. A cousin of D. N.'s, Walter (Bert) Williams, was a good old-time fiddler and, with another cousin, Floyd Williams playing old-time five-string banjo and D. N. on guitar, played square dances in the region. Bert Williams was a strong, big man, and his nickname was "Bull." Roger Williams still plays an untitled two-step dance tune he remembers "old Bull" fiddling; Bull seldom if ever announced the titles of his tunes, and no one seems to recall it.

Roger's grandfather Williams lived with the family and died in 1943. Roger learned a number of songs from their many days spent together in Roger's childhood. Among these are songs such as the old satirical ballad they called "Old Jim Stafford" and the popular sentimental song "Sweet Sunny South." "Sweet Sunny South" was Roger's first tune. Roger, who sings harmony parts in church hymns and in his bluegrass ensembles, enjoys singing verses to these songs while intermittently fiddling a chorus.

Fiddle music held special attraction for young Roger.

> Well, being a kid running around there and watching all those old-time fiddlers play—and they was a *bunch* of 'em, back then—why, I kind of wanted to learn to play *too*. So I asked my mom if I could borrow my great uncle, Emmett Williams' fiddle. And she said, "Well, I guess he'll *loan* it to you." So I asked him, and he loaned it to me. And I took it up the hill—they just lived a quarter of a mile down the hill. By the way, the elevation there at the front gate was eleven hundred feet.

Williams family ensemble, ca. 1946. *Left to right*: D. N. Williams (bass) and D. N.'s sons, Joe (with his Gibson A4 mandolin), Roger (violin), and John (Gibson SJ guitar). All had the luxury of being able to play high-quality instruments and preferred the Gibson brand. This mandolin and guitar were purchased by Joe with money he had saved during his army service. (Courtesy Roger Williams)

But anyway, I borrowed the fiddle, but she wouldn't let me *play* it, unless I set in the *middle of the bed*. Because I was too short and my feet wouldn't touch the *floor*. She said, "You'll *drop* it and break it, so you set in the middle of the bed." Well, we had a back bedroom, set off the kitchen a ways, and she put me back there, and she wouldn't let me *play* if anybody else was around. She said, "This is our secret. But when you get to where you *can* play, you can *join 'em out there*."

So I don't remember exactly *when* it was—it was in the year of forty-one—and one night, she said, "You're *ready*—go out there and *play with 'em*." And I'll tell you what, I was *scared to death*, you know. They was a bunch of good *musicians* there. And I played, and I've been playin' ever since.

I watched, and *heard the tunes*. Most of the tunes I learned were from the old-time fiddlers. And you know how they played—they didn't tell you what the *names* were. Then, I would listen to the radio and hear 'em (tunes and fiddlers).

Another of Roger's early tunes was "Beautiful, Beautiful Brown Eyes," which his grandfather John often sang. Growing up during "hard times" in the late 1930s and during World War II, he made do with the borrowed violin from his uncle Emmett

Roger Williams plays some tunes on the violin his uncle Clyde Briggs brought home from Germany after World War II, with guitarist Ed McKinney, in McKinney's basement, West Plains, June 2013. Here, Roger uses a violin bow he acquired for twenty dollars while in the US Army in 1960.

Williams and a poor-quality bow. "I had to play on the stick back when I was a kid—hoped that there was enough rosin on the stick that I could *play*, because the *hair* was all gone. I was so poor, I couldn't afford to get my bows re-haired. I used '50' size white thread to re-hair 'em. And it didn't work too good, because the thread had knots along in it, it'd *catch* every once in a while. But you could *play* with it."

His first experience as a semiprofessional musician was on radio, at age fifteen, on KLCN-AM, Blytheville, Arkansas. His two older brothers, Joe and John, were playing in a radio group called Donald Howard and the Smilin' Hillbillies, a half-hour show each morning of the workweek. "This guy [at the station] said, 'What are we going to do for a fiddle player?' And my brother said, 'We know one—if Dad'll let him *come*.' Boy, he wouldn't *think* about it. Well, they finally convinced Dad that they would be totally responsible for me, so I went down there and worked from April till September. This was in April of 1950. I would have been fifteen in August. I played there till high school started, and I had to come back."

Williams competed in his first old-time fiddlers contest in 1948, a two-night affair held at the Armory in West Plains. He won the junior division. "I was supposed to get to go to Carnegie *Hall*, but they took a full band. But anyway, that was my first contest. Won *twenty* dollars!" A number of the elite older fiddlers in the area were there, such as Charlie Hiler, Abe Weaver, Johnny Blackstock, Ansel Gore, and Lee Lasswell. Contestants played only one tune, and Roger played "Fire on the Mountain." "I called that my twenty-dollar tune." Contestants could have one accompanist, and Roger's older brother John played guitar for him. Why did he pick "Fire on the Mountain" as his tune? "Probably because it's *fast*, and I like Curly Fox's fiddling [Fox popularized the tune on Grand Ole Opry broadcasts]. World champion six or seven times."

What did the folks at home think when Roger won that contest and came home with twenty dollars?

> (I posted the twenty dollar bill) up on the wall. They was beside themselves. They were ecstatic. The thing of it was, I was always short and small, and (when I played) they put me up on a *box*, so they wouldn't have to have a special microphone for me. I wasn't but about four-and-a-half foot. I haven't growed much since then!
>
> The main judge was May Kennedy McCord from Springfield (folksong collector, Ozark culture expert, radio personality, newspaper columnist). And she wanted to talk to me after it was over. She told me, she said, "They's going to be a lot of people raise questions about why you won." She said, "I'll *tell* you why you won. You have the *makings* to be one of the best fiddlers in the country." That made me feel good.

While still a youngster, during World War II, Williams played fiddle with various ensembles as entertainment, such as performing at USO pie suppers. In the early 1950s, Williams played fiddle for dancing every Friday night at a nightspot in West Plains called the Echo Club, earning the princely sum of fifty dollars a night. Then, "after that played out" in 1954, Roger graduated West Plains High School and began performing with a Willow Springs–Mountain View ensemble, "the Collins boys." They were playing a dance near Mountain View at Crazy Cabins, a highway-junction tavern and dance hall. "I was nineteen. I wasn't old enough to *be there*. But they said, 'If you'll come play the fiddle for us, we'll *guarantee* you that nobody'll ever get *to ya*.' Well, you know, I took them up on it. I played there for about a year and a half." One of the countless nightclubs and dance halls that flourished in that time, Crazy Cabins was a "joint" where things could get rowdy as the clock ticked off the late hours on Friday and Saturday nights. "I wasn't proud of the fact that I was *there*, because I put my life at risk just about any time I went in there. They was some guys who said that they'd *see* that I wouldn't get hurt." His violin at this time was the old European violin that Clyde Briggs had left with him to play when Briggs went into the army during World War II. Years later, swapping tunes with Kenny Baker on a fiddle workshop they presented at a bluegrass festival at Eminence, Baker did not like playing Roger's Strad, because Baker's left-hand fingers were too thick to comfortably negotiate the shorter neck on the instrument.

Williams spent some time playing on television in Wichita, Kansas. He had been visiting the uncle who loaned him the "red Strad" and working at a produce company. One day Roger walked into the Milo G. Wiley music store and, having exchanged hellos, started playing a violin with the owner's daughter and a son, Bobby Wiley, sixteen, who was a pedal steel guitar player. The store owner, Milo Wiley, asked Roger to join their new band, a hillbilly ensemble of young musicians performing in the style of the *Ozark Jubilee* on the famed Springfield station KWTO. Their band played music at the end of televised movies on Wichita station KEDD-TV and filled in gaps between programs.

Soon Roger was giving violin lessons to beginning students in Wiley's music store. Milo Wiley noticed that Roger was an ear musician and offered to teach him to read music. Wiley argued that being able to read music would "keep you ahead" of his violin students, who were buying sheet music and instruction books. However, the lessons did not take. Roger kept trying to teach by ear, showing students techniques and teaching tunes that he knew by heart, but this proved unsatisfactory for all involved, especially the parents of the young would-be violinists.

> I said, well, okay, I'll give it a go. But I don't believe it can be done, because *these* things right *here* (points to his right ear) will get in the way. Because when you're playing a tune, I can hear the chord progressions and I can tell you what the next chord *is*. Because it just works right *on*. I took one lesson, but I couldn't cut the mustard. So I didn't teach the class, but I did play in the band for two or three months. But you know how kids are, I got the hot foot to come back home.

Williams returned to West Plains, happy to be home.

And then "bluegrass kind of got me hooked." Some fiddlers found bluegrass exciting; others did not like it. Some, like Roger Williams, gladly vacated the exhausting role of square-dance fiddler in favor of becoming a role player in an ensemble with other instruments. When bluegrass evolved in the 1940s (Roger dates it to 1946), he listened to *The Grand Ole Opry* and liked Bill Monroe's music as well as Flatt and Scruggs's music when they left Monroe to formed their own band in 1948. Roger Williams's list of admired professional fiddlers includes the expected names of great and innovative players—Curly Fox ("He was *amazing*. He was smooth as silk"), Benny Martin ("a genius on the fiddle"), Tommy Jackson, Dale Potter ("far ahead of his time"), and Kenny Baker. Williams knew Dale Potter and performed with him; Dale would let Roger in the back door of *The Grand Ole Opry* on visits to Nashville. Roger's own style incorporates elements from these players and emphasizes smooth bowing and rich, perfect double-stops.

While acknowledging his influences, he articulates and emphasizes that he does it his way.

> I tried to incorporate *all* the different styles. I didn't *follow nobody*. I took a little bit here, and a little bit there. Because, when I played, if I played it just *exactly* like somebody else, they could listen to the *real* thing, they wouldn't have to listen to *me*. But I played tunes a little different, you know—put a little in there, take a little away, took *away* more than I put in. . . . I tried to do my *best*. I tried to play it as *smooth* and as *close to the melody* as I could get it. And that, to *me*—if a fiddle player is playing the lead to a *song*, if he don't play the *melody*, you just got *noise*.

In the late 1940s, the Williams brothers went into an electronics store in West Plains and recorded a plastic disc of their music, for their own and the family's enjoyment. On the record, which has been preserved on CD copies, are Roger, Joe (mandolin), John (guitar), and Paul (bass) playing and singing four bluegrass-style numbers, "Will You Be Loving Another Man," "When the Echo of Your Footsteps Dies Away," "Remember the Cross," and "Kelly Waltz."[20]

How does Williams describe his style? "I'm *not* an old-time fiddler. As music progressed, I tagged along. That's a good question. I've even played jazz. I'm not very good at it, because jazz just goes every way, you don't have no *standard*. When I started playing, I tried to play all styles of music, so that when I went somewhere (to perform), I'd be able to *play it*. Because I hate to go somewhere and not be able to *play*—have to sit and *listen*. I worked on it pretty hard back then; but now, I don't even practice."

The year 1962 was a pivotal time when Roger Williams walked away from playing old-time fiddle music for square dancers. "That's my last square dance!"

> I was playing with a fellow by the name of Gene Blake up in Summersville. . . . Street dance up there. I went up there, and we played and played and *played*. *You* know that playin' for square dances is *work*. I'd about as soon *cut sprouts* as play for a square dance. . . . That's about the hardest work you'll *ever do* as a fiddler, I think it is. Because you play for five, ten, or twenty minutes or however long they want to dance. I don't know anything *about* square dancing, because I couldn't dance,

myself. But I know you're supposed to play, especially when they do the Texas Star, you're supposed to play until every man comes all the way around and does his part. Now that's *work*.

After that 1962 square dance at Summersville, Roger grew more serious about playing bluegrass, taking him away from the frustrations of dance fiddling into the bluegrass band's concert and festival state. Just as other old-time fiddlers moved to bluegrass ensemble performance, Williams concentrated on his "lead work" (brief solo breaks within songs) and the turnarounds, kickoffs, riffs, fills, and endings of his "backup work" (behind singers)—and getting the nod once per set to step to the middle of the ensemble and play an actual fiddle tune.

In 1965 Williams had a shot at going pro—sort of. Country crooner Porter Wagoner had left West Plains, passed through radio stations (where he played and sang bluegrass as well as country music) such as KWTO in Springfield, and in 1957 had begun performing on *The Grand Ole Opry* and developing a career in Nashville ("local boy makes good"). Roger Williams was in West Plains, driving a Foremost Dairies ice cream truck. Williams knew Wagoner well; both men had grown up in West Plains. Wagoner telephoned Roger one night, asking him to come to Nashville to audition for his band, the Wagonmasters, to perform and tape segments for his weekly syndicated black-and-white television show. Jack Little, the fiddler, was leaving the Wagonmasters. Porter wanted Roger there Friday to spend the weekend. Speck Rhodes (bassist and ensemble comic) met Roger at the bus station, and they went to the TV studio. The group was Buck Trent (banjo), Don Warden (guitar), Rhodes, and Wagoner. Porter told Roger he had the job. This would have been a great job, 250 dates per year. But on Saturday, when he returned to tape more TV-show segments, Porter told him that the Musicians Union was forcing him to hire Mac Magaha, who was already a union member and out of work, having left Reno and Smiley and the Tennessee Cutups. Porter paid Roger for his time off from the ice cream truck and paid his travel expenses; end of story. Williams noted, with rueful accuracy, that Mac Magaha had more experience as a professional and that Magaha was a good entertainer who jig-danced while he fiddled—while he, Roger, was comparatively inexperienced, and "I can't dance."

Williams's "number-one" violin is the German-made copy of a Stradivarius that Clyde Briggs brought home after his service in World War II. Briggs played it on the ship back from Europe, and it got damp during the trip, which caused some damage. Briggs served in the army, landed at Normandy, and fought in the Battle of the Bulge. "He found the fiddle laying up against a wall, in a case, in an old bombed-out music store." Briggs gave it to a cousin, Gus Tabor (a fiddler and violin maker), but instructed Freddie Carrington to give it to Roger in due course; Carrington presented it to Roger Williams many years later, at a Heart of the Ozarks Bluegrass Festival in West Plains. Roger was not aware of the violin until it was given to him. "It's the best 'un I ever had in my hand." Fred Stoneking did some repair work and set it up for Williams.

Williams still enjoys playing virtually all the old standards of old-time fiddling as well as the bluegrass repertoire from the classic period of the genre (into the 1980s) and a few bluegrass tunes of more recent creation. At sessions I recorded with Roger in 2013 and 2015, he chose to play tunes such as "Irish Washerwoman," "You Are My Sunshine," "Fiddler's Dream" (from Tommy Jackson), Kenny Baker's "Cheyenne" (B-flat), "Cross-Eyed Fiddler," "Ashland Breakdown," "Kelly Waltz," and, in 2015, "Sitting in the Chimney Jamb," "Julia's Waltz," "The Willies," "Roger's Waltz," and "Sweet Sunny South," as well as several old standards with Roger playing harmony over my melody (such as "Over the Waves," "Westphalia Waltz, "Red Wing," "Liberty," "Turkey in the Straw," "Golden Slippers," "Tennessee Waltz," and "Old Joe Clark"). Roger enjoys tunes in which he demonstrates his love of playing harmony (twin). Roger plays the exhibition piece "Black Mountain Rag" in chorded tuning with double-stops throughout and the addition of a "fancy part" played in pizzicato (plucking the strings). He never enjoyed fiddling jigs or schottisches.

Williams has a knack for waltzes and has composed several, such as "Julia's Waltz," composed for his wife in 1962, and "The Willies," the latter never performed in public. Roger composed "The Willies" in 1963 after his father had a life-threatening heart attack. Roger knew his father would not live much longer. "It's high and slow and lonesome." "I was kind of down in the dumps, so I wrote this tune. It's about as sad as you can get. Real slow. There's a 'drag line' at the end of each verse."

"Roger's Waltz," which he began playing in the 1960s, presents a familiar instance of an untitled older tune floating in and out of the broader active repertory. Roger Williams does not remember a title, or from whom he learned the tune, and jokes, "Maybe we ought to call it 'Waltz in F,'" keenly aware of the many tunes whose older titles have been lost in time. The tune closely echoes an untitled tune played by upper Ozarks fiddler Dallas Stamper documented in R. P. Christeson's 1973 book of transcriptions, based on Christeson's memory of Stamper fiddling the waltz at a multiday community picnic and reunion near Dixon in 1926; at this event, Christeson accompanied Stamper on piano, and his memory of the tune was accurate enough when Christeson fiddled it and had it transcribed for his University of Missouri Press tune book in 1973. Dallas Stamper seems to have shared Roger's uncle Bert's tendency—common among old-time fiddlers—to fiddle tune after tune at dances without feeling compelled to announce their titles. We do not know whether Dallas Stamper may have picked up the tune from other fiddlers in his region (conceivably fiddlers in the Williams family or circle). We do not know if Christeson was influenced by hearing other fiddlers play the waltz in the intervening years between 1926–28 and 1973.[21] Christeson gives the tune, untitled, as "Waltz."[22] We are fortunate to have Roger Williams fiddling this fine waltz today; the recording on the CD with *Fiddler's Dream* is, to date, the only known easily available published recording of "Roger's Waltz"/"Dallas Stamper's Waltz."

Roger Williams is an expert at playing twin fiddle, one of the essential skills of a bluegrass fiddler and an important ingredient in the genre. One summary by Gene Lowinger (from New York, the first Yankee brought into the Blue Grass Boys): "In most instances when playing double-stops in bluegrass fiddle, the lower note is the melody and the upper note the harmony, which can be a third, fourth, fifth, sixth or octave above the melody."[23] Roger taught himself harmony parts by making recordings and then playing with his own melody. Roger brought back a Grundig tape recorder from Germany after his army hitch and traded it for a four-track RCA reel-to-reel machine. "I try to play harmony, and I can harmonize with a steel player as long he plays a *straight melody*. . . . They're so similar—it's easy to confuse the *tones* (of violin and steel guitar). That's the reason I play a *straight* fiddle—I don't like *electrified*, because it takes the sound *away* from me; I want it right here (gestures to his ear)." Williams did not learn the older fiddle accompaniment technique of playing "second fiddle" as did many of the older generation of old-time fiddlers.

The bluegrass fiddler's repertoire differs in several ways from that of the old-time fiddler, such as in the way that a seasoned bluegrass fiddler need not have memorized a song to be able to play the expected fills and riffs and other formulaic devices of the ensemble player in bluegrass. The formulas float from tune to tune and can be added whenever desirable, and even that quasi-cadenza "kickoff" a fiddler or banjoist may play to start a tune, or a "cap" or "ending" to end a tune, follows one of the several

Roger's Waltz

As played by Roger Williams

Transcribed by Amber Gaddy

"Roger's Waltz," as played by Roger Williams, West Plains, Missouri, September 2015 (hear on the companion CD). As transcriber Amber Gaddy notes, "What transcription cannot capture is the variety of expressive bowing that Roger adds, and the stately pace of his playing."

The Bressler Brothers bluegrass band at the Summersville opry, 2008. *Left to right*: Roger Williams, Clyde Williams, Andy Bressler (guitar), and Alvin Bressler (bass). Roger's younger brother Clyde, who lives in Springfield, was on the show on this occasion and fiddled the melody line to songs while Roger played harmony ("twin"). (Courtesy Roger Williams)

traditional patterns that recur in many different tunes. However, like the old-time fiddler's repertoire, a player needs to actively practice or perform tunes in order to keep them active in his or her personal repertoire. "If you don't play the tunes you don't use, you *lose them*" and may "have trouble bringing 'em *up*, you know."

In 1976 Williams began teaching members of the Eldringhoff family in the West Plains area, and they are a successful family band. Roger taught various members of the family for twenty-four years. Williams often performed with the family band at bluegrass festivals in West Plains hosted by the Heart of the Ozarks Bluegrass Association and in addition fiddled in a bluegrass band with his brother-in-law Eric Lewis. Perhaps the best-known bluegrass band Williams has performed with is the Bressler Brothers, from the Eminence area. The Bresslers (Andy and Alvin) are known for their "brother duet" singing and instrumental work and have been performing country and bluegrass since the 1950s. Roger became the Bresslers' fiddler in 2000. The Bressler Brothers won the SPBGMA award for the Midwest's top "traditional bluegrass band."

Roger continues to perform with the Bresslers, typically at the Summersville opry in the VFW Hall, and takes part in jam sessions around West Plains. To the question "Roger, what is the future of fiddle music?" he replies, "The future of fiddle music as it is now, as it *always* has been, is the *young people*. Just like anything . . . , if you don't have the young people coming on, it won't continue. You've got to have the young people and you've got to take interest in the young people and bring 'em *on*."

Cecil Goforth, Shannon County Southpaw

Another of the well-known clans of fiddlers in Missouri through the last century and a half is the Goforths, who came from Tennessee in the 1800s. Many have noticed the strength of the Missouri Ozarks in producing generations of outstanding musicians and traditional artisans, many of whom appear in *Play Me Something Quick and Devilish* and the present volume. The first of the Goforth family in the Eminence area of Shannon County was Joshua (Josh) Goforth, who had lived near Ava, two counties to the west in Douglas County.

Cecil's father, Richard (Dink) Goforth, was born in Douglas County and, reaching fifteen, the age when young men often branched out on their own, left Douglas County and moved to eastern Shannon County, where he married Elizabeth (Ida) Counts and inaugurated his branch of the family on Thompson Creek. Thompson Creek empties into the Current River from the north, near "the junction" with the Jacks Fork River, and Prairie Hollow joins the Current from the south on the other side of the junction. Today, most of the land along and south of the Current River is part of Ozark Scenic Riverways National Park, while land on the north side of the Current in part of Shannon County continues to be managed as part of ninety thousand acres purchased by Leo Drey in 1954 and incorporated in Drey's Pioneer Forest.

This was typical mountainous Ozark living on very small subsistence acreages. Virtually everyone in earlier times had to find jobs off the farm, usually in the timber and cooperage industry that dominated the region from mid-1800s settlement until the 1950s. In earlier times, people crossed back and forth along ridges, along the Current and Jacks Fork Rivers on the many fords and shoals, and at points where someone would operate a ferry crossing with a jon boat. As timber industry historian Terry Cunningham writes, "The river wasn't the barrier that it is now. People travelled by wagon or by horseback or walked and they moved back and forth across the river frequently chasing a job or trying to scratch out a living. Farming in these valleys consisted of a garden or a small corn patch. It was open range so people let livestock roam and subsidized what they raised with wild game and fish from the river. They moved frequently."[24]

A good deal of the timber work, where some of the men in the Goforth family found employment, was one of the several roles in producing barrel staves for whiskey distilling companies. In the 1940s, the Pioneer Cooperage Company (St. Louis) operated a stave mill on Brushy Creek (a tributary of the Current River north of Eminence), where Dink and Ida Goforth lived for a time. Men in the area found employment in various labor roles, and a small workers' village grew up near the mill. Some men had hourly jobs at the mill. Others worked piecemeal to "cut company timber on company land," and these workers were paid per "stave bolt" of white oak they brought to the mill, which they had cross-sawed into stave lengths and then split into quarters. The Brushy Creek Mill was sold to National Distillers and shuttered in 1950, but other stave mills in the region continue in operation. Some workers became independent contractors, purchasing timber from landowners and selling harvested timber to outlying stave mills and sawmills.[25]

Josh Goforth worked in the timber industry and was an old-time fiddler who passed the fire to his equally strong fiddling sons, Richard Doris (Dink) Goforth (1882–1957) and Lawrence Don (Dee) Goforth (1889–1964). Dee never married. He worked as an auto mechanic, moved to Colorado and other places, and died of leukemia in a hospital in Mount Vernon, Missouri.

Dink and Ida Goforth had nine children (Earl, Gene, Goldie, Houston, Ruby, Betty, Cecil, Wanda, and Lonnie), and all were musical to some degree. The boys considered to be the most musical were Gene, Cecil, and Lonnie, and among the girls so were Ruby and Wanda. The second eldest child, Gene (born 1921), was well known outside Missouri thanks to his fiddling in bluegrass bands, friendship and tune-swapping with Kenny Baker, recordings, appearances in publications, mentoring of young fiddlers such as John Hartford, and, decades later, teaching players such as Al Murphy and Matt Wyatt.[26] Gene was the forceful older sibling, larger in stature and intensity. Lonnie Goforth (born 1945) is primarily a banjo player but also plays fiddle and guitar. Cecil, born in 1936, is of a quiet temperament and did not claim as much of the limelight.

Cecil Goforth was born at the family farm in Matthews ("Mathis") Hollow, March 1936, on the north side of the Current River. When he was four, the family moved closer to the river, and when he was seven they moved across the river to Prairie Hollow. Cecil attended the Prairie Hollow one-room country school, later attended school in Eminence, and returned to the Prairie Hollow school, where he graduated from grade school. He chose not to attend high school, preferring to look for a job. Through the years, family and various family members lived on both sides of the river. Like most families in the area, Dink and Ida raised a garden and small cornfield. Dink worked off the farm in a variety of jobs in the timber industry, at saw mills, and at stave mills.

Cecil was born into a household where music making was a daily pastime and joy. Music parties, pie suppers, and dances were the family nurseries. Fiddles, banjos, and guitars seem to have been in perpetual motion, with regular house parties and one or another member of the family playing music practically every day. He remembers knowing how to tune a violin before he knew how to play one. "Dad kept his fiddle on the wall, and we'd go by and pluck strings on it—and I knew when it was in tune and when it wasn't." "Oh, I was probably ten years old before I could play anything—that you could tell what it was," (smiles, little laugh). His first fiddle tune was "Cindy" in the key of A, a venerable square-dance tune that Cecil had learned from his father's fiddling.

In his first years, the left-handed Cecil played mostly at home. When he fiddled for his first square dance as a teenager, the first tune he played was "The Eighth of

January," and he also played many of the standards such as "Arkansas Traveler," "Ragtime Annie," and the tune with a thousand names "Lead Out" (which Cecil calls "Love Somebody"). While Cecil played for dances, his principal fiddling was done in house parties, jam sessions, and bands. His next instrument was guitar, with which he played "rhythm" (accompaniment) for his father, uncle, and other fiddlers.

In addition to the fiddling of his father, Dink, Cecil points to the early bluegrass fiddling of Benny Martin as his inspiration. "When he played with Flatt and Scruggs, he was shining. He'd really wake 'em up." Cecil plays Martin's version of "Grey Eagle." Cecil also likes bluegrass fiddler Joe Greene's fiddling and plays a version of Greene's "Cattle in the Corn" (hear on the companion CD) from *Joe Greene's Fiddle Album* (County 722, 1969). In Missouri contest fiddlers usually play the Texas version, called "Cattle in the Cane," while bluegrass fiddlers (and most old-time fiddlers) prefer the former.

In 1954 Cecil moved to St. Louis to seek employment as a concrete laborer in the construction business. He was married at nineteen to Vivian McAll of the Winona area; they had four children, none of whom are musicians. A year younger than the cutoff at twenty for the military draft and married, he was not drafted. The St. Louis–area location helped put Cecil into the robust bluegrass music scene in the 1960s and 1970s, and he became acquainted with, and performed with, such stalwarts as Norman Ford, the Hawthorne boys (Marvin and Clifford), Don Brown (Cecil's cousin and a starring Bill Monroe–style bluegrass mandolinist and singer), and young John Hartford. These and other musicians appeared on local opry shows such as Roy Queen's Queen-Arena in Warrenton and other radio shows as well as the bluegrass festival and fiddlers contest scene. After several years in construction, Cecil worked

Richard (Dink) Goforth with sons Lonnie (with "juice harp") and Cecil (guitar), at the Prairie Hollow farm near the Current River, 1952. Sitting next to her grandpa is Beverly Young, Ruby Goforth Young's daughter. (Photo by "Toots" Goforth, Mrs. Houston Goforth, Dink's daughter-in-law; courtesy Cecil Goforth)

in sheet metal for several years and then moved to Salem to work in a shoe factory for two years. He then worked in a garment factory for twenty years and, when the factory closed, took a position driving petroleum tanker trucks for the Hocker Oil Company in Salem. He drove tankers for fifteen years and retired in 2002.

Although too busy making a living to work as a regular in bluegrass bands or shows, Cecil did several guest appearances on the Current River Opry in Eminence in the later 1960s. He was typically featured playing a big breakdown such as "Sally Goodin," and then, for the rest of the set, he stepped back and accompanied the singers and other performers. Similarly, Cecil's employment schedules kept him from participating in many fiddlers contests, but when he was able to do so, he fared well. He participated in a number of major contests, including several of the state contests developed by the Missouri State Old Time Fiddlers Association, held first in Columbia and then Sedalia, in the 1980s in which his tunes were such standards as "Dance around Molly," "Bitter Creek," and "Sally Goodin." Cecil lists as his favorite tunes "Dance around Molly," "Bill Cheatem," "Tom and Jerry," "Sally Goodin," "Grey Eagle," and "Jerusalem Ridge," all of them popular in Missouri and what people call "big tunes" and powerful choices, whether fiddling for dancers, in a jam session, or in front of audiences in a contest. Cecil also fiddles some of the iconic, moody, and difficult tunes Bill Monroe composed and released late in his life, such as "Old Ebenezer Scrooge."[27]

Cecil says his favorite contest was the October 1984 "WOS Radio Reunion and Fiddling Championship" in Jefferson City in the dome of the state capitol, organized by the Missouri State Old Time Fiddlers Association and bringing to the event a number of fiddlers who had competed in similar events in the late 1920s. Cecil played well, in the toughest division, the Open Division, and took second place, behind Travis Inman, who won first (Henry Thompson won third place). In the contest, Cecil played "Katy Hill" and "Waltz across Texas" in the elimination round and in the finals "Laughing Boy" and "Festival Waltz," with Jim Lindsey of Newark as his guitarist (who won a prize for best accompanist).[28]

"Festival Waltz" has been Cecil's default waltz for many years; not being a fan of waltzes, he says, "I'm very slim on waltzes." This is a sentiment of many Ozark fiddlers, who in my experience have fewer waltzes in their repertoires than their counterparts in other Missouri cultural-geographic regions to the north.

Cecil took up the five-string banjo during the popularity of bluegrass in the 1950s and 1960s and worked for a year as the banjoist with the highly regarded upper Ozarks bluegrass band the Bluegrass Five in Dixon. He also plays Dobro guitar.

Cecil Goforth plays a number of tunes, such as "Rye Whisky," in scordatura (open tuning, cross-tuning, dischord, chorded tuning), with the violin strings tuned A–E–A–C# (low to high string). Cecil calls this tuning "sawmill key," "A tuning," "open tuning," and "Black Mountain Rag tuning."[29] He plays one of the more interesting versions of this old British Isles tune, "Rye Whisky," in waltz time, among the earliest melodies documented that fiddlers still play. Goforth learned it this way from listening to his father, Dink. Among other titles one hears for this great tune in Missouri is

"Drunken Hiccups."[30] Dink also played "White River" in sawmill key, but Cecil says he never quite mastered the plucking (pizzicato) on the open strings while bowing them at the same time that his father included in his version (perhaps the plucking came easier for a right-handed player such as his father). There is also an Ozarks tune called "Black River" played by the Goforth family fiddlers. (Goforth's "Black River" can be heard on the companion CD.)

Other chorded tunings Cecil uses include A–E–A–E and D–A–D–D. Many fiddlers play in such tuning and particular tunes that match well with particular tunings. Cecil Goforth keeps a violin in sawmill key and another in standard tuning and carries them in a double violin case in order to have one ready to play (in sawmill key). Most fiddlers dislike having to retune their violins for special tunings, because of the potential stress on the instrument and strings, so those who like to play in cross-tunings often carry two violins.

There are two tunes in the common repertoire of Missouri fiddlers with "Rye" in the title. The other one is "Rye Straw" and played in standard (concert) tuning in square-dance tempo. Dink often played this tune when Cecil was a child, but years

Cecil Goforth plays "Rye Whisky" on his father Dink's 1942 W. Wilkanowski violin. His uncle Dee had ordered it from a mail-order catalog and soon after traded it to his brother Dink. Willie Wilkanowski, a Polish immigrant luthier in Brooklyn, made guitars, violins, and violas, some entirely himself and others with assistants. In the 1940s Wilkanowski violins were being marketed by the Gretsch firm. (Photo by Russell D. Ravert, July 2015)

Lawrence (Dee) Goforth with his 1939 Chevrolet. (Courtesy Cecil Goforth)

later when Cecil worked it up, he incorporated into his version elements of Howdy Forrester's version, which Forrester called "Dog in the Rye Straw," and there are other titles in Missouri, such as "The Unfortunate Dog."[31] Christeson's annotation (for Bob Walters's 1950 version) is as follows: "The title given here is a polite substitution for use in mixed company. . . . The three parts of this tune purportedly depict a constipated canine (1) suffering in labor following the unwise ingestion of too many rye straws; (2) howling in agony prior to relief; (3) yelping while leaving the scene after the ordeal." Some versions have the violin produce doglike sounds.

Howdy Forrester's "Dog in the Rye Straw" (arranged to fit time allowed for the track on the LP record) starts with two parts in D, then has two parts in A, and completes the version with two different and lower parts in A. Many fiddlers play the three parts, and some play four different parts, and many players vary their repetitions and sometimes the order of the parts. "Rye Straw" is an important tune in Missouri and across the South, but it is seldom heard in contests, shows, or even music parties because of the several and variable parts, which make accompaniment challenging; fiddlers may indeed alter the number of parts, and the order of the parts, in the course of playing the tune on any given occasion. So the tune has the reputation as a "jam buster," but its magnificence argues for an increased presence.

Cecil's fiddle style first and foremost drew on the examples set of his father, Dink Goforth, and his uncle Dee. Although they were brothers and shared tunes and musical environment, their styles were somewhat different, and each had his strengths. Cecil says that Uncle Dee, a little younger than Dink, "played more modern" kinds of music, including some western swing, and that his father, Dink, was always said to have "the smoother style." Both were mainly dance fiddlers. In their time, there were no oprys or shows to be part of and few if any fiddlers contests in their eastern

Rye Whiskey

Transcribed by Sharon Graf

as played by Cecil Goforth 2015

Tuning low to high: A E A C#

"Rye Whisky," by Cecil Goforth, St. James, Missouri, 2015. (Transcription by Sharon Graf)

Shannon County neighborhood. Cecil also remembers being inspired by his older cousin Don Brown, who was developing as a first-rate Bill Monroe–style mandolin player and singer who would later lead the Ozark Mountain Trio as one of Missouri's top bluegrass bands.

Being left-handed in a right-handed world does not faze Cecil Goforth. Another well-known southpaw Missouri fiddler is Kathy Summers of Bourbon (Crawford County), northeast of Salem. Summers learned "Canadian Waltz" from Cecil, as well as other tunes, and like Cecil she plays a few tunes passed down from old-time fiddler Walter Alexander of Leasburg (recorded by John Hartford in the late 1950s). Summers admires Goforth's playing, and they both feel that the southpaw sometimes has a challenge when shifting up to the higher positions to "get" the high notes just right;[32] Goforth agrees that is "the hardest part" for a left-handed fiddler. Some fiddle experts consider lefties to have a bit of an advantage when playing the lower parts of complex hornpipes (many of them in the key of A), but Cecil has no opinion on that point.

Other Missouri lefties include names such as Allen Jennings (Theodosia), John Lewellen (Florida, MO), Albert Spray (Winigan), Jake Hockemeyer (Mokane), Lacy Hartje (Brookline), Cyril Stinnett (Oregon), Dickie Phillips (Sedalia), and Harry Wagganer. Like almost all left-handed fiddlers of my acquaintance, Goforth plays violins (guitars and banjos, too) set up normally and does not play instruments "reversed" by luthiers just for left-handed players. The flat keys are no problem for Cecil Goforth, and he plays a number of comparatively difficult tunes in F (for example, "Fisher's Hornpipe," "Fiddler's Shuffle") and B-flat ("Daly's Reel," "College Hornpipe").

Today Cecil Goforth lives in St. James. In recent years, he has come to wider attention thanks to inclusion in the Rounder Records compilation project *Traditional Fiddle Music of the Ozarks*, volume 1, *Along the Eastern Crescent*, as well as the 2008 Beisswenger and McCann *Ozarks Fiddle Music*, in which his "New Five Cents" and "Hamilton Ironworks" appear.[33] Cecil attends an occasional music party and fiddlers contest but feels that his "chops" are not as sharp as he would like them to be. His brother Lonnie, who lives in Belle, north of Rolla, is a fine banjo player and guitarist, as well as a fiddler, but these days they rarely get together for music parties; both men are feeling the inevitable challenges that age brings to the hands and joints of a musician. Cecil works part-time as a volunteer at the Missouri Veterans Home in St. James.

When Cecil Goforth is asked what style he plays, like many Missouri fiddlers, he pauses and thinks about it. "I don't know. Depends on what I'm playing I guess, what I was gonna play. Old-time or bluegrass." In other words, when fiddling in a bluegrass session or band, he would be considered a bluegrass fiddler; at a square dance or other venues, he's an old-time fiddler. This logical answer of Cecil Goforth's to the question that scholars, collectors, and arts-council grant panels always ask fiddlers makes good sense, and, once again, Cecil's answer testifies to the fact that fiddlers themselves spend very little effort in self-analysis and categorization of the music they play. No better reply can be imagined than Cecil's: "Depends on what I'm playing."

Cecil Goforth with the "lion's head fiddle" inherited when his brother Gene died in 2002. Gene bought the violin from Kenny Baker, who had acquired it from Jackie Phelps. Phelps performed on *The Grand Ole Opry* with Roy Acuff's Smoky Mountain Boys and played guitar and banjo as a member of Bill Monroe's Blue Grass Boys in the 1950s, but is remembered more for his comedy routines with Jimmy Riddle on television's *Hee Haw*. Violins with scrolls carved as heads of lions, mythical creatures, and people have been made since the 1600s, and between ca. 1870 and 1930 many were imported from European shops. (Photo by Russell D. Ravert, July 2015)

The 1960s and Beyond

Although up and running in the early 1960s, bluegrass came into its own as the decade ensued, an important and troubled one in American social and cultural history. While Bill Monroe and His Blue Grass Boys remain the acknowledged original bluegrass band from *The Grand Ole Opry*'s heyday in the World War II era, the jump in popularity of the music in the 1960s will substantially be due to the music of Lester Flatt and Earl Scruggs, whose banjo player would attain demigod status among young people and as a band whose smoother sound and approach to the music and vocals were more easily accepted by new audiences.

An additional factor helping spread bluegrass music and Bill Monroe's band's influence, especially among young people on college campuses, was Monroe's hiring of Bill Keith to play banjo in 1963. Monroe had overheard Keith playing the melody of the fiddle tune "Devil's Dream" backstage at *The Grand Ole Opry* and offered him a job. Called "Brad" as a Blue Grass Boy (there could be only one "Bill" in Bill Monroe's band), Bill Keith brought to immediate acclaim a style of banjo playing in which he picked linear melodies, especially fiddle tunes. "Keith style" would become as famous among many bluegrass fans and banjo enthusiasts as the iconic "Scruggs style."[34]

But the key element that had been missing in the widening of bluegrass's acceptance was the bluegrass festival, the first of which is said to have been established by Carlton Haney at a horse farm in the Shenandoah Valley of Virginia in September 1965. Discussion of these and related matters must await a future time.

Among bluegrass stalwarts today are Gerald Jones (Rolla) and cousins Rob Collins and Dale Collins (Kansas City, Blue Springs), who participate in a variety of bands and carry on appreciation of influential bluegrass fiddlers such as Lyman Enloe, Delbert Spray, and Cecil and Gene Goforth. At a music session at Jones's campsite at the Back Forty Bluegrass Festival, near Curryville, Missouri, May 2015. (Photo by Russell D. Ravert)

H. K. Silvey of Theodosia is among the respected elder masters of the fiddle in Missouri who have taken the time and effort to encourage the passing along of the music and its cultural heritage to young people. (The Historium, Gainesville, Missouri, September 2014)

Conclusion

In a larger sense the past never wholly dies: it lives on buried in the minds of men and in the landscapes they have fashioned.

—Estyn Evans, *Irish Folk Ways* (1957)

Why End *Fiddler's Dream* in the 1960s?

In the 1960s, traditional fiddle and dance music ventured into uncharted territory. Swing fiddling was well established as a plank in country music's platform as well as among more traditional or old-time fiddlers who relished the old Bob Wills–influenced dance-hall music. Bluegrass was finding its place on the musical landscape and attracting to it a creative group of young people who were immersed in, or comfortable standing next to, the counterculture and hippie movement. Nashville-based pop- and rock-influenced country music was evolving and in some ways eroding older traditions; commercial records and radio had been doing this since the early 1900s. With the help of fiddlers' organizations rushing to mark off territory, and commercial firms, the contest scene would be influenced heavily by nonregional fiddle styles of charismatic champions from Texas, Oklahoma, Alabama, and places far to the west, as a swing- and rhythm-influenced "National Contest style" evolved.[1]

The era of growing change in fiddlers contest styles and repertoires in the 1960s, and gaining speed and complexity from the 1970s on, is planned for a future publication. But change was nothing really new, either, because those early 1900s records, radio shows, and fiddlers contests had a similar effect in earlier times in drowning out certain older and local fiddling styles and repertories.

In the 1960s the Folk Music Revival came to maturity, with the popularity of collecting folk music "in the field" (whether a prairie, hollow, or city neighborhood). Scholars were analyzing music and cultural traditions in newly formed programs at universities. Federal and state arts agencies, folk festivals, and federal cultural agencies, such as the Library of Congress and the Smithsonian Institution, dramatically increased programming to highlight traditional music of all kinds.

Swing and country music would take their own paths in the sixties. With the new role of electric instruments, and country music's strange meld with rock and roll, these genres would remain popular among many old-time fiddlers. Fortunately, people dance to swing music, and in dance halls they may well have a chance to dance a schottische or polka, or even square dance, in the course of an evening mainly of fox-trots. And fortunately, people still like to go to square dances in Missouri and, if given the chance, will support them.

In the shape-shifting sixties, fiddlers contests occasionally rose to the lofty level of the big 1920s contests at Paris. While newspapers promoted the 1920s contests, in 1961 it was the MFA Oil Company, whose state championship in Columbia was preceded by hard-fought "regional" contests at selected MFA dealerships around Missouri. Here are the MFA grand championship winners in Columbia, 1961 (*left to right*): Leroy Canaday, LeRoy Haslag, Maurice Evans, Dick Logan, and Earl Morgan. (Courtesy LeRoy Haslag)

Bluegrass became a recognizable genre of folk music to which a musician could devote him- or herself entirely. While Bill Monroe stood on the mountaintop as the acknowledged mastermind, the popularity of bluegrass was substantially due to Lester Flatt and Earl Scruggs (former Bluegrass Boys). Their smooth sound and approach to the music were more easily accepted by audiences without roots in old-time singing, fiddling, and banjo playing. Bluegrass ensembles emerged as part of the Folk Music Revival and "hootenanny" movement on college campuses and among the counterculture. Flatt and Scruggs's appearances on television's *Beverly Hillbillies* and in the soundtrack for the hit movie *Bonnie and Clyde* made bluegrass familiar across regions and cultures, as did Missouri's Dillards band on *The Andy Griffith Show.*

One of the good things about modern times is that a musician may choose which path, or how many paths, to follow. In the second decade of the 2000s, we may choose to concentrate our talents and energies on any style or genre of fiddle music; just click on YouTube or Google and search for "fiddle music." We do not know what tomorrow's musicians may want to learn and carry on, so recordings, books, articles, videos, films—all kinds of documentation of music—are essential if the future can hear and see what has come before as they figure out what they like and create their own variations, if not whole new brands.

Many styles of music arrived, found a niche, and faded, to be blended into or completely replaced by the next big thing. Traditional fiddlers possess a legacy reaching back centuries. Old-time, swing, bluegrass, contest style—whatever old or new school they espouse—are expressed in performance oscillating between conservative acceptance and innovative change. This is perhaps why a young fiddler with many options may lie awake all night with headphones listening to Eck Robertson play "Sail Away Ladies" on a 1924 78 rpm record. It was good then, and it is good now.

Traditions are resilient, but they die if enough people forget. Fiddle tunes die if they are kept only in one player's memory and are not handed down or left unrecorded in any archive. Thankfully for those who enjoy homemade music and the artistic expressions of families and local communities, many old customs and habits somehow keep going.

But the real promise of tradition is change. The 1960s were a time of change, but, in retrospect, big changes may appear as crests in the rising and falling waves of time. Not stasis, not perfect copies of a certain famous recording, but music as rivers of melody and chord as a tune takes shape is shared, danced to, fussed over, passed around and altered, and sent on its way downstream to the future. This magic happens with fiddle music that lives in oral and aural tradition, handed from musician to musician in the old channels of listening, imitation, apprenticeship, and mastery. The main ambition for this book and its precursor volume is that they may, through documentation of the people who make this music and conservation of some of their music, help nourish a future that includes "fiddling" in the minds and imaginations of people to come.

"Gilsaw," a Lost Tune Returned

A storehouse of local and largely unwritten history is out there, waiting. Much of this book has attempted to fill in some of the gaps in our understanding of major themes in the continually evolving traditional music and cultural heritage of the 1920s into the 1960s. If we are able to visit with people whose ideas we respect, and whose music and oral traditions we value, sometimes we are able to come to new insights into the music. One might even say that the arc and purpose of this book has been to listen, record, and offer to explain. One more example: "Gilsaw."

"Gilsaw" is a largely forgotten tune from the 1930s that had drifted into the vast inactive repertoire of melodies neglected or forgotten in their communities. Fortunately for us, "Gilsaw" was brought back into the active repertoire in the 1980s through the filtered, purposeful recollections of Pete McMahan in old age. The title has confused people, and its story eluded me since enjoying Pete playing it in the mid-1980s—when he happened to dredge the tune from his memory. Charlie Walden, who at that time was performing with McMahan in arts-council and Missouri Cultural Heritage Center programs, along with McMahan's student John Griffin, helped spread "Gilsaw" around our area.

We wondered about the meaning of the title. Was Gilsaw a person? Some supposed it was an implement for dressing fish or a mishearing of the words "skill saw" (a generic for portable electric circular saws). With new research made possible by the Internet discussion group FiddleHangout.com, and preliminary information about the family, it can be suggested that Gilsaw is a family name in Callaway County. There were families named Gilsaw in Callaway and neighboring Audrain County in the late 1800s.

Pete McMahan grew up in the same part of east-central Missouri and recollected that "Gilsaw" was the name of a "tramp" fiddler who played the fiddle melody at the Wabash Railroad depot in Montgomery City (Montgomery County), ca. 1933–35. The Montgomery County sheriff at the time, Claude Gregory—a fiddler and uncle of Pete McMahan—seems to have heard the man play it and absorbed the tune on the spot. As the man left, Sheriff Gregory heard the man say "Gilsaw" (the tune title? the man's name?), but until now we have been unsure of the spelling.

Apparently, the "old bum" Pete's uncle told him about played a few fiddle tunes, perhaps with a hat or tin can at his feet for the donation of a coin from passersby, and hopped on the next freight train. It is possible that Mr. Gilsaw's rapid departure from the depot had something to do with Gregory wearing the county sheriff uniform and badge, during the height of the Great Depression, when law enforcement and public agencies spent a lot of time dealing with the Depression-driven numbers of hoboes and tramps moving through their territory looking for a job or a safe place to rest for the night. Mr. Gilsaw may not have realized that this sheriff played the fiddle and that his close attention to Gilsaw's fiddling was due not to the presence of a vagrant or busker to roust but to the fiddling the sheriff was hearing. Sheriff Claude Gregory soon thereafter taught the tune to his teenage nephew, and aspiring fiddler, Pete McMahan.

In December 1986, McMahan was recorded playing "Gilsaw" (with Mickey Soltys, guitar) on the University of Missouri campus in Columbia for the 1989 documentary *"Now That's a Good Tune": Masters of Traditional Missouri Fiddling*. Soon after, Charlie Walden and Bill Shull issued our 1986 *"Good Tune"* session recording of "Gilsaw" and other tunes from the session on a 1987 cassette of McMahan's fiddling called *Ozark Mountain Waltz*. This 1987 cassette reissue of McMahan's "Gilsaw," a recording of the powerful fiddler in his prime, helped spread the tune across the map, as did Pete's appearance as a master fiddler at the Festival of American Fiddle Tunes in Port Townsend, Washington, in 1996, as well as other festivals where he played the tune.[2] "Gilsaw" has been recorded by several fiddlers, including John Williams of Madison, Pete McMahan's last student. Williams plays the tune in true McMahan style and now teaches it to his own fiddle students.[3] (Hear John Williams's "Gilsaw" on the companion CD.)

Gilsaw
as played by PeteMcMahan

Transcribed by Sharon Graf

* Finger numbers 4 and 0 indicate that the pitch is being produced on both strings—one stopped with the fourth finger and one open string. Alternately, the fingered string could be stopped with the second or third finger instead of the fourth.

As played by Pete McMahan, Columbia, Missouri, December 1986, recorded by Amy Skillman and Howard Marshall, issued on McMahan, Ozark Mountain Waltz (MSOTFA 001, cassette, 1987).

Pete McMahan's "Gilsaw," December 1986, Columbia. Such rare birds, linked to evocative times, their landscapes, and interesting people, richly increase our enjoyment and appreciation for traditional music in all its oral and aural contexts. (Transcription by Sharon Graf)

Pete McMahan excavated "Gilsaw" from the dustbins of forgotten melody. Through his influence and through other fiddlers such as Fred Stoneking and Charlie Walden, and because of the tune's innate musical interest, "Gilsaw" has become part of the national and international fiddle repertoire. It is a fine hoedown for square dancing. Pete felt that it did not meet his requirements for a "contest tune," but other fiddlers find "Gilsaw" effective in that performance context. In the twenty-first century, a number of fiddlers, many of them McMahan students or fans, fiddle this great tune at square dances and sessions and in fiddlers contests. And it was almost lost.

In local history and ethnography, research is tantalizing. Further study may tell us more about Mr. Gilsaw and his family in central Missouri; people with the name appear in the 1900 Missouri census in Callaway County. The family is of Swiss-German descent and came to Missouri spelling their name "Gueltzau." Nicolaus and Lottie Gueltzau established a farm in the Portland area of southern Callaway County, along the north bank of the Missouri River. Their three sons were John Gueltzau (1870–1954), Fritz Gueltzau (1872–1947), and Luther Herman Gueltzau (1880–1937).[4] By the late 1800s, the name was being spelled in public records as "Gilsaw" as well as "Gueltzau," and the brothers seem to have disagreed over which spelling now should be used. It is probable that Fritz or Luther Herman, somehow having come under financial difficulties and taken to the road, was the Gilsaw who played the fiddle tune that day in the 1930s, waiting for a train at the Montgomery City railroad depot. Where Gilsaw finally settled, and what his life became, we do not know. But we are still playing his tune.

Pete McMahan (1918–2000, *left*) and Taylor McBaine (1910–94) were two giants of central Missouri fiddling whose lives and music continue to thrill and impress long after their passing. At a session at the Chez coffeehouse, Columbia. (1993)

In a visit in St. James with Cecil Goforth, Howard Marshall (*left*) checks a draft of his profile of Goforth for *Fiddler's Dream*. (July 29, 2015; photo by Russell D. Ravert)

Interviews

Interviews except those noted as "letter," "e-mail," "telephone," and "unrecorded" were recorded by the author and will be archived at the State Historical Society of Missouri.

Ball, Earl. December 6, 2007; February 18, 2008.
Beisswenger, Drew. November 12, 2011 (e-mail); February 21, 2012 (e-mail).
Breid, Michael. April 1967 (unrecorded); March 17, 1969 (DeMaire recording); June 9, 2010; October 19, 20, 22, 23, 24, 2014 (e-mail); April 2 (e-mail), May 20 (e-mail), June 11, 2015 (e-mail).
Brown, Kyle. November 16, 2010 (e-mail).
Caldwell, Bobby Joe. April 4, 2007; October 1, 2009; October 22, 2010.
Canaday, Leroy. October 6, December 9, 2000; February 15, March 10, 2001.
Christeson, R. P. August 21, 1982 (unrecorded); December 1985.
Clatterbuck, Vernon. May 1, 2002.
Craighead, Bill. June 29, 2013 (not recorded).
Cunningham, Terry. December 30, 2014 (e-mail); March 30, April 2 (e-mail), July 6, 2015 (e-mail).
Davidson, Patricia Spray. March 19 (e-mail), April 1, 2015 (e-mail).
Dittemore, Dennis. June 29, 2015 (e-mail).
Ellis, Larry. April 25, 28 (e-mail), May 6, 8 (e-mail), June 19 (e-mail), June 27, July 3, 2015 (telephone).
Enloe, Forrest. February 18, 2008.
Enloe, Lyman. November 22, 1986.
Fast, Dulcie (Mrs. Robert). June 2013 (letter, courtesy Judith Smith Scheurer); July 25, 2013 (letter, courtesy Lew Holt).
Garelick, Gus. November 24 (e-mail), December 18, 2009 (e-mail); January 15, 2010 (e-mail); May 19, 2015 (e-mail).
Gillmore, Jim. July 15, 1987.
Goforth, Cecil. July 1, 9 (telephone), July 29, 2015.
Grotewohl, Dan. November 9, 2001; March 22, 2015 (e-mail).
Haddix, Chuck. January 29, 2015 (e-mail).
Hagan, Bob. October 16, 2014 (e-mail).
Harmon, Greg. October 27, 2014.
Hartford, John. March 29 (e-mail), April 17 (e-mail), July 4 (e-mail), July 17 (e-mail), November 20, 2000.
Helton, Elzie. June 2, May 23, 2008.
Helton, Warren. October 18, 2010; March 29, April 6 (telephone), May 28, 2011 (telephone).

Helton, Wayne. October 3 (unrecorded), October 12, 18, 2010; March 27, 2011.
Hoppers, Lonnie. May 23, June 17, 2013 (telephone); October 13, 2014 (telephone); February 16 (e-mail), February 21 (unrecorded), February 26 (e-mail), March 29, April 24 (e-mail), June 23 (e-mail), November 15, 2015 (e-mail).
Huddleston, Barb. April 14, 2013 (e-mail).
Lee, Billy. January 28, 1989; May 15, 2001; January 3, 2002.
Luke, Belinda. February 2, July 11, 17, 2012 (e-mail); March 8, 2015 (e-mail).
Lutz, Ron. May 8, 2003; October 5, 2010.
Marriott, Sharon Heath. February 13, 2008 (e-mail); February 10, 2015 (e-mail).
Matney, Mike. November 2, 2007; January 1, 2010 (e-mail).
McCann, Gordon. February 24, 2005 (e-mail); September 2014; October 9 (unrecorded), October 29 (unrecorded), November 3, 2014 (letter); January 12 (unrecorded), June 20, 2015 (telephone).
McGeorge, Henry. July 5, 2014 (unrecorded); July 4, 12, 2015.
McGreevy, Jim. March 28, 2015 (e-mail).
McKinney, Ed. February 21, 2008; October 26, 2010 (e-mail); June 10, 12, 14, 2015 (e-mail).
McMahan, Pete. December 17, 1986; May 1992; September 18 (unrecorded), September 25, 1997.
Murphy, Al. January 28, 2005 (e-mail).
Nelson, Jim. March 16, 2015 (e-mail); June 17, 2015 (e-mail).
Oliver, Jack E. April 18, 2013.
Olson, Mark. October 12, 2010 (e-mail).
Orchard, Jim. June 6, 11, 16, 28, 2015 (telephone).
Para, Dave. May 15, 2009 (e-mail).
Pauley, Dale. November 19, 2009; April 29, 2013 (unrecorded); April 15, 2014 (unrecorded); November 17, 2015 (unrecorded).
Peek, Dan William. September 22, 2010 (unrecorded); January 5, 2015 (unrecorded).
Reiner, Dave. March 15, 2015 (e-mail).
Reser, Gladys Lewis. February 10 (unrecorded), February 21, 2015.
Robertson, Lonnie. November 1975.
Russell, Jim. March 6, 7, 28, 30 (e-mail), April 2, 2015 (e-mail).
Ruth, Jim. December 31, 2004 (unrecorded); April 2, 2015 (e-mail).
Scheurer, Judith Smith. April 17 (unrecorded), July 10, August 28, 2013 (letter).
Schmutzler, Gary. October 7, 12, 14, 2015 (e-mail).
Seaman, Kenny. June 15 (e-mail), June 20 (correspondence), July 11, 2015 (e-mail).
Silvey, H. K. September 20, 2014.
Skaggs, Bob. November 19, 2010; November 8, 2013.
Sledge, Larry. March 12, 14 (e-mail), March 28, 2015.
Smith, Virgil. November 18, 2001.
Spray, Delbert. November 17, 1990 (unrecorded).

Stewart, John G. November 12, 2009; March 8, 2010; September 30, October 1, 2015.

Stoneking, Lee Roy. November 17, 1975.

Summers, Kathy. April 25, May 29, 2010 (unrecorded); November 8, 2013.

Teague, Larry. July 11, 2010 (e-mail).

West, Tom. September 6, 2006 (e-mail); December 3, 2015 (e-mail)

White, John (Blue Springs). November 20 (unrecorded), November 21 (e-mail), December 22, 2014 (e-mail); January 3, 2015 (unrecorded).

Williams, Claude. September 1985.

Williams, Phil. June 16, 2005; March 31, 2008 (telephone); June 26, July 16 (unrecorded), November 2 (e-mail), November 29, 2009 (e-mail); May 27 (e-mail), July 15 (e-mail), July 20, 2013 (e-mail).

Williams, Roger. September 23, 2011 (unrecorded); June 15, 2013; September 18, 24, 2015.

Williams, Vivian. June 22, 2006 (unrecorded); January 4, 2007 (e-mail); December 1, 2009 (e-mail); August 5, 2011 (e-mail).

Wyatt, Allen. August 26, 2000 (e-mail); March 11, 2008 (e-mail); June 16, 2009 (e-mail); January 12, 2010 (e-mail); August 5, 2014 (e-mail).

Wyatt, Bud. October 15, 2015.

Wyatt, Matt. March 31, 2008; October 2, 2010; May 9 (e-mail), August 20, 2011 (e-mail); September 10, 2015 (e-mail).

Transcriptions

AG	Amber Gaddy, Columbia
GG	Gus Garelick, Santa Rosa, CA
JT	Jack Tuttle, Palo Alto, CA
MW	Matthew Wyatt, Independence
PKV	Philip K. Vinyard, Columbia
SG	Sharon Graf, Springfield, IL
SW	Stuart Williams, Seattle, WA

Notes

Preface

1. We now know that "Turkey in the Straw" is a reel ultimately of British Isles and eighteenth-century origins; to bandmaster Sousa, it exemplified the fiddle and dance music of the African American minstrel stage that he respected.

2. While the wire recorder had been available, like those employed by R. P. Christeson in the 1940s and 1950s to make field recordings of fiddling, their cost and complexity and the fragility of the wires made them destined to become obsolete. Similarly, home recording machines of the 1940s and 1950s that recorded onto discs (wax, plastic) to be played on a phonograph were expensive enough that few could afford them; they were also replaced by the new, inexpensive, and convenient reel-to-reel tape recorder and then the cassette recorder.

3. Nat Hentoff, *Jazz Is*, 9.

1. Radio Fiddlers

1. I appreciate the assistance of Heather Roberson, Jim Nelson, Bob Hagan, Ed and Blanche McKinney, and Russell D. Ravert in preparing this chapter.

2. Edgar D. McKinney, "Images, Realities, and Cultural Transformations in the Missouri Ozarks, 1920–1960," app. B; Patrick Huber, "The Interstate Old Fiddlers Contest of 1926: WOS, Rural Radio Audiences, and Music Making in the Missouri State Capitol," *Missouri Historical Review* 10, no. 1 (2005): 3. Among introductions to the history of radio is Erik Barnouw, *A Tower in Babel: A History of Broadcasting in the United States* (New York: Oxford University Press, 1966), vol. 1. See also Frederick Lewis Allen, *Only Yesterday: An Informal History of the Nineteen-Twenties* (New York: Harper, 1957), 67ff; and James S. Olson, *Historical Dictionary of the 1920s: From World War I to the New Deal, 1919–1933*. Radio owes much of its success to the tinkerers and amateur electricians who figured out their own sets. Sydney W. Head and Christopher H. Sterling, *Broadcasting in America: A Survey of Electronic Media* (Boston: Houghton Mifflin, 1987), 54ff; Barnouw, *Tower in Babel*, 71ff.

3. For suggestive examples, see "Condenser Acts as Storage Tank: How the Fixed and Variable Types Are Constructed and What They Do," *Madison (MO) Times*, January 4, 1932, 2. Also, Barnouw, *Tower in Babel*; Hugh G. J. Aitken, *The Continuous Wave: Technology and the American Radio, 1900–1932*; Lawrence W. Lichty and Malachi C. Topping, eds., *American Broadcasting: A Source Book on the History of Radio and Television* (New York: Hastings House, 1975); and Anthony Rudel, *A Journey across the Dial: The Dawn of American Radio* (New York: Harcourt, 2008).

4. "Runs Radio with His Ford," *Monroe County (MO) Appeal*, March 2, 1923, 6.

5. E. P. J. Shurick, *The First Quarter-Century of American Broadcasting* (Kansas City: Midland, 1946), 56. Of course, phonograph records were also an immediate success. The first classical music broadcast in Missouri seems to have been a program of light opera beamed live from the Municipal Theatre in Forest Park, St. Louis, over station KSD, June 25, 1922 (ibid., 67). McCormack is credited by Shurick with a breakthrough performance in the spread of popular music, January 1, 1925, over New York's WEAH (ibid., 67). Among first broadcasts of dance music was Paul Specht and the WWJ radio orchestra, Detroit, September 14, 1920

(ibid., 70). See also part 2 in Irving Settel, *A Pictorial History of Radio* (New York: Bonanza Books, 1960).

6. For one citation, Wayne W. Daniel, *Pickin' on Peachtree: A History of Country Music in Atlanta, Georgia* (Urbana: University of Illinois Press, 1990), 68.

7. Fans, fiddlers, and scholars will have their own lists of favorite influential players in the formative years. For example, L. Scott Miller, "Eddie Stubbs, Part 2: Recommended Listening—Fiddlers with Soul," *Fiddler Magazine* 19, no. 4 (2012–13): 4–9.

8. See, for instance, Paul Shelasky, "Bluegrass Fiddling: Learning Bluegrass Backup with Chubby Wise," *Fiddler Magazine* 8, no. 1 (2001): 38–39; and Jay Orr, "Chubby Bows Out," *Devil's Box* 30, no. 1 (1996): 21–23.

9. Smith toured and performed live and was a staple on the early *Grand Ole Opry* from 1927 through the 1930s. He formed an *Opry* band with Sam and Kirk McGee called the Dixieliners and later made records on the Bluebird label with the Delmore Brothers. A few of these recordings include twin fiddling with his colleague Tommy Magness. Smith's fiddling has been reissued on CD by County and is important listening for young and aspiring fiddlers; for example, *Nashville: The Early String Bands*, vol. 1; and *Fiddlin' Arthur Smith & His Dixieliners*, vols. 1–2.

10. The correct spelling is "Cheatham," for Cheatham County, Tennessee, but the accepted spelling in the fiddle world is "Cheatem" or even "Cheatum" (but not "Cheat 'Em"). Smith is profiled in Wayne Erbson, *Rural Roots of Bluegrass: Songs, Stories & History* (Pacific, MO: Mel Bay, 2003). Erbson repeats fiddler Dick Burnett's quip that "Arthur Smith played 'Mocking Bird' so clear you could see the feathers" (93). In addition to references elsewhere, see http://www.answers.com/topic/fiddlin-arthur-smith.

11. Jim Nelson, June 17, 2015.

12. Arthur Smith, *Songs from the Hills of Tennessee* and *Arthur Smith's Original Song Folio No. 1* (Hollywood: American Music, 1943).

13. *"That's My Rabbit, My Dog Caught It": Traditional Southern Instrumental Styles* (New World Records 226, 1978). Smith's "Hell among the Yearlings" and "Pig in a Pen" from his appearance at the Newport Folk Festival in 1965 with Sam and Kirk McGee are included, along with three vocal numbers, in a sampler, *Nashville at Newport* (reissue, Santa Monica: Vanguard, 1995). Other music from Smith's later career, recorded by Mike Seeger, appeared on an LP in 1962 called *Rare Old Time Fiddle Tunes* (Starday SLP 202, 1963).

14. Jackson fiddled briefly in 1956 with Bob Wills's Texas Playboys.

15. Charles Wolfe, "Tommy Jackson: Nashville Fiddler," *Bluegrass Unlimited* (September 1980): 46. See also Wolfe, "In Memoriam: Tommy Jackson," *Devil's Box* 14, no. 1 (1980): 20–21, and "Tommy Jackson: Portrait of a Nashville Session Fiddler," in *Devil's Box: Masters of Southern Fiddling*, by Wolfe, 186–96. Among many other references to Jackson, see Stacy Phillips, *The Complete Country Fiddler*.

16. Wolfe, "Tommy Jackson: Nashville Fiddler," 43.

17. Frank Maloy, "Fiddle Tablature: Tommy Jackson's Fiddle Style," *Devil's Box* 14, no. 1 (1980): 21 ("Tennessee Wagoner" and "Hoedown Polka"). See also Maloy, "'Lead Out' and 'Paddy on the Turnpike' as Played by Tommy Jackson," *Devil's Box* 21, no. 1 (1980): 53–56. Paul Shelasky describes Jackson's "exuberance and verve" as "the quintessential hoedown fiddler" in "The Bluegrass Fiddle Style of Tommy Jackson," *Fiddler Magazine* 17, no. 1 (2010):

21, and "Tommy Jackson Plays a Hoedown," *Fiddler Magazine* 17, no. 4 (2010–11): 47. See also Charles K. Wolfe, *Classic Country: Legends of Country Music*, chap. 4, and "Tommy Jackson: King of the '50s Country Fiddlers," http://www.nativeground.com.

18. Richard Kienzle, *Southwest Shuffle: Pioneers of Honky-Tonk, Western Swing, and Country Jazz*, 167.

19. "Tommy Jackson," http://www.country-music-archive.com.

20. A view of Howdy Forrester's story is Gayel Pitchford, *Fiddler of the Opry: The Howdy Forrester Story* (Tehachapi, CA: Viewpoint Press, 2007). See also Bill Harrison, "Howdy Forrester," *Devil's Box* 15, no. 3 (1981): 11–15.

21. In the early era, the band was called Bill Monroe and His Blue Grass Boys, and "Blue Grass" signified the Monroes' home region in Kentucky; eventually, "bluegrass" solidified as one word and widened in meaning to indicate the style of music itself.

22. Roy Acuff and His Smoky Mountain Boys; Columbia CL9010 (Magness is not mentioned on the album cover). Acuff here was appealing to the nationwide fashion for square dancing that emerged after World War II and lasted into the late 1950s. For Magness, see Wolfe, *Classic Country*, chap. 4.

23. Murphy H. Henry, "Come Prepared to Stay, Bring Fiddle: The Story of Sally Ann Forrester, the Original Bluegrass Girl," in *Country Music Annual, 2001*, ed. by Charles K. Wolfe and James E. Akenson (Lexington: University Press of Kentucky, 2001), 92–120. Sally Ann was a successful fiddler, but played the "non-bluegrass" accordion with Monroe's band from 1943 to 1945, recording several important records, including the iconic 1946 hits "Kentucky Waltz" and "Footprints in the Snow" (ibid., 93, 109). Monroe pegged her with the stage name "Sally Ann" (her name was Goldie Sue, and she went by "Billie"); (ibid., 95ff). Sally Ann Forrester was born in New Mexico, raised in Oklahoma (where she enjoyed hearing Bob Wills and His Texas Playboys play swing at Cain's Ballroom in Tulsa), and attended the high school academy at Southwest Baptist College in Bolivar, Missouri, where she played violin in the orchestra and took voice and piano lessons (ibid., 95). Howdy and Sally Ann married in 1940 in Oklahoma; they had met playing barn-dance radio shows and dances in Texas.

24. *Raw Fiddle* (Kanawha 325, 1976, CD reissue, 2008).

25. Charlie Walden, "The 1925 Missouri 'Mythical' Fiddle Championship," 4; Walden, "Radiophone WOS and WOS Radio Reunion and Fiddling Championship." See also Huber, "Interstate Old Fiddlers Contest of 1926," 2–18. After 1928 stations east of the Mississippi were required to begin with a *W* and those west of the river with a *K*. Important Ozarks references include McKinney, "Images, Realities, and Cultural Transformations" and "Like Family: Kinship Perceptions of Ozarks Radio Entertainers and the Spread of Consumer Culture, 1934–1959."

26. Gary Schmutzler, October 12, 2015.

27. The year is not certain, but the contest they entered probably was the two-day event December 31, 1925–January 1, 1926, that attracted many musicians.

28. Gary Schmutzler, October 12, 2015.

29. Crystal Payton, *The Story of Silver Dollar City: A Pictorial History of Branson's Famous Ozark Mountain Village Theme Park (*Branson, MO: Silver Dollar City, 1997), 51ff; Helen Townsend and Godsey Townsend, *Flight of the Phoenix: The Biography of the School of the Ozarks, a Unique American College (*Point Lookout, MO: School of the Ozarks Press, 1984);

Bill Earngey, *Missouri Roadsides: The Traveler's Companion* (Columbia: University of Missouri Press, 1995); http://www.projecttaney.org. For Missouri caves, see also J. Harlan Bretz, *Caves of Missouri* (Jefferson City: Missouri Division of Geological Survey and Water Resources, 1956); and H. Dwight Weaver, *Missouri Caves in History and Legend* (Columbia: University of Missouri Press, 2008).

30. *Ozarks Mountaineer* 54, no. 3 (1966). The first Americans to explore the cave were twelve members of the Springfield Women's Athletic Club in the 1860s.

31. Terry Cunningham, April 1, 2015.

32. See, among many references, Wayne W. Daniel, "The National Barn Dance on Network Radio: The 1930s," *Journal of Country Music* 9, no. 3 (1983): 47–62; and John Dunning, *Tune in Yesterday: The Ultimate Encyclopedia of Old-Time Radio, 1925–1976* (Englewood Cliffs, NJ: Prentice Hall, 1976), 435–37.

33. Shurick, *First Quarter-Century*, 279.

34. C. H. Hohmann, *Practical Violin School* (Boston: White-Smith, 1892), with text in German and English; Albert Harvey, *Progressive Course for the Violin* (Toronto: Whaley, Royer, 1925).

35. The Buseer farm was listed under Anna Buseer, and the Adams farm listed as Charles W. Adams, in 1931. *Atlas of Jackson County, Missouri* (Kansas City: Gallup Map & Supply, 1931), 46.

36. John R. White, November 21, 2014.

37. Jim McGreevy, March 28, 2015.

38. Robert L. Ramsay, *Our Storehouse of Missouri Place Names*, 83; Union Historical Company, *A History of Jackson County, Missouri* (Kansas City: Union Historical, 1881), 71, 105ff; Anne Atchison, "Place Names of Five West Central Counties of Missouri" (master's thesis, University of Missouri, 1937).

39. "Elevations and Distances in the United States," http://www.egsu.usgs.gov.

40. Daniel, *Pickin' on Peachtree*, 166ff.

41. Greg Harmon, October 27, 2014. Wanda Smith married Ted Henderson and performed on radio as "Wanda and Ted."

42. "Arkansas Boogie," Whitkay W-1001-B; on verso is another Kay Smith composition, "Life Is Not a Bed of Roses."

43. For photos of Emmy and other hillbilly radio performers, see Frank Absher, *KMOX: The Voice of St. Louis* (Charleston, SC: Arcadia Press, 2012), 42ff.

44. Elzie Helton, May 23, 2008. Elzie Helton's father was fiddler George Helton, and his grandfather was fiddler Jesse Helton; this is a clan of fiddlers and musicians in Maries County whose music is represented in Christeson's tune books and Beisswenger and McCann.

45. Michael Breid, June 9, 2010.

46. A. B. McDonald, "Missouri Goes in for Wireless: Farmers Get the Latest News from the Capitol Dome," *Country Gentleman* (May 17, 1922): 16.

47. Vernon Clatterbuck, September 14, 2004. Fiddle contests had been held occasionally among African American fiddlers just as among white fiddlers in the Civil War era, a topic worthy of further research in Missouri. Paul Cimbala, "Black Musicians from Slavery to Freedom: An Exploration of an African-American Folk Elite and Cultural Continuity in the Nineteenth-Century Rural South," *Journal of Negro History* 80, no. 1 (1995): 17ff.

48. Dr. Joe Pryor, Miller County Historical Society, http://www.millercountymuseum.org.

49. Walden, "'Mythical' Fiddle Championship," 4. See also Huber, "Interstate Old Fiddlers Contest of 1926."

50. Walden, "'Mythical' Fiddle Championship" and "Radiophone WOS"; Huber, "Interstate Old Fiddlers Contest of 1926."

51. Walden, "Radiophone WOS"; Huber, "Interstate Old Fiddlers Contest of 1926."

52. Virgil Smith, November 18, 2001.

53. "1,000 Votes Coming in for Favorites in Fiddling Contest," *Jefferson City Daily Post*, April 3, 1926, 1. Winners were, first place (fifty dollars in merchandise), Thomas Jasper Massie of Nevada; second place (forty in merchandise), Daniel Boone Jones of Stephens; third place (thirty-five in merchandise), Louie Barton; fourth place (thirty in merchandise), Jesse Burgess of Stoutland; fifth place (twenty-five in merchandise), J. A. (Aaron) Oliver of Columbia. *Jefferson City Daily Capitol Post*, January 14, 1926, 1.

54. First prize went to Thomas Jasper Massie (a Kentucky native who had moved to Nevada, Missouri), second to Daniel Boone Jones (Columbia), and third to Louie Barton (Barton, a local favorite, had been the first fiddler to play on the first live radio broadcast of fiddle music, June 24, 1923, two years before WSM in Nashville began similar broadcasts). See Walden, "'Mythical' Fiddle Championship" and "Radiophone WOS"; and Huber, "Interstate Old Fiddlers Contest of 1926." The record is somewhat confused about the winners' names in the 1925 contest following the first three winners.

55. "Old Fiddlers Contest," *Houston (MO) Herald*, January 7, 1926, 7.

56. Ed and Blanche McKinney, March 12, 2009.

57. Ed McKinney, March 11, 2009.

58. For Long, see Spencer Galloway, "Sam Long: 'Echoes of the Ozarks,'" *Devil's Box* 23, no. 1 (1989): 39–40.

59. Walden, "Radiophone WOS." Today's KWOS-AM station (which opened in 1937 and is located in West Jefferson City) is not officially an extension of the original WOS, but KWOS retains the historical call letters and continues to present significant local programming by people such as Warren Kretch, who is interested in history and fiddling.

60. Learned from their competitors, newspaper publishers.

61. Huber, "Interstate Old Fiddlers Contest of 1926," 3.

62. "Cobbler Becomes Premier Fiddler," *Chattanooga* (TN) *Times*, February 7, 1926, 14 (courtesy Jack Burlison).

63. Gifford, July 25, 2006. See also Art Menius, "Our Ford: Old-Time Fiddle and Dancing." Gifford has done extensive research on Ford and fiddling, discovering that no contests were actually paid for or sponsored by the Ford Motor Company or Mr. Ford; e.g., July 25, 2005, 3, February 7, 2009, postings to FIDDLE-L@LISTSERVE.BROWN.EDU. Gifford notes that several academic publications have, perhaps inadvertently, added to the confusion; e.g., Malone, *Country Music, U.S.A.*, and Tony Russell, *Blacks, Whites, and Blues* (New York: Stein and Day, 1970); Wolfe, *The Devil's Box*, passim; and Guthrie T. Meade, "Fiddles and Fords: Photographs from Louisville's Caulfield & Shook Studio," *Journal of Country Music* 12:3 (Fall 1989), who confirms our understanding that the major contests in Louisville were staged by the Ford company's "district headquarters" and not by Mr. Ford himself (37 ff.); Iowa fiddler and fiddle scholar Nate Kemperman wrote a valuable research paper at Iowa State University, "Fiddling for Ford" (spring 2001).

64. *Houston (MO) Herald*, January 28, 1926, 1; Guthrie T. Meade, "Fiddles and Fords: Photographs from Louisville's Caulfield & Shook Studio," 38. Meade's article implies that Elmore planned to play the same tunes in the finals in Detroit, Michigan.

65. Among the other regional contests sending their champions to Detroit for similar red-carpet treatment was an impressive-sounding "World-Wide/International Fiddlers Contest" held in Lewiston, Maine, in April 1926. Michigan saw a large number of preliminary rounds, with a state championship "Henry Ford contest" held in January 1926. The Ohio finals were held in Cleveland in February, and the Massachusetts state championship was held in Boston in March. Paul Gifford, July 25, 2005, Internet discussion group FIDDLE-L@LISTSERV.BROWN.EDU; the international contest in Maine had contestants from Ireland (John Wiseman, Bantry) and Scotland—none other than the famous composer and fiddler J. Scott Skinner (who seems to have become dissatisfied with his accompanist and walked off the stage).

66. *Houston (MO) Herald*, April 1, 1926, 5. See also McKinney, "Images, Realities, and Cultural Transformations," 93–94.

67. "Henry Elmore Wins Big Fiddling Honors," *Houston (MO) Herald*, January 21, 1926. To outsiders, everything about the Ozarks is "high up," but Houston is in an Ozarks plateau landscape of rolling timber and farmland; Elmore's new home in southern Indiana was a good deal more hilly.

68. *Houston (MO) Herald*, February 25, 1926, 1.

69. Ibid.

70. Ed McKinney, March 3, 2009. A photo of the Harmoniers appears in Wayne Glenn's valuable photopictorial, *The Ozarks' Greatest Hits: A Photo History of Music in the Ozarks*, 356. Other members of the group were Duane Sutton, Max Burkhead, and Edna Oxley (piano).

71. "D. B. Jones Plays for Henry Ford," *Columbia (MO) Daily Tribune*, February 1, 1929, 1. For more on this influential fiddler, see Howard Wight Marshall, *Play Me Something Quick and Devilish: Old-Time Fiddlers in Missouri*.

72. "Big Crowd Attends Birthday Party at Madison School," *Moberly (MO) Monitor-Index and Evening Democrat*, February 1, 1944, 2. FDR was born January 30, 1882.

73. "Amateur and Fiddlers Day at Fall Festival," *Dexter (MO) Statesman*, August 26, 1938, 1.

74. "Old Fiddlers Contest," *Dexter (MO) Statesman*, September 22, 1938, 1.

75. Jim Nelson interview with Howe Teague, September 2000 (courtesy Nelson).

76. Ivan Tribe has brought Natchee and the mock fiddlers contests into more vivid profile. See Tribe, *Mountaineer Jamboree: Country Music in West Virginia* (Lexington: University Press of Kentucky, 1984), 78, 83–84ff; and Wolfe, *Devil's Box*, 94ff.

77. For example, popular radio and record fiddler Clayton McMichen was upset to be bested by Natchee the Indian, who was more of a vaudeville act than a bona fide old-time fiddler. Wolfe, *Devil's Box*, 94. See also, for Natchee, Tribe, *Mountaineer Jamboree*.

78. McMahan, May 8, 1992. Similar recollections were communicated to me over the years by Leroy Canaday, Taylor McBaine, and Nile Wilson.

79. Pete McMahan, September 11, 1997.

80. For example, in September 1948, Charlie Cook won the Boone County Fair fiddlers contest, sponsored by the Odd Fellows Lodge, with other familiar names placing high: second place, Cleo Persinger; third, Nolan Boone; fourth, Tony Gilmore; fifth, Claude Stearns (Glasgow); and sixth, Roy Raines (New Franklin). "Charles Cook Wins Fiddling Contest," *Columbia Missourian*, September 7, 1948, 1.

2. Lonnie Robertson

1. Charles K. Wolfe, "Caney Mountain Fiddler: The Lonnie Robertson Story," 34. I discussed Robertson on several occasions with Wolfe in the 1970s. I appreciate the encouragement and advice of Gordon McCann in my discussion of Lonnie Robertson. See also Allen Gage, "Old-Time Fiddling: A Traditional Folk Art with Four Ozark Musicians."

2. Christeson 2, xvi.

3. Mary Ruth Luna Sparks, "Two Ozark Countians Were Early Radio Stars—Lonnie and Thelma Robertson," 5.

4. Janet Taber, *Just Down Home Folks*. Taber is a leading light in the conservation of local heritage.

5. Wolfe, "Caney Mountain Fiddler," 35; H. K. Silvey, September 20, 2014.

6. Marshall, *Play Me Something Quick and Devilish*, 90, 105, 126ff.

7. Paul Roberts, "Missouri Fiddling—Stinnett, Robertson & Stoneking," http://www.mustrad.org.uk.

8. Jim Orchard, June 6, 2015.

9. Howard Wight Marshall and Vivian Williams, *Fiddle Seconding Missouri Style, Chords and Bowing Techniques* (Seattle: Voyager Recordings and Publications, VR-DVD1001, 2012, instructional DVD with historical commentary).

10. H. K. Silvey, September 20, 2014.

11. Don Harvey, album notes, Robertson, *Country Fiddling* (Caney Mountain CLP229).

12. Mrs. Roy (Ruby) McGeorge, letter to Henry McGeorge, September 23, 1985 (courtesy Henry McGeorge); Wolfe, "Caney Mountain Fiddler," 34. Roy McGeorge's family and fans called the duo "Roy and Lonnie."

13. See, for example, Charles K. Wolfe, *Kentucky Music: Folk and Country Music of Kentucky* (Lexington: University Press of Kentucky, 1982), 100; Walter V. Saunders, "Notes and Queries," *Bluegrass Unlimited* (October 1991): 10; and Neil V. Rosenberg, *Bluegrass: A History*, 21ff.

14. Henry McGeorge, July 5, 2014.

15. "Kohala March" was recorded in 1914 by guitar duo Pale K. Lua and David K. Kaili (of the Irene West Royal Hawaiian Troupe) on Victor B-15493, in 1918 on Edison Cylinder as "Kahala March" by the Ford Hawaiians (Blue Amberol 3446), and as "Kohala March" in 1920 by Franchini and Dettborn (Supreme 4114). Phil and Vivian Williams, July 8, 2014. Note that the Nashville resophonic guitarist and comedian Brother Oswald (Pete Kirby), a frequent performer on *The Grand Ole Opry*, played a version of this "Kahola March." Discographer Jim Nelson reports that another recording of the tune, spelled "Kahala March," was recorded later by the Hawaiian ensemble Sol Hoopi and the Novelty Four, on Los Angeles label Eldee Records (78 rpm, 133-A, ca. 1950). Nelson, July 8, 2014. Hoopi recorded with an electric lap steel guitar tuned in scordatura tunings, and his playing reflects the influences of swing and jazz.

16. Sparks, "Two Ozark Countians," 6; Gordon McCann, October 29, 2014.

17. Henry McGeorge, July 5, 2014; Saunders, "Notes and Queries," 10. There may also be some cassettes of home recordings of jam sessions.

18. Mrs. Roy (Ruby) McGeorge, letter to Henry McGeorge, September 23, 1985 (courtesy Henry McGeorge); album notes, *Country Fiddling* (CLP229).

19. McCann, October 29, 2014.

20. In 1990 KWTO radio's historic identity with Ozarks people and music evaporated when it changed into a mass-culture talk radio–format station.

21. See McKinney, "Images, Realities, and Cultural Transformations," 173ff, and "Like Family."

22. Taber, *Just Down Home Folks*.

23. Kim Lansford, "'Boy! He Sure Had Some Good Tunes!' The Music of Lonnie Robertson," 38; Paul Roberts, "Midwestern Fiddling—Stinnett, Robertson, and Stoneking," http://www.mustad.org.uk (July 7, 2014); Gordon McCann, June 20, 2015. Among commercial releases where we can hear Casey Jones and Cyril Stinnett, as well as their contemporary Lyman Enloe, is a reissue project by County Records, *Three Fiddlers from the Show-Me State* (County CO-2739-CD, 2005).

24. Gordon McCann, June 20, 2015.

25. Bob Walter's version of "Tunes from Home" is in Christeson 1, 158. A 1929 78 rpm recording by the Jahrl Instrumental Quintet (Victor V-10) circulated in the Midwest. Eddie Jahrl was a Swedish immigrant accordionist who recorded "ethnic" dance music extensively. Victor Greene, *A Passion for Polka: Old-Time Ethnic Music in America* (Berkeley: University of California Press, 1992), 185.

26. Album notes, *Lonnie's Breakdown: Classic Fiddle Music from Missouri* (Rounder CD0375, 1996); Gordon McCann, "Lonnie Robertson," 12; Beisswenger and McCann, 113. The "EP" (extended play) was an evolution of the seven-inch 45 rpm record in the 1950s that provided more listening time than a standard 45 that, like the precursor 78 rpm records, typically were "singles" with one performance per side. Competing with the new and popular LP (long play) record format, the EP soon went out of production.

27. The Rounder CD *Lonnie's Breakdown* is the essential compilation of Robertson's fiddling; there are Robertson tunes in the Rounder compilation *Traditional Fiddle Music of the Ozarks*, vol. 3, *Down in the Border Counties*, and several are transcribed in the Milliner-Koken Collection, available on Larry Warren's website, http://www.slippery-hill.com, where one can hear "Fiddler's Blues," "Saddle Old Kate," "Ozark Mountain Waltz," "Arkansas Stomp," "Kaiser Waltz," "Lonnie's Breakdown," "Rock All the Babies to Sleep," and "Bonaparte's Retreat" (played in a dischord D tuning). Clare Milliner and Walt Koken, *The Milliner-Koken Collection of American Fiddle Tunes*. According to Jim Nelson, Ozark County fiddler Alton Jones, a carrier of many rare tunes, was the main source for "Saddle Old Kate," having learned it from a whistling blacksmith; Jones taught the tune to Bob Holt, Lonnie Roberson, and others (Nelson, June 17, 2015). Jones in his elder years may be heard on the Gordon McCann–Mark Wilson documentary, *Traditional Fiddle Music of the Ozarks*.

28. Wolfe, "Caney Mountain Fiddler," 35.

29. Holt's famous version of "The Eighth of January" as "The Ninth of January" is available on the compilation CD enclosed with *Play Me Something Quick and Devilish*; transcribed in Beisswenger and McCann, 124.

30. Hull Forest of Springfield and Scrivner of Forsyth often attend jam sessions and play for dances together, and both began playing Ozarks fiddle music as young children. Scrivner, Bob Holt's final apprentice in the Missouri Folk Arts Apprenticeship Program in 2001, appears on *Hangin' around the Kitchen* with Holt's longtime guitarist, Alvie Dooms, and claw-hammer banjoist Karen Kraft (self-produced, 2007). Liz Amos, a few years older, was Holt's fiddle apprentice in 1998 and 1999 and spent much time in Ava to acquire his tunes and tempos; she currently is a fiddle instructor at the annual Bethel Fiddle Camp. The favored session where these and other fiddlers congregate is the Monday-evening McClurg store session in northeastern Taney County,

where Bob Holt and Alvie Dooms held forth for decades. See Jeremy Myers, "McClurg: The Ozark Tradition Lives On," *Ozarks Mountaineer* (November–December 2011): 13–15.

31. McCann, October 29, 2014.

32. Precise determination of beats per minute can be difficult (counting how many beats are given in one minute), with different devices presenting slightly different data; here, a Korg TM-50 digital metronome was used, and BPMs were cross-checked with a Korg MA-20. Lincoln Lewis described Arkansas Ozarks square-dance tempos in "Tempo of Old Square Dances Reveals Differences in Regional Ways of Life," *Kansas City Star*, May 17, 1944.

33. McCann, "Lonnie Robertson," 13.

34. "Rosebud Reel" (a.k.a. "Mountain Ranger Hornpipe") is virtually unknown in Missouri tradition except among northern fiddlers such as Walters, Casey Jones, and Stinnett, and the tune, evolving from an 1847 New England publication, was no doubt picked up from tune books such as the 1940 Cole's, 10, a reprint of Ryan's; transcriptions appear in Christeson 2, 26–27; and Beisswenger and McCann, 125. See *Fiddler's Companion*, http://www.ibiblio.org (October 1, 2014).

35. Just as with other tunes that began as dotted-rhythm hornpipes a century and a half or more in the past and that were accompaniment for the solo step dance (hornpipe), or with tunes of recent development that fiddlers may call "hornpipes," "Lonnie's Hornpipe" is played as a reel (breakdown, hoedown) for square dancing. See Marshall, *Play Me Something Quick and Devilish*.

36. Lonnie Hoppers, May 23, 2013.

3. Music Parties

1. I appreciate the assistance of Jim Nelson and Terry Cunningham in preparing this chapter.

2. Among studies of the jam session, see Michelle Kisliuk, "'A Special Kind of Courtesy': Action at a Bluegrass Festival Jam Session," 141. Jam-session etiquette varies substantially not only from genre to genre (for example, old-time fiddling versus bluegrass versus Irish fiddling versus jazz fiddling) but regionally and even from session to session in the same community.

3. I thank Gladys Lewis Reser, Alice Reser Carneal, and Lonnie Hoppers for their help documenting the Bert Lewis story. I became acquainted with Lewis's fiddling in 2013, thanks to Hoppers, who, in his childhood, chorded plectrum banjo behind Lewis's fiddling in and around the Urbana community.

4. Hoppers, October 13, 2014.

5. Ibid., May 23, 2013.

6. The category reels (hoedown, breakdown) include many old British Isles dance tunes, the majority Scottish and Irish in provenance, handed down in America since colonial times; by the early twentieth century, British Isles dotted-rhythm hornpipes were being evened out and played much as reels suitable for square dancing. The waltz came to the United States in the early 1800s largely from German-speaking Europe. Like the waltz, many reels and hornpipes can be traced to known books of transcribed tunes, if not to authors.

7. See Beisswenger and McCann, 112.

8. Eldridge was the home of Mrs. Harriet Waterman, who inspired young Floyd Smith to play the fiddle; Mrs. Waterman was a rare young woman (and preacher's wife) competing in and winning fiddlers contests in the 1920s. See previous chapter, and Marshall, *Play Me Something Quick and Devilish*.

9. Floyd Smith, July 30, 1985; Gordon McCann video recording of Smith fiddle session, Buffalo (courtesy Greg Harman, April 2014).

10. A 1955 home recording of a music party with Bert Lewis and others, courtesy Alice Carneal.

11. Frances Smith, 1955 home recording.

12. Reser, February 10, 20, 2015.

13. The death certificate spells it "Cassidy," as do album notes for *Traditional Fiddle Music of the Ozarks*, vol. 1, *Along the Eastern Crescent* (Rounder, CD 0435, 1999). However, Larry Teague states that the name is spelled "Cassity" (July 11, 2010), and it appears as "Cassity" in Salem artist L. L. Broadfoot's interview.

14. Howe Teague speaking about his mentor, Orville Cassity; interview with Jim Nelson, September 9, 2000; see also album notes, *Traditional Fiddle Music of the Ozarks*, vol. 1.

15. Walden, "'Mythical' Fiddle Championship" and "Radiophone WOS." The top five winners were Thomas Massie (Nevada), Daniel Boone Jones (Stephens), Louie Barton (Jefferson City), Jess Burgess (Stoutland), and Aaron Oliver (Columbia).

16. *Traditional Fiddle Music of the Ozarks*, vol. 1.

17. L. L. Broadfoot, "The Champion Fiddler of the Ozarks," in *Pioneers of the Ozarks* (1977; reprint, Salem: L. L. Broadfoot, 1944), 111. "Billy in the Lowlands" is usually called "Billy in the Low Ground" in Missouri. "Stoney Mountain" was probably Cassity's title for "Stony Point." Broadfoot's papers are archived in the State Historical Society of Missouri, Columbia. The Harlin Museum in West Plains maintains an important collection.

18. Russell L. Gerlach, *Settlement Patterns in Missouri* (Columbia: University of Missouri Press, 1986), 24ff.

19. Nelson interview with Teague, September 9, 2000 (courtesy Nelson). Unless otherwise noted, all Teague quotes are from the Nelson interview. For this important house type in Missouri, with antecedents in Kentucky, Tennessee, the Carolinas, and Virginia and prior to that in the British Isles, see Howard Wight Marshall, *Folk Architecture in Little Dixie: A Regional Culture in Missouri* and *Vernacular Architecture in Rural and Small Town Missouri: An Introduction.*

20. Beisswenger and McCann, 146.

21. Among several scholarly explications of the cornstalk fiddle in the American Midwest is Roger L. Welsch, "The Cornstalk Fiddle," *Journal of American Folklore* 77, no. 30 (1964): 262–63. Similar instruments are known in middle European traditions as well as in some Native American tribal music traditions that incorporated European traditions.

22. Beisswenger and McCann, 146. I had the same shocking experience of finding myself the only fiddler in front of a roomful of waiting dancers when the principal fiddler Johnny Bruce failed to make it to a dance at the Knights of Pythias Hall in Boonville, ca. 1984, but I was forty years old and accompanied by a strong piano player, Musial Wolfe.

23. http://www.redhotjazz.com (December 25, 2014).

24. The "97" was a Southern Railway "fast mail" steam train that derailed at high speed near Danville, Virginia, in 1903, causing death and destruction worthy of the ballad that commemorated the tragedy. Born on the family cattle ranch in northeastern Texas, Vernon Dalhart (Marion Try Slaughter, 1883–1948) was one of the earliest and most successful of the "hillbilly" balladeers and recording stars. His stage name (Vernon Dalhart) was derived from

two towns in the Texas panhandle, where he had worked as a cowboy. A trained singer, Dalhart moved with his family to New York in 1910, where he found work in a piano warehouse and sang opera. Dalhart won a recording contract with Edison and made hundreds of records from 1916 through the 1920s. "Wreck of the Old 97" is often considered the first record to sell a million copies. See, for example, Tony Russell, *Country Music Originals: The Legends and the Lost*; and Frank Hoffman, *Encyclopedia of Recorded Sound* (New York: Routledge, 2005).

25. The author uses the word "violin" for the instrument itself; the word "fiddle" is used, but most often applies to the manner of performance ("fiddling").

26. Margot Roberson and Howard Wight Marshall, "Howe Kenneth Teague, Dent County Ozark Fiddler," in *The Masters: Traditional Arts Apprenticeship Program*, by Roberson and Marshall, 49.

27. In rural Missouri vernacular, "dinner" means lunch, while "supper" is the evening meal, except in the specific usage for "basket dinner" and "carry-in dinner."

28. Among many references, see Joseph Nelson [pseud.], "Box Supper," in *Missouri Reader*, edited by Frank Luther Mott, 281–88; Suzanne Carr, "Pie Supper," *Missouri Bittersweet* 1, no. 1 (1973): 45–49; and especially Robert K. Gilmore, *Ozark Baptizings, Hangings, and Other Diversions: Theatrical Folkways of Rural Missouri, 1885–1910*, 103–10.

29. Howe Teague, recorded by Amy Skillman for *"Now That's a Good Tune,"* January 17, 1988, Salem.

30. Orchard, June 6, 2015.

31. "Roy Wooliver (Dent), Discharged under 7/12 Merit Time," July 21, 1932, in Missouri State Archives, *Missouri State Penitentiary Register of Inmates*, Box S-209, 250.

32. Teague, Nelson interview, 2000; Nelson, March 16, 2015.

33. Howe Teague, "Ozark Mountain Fox Chase" (Nashville: Zeke Clements); *Square Dance Music/Ozark Fiddlin'* (Gold Standard GS-SQ D.LP1 [1964]); *Ozark Memories: Fiddle Tunes by Howe Teague* (OMHT-001 [1986]).

34. Howe Teague's mentoring of the Dillard brothers as musicians and radio performers and his influence on Mitch Jayne (the Dillards' wry, comic-storytelling emcee) are recounted, among other places, in Lee Grant, *Everybody on the Truck! The Story of the Dillards, by Lee Grant with the Original Dillards* (Nashville: Eggman, 1995).

35. Roberson and Marshall, "Howe Kenneth Teague."

36. Ken Fiebelman, *Ozark Hills and Neighbors, 1829–2000: East Central Missouri Ozarks* (Paducah, KY: Turner, 2001), 1:43; Dent County Historical Society, *Ozark Heritage: Dent County, Missouri* (Salem, 1978), 1:397, 582ff.

37. Marshall, *Play Me Something Quick and Devilish*, 198, 242.

38. "Old-Time Dance Music by Wooliver and Coppage," with "Square Dancing by Selected Sets" (newspaper ad), *Salem News* June 23, 1938.

39. "Roy Wooliver (Dent), Discharged 1920," Missouri State Archives, *Missouri State Penitentiary Register of Inmates*, Box S-209, 250.

40. Secretary of State, *Index of Penal Records (State Penitentiary), 1837–1939*, vol. 3, June 1920, Box S-209, 253.

41. November 17, 1987, Hannibal; recounted by Goforth on his CD *Hamilton Ironworks*. John Hartford repeats the thread of the story on his *Eminence Breakdown* CD (Rounder 0388, 1997).

42. "Roy Wolliver [*sic*] Arrested for Burglary, Reynolds County, CMS 5-14-1926," Secretary of State, *Index of Penal Records (State Penitentiary)*, vol. 3 (n.d.); "Roy Wooliver (Reynolds), Discharged under 7/12 Merit Time," May 17, 1926, 247; Nelson, Teague interview.

43. "Roy Wooliver (Dent), Discharged under 7/12 Merit Time," July 21, 1932, 263.

44. "James Christopher LeRoy Wooliver (Reynolds), Discharged February 15, 1952," *Missouri State Penitentiary Register of Inmates*, Box S-210, 382.

45. In 2015 some 1940s recordings of Howe Teague fiddling with Wooliver playing guitar and recordings of Roy Wooliver's fiddling that Gordon McCann obtained from Teague are being made available on the Internet by Missouri State University, as part of the McCann Collection of Ozarks fiddle music (http://www.digitalcollections.missouristate.edu).

46. Spoken narrative, *Hamilton Ironworks*.

47. Jim Nelson and Mike Seeger produced a CD reissue of some Cousin Emmy performances: *Cousin Emmy and Her Kinfolks, 1937–1949* (Bear Family, 2007).

48. Spoken narrative, *Hamilton Ironworks* CD. There is a common folk expression in Missouri to describe poor fiddling, that one is fiddling "like you're fighting snakes" (Pete McMahan, Taylor McBaine).

49. For example, John Hartford, "Old Time Tunes: 'Wolves a-Howlin'"; "John Hartford Tune Transcriptions: 'Hamilton Iron Works.'"

50. Jim Nelson writes that fiddle scholar and English professor at Middle Tennessee State University Charles Wolfe, an acquaintance of Hartford's, had obtained the original reels of tape from Hartford and around 1999 sent them to Nelson in St. Louis. A friend of Nelson's digitized the tapes and made CD copies for several interested people (including me); the original tapes are now archived at the Center for Popular Music at Middle Tennessee State. Hartford's transcription of a tune from Walter Alexander, "Knocking at Your Door," is in "John Hartford Tune Transcriptions: 'Darkie's Curly Hair,' 'Knocking at Your Door,' 'Maysville,' 'Better Get Outa My Way.'" Cyril Stinnett's version is in Christeson 2, 44.

51. Goodspeed, *History of Franklin, Jefferson, Washington, Crawford, and Gasconade Counties, Missouri* (Chicago: Goodspeed, 1888), 476; *Hand-Book of Missouri* (St. Louis: Missouri Immigration Society, 1880), 137.

52. Beisswenger and McCann, 186; Ryan's, 30. Cole's is commonly found among Missouri fiddlers (Cole's, 15). Hartford's version is in Stacy Phillips, *The Phillips Collection of Traditional American Fiddle Tunes*, vol. 1, *Hoedowns, Breakdowns, & Reels*, 107.

53. Fiebelman, *Ozark Hills and Neighbors*, 1:43.

4. Missourians Out West

1. I appreciate the advice of Phil and Vivian Williams, Stuart Williams, Gus Garelick, Lew Holt, Belinda Luke, and Tom West.

2. R. D. Lunceford, *Old Blue Tick: Traditional Fiddle Tunes from Missouri* (Santa Rosa, CA: Ceilidh Brothers Music, 1997). Lunceford grew up in Southern California, listening to his father's stories and music brought from Chariton County and learning fiddle tunes from Earl Collins, the expatriate Missouri fiddler who had moved to California. Lunceford lives in Washington State and is a contributor to Internet discussion groups.

3. Linda Danielson, "Fiddling," in *Oregon Folklore*, ed. by Suzi Jones (Eugene: University of Oregon and Oregon Arts Commission, 1977), 84.

4. Kenneth Leivers, "A Short History of Fiddling and of the California State Old-Time Fiddler's Association" (manuscript, spring 1974, retyped by Ernest C. Yoes in 2004); http://www.sandiegofiddler.com.

5. Winchester (Jefferson County) is around twenty-five miles west of Leavenworth on the Missouri River, some fifty miles northwest of Kansas City, Missouri.

6. Mike Matney, November 2, 2007, January 1, 2010.

7. John Howard Reid, *Movie Westerns: Hollywood Films the Wild, Wild West* (Raleigh, NC: LuLu Press, 2006), 191.

8. Danielson, "Fiddling," 84. Other areas are the upper Plains states of Minnesota, North Dakota, South Dakota, and Nebraska as well as Canada. Oregon and Washington State are especially interesting for the imprint of Missouri-derived fiddle music as it moved west because much research has been done there by Danielson, Lew Holt, Phil and Vivian Williams, and Stuart Williams.

9. This and other Earl Willis quotes are from a transcription of Danielson interviews for the Oregon Old-Time Fiddlers Project, June 1976 (courtesy Lew Holt); edits have been made for readability. The conflating of Missouri's different cultural-geographic regions into "the Ozarks" is a common occurrence, just as Missourians might think Oregon is made up entirely of forests, extinct volcanoes, and beaches.

10. Steve Young, November 8, 2009; Lloyd Shaw, *Cowboy Dances* (Caldwell, ID: Caxton, 1952) was a popular guide in the revival of square dancing in the 1940s and 1950s, particularly in the Midwest and West: "Swing at the Wall," 178.

11. An example of "Sally Goodin" as a square-dance figure is in Karen Mulrenin, Rita Saeger, and Terry Brandt, "Old-Time Ozark Square Dancing," *OzarksWatch* 2, no. 1 (1974): 22–37.

12. Willis, November 11, 1980, Eugene, Oregon, program, hosted by Danielson (recorded by Lew Holt).

13. Walter D. McQuie Jr. via Marjorie Miller, Montgomery County Historical Society, Wellsville, February 5, 2009.

14. The German band, with several accordions, was probably from one of the German-speaking communities along the Missouri River in southern Montgomery, Warren, and Callaway Counties or across the river in Osage, Gasconade, or Franklin Counties.

15. Pete McMahan, who was from a few miles south of Mineola, often told me that as a teenager in the mid-1930s, he watched a neighboring farmer drive his emaciated and weakened cattle into the Missouri River rather than continue to see them stumble and die in barren pastures; the farmer reasoned that perhaps a few of the calves could swim and survive long enough to be pulled to shore by someone downstream who would be able to feed them.

16. Thirteenth Census of the United States for Carter Township, village of Van Buren, 1910, courtesy Vivian Williams.

17. Vivian Williams, November 22, 2009.

18. Ibid., May 11, 2016.

19. See Phillips, *Phillips Collection*, 1:169; and Gene Silberberg, *Fiddle Tunes I Either Did or Did Not Learn at the Tractor Tavern*, 109. Jim Herd's version is on *Jim Herd: Old Time Ozark Fiddling* (Voyager VRCD340).

20. The 1969 LP *Comin' Round the Mountain: Old-Time Southern Singing and Playing in Western Washington* (Voyager VRCD302), http://www.voyagerrecords.com.

21. Osage genes indicate blood ties to Native Americans before the Trail of Tears brought Cherokee and other tribes to Missouri. The Osage were encountered by French explorers and priests coming from Canada to explore the Upper Mississippi in the 1600s and to claim territory for France. The early Osage men were unusually tall for the time and place (averaging well over six feet tall) and famous for their strength and fighting abilities, particularly in combat on foot against adversaries on horseback. The Osage assimilated into the European community and were prominent in early St. Louis and development of the fur trade. Eventually, the tribe was pushed to a reservation in Oklahoma. See Marshall, *Play Me Something Quick and Devilish*, chap. 8.

22. Shrum's first movie job was in Gene Autry's movie *The Old Barn Dance* (Republic, 1938). The Rhythm Rangers appeared in movies by cowboy actors such as Charles Starrett, Tex Ritter, and Johnny Mack Brown. http://www.b-westerns.com.

23. *Dial*, June 1947, 1, 8.

24. The lead comment in album notes by M. Bryan Baker for *Ron Hughey: Country Fiddlin' Ozark Style* (Caldwell, ID: American Heritage AH-402-511, 1973). I thank Gus Garelick for improving these pages on Hughey and Horace (Tom) Riddle. Hughey's accompanists on the LP were John Davis (banjo), Ron Trammell (guitar), Steve Duncan (snare drum), and Norman Belt (bass).

25. Baker album notes, *Ron Hughey*. See Hank Bradley, "Ron Hughey—Some Memories," *Old-Time Herald* 6, no. 3 (1998): 26–27, 56; and Beisswenger and McCann, "Ron Hughey," in Beisswenger and McCann, 192.

26. Gus Garelick interview with Hughey, July 1973; Garelick, December 18, 2009.

27. Garelick, November 24, 2009; Hugh Farr was an influential swing and jazz fiddler in the early days of western swing on the West Coast and recorded numerous records. Gus Garelick, "Hugh Farr," *Fiddler Magazine* 21, no. 1 (2014): 54–55.

28. *Country Fiddlin' Ozark Style*. While some fiddlers' "Cricket on the Hearth" is more like the bluegrass version as popularized by Kenny Baker, Hughey's version hews to the traditional Missouri tune "Marmaduke's Hornpipe."

29. "Sally in the Garden" is an A-minor tune learned from Dad Crockett, leader of "Crockett's Mountaineers," a Kentucky family string band who recorded in the late 1920s and who also had moved to California and lived near Hughey in the Fresno area. Another of Hughey's tunes, "Pig Ankle Rag," is notated in David Brody, *The Fiddler's Fakebook*, 217; and Stacy Phillips, *The Phillips Collection of Traditional American Fiddle Tunes*, vol. 2, *Rags, Blues, Hornpipes, Waltzes, Polkas, Jigs, Etc.*, 100. For "Missouri Waltz" (originally called "The Graveyard Waltz"), see Marshall, *Play Me Something Quick and Devilish*, chap. 10.

30. *Country Fiddlin' Ozark Style*; "Yellow Gals," in Carl Baron, "Workshop," 37; Beisswenger and McCann, 192.

31. Recorded July 1973, Hughey home, Fowler, CA, courtesy Garelick, December 18, 2009. Other titles for "Stony Point," once common across Missouri and dating from colonial times, include "Wild Horse on Stony Point" and Gene Goforth's title "Hop Skip Squirrel" (Goforth, *Eminence Breakdown*, Rounder 0388, 1997). Lyman Enloe's version (as "Stony Point") is on his LP *Fiddle Tunes I Recall* (1978; reissue, County CO-CD-2702, 1993). "Stony Point" is in Christeson 1 as played by Bob Walter (99).

32. Gus Garelick, email, January 15, 2010.

33. Leivers, "Short History of Fiddling."

34. Marshall, *Play Me Something Quick and Devilish*, 193–200.

35. Judy Smith Schuerer, August 28, 2013.

36. Portland, Fast birthday party, 1998; courtesy Lew Holt, November 2007.

37. Minnie Bennett, "Bob Fast: Fiddler of the Month, for December 1978," in *The Hoedowner* (Oregon Old-Time Fiddlers Association, courtesy Lew Holt). See also Linda Danielson interview with Fast, Oregon Old-Time Fiddlers Project, ca. 1976.

38. Dulcie Fast, letter to Lew Holt, July 25, 2013.

39. Ibid.

40. Ibid.

41. D. Fast, notes for Judith Scheurer, June 2013. These are big names in fiddle music and swing music in the Northwest. Bob Fast joined the Oregon State Oldtime Fiddlers' Association in 1971, and this organization hosted many events.

42. The gold standard for "Fisher's Hornpipe" (composed in the United States in the late eighteenth century) in the key of F is by Callaway County fiddler Jake Hockemeyer (1965), on the companion CD with *Play Me Something Quick and Devilish.*

43. "Autumn Waltz" was transcribed and arranged by Susie Anderson, and Stacy Phillips's transcription appears in *Phillips Collection*, 2:239. Gayle Clarity notated several Bob Fast tunes in 2001.

44. Tom West, December 3, 2005.

45. Eastview was the name of the rural community several miles southeast of Brown Branch and south of McClurg; a post office existed from 1901 to 1908. Arthur Pat Moser, comp., "A Directory of Towns, Villages, and Hamlets Past and Present of Taney County, Missouri" (manuscript, Springfield Library); Elmo Ingenthron, *The Land of Taney: A History of an Ozark Commonwealth* (Point Lookout, MO: School of the Ozarks Press, 1974), 468. The land having been taken into Mark Twain National Forest and most of the families removed, Eastview no longer appears on maps.

46. Album notes, *Old Time Ozark Fiddling*: "The Washington Traditional Fiddlers Project was a research project funded by the National Endowment for the Arts and the Washington State Arts Commission, initiated by the Centrum Foundation and continued by the Seattle Folklore Society and Northwest Folklife."

47. Beisswenger and McCann, 58ff; V. Williams, album notes, Herd, *Old Time Ozark Fiddling.*

48. *Traditional Fiddle Music of the Ozarks*, vol. 1 (see chap. 3, n. 13).

49. Album notes, Herd, *Old Time Ozark Fiddling.*

50. "Tennessee Gray Eagle" is transcribed in Stuart Williams, comp., *Evergreen Fiddler Tune Book*, vol. 1; "Monkey in the Dog Cart" is in *Evergreen Fiddler*, vols. 2–3, and is on the companion CD with Marshall, *Play Me Something Quick and Devilish.*

51. Album notes, *Old Time Ozark Fiddling.*

52. Notes, *Old Time Ozark Fiddling.*

53. "Zenda" is an alternate title for "La Zenda Waltz," a.k.a. "Lucenda Waltz," a Canadian tune composed by Frank M. Witmark, ca. 1896, as music for a staged version of the novel by Anthony Hope *The Prisoner of Zenda*. Notated in Don Messer, *Anthology of Favorite Fiddle Tunes* (Pacific, MO: Mel Bay, 1980), 114–15; and Phillips, *Phillips Collection*, 2:330.

5. Contests

1. My experiences in fiddling contests run the gamut from curious observer to photographer, sound recordist, guitar accompanist, contestant, emcee, judge, organizer, donor, and custodian. I began by playing backup guitar for fiddlers in contests in the late 1960s and soon started trudging up the path of competing and judging.

2. See Steve Kirtley, "Fiddle Contests through the Years," *Fiddler Magazine* 1, no. 2 (1994): 36–37; *Virginia Gazette* 17 (November 19–November 26, 1736). Eighteenth-century spellings have been adjusted for contemporary reading (*s* for *ſ*).

3. As seen in various editions of the *Virginia Gazette*. See Helen Cripe, *Thomas Jefferson and Music* (Charlottesville: University Press of Virginia, 1974), 10, quoting Albert L. Stoutamire, "A History of Music in Richmond, Virginia, from 1742 to 1865" (PhD diss., Florida State University, 1960), 10–11. Among other contests in this period reported in the *Virginia Gazette* (Williamsburg) was one in October 1737 announcing a singing contest ("a quire of ballads [to be] sung for"), a dancing contest ("a pair of handsome shoes danced for"), and a fiddlers contest: "that a violin be played for by 20 fiddlers and be given to him that be adjudged to play the best. After the prize is won they are all to play together and each a different tune, and to be treated by the company" (FIDDLE-L Internet discussion group posting by Scott O'Dell, January 20, 2005).

4. Robin Burnett and Ken Luebbering, *German Settlement in Missouri: New Land, Old Ways* (Columbia: University of Missouri Press, 1996), 89–90.

5. "Jones Is Champion," *Monroe County (MO) Appeal*, February 16, 1923, 1.

6. This division of the state has been echoed in many ways, with the central section of Missouri targeted by both cities. In the central sections of Missouri, papers from both cities were read, and fans were sought by baseball teams in St. Louis and Kansas City, bracketing the state geographically. For example, in the north-central Missouri town of Moberly where I grew up, near Paris, Mexico, Columbia, and Macon, the St. Louis Cardinals were the best-loved baseball team. It is hard for us today to appreciate the importance and relevance that the daily newspapers from St. Louis and Kansas City as well as local papers had in people's lives.

7. This was a well-known novelty tune in former times and allowed the fiddler to interject some fun and audience appeal into a performance. Like "Indian War Whoop," "Lost Indian" could be impressively delivered, with a fiddler imitating war cries or lonesome wails by careful bowing, augmented by the fiddler's vocal effects.

8. Most likely, Lewellen was "pulling the leg" of the uninformed or misinformed reporter from the big city.

9. "Old Time Fiddlers 'Hit 'Er Up' on Forefathers Tunes," *Moberly (MO) Monitor-Index and Evening Democrat*, December 27, 1921, 1–3. According to Andrew Kuntz, "Mulberry Gap" is a tune known in Kentucky and Georgia (http://www.celtic.stanford.edu/pub/tunes). This title and "Matches from the Wood" are unfamiliar titles today and may have been in the 1920s as well. Oregon fiddler Earl Willis from Mineola, Missouri, recalled that at central Missouri fiddlers contests in the 1920s, "Whoever played 'Grey Eagle' the best usually won." Willis, November 11, 1980, Eugene, OR, program hosted by Linda Danielson, recorded by Lew Holt.

10. In the many newspaper articles of the time, Oliver's initials appear variously as J. L., J. J., J. O., and J. A. "J. A." is correct; he went by the name "Aaron." *Monroe County (MO) Appeal*, May 11, 1923, 1. R. I. (Si) Colburn was Nipps's colleague in developing the contests at Paris; it is believed that some of the fiddlers writing letters to contest administrator Paul

Nipps for entry lived in places that did not put on a qualifying contest. Some of the contestants apparently gained admission to the fracas by reputation alone, as established players with credentials in the region, because the Paris administrators attempted to attract as many of the best fiddlers in Missouri as they could.

11. "Taylor Defies Brown," *Monroe County (MO) Appeal*, May 18, 1923, 1.

12. Ibid. The same article gives additional names of fiddlers entered in the contest: A. O. Porter (Coatesville, Schuyler County), J. Wesley Murphy (Mexico, Audrain County), and "the winner of the *St. Louis Times* contest, whose name has not been announced."

13. "After Wood Brown Scalp," *Monroe County (MO) Appeal*, March 23, 1923, 1.

14. "Ready for Fiddle Feast: Old-Time Artists from Far and Near Are Tuning Up for the State Championship Contest at Paris," *Monroe County (MO) Appeal*, April 13, 1923, 1.

15. "Noted Men Coming," *Monroe County (MO) Appeal*, April 27, 1923, 3. Daniel Boone Jones at this time lived in northeastern Callaway County, across Cedar Creek from Boone County, his later residence.

16. "Ready for the Fiddlingfest," *Monroe County (MO) Appeal*, May 23, 1923, 1. We cannot determine whether the film footage was produced and shown at movie theaters as part of the weekly Pathé newsreels. An article in the *Appeal* on June 15, 1923 (1), "Showing Fiddling Films This Week," announces that a film made at the request of the Opera House (Paris's stage and movie venue) would be shown in the coming days, along with Rudolph Valentino starring in the Hollywood movie *The Young Raja*.

17. "Henry Taylor Wins in Tuneful Triumph," *Monroe County (MO) Appeal*, June 1, 1923, 3.

18. Charlie Walden, "Henry Taylor: A Fiddle Champ from Yesteryear." Louie Barton was a popular fiddler who had developed a live radio program called *Barn Dance* on WOS in 1924, before fiddling was programmed on Nashville's WSM. Walden, "'Mythical' Fiddle Championship," 4.

19. The key articles on Morris are Walden, "Tracking Down the Legendary 'Sheriff'" and "The Life and Legacy of George Morris, the 'Fiddling Sheriff.'"

20. "Henry Taylor Wins in Tuneful Triumph."

21. Betty Ransdell Canaday (Mrs. Leroy Canaday) was a nephew of Clate Ransdell, whose Cherokee ancestors came to Missouri on the Trail of Tears in the early nineteenth century. "Uncle Clate'd play Lost Indian, made the hair stand up on your head." Among Ransdell's first-place wins was a major contest featuring fiddlers from Missouri, Iowa, and Illinois, sometime in the 1930s (personal communication, Moberly, October 28, 2000). Among fiddlers who learned much from Ransdell was Frank Reed of Overland (originally Huntsville). Reed's father, fiddler Thomas Reed, was a good friend of Ransdell's. Frank Reed plays "Fox Chase," learned from Clate Ransdell, on his 1976 LP record, *Ole Tyme Fiddlin'* (Overland, Frank Reed, TS76-922-923).

22. There are many "Lost Indian" fiddle tunes. This one, played at Paris by several fiddlers in the 1920s, is not the same tune as "Lonesome Indian," a familiar tune today that is related to "Cherokee Shuffle," which was popularized by radio fiddlers in the 1930s and 1940s. One example of the older "Lost Indian" tune, as played by Bob Holt, is in Beisswenger and McCann, 63 (on *Holt's Got a Little Home to Go To* recording). Most Missouri fiddlers play the "Cherokee Shuffle"–related "Lost Indian" in part thanks to popular recordings of the tune by Kenny Baker. Some of the titles reported were inaccurate, some may be personal title variations, and

some titles have become confused over the years. The tune most people play today, titled "Lost Indian" by Kenny Baker and others, is historically titled "Lonesome Indian."

23. It cannot be known whether Taylor was actually playing "Sally Gooden" with an alternate title, but, based on the words he sang, it seems likely. No such tune by the title given is familiar in my experience.

24. "Henry Taylor Wins in Tuneful Triumph."

25. "It Never Fails," *Monroe County (MO) Appeal*, June 1, 1923, 2.

26. This photo-feature page appears to have been lost; it does not appear in the June 10, 1923, edition of the *Globe-Democrat* in The State Historical Society of Missouri's microfilmed newspaper collection.

27. "Wood All Tuned and Ready," *Monroe County (MO) Appeal*, April 9, 1926, 1.

28. Other fiddlers were promoted in the paper as well, such as "Fiddlin' Dave Hanna," Frank Tanzy, William Taft, and Jim Clark. "Fiddlers Are Gettin' In," *Monroe County (MO) Appeal*, April 9, 1926, 1.

29. "Brown Retains Wreath," *Monroe County (MO) Appeal*, April 23, 1926, 1.

30. "Fiddlin' and Then Some," *Monroe County (MO) Appeal*, April 2, 1926, 3.

31. Ibid.

32. "A Battle of Champions: Nothing but Champions Will Enter State Contest Here Saturday," *Monroe County (MO) Appeal*, April 30, 1926, 1.

33. *Monroe County (MO) Appeal*, May 7, 1926, 1. The judges for the elimination round were J. O. Oliver, Lloyd Heathman of Hannibal, and Gus Trusdell (Truesdell) of Bates County, all of them respected fiddlers.

34. Contestants who did not make the finals included one or two familiar names, but many we know only through the newspaper articles; W. O. Rigney (Marion County), J. W. Parr (Barton County), Z. A. Coleman (Jefferson County, undoubtedly Isadore [Zedore] Coleman, the legendary French American fiddler from Cadet), Jack Shaneyfelt (Johnson County), O. M. Sebers (Ralls County), William Miller (Knox County), Joe Hicks (Scotland County), William Stalcup (Shelby County), W. D. Settle (Howard County), Albert Claybrook (Macon County), and Clyde Fox (Audrain County).

35. "Taylor Won State Fiddling Contest," *Monroe County (MO) Appeal*, May 7, 1926, 1.

36. Walden, "Life and Legacy of George Morris" (1985), 8. It appears that Morris had won a preliminary contest in Joplin, with some 102 contestants, to gain entry to the state contest in Paris.

37. "Taylor Won State Fiddling Contest." For the celebrated interstate contest in Jeff City over WOS radio, see Huber, "Interstate Old Fiddlers Contest of 1926" (see chap. 1, n. 2).

38. Walden, "Life and Legacy of George Morris" (1985), 8. See also Galloway, "Sam Long" (see chap. 1, n. 58).

39. Here Woods calls upon popular notions of industrialist Henry Ford as a lover of old-time fiddling and knowledgeable judge of the music.

40. "Wood Brown Wants to Meet H'y Taylor," *Monroe County (MO) Appeal*, May 14, 1926, 1.

41. Donna Taylor Hook, October 30, 2000, April 23, 2001. I appreciate Ms. Hook's assistance and guidance regarding her grandfather Henry Taylor.

42. When Henry Taylor died at age seventy-five in a highway accident in December 1940 (an intoxicated person was driving the Taylor Chevrolet pickup truck; Henry was a passenger)

on US 24, east of Milton, my father, Charles Marshall, witnessed the accident and testified at the coroner's inquest. *Moberly (MO) Monitor-Index and Evening Democrat*, December 28, 1940, 1; *Macon (MO) Chronicle-Herald*, December 30, 1940. Henry Taylor's father, James B. Taylor, came from Fayette County, Kentucky, to Randolph County in the same time period (1830s) as my mother's great-grandfather James F. R. Wight, who founded the farm along the highway (originally a plan road from Hannibal to Glasgow) where Henry Taylor died in the 1940 automobile accident.

43. Marshall, *Folk Architecture in Little Dixie*.

44. R. Douglas Hurt, *Agriculture and Slavery in Missouri's Little Dixie* (Columbia: University of Missouri Press, 1992); and Marshall, *Folk Architecture in Little Dixie* and "Little Dixie," in *Encyclopedia of Southern Culture*, edited by C. Wilson and W. Ferris (Chapel Hill: University of North Carolina Press, 1989), 572–73.

45. These central Missouri races were a distinctive link to horse racing and specific horses back in Kentucky. To be asked to start a county fair horse race was a great honor, and at Little Dixie races, the invited starters triggering the pistol tended to include former Confederate army heroes and pro-South politicians, and even Frank James, the former Confederate guerrilla and retired bank robber, did the honors at several races near Paris, Huntsville, and Moberly, while being sought by the Pinkertons at the time.

46. *Macon (MO) Daily Chronicle-Herald*, July 5, 1922, 1.

47. *Macon (MO) Daily Chronicle-Herald*, September 5, 1922, 1.

48. *Macon (MO) Daily Chronicle-Herald*, September 28, 1922, 1. Many knew of Bob Taylor. Robert L. Taylor was a senator and three-time Democratic Tennessee governor in the later nineteenth century. His brother Alfred (Alf) Taylor was a Republican and competed for the same office. Bob and Alf Taylor were both old-time fiddlers who competed in contests. Bob Taylor's fiddling against the well-known Fiddlin' John Carson at a famous Atlanta fiddlers' convention contest in the 1920s was the inspiration for Stephen Vincent Benet's "The Mountain Whippoorwill; or, How Hill-Billy Jim Won the Great Fiddler's Prize," which in turn inspired the late-twentieth-century country music recording by Charlie Daniels, "The Devil Went Down to Georgia." See Gene Wiggins, *Fiddlin' Georgia Crazy: Fiddlin' John Carson, His Real World, and the World of His Songs* (Urbana: University of Illinois Press, 1987). Other fiddling politicians have ranged from President Thomas Jefferson and David Crockett to Senators Albert Gore Sr. and Robert Byrd. See also Guthrie T. Meade, *Fiddle Contests and Conventions* (program booklet, Festival of American Folklife, Smithsonian Institution, 1968), 33.

49. "Arkansas Traveler" is taken up elsewhere.

50. Entrants in the September 5, 1922, Macon Old Settlers contest included Bill Harris (Kirksville, Adair County, a blind fiddler), S. D. Shoemaker (New Cambria, Macon County), M. D. Richardson (Clarence, Monroe County), Douglas Cook (Macon County), S. S. Phipps (Callao, Macon County), J. (James) T. Miles (Macon), J. H. Tracy (Macon), John N. Johnson (Macon), F. G. Turner (Ethel, Macon County), and C. A. Terry (College Mound, Macon County).

51. "Men of the Fiddle and Bow," *Macon (MO) Daily Chronicle-Herald*, October 4, 1922, 1–3; "Henry Taylor Some Fiddler," *Moberly (MO) Weekly*, November 16, 1922, 6.

52. This word "welkin" may be unfamiliar to readers today but in former times was a common vernacular usage meaning the sky, the heavens.

53. This comment is confusing, because "Tennessee Wagner" was an ironclad in the central and northern Missouri fiddler's tune kit, and virtually every old-time fiddler had a version of it. The title given here, "Wagoner," may be the source of the confusion, a title often used instead of the more historically correct "Wagner" ("Tennessee Wagner").

54. "Men of the Fiddle and Bow." This is almost exactly the same article (also signed "From the St. Louis Star") in "Henry Taylor Some Fiddler."

55. Edgar White, "Jazz v. the Arkansaw Traveler," *Musical Courier* (November 20, 1924), reprinted in Karl Koenig, ed., *Jazz in Print (1856–1929): An Anthology of Selected Early Readings in Jazz History* (Hillsdale, NY: Pendragon Press, 2002), 363–64.

56. "Wood Brown Wins Fiddling Contest," *Moberly (MO) Monitor-Index and Evening Democrat*, October 11, 1929.

6. Shows

1. See Thomas A. Adler, *Bean Blossom: The Brown County Jamboree and Bill Monroe's Bluegrass Festival*, chap. 4. After acquiring official ownership of the existing park in 1976, "Monroe began immediately to call the whole place 'Brown County Jamboree Park'" (53).

2. I appreciate the assistance of Ed McKinney, Gordon McCann, Michael Breid, Mark Olson, Bob Hagan, Jim Orchard, Kenny Seaman, and Tom Adler in the preparation of this chapter.

3. "Opry" is more inclusive, while "barn dance" emits a more exclusive air. The word "opry" cannot be copyrighted, as proved in a failed case by WSM's *Grand Ole Opry* owners against Dennis Hilton (who operated an opry hall at the Lake of the Ozarks) in the early 1980s. Lee Mace testified for Hilton as a witness (Dan William Peek, July 7, 2010). Numerous *Grand Ole Opry* stars testified for WSM (Roy Acuff, Minnie Pearl, Porter Wagoner). As recalled by Judge Scott O. Wright, who adjudicated the case in Kansas City federal court, "Hilton's lawyers did a good job of putting on evidence about how 'opry' had been used in a countrified version of the word 'opera' dating back to the 1700s and how it had been used to describe a show consisting of country music, dancing, and comedy routines. . . . As I saw it, no one who attended Hilton's show at the Lake of the Ozarks would mistakenly think they were at the Grand Ole Opry in Nashville. As I saw it, the word 'opry' was part of the public domain and could not be trademarked by anybody." Scott O. Wright with Larry M. Schumaker, *Never in Doubt: Memoirs of an Uncommon Judge* (Kansas City: Kansas City Star Books, 2007), 105. Among works on the country music industry, see Richard A. Peterson, *Creating Country Music: Fabricating Authenticity* (Chicago: University of Chicago Press, 1997); Richard Peterson and Paul Di Maggio, "The Early Opry: Its Hillbilly Image in Fact and Fancy"; and Charles Wolfe's several works cited elsewhere. McKinney discusses radio and traditional music in chap. 6 of "Images, Realities, and Cultural Transformations."

4. Glenn, *Ozarks' Greatest Hits*, 266. For the Jubilee (1954–60), see McKinney, "Images, Realities, and Cultural Transformations," 94, 368ff; and Reta Spears-Stewart, *Remembering the Ozark Jubilee "Starring Red Foley."*

5. Rebecca L. Snider discusses the Farris Theatre in "The Show Must Go On! A Plan for Rehabilitating an Historic Theatre: Case Studies of Three Historic Theatre Rehabilitations in Missouri" (PhD diss., University of Missouri, 1999), 87ff.

6. Dawn L. Niceley, "The Corn Crib Theatre, a Long Surviving Professional Toby Company," *Mid-America Folklore* 22, no. 1 (1994): 1. "The term 'Toby show,' in its heyday, denoted a traveling vaudeville-type melodramatic tent show. It was basically a vaudeville show with a plot that

included one dominant character Toby. Toby is defined . . . as 'a stock character in the folk theatre of the United States, a bucolic comedy juvenile leading man in provincial repertoire companies of the Mississippi Valley and the Great Southwest.'" Elbert Bowen's *Theatrical Entertainments in Rural Missouri before the Civil War* (Columbia: University of Missouri Press, 1959) offers background to today's stage shows and oprys but does not include the vernacular figure Toby.

7. An elephant was the drawing card for traveling circuses and led to the vernacular expression in everyday speech, to express wonder at having seen a remarkable thing or summarize a person's unusual experiences and hardships: "I've seen the elephant."

8. Bowen, *Theatrical Entertainments in Rural Missouri*, 19.

9. "By leaving the hopelessly compromised word 'country' behind and exclusively using the term 'Ameripolitan', our intention is to reestablish this music's own unique identity, elevate its significance and help reinvigorate it creatively. Also, because of our place in history, we have the privilege and responsibility to pass a great musical tradition on to future generations who will otherwise have no direct connection to this music" (http://www.ameripolitan.com, June 28, 2015).

10. http://www.bransonshows.com, June 28, 2015.

11. Drew Beisswenger, "Jam Sessions in Southwest Missouri," 2006 video series, http://www.library,missouristate.edu.

12. Some of this material appears in Howard Wight Marshall, "Live! At the Ozark Opry: An Appreciation of Vaudeville and 'Show Fiddler' LeRoy Haslag" as well as *Play Me Something Quick and Devilish* (154–59ff). See Peek, *Live! At the Ozark Opry*. Television footage and a biography of Lee Mace are available from the Miller County Historical Society at http://www.millercountymuseum.org.

13. Peek, *Live! At the Ozark Opry*, 53; Peek, "Memories of That Mountain Music: Lee Mace's Ozark Opry Is the Birthplace of 'Branson-Style' Entertainment," *Rural Missouri Magazine* (April 2011): 10–11; Glenn, *Ozarks' Greatest Hits*, and *Down the Road from Nixa* (Cassville: Litho Printers 2007). For the lake area, see H. Dwight Weaver, *History & Geography of the Lake of the Ozarks*, 2 vols. (Eldon, MO: Osage River Trails, 2005), and *Lake of the Ozarks: The Early Years* (Chicago: Arcadia, 2000). For the Springfield area, see McKinney, "Images, Realities, and Cultural Transformations" and "Like Family."

14. Bill Monroe and His Bluegrass Boys, "Pike County Breakdown" (45 rpm, Decca 28352, 1952).

15. Lonnie Hoppers, May 23, 2013.

16. Les Gotcher appears in 1950s square-dance association newsletters in New England, such as the *Square Dance Caller*. A 1962 talk by Gotcher on his style of "Modern Western" calling style is archived in the Square Dance History Project, http://www.squaredancehistory.org (April 2, 2016). In Hollywood, California, Gotcher issued 78 rpm records on the McGregor Records label with his calls and accompaniment by the Circle 8 Ranch Boys; Gotcher also published a dance instructor titled *Les Gotcher on Sight Calling*.

17. McCoy and Stamper played acoustic guitars, Penny a Gibson electric guitar or Gibson A model mandolin, and Newman played a Fender electric steel guitar (the first steel guitarist on *The Ozark Opry*). Lonnie Hoppers, April 1, 2016.

18. Howard Wight Marshall, "Keep on the Sunny Side of Life: Pattern and Religious Expression in Bluegrass Gospel Music," 1–43, reprinted in Special Studies #30, John Edwards Memorial Foundation, UCLA. I indicate how the gospel number has been a necessary part of performances since the 1920s.

19. Peek, *Live! At the Ozark Opry*, 47.

20. Peek, October 16, 2010.

21. I thank Phil Williams for pointing out this anecdote and book. Lawrence Welk with Bernice McGeehan, *Wunnerful, Wunnerful! The Autobiography of Lawrence Welk* (Englewood Cliffs, NJ: Prentice Hall, 1971), 70–71. Part of what Kelly told Welk was "Lawrence, wherever you go you leave an impression. Now it's up to you whether you leave a good one or a bad one" (71).

22. Soon after, Welk invited the *Opry*'s multi-instrumentalist and comedian Bill Atterberry to join his orchestra, but Atterberry declined (LeRoy Haslag, September 17, 2010).

23. *Hillbilly music* has become an acceptable term to many insiders, even while most Ozarkers reject the term *hillbilly* to describe their region and culture; *hill people* is more acceptable. "'Hillbilly' carries within the word a connotation of condescension; the term is universally anathema to native hill people of the Ozarks." McKinney, "Images, Realities, and Cultural Transformations," 38; on tourism, 273ff.

24. Breid, October 13, 2013; Hartford, preface to *Fiddler's Curse: The Untold Story of Ervin T. Rouse, Chubby Wise, Johnny Cash, and the Orange Blossom Special*, by Randy Noles, iv.

25. Breid, September 6, 2010.

26. Peek, October 16, 2010.

27. Jim Russell, March 6, 2015.

28. Porter Waggoner departed to seek fame and fortune in Nashville, where he dropped one *g* from his name.

29. Orchard, June 6, 2015.

30. Hoppers, May 23, 2013.

31. Lee Mace and His Ozark Opry Gang, Starday SEP152, EP, 1960 (courtesy Jim Russell). Starday was a small but influential independent label that issued country music and bluegrass from 1953 to 1968. See Nathan D. Gibson and Don Pierce, *The Starday Story: The House That Country Music Built* (Jackson: University Press of Mississippi, 2011).

32. Peek, *Live! At the Ozark Opry*, 65.

33. Canaday, October 6, 2000.

34. Ibid.

35. The band this evening was composed of seasoned musicians in the region, none of them a full-time professional: Bill Potts (lead guitar and leader), Ron Pashia (drums, vocals), "Grandma" (Adelaide Minor, vocals, keyboard), Bill Cornelius (bass guitar), Glen Cornelius (Bill's brother, electric guitar), and Adelaide and J. W. Minor's daughter, Sheila (lead singer, rhythm guitar).

36. In 2001 Canaday recorded a fiddle CD, *Old Dan Tucker Was a Fine Old Man: Missouri Fiddler Leroy Canaday* (Voyager VRCD353).

37. Ron Lutz checked this discussion and made improvements (October 5, 2010). I also appreciate the guidance of Bob Hagan, Mark Olson, Heather Roberson, and Margot Ford McMillen in the *Rooster Creek* story.

38. Lutz, May 8, 2003.

39. As indicated in a promotional photo while Ron was a deejay on the Brookfield radio station. See Woody Adkins, "Ron Lutz," on *Midnight Country*, KOPN 89.5 FM, http://www.midnightcountry.org (October 8, 2010). The website includes historical photos and

recollections. Ron telephoned Woody on the air during *Midnight Country* and visited about music and old times, and Ron mentored Woody as a deejay. Eventually, Lutz's weight increased to more than four hundred pounds.

40. Hagan, October 16, 2014.

41. Around 2006 an all-female string band of Fulton and Columbia musicians, several of whom had been guests at *Rooster Creek* sessions, called themselves the Rooster Creek Girls: Karen Howard, Margot McMillen, Pippa Letsky, and guests Emily Parsons and Laura Idle.

42. "Seth Bradley, of Mokane, Won First Prize in the Fiddler's Contest Held in the Fulton Theatre," in "Callaway Memoirs," *Fulton (MO) Sun*, June 17, 2007, 6, reprinted from *Fulton (MO) Daily Sun-Gazette*, June 17, 1932.

43. Photos of Haley, Pappy Cheshire, and others appear in Absher, *KMOX*, 28, 47, 70ff (see chap. 1, n. 43).

44. "Callaway Memoirs," *Fulton (MO) Sun*, June 5, 2006, 5, reprinted from *Fulton (MO) Daily Sun-Gazette*, June 5, 1981.

45. Howard Hinckley, *Midnight Country*, KOPN 89.5 FM, http://www.midnightcountry.org (October 9, 2010).

46. Station break, KFAL, July 12, 2008. There are exceptions, such as community FM stations, such as Columbia's KOPN, Rolla's KUMR, and KDHX in St. Louis. The digital revolution has brought numerous satellite-feed programs that do indeed feature classic country music and old-time fiddling. In fact, the Internet allows and encourages programming in discrete and sometimes arcane listening preferences.

47. Ron Lutz, *Jack of Diamonds*, produced by Kirby Crane (Jefferson City: Hot City Productions, 2007).

7. Opry Entrepreneurs and Born Showmen

1. In other parts of Missouri, particularly central and northern areas, the country church fellowship hall also provided space for various community events, including music parties and dances. In the Carter and Shannon Counties area, the generally conservative Protestant tenor of the community augured against dancing, especially on church property.

2. Jim Orchard, June 26, 2015.

3. I thank Jim Orchard, Ed McKinney, Clarence Crider, and Kenny Seaman for their assistance in piecing together the chronology and details in this discussion.

4. Kenny Seaman, July 11, 2015. Many cultural ties existed (and still exist) between the eastern Ozarks region around Eminence. Numerous young men have had to leave to seek employment in the city.

5. Among members of the Current River Drifters (Seaman, banjo) were Andy Bressler (guitar), Don Millinger (bass), Jim Orchard (mandolin), and Clark Weaver and Charley Martin (violin). The band appears on the 1974 compilation LP *Grass Cuttin' Time in Missouri* (St. Louis: Missouri Area Bluegrass Committee, MABC-LP101): Jim Orchard's brother Rich, Frank Ray, and the Ramblin' Bluegrass Boys (Orchard, guitar; Ray, mandolin; Norman Clark, banjo; Stan Wagganer, violin; and Woody Woods, bass), and they also appear on *Grass Cuttin' Time in Missouri*. Among newspaper features about the Current River Opry and Seaman, see James P. Sterba, "Bluegrass Music Thrives in the Ozarks," *Springfield (MO) News-Leader*, June

20, 1969, B5 (reprinted from *New York Times*); and Jim Creighton, "In Shannon County, Almost Any Day Is Country Music Day," *St. Louis Post-Dispatch*, April 22, 1973, Sunday Pictures section, 1–11 (courtesy Kenny Seaman).

6. In Colorado banjoist Kenny Seaman helped popularize bluegrass music through his encouragement of bluegrass festivals and his influential band formed in 1980, the Bluegrass Patriots. http://www.bluegrasspatriots.org; http://www.encyclopedia.com.

7. Weaver's RV Park and Campground also supported informal bluegrass and country music jam sessions; a video of one of the jam sessions is featured on a series produced several years ago by Drew Beisswenger (then librarian at Missouri State University, Springfield), http://www.library.missouristate.edu/projects.

8. Ed McKinney, June 16, 2015.

9. Jim Orchard pronounces "hollow" as "holla," although prevailing Missouri pronunciation seems to be "holler." Ink is a humorous name, chosen when village founders could not decide what to send the Post Office Department in the 1880s (as their post office was being planned); they wanted a short name and were paging through a children's book, and someone spilled ink, and they just decided to call the place "Ink." Margot Ford McMillen, *Paris, Tightwad, and Peculiar: Missouri Place Names*, 5.

10. Jim first heard Bill Monroe on *The Grand Ole Opry* radio show in the late 1940s; he would later become acquainted with Monroe and visit Monroe at his farm, and when Monroe died in 1996, he was asked to be an honorary pallbearer at Monroe's funeral in Kentucky.

11. Unless otherwise indicated, quotes are from Jim Orchard, June 6, 2015.

12. Jack Shockley and many other people from the area, including Orchard's uncle Arthur Deatherage, eventually moved to California and other West Coast states to seek a better income and life for their families. According to Jim Orchard, "Lots of starved-out Ozarkians moved out west." "Uncle Arth," a county judge and respected man in Shannon County, settled in Crescent City, California, in 1948, where his brother Clarence had settled during the Great Depression in the 1930s. When Uncle Arth "sold out" (auctioned) the farm and unneeded possessions, he kept his violin out of the sale and gave to young Jim the Stradivarius-copy violin, bow, and canvas case he had ordered from Montgomery Ward in 1922 for five dollars.

13. In 1958 Orchard became a country schoolmaster just as the consolidation of single-teacher rural schools was being completed across the nation.

14. Orchard, June 16, 2015.

15. The substantial theme of the rise and (perhaps) the decline of bluegrass festivals will be treated in a future publication.

16. Orchard has been my guide through the many chambers of Current River Opry history and local lore; Orchard's recordings include Jimmy Orchard and the Ozark Bluegrass Boys, "Longing for the Ozarks"/"Trouble in B" (Cherry Records CH 014, 1972), Orchard, mandolin; Odie Mullins, violin; and Hubert Woolsey, Lew Broadfoot, Guy Stevenson; Jim Orchard, *Front Porch Fiddlin'* (Birch Tree, MO: Jim Orchard, 2003); *Ozarks Fiddlin' from Hartshorn to Low Wassie* (Birch Tree, MO: Orchard, n.d.); Jim Orchard and Devin Quick, *Today and Tomorrow* (Birch Tree, MO, ca. 1999); Orchard Brothers, *McHenry Hollow Fiddlin* (Birch Tree, MO: Jim Orchard, 1995); and Edward James Richard and Friends, *Jimmy Brown the Newsboy* (Mission Music, 2002; Orchard, violin). "Low wassie" (derived from a Native American word) is a dialect term for a rainy spot or a swamp and may have connections to Scots Gaelic. There are "Hiwassie" place-names in North Carolina and Tennessee, from whence came many Ozark

settlers; there is a High Wassie Creek in Oregon County. Margot Ford McMillen, *A to Z Missouri: The Dictionary of Missouri Place Names*, 75.

17. Lennis Leonard Broadfoot, "Pete Counts: 'The Hill Comedian,'" in *Pioneers of the Ozarks*, 68–69 (see chap. 3, n. 17). Broadfoot was an artist in Salem whose charcoal drawings and essays depict Ozark daily life, people, and events. Broadfoot's life and art are featured in the Harlin Museum in West Plains, http://www.harlinmuseum.com.

18. On the companion CD, Ellis's swing fiddling and his twin fiddling in bluegrass bands are represented. Unless otherwise noted, Larry Ellis quotes are from May 5, 2015.

19. Those able to prove allegiance to the United States were also driven from their homes but were allowed to relocate in one of the several towns with Union army garrisons. Bates and Cass Counties are still known as "the Burnt District." For summary of this history, see Duane G. Meyer, *The Heritage of Missouri*, chaps. 10–11; and the Burnt District Museum and Archives in Harrisonville, http://www.casscountyhistoricalsociety.com.

20. Ellis, April 25, 2015; "That Fiddler from Adak," *Missouri Life* 3, no. 3 (1975): 18–23 (courtesy Laura Jolley). A few years after Ellis was on Adak, I was a Marine stationed on Kodiak Island at Marine Barracks, and I share much with Ellis about playing music on military bases and local venues in that period, just before the Vietnam War opened up.

21. Jack Deck was a multi-instrumentalist whose banjo playing can be heard on Pete McMahan's recordings. See McMahan, *50 Old-Time Fiddle Gems* (Voyager VRCD366, 2005).

22. Kansas City Area Bluegrass Music Club, http://www.kcabmc.org. Early Kansas City bluegrass bands such as the Drifters (the Collins family with others), the Bluegrass Brigade, and Green Side Up are discussed in Alison Campbell, "The Tradition of Kansas City Bluegrass," *Bluegrass Unlimited* (November 2008): 40–43, http://www.elkcreekcc.org/files/KC_Bluegrass_2009.pdf. Kansas City has an additional bluegrass and country music group, founded ca. 1990, the Heart of American Bluegrass and Old-Time Music association, which meets in North Kansas City every third Friday of the month (http://www.habot.org).

23. Campbell, "Kansas City Bluegrass," 40.

24. Green Side Up, *How Does Bluegrass Grow?* (eight-track tape, Kansas City: George's Music Service, 1975); *Green Side Up* (Kansas City: Chapman Studios, 1988); *The Missouri Session: A Studio Jam Session with Years of Memories* (Macks Creek: Audio Loft Studios TMS 3033CD, 1990).

25. http://www.bigcreekcountry.com. The show is owned by Cindy and Dennis Dittemore together with Cindy's parents, Glen and Betty Crowell. Cindy sings and plays fiddle on the show; Dennis plays saxophone and emcees.

26. Dennis Dittemore, June 29, 2015.

27. Ellis, July 3, 2015.

28. Ibid., May 1, 2015.

8. Jazz / Swing / Western Swing

1. For contributions to this chapter's discussion, I thank John G. Stewart, Bobby Joe Caldwell, Michael Mendelson, Paul Anastasio, Chuck Haddix, Kelly Jones, Deena Bistodeau, Rich Levine, Derwood Brown, and Phil Williams.

2. Gunther Schuller, *The Swing Era: The Development of Jazz, 1930–1945*, 867 and *passim*. See also John Szwed, *Jazz 101: A Complete Guide to Learning and Loving Jazz*; and Hentoff, *Jazz Is*. A good introduction is Stacy Phillips, *Western Swing Fiddle*.

3. Jean Ann Boyd, *The Jazz of the Southwest: An Oral History of Western Swing*, 32.

4. Cary Ginell, *Milton Brown and the Founding of Western Swing* (Urbana: University of Illinois Press, 1994), 41–42. Ginell notes that swing fiddlers sometimes use the term *hokum fiddling* for takeoff fiddling.

5. James A. Poling, "Swing," in *Music Lover's Encyclopedia*, edited by Deems Taylor and Russell Kerr (New York: Knopf Doubleday, 1957), 818. For Cliff Bruner, a pioneer of the swing solo, see, for example, Paul Anastasio, "Cliff Bruner: Swingin' from the Golden Triangle to Houston," *Fiddler Magazine* 6, no. 42 (1999–2000): 16–20; and Stacy Phillips, "The History of Western Swing Fiddling," *Fiddler Magazine* 2, no. 1 (1995): 10–14.

6. Szwed, *Jazz 101*, 43.

7. Paul Anastasio's articles for *Fiddler Magazine* offer insights. Paul played with Venuti and Bruner as well as Merle Haggard and Asleep at the Wheel. "Playing truly creative ideas within an established style can, and often does, take a lifetime. The trick is to enjoy the journey." Anastasio, "On Improvisation: Improvising in a Specific Style," *Fiddler Magazine* 10, no. 1 (2003): 39; "On Improvisation: Taking the Plunge into Swing"; and "On Improvisation: Learning by Ear—Demystified," 42–43. Among many treatments of improvisation in jazz and swing relevant to fiddling is Henry Martin, *Charlie Parker and Thematic Improvisation* (Lanham, MD: Scarecrow Press, 1996).

8. For Venuti, for example, Eddy Noordijk, ed., *Joe Venuti Violin Rhythm: A School of Modern Rhythmic Violin Playing*; Richard M. Sudhalter, *Lost Chords: White Musicians and Their Contribution to Jazz, 1915–1945* (New York: Oxford University Press, 1999); Richard Niles Romano, ed., *Joe Venuti: Never Before . . . Never Again*; and *Village Voice* (1978), in *Riding on a Blue Note: Jazz and American Pop*, 79–84. Eddie Lang died young in 1933, and Venuti went through a dark period before resuming his career and becoming a venerated master. Lang's marvelous takeoff guitar solos influenced and inspired the legendary gypsy player Django Reinhardt; these players fostered an entire subgenre of jazz carried on today by young musicians.

9. Giddins, "Penchant for Mayhem," 80.

10. Noordijk, foreword to *Joe Venuti Violin Rhythm*. Venuti's examples include a fiddler's favorite of earlier generations, "Darktown Strutters' Ball" (composed by Shelton Brooks and published in New York by Leo Feist, 1917), 94. I thank Rich Levine for bringing this publication to my attention. Nothing we find suggests that Venuti's book was banned by the Nazis; perhaps it passed due to his Italian name. Another early jazz tutor is Axel Christensen, *Axel Christensen's New Instruction Book for Rag and Jazz* (Chicago: Christensen School of Popular Music, 1920). Among many references for Grappelli, see Jack Tuttle and Mary Larsen, "Stéphane Grappelli: Master of Jazz Violin," *Fiddler Magazine* 2, no. 4 (1995–96): 19–24.

11. Noordijk, *Joe Venuti Violin Rhythm*, 77–90.

12. Ibid., 68.

13. Ibid., 73, 75; Roger Williams, September 18, 2015.

14. Experiments in improvisation on the chords would lead in the later 1940s to a non-danceable substyle of jazz called "bebop," the extreme frontier of improvising on the chords developed by Parker, Charlie Christian, Dizzy Gillespie, Thelonious Monk, and others. Bebop emphasizes technical brilliance but could, at times, obscure or abandon the essential tune to such an extent that many people lost interest in this form of early modern jazz. The violin was virtually left out of bebop, although a few fiddlers, like Claude Williams, did play bebop.

15. Massey in Romano, *Joe Venuti*, 43.

16. Deena Bistodeau, "Texas Style Controlled Improvisation and the American Fiddle Contest," 18; ibid., "Part II," 18; ibid., "Part III"; ibid., "Part IV." Bistodeau's 2001 senior thesis for the bachelor's degree in music from the University of Minnesota bears the same title. http://www.skypefiddle.com.

17. Ginell, *Milton Brown*, 31; Richard Kienzle, "The Checkered Career of Hank Penny," *Journal of Country Music* 8, no. 2 (1980): 61. For Spade Cooley, who early in his career was a square-dance fiddler (with classical training), see also Kienzle, "Jekyl and Hyde: Spade Cooley," in *Southwest Shuffle*, 2–25.

18. Russell, *Country Music Originals*, 207. See also Charles Gardner, "Bob Wills: Texas Fiddler or Fiddler from Texas," *Texas Fiddler* 31, no. 8 (2003): 1. Cooley issued a song folio of the times, *Spade Cooley's Western Swing Song Folio for Voice, Piano, and Guitar* (New York: Hill and Range Songs, 1945).

19. Kevin Reed Coffey, "Who Is Western Swing's Father?" *Journal of Country Music* 17, no. 1 (1995): 60. For Coffey, the jury is still out. For the Light Crust Doughboys, see John Mark Dempsey, *The Light Crust Doughboys Are on the Air: Celebrating Seventy Years of Texas Music* (Denton: University of North Texas Press, 2002); and Jean Ann Boyd, *"We're the Light Crust Doughboys from Burrus Mill": An Oral History* (Austin: University of Texas Press, 2003). See also Ginell, *Milton Brown*; and Kienzle, *Southwest Shuffle*.

20. Boyd, *"We're the Light Crust Doughboys,"* 43.

21. Phillips, "History of Western Swing Fiddling"; Anastasio, "On Improvisation: Two Great Fiddlers Play 'Crafton Blues,'" *Fiddler Magazine* 7, no. 2 (2000): 32.

22. Anastasio, "Two Great Fiddlers Play 'Crafton Blues,'" 32. Anastasio notes that "Crafton Blues" is actually a rag and incorporates an old tune, "I Don't Love Nobody." Among other sources, see Malone, *Country Music, USA*; and Ginell's *Milton Brown*. For Cliff Bruner, see Tony Russell, *Country Music Originals*, 216–18.

23. This history is complicated, and different views exist. Works such as Boyd's *Jazz of the Southwest* and Ginell's *Milton Brown* offer readable entry points.

24. Partial lyrics from Milton Brown and His Musical Brownies, "Easy Ridin' Papa," adapted from a 1930 Banner record by the Hokum Boys (Big Bill Broonzy, Georgia Tom Dorsey, and Frank Brasswell). Although Brown copyrighted the song, Bob Wills adopted it as his theme. See Ginell, *Milton Brown*, 299; and Tony Russell and Bob Pinson, *Country Music Records: A Discography, 1921–1942* (New York: Oxford University Press, 2004), 137.

25. Derwood Brown kept the Brownies together for a year, issuing recordings, but by 1937 the band had dispersed, with several Brownies migrating to the Texas Playboys. For Wills, see Charles R. Townsend, *San Antonio Rose: The Life and Music of Bob Wills*; Duncan McLean's delightful *Lone Star Swing: On the Trail of Bob Wills and the Texas Playboys*; and Ronny S. Schiff, ed., *Bob Wills: King of Western Swing* (Milwaukee: Hal Leonard, n.d.).

26. In addition to several western songs, in *The Last Horseman* (Columbia Pictures, 1944) Wills and the Playboys play "Dreamy-Eyed Waltz" (Wills's version of "Wednesday Night Waltz"). Instrumentation is two or three violins, acoustic guitar, acoustic tenor guitar, electric lap steel (the electric instrument replaced for the camera by a six-string flattop guitar played on the knees), and upright bass.

27. Charles K. Wolfe, "Bob Wills, Fiddler," *Devil's Box* 16, no. 2 (1982): 16.

28. Schuller, *Early Jazz*, 564–65.

29. Canaday, October 2000.

30. Debbie Holley, "Billy Byrd: The Jazzman Wore Cowboy Boots," *Journal of Country Music* 12, no. 1 (1987): 44, 45. Byrd was typical of early country guitarists with respect to his enjoyment of old-time fiddling. Byrd's brother was a fiddler. Byrd played for a time in the late 1930s with the Herald Goodman band on *The Grand Ole Opry*. Goodman's fiddler at the time was Howdy Forrester.

31. Claude Williams, September 1985; John G. Stewart, March 8, 2010, October 1, 2015.

32. See Marshall, *Play Me Something Quick and Devilish*, for more on Warren Helton. Unless otherwise noted, quotes are from Helton interviews, October 12 and 18, 2010. Vienna is the seat of Maries County; originally pronounced "Vi'anny," the town was named not for the Austrian capital but for a local girl. McMillen, *A to Z Missouri*, 184.

33. Helton, March 27, 2011.

34. Tiny Moore and Merle Haggard, *Swinging Texas Fiddlin': A Study of Traditional and Modern Breakdown and Hoedown Fiddling*, 47–40.

35. For example, *Tiny Moore Music* (1975) was an album of instrumental jazz and swing featuring Moore (playing fiddle as well as his custom-made solid-body five-string electric mandolin) with Shamblin, Merle Haggard (second lead electric guitar), and jazz all-stars bassist Ray Brown and drummer Shelly Manne. Moore and Haggard, *Swinging Texas Fiddlin'*; Merle Haggard, *A Tribute to the Best Damn Fiddle Player in the World; or, My Salute to Bob Wills* (Capitol Records). Moore also recorded a jazz album in 1979 with mandolinist Jethro Burns, *Back to Back*.

36. *Swinging Texas Fiddlin'*, 47.

37. McCann, March 11, 2008.

38. "Lowell F. (Zed) Tennis" (obituary), *Springfield (MO) Leader-Press*, August 4, 1972, 23.

39. Malone, *Country Music, USA*, 102, 122. See also Ginell, "Development of Western Swing," 31–35; Ken Griffis, "Hank Penny: The Original Outlaw," *John Edwards Memorial Foundation Quarterly* 18, nos. 65–66 (1982): 5–13; and Daniel, *Pickin' on Peachtree*, chap. 8 (see chap. 1, n. 6). Penny, born in Alabama and eventually settling in California, pops in and out of the history of western swing.

40. Richard Kienzle, *Southwest Shuffle: Pioneers of Honky-Tonk, Western Swing, and Country Jazz*, 26–53.

41. Townsend, *San Antonio Rose*, 102; Kienzle, *Southwest Shuffle*, 254ff. Hank Penny was blunt in his disapproval of the Nashville-controlled music business. Kienzle writes that Penny "never played the game" and that to Penny, in words that could describe some of today's Branson music shows, "Nashville is too hokey. Nothing is real. Everybody has to do everything with a flourish and consequently the simplicity, the charm of country music is gone." Kienzle, "Checkered Career of Hank Penny," 43. See also Richard Carlin, *Country Music: A Biographical Dictionary* (New York: Routledge, 2014).

42. Kienzle, *Southwest Shuffle*, 35–36. "Lanham, who played a mixture of chord melodies and single-string licks a la Chicago jazzman George Barns, gave them as strong or stronger a swing content than the Cowboys. Tennis further enhanced the sound." For Penny, see also Kienzle, "Checkered Career of Hank Penny," 42–48, 61–77; T. Russell, *Country Music Originals*, 219–20; and Guy Logsdon, Mary Rogers, and William Jacobson, *Saddle Serenaders* (Salt Lake City: Gibbs-Smith, 1995), 115.

43. Kienzle, "Checkered Career of Hank Penny," 62.

44. Ed McKinney, February 21, 2008. See also McKinney, "Images, Realities, and Cultural Transformations," 180ff.

45. Gordon McCann, April 30, 2008. Rickman's version of "Finley Creek Blues" (to my ears a tune resembling Kerry Mills's 1897 cakewalk "At a Georgia Camp Meeting") is in Beisswenger and McCann, 111; Holt's version is on his CD *Got a Little Home to Go To*. Forsyth fiddler Jim Beeler's is on the Rounder project *Traditional Fiddle Music of the Ozarks*, vol. 3 (see chap. 2, n. 27), and Rickman's is on the CD accompanying Beisswenger and McCann.

46. McKinney, February 21, 2008.

47. McKinney, "Images, Realities, and Cultural Transformations," 182. As with other radio programs, the band was recorded live on large aluminum discs, and the resulting recordings were called "transcriptions." The transcriptions were then copied by the radio station and mailed to other radio stations that had subscribed to their service, were part of a network of sister stations, or were part of one of the major networks such as CBS and NBC. This way, live radio shows were recorded but could be disseminated to other towns and other parts of the United States, with the airings often presented as "live" programming.

48. "Ida Red" appears in, among other publications, Miles Krassen, *Appalachian Fiddle* (New York: Oak, 1973), 16; Phillips, *Phillips Collection*, 1:117 (by Wills and Sleepy Johnson); and Marion Unger Thede, *The Fiddle Book*, 60–61. "Ida Red" continues to appear in popular songbooks and has been reissued on compilation CDs.

49. Bob Wills's 1938 recording of "Ida Red" with vocals by Tommy Duncan is on Vocalion 05079. "Ida Red" also relates to songs in the African American tradition. Andrew Kuntz writes that "Ida Red" was, in some legends, an African American outlaw, but "the gender of the character in most versions is feminine or androgynous." Fiddler's Companion, http://ibiblio.org/fiddlers/FChomepage.htm.

50. September 5, 1952, radio transcription. "Yes Sir, That's My Baby" was a hit song written in 1925 by Gus Kahn and Walter Donaldson and recorded by Eddie Cantor in 1930.

51. Michael Breid, March 7, 2008, October 24, 2014. "Sunrise on a [the] Guinea Farm" is played today by some Missouri swing fiddlers. Early recordings include Al Clauser and His Oklahoma Outlaws, ca. 1940, reissued as *Al Clauser and His Oklahoma Outlaws: Hot Western Swing, 1937–1948* (with singer Patti Page) on Krazy Kat KKCD 32 (2004). It is probable that Tennis was acquainted with the Clauser band.

52. Paul Shelasky, "Bluegrass Fiddling: Dale Potter's Bluegrass," *Fiddler Magazine* 14, no. 4 (2007–8): 41. Some feel Potter's twin-fiddle exhibition with Benny Martin on Monroe's 1959 "Stoney Lonesome" is among the best bluegrass fiddling exhibitions on record: "The master of the double-stop . . . his influence on all the famous fiddlers of his day cannot be over-estimated. Monroe obviously thought highly of his talents—he was often featured on Bill's recordings, usually combined with one or two other fiddlers." Examples of Potter's fiddling are included in Stacy Phillips and Kenny Kosek, *Bluegrass Fiddle Styles*; and Phillips, *The Complete Country Fiddler*.

53. Shelasky, "Dale Potter's Bluegrass," 41.

54. Quoted by Barry Willis in his album notes for the Potter compilation CD *24 Fiddle Favorites* (Rural Rhythm Classics RHY-253, 1997).

55. McMillen, *A to Z Missouri*, 148.

56. Nancy Cardwell, "Bobby Hicks: The Next Chapter," *Bluegrass Now* (July 2005): 40; Walden website, http://www.missourifiddling.com; "Great Fiddler Dale Potter Is Dead at 66," *Puxico (MO) Press*, March 20, 1996, 1.

57. For example, "Puxico Is Welcoming Homecomers," *Poplar Bluff (MO) Daily American Republic*, August 14, 1939, 1, announces the forthcoming WPA Band concert, bicycle

float parade, Miss Puxico contest, Poplar Bluff Municipal Band concert, hog-calling contest, American Legion Drum and Bugle Corps concert, Amateur Contest, and Old Time Fiddlers Contest, but there was no follow-up reporting of contest results. The 1940 event is announced in "Day of Music at Puxico Homecoming," *Poplar Bluff (MO) Daily American Republic*, August 15, 1940, 1, again with no follow-up story. A fiddlers contest that would have drawn Dale Potter's participation, as well as a performance by Millage Gaines (and his) Hillbilly Band, was advertised in "Fall Festival in Full Swing Here," *Dexter (MO) Messenger*, October 19, 1939, 1, reporting on the Stoddard County Fall Festival and Agricultural Fair, but no follow-up article reported the results of the fiddling competition.

58. El Freda Cox, "Fiddler Is Put to Rest," *Puxico (MO) Press*, March 27, 1996, 1.

59. "Dale Potter," *Dexter (MO) Daily Statesman*, March 17, 1996 (courtesy Noreen Hyslop).

60. These recordings have been reissued numerous times on compilation projects—for example, "Mind Your Own Business" (recorded March 1949 for MGM Records), which offers an excellent sample of Potter's backup fiddling and "fills," and "Lost Highway (recorded at WSM Radio, October 1949), on *Hank Williams Gold* (Mercury Records CD, 2005).

61. Transcribed in Phillips, *The Complete Country Fiddler*.

62. Phillips and Kosek, *Bluegrass Fiddle Styles*, 89–92. The authors note that "Fiddle Patch" is a reworking of steel guitarist Joaquin Murphy's "Oklahoma Stomp."

63. Cardwell, "Bobby Hicks," 39–40.

64. Hank Jones recalled that Potter was fiddling with Patsy Cline's road band at the time of Cline's death in a plane crash near Camden, Tennessee, in 1963 along with her fellow *Grand Ole Opry* stars Hawkshaw Hawkins, Cowboy Copas, and her manager, Randy Hughes; the band took ground transportation back to Nashville, while Cline et al. chose to take the ill-fated airplane flight in a light aircraft.

65. *24 Fiddle Favorites*. "Fiddle Patch" is also on a Rural Rhythm compilation CD, *Burnin' Up the Strings (the Best of Bluegrass)* (RH-309).

66. *Mr. Bluegrass* (Decca, 1960), reissued in a Bear Family 1991 boxed compilation set of CDs, *Blue Grass, 1959–1969*. Other examples include Potter doing the fiddle work on "Time Changes Everything" on the reissued set *Bill Monroe Anthology* (Decca 088 113 207-2). For Spicher, see Jim Wood, "The Legacy of Buddy Spicher," *Fiddler Magazine* 14, no. 1 (2007): 17–19.

67. *Dale Potter: World's Champion Country & Western Fiddler, Hoe Down!*, vol. 1 (Rural Rhythm RRDP 179, 1963, reissued in 1994 on cassette as *Dale Potter and Shot Jackson: Twenty Fiddle Favorites*). On the album are Dobro player Jackson and Jim Murphy, a pedal steel guitarist from Jefferson City who was a valued session player and sideman in Nashville.

68. Paul Wadey, "Obituary: Dale Potter," *Independent* (London), May 10, 1996.

9. Born to Play Swing

1. Mary Lee Hester, "The Cat's in the Fiddle," in *Going to Kansas City* (Sherman, TX: Early Bird Press, 1980), 158. Tenor saxophonist Buddy Tate, from Texas, played with the Andy Kirk band in Kansas City before joining the Count Basie orchestra in New York, performing with Basie from 1939 to 1948. See, for example, Schuller, *Swing Era*.

2. John Brisbin, "Claude Williams," *Living Blues* 173 (July–August 2004): 89; Chuck Haddix, "Claude Williams: The Fiddler's Triumph," 32. Williams is also said to have played ukuleles

with Charlie Christian on the streets of Muscogee. Christian later achieved fame as an innovative swing guitarist (John G. Stewart, November 12, 2009). I appreciate the assistance of John G. Stewart, Chuck Haddix, and Mary Larsen in preparing this material on Claude Williams.

3. Susan Newstead interview. In my research, the exact chronology of Claude's taking up guitar and cello (before learning violin) is unclear.

4. Susan Newstead, "Claude Williams, Jazz Violinist," segment 8, on *Missouri Legacy: Fiddlers Plus* (1988); Margot Roberson and Howard Wight Marshall, "Claude G. Williams, Kansas City Jazz Violinist," in *The Masters*, by Roberson and Marshall, 46. The same pronunciation and similar traditions were commonplace across Missouri; by the time of Williams's death in 2004, the old use of "bass" for cello had been largely forgotten. In an obituary, Claude was remembered as playing the "bass" rather than the cello ("sello"), which will add confusion to future biographies. Lee Hill Kavanaugh and Eric Adler, "Claude 'Fiddler' Williams, 1908–2004: 'He Lived for His Music,'" *Kansas City Star*, April 26, 2004, 6.

5. Roberson and Marshall, "Claude G. Williams," 46.

6. Song by Billy Rose and Con Conrad; it was a popular dance number played by old-time fiddlers of Claude Williams's generation (for example, Pete McMahan) as well as swing and jazz players. Mary Larsen, "Claude 'Fiddler' Williams: Kansas City Swing!," 25.

7. Haddix, "Claude Williams," 32; Larsen, "Claude 'Fiddler' Williams," 26.

8. Forrest Rose, "Jamming with the County Spices Memories of Top Jazz Fiddler," *Columbia (MO) Daily Tribune*, May 10, 1984, 1. For jitney dances, sometimes called "taxi dances," see, for example, Jonathon Green, *Cassell's Dictionary of Slang* (London: Cassell, 2000), 803.

9. Haddix, "18th and Vine: Streets of Dreams," http://www.library.umkc.edu/spec-col.

10. For Kansas City, see Marc Rice, "Break o' Day Blues: The 1923 Recordings of the Bennie Moten Orchestra," *Musical Quarterly* 86, no. 2 (2002): 283–85; Frank S. Driggs, "Kansas City and the Southwest," in *Jazz: New Perspectives on the History of Jazz*, edited by Nat Hentoff and Albert J. McCarthy (New York: Da Capo Press, 1959), 189ff; Driggs and Chuck Haddix, *Kansas City Jazz: From Ragtime to Bebop—a History*; Burton Peretti, *Jazz in American Culture* (Chicago: Ivan R. Dee, 1997), 54–55; Delia C. Gillis, *Kansas City* (Charleston, SC: Arcadia, 2007); and Hester, "Cat's in the Fiddle."

11. Chuck Haddix, January 27, 2015.

12. Nathan W. Pearson Jr., *Goin' to Kansas City*, 33.

13. Newstead, "Claude Williams, Jazz Violinist."

14. Martin Williams, "What Happened in Kansas City?," *American Music* 3, no. 2 (1985): 172; Rice, "Break o' Day Blues," 282–306. See also Leonard Brown, *Kansas City . . . and All That's Jazz* (Kansas City: Andrews McMeel, 1999). Marc Rice has documented Moten's career in Kansas City in "Break o' Day Blues." Jazz musicians were "heroes" in the neighborhood (282). See also Rice, "Prelude to Swing: The 1920s Recordings of the Benny Moten Orchestra," *American Music* 25, no. 3 (2007): 259–81, 206.

15. Newstead, "Claude Williams, Jazz Violinist."

16. *Sunday Morning* (CBS Television), September 16, 1990.

17. Molly Murphy, producer, "Jazz Profiles: Claude 'Fiddler' Williams (1908–2004)," National Public Radio, April 2006, http://www.npr.org/programs/jazzprofiles/archive/williams_c.html.

18. Carney Lovelass Jr., "Claude 'Fiddler' Williams Will Bow for the Festival," *St. Louis Argus*, September 20, 1984, 5; Haddix, "Claude Williams," 32.

19. Stanley Crouch, "Swing on Top" and *Kansas City Lightning: The Rise and Times of Charlie Parker*. Among many treatments of Charlie Parker, see Martin Williams, "Charlie Parker: The Burden of Innovation," in *The Jazz Tradition*, by Williams, 135–53; Ross Russell, *Bird Lives: The High Life and Hard Times of Charlie (Yardbird) Parker*; and Chuck Haddix, *Bird: The Life and Music of Charlie Parker*.

20. "Honeysuckle Rose" was one of Williams's signature tunes. Composed by Fats Waller in 1933, it was a mainstay of the Benny Goodman orchestra. Williams, *Call for the Fiddler* (SteepleChase, 1994). John Intrator's transcription of Williams's version of "Honeysuckle Rose" is in Intrator, "Claude Williams Live: That Kansas City Spell," 12.

21. Kavanaugh and Adler, "Claude 'Fiddler' Williams," 1; Colin Larkin, "Williams, Claude," in *The Virgin Encyclopedia of Jazz*, edited by Larkin (London: Virgin Books 2004), 932.

22. Hester, "Cat's in the Fiddle," 158; Schuller, *The Swing Era*, 237. Research has shown that the popular belief that Claude Williams was named guitarist of the year by *DownBeat* is not true (Chuck Haddix, January 27, 2015).

23. More references for Williams include Larsen, "Claude 'Fiddler' Williams"; Boyd, *Jazz of the Southwest*, 34; Roberson and Marshall, "Claude G. Williams," 46–47; "Williams, Claude," in *Who's Who of Jazz: Storyville to Swing Street*, edited by John Chilton (Philadelphia: Chilton, 1978), 355; "Williams, Claude," in *The Biographical Encyclopedia of Jazz*, edited by Leonard Feather and Ira Gitler, 694; Colin Larkin, "Williams, Claude," in *The Virgin Encyclopedia of Jazz*, edited by Larkin (London: Virgin Books, 2004), 932; Julie Lyonn Lieberman, "Fiddling the Blues," *Fiddler Magazine* 3, no. 4 (1996–97): 6; Haddix, "Claude Williams"; and Intrator, "Claude Williams Live." The principal archive for Williams is the Claude "Fiddler" Williams Collection, LaBudde Special Collections, Miller Nichols Library, University of Missouri–Kansas City, http://www.library.umkc.edu.

24. Among sources, see Kevin Fox Gotham, "City without Slums: Urban Renewal, Public Housing and Downtown Revitalization in Kansas City, Missouri," *American Journal of Economics and Sociology* 60, no. 1 (2003): 285–316; James R. Shortridge, *Kansas City and How It Grew* (Lawrence: University Press of Kansas, 2012); and http://www.mutualmusiciansfoundation.org.

25. For example, the Brubeck quartet's *Time Out* LP and Miles Davis's *Kind of Blue* were best sellers across the country in 1959—even in the Reed Street record shop in my hometown of Moberly, Missouri—and drew white teenagers like myself to jazz.

26. Bob Porter, album notes, *Swingin' the Blues* (Bullseye BB 9627, 2000).

27. Art Galbraith often fiddled "You've Got to See Your Momma," with his group the Fiddlers Four at Silver Dollar City in the 1970s.

28. Williams plays "Smooth Sailing" and "You've Got to See Your Momma Every Night" on a sampler from the tour, *Masters of the Folk Violin* (Arhoolie CD 434, 1995). A transcription of Williams's "Back Home in Indiana" by Jack Tuttle is included in the book and CD *Fiddler Magazine's Favorites* (Pacific, MO: Mel Bay, 1999), 105–7.

29. Stewart, November 12, 2009.

30. *Sunday Morning*.

31. A usable recording of Claude Williams for the companion CD was not available at the time this book was in preparation. Williams's recordings are numerous and easily accessible on the Internet and elsewhere.

32. Parker, "Cherokee," with guitarist Efferge Ware and drummer Little Phil Phillips (reissued on Stash SCD 35); Barnet, "Cherokee" (RCA Victor 20-1756); Schuller, *The Swing Era*.

Transcribed by Matt Glaser in "Claude Williams on the Warpath: A Jazz Great Plays 'Cherokee,'" *Strings* (September–October 1989): 28–29.

33. "Indiana" and "Darktown Strutter's Ball" are reissued on the CD *Original Dixieland Jazz Band: The Creators of Jazz* (Avid Records, 2006).

34. Julie Lyonn Lieberman, "A Brief History of Jazz Violin," *American String Teacher* 52, no. 4 (2002): 83.

35. John Brisbin, quoting Russ Dantzler, who produced several Williams albums, in "Claude Williams," *Living Blues* 173 (July–August 2004): 88.

36. January 21, 2010, Missouri Theater, Columbia. "Fiddler Going Home" is on the CD *Mark O'Connor's Hot Swing Trio Live from New York* (OMAC, 2005).

37. "Son, 15, Is Right-Hand Man of One-Armed Fiddle Player Who Will Play at the Fair," *Columbia (MO) Daily Tribune*, ca. 1948. Digital downloads of Luther Caldwell's fiddling are available on *Luther Caldwell—One Armed Fiddler of Boone County, MO* (MSOTFA Recordings 107, 2015).

38. Merle Lutes, "Fiddler Turns Bad Luck into Good," *Columbia Missourian*, July 7, 1968, 3.

39. Caldwell, October 22, 2010.

40. As Bud Wyatt and others recall, Bill Perkins (also known as Junior), of the Columbia area, was a hard-swinging, fine fiddler whose versatility and interest in hoedowns as well as pop tunes made him and his band a mainstay in the 1940s and 1950s (Wyatt, October 15, 2015). Perkins and his group the Midwesterners recorded a private-label LP that is worth searching out, *Pickin' at Liberty* (Camdenton, MO: Ozark Records, 1978), featuring lead electric guitarist Bill Potts, Jackie Kimsey (piano), Chuck Kimsey (bass), Gene Barnes (pedal steel guitar), and Eddie Reno (drums).

41. Caldwell, October 1, 2009.

42. "Charmaine" (composed by Erno Rapee, lyrics by Lew Pollock) in *What Price Glory?* (Fox Films). Champion Missouri old-time fiddler Travis Inman included the tune in his 2012 CD, *John Swearingen's Hornpipe* (Voyager VRCD376), with swing guitar backup by Charlie Walden and piano by Patt Plunkett.

43. "Kansas City Kitty" (New York: Donaldson-Douglas and Gumble, 1929). Tin Pan Alley composer Donaldson wrote songs familiar to swing and pop fiddlers, such as "At Sundown," "Sioux City Sue," "Thousand Goodnights," and "My Blue Heaven." Among early recordings are a 1929 version by Juice Wilson with Noble Sissle's orchestra, reissued on *Jazz Violin, 1926–1942* (Jazz Archives no. 71); Noble Sissle and His Orchestra, in England (Victor 5731); and the Cotton Pickers (Brunswick 4325). In 1944 there was a Hollywood movie called *Kansas City Kitty* (Columbia Pictures), a musical comedy in which a fable of the song's creation was depicted. Country singer Johnny Bond plays a cowboy called Chaps Whiliker who says to a young woman piano teacher named Polly (Joan Davis), "I cooked up a little ditty," and then sings it for her; confusion, misdirection, and movie funny business ensue. See Chuck Haddix, "Coon-Sanders Original Nighthawk Orchestra: Radio Aces"; Bob Harrington and Rex Downing, "Tales of Coon-Sanders," *Mississippi Rag (*April 1991): 10–14. Phillips's version of "Kansas City Kitty" is in *Phillips Collection*, 2:70.

10. Bluegrass Time in the Show-Me State

1. I appreciate the assistance of Patricia Spray Davidson, Jim Russell, Al Murphy, Dan Grotewohl, Dan William Peek, Ed McKinney, Jim Orchard, and Lonnie and Charlene Hoppers in preparing this chapter.

2. Lomax in a documentary film tracing his career collecting and studying music and dancing in the Upper South between 1978 and 1985, *Appalachian Journey* (New York: Association for Cultural Equity, 1991). Earlier, Lomax had coined the description of bluegrass as "folk music with overdrive," in Alan Lomax, "Bluegrass Background: Folk Music with Overdrive," *Esquire*, (October 1959), 108. For bluegrass, see Ronald D. Cohen, ed., *Alan Lomax: Selected Writings, 1933–1997* (New York: Routledge, 2003); Malone, *Country Music, USA*, 323–24; Robert Cantwell, *Bluegrass Breakdown: The Making of the Old Southern Sound* (Urbana: University of Illinois Press, 1984), 61; Jim Rooney, *Bossmen: Bill Monroe and Muddy Waters*; Ralph Rinzler, "Bill Monroe—the Daddy of Blue Grass Music," *Sing Out!* 13, no. 1 (1963): 5–8; Thomas A. Adler, "Manual Formulaic Composition: Innovation in Bluegrass Banjo Styles"; Rosenberg, *Bluegrass: A History*; Neil V. Rosenberg and Charles K. Wolfe, *The Music of Bill Monroe*; Richard D. Smith, *Bluegrass: An Informal Guide* (New York: A Capella Books, 1995) and *Can't You Hear Me Callin': The Life of Bill Monroe, Father of Bluegrass* (Boston: Little, Brown, 2000); Carl Fleischhauer and Neil V. Rosenberg, *Bluegrass Odyssey* (Urbana: University of Illinois Press, 2001); Tom Ewing, ed., *The Bill Monroe Reader* (Urbana: University of Illinois Press, 2000); and Bob Black, *Come Hither to Go Yonder: Playing Bluegrass with Bill Monroe*. Peek offers a summary of bluegrass, in relation to *The Ozark Opry*, in *Live! At the Ozark Opry*.

3. Marshall, "Keep on the Sunny Side of Life," 1–43.

4. Monroe learned the guitar "G run" (a bass run beginning on the low E string in an open G chord) from Shultz, and today the G run, later made famous by Lester Flatt in Monroe's band, is an essential ingredient in bluegrass guitar traditions and sounds. The G run is as follows, as analyzed by Neil V. Rosenberg: The key is G and the run moves "from F# to G on the sixth string, then from A to B on the fifth string, then from D to E on the fourth and ends up with a ringing open G note on the third string." Rosenberg, "Lester Flatt and Earl Scruggs," in *Stars of Country Music: From Uncle Dave Macon to Johnny Rodriguez*, edited by Bill C. Malone and Judith McCulloh (Urbana: University of Illinois Press, 1975), 260.

5. Chubby Wise in the documentary film *Bill Monroe: Father of Bluegrass Music* (Steve Gebhardt, WinStar Home Entertainment, VHS1176, 1993, 1999).

6. The cultural-geographic region known as "Bluegrass Kentucky" consists of a cluster of counties in northern Kentucky, featuring key early settlement, dependence on tobacco and slave labor in early times, and the state's major urban areas. It is not the mountainous region of eastern Kentucky that is stereotypically linked with old-time music. Monroe was from the Rosine community in western Kentucky.

7. For more on this, see Neil V. Rosenberg, "Into Bluegrass: The History of the Word," in *The Bluegrass Reader*, edited by Thomas Goldsmith (Urbana: University of Illinois Press, 2004), 93–101.

8. Howard Wight Marshall, "Country Music Interviews: Lester Flatt," *Country Music Magazine* 1, no. 3 (1972): 53. Flatt stated that to use electricity would not be "real" and would take away from the heritage of the music.

9. Howdy Forrester left the band to serve in the army in World War II. Billie (Sally Ann) remained and performed and recorded several records as a Blue Grass Boy, but after the war left the band to perform with her husband and brother-in-law, Joe Forrester. Henry, "Come Prepared to Stay," 92–93ff (see chap. 1, n. 23).

10. Over the years, the band name changed from "Bill Monroe and His Blue Grass Boys" to "Bill Monroe and the Bluegrass Boys."

11. Several companies made "Open Road"–style hats. The Langenberg family firm in New Haven, MO, like other small firms, made this style of felted-rabbit fur hats they called Beaver Brand, undistinguishable to the unpracticed eye to Stetsons, sold as generic Open Roads to western-wear stores that then stamped them with their own logo.

12. Lonnie Hoppers, February 24, 2015.

13. President John F. Kennedy would effectively spell the end of formal hats for men when he arrived hatless at his inauguration at the White House on a cold winter day in January 1961. JFK's hatless look caught on.

14. Gene Lowinger, *I Hear a Voice Calling: A Bluegrass Memoir*; Rooney, *Bossmen*; Black, *Come Hither to Go Yonder*; Lowinger's *Bluegrass Fiddle* includes transcriptions of tunes in the bluegrass repertory.

15. See Thomas A. Adler, "The Physical Development of the Banjo." For banjo history, see also Dena Epstein, *Sinful Tunes and Spirituals: Black Folk Music to the Civil War* (Urbana: University of Illinois Press, 1977); Karen Linn, *That Half-Barbaric Twang: The Banjo in American Popular Culture* (Chicago: University of Chicago Press, 1991); Philip F. Gura and James F. Bollman, *America's Instrument: The Banjo in the Nineteenth Century* (Chapel Hill: University of North Carolina Press, 1999); Bob Carlin, *The Birth of the Banjo: Joel Walker Sweeney and Early Minstrelsy* (Jefferson, NC: McFarland, 2007); and Jay Scott O'Dell, "Banjo," in *The New Grove Dictionary of Musical Instruments*, edited by S. Sadie (New York: Macmillan, 1984), 151–54.

16. It is possible that "High Lonesome" is at least in part a comic place-name Morrison used in his shows.

17. Hoppers, February 16, 2015.

18. Ibid., May 23, 2013.

19. Newstead, *Missouri Legacy: Fiddlers Plus*, "Don Brown: Bluegrass Musician" segment.

20. Jimmie Rodgers's "Blue Yodel #8" was also known as "Mule Skinner Blues," recorded by Rodgers in 1930. Monroe's 1940 record featured an early version of the Blue Grass Boys (with Tommy Magness, fiddle). A year before, Monroe had successfully auditioned for a job on *The Grand Ole Opry* singing "Mule Skinner Blues." Among many sources for the story of "Mule Skinner Blues," which helped establish the driving, bluesy, syncopated beat of bluegrass music, see Smith, *Bluegrass: An Informal Guide*; and Ewing, *Bill Monroe Reader*.

21. McKinney, October 26, 2010.

22. I appreciate the assistance of Patricia Spray Davidson in preparing this section. Howard Wight Marshall and Margot Roberson, "Delbert Spray, North Missouri Old-Time and Bluegrass Fiddler," in *Masters*, by Roberson and Marshall, 32. See also Howard Wight Marshall, "Portrait of a Bluegrass Fiddler: Delbert Spray, 1923–2001," *Missouri Folklore Society Newsletter* 26, no. 102 (2002): 7–11; and "Delbert E. Spray, 1923–2001," *Bluegrass Music News* (Spring 2000): 5–6.

23. "Clark County Fair Board Plans Evening at Fair Dedicated to 'Master Fiddler' Delbert Spray," *Media* (Kahoka), April 10, 2002, 16–17. Among his military decorations was the Philippine Liberation Ribbon with one bronze star for saving the lives of schoolchildren when their school was shelled (Pat Davidson, April 1, 2015).

24. "Delbert E. Spray, 1923–2001," 6.

25. Tri-State Bluegrass Association, http://www.tsbafestivals.org. Other founding members of the TSBA were Larry Peck, Richard Bunch, Daryl Stephenson, Roy Brosi, Richard and Gertrude Bridgett, Dave Majors, Charlie Wade, Mary Jo Hamilton, and Larry Dudding.

26. *Live! From the Kahoka Festival of Bluegrass Music* (Kahoka: Delbert Spray OS16396, ca. 1980).

27. Alan Murphy, *Through the Fields* (Global Village LP 305, 1987).

28. Bob Skaggs, November 19, 2010.

29. Monroe assigned part of the royalties to Delbert. Delbert later "gave" the tune to Karl Shiflett's band in 1998, and it was recorded by the Karl Shiflett and Big Country Show on *The Karl Shiflett & Big Country Show* (Rebel 1752 CD, 1999). The fiddler in the band is Kirk Brandenberger, from Keokuk, Iowa, and an old friend of Delbert's. Bill Monroe often called Delbert and Erma to visit about cattle and reminisce about the old days. His favorite topics were always the same, how the times have changed, cattle, and foxhounds. Around Christmastime Monroe would phone and just sing into the phone, "Christmas time's a-comin' . . . ," and they knew it was Bill on the phone. Marshall, "Portrait of a Bluegrass Fiddler." See also Erma Spray, "Bill Monroe Honors Delbert Spray with a Tune Named after Him," in *"The Blue Book" Band and Festival Guide*, edited by Patricia Spray Davidson (Williamstown, MO: Tri-State Bluegrass Association, 2011), 43.

30. "Christmas Time's a-Comin'" was on an early Bill Monroe 45 rpm record, composed by bluegrass fiddler and Columbia University PhD electrical engineer Tex Logan. Decca 45386 (1951), with fiddle by Gordon Terry.

11. Family Tradition

1. See *Good Tune*, 43–46, 84. Unless otherwise noted, quotes are from this publication. See also Gordon McCann, "Missouri Fiddler Lyman Enloe to Receive National Heritage Fellowship," *Devil's Box* 29, no. 3 (1995): 51–52; Nancy Cardwell, "Lyman Enloe: A Stylist of the Old-Time Fiddle," *Bluegrass Unlimited* (January 1989): 61–64; and Bill Shull, ed., *"Uncle Pink" and Other Central Missouri Fiddle Tunes from Lyman Enloe*, 5ff.

2. Forrest Enloe, February 18, 2008.

3. My favorite examples of the difficulty of categorizing fiddlers in the real world can include the renowned "old-time fiddler" Pete McMahan (whom I knew well for thirty years), a man of fierce opinions who played bluegrass tunes learned from records (particularly those of Kenny Baker and Bill Monroe and the Bluegrass Boys), Texas-style contest tunes from records by Jim Chancellor (Texas Shorty) and others, as well as many pop tunes from the big-band era, and as a young man flirted with becoming a "bluegrass fiddler," but McMahan would quickly and clearly set one straight if one were careless enough to address him as a "bluegrass fiddler" or a "Texas fiddler."

4. Clifford Hill, November 4, 2010. Baker copyrighted the tune in 1972, and it appeared on his LP *Kenny Baker Country* (County 736) and CD *Kenny Baker: Master Fiddler* (County 2705, 1993). "Festival Waltz" is one of the few bluegrass standards ensconced in old-time fiddle circles and contest fiddling.

5. Cardwell, "Lyman Enloe," 64.

6. The Bluegrass Association eventually became the Bluegrass Brigade, with Montgomery (violin), McGreevy, and Jack and Mae Burlison (guitar, bass); among their LPs are *Happy I'll Be* (Ozark Opry OOR 81 104,1981) and *Festival Favorites* (BBR 84–105, 1984).

7. *Fiddle Tunes I Recall*, one of the best-known old-time fiddle records of all time, was originally released on LP by Cavern Custom 41308 (1973), then rereleased on LP County Records (County 762, 1978), and then reissued on CD by County in 1993.

8. Cardwell, "Lyman Enloe," 64.

9. *Good Tune*, 31.

10. An alternate title for the mid-1800s "Richmond Polka." See Ira W. Ford, *Traditional Music of America*, 114; and Phillips, *Phillips Collection*, 1:198. Phillips has it under "Richmond Cotillion" (à la Clark Kessinger) in *Phillips Collection*, 2:350. Enloe's setting is in Shull, *"Uncle Pink,"* 33. Jim Herd's version as "Hanging around the Kitchen till the Cook Comes Home" is in Beisswenger and McCann, 56–57; numerous fiddlers learned the tune as "Richmond Polka" from the 1929 78 rpm record by the Kessinger Brothers (Brunswick 309).

11. Due to an inadvertent error speaking the title of "Snow Shoes" as "Spotted Pony" by Pete McMahan in a jam session at the National Oldtime Fiddlers Contest in Weiser, Idaho, in June 1968, in which the tune was recorded by several listeners and later published, today many fiddlers use "Spotted Pony" for the other tune "Snow Shoes." Pete's fiddling of "Snow Shoes" was issued with the misspoken title "Spotted Pony" on a 1972 compilation Voyager LP, *More Fiddle Jam Sessions* (reissued on CD as VRCD301). The continuing confusion represents an example of the folk process and the dynamics of oral tradition in which a tune may acquire a new title. Examples of the authentic "Snow Shoes" include Brody, *The Fiddler's Fakebook*, 263. Versions of "Snow Shoes" titled "Spotted Pony" are in Phil Williams, *The Mandolin Player's Pastime* (Seattle: Voyager Recordings and Publications, 1991), 8; and Gene Silberberg, *The Complete Fiddle Tunes I Either Did or Did Not Learn at the Tractor Tavern*, 184. Exemplary versions of the "real" "Spotted Pony" include Carol Hascall on the *Good Tune* documentary project and Earl Ball on *Traditional Fiddle Music of the Ozarks*, vol. 2, *On the Springfield Plain.*

12. See Shull, *"Uncle Pink,"* 16.

13. Enloe's version of "Old Melinda" ("Malindy") was recorded by Jake Hughes in 1965 and was put on Jake Hughes's "best fiddlers tape" with a number of other Missouri fiddlers. I deposited the copy Hughes gave me in 1973 in the Archive of Folk Song in the Library of Congress.

14. *The Missouri Session* (HMS-3033-CD, 1990), recorded at the Audio Loft, Mack's Creek. I was fortunate to be among listeners at sessions at the Dixon festivals, on the board porch of Frank Ray's roughhewn music shop, when this CD was being formulated. The project is mentioned in Neil V. Rosenberg, "From the Sound Recordings Review Editor: Bluegrass Today," *Journal of American Folklore* 105, no. 418 (1992): 467–68.

15. McCann, "Missouri Fiddler Lyman Enloe."

16. Hill, November 4, 2010.

17. November 9, 2001. In 2000 Grotewohl released a CD of his fiddling called *Bear in the Greengrass*, with tunes from Enloe and Dan's own compositions, reflecting his wide-ranging interests, and accompaniment including his brother Chris Grotewohl (banjo, bouzouki), Zan McLeod (guitar, bass, electric slide), Paddy League (percussion), Roger Landes (uilleann pipe drones), and Jimmy Stadler (keyboard). Dan moved to Colorado, where he became a ski instructor, and later moved to Lawrence, Kansas, to teach fiddling at the Tallgrass Prairie Folk School and at the American Music Academy. In 2016 Grotewohl is in Lawrence, employed by the University of Kansas. Dan Grotewohl became adept at a variety of fiddle styles, including Irish styles, and traveled to perform and teach in Ireland as part of a US State Department exchange program. In a presentation on his experiences with Enloe at the 2001 Missouri Folklore Society conference in Kansas City, Dan remarked that, while he mastered such Enloe classic versions of tunes as the demanding "Brickyard Joe" and "Florida Blues" ("They sound

simple, but they actually have a lot of complexity hidden in them"), his own lights led him to formulate his own take on old-time fiddling, which he called "greengrass style" in which the flow of his own compositions is evident as well as his interest in Celtic fiddling. "I come purely from the emotional side of music. I didn't want to continue rehashing old tunes. I play a lot of originals. I just play from the heart."

18. Cardwell, "Lyman Enloe," 64.

19. Fiddlers with Native American heritage are discussed in Marshall, *Play Me Something Quick and Devilish*. Williams: "My grandma came from *Tennessee*, and her name was *McGoldrick*, and some of the McGoldricks, on *back*, were *dipped in Indian*." Williams quotes come from interviews, June 24, 2013, and September 18, 24, 2015.

20. "Will You Be Loving Another Man" was released in 1947 by Bill Monroe and His Blue Grass Boys (Rosenberg and Wolfe, *Music of Bill Monroe*, 59; Rosenberg, *Bluegrass: A History*, 93). John Williams sings the vocal lead in the style and cast of Lester Flatt on the 1947 record. "When the Echo of Your Footsteps Dies Away" was recorded by country crooner Eddie Arnold in 1949. Irwin Stambler and Grelun Landon, *Country Music: The Encyclopedia*, rev. ed. (New York: St. Martin's Press, 1982), 17. "Remember the Cross" was a gospel song on a Bill Monroe record. "Kelly Waltz" ("Brown Kelly Waltz") was popularized by Texas fiddler Eck Robertson on a 78 rpm record in 1929 and further released by others. Charles Gardner, "The Origins of the Texas Style of Old-Time Fiddling," in *2001: A Texas Folklore Odyssey*, edited by Francis Edward Abernathy (Denton: University of North Texas Press, 2001), 61.

21. Christeson and Stamper played the Dixon picnic in 1926, with Pat Scott, old-time banjo; it is unclear whether Christeson's recollection of the waltz is based on the 1926 event or his visit with Stamper in 1928. Stamper, of Brumley (Miller County), was much admired by Christeson (Christeson 1, xiv; *Good Tune*, 81). Stamper died in 1944. Recently, the waltz was learned from "the book" (Christeson) by South Dakota fiddler Bill Peterson and then picked up by his colleagues, including Iowa fiddlers Nate Kemperman and Dwight Lamb and Amber Gaddy of Columbia, MO; they call it "Dallas Stamper's Waltz" ("It is a good one and I was looking for F tunes to learn and found it in the book" [Bill Peterson, October 2, 2015]). The tune can be heard as obtained from Christeson's collection in the State Historical Society of Missouri by Larry Warren for his website, http://www.slippery-hill.com. Moreover, the initial strains of this tune are like those in "Merry Widow Waltz" as played by Texas Shorty (Jim Chancellor) on his 1980s LP *The Best of Texas Shorty*, but Chancellor's version is not the same tune as classical composer Franz Lehar's "The Merry Widow" ("Merry Widow Waltz") released on a Victor 78 rpm record in 1907 and a standard in the light classical repertory.

22. Tune 226, Christeson 1, 184.

23. Lowinger, *Bluegrass Fiddle*, 32ff. See also Stacy Phillips and Kenny Kosek, *Bluegrass Fiddle Styles* (New York: Oak, 1978); and Phillips, *Hot Licks for Bluegrass Fiddle* (New York: Oak, 1984).

24. Terry Cunningham, July 6, 2015. Cunningham is the retired chief forester for the Drey Pioneer Forest and a bluegrass musician.

25. Ibid., July 7, 2015. The stave companies "did buy staves off private lands and had buying yards and mills at Eminence, Salem, Timber, Van Buren etc., but the haul distance was too great for staves to be taken from this area to another mill." In the previous century, much of

the old-growth timber had been taken by "cut and run" loggers for railroad ties, mine timbers, fence posts, lumber, and fuel.

26. Cecil's brother Gene, some fifteen years older and with a different and more assertive personality, performed in various bands, played dances and sessions, and traveled to festivals, where he became acquainted with a wide swath of professional musicians. For Gene Goforth, see Marshall, "Done Gone: Gene Goforth, 1921–2002," *Fiddler Magazine* 10, no. 3 (2003): 25; *Good Tune*; and Marshall, *Play Me Something Quick and Devilish* (the CD has Gene's "Leather Britches," transcribed in the text, and "Rye Straw"). Both Gene and Cecil appear in Beisswenger and McCann and on the Rounder CD *Traditional Fiddle Music of the Ozarks*, vol. 1 (see chap. 3, n. 13). Hartford's elegant transcriptions of Goforth family tunes appear in issues of the *Devil's Box*.

27. The standard for this fine mandolin tune was set in its initial recording by Monroe's longtime fiddler, Kenny Baker, on the MCA LP *Master of Bluegrass*. More accessible is the 1996 recording by Jimmy Campbell, one of few young fiddlers Monroe considered up to the job of learning and passing on Monroe's special instrumental compositions. Campbell, *Pieces of Time* (Red Clay RC-RD-113, 1996). Campbell died young in 2003, three years before Monroe's death.

28. The open-division contestants who made it through the preliminaries and competed in the finals were Spencer Galloway, John Griffin, Wayne Helton, Henry Thompson, Michelle Ogle, Travis Inman, Junior Marriott, Donna Kirksey, and Jake Hockemeyer. Howe Teague won the senior division, followed by Pete McMahan and Taylor McBaine (courtesy Charlie Walden).

29. The term *sawmill key* is not common in Missouri and may have filtered down through the generations of Scotch-Irish fiddlers in this part of the Ozarks whose people, like the Goforths, came from Scotch-Irish regions of Tennessee, Kentucky, Virginia, and North Carolina. "Sawmill tuning" (or "G modal tuning") is common in the southern Appalachians for banjo tunings (made famous by banjoists such as Clarence Ashley of North Carolina) and fiddlers. Violin scordatura tunings such as A–E–A–E and G–D–G–D are also sometimes called sawmill tuning or sawmill key.

30. "Rye Whisky" traces back to a seventeenth-century Irish tune, "Bacah Buidhe." Among recordings are a version by Vivian Williams and Howard Marshall, *Fiddle Tunes of the Lewis & Clark Era* (Voyager VRCD358, 2002).

31. "Dog in the Rye Straw," on *Fancy Fiddlin' Country Style* (MGM, Cub 8008, 1960). Versions from elsewhere appear in books such as Brody, *The Fiddler's Fakebook*, 241; Ford, *Traditional Music of America*, 47; David Reiner and Peter Anick, *Mel Bay's Fiddling across America*, 123; Phillips, *Phillips Collection*, 1:205–6; and Christeson 1, 17 (Bob Walters's version). Gene Goforth's version is on the companion CD with Marshall, *Play Me Something Quick and Devilish*.

32. Kathy Summers, November 8, 2013.

33. Beisswenger and McCann, 186.

34. For one reference for Bill Keith, Derek Halsey, "A Tribute to Bill Keith: Give Me Flowers While I'm Living," *Bluegrass Unlimited* 50, no. 6 (2015): 14–17. Like Lonnie Hoppers and others masters of the five-string, Bill Keith began his banjo journey on a four-stringed instrument (tenor banjo).

Conclusion

1. For example, in Texas, such creative and powerful fiddlers can be listed, such as Vernon and Norman Solomon, Major Franklin, Jim (Texas Shorty) Chancellor, Orville Burns, Dick Barrett, Benny Thomasson; for Oklahoma, Herman Johnson and Ace Sewell; for Alabama, J. T. Perkins and Jack Weeks. No one of their generation in Missouri had such impact as "Texas"-style fiddlers in contests.

2. McMahan's "Gilsaw" (December 1986) can be heard on Larry Warren's fiddle music website, http://www.slippery-hill.com (tune 795).

3. The tune, as played by Fred Stoneking, a friend of McMahan's, is included in Seattle fiddler Gene Silberberg's book *The Complete Tunes I Either Did or Did Not Learn at the Tractor Tavern*, 65, titled "Gill Saw." Stoneking was a master artist at the Festival of American Fiddle Tunes ca. 2002 and may well have played "Gilsaw" in one of his performances there. Silberberg's is a solid transcription of the basic tune, and it has helped the tune travel (he does not recall where he first heard it [February 2013]). The tune appears in *The Milliner-Koken Collection of American Fiddle Tunes*, based on our 1986 recording of Pete in Columbia for the *Good Tune* documentary. Other Missouri fiddlers have versions: Junior and Cody Marriott, "Gill Saw," *Cody & Jr. Marriott* CD (Ava, MO, 2004); Hugh Strawn of Springfield published tablature for "Gilsaw" in the online *Banjo Newsletter* (http://courses.missouristate.edu/HStrawn/music); McMahan's last student, John Williams, plays "Gilsaw" on his 2004 CD, *Monroe County Influences* (visit YouTube for the video recording); also on YouTube is a performance by John Williams (with Cathy Barton, banjo; Heinrich Leonhard, guitar; and Howard Marshall, violin) at the Big Muddy Folk Festival in Boonville, April 2014; and a version is on the "Soundcloud" Internet site, as Williams played it March 9, 2013, at a dance in Hallsville with fiddlers Howard Marshall and Roger Netherton (St. Louis), joining in, https://soundcloud.com/john-williams-26/gilsaw..

4. Barb Huddleston, Kingdom of Callaway Historical Society, April 14, 2013.

Index to the Voyager Companion CD

1. The theme tune Lonnie fiddles on this occasion is much the same as "Old Parnell," a popular two-step in the "Georgia Camp Meeting" (composed and published by Kerry Mills 1897) and "Whistling Rufus" (Kerry Mills 1899), circles of minstrel-era country rags. Down Texas way, it tends to be called "Hot Foot" and played in C; transcribed in books such as Christeson 1, 162; and Beisswenger and McCann, 123. "Frisky Jim" is an unusual tune rarely played today, and it resembles a number of reels and hornpipes in the key of A. Printed versions appear in Christeson 1, 4; Phillips, *Phillips Collection*, 1:92; and Beisswenger and McCann, 75 (from Dean Johnston's version on *Traditional Fiddle Music of the Ozarks*, vol. 2, Rounder CD 82161, 2000). Here Lonnie Robertson fiddles at a fast breakdown tempo well suited for Ozark square dancing.

2. Tony Gilmore's 1950 version of "Brickyard Joe," recorded by Christeson, is on his double-cassette album *Old-Time Fiddler's Repertory: Historic Field Recordings* (Columbia: University of Missouri Press, 1976; reissued, 2011, MSOTFA). Lyman Enloe, who learned it from Gilmore, has it on his 1978 County LP, *Fiddle Tunes I Recall* (and see Beisswenger and McCann, 27). Dan Grotewohl, who learned it from Lyman Enloe, has it on his 2000 CD,

Bear in the Greengrass. Published examples include Gilmore's in Christeson 1, no. 124, p. 89; Charlie Walden's arrangement in *Missouri Fiddle Tunes*, 11; Brody, *The Fiddler's Fakebook*, 56; and Phillips, *Phillips Collection*, 1:36.

Selected Bibliography

This list is intended as a guide for readers who would like to learn more. The list is not exhaustive but a selection of pertinent works as well as personal favorites. Additional references appear in the endnotes.

Adam, E. F. *Old-Time Fiddlers' Favorite Barn Dance Tunes for the Violin.* St. Louis: Louis Retter, 1927. Reissued as *Mel Bay's Old Time Fiddle Solos.* Pacific, MO: Mel Bay, 1977.

Adler, Thomas A. *Bean Blossom: The Brown County Jamboree and Bill Monroe's Bluegrass Festival.* Urbana: University of Illinois Press, 2011.

———. "Manual Formulaic Composition: Innovation in Bluegrass Banjo Styles." *Journal of Country Music* 5, no. 2 (1974): 55–64.

———. "The Physical Development of the Banjo." *New York Folklore Quarterly* 28, no. 3 (1972): 187–208.

Aitken, Hugh G. J. *The Continuous Wave: Technology and the American Radio, 1900–1932.* Princeton, NJ: Princeton University Press, 1985.

Anastasio, Paul. "On Improvisation." *Fiddler Magazine* 4, no. 3 (1997): 39.

———. "On Improvisation: How to Play in a Pickup Band." *Fiddler Magazine* 12, no. 3 (2005): 40–41.

———. "On Improvisation: Learning by Ear—Demystified." *Fiddler Magazine* 9, no. 3 (2002): 42–44.

———. "On Improvisation: Taking the Plunge into Swing." *Fiddler Magazine* 6, no. 1 (1999): 37–39.

———. "On Improvisation: Thinking on Your Feet." *Fiddler Magazine* 8, no. 4 (2000–2001): 46–47.

———. "Order Out of Chaos; or, How to Play in a Group." *Fiddler Magazine* 8, no. 3 (2001): 40–41.

———. *Swing Fiddle by Paul Anastasio.* Instructional DVD. Seattle: Swing Cat Enterprises, 2009.

Baron, Carl. "Workshop" [transcriptions of Ron Hughey tunes]. *Old-Time Herald* (Spring 1998): 37–38.

Beisswenger, Drew. "Gordon McCann: The Improbable Ascent of the Ozarks Fiddle Man." *Old-Time Herald* 10, no. 4 (2006): 32–36.

Beisswenger, Drew, and Gordon McCann. *Ozarks Fiddle Music: 308 Tunes Featuring 30 Legendary Fiddlers with Selections from 50 Other Great Ozarks Fiddlers.* Pacific, MO: Mel Bay, 2008.

Benson, Doug. "Bill Monroe, King of Blue Grass Music." In *The Bill Monroe Reader*, edited by Tom Ewing. Urbana: University of Illinois Press, 2000.

Bistodeau, Deena. "Texas Style Controlled Improvisation and the American Fiddle Contest." *National Oldtime Fiddler* (October–December 2011): 18–19.

———. "Texas Style Controlled Improvisation and the American Fiddle Contest, Part II." *National Oldtime Fiddler* (January–March 2012): 19–20.

———. "Texas Style Controlled Improvisation and the American Fiddle Contest, Part III." *National Oldtime Fiddler* (Summer 2012): 21–23.

———. "Texas Style Controlled Improvisation and the American Fiddle Contest, Part IV." *National Oldtime Fiddler* (October–December 2012): 20–22.

Black, Bob. *Come Hither to Go Yonder: Playing Music with Bill Monroe*. Urbana: University of Illinois Press, 2005.

Boyd, Jean Ann. *The Jazz of the Southwest: An Oral History of Western Swing*. Austin: University of Texas Press, 1998.

Brody, David. *The Fiddler's Fakebook*. New York: Oak, 1983.

Burman-Hall, Linda C. "Southern American Folk Fiddle Styles." *Ethnomusicology* 19, no. 1 (1975): 47–65.

Cardwell, Nancy. "The Fiddle Music of Art Galbraith: An Ozark Family Legacy Passed Down Four Generations." *Bluegrass Unlimited* (January 1984): 16–19.

———. "Lyman Enloe: A Stylist of the Old-Time Fiddle." *Bluegrass Unlimited* (January 1989): 61–64.

Cauthen, Joyce. *With Fiddle and Well-Rosined Bow: Old-Time Fiddling in Alabama*. Tuscaloosa: University of Alabama Press, 1989.

Christeson, R. P. *The Old-Time Fiddlers Repertory*. 2 vols., 1973, 1984. Reprint, Columbia: University of Missouri Press, 2010.

———. "Old-Time Fiddling in Missouri: A Workshop." *Missouri Folklore Society Journal* 20 (1998): 1–24.

Cole, M. M. *One Thousand Fiddle Tunes*. 1883. Reprint of *Ryan's Mammoth Collection*. Chicago: Cole, 1940.

Crouch, Stanley. *Kansas City Lightning: The Rise and Times of Charlie Parker*. New York: Harper, 2013.

———. "Swing on Top" [about Claude Williams]. *Village Voice*, January 22, 1985, 91, 92, 96.

Driggs, Frank, and Chuck Haddix. *Kansas City Jazz: From Ragtime to Bebop—a History*. New York: Oxford University Press, 2005.

Evans, E. Estyn. *Irish Folk Ways*. London: Routledge and Kegan Paul, 1957.

Feather, Leonard, and Ira Gitler. *The Biographical Encyclopedia of Jazz*. New York: Oxford University Press 1999.

Ford, Ira W. *Traditional Music of America*. New York: E. P. Dutton, 1940.

Gage, Allen. "Old-Time Fiddling: A Traditional Folk Art with Four Ozark Musicians." *Bittersweet* 9, no. 3 (1982): 48–64.

Galbraith, Arthur. "Autobiography." On *Dixie Blossoms*. LP 0133. Somerville, MA: Rounder Records, 1980.

———. "The Devil's Own Box." *Bittersweet* 9, no. 3 (1982): 58–60.

———. "The Devil's Own Instrument." *Ozarks Mountaineer* 25, no. 9 (1977): 21.

———. "Music Parties in the Ozarks." *Ozarks Mountaineer* 28, nos. 6–7 (1980): 35, 50.

Galloway, Spencer. "Missouri Fiddling Styles." In *Old-Time Fiddling: Traditional American Music*, edited by Margot Ford McMillen, 5–6. Columbia: University of Missouri Cultural Heritage Center, 1986.

Gardner, Howard. *Frames of Mind: The Theory of Multiple Intelligences*. 1983. Reprint, New York: Basic Books, 2011.

Giddins, Gary. *Riding on a Blue Note: Jazz and American Pop*. New York: Oxford University Press, 1981.

Gilmore, Robert K. *Ozark Baptizings, Hangings, and Other Diversions: Theatrical Folkways of Rural Missouri, 1885–1910*. Norman: University of Oklahoma Press, 1984.

Glenn, Wayne. *The Ozarks' Greatest Hits: A Photo History of Music in the Ozarks*. Nixa, MO: Wayne Glenn, 2005.

Haddix, Chuck. *Bird: The Life and Music of Charlie Parker*. Urbana: University of Illinois Press, 2013.

———. "Claude Williams: The Fiddler's Triumph." *Down Beat* (March 1999): 32–34.

———. "Coon-Sanders Original Nighthawk Orchestra: Radio Aces." http://www.library.umc.edu.

Harding's Original Collection of Jigs and Reels: 200 Jigs, Reels and Country Dances for Piano, Violin, Flute, or Mandolin. New York: Paull-Pioneer Music, 1928.

Hartford, John. "John Hartford Tune Transcriptions: 'Coming Down from Denver on a Trip to Galway Here and There,' 'Flannery's Dream.'" *Devil's Box* 29, no. 1 (1995): 12–14.

———. "John Hartford Tune Transcriptions: 'Darkie's Curly Hair,' 'Knocking at Your Door,' 'Maysville,' 'Better Get Outa My Way.'" *Devil's Box* 29, no. 4 (1995): 17–19.

———. "John Hartford Tune Transcriptions: 'Hamilton Iron Works.'" *Devil's Box* 32, no. 4 (1998): 53.

———. "John Hartford Tune Transcriptions: 'Whoa Mule,' 'Boone County Rag.'" *Devil's Box* 28, no. 4 (1994): 11–13.

———. "Old Time Tunes: 'Wolves a-Howlin'.'" *Fiddler Magazine* 4, no. 4 (1997–98): 37.

———. "On the Study of Fiddle Tunes: Reassurance That There Is No Frivolous Design behind This Seemingly 'Goofy' Maneuver." *Fiddler Magazine* 6, no. 2 (1999): 38–40.

Hentoff, Nat. *Jazz Is*. New York: Limelight, 1984.

Hickerson, Joseph C., comp. *A Bibliography of Fiddling, Fiddle Tunes, and Related Dance Tune Collections in North America*. . . . Washington, DC: Archive of Folk Song, Library of Congress, 1974.

Higgins, Lisa L., et al. *Work Is Art; Art Is Work: Interviews with Missouri Luthiers*. Videodocumentary. Columbia: Missouri Folk Arts Program, 2007.

Howe, Elias. *Howe's 1,000 Jigs and Reels, Clog Dances, Contra Dances, Fancy Dances, Hornpipes, Strathspeys, Breakdowns, Irish Dances, Scotch Dances, and More*. . . .

1867. Reprinted as *Mel Bay Presents Howe's 1,000 . . .*, edited by Patrick Sky. Pacific, MO: Mel Bay, 2001.

Intrator, John. "Claude Williams Live: That Kansas City Spell." *Fiddler Magazine* 7, no. 2 (2000): 9–12.

Johnson, Kenneth. *Moonlight Serenade to City Lights: Rare Images of Bands and Orchestras in the Dance Hall Era in Missouri*. St. Louis: Reedy Press, 2015.

Kemperman, Nate. "Fiddling for Ford." Research paper, Iowa State University, History of American Popular Culture, 2001.

Kienzle, Richard. *Southwest Shuffle: Pioneers of Honky-Tonk, Western Swing, and Country Jazz*. New York: Routledge, 2003.

Kisliuk, Michelle. "'A Special Kind of Courtesy': Action at a Bluegrass Festival Jam Session." *TDR: The Drama Review* 32, no. 3 (1988): 141–55.

Kuntz, Andrew. "The Fiddler's Companion: A Descriptive Index of North American and British Isles Music for the Folk Violin." http://ibiblio.org/fiddlers/FChomepage.htm

Lansford, Kim. "'Boy! He Sure Had Some Good Tunes!' The Music of Lonnie Robertson." *Ozarks Mountaineer* (July–August 2012): 38–39.

Larsen, Mary. "Claude 'Fiddler' Williams: Kansas City Swing!" *Fiddler Magazine* 3, no. 4 (1994–95): 24–30.

Levi, Peter, ed. *A Journey to the Western Islands of Scotland: James Boswell, the Journal of a Tour to the Hebrides*. 1775. Reprint, London: Penguin Books, 1984.

Linn, Karen. *That Half-Barbaric Twang: The Banjo in American Popular Culture*. Chicago: University of Chicago Press, 1991.

Lowinger, Gene. *Bluegrass Fiddle*. New York: Oak, 1974.

———. *I Hear a Voice Calling: A Bluegrass Memoir*. Urbana: University of Illinois Press, 2009.

Malone, Bill C. *Country Music, USA*. 2nd ed. Austin: University of Texas Press, 2002.

Marshall, Howard Wight. *Barns of Missouri: Storehouses of History*. Marceline, MO: Donning, 2003.

———. "Cyril Stinnett, Legendary Missouri Fiddler: Home Videos from the Dwight Lamb Collection." *Old-Time Herald* 13, no. 11 (2015): 43–47.

———. "Evansville (Missouri, That Is)." *MSOTFA Journal* (1994): 3.

———. "An Evening with Lee Roy Stoneking, with a Few Unexpurgated and Incomplete Comments on Field Recording Traditional Artists during the Heyday of the Folk Festival and Fiddlers' Contest Revival." Online notes. Brad Leftwich and Linda Higginbotham. *Lee Stoneking: Missouri Fiddling and Banjo Playing*. Ravenna, OH: Field Recorders' Collective FRC 708, 2014. http://www.fieldrecorder.com.

———. *Folk Architecture in Little Dixie: A Regional Culture in Missouri*. Columbia: University of Missouri Press, 1981.

———. "In Memory: Taylor Franklin McBaine (1910–1994)." *Devil's Box* 28, no. 4 (1994): 33–35.

———. "Jake Hockemeyer and the Legacy of Missouri Traditional Fiddling." *Devil's Box* 32, no. 4 (1997): 14–21.

———. "Keep on the Sunny Side of Life: Pattern and Religious Expression in Bluegrass Gospel Music." *New York Folklore Quarterly* 30, no. 1 (1974): 1–43.

———. "'King of the Folks': R. P. Christeson and His *Old-Time Repertory*." *Old-Time Herald* 13, no. 3 (2012): 22–35.

———. "Leroy Canaday." *Old-Time Herald* 1, no. 4 (1994–95): 17–18.

———. "Live! At the Ozark Opry: An Appreciation of Vaudeville and 'Show Fiddler' LeRoy Haslag." *Old-Time Herald* 12, no. 9 (2011): 24–35.

———. "Lloyd Lalumondier, 1924–2005." Missouri Folklore Society, July 2015. http://www.missourifolkloresociety.truman.edu.

———. "Lonnie Robertson, Radio Fiddler." *Fiddler Magazine* (in press).

———. "'Play Me Something Quick and Devilish': Adventures in the Documentation and Conservation of Missouri's Heritage of Traditional Fiddle and Dance Music." *Missouri Historical Review* 108, no. 2 (2014): 105–22.

———. *Play Me Something Quick and Devilish: Old-Time Fiddlers in Missouri.* Columbia: University of Missouri Press, 2012.

———. "Rattlesnake Buttons." *MSOTFA Quarterly* 13, no. 1 (1995): 3.

———. "Remembering Jake Hockemeyer." *MSOTFA Quarterly* 16, no. 1 (1999): 1–2.

———. "Rhonda Vincent and Missouri's Old-Time and Bluegrass Crossroads." *Old-Time Herald* 13, no. 8 (2014): 10–21.

———. *Vernacular Architecture in Rural and Small Town Missouri: An Introduction*. Columbia: University of Missouri Extension Division, 1984.

———. "'Where Did You Come From, Where Did You Go?' The Split Personality of Cotton-Eyed Joe, Part Two." July 2010. http://www.fiddlesessions.com.

———, et. al., eds. *"Now That's a Good Tune": Masters of Traditional Missouri Fiddling.* Rev. ed. 1989. Reprint, Seattle: Voyager Recordings and Publications, 2008.

McCann, Gordon. "Bob Walsh." *Old-Time Herald* 4, no. 9 (1994): 13.

———. "Lonnie Robertson." *Old-Time Herald* 4, no. 9 (1994): 12–13.

McKinney, Edgar D. "Images, Realities, and Cultural Transformations in the Missouri Ozarks, 1920–1960." PhD diss., University of Missouri, 1990.

———. "Like Family: Kinship Perceptions of Ozarks Radio Entertainers and the Spread of Consumer Culture, 1934–1959." *Gateway Heritage* 11, no. 4 (1991): 26–39.

McLean, Duncan. *Lone Star Swing: On the Trail of Bob Wills and the Texas Playboys*. New York: W. W. Norton, 1997.

McMillen, Margot Ford. *A to Z Missouri: The Dictionary of Missouri Place Names.* 1996. Reprint, Columbia, MO: Pebble, 2014.

———, ed. *Old-Time Fiddling: Traditional American Music.* Columbia: University of Missouri Cultural Heritage Center, 1986.

———. *Paris, Tightwad, and Peculiar: Missouri Place Names*. Columbia: University of Missouri Press, 1994.

Meade, Guthrie T. "Fiddles and Fords: Photographs from Louisville's Caufield & Shook Studio." *Journal of Country Music* 12, no. 3 (1989): 37–45.

Menius, Art. "Our Ford: Old Time Fiddle and Dancing." *Bluegrass Unlimited* (February 1992): 36–39.

Meyer, Duane G. *The Heritage of Missouri*. 3rd ed. 1963. Reprint, St. Louis: River City, 1982.

Milliner, Clare, and Walt Koken. *The Milliner-Koken Collection of American Fiddle Tunes*. Kennett Square, PA: Mudthumper Music, 2011.

Moore, Tiny, and Merle Haggard. *Merle Haggard Presents Swinging Texas Fiddlin' by Tiny Moore with Warren Helton and Vernon Solomon: A Study of Traditional and Modern Breakdown and Hoedown Fiddling*. New York: Peer International, 1982.

Morris, W. H. *Old-Time Violin Melodies*. 1927. Reprint, St. Joseph: Missouri State Old Time Fiddlers Association, 1992.

Mott, Frank Luther, ed. *Missouri Reader*. Columbia: University of Missouri Press, 1964.

Nolan, Brid, and Stuart Williams. *Rose in Winter: A Celebration of Fiddlers in Washington State*. Seattle: Washington State Old Time Fiddlers Association, 2006.

Noles, Randy. *Fiddler's Curse: The Untold Story of Ervin T. Rouse, Chubby Wise, Johnny Cash, and the Orange Blossom Special*. Anaheim Hills, CA: Centerstream, 2007.

Noordijk, Eddy, ed. *Joe Venuti Violin Rhythm: A School of Modern Rhythmic Violin Playing*. New York: Robbins Music, 1937.

O'Neill, Francis. *The Dance Music of Ireland: 1001 Gems*. Chicago: Lyon & Healy, 1907. Reprint, Dublin: Walton's, 2004.

Pearson, Nathan W., Jr. *Goin' to Kansas City*. Urbana: University of Illinois Press, 1987.

Peek, Dan William. *Live! At the Ozark Opry*. Charleston, SC: History Press, 2010.

Phillips, Stacy. *The Complete Country Fiddler*. Pacific, MO: Mel Bay, 1992.

———. *The Phillips Collection of Traditional American Fiddle Tunes*. Vol. 1, *Hoedowns, Breakdowns, & Reels*. Pacific, MO: Mel Bay, 1994.

———. *The Phillips Collection of Traditional American Fiddle Tunes*. Vol. 2, *Rags, Blues, Hornpipes, Waltzes, Polkas, Jigs, Etc*. Pacific, MO: Mel Bay, 1995.

———. *Western Swing Fiddle*. New York: Western Sales, 1997.

Phillips, Stacy, and Kenny Kosek. *Bluegrass Fiddle Styles*. New York: Oak, 1978.

Ramsay, Robert L. *Our Storehouse of Missouri Place Names*. Columbia: University of Missouri Press, 1952.

Randolph, Vance. "The Names of Ozark Fiddle Tunes." *Midwest Folklore* 4, no. 2 (1954): 81–86.

Reiner, David, and Peter Anick. *Mel Bay's Fiddling across America*. Pacific, MO: Mel Bay, 1989.

Roberson, Margot, and Howard Marshall. *The Masters: Traditional Arts Apprenticeship Program*. Columbia: University of Missouri Cultural Heritage Center, 1986.

Romano, Richard Niles, ed. *Joe Venuti: Never Before . . . Never Again*. Pacific, MO: Mel Bay, 2005.

Rooney, Jim. *Bossmen: Bill Monroe and Muddy Waters*. New York: Dial Press, 1971.

Rosenberg, Neil V. *Bluegrass: A History*. Urbana: University of Illinois Press, 1985.

———, ed. *Transforming Tradition: Folk Music Revivals Examined*. Urbana: University of Illinois Press, 1993.

Rosenberg, Neil V., and Charles K. Wolfe. *The Music of Bill Monroe*. Urbana: University of Illinois Press, 2007.

Russell, Ross. *Bird Lives: The High Life and Hard Times of Charlie (Yardbird) Parker*. New York: Da Capo Press, 1996.

Russell, Tony. *Country Music Originals: The Legends and the Lost*. New York: Oxford University Press, 2007.

Ryan, William Bradbury. *Ryan's Mammoth Collection of 1050 Reels and Jigs*. 1883. Reprinted as *Mel Bay Presents Ryan's Mammoth Collection . . .* , edited by Patrick Sky. Pacific, MO: Mel Bay, 1995.

Schmidt, Claire. "Vesta Johnson, Award-Winning Old-Time Missouri Fiddler." *Museum Magazine* 63 (Fall 2013): 8–9.

Scholes, Percy Alfred. *The Oxford Companion to Music*. London and New York: Oxford University Press, 1938.

Schuller, Gunther. *The Swing Era: The Development of Jazz, 1930–1945*. New York: Oxford University Press, 1981.

Shull, Bill. *Cross-Tuning Your Fiddle: History, Techniques, & Transcriptions*. Pacific, MO: Mel Bay, 1994.

———, ed. *"Uncle Pink" and Other Central Missouri Fiddle Tunes from Lyman Enloe*. Columbia: Missouri State Old Time Fiddlers Association, 1993.

Silberberg, Gene. *The Complete Fiddle Tunes I Either Did or Did Not Learn at the Tractor Tavern*. Seattle: Gene Silberberg, 2007.

———. *Fiddle Tunes I Either Did or Did Not Learn at the Tractor Tavern*. Seattle: Gene Silberberg, 2002.

Sky, Patrick, ed. *Mel Bay Presents Howe's 1,000 Jigs and Reels, Clog Dances, Contra Dances, Fancy Dances, Hornpipes, Strathspeys, Breakdowns, Irish Dances, Scotch Dances, and More. . . .* 1867. Reprint, Pacific, MO: Mel Bay, 2001.

———. *Mel Bay Presents Ryan's Mammoth Collection. . . .* 1883. Reprint, Pacific, MO: Mel Bay, 1995.

Sparks, Mary Ruth Luna. "Two Ozark Countians Were Early Radio Stars—Lonnie and Thelma Robertson." *Old Mill Run* (October 2007): 5–7.

Spears-Stewart, Reta. *Remembering the Ozark Jubilee "Starring Red Foley."* Springfield, MO: Stewart, Dilbeck, and White, 1993.

Szwed, John. F. *Jazz 101: A Complete Guide to Learning and Loving Jazz*. New York: Hyperion, 2000.

Taber, Janet. *Just Down Home Folks* [exhibition text]. Gainesville: Ozark County Historium, 2014.

Taylor, Deems, and Russell Kerr, eds. *Music Lover's Encyclopedia by Rupert Hughes.* New York: Knopf Doubleday, 1957.
Thede, Marion Unger. *The Fiddle Book.* New York: Oak, 1967.
Townsend, Charles R. *San Antonio Rose: The Life and Music of Bob Wills.* Urbana: University of Chicago Press, 1986.
Walden, Charlie. "The 1925 Missouri 'Mythical' Fiddle Championship." *MSOTFA Contest Calendar* (1983): 4–5.
———. "Chief Francis O'Neill in Missouri." N.d. http://www.missourifiddling.com.
———. "Cyril Winfield Stinnett: Master of Hornpipe and Hoedown." *Old-Time Herald* 4, no. 6 (1994–95): 10–11.
———. "Dance Fiddling in Missouri." In *Traditional Dance in Missouri: Southern Missouri Jig Dancing*, by Peter Lippincott and Margot Lippincott, 1:4–6. St. Louis: Childgrove Country Dancers, 1984.
———. "Daniel Boone Jones: Early Radio Fiddler." *Devil's Box* 23, no. 1 (1989): 34–35.
———. "Geoff Seitz: "The Last of the Great Lemay Fiddlers." *Old-Time Herald* 4, no. 6 (1994–95): 32–34.
———. "Henry Taylor: A Fiddle Champ from Yesteryear." *MSOTFA Quarterly* 12, no. 1 (1994): 1.
———. *Hoe-Downs, Hornpipes & Hokum.* Evanston, IL: Charlie Walden Music, 2011.
———. "The Life and Legacy of George Morris, the 'Fiddling Sheriff.'" *MSOTFA Contest Calendar* (1985): 6–11.
———. "The Life and Legacy of George Morris: The Fiddlin' Sheriff." *Devil's Box* 18, no. 4 (1984): 3–14.
———. "Missouri Fiddle Tune Collections." N.d. http://www.missourifiddling.com.
———. *Missouri Fiddle Tunes.* Vols. 1–2, *Fast & Slow for Learning.* Evanston, IL: Charlie Walden Music, 2010.
———. "The Missouri-Irish Connection?" *MSOTFA Quarterly* 2, no. 1 (1984): 3–4.
———. "Missouri Old-Time Fiddling Traditions." N.d. http://www.missourifiddling.com.
———. "Missouri Old-Time Fiddling Traditions." *Fiddler Magazine* 3, no. 3 (1996): 5–11.
———. "Nile Wilson—Old-Time Fiddler." *MSOTFA Quarterly* 13, no. 1 (1995): 1.
———. "One Hundred Essential Missouri Fiddle Tunes." N.d. http://www.missourifiddling.com.
———. "Radiophone WOS and WOS Radio Reunion and Fiddling Championship." N.d. http://www.missourifiddling.com.
———. "Tracking Down the Legendary 'Sheriff.'" *MSOTFA Contest Calendar* (1984): 4–5.
Warner, Judy Mae. "Ozark Old-Time Fiddling." Master's thesis, University of Arkansas, 2010.

Weil, Gordon Lee. *Sears, Roebuck, U.S.A.: The Great American Catalog Store and How It Grew*. Briarcliff Manor, NY: Stein and Day, 1977.

Williams, Martin. *The Jazz Tradition*. New York: Oxford University Press, 1983.

Williams, Phil, and Vivian Williams. *Fiddler Magazine* 21, no. 2 (2014): 10–14.

Williams, Stuart, comp. *Evergreen Fiddler Tune Book*. Vols. 1–3. N.p.: Washington Old Time Fiddlers Association, 2005, 2006, 2008. http://www.wotfa.org.

———. "Tune of the Month: Crystal Stream Waltz." *Washington State Old Time Fiddlers Association Newsletter* (February 2013).

Williams, Vivian T. "The Essential Fiddle Tune Books." http://www.voyagerrecords.com.

———. *The Haynes Family Manuscript: Pioneer Dance Music from the Willamette Valley of Oregon*. Seattle: Voyager Recordings and Publications, 2009.

———. "Jam Session Etiquette." http://voyagerrecords.com/arjam.htm

———. "Northwest Pioneer Fiddlers." http://www.voyagerrecords.com, 2010.

———. *The Peter Beemer Manuscript: Dance Music Collected in the Mining Camp of Warren's Diggins, Idaho, in the 1860s*. Seattle: Voyager Recordings and Publications, 2007.

Williams, Vivian T., and Phil Williams. "Contra and Square Dance Playing." 1998. http://www.voyagerrecords.com.

———. *Songs and Dances of the Oregon Trail*. Seattle: Voyager Records, 2012.

———. "Stuart Williams, Northwest Fiddler." *Fiddler Magazine* 21, no. 2 (2014): 10–14.

Wolfe, Charles K. "Caney Mountain Fiddler: The Lonnie Robertson Story." *Devil's Box* 12, no. 3 (1978): 34–36.

———. *Classic Country: Legends of Country Music*. New York and London: Routledge, 2001.

———. *The Devil's Box: Masters of Southern Fiddling*. Nashville: Vanderbilt University Press, 1997.

"Over the Waves" has been a favorite waltz among Missouri fiddlers since it appeared in the late 1800s. It was composed by Mexican dance band leader Juventino Rosas in 1884. Rosas toured extensively with his orchestra, including concerts at the 1893 Chicago World's Fair (see *Play Me Something Quick and Devilish*). The waltz has been recorded across the spectrum; this example from a local attic is a 78 rpm record ca. 1918 by the Paramount Military Band (Paramount 2017-A).

Discography

This discography is only a sampling of recordings, most of which can be located by interested parties.

Field recordings of Missouri fiddlers may be found archived in the Library of Congress, Smithsonian Institution (Festival of American Folklife), National Council for the Traditional Arts, Greene County Library in Springfield, Meyer Library at Missouri State University, Missouri Folk Arts Program (University of Missouri, Columbia), State Historical Society of Missouri, and other institutions, including local museums and county historical societies.

An untold number of important informal field recordings and home recordings have been made since the 1940s, and especially during the golden age of the inexpensive portable cassette recorder (from the 1960s into the 1990s), with vast personal collections existing today, in many cases lovingly accumulated by now unknown or undocumented collectors and fans of fiddle music. In most instances, these troves of informal recordings never come to light and are never heard again once their originators and owners pass away and the old tapes get stored in an attic or back of a closet, someday to turn up at a garage sale or end up in a public landfill. Now in the 2010s, proliferation of inexpensive digital recorders of all kinds (including "smart phones") is giving us a new era of informal recording, much of which will never be archived, kept, or available to the future.

Ball, Earl. *Family Favorites.* Humansville, MO: private-label CD (ca. 2003).

Barton, Cathy, and Dave Para. *Ballad of the Boonslick.* 1982, CD reissue, Barton and Para, http://www.bartonandpara.com, 2003.

———. *Crazy Quilt.* Big Canoe Records (1998).

———. *Rebel in the Woods: Civil War Songs from the Western Border.* Vol. 2. Boonville, MO: Big Canoe Records (1995).

Barton, Cathy, Dave Para, and Bob Dyer. *Johnny Whistletrigger: Civil War Songs from the Western Border.* Big Canoe Records (1993).

Beisswenger, Drew, and Gordon McCann. *Ozarks Fiddle Music: 308 Tunes Featuring 30 Legendary Fiddlers with Selections from 50 Other Great Ozarks Fiddlers.* Mel Bay (2008).

Bill Perkins and the Midwesterners. *Pickin' at Liberty.* Ozark Records LP (1978). [Bill Perkins, violin]

Bluegrass Association. *Festival Favorites.* BBR 84-105 (1984). [Don Montgomery, violin]

———. *Happy I'll Be.* Ozark Opry OOR 81 104 (1981). [Don Montgomery, violin]

———. *One Tin Soldier.* Cavern Custom USR 4122 (1973). [Lyman Enloe, violin]

———. *Strings Today . . . and Yesterday.* Cavern Custom 42419 (1974). [Lyman Enloe, violin]

Bressler Brothers. *Heroes*. Shan-Co-Mo Records 4001 (1998).

Brown, Don, and Ozark Mountain Trio. *Recorded Live on Stage*. K-Ark 6017 (1972). [Bobby Puckett, violin]

Bruce, Johnny. *Carroll County Fiddler*. Bosworth, MO: private-label cassette (ca. 1977).

Bryan, Cliff. *Got a Little Home to Go To*. Voyager VRCD378 (2015).

Caldwell, Luther. *Luther Caldwell—One Armed Fiddler of Boone County MO*. MSOTFA Recordings 107 (digital download, 2015).

Canaday, Leroy. *Old Dan Tucker Was a Fine Old Man: Missouri Fiddler Leroy Canaday*. Voyager VRCD353 (2001).

Collins, Earl. *"That's Earl": Collins Family Fiddling*. Briar Recordings LP 4204 (1975).

County Line. *Sweet Prairie Hay*. Grass Mountain Records GM1001 (1975). [Dale Hopkins, violin]

Currey, Sadie. *Sadie Caroline*. Columbia, MO: private-label CD, Curreykorn (2010).

Cyril Stinnett, Legendary Missouri Fiddler: Home Videos from the Dwight Lamb Collection. Missouri Valley Music, 2013. [DVD]

The Dillards. *Back Porch Bluegrass*. Elektra EKS-7231 (1963).

———. *Live! Almost!* Elektra EKL-265 (1964).

———. *Pickin' and Fiddlin'*. Elektra EKS-7285 (1965).

Draper, Rusty, with Ozark Red Loveall. *Rusty and Red: The Early Recordings of Rusty Draper Featuring Ozark Red Loveall*. British Archive of Country Music, CD D334 (2011).

Drifters. *Live from Everywhere*. Driftime DTP001 (ca. 1980). [cassette] [Gary Brown, violin]

Ellis, Larry. *Larry Ellis Fiddle CD #1*. Lee's Summit: private label, 2012.

Enloe, Lyman. *Fiddle Tunes I Recall*. 1978. Reissue, County CO-CD-2702 (1993). [with the Bluegrass Association]

———. *Rugged Road*. Society for the Preservation of Blue Grass Music in America, 1976. Reissue, Missouri State Old Time Fiddlers Association, MSOTFA 004 (1989). [with the Bluegrass Association]

Enloe, Lyman, Casey Jones, and Cyril Stinnett. *Three Fiddlers from the Show-Me State*. County CO-2739-CD (2005).

Esloo, Jeff, and Matt Wyatt. *Banjo & Fiddle*. Fiddlesong Records (2005).

Fiddle Farts. *Fiddle Farts: Old Time Country Favorites*. Russellville, MO: private-label CD (2001). [Herschel West, Gerald Steenbergen, Gene Steenbergen, Lige Enloe, Bill Bertucci]

Galbraith, Art. *Dixie Blossoms*. Rounder Records LP 0133 (1980). Reissue, Musical Traditions Records (England), with additional tracks, MTCD509 (2010).

———. *Simple Pleasures: Old-Time Fiddling from the Ozarks*. Rounder LP 0157 (198?).

Goforth, Gene. *Eminence Breakdown*. Rounder Records 0388 (1997).
———. *Strike Up the Bow*. Professional Artists PAS 7433-21 (1974).
Graves, Bill. *Sugar in the Coffee*. Missouri State Old Time Fiddlers Association 301-CD (1997).
Green Side Up. *Green Side Up*. Kansas City: Chapman Studios (1988). [cassette] [Larry Ellis, violin]
———. *How Does Bluegrass Grow? Green Side Up*. Kansas City: George's Music Service, 1975. [eight-track tape] [Larry Ellis, violin]
Grotewohl, Dan. *Bear in the Greengrass*. Orchard (2000).
Hartford, John. *Hamilton Ironworks*. Rounder 0442 (2001).
Haslag, LeRoy. *Reflections of a Missouri Fiddler*. Jefferson City, MO: private label, NR 21420 (2001).
Helton, Warren. *Warren Helton: Old Tyme Fiddler*. Vienna, MO: private label, Warren Helton Music, 2014.
Herd, Jim. *Old Time Ozark Fiddling*. Voyager VRCD340 (1999).
Holt, Bob. *Got a Little Home to Go To*. Rounder CD 0432 (1998).
———. *Rabbit in the Pea Patch: Traditional South Missouri Dance Tunes*. Ava, MO: private–label cassette (ca. 1992).
———. *The Way I Heard It*. [Bob Holt, 1993].
Hopkins, Dale. *Old'n in the Way*. Reissue CD, Macks Creek, MO: Nearly Famous Records (2001).
Hoppers, Lonnie. *The Old Country Church: Instrumentals Featuring Five-String Banjo*. Urbana, MO: private-label CD, Hoppers (n.d.). [Jamie Haage, violin]
Hoppers, Lonnie, and Dan Crary. *Lonnie Hoppers and Dan Crary and Their American Band*. Pinecastle PRC-CD-100 (2000). [Jamie Haage, principal; also Dale Hopkins]
Hoppers, Lonnie, and Friends. *Pickin' for Fun*. Dungeon 2041 (LP). Reissue, Urbana, MO: private-label CD, Hoppers (1980). [Mark Pearman, principal fiddler; also David Wilson, Randy Newman]
Hoppers, Lonnie, and New Union. *Grass Hoppin'*. Haage Studio (2000). [Jamie Haage, violin]
———. *Lifetime Harvest*. Urbana, MO: private-label CD, Franklin Ridge Records (2005). [Kelly Jones, violin]
Hughes, Lena. *Lena Hughes, Queen of the Guitar Pickers and Her Flat Top Guitar*. Power Records PLR185 (ca. 1965). CD reissue, Tompkins Square (2013).
Hughey, Ron. *Country Fiddlin' Ozark Style*. American Heritage AH-402-511 (1973).
Jimmy Orchard and the Ozark Bluegrass Boys. "Longing for the Ozarks," "Trouble in B." Cherry Records CH 014 (1972). [Odie Mullins, violin]
Johnson, Ray "Pick." *Tunes I Learned from My Uncle Cleve from Big Springs, Missouri*. Graphic Recording LP GR-1004 (ca. 1980).
Johnson, Vesta. *Blue Flame*. Marimac 9057 (1994). [cassette]

———. *Down Home Rag*. Marimac 9017 (1988). [cassette]

———. *Indian Creek*. Kirkwood, MO: private-label CD (1999).

Johnston, Herbie. *Fiddlin' around with Herbie Johnston*. N.d., n.p., private-label cassette (ca. 1985).

Jones, Casey. *Rocky Road to Jordan*. Missouri State Old Time Fiddlers Association 102 (1987). [cassette]

Jones, Kelly. *Authentic Old-Time Fiddle Tunes*. Cavern Custom Recording, USR7714 (1975). Reissue, Missouri State Old Time Fiddlers Association 006 (1990). [cassette]

———. *"Through the Years."* Vol. 1. Stover, MO: private-label CD (2001). [compilation]

The Karl Shiflett & Big Country Show. Rebel Reb-CD-1752 (1999). [Kirk Brandenberger, violin]

Latty, Vee. *Fever in the South*. Columbia: Missouri State Old Time Fiddlers Association (ca. 1990). [cassette]

Lee, Billy. *Up Jumped the Devil*. Voyager VRCD357 (2003).

Lee Mace and His Ozark Opry Gang. "Resurrection Morning" / "Someday We'll Know." Starday SEP152A EP (1960). [Don Russell, violin]

———. "Steppin' in the Straw" / "Ozark Fiddler." Starday SEP152B EP (1960). [Don Russell, violin]

Lutz, Ron. *Jack of Diamonds*. Jefferson City, MO: private-label CD, Hot City (2007). [Harold Leake, violin]

Marshall, Howard, and John Williams. *Fiddling Missouri*. Voyager VRCD344 (1999).

Marshall, Howard, and Vivian Williams. *Fiddle Seconding Missouri Style, Chords and Bowing Techniques*. Seattle: Voyager Recordings and Publications, VR-DVD1001 (2012). [instructional DVD with historical commentary]

McBaine, Taylor. *Boone County Fiddler*. Missouri State Old Time Fiddlers Association, 002 (1987). [cassette]

McMahan, Pete. *50 Old-Time Fiddle Gems*. Reissue of *Missouri Fiddlin'* series (four LPs), Voyager VRCD366 (2005).

———. *Kansas City Rag*. Reissue of *Missouri Fiddlin' #3*, Missouri State Old Time Fiddlers Association 003 (1989). [cassette]

———. *Missouri Fiddlin'*. Graphic Recording, MLP 534 (1972).

———. *Missouri Fiddlin' #2*. Graphic Recording, MLP-538 (ca. 1976).

———. *Missouri Fiddlin' #3*. Graphic Recording (ca. 1977).

———. *Missouri Fiddlin' #4*. Graphic Recording (ca. 1978).

———. *Ozark Mountain Waltz*. Missouri State Old Time Fiddlers Association 001 (1987). [cassette]

Miller, Shorty. *Fiddling Around*. Lebanon, MO: private-label cassette, NQD14381 (1996).

Mona Jones and the Bluegrass Travelers. *Live at Starvy Creek: A Tribute to Bill Jones*. Dixon, MO: private-label CD, M. Jones (2009). [Joe Wieneman, violin]

Morrow Sisters Band. *Yesterday, Today, and Two Morrows*. Rosa Stringworks CD (ca. 2005). [Patty Morrow Chandler, violin]

Murphy, Al. *Through the Fields*. Global Village LP 305 (1987).

Orchard, Jim. *Front Porch Fiddlin'*. Birch Tree, MO: private-label CD (2003).

———. *Old 'Ens an' New 'Ens*. Birch Tree, MO: private-label CD (n.d.).

Orchard, Jim, and Devin Quick. *Ozarks Fiddlin' from Hartshorn to Low Wassie*. Birch Tree, MO: private-label CD (n.d.).

———. *Today and Tomorrow*. Birch Tree, MO: private-label CD (ca. 1999).

Orchard Brothers. *McHenry Hollow Fiddlin*. Birch Tree, MO: private-label CD, Jim Orchard (1995). [Jim Orchard, violin; Rich Orchard, guitar]

Ozark Opry. *Lee Mace's Ozark Opry: On Stage*. Century Records 25163/5 (ca. 1964).

———. *A Night at Lee Mace's Ozark Opry*. Vol. 2. Lee Mace's Ozark Opry SoN 115591 (ca. 1964).

Ozark Originals. "Please Pass the Biscuits" / "Home Sweet Home." Sure 8100-6262 (1963). [Don Russell, violin]

Potter, Dale. *Dale Potter: World's Champion Country & Western Fiddler, Hoe Down!* Vol. 1. Rural Rhythm RRDP 179, 1963, cassette reissue, *Dale Potter and Shot Jackson: Twenty Fiddle Favorites* (1994).

———. *Jazz from the Hills*. 1953, RCA. Reissued on CD with the Country All-Stars (Jethro Burns, Chet Atkins, Homer Haynes, Jerry Byrd).

Puckett, Bobby. *Bobby Puckett and Elmer Jones: Just Bobby & Elmer*. Caney, KS: private-label cassette (1986). CD reissue, ca. 1995.

———. "Eminence" / "Squaws along the Illinois." St. Louis: DB 643 (1972). [45 rpm]

———. "Indian Council" / "Van Buren Reel." St. Louis: DB label (no number) (ca. 1972). [45 rpm]

Reed, Frank. *Ole Tyme Fiddlin'*. Overland, MO: private-label LP, Frank Reed, TS76-922-923 (1976).

Rhodes, Dusty. *Rosin Dust*. Dungeon LP D-2029.

Richard, Edward James, and Friends. *Jimmy Brown the Newsboy*. Mission Music (2002).

Robertson, Lonnie. *Country Fiddling*. Caney Mountain CLP-229 (ca. 1975).

———. *Fiddle Tune Favorites*. Caney Mountain CLP-228 (1972).

———. *Fiddle Tunes Ozark Style by Lonnie Robertson*. Caney Mountain CLP-232 (n.d.).

———. *Fiddle Tunes Ozark Style by Lonnie Robertson*. Vol. 2. Caney Mountain CLP-233 (n.d.).

———. *Fiddling by Lonnie Robertson*. CEP-211 (ca. 1965). ("Old Frisky Jim," "Wednesday Night Waltz" "Twinkle Little Star" / "Durang's Hornpipe," "Smith's Waltz," "Dill Pickle Rag")

———. *Fiddling by Lonnie Robertson*. CEP-212 (ca. 1965). ("Ragtime Annie," "Florida Blues," "Fisher's Hornpipe" / "Saturday Night Rag," "Dry and Dusty")

———. *Fiddling by Lonnie Robertson*. CEP-213 LP (ca. 1965). ("Katy Hill," "Darkie's Dream," "Brown Leaf Rag" / "Mahoney's Reel," "Waldo," "Cotton Eyed Joe")
———. *Home Folks Get Together*. Caney Mountain CEP-211 (ca. 1969). [Lonnie Robertson, violin; Roy McGeorge, Thelma Robertson, Jarrett Robertson]
———. *Missouri Fiddling by Lonnie Robertson*. Caney Mountain Record Co., CEP-102 (ca. 1965). ("Lonnie's Breakdown," "Arkansas Stomp," "A & E Rag," "Caney Mt. Hornpipe," "Ozark Mt. Waltz" / "Taney Co. Breakdown")
———. *Missouri Fiddling by Lonnie Robertson*. CEP-207 (ca. 1965). ("Coming Down from Denver," "Lonesome Valley Waltz," "My Little Home in the Hills" / "Turnpike Reel," "Blue Bird Waltz," "Little Creek Rag")
———. *Missouri Fiddling by Lonnie Robertson*. CEP-208 (ca. 1965). ("Eagle Hornpipe," "Sunrise Waltz," "Mountain Reel" / "Star Light Hornpipe," "Lazy Hills Waltz," "Brush Creek")
———. *Missouri Fiddling by Lonnie Robertson*. CEP-210 (ca. 1965). ("Sally Goodin," "Soldier's Joy," "Miller's Reel" / "Wagoner," "Country Man's Hornpipe," "Leather Britches")
———. *Old-Time Fiddle Tunes*. Caney Mountain CLP230 (ca. 1976).
———. *Square Dance Fiddlin'*. Caney Mountain CEP-213 (ca. 1971).
Robertson, Lonnie, and Thelma Jarrett. *Favorite Hymns by the Down Home Folks*. Caney Mountain CS-301 (ca. 1965). ("Take Up the Cross," "Rank Strangers to Me")
———. *Lonnie's Breakdown: Classic Fiddle Music from Missouri*. Compilation, reissue CD, Rounder 0375 (1996).
Robertson, Lonnie, and Thelma Robertson. *Favorite Gospel and Country Songs*. Caney Mountain CLP-231 (1976).
Schoenberger, Liesl. *Amazing Grace of the Fiddler's Touch*. Sugar Bear Records CD (ca. 2000).
———. *Classic Fiddle*. Sugar Bear Records CD (1997).
———. *Say Old Man*. Sugar Bear Records CD (2005).
Scrivner, David, Alvie Dooms, and Karen Kraft. *Hangin' around the Kitchen*. Mansfield, MO: private-label CD (2007).
Seitz, Geoff. *Common Fiddle Tunes Fast and Slow*. St. Louis: private-label cassette, Seitz (1994).
———. *The Good Old Days Are Here*. Oceana Productions OP003 (1995).
Shaw, John and Jason. *Flowers from Heaven*. Startracker (1989) [cassette]
Silvey, H. K. *H. K. Silvey, Traditional Ozarks Fiddlin'*. D&D Studio (n.d.). [cassette]
Stephens, Gene. *Gene Stephens: A Musical Legacy*. Fulton, MO: private-label CD (2005).
Stinnett, Cyril. *Cyril Stinnett Plays His Favorite Old Time Fiddle Tunes*. Stinnett Records, Slp-234 (ca. 1971).
———. *Fiddler's Dream*. Stinnett Records, Slp-1012 (ca. 1973).
———. *Grey Eagle in C*. Missouri State Old Time Fiddlers Association, 103 (1992). [cassette]

———. *Mahoney's Reel.* Missouri State Old Time Fiddlers Association, 105 (1992). [cassette]
———. *Plain Old Time Fiddlin'.* Stinnett Records, Slp-1013 (ca. 1975).
———. *Salty River Reel.* Missouri State Old Time Fiddlers Association, 104 (1992). [cassette]
Stoneking, Fred. *Saddle Old Spike: Fiddle Music from Missouri.* Rounder 0381 (1996).
Stoneking, Lee R., & Sons. *Missouri Old Time Fiddlin'.* Graphic Recording, NR11285 (ca. 1976).
———. *Rainbow of Fiddle Tunes.* Graphic recording, NR13168 (ca. 1976).
Sunny Side Up. *Sunny Side Up.* West Plains, MO: private-label CD (2004). [Dean Von Allmen, violin]
Swing Deville. *Swing Deville: Salt Up the Dance Floor.* http://www.swingdeville.com (2010).
———. *Western Swing Deville.* Fiddlesong Music (2009). [Matt Wyatt, Justin Branum, violins]
Teague, Howe. *Ozark Memories: Fiddle Tunes by Howe Teague.* OMHT-001 (1986).
———. "Ozark Mountain Fox Chase." Salem, MO: private-label 45 rpm record.
———. *Square Dance Music / Ozark Fiddlin'.* Gold Standard GS-SQ D.LP1 (1964).
Various Artists. *24 Fiddle Favorites.* Rural Rhythm Classics RHY-253 (1997). [Dale Potter, violin]
Various Artists. *Art of Traditional Fiddle.* Rounder 11592 (2001). [Jim Herd, Fred Stoneking, Art Galbraith, Lonnie Robertson, Ray Curbow, Alton Jones, Bob Holt, Howe Teague, violins]
Various Artists. *Fiddlers of the Tennessee Valley* [ca. 1965]. Reissue, Spring Fed SFR-DU-33004 (ca. 2007). [Lena Hughes, violin]
Various Artists. *Grass Cuttin' Time in Missouri.* St. Louis: Missouri Area Bluegrass Committee, MABC-LP101 (1970). [Don Brown, Bob Wagganer, Stan Wagganer, Clark Weaver, violins]
Various Artists. *Live! From the Kahoka Festival of Bluegrass Music.* Kahoka, MO: Delbert Spray OS16396 (ca. 1980). [Darrin Vincent, Gerald Jones, violins]
Various Artists. *Masters of the Folk Violin.* Arhoolie CD 434 (1995). [Claude Williams and others, violin]
Various Artists. *The Missouri Session: A Studio Jam Session with Years of Memories.* Audio Loft, TMS-3033-CD (1990). [Lyman Enloe, Larry Ellis, Kirk Brandenberger, Joe Wieneman, violins]
Various Artists. *"Now That's a Good Tune": Masters of Traditional Missouri Fiddling.* University of Missouri Cultural Heritage Center and Extension Division, 1989 (LPs and book). Reissue, Voyager Recordings and Publications, CDs and book (2008). [R. P. Christeson, Bill Eddy, Lyman Enloe, Gene Goforth, Carol Hascall, Vesta Johnson, Dean Johnston, Pete McMahan, Cyril Stinnett, Howe Teague, Charlie Walden, Bob Walsh, Nile Wilson, violins]

Various Artists. *Three Fiddlers from the Show-Me State*. County CO-CD-2739 (2005). [Lyman Enloe, Cyril Stinnett, Casey Jones, violins]

Various Artists. *Traditional Fiddle Music of the Ozarks*. Vol. 1, *Along the Eastern Crescent*. Rounder 0435 (1999). [Cecil Goforth, Gene Goforth, Aubrey Haynie, Violet Hensley, Bob Holt, Stan Jackson, Howe Teague, Jesse Wallace, Sam Younger, violins]

———. *Traditional Fiddle Music of the Ozarks*. Vol. 2, *On the Springfield Plain*. Rounder 0436 (2000). [Earl Ball, Ray Curbow, Art Galbraith, Bill Graves, Lacy Hartje, Ruth Hawkins, Dean Johnston, Gary Johnston, Bill Mustain, Leonard Smith, Fred Stoneking, Raymond Thomas, violins]

———. *Traditional Fiddle Music of the Ozarks*. Vol. 3, *Down in the Border Counties*. Rounder 0437 (2000). [Jim Beeler, Bill Conley, Alton Jones, Jim Herd, Noel Scott, Jess Silvey, H. K. Silvey, violins]

Von Allmen, Dean. *Country Fiddlin'*. West Plains, MO: private-label CD (2005).

Walden, Charlie. *Draggin' the Bow*. Missouri State Old Time Fiddlers Association 007 (1996). [cassette]

———. *Missouri Fiddle Tunes Fast & Slow*. 2 vols. Evanston, IL (2010). http://www.charliewalden.com (to be purchased with book), CWM 004, CWM 005.

———. *Patt & Possum: Hoe-Downs, Hornpipes, & Hokum*. Marimac Recordings 5062C (1994). [cassette]

———. *Traditional Fiddle Music of Missouri*. Marimac Recordings 9011 (1987). [cassette]

Williams, Claude. *Claude Williams Quintet: Call for the Fiddler*. SCCD 31051 (1994).

———. *Live at J's—Part 1*. Arhoolie CD 405 (n.d.).

———. *Live at J's—Part 2*. Arhoolie CD 406 (1989).

Williams, Vivian, Howard Marshall, Phil Williams, and John Williams. *Fiddle Tunes of the Lewis & Clark Era*. Voyager CD358 (2002).

Williams, Vivian, and Phil Williams. *Dance Music of the Oregon Trail*. Voyager VRCD350 (2009).

———. *Pioneer Dance Tunes of the Far West*. Voyager VRCD371 (2009).

Wilson, Nile. *Tie Hacker Hoe-Down*. Missouri State Old Time Fiddlers Association 202-CD (1995).

Wyatt, Matt, and Justin Branum. *The Good-Bye Waltz*. Fiddlesong Music (2003). [Matt Wyatt, violin]

Index to Text

Index to the Voyager Records Companion CD

The time period covered ranges from 1939 to 2015. The selections are drawn from informal home recordings as well as polished performances on live radio programs and records. Like the CD with the 2012 volume, this one was produced for the University of Missouri Press by Phil and Vivian Williams of Voyager Recordings and Publications, 424 Thirty-Fifth Avenue, Seattle, WA 98122. Visit http://www.voyagerrecords.com. Telephone: (206) 323-1112.

The recorded music is integral to the book, offering examples of certain fiddlers' music and to give audible representations of various themes in the discussion. Taken overall, and especially in league with the music CD that accompanied the 2012 book, the CD gives an overview of the styles and repertoires of seasoned fiddlers active in Missouri from the 1920s into the early 1960s. Some heretofore little-known fiddlers are emphasized to bring them to wider attention. Some better-known fiddlers (especially those with available recordings) may only nominally be represented.

No attempt is made to present a player's "best" recorded examples. The recordings vary in audio quality, from informal home sessions and low-fidelity copies from AM radio program transcriptions to polished studio productions, and they span the years 1939 to 2015. As with the 2012 project *Play Me Something Quick and Devilish*, the CD endeavors to give readers and listeners a reasonably good glimpse of the broad range of "fiddling" in that time period, which runs the gamut from old-time and archaic styles through western swing and early jazz to bluegrass, contest fiddling, and show fiddling. Some of the tracks represent fiddlers in their absolute prime, while others are home recordings of fiddlers in their elder years when their violin "chops," memory, and health were in decline.

Writing annotations for fiddle tunes can consume many pages. In this book, some less familiar tunes receive extensive attention in the text, endnotes, and annotations, as with "Brickyard Joe" and "Roger's Waltz." Due to space limitations, many of the well-known tunes on the CD, such as "Black Mountain Rag," are given only basic information.

Track 1. "Theme tune" and "Frisky Jim," by Lonnie Robertson, 1939, KFAB radio. Lonnie Robertson played "Etherham Hobbs" with his partner, guitarist Roy (Uncle Enoch) McGeorge, on their radio show at KFAB, Lincoln, Nebraska. They did back-to-back shows; the first was straight, with duet singing (mandolin and guitar) with a fiddle tune or two; the second was a parody of hillbilly comedy acts such as "Lum and Abner," with mock dialect but serious music. Recorded by Dick Hill (Hastings, Nebraska) and sent to Henry McGeorge (Roy's son). Theme tunes to launch radio shows typically were not announced or named on the air.[1] (Courtesy Henry McGeorge)

Track 2. "Marmaduke's Hornpipe," by Lonnie Robertson and Roy McGeorge (guitar), 1939, KFAB radio, continued; singing square-dance call by McGeorge. The version Robertson (who learned his fiddling deep in the Ozarks and on radio stations in western Missouri, Nebraska, and Kansas) played in 1939 did not exhibit the "hokum" bowing on the G and D strings in the first part that had been popularized in the Columbia area of central Missouri by fiddlers such as Daniel Boone Jones, Ed Tharp, and Cleo Persinger. Extensive discussion of this tune is in *Play Me Something Quick and Devilish*. (Courtesy Henry McGeorge)

Track 3. "Wabash Fox Trot," by Howe Teague, 1986. A rolling two-step in three parts, related to "Twinkle, Twinkle" and "I Don't Love Nobody," as well as the "Georgia Camp Meeting" circle of country rags (see track 1). This is the sort of tune that can work when couples ask for a schottische; Missouri fiddlers play very few schottisches. No known composer has been discovered; as a two-step couple dance popular in Missouri, "Wabash" presumably refers to the railroad (significant in Missouri history), although the title may refer to the river (important in settlement of the Old Northwest) that rises in western Ohio to angle across Indiana, eventually to divide southern Indiana from Illinois near Terre Haute and then flow into the Ohio River. From Teague's *Ozark Memories* LP with his son Larry Teague, guitar and bass. A version by Teague in 1942 with guitar by Roy Wooliver is in the splendid online Gordon McCann collection of Ozarks fiddle music (Missouri State University Libraries). See also the 2001 Rounder compilation CD *The Art of Traditional Fiddle*. (Courtesy Jim Nelson)

Track 4. "Fiddler's Hornpipe," by Roy Wooliver, 1958. Marvin Hawthorn, guitar, John Hartford, banjo; recorded by Hartford. An interesting B-flat hornpipe familiar in the upper Ozarks and central Missouri but unusual elsewhere. Gene Goforth's version, learned from Wooliver, is on Goforth's CD *Eminence Breakdown* (Rounder 0388, 1997) and Hartford's *Hamilton Ironworks* CD (0442, 1991), and the tune was a favorite among central Missouri B-flat fiddlers of former times such as Cleo Persinger, Ed Tharp, and Taylor McBaine and those today such as Bob Hagan and John Williams. (Recorded by John Hartford; courtesy Hartford, 2000)

Track 5. "Grasshopper Rag," by Bert Lewis, with the Ozark Drifters, 1954. A solid, hard-driving breakdown apparently of local evolution, excellent for square dancing. The Ozark Drifters were a short-lived local band that played a few live radio shows and many dances; Lewis with Truman Bridges (plectrum banjo), Don Agee (guitar), George Hoppers (guitar), Bobby Crabtree (bass), and Bob Pitts (guitar). (Courtesy Gladys Reser)

Track 6. "Brickyard Joe," by Earl Willis, ca. 1976. One of Willis's favorite old-time breakdowns, this is known as a central Missouri tune as well as a Kentucky tune. Willis may have heard it fiddled by players such as Tony Gilmore, who performed on

WOS radio in the late 1920s; Willis himself fiddled over WOS in the same era, with his band the Beacon Camp Fiddlers.[2] (Courtesy Linda Daniels, Oregon Old-Time Fiddlers Project; and Stuart Williams)

Track 7. "Walk Along John," by Ellis Cowin, 1966, at the "Missouri Picnic" near Lynden, Washington, a tune and style basic to Missouri fiddlers then and now. Accompaniment by Phil Williams (bluegrass banjo) and Ivan Hart (guitar, another Missouri emigrant musician). (Courtesy Phil Williams)

Track 8. "Ozark Kitchen Sweat," by Ishmael (Ozark Red) Loveall, 1939, Chicago. Loveall fiddles a hot square-dance set with the Sons of the Ozarks. Loveall's "Ozark Kitchen Sweat" is a medley worked up for the recording session and radio shows ("Red-Haired Boy," "Devil's Dream," "Grey Eagle") and represents the hard-core square-dance fiddling back in Missouri. Rusty Draper (a native of Kirksville, Missouri) provides closed-chord guitar accompaniment. A "kitchen sweat" is a music party, usually with some square dancing (furniture moved to the porch or another room). From *Rusty and Red: The Early Recordings of Rusty Draper Featuring Ozark Red Loveall* (British Archive of Country Music, CD D334, 2011; courtesy Dave Barnes).

Track 9. "Yellow Gals," by Ron Hughey, 1973. A tune Hughey identified as a melody from his family in Dade County, Missouri. From the acclaimed LP *Country Fiddlin' Ozark Style* (American Heritage AH-402-511), with Ron Trammell (guitar), John Davis (banjo), Norman Belt (bass), and Steve Duncan (snare drum). The tune is "crooked" (see text), but old-time Missouri square dancers have no problem dancing to crooked tunes (in contrast to today's contra dancers). While it may be anathema to old-time fiddle purists, in this case a drum adds value and interesting rhythm. (Courtesy Phil Williams)

Track 10. "Rosebuds of Avondale," by Bob Fast, 1970, with Russ Phillips and Stan Gleason (guitars) and an unnamed bassist. Published as "Rosebud of Allenvale" by Scottish composer-violinist J. Scott Skinner, ca. 1920. Other titles include "Rosebuds of Avonmore," "Rosebuds of Evermore," "Rosebuds of Nevermore," and "Rose of Sharon" (Howdy Forrester's title, who played it in A). (Courtesy Judy Scheurer)

Track 11. "Sally Goodin," by Billy Moore, *The Ozark Opry*, May 1955, KRMS-AM, Osage Beach. Lee Mace (emcee, bass), Lonnie Hoppers (banjo), Dale Sledd (Dobro), Bob McCoy (guitar), and Bob Penny (electric guitar). Mace introduces the tune.

Track 12. "Ozark Fiddler," by Don Russell, 1960, with Lee Mace and His Ozark Opry Gang (Starday SEP152B); this is the band's title for "Bill Cheatem." Russell (violin), Bob McCoy (guitar), Dale Sledd (mandolin), and Lee Mace (bass, jig dancing). A driving, exemplary version of an ironclad in the old-time and bluegrass fiddle repertoire. (Courtesy Jim Russell)

Track 13. "Charlie Cook's Waltz," by Leroy Canaday, 2001, with Norman Canaday (guitar) and Forrest Rose (bowed bass). Rose's judicious application of a bow to the usually plucked upright bass adds warmth and richness to the accompaniment for waltzes. A fine intricate waltz composed by Cook, sometimes called "The G Waltz" and "Cook's Waltz." Canaday learned the tune in a jam session with Cook in the 1950s in Boone County; both men loved to play waltzes with abundant, opulent double-stops, a trait common in central Missouri. From Canaday's *Old Dan Tucker Was a Fine Old Man* Voyager CD. (Recorded by Howard Marshall)

Track 14. "Black Mountain Rag," by Leroy Canaday, 2001. It is probable that most if not all show fiddlers from the 1940s to the present time have a version of this crowd-pleasing exhibition piece credited to Leslie Keith in the 1930s and popularized by Nashville stars such as Curly Fox and Tommy Jackson; Canaday had it from Fox. In chorded tuning (A–E–A–C#), this is one of the three tunes banned in contests in the 1960s when overenthusiastic fiddlers' association cognoscenti invented rules for contests (the other two banned tunes were the florid show tune "Orange Blossom Special" and the venerable Civil War sentimental song cum instrumental exhibition piece "Listen to the Mocking Bird"). From Canaday's *Old Dan Tucker Was a Fine Old Man* Voyager CD. (Recorded by Howard Marshall)

Track 15. "The Cuckoo's Nest," by Larry Ellis, 1988, with Green Side Up (cassette, *Green Side Up*). Don Hoglen (melody fiddle), Larry Ellis (harmony fiddle), Jon Porter (bass), Marty McIntosh (banjo), and Andy McIntosh (guitar). Ellis's love for playing "harmony" over Don Hoglen's melody line is nicely on display and a hallmark of Green Side Up and other bluegrass bands. One of the oldest tunes in the fiddler's kit, this is from eighteenth-century England and found across the globe; first publication seems to have been in Scottish collector James Aird, *A Selection of 200 Scots, English, Irish, and Foreign Airs: Adapted to the Fife, Violin, or German Flute* (Glasgow, 1782), 66; appearances in tune collections since then are too numerous to list here. (Courtesy Larry Ellis)

Track 16. "September Waltz," by Larry Ellis, 2012 (Larry *Ellis CD #1*), with Jim Lower (guitars, bass; active in the Kansas City–area music scene). This illustrates Ellis's professional and studio work employing electric instruments, including Larry's Zeta Classic electric violin. Larry learned this Blaine Sprouse composition from the Sprouse 1989 Rounder CD of twin fiddling with Kenny Baker, *Indian Springs* (CD0259), a project combining bluegrass and swing. (Courtesy Larry Ellis)

Track 17. "South," by Luther Caldwell, 1940, Columbia, with Roy Ethington (guitar). A favorite swing tune played by many old-time fiddlers at dances as a "round dance" (fox-trot or two-step), composed by Thamon Hayes and Bennie Moten. Thamon Hays was an early jazz trombonist in the Kansas City "Eighteenth and Vine" music scene; his collaborator Bennie Moten recorded "South" with his orchestra in

1924 and 1928 and popularized it in Kansas City nightclubs, dance halls, and radio broadcasts. (Recorded by Roy Ethington; courtesy Jack Oliver)

Track 18. "Sweet Georgia Brown," by Emmett Heath, ca. 1952, with guitar and strummed tenor banjo, the 1925 jazz composition by Ben Bernie, Maceo Pinkard, and Kenneth Casey. Most seasoned fiddlers of my acquaintance play this old favorite; Heath's 1952 version sounds much like versions on historic 78 rpm records we have heard. (Courtesy Sharon Heath Marriott)

Track 19. "Ida Red," by Zed Tennis ("the flash from Nixa"), 1952, with Doc Martin and the Haden Family, August 29, 1952, broadcast from a prerecorded radio transcription (disc) over Omaha, Nebraska, station WOW-AM. This is one of the Texas dance-hall tunes most fiddlers play, and most base their version on the 1938 recording by Bob Wills and His Texas Playboys. There are countless varieties of this melody. (Courtesy Ed McKinney)

Track 20. "Under the Silvery Moon," by Bobby Joe Caldwell, 2006, with Matt Wyatt (guitar). Learned from his father, Luther, this subtle waltz was played by other Columbia-area fiddlers such as Ed Tharp and Bill (Junior) Perkins. This track nicely represents the strongly melody-centric playing and smooth bowing for which Bobby Joe was famous. Recorded at the Caldwell home in Columbia by Matt Wyatt; Matt plays rhythm on a 1949 Epiphone Triumph archtop guitar. (Recorded by Matt Wyatt)

Track 21. "Anniversary Waltz," by Dale Pauley, 2008, Columbia, with Bobby Joe Caldwell and Brad Roby (guitars) and Kathy Gordon (bass). Composed by Dave Franklin and Al Dubin, 1941. Not to be confused with "The Anniversary Song" ("Oh, how we danced on the night we were wed"), "Golden Anniversary Waltz," or "50-Years Ago Waltz," this is the one recorded by pop crooners such as Bing Crosby and Vera Lynn. Dale learned it from Bobby Joe Caldwell. (Recorded by Kathy Gordon)

Track 22. "Unclouded Day," by Jamie Haage (Kirbyville), 1992, with Lonnie Hoppers; a favorite gospel song in the evocative fiddle-and-banjo duet, bluegrass style. From *Lonnie Hoppers: Old Country Church* (CD reissue, 2000), the pace and presentation represent the tradition well. Recorded at Haage's studio at Kirbyville (now in Branson), Haage adds Fender electric bass accompaniment and a harmony violin track, and Hoppers provides accompaniment on a 1950 Gibson J-45 guitar as well as playing his 1954 Gibson RB250 five-string banjo. Composed by Ohio circuit-rider preacher Joseph K. Alwood as "The Unclouded Day" in 1885, the hymn is a staple of Protestant congregations as well as camp-meeting folios and commercial songbooks. (Courtesy Lonnie Hoppers)

Track 23. "Dixie Hoedown," by Lyman Enloe, 1990 (with Kirk Brandenberger and Larry Ellis, harmony fiddle parts). On a Midwest bluegrass project produced by Joe

Wieneman and Irl Hees, *The Missouri Session*, conceived to give listeners a feeling for the pickin' parties that have always been the heart of the bluegrass-festival scene. Brandenberger and Ellis were great admirers of Enloe. Composed by bluegrass mandolin innovator Jesse McReynolds, of Jim and Jesse and the Virginia Boys, in the 1950s. A tune popular among old-time as well as bluegrass fiddlers; Cyril Stinnett's interesting setting under his title "Hillbilly Hoedown" is on one of Stinnett's 1970s LPs. With Rusty Dutton, Joe Wieneman (guitars), Jim McGreevy (banjo), Harry Wagganer (mandolin), and Irl Hees (bass). (Courtesy Joey Wieneman)

Track 24. "Sadie's in the Kitchen," by Delbert Spray, 1990; a northern Missouri breakdown from Delbert's father, Albert Spray. With the Iowa City guitarist (and fiddler) Al Murphy, recorded by a music party ca. 1990 at a Tri-State Bluegrass Association festival at Kahoka, Missouri or Aledo, Illinois. Note the strong, straight guitar accompaniment and the chord sequence by Murphy, whose style and taste are a model for old-time fiddle accompanists. (Courtesy Al Murphy)

Track 25. "Take Me Back to Tulsa," by Warren Helton, 2011, with David Cavins (guitar) and Howard Marshall (banjo). A classic of western swing from the golden age of Bob Wills and His Texas Playboys. In a pleasurable, laid-back session of old-time fiddling and storytelling at his home just west of Vienna, Helton suddenly took off into this favorite swing piece, and the good vibes carried David and me right along. (Recorded by David Cavins)

Track 26. "Roger's Waltz," by Roger Williams, 2015. A fine waltz Roger worked up in the 1960s that echoes an untitled tune R. P. Christeson remembered upper Ozarks fiddler Dallas Stamper playing at a community picnic in 1928 (published untitled in Christeson's 1973 book as "Waltz," tune 226). Ed McKinney provides guitar accompaniment on a 1940s Gibson J-45 he recently made playable again. Roger Williams is among many Missouri fiddlers who regard old Gibson guitars as their favorites for accompaniment (most others vote for Martin guitars). (Recorded by Howard Marshall)

Track 27. "Cattle in the Corn," by Cecil Goforth, 2015. Cecil obtained the essence of this tune from a laudable LP by bluegrass fiddler Joe Green (*Joe Greene's Fiddle Album*). This is one of several archaic-sounding fiddle tunes that seem to wander between major and minor chords, sometimes to the dismay of unfamiliar accompanists trying to figure out the fiddler's preferences. This is a similar but different tune, as they say, from its cousin "Cattle in the *Cane*." (Recorded by Howard Marshall)

Track 28. "Black River," by Cecil Goforth, 2015. The Black River rises in the southeastern Missouri Ozarks and winds its way south through mountains and valleys, eventually passing through northeastern Arkansas to empty into the Mississippi River. (Recorded by Howard Marshall; courtesy Cecil Goforth)

Track 29. "Gilsaw," by John Williams, 2013, solo violin. The hard-driving Missouri breakdown from Pete McMahan via his uncle Claude Gregory, 1930s. Williams plays it much as Pete taught him in the late 1990s (complete with heel-stomp accent). John recorded the tune for his student Bob Cathey (Centralia) at the Williams family farm near Madison; video-recorded by John's mother, Tammy Williams, with a cell phone. Listed in Charlie Walden's "One Hundred Essential Missouri Fiddle Tunes" (www.missourifiddling.com). (Courtesy John Williams)

Track 30. "Fiddler's Dream," by Pete McMahan, 1970s (2005 reissue, *50 Old-Time Fiddle Gems*). This is the Fiddlin' Arthur Smith chestnut from radio and records when Pete was a teenager in the 1930s and recorded by other show fiddlers Pete admired (Benny Martin, Tommy Jackson). For many years, this was Pete McMahan's signature piece, and this recording is among the most compelling and instructive examples of central Missouri traditional fiddling. The spare yet powerful and appropriate old-time guitar accompaniment by Fred Stoneking is equally stellar.